Cases on the Interplay Between Family, Society, and Entrepreneurship

Ethel Ndidiamaka Abe
SashBM LLC, USA

Isaac Idowu Abe
SashBM LLC, USA

IGI Global
PUBLISHER of TIMELY KNOWLEDGE

A volume in the Advances in Human Resources Management and Organizational Development (AHRMOD) Book Series

Published in the United States of America by
IGI Global
Business Science Reference (an imprint of IGI Global)
701 E. Chocolate Avenue
Hershey PA, USA 17033
Tel: 717-533-8845
Fax: 717-533-8661
E-mail: cust@igi-global.com
Web site: http://www.igi-global.com

Library of Congress Cataloging-in-Publication Data

Names: Abe, Ethel Ndidiamaka, 1966- editor. | Abe, Isaac Idowu, 1963- editor.
Title: Cases on the interplay between family, society, and entrepreneurship / edited by Ethel Ndidiamaka Abe, and Isaac Idowu Abe.
Description: Hershey, PA : Business Science Reference, [2024] | Includes bibliographical references and index. | Summary: "The proposed book will adopt a multi-disciplinary approach to appraising and managing the subject matter. Contributions from scholars in the Humanities, Business Management, Entrepreneurship, Human Resource Management, Innovations and Technology, Psychology, Governance, and Law are acceptable for the proposed book. The 'teaching case' approach to writing should be adopted by contributors to this book"-- Provided by publisher.
Identifiers: LCCN 2023025856 (print) | LCCN 2023025857 (ebook) | ISBN 9781668487488 (hardcover) | ISBN 9781668487495 (paperback) | ISBN 9781668487501 (ebook)
Subjects: LCSH: Entrepreneurship--Social aspects. | Work and family. | Businesspeople--Family relationships. | Family-owned business enterprises.
Classification: LCC HB615 .C34 2024 (print) | LCC HB615 (ebook) | DDC 338/.04--dc23/eng/20230623
LC record available at https://lccn.loc.gov/2023025856
LC ebook record available at https://lccn.loc.gov/2023025857

This book is published in the IGI Global book series Advances in Human Resources Management and Organizational Development (AHRMOD) (ISSN: 2327-3372; eISSN: 2327-3380)

British Cataloguing in Publication Data
A Cataloguing in Publication record for this book is available from the British Library.
All work contributed to this book is new, previously-unpublished material.
The views expressed in this book are those of the authors, but not necessarily of the publisher.
For electronic access to this publication, please contact: eresources@igi-global.com.

Advances in Human Resources Management and Organizational Development (AHRMOD) Book Series

ISSN:2327-3372
EISSN:2327-3380

Editor-in-Chief: Patricia Ordóñez de Pablos, Universidad de Oviedo, Spain

MISSION

A solid foundation is essential to the development and success of any organization and can be accomplished through the effective and careful management of an organization's human capital. Research in human resources management and organizational development is necessary in providing business leaders with the tools and methodologies which will assist in the development and maintenance of their organizational structure.

The **Advances in Human Resources Management and Organizational Development (AHRMOD) Book Series** aims to publish the latest research on all aspects of human resources as well as the latest methodologies, tools, and theories regarding organizational development and sustainability. The **AHRMOD Book Series** intends to provide business professionals, managers, researchers, and students with the necessary resources to effectively develop and implement organizational strategies.

COVERAGE

- Employee Communications
- Disputes Resolution
- Coaching and Mentoring
- Talent Identification and Management
- Collaborative Method
- Process Improvement
- Human Relations Movement
- Change Management
- Recruitment Process
- Training and Development

IGI Global is currently accepting manuscripts for publication within this series. To submit a proposal for a volume in this series, please contact our Acquisition Editors at Acquisitions@igi-global.com or visit: http://www.igi-global.com/publish/.

The Advances in Human Resources Management and Organizational Development (AHRMOD) Book Series (ISSN 2327-3372) is published by IGI Global, 701 E. Chocolate Avenue, Hershey, PA 17033-1240, USA, www.igi-global.com. This series is composed of titles available for purchase individually; each title is edited to be contextually exclusive from any other title within the series. For pricing and ordering information please visit http://www.igi-global.com/book-series/advances-human-resources-management-organizational/73670. Postmaster: Send all address changes to above address.

Titles in this Series

For a list of additional titles in this series, please visit:
http://www.igi-global.com/book-series/advances-human-resources-management-organizational/73670

Managing Successful and Ethical Organizational Change
Dimitrios Belias (University of Thessaly, Greece) Ioannis Rossidis (Hellenic Open University, Greece) Christos Papademetriou (Neapolis University, Cyprus) Andreas Masouras (Neapolis University, Cyprus) and Sofia Anastasiadou (University of Western Macedonia, Greece)
Business Science Reference • © 2023 • 396pp • H/C (ISBN: 9798369302354) • US $250.00

Women of Color and Hair Bias in the Work Environment
Kula A. Francis (University of the Virgin Islands, US Virgin Islands) and Anna M. Clarke (University of the Virgin Islands, US Virgin Islands)
Business Science Reference • © 2023 • 320pp • H/C (ISBN: 9781668487907) • US $245.00

Addressing Corporate Scandals and Transgressions Through Governance and Social Responsibility
Carlos Flórido Lopes (DEGEIT, University of Aveiro, Portugal & Research Centre on Accounting and Taxation (CICF-IPCA), Polytechnic Institute of Cávado and Ave, Portugal) Augusta Ferreira (ISCA-UA, University of Aveiro, Portugal & Research Centre on Accounting and Taxation (CICF-IPCA), Polytechnic Institute of Cávado and Ave, Portugal) Carlos Ferreira (DEGEIT and LASI/IEETA, University of Aveiro, Portugal) Helena Inácio (ISCA-UA and GOVCOPP, University of Aveiro, Portugal) and Carlos Santos (ISCA-UA, University of Aveiro, Portugal & Research Centre on Accounting and Taxation (CICF-IPCA), Polytechnic Institute of Cávado and Ave, Portugal)
Business Science Reference • © 2023 • 311pp • H/C (ISBN: 9781668478851) • US $250.00

Promoting Regional Industries Through Cross-Sectoral Collaborations Regional System, Management, and the Management Body
Yuki Kawabata (Chukyo University, Japan)
Business Science Reference • © 2023 • 277pp • H/C (ISBN: 9781668484944) • US $100.00

For an entire list of titles in this series, please visit:
http://www.igi-global.com/book-series/advances-human-resources-management-organizational/73670

IGI Global
PUBLISHER of TIMELY KNOWLEDGE

701 East Chocolate Avenue, Hershey, PA 17033, USA
Tel: 717-533-8845 x100 • Fax: 717-533-8661
E-Mail: cust@igi-global.com • www.igi-global.com

Table of Contents

Foreword xv

Preface xvii

Chapter 1
Entrepreneurship and the Family: Panacea for Resilience, Sustainability, and Socioeconomic Development 1
Ethel Ndidiamaka Abe, SashBM LLC, USA
Chidi Idi Eke, Mangosuthu University of Technology, Nigeria

Chapter 2
Influence of Family Environment in Promoting Entrepreneurial Intentions and the Proliferation of Entrepreneurs 34
Dagogo William Legg-Jack, Walter Sisulu University, South Africa
Clever Ndebele, Walter Sisulu University, South Africa

Chapter 3
Family Processes, Entrepreneurial Resilience, and Socio-Economic Crisis: Case of an Entertainment and Attraction Enterprise 57
Isaac Idowu Abe, SashBM LLC, USA
Eke Idi Chidi, Mangosuthu University of Technology, South Africa

Chapter 4
Fostering Psychological Safety for Team Effectiveness in Family Businesses: Insights From Royal Savoy Hotel 84
Sulaiman Olusegun Atiku, Namibia University of Science and Technology, Namibia & Walter Sisulu University, South Africa
Funmilola Aderayo Soneye, Namibia University of Science and Technology, Namibia
Richmond Anane-Simon, Independent Researcher, Ghana

Chapter 5
Psychosocial Wellbeing of Entrepreneurs: The Interplay of Business-Family Life Stressors and Social Support 122
Ethel Ndidiamaka Abe, SashBM LLC, USA
Doreen Mukuku, Varsity College, South Africa
Mercy Okoli, Durban University of Technology, South Africa

Chapter 6
The Influence of Family Dynamics on Entrepreneurial Intentions and Self-Efficacy 146
Taiwo Hassan Ajadi, University of KwaZulu-Natal, South Africa
Olalekan Adisa, University of Northampton, UK
Al-Amin Abba Dabo, University of Northampton, UK
Olushola Margaret Adisa, University of Zululand, South Africa

Chapter 7
Authentic Leadership, Entrepreneurial Self-Efficacy, and Family Values 182
Isaac Idowu Abe, SashBM LLC, USA
Ethel Ndidiamaka Abe, SashBM LLC, USA

Chapter 8
Can Entrepreneurial Skills Development Mitigate Poverty Among Dropped Out High School Teenage Mothers in North-Central Nigeria? 210
Louis Okon Akpan, National Open University of Nigeria, Nigeria

Chapter 9
Succession and Survival Plan for Family Business: Lessons Learnt From Houshi Ryokan's Family Business 227
Ayansola Olatunji Ayandibu, University of Zululand, South Africa

Chapter 10
Knowledge Management in Family Firms: Perspectives From Management Research 250
Nelson Andres Andrade-Valbuena, Universidad Católica de la Santísima Concepción, Chile
Sergio A. Olavarrieta Soto, University of Chile, Chile
Miguel Zapata Perez, University of Chile, Chile

Chapter 11
Appraising the Influence of Social Support on Entrepreneurial Success and Sustainability 286
Olalekan Adisa, University of Northampton, UK

Chapter 12
Empirical Investigation for Assessing the Causality of Entrepreneurship Ecosystem With Entrepreneurial Behavior and Attitudes Across Countries.....315
Ajay Kumar Singh, Department of Economics, School of Liberal Arts and Management, DIT University, Dehradun, India
Bhim Jyoti, Department of Seed Science and Technology, College of Forestry, Veer Chandra Singh Garhwali Uttarakhand University of Horticulture and Forestry, Ranichauri, India

Compilation of References 354

About the Contributors 424

Index 432

Detailed Table of Contents

Foreword xv

Preface xvii

Chapter 1
Entrepreneurship and the Family: Panacea for Resilience, Sustainability, and Socioeconomic Development 1
Ethel Ndidiamaka Abe, SashBM LLC, USA
Chidi Idi Eke, Mangosuthu University of Technology, Nigeria

Entrepreneurship and the family are fast becoming the linchpin of contemporary societies, especially since the global economic crisis of 2008 and the COVID-19 pandemic. Entrepreneurs confirm that support from family in addition to resources developed by the family has contributed to their ability to be resilient in crises and grow sustainable businesses. Policymakers thus need to create a favourable environment to enable societies to derive the benefits of the interplay between entrepreneurial activities and family support in times of crisis. This chapter aims to contribute to an understanding of how an integration of family resources into entrepreneurship positively influences socioeconomic development and fuels resilience and sustainability. As the environment continues to be volatile, uncertain, complex, and ambiguous globally, this chapter provides a theoretical and practical understanding of the interplay between family and entrepreneurship, in generating socioeconomic development, through resilient and sustainable entrepreneurial activities.

Chapter 2
Influence of Family Environment in Promoting Entrepreneurial Intentions and the Proliferation of Entrepreneurs 34
Dagogo William Legg-Jack, Walter Sisulu University, South Africa
Clever Ndebele, Walter Sisulu University, South Africa

Research has shown that the family environment is one of the factors that shapes a person's entrepreneurial intentions, thereby leading to the production of entrepreneurs. Although several studies exist, none seem to have adopted the approach employed in this chapter. Premised on that, the chapter employed a teaching case approach to explain the influence of family environment in promoting entrepreneurial intentions and the proliferation of entrepreneurs. Guided by one research question, namely "How does the family environment promote entrepreneurial intention?" the chapter analysed three cases from Chinese Indonesia, Turkey, and Tunisia building on the theoretical strengths of the theory of planned behaviour and social cognitive theory. These theories were employed to analyse how family environment promoted entrepreneurial intentions in the countries mentioned. Findings from the analysis in the three cases highlighted revealed that the family environment through the instrumentality of role modelling and support for autonomy promotes entrepreneurial intentions.

Chapter 3
Family Processes, Entrepreneurial Resilience, and Socio-Economic Crisis: Case of an Entertainment and Attraction Enterprise 57
Isaac Idowu Abe, SashBM LLC, USA
Eke Idi Chidi, Mangosuthu University of Technology, South Africa

Resilience in entrepreneurship has been shown to mean more than the capacity of individuals to cope well under adversity. It is also the ability of the business to effectively navigate psychologically, socially, culturally, and physically, and turn hostile and uncertain situations into long-term opportunities. The aim of this chapter is to consider the possibilities of turning socio-economic adversity into opportunities through the functionality of family processes and entrepreneurial resilience. The chapter will examine the case of a successful entrepreneurial company that faced adversity during the pandemic and how the company turned adversity into opportunity. The strategies of the company are further analyzed from the lens of different theories that support her actions. Leadership flexibility in approach, techniques, and strategies emerged as a dominant factor for problem-solving in coping with family business during adverse socio-economic conditions. Stress and vulnerability in high-risk situations will foster growth and empower entrepreneurship in crisis.

Chapter 4
Fostering Psychological Safety for Team Effectiveness in Family Businesses: Insights From Royal Savoy Hotel 84
Sulaiman Olusegun Atiku, Namibia University of Science and Technology, Namibia & Walter Sisulu University, South Africa
Funmilola Aderayo Soneye, Namibia University of Science and Technology, Namibia
Richmond Anane-Simon, Independent Researcher, Ghana

This chapter examines the relationship between psychological safety and team effectiveness. Psychological safety is the perception and belief held by members of a team that interpersonal risk-taking is supported and encouraged in the workplace. A literature review was conducted to establish the relationships between psychological safety and employee engagement, satisfaction, performance, as well as team effectiveness in family businesses. The results showed that teams with a prominent level of psychological safety were significantly more effective than teams with a low level of psychological safety. Psychological safety has a significant effect on teams' performance and business effectiveness. This research holds that psychological safety is essential for team effectiveness and should be considered in building effective teams for innovative performance and sustainable competitive advantage in family businesses.

Chapter 5
Psychosocial Wellbeing of Entrepreneurs: The Interplay of Business-Family Life Stressors and Social Support 122
Ethel Ndidiamaka Abe, SashBM LLC, USA
Doreen Mukuku, Varsity College, South Africa
Mercy Okoli, Durban University of Technology, South Africa

Entrepreneurship engages every aspect of the entrepreneur's being in conducting work and engaging with family life. The entrepreneurial process, from beginning to completion, comprises transition stages, which are all distinctively stressful. Unlike people who are employees in the public or private sectors of any economy, the entrepreneur may not be able to draw boundaries between business life and family life as their business traverses both domains. These scholars argue that the resultant effect of the boundary-crossing activities of the entrepreneur will result in stress and conversely affect their psychosocial well-being. Amid their entrepreneurial activities and family responsibilities, the chaos unfolding opens the entrepreneur to needing balance. This chapter explores the role that business-family life strategies and social support could play in assisting entrepreneurs to achieve and maintain psychosocial well-being. The findings of the chapter from the review of extant literature will have practical and theoretical implications.

Chapter 6
The Influence of Family Dynamics on Entrepreneurial Intentions and Self-Efficacy 146
Taiwo Hassan Ajadi, University of KwaZulu-Natal, South Africa
Olalekan Adisa, University of Northampton, UK
Al-Amin Abba Dabo, University of Northampton, UK
Olushola Margaret Adisa, University of Zululand, South Africa

This chapter explores the complex relationship between family dynamics and entrepreneurship, particularly in the context of evolving societal norms and the COVID-19 pandemic. It critically examines the role of parental influence, family support, and the family environment in shaping entrepreneurial intentions and self-efficacy. It also discusses the challenges and strategies that entrepreneurs face due to family dynamics, drawing on real-world case studies. The chapter provides a comprehensive theoretical framework that integrates various perspectives on how family interactions influence entrepreneurial decisions. It also highlights the practical implications of the findings and suggests areas for future research.

Chapter 7
Authentic Leadership, Entrepreneurial Self-Efficacy, and Family Values.........182
Isaac Idowu Abe, SashBM LLC, USA
Ethel Ndidiamaka Abe, SashBM LLC, USA

The case study of this chapter disposes of the notion of profit maximization as the major driving factor of an organization. There are other salient visions that should drive profit maximization. Making a profit becomes the means to an end, not an end. The aim of this chapter is to find the probable connector between entrepreneurial self-efficacy, strong family values, and the kind of leader who possesses these combinations. The knowledge search revealed that a strong interpersonal relationship between the authentic leader to all stakeholders in the organization and the response to the same from the stakeholders to the leader is key to the success of the organization and authentic leadership. Effective leadership performance is linked to high competencies, skills, characteristics, and behaviors in meeting an organization's strategic objectives. The leader must be willing to communicate with employees within and relate to the external stakeholders in holding high the flagship of leadership.

Chapter 8
Can Entrepreneurial Skills Development Mitigate Poverty Among Dropped Out High School Teenage Mothers in North-Central Nigeria? 210
Louis Okon Akpan, National Open University of Nigeria, Nigeria

Recently, it was observed that a majority of girls dropped out of high schools due to early marriage, pregnancy, and poverty in North Central Zone of Nigeria. This led to the increase of out-of-school children which is now put at 12 million. Based on the conversation, the researcher seeks to examine whether entrepreneurial skills development do mitigate poverty among now teenage mothers in the zone. Two research questions guided the study. Furthermore, qualitative approach was used as research design for the study. Six focus groups were formed to elicit information for the study. Additionally, semi-structured interview was developed; thereafter, narrative analysis was adopted to analyse the data. It was discovered that teenage mothers were engaged in sewing and needle work, laali design, and mobile phone repairs. Similarly, it was also found that teenage mothers' acquisition of entrepreneurial skills has a great impact on their financial autonomy, poverty reduction, and improving the Nigerian economy.

Chapter 9
Succession and Survival Plan for Family Business: Lessons Learnt From Houshi Ryokan's Family Business..227
Ayansola Olatunji Ayandibu, University of Zululand, South Africa

This chapter explores the crucial aspect of succession planning and survival strategies for family businesses, drawing inspiration from the remarkable story of Houshi Ryokan, a traditional Japanese inn with a history spanning over a millennium. The chapter delves into the challenges faced by family-owned enterprises when transitioning leadership to the next generation and offers valuable insights into effective succession planning models. Finally, the chapter draws insightful lessons from Houshi Ryokan's family business journey, distilling key success factors and actionable strategies that can be applied by other family businesses seeking longevity and prosperity. By examining the exemplary case of Houshi Ryokan, this chapter provides invaluable insights for family business owners, managers, and advisors, offering practical guidance on navigating the complexities of succession planning and developing robust survival strategies to safeguard the legacy and prosperity of their enterprises.

Chapter 10
Knowledge Management in Family Firms: Perspectives From Management Research 250
Nelson Andres Andrade-Valbuena, Universidad Católica de la Santísima Concepción, Chile
Sergio A. Olavarrieta Soto, University of Chile, Chile
Miguel Zapata Perez, University of Chile, Chile

Knowledge management has received increasing attention from scholars. However, the understanding of this literature in the context of family firms remains fragmented. Different positions suggest that the inherent features of family businesses indicate the importance of considering the context. In this chapter, the authors aim to extend the understanding of knowledge management in the context of family firms. They achieve this by identifying the intellectual structure and evolution of the knowledge management corpus using bibliometric techniques applied to authors, universities, countries, and supranational regions. The analysis is complemented by the application of distance-based mapping techniques at the level of authors and publishers, enabling exploration of the historical dynamics and knowledge flows among management disciplines. The contribution of this chapter to the management literature lies in the provision of deep insights into this young and fertile stream of research, ultimately building bridges between both fields of research.

Chapter 11
Appraising the Influence of Social Support on Entrepreneurial Success and Sustainability 286
Olalekan Adisa, University of Northampton, UK

This chapter critically explores the intricate relationship between social support and entrepreneurial success, examining the profound impact that various sociocultural norms and factors have on the experiences of entrepreneurs. It delves into the distinctive roles of both individualistic and collectivistic cultures in shaping the availability and utilization of social support. The chapter concludes by underscoring the profound influence of social support on entrepreneurial success and sustainability. It highlights a range of strategies for optimizing social support, including proactive network building, promoting inclusivity, managing reliance on social support, and effective time management. It concludes by examining the significant influence of cultural and societal norms on entrepreneurial activities, with suggestions on future research on how to integrate theories or develop new theoretical frameworks for a more comprehensive understanding of the dynamics between social support and entrepreneurship.

Chapter 12
Empirical Investigation for Assessing the Causality of Entrepreneurship Ecosystem With Entrepreneurial Behavior and Attitudes Across Countries.....315
Ajay Kumar Singh, Department of Economics, School of Liberal Arts and Management, DIT University, Dehradun, India
Bhim Jyoti, Department of Seed Science and Technology, College of Forestry, Veer Chandra Singh Garhwali Uttarakhand University of Horticulture and Forestry, Ranichauri, India

This chapter measures the causal association of the entrepreneurship ecosystem (EE) with entrepreneurial behavior and attitudes (EBA) in 47 countries using log-linear regression equations. Entrepreneurship ecosystem index (ENECIN) and entrepreneurial behavior and attitudes index (ENBEATIN) are used as representative variables for EE and EBA, respectively, in regression analysis while ENECIN and ENBEATIN are the composite indexes of 12 and 11 indicators, respectively, using principal component analysis. These indicators are reported as key determinants of EE and EBA as per the global entrepreneurship monitor (GEM). There was a high level of diversity in EE and EBA across countries. EE has a positive impact on EBA and vice versa. The causation of EE and EBA with control variables is detected using the Granger causality test. The findings of this chapter are beneficial for global policymakers to implement appropriate policies to reinforce EE and EBA.

Compilation of References 354

About the Contributors 424

Index 432

Foreword

The family is the oldest institution in the history of human life on earth. Every individual born into the world comes from a family. Societies are formed by growing clusters of families; hence, the family is the core and microcosm of society. As a primary institution in the entrepreneurship ecosystem, it plays significant roles in stimulating entrepreneurial intentions and entrepreneurship in general. It significantly serves as a nurture-bed for support, building, rebuilding, and sustaining family businesses, globally. It is on record that over 80% of corporations and SMEs are family owned and/or managed.

The family among all other entities in the entrepreneurship ecosystem (such as business development cells, technology transfer offices, research organizations, marketing, and government initiatives) is the least understood as it is typically neither taught in colleges and universities nor even discussed in corporate training, leadership, and entrepreneurship development settings. Nevertheless, prior to, during, and after the 2008 global economic downturn and the novel Covid 19 pandemic, entrepreneurs made recourse to the family in times of business distresses.

For instance, entrepreneurs experienced a devastating impact on productivity, functionality of their businesses, sustainability, and on a personal level during COVID-19. The various conventions to curtail the effect of the rampaging virus dealt severe blows on entrepreneurship and entrepreneurs in more than describable dimensions. Entrepreneurs, forced to rethink their business models, to include the inevitable digitalization, about which, most of them were either not capable or ready to do, made recourse to support from their family members to raise funds and human capacity.

The interplay between family and entrepreneurship became increasingly realized. Even now, entrepreneurs and families need each other to become and remain resilient, successful, and sustainable in the ever-changing and challenging business environment. This book confirms that the family environment promotes entrepreneurial intentions through the instrumentality of role modelling and support for autonomy. It highlights the importance of navigating psychological, social, cultural, and physical support to turn hostile and uncertain situations into long-term opportunities. The needed range of strategies for optimizing social support, including initiative-taking network building, promoting inclusivity, managing reliance on social support, and effective time management, are discussed.

Regarding family businesses, this book strengthens the view that fostering psychological safety for team effectiveness is crucial because it significantly affects teams' performance, business effectiveness, innovative performance, and sustainable competitive advantage. Leadership flexibility emerged as a dominant factor for problem-solving in coping with family business during adverse socio-economic conditions. The forward-looking book goes further to explore the psychosocial challenges that entrepreneurs face while starting and/or running a business. It further shows how business-family life strategies and social support assist entrepreneurs to achieve and maintain psychosocial well-being. Succession planning remains vital to safeguarding a family business's legacy and prosperity.

The book displays the intricate interplay among the family, entrepreneurship and society in the manner that significantly highlights the influence of the family dynamics and processes in the development and sustainability of entrepreneurship that gender socio-economic development.

The writers meticulously display interesting cases that enhance understanding of entrepreneurship, family businesses, and family dynamics in a volatile environment and uncertain times. The focus of this book makes it a valuable source because twelve authors contributed from seven countries on five continents.

Ziska Fields
University of Johannesburg, South Africa

Preface

In the ever-evolving tapestry of human existence, there are moments that etch themselves into our collective memory, forever altering the way we perceive the world. The year 2020 is undoubtedly one such moment. It was a year that brought our bustling societies to an abrupt standstill, pushing us into uncharted territories. A silent adversary, in the form of an unknown pandemic, swept across the globe, grinding economic, social, and institutional activities to a halt. Governments took drastic measures to curtail its spread, instructing millions to "stay at home" for what seemed like an eternity.

But what is home, exactly? For many, it had become a place they rarely spent significant time in, as the relentless grind of work or business had kept them away from their families. The very concept of family and its interplay with the dynamics of society and entrepreneurship came into sharp focus during this period of isolation and uncertainty.

The journey of families during this time was not without its challenges. Reports emerged of increased domestic violence, declines in child well-being, parental depression, and disruptions in co-parenting quality. The toll on the mental and emotional well-being of parents and children was undeniable. Likewise, the world of entrepreneurship was not spared. Small and medium-scale entrepreneurs, whose livelihoods depended on daily, weekly, or monthly income from their businesses, were left grappling with uncertainty. What were once opportunistic ventures turned into necessities, as the pandemic reshaped the entrepreneurial landscape. Many small and medium-sized enterprises (SMEs) struggled, and their financial performance suffered as a result.

Yet, amidst the trials and tribulations, both families and SMEs displayed remarkable resilience. Families, often the bedrock of support and stability, proved their adaptability. SMEs, too, demonstrated an ability to pivot and weather the storm. It became apparent that there was an intricate interplay between family, society, and entrepreneurship that could be harnessed to drive recovery in a world forever altered by the COVID-19 pandemic.

It is against this backdrop that we present this edited reference book, *Cases on the Interplay Between Family, Society, and Entrepreneurship*. Our aim is to take a multi-disciplinary approach, inviting contributions from scholars in various fields, including Humanities, Business Management, Entrepreneurship, Human Resource Management, Innovations and Technology, Psychology, Governance, and Law. We encourage the use of the "teaching case" approach, as it allows us to explore real-world scenarios that shed light on the complex relationship between family, society, and entrepreneurship.

Our objectives in assembling this volume are manifold:

To provide valuable insights for policymakers at all levels, from organizations to governments, SMEs, and communities, on leveraging family and entrepreneurship for societal growth and enhancement.

To showcase the roles that family and entrepreneurship play in sustaining societal cohesion and coherence during challenging times.

To elucidate the intricate connections among family, enterprise, and societal development and sustainability.

To unravel the interplay between family dynamics and the formation of entrepreneurial intent, orientation, efficacy, development, and success.

To examine the impact of family on entrepreneurial resilience and socio-economic development.

To raise awareness about the crucial role of family and family support in fostering entrepreneurship and societal well-being.

To assist governments in proactively detecting adverse environmental and psychosocial changes, allowing them to implement policies that strengthen the family unit and address issues like mental health, substance abuse, and domestic violence in real-time.

To explore the potential synergies between family and entrepreneurship as a means to navigate future uncertainties.

This book is intended for a diverse audience, including entrepreneurs, scholars, governments, opinion leaders, human resource managers, educators, psychologists, psychotherapists, university and college students, consultants, family experts, legal practitioners, policymakers, and software developers.

The chapters in this book span a wide range of topics, each shedding light on different facets of the interplay between family, society, and entrepreneurship. From the role of families in entrepreneurial development to the effects of gender bias on self-efficacy, from the impact of COVID-19 on entrepreneurial activities to the historical and economic roles of families in turbulent times, these chapters offer a comprehensive exploration of this multifaceted relationship.

ORGANIZATION OF BOOK

Chapter 1

In this chapter, we delve into the crucial relationship between family support and entrepreneurial resilience, especially in the wake of global economic crises and the COVID-19 pandemic. Entrepreneurs have long acknowledged the significance of family resources in weathering crises and building sustainable businesses. This chapter seeks to shed light on how the integration of family resources into entrepreneurship can positively impact socioeconomic development and foster resilience. In an ever-volatile world, this chapter provides both theoretical insights and practical wisdom, illuminating the role of family in generating socioeconomic development through resilient and sustainable entrepreneurial activities.

Chapter 2

This chapter takes a unique approach to understanding the role of the family environment in shaping entrepreneurial intentions. Using a teaching case approach, it explores how family dynamics promote entrepreneurial intentions in diverse cultural contexts, including Chinese Indonesia, Turkey, and Tunisia. Guided by the Theory of Planned Behavior and Social Cognitive Theory, this chapter unveils the mechanisms through which the family environment, particularly role modeling and support for autonomy, influences individuals' entrepreneurial aspirations. By analyzing these cases, we gain valuable insights into the complex interplay between family and entrepreneurial intent.

Chapter 3

Resilience in entrepreneurship extends beyond individual coping abilities; it encompasses the capacity of businesses to thrive in adverse circumstances. This chapter presents a case study of a successful entrepreneurial company that navigated the challenges posed by the COVID-19 pandemic. It examines the strategies employed by the company from the perspectives of various resilience theories. Notably, leadership flexibility emerges as a key factor in effectively addressing family business challenges during socio-economic adversity. This chapter demonstrates how stress and vulnerability in high-risk situations can catalyze growth and empower entrepreneurship.

Chapter 4

Psychological safety within teams is a critical factor for effective performance in family businesses. This chapter reviews the literature to establish the link between psychological safety and employee engagement, satisfaction, performance, and team effectiveness in family firms. The findings underscore the importance of fostering psychological safety within family business teams. Teams that embrace high levels of psychological safety are shown to be significantly more effective than those lacking this critical element. This research highlights the essential role of psychological safety in building effective teams and achieving sustainable competitive advantage in family businesses.

Chapter 5

Entrepreneurship can be a relentless journey, blurring the boundaries between business and family life. This chapter explores the stress and challenges entrepreneurs face as they navigate these dual responsibilities. It delves into the importance of achieving balance and examines the role of business-family life strategies and social support in promoting entrepreneurs' psychosocial well-being. Drawing from existing literature, this chapter offers both practical and theoretical insights into addressing the psychosocial well-being of entrepreneurs in the context of their multifaceted lives.

Chapter 6

This chapter offers a comprehensive exploration of the intricate relationship between family dynamics and entrepreneurship. It critically examines the role of parental influence, family support, and the family environment in shaping entrepreneurial intentions and self-efficacy. Real-world case studies are used to illustrate the challenges and strategies entrepreneurs face due to family dynamics. The chapter provides a theoretical framework that integrates various perspectives on how family interactions influence entrepreneurial decisions. It also discusses the practical implications of these findings and identifies areas for future research.

Chapter 7

Profit maximization is not the sole driving force of successful organizations. This chapter challenges conventional wisdom by emphasizing the importance of strong family values and authentic leadership in achieving organizational success. It explores the interplay between entrepreneurial self-efficacy, family values, and authentic leadership, highlighting the significance of interpersonal relationships between leaders and stakeholders. The chapter offers recommendations for effective leadership and suggests that authentic leadership, marked by high competencies, skills, characteristics, and behaviors, plays a pivotal role in meeting strategic objectives.

Chapter 8

This chapter investigates the impact of entrepreneurial skills development on poverty reduction among teenage mothers in the North Central Zone of Nigeria. Through qualitative research, it explores the skills acquired by teenage mothers and their effect on financial autonomy and poverty reduction. The findings reveal that entrepreneurial skills significantly empower teenage mothers, contributing to both individual and societal economic improvement. This research highlights the potential of entrepreneurship as a means to uplift marginalized individuals and stimulate economic growth.

Chapter 9

Drawing inspiration from the resilient journey of Houshi Ryokan, a traditional Japanese inn with a history spanning over a millennium, this chapter explores the challenges of succession planning in family-owned enterprises. It provides valuable insights into effective succession planning models and survival strategies for family businesses. By examining the exceptional case of Houshi Ryokan, the chapter distills key success factors and actionable strategies that can guide other family businesses in safeguarding their legacies and prosperity.

Chapter 10

This chapter contributes to the understanding of knowledge management in the context of family firms. It employs bibliometric techniques to analyze the intellectual structure and evolution of knowledge management research in family firms. The analysis explores the historical dynamics and knowledge flows among management disciplines. By building bridges between knowledge management and family business research, this chapter offers deep insights into this fertile research domain, shedding light on the unique challenges and opportunities faced by family firms in managing knowledge effectively.

Chapter 11

This chapter delves into the intricate relationship between sociocultural norms, social support, and entrepreneurial success. It explores how individualistic and collectivistic cultures influence the availability and utilization of social support for entrepreneurs. The chapter emphasizes the profound impact of sociocultural factors on the entrepreneurial experience and offers strategies for optimizing social support. It highlights the influence of cultural and societal norms on entrepreneurial activities, paving the way for future research to develop a comprehensive understanding of the dynamics between social support and entrepreneurship.

Chapter 12

This chapter conducts a global analysis to measure the causal association between the entrepreneurship ecosystem and entrepreneurial behavior and attitudes in 47 countries. Through log-linear regression equations and the Granger causality test, it explores the impact of the entrepreneurship ecosystem on entrepreneurial behavior and vice versa. The findings offer valuable insights for global policymakers aiming to strengthen entrepreneurship ecosystems and enhance entrepreneurial behavior for economic growth and innovation.

As editors, we extend our gratitude to the contributors for their invaluable insights and dedication to this project. We hope that this book serves as a compass, guiding us through the intricate landscape of family, society, and entrepreneurship, helping us make sense of the challenges we face and illuminating the path toward a more resilient and prosperous future.

Ethel Ndidiamaka Abe
SashBM LLC, USA

Isaac Idowu Abe
SashBM LLC, USA

Chapter 1
Entrepreneurship and the Family:
Panacea for Resilience, Sustainability, and Socioeconomic Development

Ethel Ndidiamaka Abe
https://orcid.org/0000-0003-1670-6801
SashBM LLC, USA

Chidi Idi Eke
https://orcid.org/0000-0003-1407-7706
Mangosuthu University of Technology, Nigeria

EXECUTIVE SUMMARY

Entrepreneurship and the family are fast becoming the linchpin of contemporary societies, especially since the global economic crisis of 2008 and the COVID-19 pandemic. Entrepreneurs confirm that support from family in addition to resources developed by the family has contributed to their ability to be resilient in crises and grow sustainable businesses. Policymakers thus need to create a favourable environment to enable societies to derive the benefits of the interplay between entrepreneurial activities and family support in times of crisis. This chapter aims to contribute to an understanding of how an integration of family resources into entrepreneurship positively influences socioeconomic development and fuels resilience and sustainability. As the environment continues to be volatile, uncertain, complex, and ambiguous globally, this chapter provides a theoretical and practical understanding of the interplay between family and entrepreneurship, in generating socioeconomic development, through resilient and sustainable entrepreneurial activities.

DOI: 10.4018/978-1-6684-8748-8.ch001

SECTION 1: BACKGROUND OF ENTREPRENEURSHIP AND THE FAMILY

Introduction

This chapter examines the interplay among family and entrepreneurship to produce resilient and sustainable businesses (family enterprises) that contribute to socioeconomic development in economies. A family-based enterprise or business is a proprietary business (one-man-owned), joint venture, company, or any type of firm association whose control is in the hands of a specific family (Neubauer & Lank, 2016). In simple terms, family-based enterprises are owned, directed, and controlled by a family. This includes family businesses not entirely owned, controlled, or directed by a particular family but are influenced by the name of the enterprise as well as their traditions that have explicit or implicit influence on the enterprise through third parties. Even though the family does not control these enterprises, family strongly influences them, e.g., Siemens. The Siemens family holds about 10% of the equity of the company while over 600,000 other individuals and non-family equity holders hold the rest 90% equity.

This section will discuss entrepreneurship in history and the meaning and influence of family in entrepreneurship.

Entrepreneurship

Entrepreneurship involves assessing options and making decisions regarding opportunities to provide solutions to problems in the society (Santos, 2012). Chandler (1990) views it as engaging with ambiguities and separating between risks that are assessable and others which cannot. Scholars have variously described an entrepreneur as an innovator (Fang, Razzaq, Mohsin, & Irfan, 2022; Schumpeter, 1934); a person willing to use resources and capital for a new venture in the pursuit of profit (Drucker, Khan, Li, Safdar, & Khan, 2019; 1985); and a zealous individual with the ability to appraise opportunities vis-à-vis seen and unseen risks (Okpara, 2000). Entrepreneurship fosters a sense of tenure, long-term loyalty, understanding and calculated thinking and enables decision making in uncertain times (Ylijoki & Henriksson, 2017; Shapiro & Gross, 2008)

Entrepreneurship has been reported as an immense contributor to the socio-economic development of nations and vital provider of employment, innovations, and market competition (Anekwe, Ndubuisi-Okolo, & Nwanah, 2020). It evokes the sense of ownership, lasting commitment, learning and tactical thinking, and making of decisions under ambiguous circumstances. Entrepreneurs tailor their actions to produce benefits for society and the benefit of their businesses. They often start from seeing a gap or need/issue in the society that they can fill or address.

History of Entrepreneurship

Entrepreneurship originated since man's history when needs and resources were not in equilibrium. It began with finding help or solutions to needs of people which resulted to bartering of resources. In the days of trade by barter, individuals had needs as well as resources but the resource available to everyone were not sufficient to meet every need. For instance, an individual could have need for warm clothing but have abundant food, hence, he needed to identify someone who had warm clothing to exchange for food. The value of what was to be bartered was not considered then but the meeting of needs was supreme. The existence of the inequality led to other forms of exchanges which culminated in the development of money. Money, therefore, became a means of exchange for value.

The study of entrepreneurship dates to the 17th and early 18th centuries via the work of Richard Cantillon, an Irish - French economist. Additionally, Joseph Schumpeter (1883-1950) an Austrian-trained economic historian reputed as one of the 20th century proponents of the concept of entrepreneurship, theories on *business cycles* and the development of *capitalist economies* also contributed immensely to the discussion. He saw the entrepreneur as the foundation of capitalism – the supplier of the creativity that drives a capitalist financial system. Although, much of what was then known as entrepreneurship originated from business historians, research into the concept ran into serious methodological challenges giving room for attention to be given to corporations.

Business historians concentrated on comprehending the fundamental nature and reasons of the historical transformation of corporations, businesses, and markets. Schumpeterian explanation of entrepreneurship, unlike the contemporary management knowledge, does not focus primarily on new business formation, but rather on the several forms that innovative effort has led to and the part that innovative entrepreneurship plays in fostering transformation in the historical setting of business, commerce, and the economy (Jones & Wadhwani, 2006).

Historical sociologists from Germany investigated the role that religion and public relations played in the advancement of contemporary entrepreneurial attitudes to monetary gain and economic opportunity (Weber 1904, English translation 1930; Simmel 1908, English translation 1950; Sombart 1911). In the mid-1930s, economic and business historians examined the occupations of prominent eighteenth-century entrepreneurs to understand the reasons behind the Industrial Revolution (Ashton 1939; Wilson 1955). Their attention was focused on the innovative agency and subjective roles of people in the process of economic transformation (Jones & Wadhwani, 2006).

In the 1980s, entrepreneurship grew in legitimacy, especially in business schools (Cooper, 2005) with the energetic start-ups in technological sector, growth of venture capital funding, and the notable achievements of regional groups like the Silicon Valley in the United States. This is in line with Schumpeter's (1940) theorizing that entrepreneurship is the foundation for development in capitalist economies. Other early scholars of the concept of entrepreneurship had explained that the entrepreneur is someone whose attributes are somewhat underpinned by their socio-cultural (including family) and their innovation is a mixture of influences and elements already within reach (Jenks 1944, 1949).

Landes (1953) contended that culture consistently determined the supply of entrepreneurship and conversely sustainable economic development of certain nations. He had argued for instance, that although the family was contributory to France's business development the French entrepreneurs of the 19th century saw business as an inherent component of the family status instead of an end in itself (1949). This, he said, made the French entrepreneurs laid back, resulting in the poor performance of the French national economic performance. Several studies attributed to Landes for over half a century continued to argue for the significance of cultural factors, worth, and social approaches in the growth of entrepreneurial activity and conversely economic productivity of national economies (Landes 1969, 1999, 2003). However, recent historical studies have confounded Landes' claims about the French industry through the discovery that French enterprise was more industrially developed than was imagined (Smith 2006)

Business historians have posed arguments for (Sawyer 1954; Wiener 1981; Hannah 1984) and against (Gerschenkron 1962b, 1966) the role of national culture on the provision of entrepreneurship. In various instances, the fundamental assumption of research agenda has been found to be doubtful. Nevertheless, culture teaches the way that things should be done among people of that inkling. Cultural behaviours are handed down and learnt from the family right from cradle, though acculturation can occur during life. For instance, Godley (2001) in a comparative study using samples from migrant eastern European Jews who moved to London and New York found that those who migrated to New York were more likely to engage in entrepreneurial activities than those who moved to London. He explained that in the two host countries, the Jews embraced some new values which influenced their home culture. This finding indicated that the way the Americans and British valued entrepreneurship was different.

In an Uncertain Contemporary Time: A Summarised Vicissitude

Entrepreneurship goes beyond starting and running a business. The world has changed forever because of the Covid 19 pandemic and a new world id fast emerging. The question is what does it take to thrive in that world? Our post-Covid experiences should tell us that it is more than starting a business. This chapter suggests that there are phenomenal opportunities for investigating the relevance of entrepreneurship vis-à-vis the family and the formidable roots in place, in gendering further societal development, resilience and sustainability in present and emerging times. There are prospects for developing insight on the historical role of the family in the development of entrepreneurial mindset, intention, orientation, self-efficacy, and resilience, among others. Other prospects exist in the interplay between entrepreneurship and family in socioeconomic development, societal sustainability, and entrepreneurial resilience.

Family

Abe (2015) describes a family as the relationship existing among individuals found in a household. To be meaningful, this relationship must be influential in forming and shaping the behaviour of members in certain directions. Family members include *spouses, parents, adult children, and other relatives.* History documents the agreeable cyclical existence among families and entrepreneurship (Hamilton, Cruz, & Jack, 2017; Morck & Yeung, 2002; Narva, 2001). Entrepreneurship in the families is underpinned by the need to earn a living to support the family (Constantinidis, Lebègue, El Abboubi, & Salman, 2018; Winter, Fitzgerald, Heck, Haynes & Danes 1998). Other factors that play significant role in the inspiration of families to engage in entrepreneurial activities are the desire to amass wealth and lifestyle goals. Families are reported to be the clear incubators for the sprouting of business ideas and ventures and the origin of entrepreneurial endeavours is often in the family (Heck, Danes, Fitzgerald, Haynes, Jasper, Schrank, & Winter, 2006).

Some scholars report that a connection exists between family and entrepreneurship (Goel & Jones III, 2016; Gartner, 2001; Upton & Heck, 1997). Heck et al. (2006) observes that studies in the entrepreneurship field rarely recognises the fundamental family dynamics in family business ownership and its impacts on the business. A few recent interests have been shown to family ownership and its connection to the continuing result in existing businesses (Ward, 2016; Anderson & Reeb, 2003). Conversely, the interchange among the business and the family have been completely overlooked by most entrepreneurship studies (Aldrich & Cliff, 2003; Rogoff & Heck, 2003). Nevertheless, the Sustainable Family Business Model (SFBM) developed by Stafford et al. (1999) and empirically tested by Olson et al. (2003), fully incorporates the viewpoint of the family in connection to entrepreneurship and vice versa.

The SFBM portrays the family and entrepreneurial activities as inseparable, having intersecting systems that run concurrently to a reciprocal sustainability. Olson and her colleagues (2003) agree that the success in entrepreneurship can be traced to success in family, and that challenges in one will lead to challenges in the other. Aldrich's (1999) Networking theory supports this by positing that knowledge, resources, and collective support that people acquire are obtained via the web of social relationships. Contemporary entrepreneurship literature reports that entrepreneurs are found in a social background that is most likely, the family. For instance, a study conducted among women entrepreneurs in Morocco found that the entrepreneurial practices and family support given to participants in the study were influential in their entrepreneurial success (Constantinidis, et al., 2019). Aldrich and Cliff (2003) report that the family system traits like changes, assets, and customs are embedded in entrepreneurial development.

Nevertheless, several scholars have suggested that family responsibilities and values are usually placed contrary to those of the enterprise (Danes et al., 2005; Danes & Olson, 2003). This has led to the tendency to think the family as a structure that hinders the operation of the enterprise, and therefore, family should be seen a situation that needs to be managed (Danes et al., 2002; Ward, 1997). The SFBM allows an unbiased approach and does not suppose that the family is in contest with the enterprise. Instead, the SFBM accepts that interruptions generated by change are common and happen at the connexion of family and enterprise. The model further advises that addressing the challenges arising from disruptions could serve to lead the family or enterprise into needed constructive change that fosters sustainability rather than assuming conflict progresses into purely damaging skirmish that would adversely affect resilience and sustainability (Danes & Morgan, 2004; Danes et al., 1999).

In conclusion, every family enterprise mirrors the family that started and owns it, therefore, to understand an enterprise, the family behind it needs to be understood (Fukuyama, 1999).

SECTION 2. SOCIOECONOMIC DEVELOPMENT, RESILIENCE, AND SUSTAINABILITY

Introduction

The report that family enterprises account for approximately 80 per cent of the total global businesses (Gagné, Marwick, Brun de Pontet, & Wrosch, 2021; Sonfield & Lussier, 2003) is vital in strengthening the claim that families are pivotal in socioeconomic development of any nation. Neubauer and Lak (2013) are of the opinion that families build enterprises that develop quickly and live longer. They further report that in the annals of economic history, no establishment has powered economic growth like businesses that are family-based have. Metaphorically represented as a locomotive which through the snow moves powerfully, enterprises that are family-rooted in family play significant roles in nations. These roles played by family in entrepreneurship date back to the early days of Western civilisation.

One of the articles found among Aristotle's writings was a brief document on commercial activities of the Helenic Era, stating that the economic activities of individuals during those days were family-based. The situation did not change through the Roman Empire and the following Middle ages. It remained the same through to the emergence of the New World. Family-based enterprises were also influential in driving the early stages of economic growth practices in the industrialisation era. Copious proof to support this is provided by the expanse of fortunes amassed by families that were entrepreneurial during the early years of the United States, for example. Wealth from owning land (e.g., Astor family), invaluable riches from constructing railroad (e.g., the Vanderbilt family), wealth from baking (e.g., J. P. Morgan), and industry (e.g., Ford, Carnegie, and Rockefeller) were all respectively managed and led by powerful persons who equally strongly rooted in their various family clans.

Similarly, the post capital and management split of the 19th century witnessed the sustained leadership of family-owned enterprises in the way businesses were directed at the topmost levels. Furthermore, even though most of the well-known corporations of the contemporary times are owned by vast array of diverse and unnamed shareholders (I.e., they have lost the characteristic family-ownership look), enterprises that are family owned still create about 45% to 70% of the Gross National Product (GNP) of their individual nations (Neubauer & Lank, 2013).

The profound effect of family-owned enterprises in the recent decades has been highlighted again. During the recessions of the 80's and 90's on the two sides of the North Atlantic, family-rooted enterprises were identified as some of the most efficient 'locomotives' of their respective national economies because they were resilient in creating jobs, consistently paid taxes because they were successful enough to do so. Moreover, the family-based enterprises showed the swiftness and flexibility needed to navigate the troubled economic waters of their respective country economies effectively.

Similarly, Asian countries have experienced global admiration in the successful thriving of their economies because of the energetic, resilient, and flexibility of their family-based enterprises (especially in years before 1997).

The main aim of this chapter is to showcase how family and entrepreneurship contribute to socioeconomic development, and resiliently and sustainably drive national economies in and through turbulent times.

Socioeconomic Development

The family is at the centre of society, meaning that the way society develops are formed from the systems and practices of families. The number and size of families in a society is one of the indicators of the development of that society. Socioeconomic development integrates public interests in improving social policy and economic enterprises (Rahman, 2009). The fundamental goal of socioeconomic development is to foster sustained development in the well-being of individuals, groups, families, neighbourhoods, and the society. It encompasses consistent growth in the standard of living of national population, usually achieved by improving its stocks of human capital and technology.

For the past 25 years entrepreneurship has demonstrated itself as one of the major causes of macroeconomic growth in nations (Neumann, 2021). The possible socioeconomic effect of entrepreneurship has been widely investigated for over two decades, yet this field of research continues to grow. Most studies from several scientific fields provide empirical proofs that substantial positive macroeconomic effect of entrepreneurship exists (Atems & Shand, 2018; Audretsch & Keilbach, 2004a; Fritsch & Mueller, 2008). However, other empirical studies report that the macroeconomic effect of entrepreneurship may also be negative in some situations (Carree & Thurik, 2008; Andersson & Noseleit, 2011; Fritsch & Mueller, 2008). Possible reasons for these conflicting outcomes could be attributed to the complicated relationship among entrepreneurship and economic development. Factors such as business affiliation (Fritsch, 1996), the nation's level of advancement and the domestic bulk of small business owners (Carree et al., 2002) considerably affect the effect of entrepreneurship on socioeconomic development.

Nevertheless, scholars agree that the significant growth in entrepreneurship has made notable contribution to the output worth, increase in exports, employment, and tax in China, They also report that from year 2010 to 2014, tech entrepreneurship generated and accounted for 41.49% of the Chinese average GDP growth (Shan, Jia, Zheng, & Xu, 2018). In contributing to wellbeing of the population, Shan et al. (2018) report that invention patents developed by entrepreneurs represents almost 71% of national invention patents. Neumann (2021 also provides evidence that entrepreneurship mostly has positive impact on regional and socioeconomic development.

Resilience

For entrepreneurship to be consistently successful on the long run, entrepreneurs must be resilient to surmount challenging circumstances and surf from failures and disasters better than before. Resilience underscores the adaptive capability for rejuvenation after crisis (Larsson, Milestad, Hahn, & von Oelreich, 2016). The level of resilience of an organisation can only be determined after a severe disaster hence, for an enterprise to be said to be resilient, it must be able to renew itself after crisis (Linnenluecke, Griffiths, & Winn, 2012). According to Hamel and Valikangas, (2004), such ability to reinvent itself is the real result of the enterprise's natural or inherent resilience. Therefore, resilience is not just the ability to be stable, but effectively adjusting to outside influences.

Walker, Holling, Carpenter, and Kinzig, (2004) are of the view that resilience is the ability of an organization to soak up disruption and restructure while experiencing shift and yet maintain fundamentally the same role, formation, uniqueness, and feedbacks. For an environment, this can include struggling with overfishing or contamination, while for people, it entails a capability to handle all sorts of disruptions. For a business, it can include managing heightened competition or unpredictable demand. Resilience is a model for understanding how perseverance and change synchronise in living entities, organisations, and systems. Crucial to the discussion in this section is resilience as a way of grasping the dynamics of entrepreneurial business. The resilience method concentrates on the active relationship among cycles of steady and abrupt transformation and ponders on approaches to adjust to change (Folke, 2006)

The SFBM which theoretically derives from family systems theory gives equal acknowledgement to the family and entrepreneurship systems as well as the interplay among them that is vital to the attainment of mutual sustainability (Stafford et al., 1999). The family and the enterprise are both collective systems that are goal oriented and logical. They both transform accessible resources and challenges through interactive and resource activities into accomplishments. Accomplishments in the SFBM can be both tangible and subjective (Olson et al., 2003). The model also acknowledges that family and enterprise are both influenced by environmental and fundamental change, and that responses from both domains are different when changes happen. According to Stafford et al., (1999), the resilience of a family enterprise is attributable to the success of the enterprise and functioning of the family.

Family influenced enterprises create transgenerational wealth. Heck and Trent (1999) report that most of the enterprises in the United States of America are family businesses. The vision of the enterprising family's system is usually formed by a partnership that controls the entrepreneurial activities of the domestic unit, enterprise, and respective family members to realise the highest potential wealth for present and future generations of a family. Hence, the social system of an entrepreneurial family synergistically and significantly assists them to develop wealth that traverses several generations of the family (Heck et al., 2006).

Furthermore, Heck et al. (2006) report that in times of changes, family businesses re-evaluate and rebuild their systems of relationships, shared meaning, and structure to successfully navigate any changes. Where this is not done after a change, conflict, and anxiety results, adversely impacting the integration of the change and the past consolidated achievements of the enterprise's system. During changing times also, like the Covid-19 pandemic, pressures arise from the disruption, and these pressures could be innovative or disruptive. Innovative pressures highlight the present realities of an enterprise vis-à-vis the vision that members of the family enterprise hold for the business. These pressures develop momentum and enthusiasm that inspire members of the enterprise to employ productive behaviours that result in successful entrepreneurship. Disruptive pressures on the other hand, drag the entrepreneurial vision to the present reality and hinders the enterprise from going successfully forward towards its set targets.

Enterprises owned by families remain resilient (in accomplishment, strength, and camaraderie) through changing times by revisiting and rebuilding their business structures (models), assessing individual family member's connection and commitment to the enterprise, and the level of shared meaning (Danes et al., 2002). When achieved, this minimises the degree of disrupting pressures and maximises the degree of innovative pressures. Resilient enterprises view conflict as a common part of beneficial change (Danes & Morgan, 2004; Danes & Amarapurkar, 2000). These scholars further report that a certain degree of pressure functions as a creative tool capable of increasing accomplishment, vitality, and camaraderie of the family enterprise.

In conclusion, it is reported that about 90% of all incorporated businesses in the USA with about 17 million family businesses (including one-man businesses) are owned or controlled by families (Astrachan & Carey, 1994). Likewise, one-third of the entire *Fortune 500* companies are controlled by families while approximately 60% of businesses that are publicly traded are influenced by family (Bristow, 2000). Poza (2013) reports that family businesses contribute 64% of the GDP, or about $6 trillion, 85% of employment in the private sector, and approximately 86% of the total jobs generated in a decade. Similar reports are received from Germany, Spain, France, and so many other developed and developing nations. Larson et al. (2016) confirmed that a company that faced crises in 1970s and towards the end of 1990s, showed resilience because through transformation (re-organisation) and modifications (new market innovations), they boosted Sweden's organic food sector. The scholars further concluded that resilience enhanced sustainability amidst certain recognized trade-offs in that case.

Sustainability

Sustainability in entrepreneurship denotes, the advancing of a business cause beyond the accomplishment of the company. In general terms, development in economic, societal, and environmental dimensions can be said to be sustainable if the systems are able to solve present challenges without conceding the capacity of generations after to solve their own problems (Sauvé, Bernard, & Sloan, 2016). Elkington (1997) clarifies the matter about sustainability engaging the triple bottom line in addressing the sustainable factors and is explained vis-à-vis entrepreneurship. However, the United Nations designed several aggregate human development indices in addition to the Human Development Index (HDI) to measure the assessable aspects of human development. Scholars like Obraztsova and Chepurenko (2010) have combined these and the Sustainable Society Index (SSI) to define sustainable entrepreneurship.

Sustainable development has been widely accepted as, "the development that meets the needs of the present without compromising the ability of future generations to meet their own needs" (Brooks, 1990). Relating this concept to entrepreneurship, a sustainable entrepreneurship ought to:

- operate where governance is good and in an entrepreneurially pleasant environment.
- satisfy the requirements of the current entrepreneurs.
- do not negotiate the capacity of future advancement in business development,
- build the venture in a viable, but fair manner

Economic Sustainability and Entrepreneurship

Economic sustainability focuses on a firm's capacity to stay profitable to maintain its daily operations (Masocha & Fatoki, 2018), and add value to shareholders' investment (Sarango-Lalangui, Álvarez-García & del Río-Rama, 2018). The Global Reporting Index (GRI) (2019) summarily describes economic sustainability as the company's effect on the economic situations of its shareholders, the economic structures at the domestic, national, and world-wide levels. Entrepreneurship creates a stage for sustainable development to thrive. For instance, social entrepreneurial activities lead to sustainable businesses that invest major part of their excess revenue to strengthen their endeavours among communities that they work in (Jilenga, 2017). In addition to creating jobs, social entrepreneurship grows networks that constantly helps enterprises, thereby, producing new sustainable firms (Muralidharan & Pathak, 2018). The dynamic role of entrepreneurship in driving economic activity is broadly reported (Bhati, Qureshi, & Riaz, 2019). In line with the foregoing, this chapter deduces an important association between economic sustainability and entrepreneurship, and opines that entrepreneurship influences economic sustainability locally, nationally, and globally.

Societal Sustainability and Entrepreneurship

Societal sustainability factor elucidates the balance achieved by the social structures in terms of culture, tranquillity, wellness, and justice (Social Sustainability Policy, 2016). Furthermore, the concept is described as the equilibrium achieved among the firms' operations and the societal needs (Sarango-Lalangui et al., 2018). This comprises corporate social responsibility and the firm's ethically acceptable behaviour to the community in which it conducts its businesses activities.

According to Zhang and Swansona (2014), entrepreneurship performs a crucial role in the attainment of sustainable development. It is a strong facilitator of balance between business and society (Sulphey & Alkahtani, 2017), makes direct and indirect contributions to economic, social, and environmental sustainability (Forouharfar, Rowshan & Salarzehi, 2019).

According to Stenn (2016), the main driver of social entrepreneurship for instance, is societal purpose and effectiveness. Social entrepreneurs react to societal problems like gender-based violence, joblessness among young people, alcoholism and substance abuse in a socially, economically, sustainable, and environmentally responsive way. El Ebrashi (2015) posits that social entrepreneurship is different from other profit-maximising entrepreneurial activities because it contributes sustainable wealth to the public. Infact, Manyaka (2015) recognized social entrepreneurship as a remedy to the soaring levels of joblessness in South Africa. Additionally, entrepreneurial activities by social entrepreneurs leads to creation of social capital which fosters equity (Sivathanu & Bhise, 2013). In view of the scholars' opinions herein reviewed, this chapter theorises that an important association exists among entrepreneurship and societal sustainability.

Environmental Sustainability and Entrepreneurship

Environmental sustainability is the capacity of firms' systems to achieve a balance with its operations in enhancing the wellbeing of people in line with the needs of the environment (McGinn, 2009). This includes keeping emissions within the assimilative ability of the environment without harming it (Goodland & Daly, 1996). From Elkington's (1997) view, enterprises will be successful in their economic operations by using the natural resources from the environment and human resources from the community. The Triple Bottomline principles suggests that the three interconnected pillars of sustainable business practices must be wholly attended to, otherwise, the agenda to achieve sustainable development will be weakened (Amacha & Datane, 2017).

In contemporary societies, social entrepreneurs have been active in their activism against environmental degradation and should be praised for this. From climate change, to recycling, and environmental protection drives, and from new business creation to systemic entrepreneurial operations, the effect of entrepreneurship can be seen and felt locally, nationally, and globally. Van Cauwelaert (2015) applauds the effort of social entrepreneurs in initiating programs to create awareness, alleviation strategies, and pressurise policy makers to formulate policies and practices that are favourable to the environment.

Curiously, entrepreneurship cannot be induced by coercion, entrepreneurs usually are self-motivated and inspired by their personal vision to solve a problem or meet a need in the society. For instance, social entrepreneurs do not get forced by law to get involved in tackling environmental sustainability issues as part of their business but do so voluntarily unlike those in it to make profit (Muralidharan & Pathak, 2018). Hence, this chapter concludes that there is a linkage between entrepreneurship and environmental sustainability.

SECTION 3: CASE DESCRIPTION

The case of Grant Cardone as an entrepreneur, his enterprises and family, challenges and resilience are discussed below. These are evidenced information of how Grant Cardone as an individual transformed from drug addiction into an entrepreneur who grew and sustained several businesses and survived a global meltdown and a pandemic of global magnitude. He remained resilient through the challenges and mentioned at a time that he always consulted his wife and children in making decisions. The major concepts that informed the following discussion are family, entrepreneurship, challenges, and resilience. A brief introduction on Grant and his family background initiated the conversation in this section.

Grant Cardone

Grant Cardone is an American entrepreneur, motivational speaker, real estate investor, sales coach, and author. He is known for launching 10x Growth Conference. Grant is the chief executive officer of Cardone Enterprises, Cardone Capital, international speaker, entrepreneur, and author of The 10X Rule and creator of 21 best-selling business programs. Grant Cardone owns and operates seven privately held companies and a portfolio over four billion dollars in multifamily properties. Named the number one (#1) marketer by Forbes Magazine, Cardone is also the founder of the 10X Movement and The 10X Growth Conference, the world's largest business and entrepreneur conference (Cardone, 2023).

Family

Before all these, for many years Grant Cardone was addicted to drugs, and his life got worse. He was fired from jobs, overdosed, and in debt. He had lost his father when he was ten years old and this devastated him as he did not have a person to look up to for guidance, as his mother always tried to make ends meet for the family. He became rebellious and his grades dropped. He also became addicted to drugs and alcohol. Talking about his father's death and its impact on him and his school, he said

"It left a massive void in my life. The person I looked up to for guidance, success, an example of how to work, the provider, and the strength of the family was gone. My mother was left to manage three teenage boys and the little bit of money my dad had left, The family immediately went into turmoil with the loss of my dad. While my mom should have been experiencing the loss of her lifelong romance she was faced with the fear and uncertainty of raising five kids as a single mother. For many years I lived in grief, anger, and resentment over the loss of my dad. I watched in envy and resentment of other kids spending time with their dads and it enraged me. I had become openly rebellious, a problem at school, my grades dropped to just above passing levels and I turned to drugs and alcohol. I had become an outcast in the school system and a black sheep of the family. I hated everything; the schools, teachers, authority figures, my peers, and myself"

At the age of 25, he underwent rehabilitation and began focusing on his work. According to him,

"I was a good kid raised in a good family that turned bad because there was no father figure to guide, mentor, and discipline me. While treating the symptoms, treatment centers easily overlooked the root cause. The problem was not the drug for me. The problem was what got people like me to these drugs in the first place. And that was never addressed while I was in rehab. But I kept strong and left with a feeling of gratefulness, with the thought of going, just 24 hours without a drug. I have not used a drug, any kind of drug, since then".

Grant is a philanthropist and believes in giving back what you get. He is the founder of Grant Cardone Foundation, a charity that partners with community organisations, municipal agencies, corporations, and other non-profit entities to provide mentoring and financial literacy education to children in need, especially those who lack father figures in their lives. He created the foundation because of losing his father at a young age, which affected him emotionally, socially, and academically.

He considers entrepreneurs Warren Buffett and Mark Cuban and author Napoleon Hill as his mentors. Talking about mentors in his life, he said, "I have had many mentors. That does not mean I sit with them in person over coffee. I can be mentored by someone through one of their books".

Grant Carbone is a regular commentator and has made guest appearances on Fox News, Fox Business. CNBC, and MSNBC. He has written articles for publications like Forbes, Success Magazine, Business Insider, Entrepreneur.com, and Huffington Post. Grant Cardone is married and according to him, the day starts with wife and kids and getting dressed for meetings.

Entrepreneurship

After graduation, Grant Cardon did a few jobs but was fired from them soon. He was suffering from drug addiction at that time. After rehabilitation, he put his focus on sales and began working as a salesperson at the age of 25. Talking about it in an interview, he said

"I hated sales but also hated my life. I especially hated being broke, having dead-end jobs, and not being able to pay the rent. I also wanted to be sure that I didn't use drugs again. I had to channel all that into something. I used work – the crummy sales job that nobody liked. I decided I was going to get at that job".

At the age of 29, he started his first business, a consulting company for the automobile industry. Talking about his first business in an interview, he said, "I began consulting manufacturers and car dealers in the USA and Canada on how they could change their processes to be more consumer-friendly, fast, profitable, and effective with both customers and dealers. I still have that company today. I had an idea of changing the auto industry. And I think everybody could learn from this too. I went up to the auto industry and had them paying me to learn about this idea. They were essentially investors without being investors".

Soon, more people asked for more consulting sessions. People paid him to just speak about business ideas, he began traveling around countries and became a public speaker. He gives speeches on sales, marketing, branding, real estate, relationships, investments, wealth and more. In February 1989, he founded Grant Cardone Enterprises, a company that provides tools for individuals, salespeople, businesses, and executives to improve and maximise their opportunities.

In June 1990, he founded Grant Cardone Sales Training University, Miami, which offers training programs and courses on prospecting, sales, negotiations, closing, money and finances, and motivation.

In 1996, he founded a real estate company Cardone Capital in Miami/Fort Lauderdale Area. Since the mid-1990's, through his real-estate company, he has been investing in multi-family real estate across California, Arizona, Texas, North Carolina, Tennessee, Georgia, Alabama, and Florida.

In 2012, he made the single largest private acquisition in Florida, consisting of 5 properties. Along with it, Grant has worked with small and Fortune 500 companies, helping them grow their sales. Some of the famous companies he has worked with are Google, Sprint, Aflac, Toyota, GM, and Ford.

Books

In 2000, Grant Cardone turned author with his book "Control Without Confrontation: Automotive Sales Program". He wrote other sales programs and books like Maximizing Every Opportunity: Automotive Sales Program (2005), Selling: The Secret to Success (2008), Sell To Survive (2008), and If You're Not First, You are Last (2010). In 2011, he authored a book titled "The 10X Rule: The Only Difference Between Success and Failure". The best-seller book has Spanish edition and quotes and several summary versions. His other successful book is "The Millionaire Booklet: How to Get Super Rich" (2016), which has Hmong, Hebrew, and Norwegian editions.

He later published other books such as Sell or Be Sold: How to Get Your Way in Business and in Life (2011), Closer's Survival Guide (2011), Secrets of Selling (2014), Obsessed: How to Demand Business Success and Get It (2014), If You're Not First, You're Last LIB/e (2021) and Be Obsessed Or Be Average LIB/e (2021).

10X Movement

After writing the 10X Rule in 2011, he launched the 10X Growth Conference in 2017. People attend the three-day event to learn strategies from world-class entrepreneurs in one place. The event is the world's largest business and entrepreneur conference, and the phenomenon came to be known as the 10X Movement.

Television

In 2011, Grant Cardone made his television debut with his reality show 'Turnaround King", where he brings failing businesses back into track. The show aired on National Geographic. He then appeared in other television programs like Ed Mylett Show (2017), The America Dream (2017), Dhar Mann (2020), and CovAID Festival Live! (2020). In 2021, he appeared in season 2 of the reality TV show "Undercover Billionaire" broadcast on the Discovery Channel. The series features him going undercover, along with Monique Idlett-Mosley and Elaine Culotti, to a city and attempt to start a business with a valuation of one million dollars in 90 days. He also owns Grant Cardone TV, a channel where he has more than eighteen shows for entrepreneurs who want to increase their revenue, grow their brand, and create a legacy of wealth.

Grant has a self-titled YouTube channel, which he started on October 16, 2007. The channel has over six million subscribers. Although Grant Cardone is successful in business, he also faced several challenges and surmounted. The following section explicates some of these challenges, mostly, in his own words.

Challenges Faced by Grant Cardone

According to Cardone, "Before I had everything, I almost lost everything. Here is the story of how I faced lawsuits, loans, and some of the biggest challenges in my life" There have been numerous economic crashes before and Grant's businesses survived, but he predicts that nothing that happened before is to the extent of the upcoming one. In his own words, Cardone said

"One day in 2020, I got a phone call saying, "Something serious is about to happen. And it is going to roll out in stages." I made moves a few weeks before to protect myself. I learned from the 2008 recession that my mistakes cost me money and time. Moving forward, I had to plan so that when the next recession comes around, I don't fall into the same problems again".

Before the Great Recession

"Before 2007, banks would give out loans to anyone, and it did not matter. People were getting approved for million-dollar homes. At the time, I was trying to make practical and conservative investments. I used to put a lot of money down to buy a deal. If a deal were $8M, I would put $2.4M down. I had friends taking out $800K loans to get the same deal, and I thought it was mad. Nothing about it made sense except that it was too easy. Everyone was doing this".

Continuing, Cardone said, "It reminded me of the days I used to do drugs, and I could not say no. If you want to create true wealth for yourself, there are things you have to say "no" to. I did not lose one piece of property in 2007, 2008, 2009, or 2010. I never lost anything. Every one of my friends that did this nonsense lost everything they had.

"You Owe Us $50M"

I owed $50M to a bank, and the bank collapsed. The new bank says, "we need our money." They told me the value of the properties was down, and I responded with, "The value of the entire universe went down." They were trying to squeeze out every dollar of the people who had money. People that didn't have money folded so fast. The banks could not keep up"

The $60M Lawsuit

Another thing that happened to me was one of my "friends" sued me for $60M because I took an interest in possibly buying their business. I found out they were doing a bunch of shenanigans like lying to the bank and false reporting. I pulled out of that deal, and they claimed I ruined their business. The truth is their business was going to lose no matter what. But I was close… I almost lost everything.

You Cannot Sell Anything

My other two businesses were cut by two-thirds. I was living in Los Angeles and about to have my first baby. I had just married my wife, Elena. Then, I had to tell her we could not spend one penny on anything, and I didn't know how long it would last. Financially, I was terrified, and I realized how much it takes to be protected when things happen. We almost lost everything, and it was one of the most uncertain times in our lives.

How I Protected Myself

No education prepares someone for this obstacle. The only thing that I still had was my passive income. My cash flow from my rental properties kept me afloat, and the money never stopped. I talk all about how this vehicle has helped me prosper in any economy in my **Free Real Estate Training**.

Finally, this is the big takeaway: *It is easier to make money than to keep it. The more money you have, the more you need to protect it.* Make sure you have a cash-flowing asset that consistently brings you income every month, and learn how to protect that money so you do not lose everything you have" Grant Cardone

Resilience and Sustainability

Grant's story of being devastated by the 2008 recession and then turning it into a huge empire is all over the public space on the internet. In several discussions and interviews online, several factors were attributed to the reasons why the Grant Cardone empire did not sink during the 2008 global economic crisis and the Covid-19 pandemic. According to Cardone, "recession shows you how solvent/insolvent your business is". He went through grief and pain, however he started piecing in information and past experiences. He suggests that going to zero on everything and from there, determining where you are and who you are during crisis underpins how you rebuild the entire business in your mind. It is a hard thing that you confront and must go through it as an entrepreneur. You and your family (your spouse) need to make decisions on how to get bigger. It all begins with a decision.

In a recession, there are fewer people to compete with because a lot of people throw in the towel. When the business weather changes, you change too. Study successful people. Grant stated inter alia that to remain in business through the many challenges, he needed to create new challenges, refocused, and determined what needed to be done. He went on to say that out of his three businesses in 2008, two were 'slaughtered'

Grant Cardone further suggests that people in business should keep track of everything that matters to you. This is one of his finest bits of advice. To put it another way, maintain track of your progress and make sure you are on track. If you are not seeing results, it is time to rethink your approach and make some adjustments. Continue taking steps in the wrong direction is the last thing you want to do. It is lot simpler to stay motivated and push things to the next level once you know your strategy is working. That is something Grant Cardone is all too familiar with.

He further advices that businesses in a recession should "reboot" to stay solvent and keep growing. Unfortunately, most business owners get it totally wrong and that causes them to stay stuck at a low level or fail entirely at times like these. Recession is the perfect time to take risks (and Grant's story that proves it). One driving belief that helps Grant continually achieve at his highest level is to continue to thrive no matter how bad things get. When it comes to building success — even in hard times like these — Grant is a voice you want to listen.

SECTION 4: CASE ANALYSIS, DISCUSSIONS, AND CONCLUSIONS

The key factors under examination in this chapter are namely, family, entrepreneurship, socio-economic development, resilience, and sustainability. Having identified the central character in this case, i.e., Grant Cardone and his businesses through a review of online documented evidence, we found that Cardone plays multiple roles in his 7 businesses, including the role of Chief Executive Officer (CEO) and Founder. He also demonstrated his wife's and children's roles in his businesses as well as the impact that his father's death had on him, when he passed while Grant was only 10 years old. His mother's actions towards mustering sustenance him and his siblings only days after his father's death left indelible impacts in his young mind. In almost all the interviews that Mr. Carbone conducted with bloggers and others, the thread of the family showed conspicuously. The variables reviewed in the literature namely, family, entrepreneurship, socioeconomic development, sustainability and resilience will be discussed in the light of the case study below.

Family

Grant Cardone as a family member and head - implication on Grant Cardone as an Entrepreneur

Grant was a 10-year-old child whose family revolved around his father and mother. Theirs was a nuclear family where children, and both parents lived in a large town home until the father died and their mother sold their home for a smaller living space. In line with Abe (2015), the unfolding situation in addition to the precedent ones informed Grant Cardone's entrepreneurial outcome. According to Mr. Cardone, he needed his father to coach and mentor him through life, but his absence embittered him and made him angry. Seeing the mother crash their lifestyle to reduce the burden of survival broke his young mind and he determined in later life that he will never 'contract but expand' in everything he needed to do. In line with Morck and Yeung (2002) and Narva (2001), the cyclical effect of the influence of the family in shaping entrepreneurial mindset is demonstrated in Grant Cardone's entrepreneurial journey. Directly or indirectly, the family incubated the germination of business ideas (Heck et al., 2006) in Grant's life.

Mr. Cardone reported that he could not hold down employment and did not want to work for companies as he easily reached his target and saw ceilings that made no provision for growth. But when he started his own businesses, not even recessions and severe economic downturns could stop him. It is reported that during the 2008 economic recession, he was devastated but later turned it around to a huge empire (Growth, 2012). Although some scholars reported that a relationship exists between family and entrepreneurship (Anderson & Reeb, 2003; Gartner, 2001; Upton & Heck, 1997), others like Heck et al., (2006) indict literature's inability to clearly recognise the dynamic influence of family in entrepreneurship and its impact on business. This is justifiable because, as in the case of Grant Cardone, his upbringing, education, addiction, and rehabilitation can easily bring complexities to his entrepreneurial success and cofound findings. However, several scholars agree that the linkage between entrepreneurship and family have been completely ignored (Aldrich & Cliff, 2003; Rogoff & Heck, 2003).

The case in review agrees with the SFBM which demonstrates that the interplay among entrepreneurship and family is not separable, because of the intersections that run concurrently to an agreeable sustainability. The case may not be supported by Olson et al.'s (2003) claim that success in entrepreneurship is traceable to success in family as the death of the key actor's father cuts off such claims although Grant himself reported that his father saved and bough their home and he does not believe in such, rather, he believes in investing and taking risks. However, Aldrich's (1999) Networking theory could explain the knowledge, resources, and collective support that Grant Cardone drew from in his business activities. He stated that he always made decisions by primarily talking with his wife, and children (to keep them abreast of where they as a family and a business are headed to).

A man armed with the support of his wife and understanding children is a confident man. This should embolden the entrepreneur to make decisive and representative decisions bearing the interest and security of his family in mind. Grant Cardone confidently demonstrates his entrepreneurial prowess in his ability to take risks and make astute business decisions that result in success. Take for instance, how Grant Cardone turned his business into a multibillion-dollar empire in the midst of a global recession that hit businesses globally. This is in line with the findings of Constantinidis et al. (2019) and Aldrich and Cliff (2003) and confounds Danes et al. (2005) and Danes and Olson (2003) who suggest that family values and duties run contrary to that of business and needs to be managed (Danes et al., 2002; Ward, 1997). Cardone's family and business appropriately demonstrate the postulations of SFBM that the family is not in contest with the enterprise. Rather, the SFBM recognizes that interruptions generated by change are common and happen at the connexion of family and enterprise and recommends that addressing the challenges arising from disruptions could serve to lead the family or enterprise into needed constructive change that fosters sustainability, It does not assume that conflict progresses into purely damaging skirmish that would adversely affect resilience and sustainability (Danes & Morgan, 2004; Danes et al., 1999). The analysis of Grant Cardone and his businesses in this chapter is in line with Fukuyama (1999),

Entrepreneurship

Grant Cardone as an Entrepreneurship Organisation

Grant Cardone is an entrepreneur whose entrepreneurial activities align to Chandler's (1990) definition. Cardone repeatedly engaged with ambiguities during flourishing and downturn times in his business and separated assessable risks and inaccessible risks. He assessed options and made decisions regarding opportunities to provide solutions to problems in the society. In tandem with Schumpeter (1984), Grand Cardone is an innovator, a person willing to utilise resources and capital for a new venture in the pursuit of profit (Drucker, 1985); and a zealous individual with the ability to appraise opportunities vis-à-vis seen and unseen risks (Okpara, 2000).

The entrepreneurial activities of Grant Cardone businesses confirm the claims of Anekwe et al. (2020) who extol the contributions of entrepreneurship to national socioeconomic growth, employment, creativity, and competitiveness. Grant founded several business enterprises including the Grant Cardone Sales Training University in Miami. Cardone Capital a real estate company alone employs about 375 people, and invests in multi-family property across California, Arizona, Texas, North Carolina,

Tennessee, Georgia, Alabama, and Florida. These validate the contributions of Grant Cardone businesses to the national economy. The organisation and Grant employ several hundreds of people has innovatively introduced the *Unbreakable Challenge* to prepare business community for the next economic crisis. Hundreds of thousands of people globally registered and attended this online event.

Grant Cardone tailored all the entrepreneurial activities to produce benefits for society and his organisation. The company sees gaps and takes every necessary step to fill the gap. For instance, the Grant Cardone Unbreakable System is an innovative business model that offers an efficient approach to growing businesses and building a brand. This system is a blueprint for thousands of successful businesses, including many well-known brands, and aspiring entrepreneurs and small business owner. The course is not your everyday over-the-shoulder step-by-step training, it is more of a formula (approaches and strategies) to develop, expand, or scale businesses to be unbreakable. This follows the Schumpeterian explanation of entrepreneurship, unlike the contemporary management knowledge which focuses primarily on new business formation. Schumpeterian explanation rather focuses on the several forms that innovative effort can lead to and the part that innovative entrepreneurship plays in fostering transformation in the historical setting of business, commerce, and the economy (Jones & Wadhwani, 2006). Additionally, scholars have attributed the family to being a major factor underpinning innovation in an entrepreneurial setting (Jenks 1944, 1949; Cochran 1950, 1960).

The emergence of Covid-19 pandemic in the global economic space has changed the world forever. The way business is idealized and implemented has changed. Grant Cardone is positioned to answer questions relating to what it takes for businesses to thrive in the post-Covid-19 era. The business under review has succinctly shown that there are prospects for enhancing the significance of entrepreneurship vis-à-vis the family and the values in place, in fostering further societal development, resilience and sustainability. These prospects manifest from the historical role of the family in the development of entrepreneurial mindset, intention, orientation, self-efficacy, and resilience. In this new era, entrepreneurship is more than starting a business. It involves engaging with family to strengthen what it stands for to enable it influence entrepreneurship for societal rebooting, development, business resilience and sustainability.

Socioeconomic Development

Society is built up by the systems and practices of families in them. In any economy, tangible indicators are not enough to describe the contributions of entrepreneurship to development though Schumpeterian era economics scholars agree that entrepreneurship stimulates economic and societal (social) growth. Obraztsova and

Chepurenko (2010) perceive that socioeconomic development need to be assessed with measures other than the Gross Domestic Product (GDP), but in sustainable livelihood, long and satisfied healthy life, and access to good education. This is because, according to these scholars, a globally competitive economy should derive input from everyone's ability. Hence, using the GDP as a measure of entrepreneurial benefit has become debatable in developed economies.

However, the Global Entrepreneurship Monitor (GEM) provides index for assessing entrepreneurial impact on participating nations by categorising them into

a) Factor-driven economies
b) Efficiency-driven economies
c) Innovation-driven economies

The United States of America where Grant Cardone businesses are situated is categorised among the innovation-driven economies. These economies are also known as human-factor economies. Human development in entrepreneurship is concerned with the awareness of human capability. It focuses on individual potentials and what they can do to harness these potentials as well as the liberty that they can enjoy in life. As Obraztsova and Chepurenko (2010) reported, a sufficient measure for human capital development in business could be based on a comprehensive aggregate statistic, namely, Human Development Index in Entrepreneurship (HDIE), which is based on UNDP's Human Capital Development Index (HDI) (Akder, 1994).

The examined case is built from developing human capacity using every methodology. This approach focuses on not only income but on people as actors of entrepreneurship and economic development. Here, small level of human capital development reflects on the quality of social life and societal wellbeing on the one hand and predicts business activity on the other hand. Hence, there must vitally be a certain level of innovative human capital development, to explore the prospect for new businesses and to obtain necessary skills for entrepreneurship to be successful (Obraztsova & Chepurenko, 2010).

The socioeconomic contributions of entrepreneurship have also been indicated by free expression, skills, training, family structure, business background, professional history, innovativeness, inspiration and so on (Boswell, 1972; Bates, 1985, 1990; Preisendörfer & Voss, 1990; Dahl & Reichstein, 2005). But all the indicators vary very much between individuals, and between countries. However, the HDIE added three very significant dimensions of advancement namely, entrepreneurs' sustainable wellness, organisational sound health and enterprise longevity, and adequate training and entrepreneurial skills of entrepreneurs. In this context therefore, the entrepreneurial activities of Grant Cardone contribute to the national socioeconomic development because of mainly the training programmes developed and facilitated by the organisations across all levels of business organisations in the United States and elsewhere globally.

Resilience

Grant Cardone himself reported that he had three businesses that went into the 2008 recession and two were "slaughtered" leaving one. He worked tirelessly using various methodologies including going to zero and making pertinent decisions to build an empire from a recession. According to Larsson et al. (2016), the ability of a business to rejuvenate itself after a crisis is called resilience. Similarly, Linnelnluecke et al (2012) affirm that resilience is only measurable post-crisis. Grant Cardone organisation has shown resilience in bouncing back to not three businesses, but tens of them since 2008. In the view of Hamel and Valikangas, (2004), such capacity to reinvent itself can be attributed to the organisation's inherent resilience, which could be traceable to the leadership of Mr Cardone's natural resilience, in this case.

According to Heck et al. (2006) and Danes et al. (2002), family-influenced enterprises re-evaluate and restructure their systems, commitment, and values to be able to successfully navigate those times. The Grant Carbone organisation displayed how their business survived the 2008 global economic meltdown and Covid-19 pandemic era. Grant said that he usually discussed with his wife first, marshalled alternatives, made choices and together they would decide about the way forward and thereafter, call their children into the plot. This is a way of mitigating post-crises interpersonal conflicts as shared meanings and values will assist each person to take responsibility and be responsible to the future of the enterprise. Hence, it can be rightly said that resilient businesses see crises as a common enemy that must be conquered or a wild horse that must be tamed with all hands on deck. Grand Cardone businesses, from the analysis of the case, is a resilient organisation.

Sustainability

Sauvé et al. (2016) agree with the common definition of sustainable development in the economic, social, and environmental dimensions using durable systems capable of solving current problems and not compromising its capacity to assist future generations in solving their own challenges. Furthermore, Obraztsova and Chepurenko (2010) suggest that sustainable entrepreneurship is one operating in an environment where excellent governance is practiced, and the needs of current entrepreneurs are met in addition to an uncompromised capacity for future advancement in entrepreneurship in an ethical manner.

In this context, the Grant Cardone business empire can be deduced to be such a sustainable business, since the United States business environment met all the criteria needed for sustainability. In line with Sauvé et al. (2016), the organization under review demonstrates capacity to address present day challenges faced by entrepreneurs in need of training and leaving systems that can assist future generations in doing same. The Grant Cardone System attests to this and could be further explored at the Unbreakable Business System Online where the Money and Mindset System, Marketing System, Communication System, and a host of others are made available for business practitioners to access.

Scholars have also alluded to many contributors to societal development. For instance, Zhang and Swansona (2014) report the role of entrepreneurship in the achievement of sustainable social development while Sulphey and Alkahtani (2017) agree that entrepreneurship facilitates balance among business and society. Forouharfa et al (2019) conclude that entrepreneurship makes direct and indirect contributions to economic, social, and environmental sustainability. In addition to job creation, real estate, academic institution, and computer programmes and new technologies, the reviewed entity as a business organization has made tremendous sustainable contributions to socioeconomic development in the United States.

CONCLUSION

The SFBM recommends that often, exchange of resources (for e.g., uses or conversion of time, energy, and money), as well as interpersonal exchanges (for e.g., interaction, personal dealings, dispute management) from either the family or enterprise could accelerate or impair sustainability of family-based enterprises. The interpersonal dynamics in Grant Cardone's life both as a growing child who lost his father early in life and a happily married man did aggregate to result in resilient and sustainable entrepreneurship that contribute to socioeconomic development. In history, family-based enterprises showed the swiftness and flexibility needed to navigate the troubled economic waters of their respective country economies effectively. Since 2008, Grant Cardone has contributed to national and regional sustainable socioeconomic development in line with the United Nations' HDI and Obraztsova and Chepurenko's (2010) HDIE for measuring socioeconomic contribution to the economy. Over the years, Grant says, that he has seen some of his businesses got completely run over, others he learnt from, and others that he repositioned so that next time a crisis hits, he is better equipped (Grant. 2023).

Grant Cardone organisation catalysed the expansion of marketing business and leads the way by introducing range of other marketing products in the United States. He works with small companies and Fortune 500 companies like Google, Sprint, Aflac, Toyota, GM, Ford, and thousands more. Mr Grant Cardone predicts that ever business and individual will be affected in the next crisis and needs to prepare to have an unbreakable system of income. Grant Cardone online businesses has millions of customers including thousands of corporate clients; multi-unit rental business, and live-event business that could be the largest globally. He built his $5Billion portfolio of multifamily properties from scratch and named number one (#1) marketer to watch in 2017 by Forbes Magazine.

"Grant urges his followers and clients to make success their duty, responsibility, obligation, and to rise above outdated, unworkable middle-class myths and limitations to achieve true freedom for themselves and their families. His straight-shooting viewpoints on leadership, the economy, small business, retail sales, employment, and headlines have made him a valuable resource for media seeking commentary and insights on real topics that matter". Grant Cardone

Sustainability demands change after crisis, not a mere alteration. Although a case study is not generalisable, the application of the insights of Grant Cardone business development and its effects for a transformative business movement is illuminating. Teaching case studies play roles in knowledge creation around adaptive phases in resilience and sustainability of the business ecosystem that is necessary for businesses to overcome crisis. The reviewed case should help in creating a better vibrant enterprise theoretical model for business crisis management that can address the absence of useful models in this area.

REFERENCES

Abe, E. N. (2015). *The connection between work-life balance (WLB) and a sense of coherence (SOC) at a municipality in the South African public sector* [Doctoral dissertation].

Amacha, E., & Dastane, O. (2017). Sustainability Practices as Determinants of Financial Performance: A Case of Malaysian Corporations. *The Journal of Asian Finance, Economics and Business*, *4*(2), 55–68.

Andersson, M., & Noseleit, F. (2011). Start-ups and employment dynamics within and across sectors. *Small Business Economics*, *36*(4), 461–483. doi:10.100711187-009-9252-0

Anekwe, I. R., Ndubuisi-Okolo, P & Nwanah, C. P. (2020). *Entrepreneurship Management: A Panacea for Social Economic Development in Nigeria*. Academic Press.

Ashton, T. S. (1939). An eighteenth-century industrialist: Peter Stubs of Warrington, 1756-1806 (No. 13). Manchester University Press.

Astrachan, J., & Carey, M. (1994). *Family Businesses in the United States Economy*. Paper presented to the Center for the Study of Taxation, Washington, DC.

Atems, B., & Shand, G. (2018). An empirical analysis of the relationship between entrepreneurship and income inequality. *Small Business Economics*, *51*(4), 905–922. doi:10.100711187-017-9984-1

Audretsch, D., & Fritsch, M. (2003). Linking entrepreneurship to growth: The case of West Germany. *Industry and Innovation*, *10*(1), 65–73. doi:10.1080/1366271032000068104

Bates, T. (1985). Entrepreneur Human Capital Endowments and Minority Business Viability. *The Journal of Human Resources*, *20*(4), 540–554. doi:10.2307/145683

Bates, T. (1990). Entrepreneur Human Capital Inputs and Small Business Longevity. *The Review of Economics and Statistics*, *72*(4), 551–559. doi:10.2307/2109594

Bhatt, B., Qureshi, I., & Riaz, S. (2019). Social entrepreneurship in non-munificent institutional environments and implications for institutional work: Insights from China. *Journal of Business Ethics*, *154*(3), 605–630. doi:10.100710551-017-3451-4

Boswell, J. (1972). *The Rise and Decline of Small Firms*. Allen and Unwin.

Bristow, D. K. (2000). *Composition of US stock exchanges firms*. Unpublished study of the Directors Institute, Los Angeles, UCLA.

Brooks, D. B. (1990). Beyond catch phrases: What does sustainable development really mean? *The IDRC Reports / International Development Research Centre*, *18*(4), 1–2.

Cardone, G. (2022). *Before I had everything, I almost lost everything. Here's the story of how I faced lawsuits, loans, and some of the biggest challenges in my life*. https://gctv.com/almost-lost-everything/

CardoneG. (2023a). *About*. https://grantcardone.com/about/

Cardone, G. (2023b). *Grant Cardone on Learning from the 2008 Crash & Preparing for This One (Part 1)*. https://www.youtube.com/watch?v=ElE_MgDmrbY

CardoneG. (2023c). https://wikibio.in/grant-cardone/#f+71761+1+1

Carree, M., Van Stel, A., Thurik, R., & Wennekers, S. (2002). Economic development and business ownership: An analysis using data of 23 OECD countries in the period 1976–1996. *Small Business Economics*, *19*(3), 271–290. doi:10.1023/A:1019604426387

Carree, M. A., & Thurik, A. R. (2008). The lag structure of the impact of business ownership on economic performance in OECD countries. *Small Business Economics*, *30*(1), 101–110. doi:10.100711187-006-9007-0

Chandler, A. (1990). *Entrepreneurship and Economic Growth*. Harvard University Press.

Constantinidis, C., Lebègue, T., El Abboubi, M., & Salman, N. (2019). How families shape women's entrepreneurial success in Morocco: An intersectional study. *International Journal of Entrepreneurial Behaviour & Research*, *25*(8), 1786–1808. doi:10.1108/IJEBR-12-2017-0501

Dahl, M., & Reichstein, T. (2005). *Are You Experienced? Prior Experience and the Survival of New Organizations*. Aalborg: DRUID Working Paper, 05-01.

Drucker, P. F. (1985). *Innovation and Entrepreneurship. Practice and Principles*. Heinemman.

El Ebrashi, R. (2013). Social entrepreneurship theory and sustainable social impact. *Social Responsibility Journal*, *9*(2), 188–209. doi:10.1108/SRJ-07-2011-0013

Elkington, J. (1997). The triple bottom line. *Environmental management: Readings and cases, 2*, 49-66.

Fang, Z., Razzaq, A., Mohsin, M., & Irfan, M. (2022). Spatial spillovers and threshold effects of internet development and entrepreneurship on green innovation efficiency in China. *Technology in Society*, *68*, 101844. doi:10.1016/j.techsoc.2021.101844

Folke, C. (2006). Resilience: The emergence of a perspective for social–ecological systems analyses. *Global Environmental Change*, *16*(3), 253–267. doi:10.1016/j.gloenvcha.2006.04.002

Forouharfar, A., Rowshan, S. A., & Habibollah Salarzehi, H. (2019). The Relationship between Social Entrepreneurship and Sustainable Development from the Social Expertsâ Points of View. *Quarterly Journal of Environmental Education and Sustainable Development*, *7*(4), 70–82.

Fritsch, M. (1996). Turbulence and growth in West Germany: A comparison of evidence by regions and industries. *Review of Industrial Organization*, *11*(2), 231–251. doi:10.1007/BF00157669

Fritsch, M., & Mueller, P. (2008). The effect of new business formation on regional development over time: The case of Germany. *Small Business Economics*, *30*(1), 15–29. doi:10.100711187-007-9067-9

Gagné, M., Marwick, C., Brun de Pontet, S., & Wrosch, C. (2021). Family business succession: What's motivation got to do with it? *Family Business Review*, *34*(2), 154–167. doi:10.1177/0894486519894759

Gerschenkron, A. (1962a). *Economic Backwardness in Historical Perspective*. Belknap Press.

Gerschenkron, A. (1962b). Social Attitudes, Entrepreneurship, and Economic Development: A Comment. *Explorations in Entrepreneurial History, 6*, 245-72.

Gerschenkron, A. (1966). The Modernization of Entrepreneurship. InWeiner, M. (Ed.), *Modernization: The Dynamics of Growth*. Basic Books.

Gibb, A. (2004). *Effective Policies for Small Business. A Guide for the Policy Review Process and Strategic Plans for Micro, Small and Medium Enterprise Development. OECD/United Nations Industrial Development Organization*. UNIDO.

Global Reporting Index (GRI). (2019). *Sustainability reporting guidelines*. Available: https://www.globalreporting.org/Pages/default.aspx

Godley, A. (2001). *Jewish immigrant entrepreneurship in New York and London, 1880-1914*. Palgrave. doi:10.1057/9780333993866

Goel, S., & Jones, R. J. III. (2016). Entrepreneurial exploration and exploitation in family business: A systematic review and future directions. *Family Business Review*, *29*(1), 94–120. doi:10.1177/0894486515625541

Goodland, R., & Daly, H. (1996). Environmental sustainability: Universal and non-negotiable. *Ecological Applications*, *6*(4), 1002–1017. doi:10.2307/2269583

Growth, A. (2012). *Sustainability or growth? Why not both?* https://www.businessinsider.com/grant-cardone-on-why-companies-fail-2012-4

Halis Akder, A. (1994). *A Means to Closing Gaps: Disaggregated Human Development Index*. Human Development Report Office.

Hamel, G., & Valikangas, L. (2004). The quest for resilience. *icade. Revista de la Facultad de Derecho (Montevideo)*, (62), 355–358.

Hamilton, E., Cruz, A. D., & Jack, S. (2017). Re-framing the status of narrative in family business research: Towards an understanding of families in business. *Journal of Family Business Strategy*, *8*(1), 3–12. doi:10.1016/j.jfbs.2016.11.001

Hannah, L. (1984). Entrepreneurs and the Social Sciences. *Economica*, *51*(203), 219–234. doi:10.2307/2554542

Heck, R. K., Danes, S. M., Fitzgerald, M. A., Haynes, G. W., Jasper, C. R., Schrank, H. L., . . . Winter, M. (2006). The family's dynamic role within family business entrepreneurship. Handbook of research on family business, 80-105.

Jenks, L. H. (1944). Railroads as an Economic Force in American Development. *The Journal of Economic History, 4, 18-20.* doi:10.1017/S002205070008400X

Jenks, L. H. (1949). Role Structure of Entrepreneurial Personality. In Change and the Entrepreneur: Postulates and the Patterns for Entrepreneurial History. Harvard University Press. doi:10.1017/S002205070008400X

Jilenga, M. T. (2017). Social enterprise and economic growth: A theoretical approach and policy recommendations. *International Journal of Academic Research in Accounting, Finance and Management Sciences*, *7*(1), 41–49.

Jones, G., & Wadhwani, R. D. (2006). *Entrepreneurship and business history: Renewing the research agenda* (Vol. 7). Harvard Business School.

Khan, N. U., Li, S., Safdar, M. N., & Khan, Z. U. (2019). The role of entrepreneurial strategy, network ties, human and financial capital in new venture performance. *Journal of Risk and Financial Management*, *12*(1), 41. doi:10.3390/jrfm12010041

Landes, D. (1949). French Entrepreneurship and Industrial Growth in the Nineteenth Century. *Journal of Economic History, 9, 45-61.* doi:10.1017/S002205070009032X

Landes, D. (1953). Social Attitudes, Entrepreneurship, and Economic Development: A Comment. Explorations in Entrepreneurial History, 6, 245-72. doi:10.1017/S002205070009032X

Landes, D. (1998). The Wealth and Poverty of Nations. W. W. Norton. doi:10.1017/S002205070009032X

Landes, D. S. (2003). *The unbound Prometheus: technological change and industrial development in Western Europe from 1750 to the present.* Cambridge University Press. doi:10.1017/CBO9780511819957

Larsson, M., Milestad, R., Hahn, T., & Von Oelreich, J. (2016). The resilience of a sustainability entrepreneur in the Swedish food system. *Sustainability (Basel)*, *8*(6), 550. doi:10.3390u8060550

Linnenluecke, M. K., Griffiths, A., & Winn, M. (2012). Extreme weather events and the critical importance of anticipatory adaptation and organizational resilience in responding to impacts. *Business Strategy and the Environment*, *21*(1), 17–32. doi:10.1002/bse.708

Manyaka, S. J. (2015). Social entrepreneurship: A solution for transforming the disadvantaged community of Nellmapius. *Hervormde Teologiese Studies*, *71*(3), 1–7. doi:10.4102/hts.v71i3.2821

Masocha, R., & Fatoki, O. (2018). The impact of coercive pressures on sustainability practices of small businesses in South Africa. *Sustainability (Basel)*, *10*(9), 3032. doi:10.3390u10093032

Morck, R., & Yeung, B. (2002). *Family control and the rent-seeking society*. Paper presented at the 2002 Theories of the Family Enterprise Conference, Wharton Business School, Philadelphia, PA.

Muralidharan, E., & Pathak, S. (2018). Sustainability, transformational leadership, and social entrepreneurship. *Sustainability (Basel)*, *10*(2), 1–22. doi:10.3390u10020567

Narva, R. L. (2001). Heritage and tradition in family business: how family-controlled enterprises connect the experience of their past to the promise of their future. In G. K. McCann & N. Upton (Eds.), *Destroying Myths and Creating Value in Family Business* (pp. 29–38). Stetson University.

Neubauer, F., & Lank, A. G. (2016). *The family business: Its governance for sustainability*. Springer.

Neumann, T. (2021). The impact of entrepreneurship on economic, social and environmental welfare and its determinants: A systematic review. *Management Review Quarterly*, *71*(3), 553–584. doi:10.100711301-020-00193-7

Obraztsova, O., & Chepurenko, A. (2010). *Entrepreneurship and socio-economic development in cross-countries analysis. In Strategic Entrepreneurship: The promise for future entrepreneurship, family business and SME research*. KMU Verlag HSG.

Okpara, F. O. (2000). *Entrepreneurship: Test and Cases*. Precision Printers and Publishers.

Poza, E. J. (2013). *Family business*. Cengage Learning.

Preisendörfer, P., & Voss, T. (1990). Organizational Mortality of Small Firms: The Effects of Entrepreneurial Age and Human Capital. *Organization Studies*, *11*(1), 107–112. doi:10.1177/017084069001100109

Rahman, H. (2009). Network deployment for social benefits in developing countries. In *Encyclopedia of Multimedia Technology and Networking* (2nd ed., pp. 1048–1054). IGI Global. doi:10.4018/978-1-60566-014-1.ch141

Santos, F. M. (2012). A positive theory of social entrepreneurship. *Journal of Business Ethics, 111*(3), 335–351. doi:10.100710551-012-1413-4

Sarango-Lalangui, P., Álvarez-García, J., & del Río-Rama, M. D. L. C. (2018). Sustainable practices in small and medium-sized enterprises in Ecuador. *Sustainability (Basel), 10*(6), 2105. doi:10.3390u10062105

Sauvé, S., Bernard, S., & Sloan, P. (2016). Environmental sciences, sustainable development and circular economy: Alternative concepts for trans-disciplinary research. *Environmental Development, 17*, 48–56. doi:10.1016/j.envdev.2015.09.002

Sawyer, J. (1954). The Social Basis of the American System of Manufacturing. *The Journal of Economic History, 14*(4), 361–379. doi:10.1017/S0022050700077007

Schumpeter, J. (1942). *Capitalism, Socialism, and Democracy*. Harper and Brothers.

Shan, S., Jia, Y., Zheng, X., & Xu, X. (2018). Assessing relationship and contribution of China's technological entrepreneurship to socio-economic development. *Technological Forecasting and Social Change, 135*, 83–90. doi:10.1016/j.techfore.2017.12.022

Shapiro, J. P., & Gross, S. J. (2008). *Ethical educational leadership in turbulent times*. Routledge.

Simmel, G. (1908). The Stranger. In K. H. Wolff (Ed.), *The Sociology of Georg Simmel*. The Free Press.

Sivathanu, B., & Bhise, P. V. (2016). *Challenges for Social Entrepreneurship*. Available online: http://www.ijaiem.org/ RATMIG2013/MGT%2025%20Challenges%20 for%20Social %20Entrepreneurship.pdf

Smith, M. S. (2006). *The Emergence of Modern Business Enterprise in France, 1800- 1930*. Harvard University Press.

Social Sustainability Policy. (2016). *A city for all: Towards a socially just and resilient Sydney*. Available at: http://www.cityofsydney.nsw.gov.au/__data/assets/pdf_file/0 005/262346/Social-Sustainability-Policy.pdf

Sombart, W. (1911). *The Jews and Modern Capitalism*. Transaction Books.

Stenn, T. L. (2016). *Social entrepreneurship as sustainable development: Introducing the sustainability lens*. Springer.

Sulphey, M. M., & Alkahtani, N. (2017). Economic security and sustainability through social entrepreneurship: the current Saudi scenario. *Journal of Security and Sustainability Issues, 6*(3).

Vaswani, J. (2023). *Grant Cardone Net Worth: Why He Is So Successful?* https://schemaninja.com/grant-cardone-net-worth/

Walker, B., Holling, C. S., Carpenter, S. R., & Kinzig, A. (2004). Resilience, adaptability and transformability in social–ecological systems. *Ecology and Society*, *9*(2), 1–18. doi:10.5751/ES-00650-090205

Ward, J. (2016). *Keeping the family business healthy: How to plan for continuing growth, profitability, and family leadership*. Springer.

Weber, M. (1904). *The Protestant Ethic and the Spirit of Capitalism*. Scribner.

Wiener, M. (1981). English Culture and the Decline of the Industrial Spirit: 1850–1980. New York: Cambridge University Press.

Wiener, M. (Ed.). (1966). Modernization: The Dynamics of Growth. New York: Basic Books.

Wilson, C. H. (1955). The Entrepreneur in the Industrial Revolution. *Explorations in Entrepreneurial History*, *7*(3), 129–145.

Winter, M., Danes, S. M., Koh, S.-K., Fredericks, K., & Paul, J. J. (2004). Tracking family businesses and their owners over time: Panel attrition, manager departure, and business demise. *Journal of Business Venturing*, *19*(4), 535–559. doi:10.1016/S0883-9026(03)00061-2

Winter, M., Fitzgerald, M. A., Heck, R. K. Z., Haynes, G. W., & Danes, S. M. (1998). Revisiting the study of family businesses: Methodological challenges, dilemmas, and alternative approaches. *Family Business Review*, *11*(3), 239–252. doi:10.1111/j.1741-6248.1998.00239.x

Winter, M., Puspitawati, H., Heck, R. K. Z., & Stafford, K. (1993). Time-management strategies used by households with home-based work. *Journal of Family and Economic Issues*, *14*(1), 69–92. doi:10.1007/BF01013430

Ylijoki, O. H., & Henriksson, L. (2017). Tribal, proletarian and entrepreneurial career stories: Junior academics as a case in point. *Studies in Higher Education*, *42*(7), 1292–1308. doi:10.1080/03075079.2015.1092129

Zhang, D. D., & Swanson, L. A. (2014). Linking social entrepreneurship and sustainability. *Journal of Social Entrepreneurship*, *5*(2), 175–191. doi:10.1080/19420676.2014.880503

Chapter 2
Influence of Family Environment in Promoting Entrepreneurial Intentions and the Proliferation of Entrepreneurs

Dagogo William Legg-Jack
https://orcid.org/0000-0002-6739-5575
Walter Sisulu University, South Africa

Clever Ndebele
Walter Sisulu University, South Africa

EXECUTIVE SUMMARY

Research has shown that the family environment is one of the factors that shapes a person's entrepreneurial intentions, thereby leading to the production of entrepreneurs. Although several studies exist, none seem to have adopted the approach employed in this chapter. Premised on that, the chapter employed a teaching case approach to explain the influence of family environment in promoting entrepreneurial intentions and the proliferation of entrepreneurs. Guided by one research question, namely "How does the family environment promote entrepreneurial intention?" the chapter analysed three cases from Chinese Indonesia, Turkey, and Tunisia building on the theoretical strengths of the theory of planned behaviour and social cognitive theory. These theories were employed to analyse how family environment promoted entrepreneurial intentions in the countries mentioned. Findings from the analysis in the three cases highlighted revealed that the family environment through the instrumentality of role modelling and support for autonomy promotes entrepreneurial intentions.

DOI: 10.4018/978-1-6684-8748-8.ch002

INTRODUCTION

At both the European Union level and globally, a troubling trend emerges as the unemployment rate among youth aged 18 to 24 stands at three times the overall unemployment rate. This stark reality underscores the formidable challenge that unemployment poses for young individuals (Eurostat, 2020). Entrepreneurship is increasingly recognised as a vital avenue for addressing this problem (Halabisky, 2021). Statistically, it is reported that approximately 45% of young people express a preference for pursuing entrepreneurship over traditional employment, with 41% of this demographic believing in the feasibility of such a choice (Halabisky, 2021). Hence, it is argued that entrepreneurial activity is the only pathway out of poverty for young people, especially in Africa (Chigunta, 2017).

Moreover, nurturing greater entrepreneurial involvement among young people worldwide holds the potential to advance progress towards at least one of the 17 Sustainable Development Goals (SDGs) (Georgescu & Herman, 2020). Specifically, this aligns with Goal 8 of the 2030 Agenda for Sustainable Development established by the United Nations (2015), which seeks to promote "sustained, inclusive and sustainable economic growth, full and productive employment and decent work for all". Essentially, developing entrepreneurs is the potential key to achieving this lofty goal. In the development of entrepreneurs, research has shown that the family environment is considered a factor in steering one's interest in the direction of entrepreneurial activities (Mala et al., 2019; Osunde, 2017).

The family environment is an individual's closest community with whom they interact with. The first education that a child receives after birth comes from the family environment (Siregar, 2020). This implies that a child's future success or challenges can be closely linked to their family environment, which is defined by various factors. These factors encompass the way parents educate, the relationship between parents and family members, the overall home atmosphere, the family's economic situation, parental understanding, and cultural background (Muhtarom & Suyatno, 2018). Additionally, family backgrounds, including parenting style, parental support, and communication in the family environment, exert a considerable influence on an individual's interests (Mala et al., 2019).

As proposed by Sandi and Nurhayati (2020), the family environment stands as the most immediate social sphere for an entrepreneur, playing a significant role in shaping the child's character, including their entrepreneurial traits. It is within this familial context that the atmosphere for an individual's development and growth is established (Hutagalung et al., 2017). Furthermore, Lingappa et al. (2020) have affirmed that the family and its socialisation exert a profound influence on an individual's entrepreneurial attitudes and intentions, which are attributable to a number of indicators. According to Moussa and Kerkeni (2021), these indicators include parental support for autonomy, both in terms of promoting independence and fostering volitional functioning, alongside the presence of entrepreneurial role models, in addition to financial capital and social capital. This collective body of research underscores the pivotal role that the family environment plays in forecasting entrepreneurial intention (EI) (Zhou et al., 2021).

EI can be defined as an individual's mindset aimed at achieving a specific business objective shaped by their previous experiences, actions, and focus (Noor et al., 2019; Joseph, 2017). It encompasses a person's hopes, desires, and wishes, which significantly influence their decision to pursue entrepreneurship (Ismail et al., 2018). Often manifested as entrepreneurial willingness or inclination, it represents an individual's subjective attitude toward engaging in entrepreneurial activities (Jiang et al., 2022). Research has shown that EI can serve as a metric for predicting entrepreneurial behaviour and the initiation of new businesses (Taha et al., 2017), including the actions of entrepreneurs themselves.

Entrepreneurs are individuals who identify a need in the marketplace and strive to meet it (Pratt, 2018). Historically, the term has been applied to anyone who starts a venture, recognising the ability to fulfil the identified need as an economic opportunity (Pratt, 2018). This implies that an entrepreneur is someone who establishes a new business. When it comes to the creation of new businesses, the entrepreneur's initial starting point is his/her social environment which includes family, friends, and acquaintances (Le Thi Bao et al., 2020). According to these scholars, entrepreneurs appear to depend on family resources, including financial, human, experiential, and infrastructural assets, to initiate a venture (Le Thi Bao et al., 2020). This suggests that family plays a multifaceted role in influencing an entrepreneur's activities, as highlighted in the research (Sieger & Minola, 2017; Bernardon & Monticelli, 2015; Kirkwood, 2012).

Research evidence suggests the presence of a gap in the literature concerning the influence of the family environment on stimulating EI, especially in the use of the teaching case approach. Thus, the chapter focuses on the influence of the family environment in promoting EI, thereby leading to the development of entrepreneurial activities that result in the production of entrepreneurs within a given family context. Framed by two theories, namely, the Theory of Planned Behaviour (TPB) (Ajzen, 1991) and the Social Cognitive Theory (SCT) (Bandura, 1986), the chapter addresses the following question: *how does the family environment promote entrepreneurial intention?* The choice of these theories, such as the TPB, is based on its extensive use in the field of behavioural sciences, particularly in entrepreneurship-related studies, where it effectively explains people's intentional behaviour. On the other hand, the inclusion of SCT in this chapter is driven by its aptitude for elucidating how individuals acquire knowledge and skills within a social context through their interactions with the environment.

In the next section, we provide a succinct review of relevant literature covering the family environment, entrepreneurship, entrepreneurs, EIs, TPB, and SCT. Following this, we present a detailed examination and analysis of the cases and conclude with our recommendations.

REVIEW OF RELATED LITERATURE

Family Environment

The family, being the primary agent of socialisation, is widely regarded as the most influential social entity in which an individual learns to integrate and interact (Wiani et al., 2018). The family environment comprises two distinct components: the *physical aspect*, encompassing learning resources and facilities, and *the non-physical aspect,* which includes parental guidance, empathy, support, and socio-economic conditions (Indaryani et al., 2021). Both of these components impact how an individual is groomed within the family. This implies that children's education in the family environment positions the family as having a strong influence on their success (Siregar, 2020). This is because the emergence of new entrepreneurial candidates in a family is based on the belief that parents who work as entrepreneurs tend to replicate that same order (Mulyani, et al., 2018), as they are accustomed to the environment and understand the flow and methods of entrepreneurship (Rastiti et al., 2021).

Research evidence shows that the higher the motivation from an individual's family environment, the greater their interest in an entrepreneurship career (Susanto, 2018). The family plays a vital role by providing parental support for autonomy (Anil & Azize, 2014; Sharma, 2014), serving as an entrepreneurial role model (Meroka, 2023), and offering family support for entrepreneurship (Bird & Wennberg, 2016; Sharma, 2014). Thus, being a member of a family of entrepreneurs increases a person's entrepreneurial motivation and intention (Moussa & Kerkeni, 2021), thereby boosting the self-efficacy of that individual (Wibowo, 2016). This implies that the family environment acts a source of encouragement that motivates every move and decision of the child.

From the foregoing, it becomes evident that family environment plays an important role in influencing one's interest in entrepreneurship (Mala et al., 2019). Accordingly, the family environment wields influence over career choices, moulds an individual's personality and behaviour, and provides the financial support that stimulates EI (Moussa & Kerkeni, 2021). Within this context, parents, particularly the father within the family environment, are more likely to have a significant impact in motivating their children to pursue entrepreneurial paths (Mala et al.,

2019). This validates the fact that the environment in which an individual grows can either facilitate or impede their ability to embark on entrepreneurial endeavours (Moussa & Kerkeni, 2021).

Numerous studies have shown that family environment impacts the EI of an individual (Tantono et al., 2022; Siregar, 2020; Mala et al., 2019). Several compelling reasons underpin the encouragement of EI among family members. These reasons encompass the creation of opportunities for offspring, preservation of the family legacy, fostering family cohesion, attaining financial independence and assets, facilitating self-retirement and personal plans, protection of efficient employees, ensuring the financial well-being of the family, and promoting benevolence (Diken & Erdirençelebi, 2016). All of these factors collectively serve the overarching goal of perpetuating the family legacy through the cultivation and development of entrepreneurs.

Entrepreneurs

Entrepreneurs are the products of EIs. This underscores the notion that, when compared to various other factors and variables, EI holds significant importance in fostering the level of readiness and creativity necessary for the emergence of an entrepreneur (Sabah, 2016). While numerous definitions exist for "entrepreneurs", particularly in less developed nations, entrepreneurs are often characterised as individuals who actively engage in and contribute to a country's economic growth by nurturing individual initiatives that lead to the creation of valuable assets through new business ventures (Vodă & Florea, 2019).

Moreover, others have described entrepreneurs as individuals who seize opportunities and exhibit vigorous and persistent efforts to transform their ideas and visions into viable, profit-generating businesses (Gieure et al., 2020). Being an entrepreneur entails the ability to not only create and diversify but also to intervene in established organisational processes (Ratten & Tajeddini, 2019). For instance, entrepreneurs create jobs for the jobless with the intention of tackling the menace of unemployment (Klofsten et al., 2019; Cao & Shi, 2021; Khan et al., 2022). This substantiates the claim made by some scholars that the establishment of new enterprises is frequently proposed as a possible solution to unemployment (Vodă & Florea, 2019), serving as an important economic stimulus at the regional level (Bosma & Kelley, 2019). Entrepreneurs act as catalysts for societal change by introducing innovative products and services (Aktaş, 2019). They don't merely create something new but provide services distinct from what is already known to customers (Kerr et al., 2018), employing a diverse set of characteristic features in the process.

The success of entrepreneurs is dependent on unique inherent traits and qualities. They require specific attributes as they pursue their goals (Franco & Prata, 2019).

These characteristics include internal locus of control, motivation to achieve goals, a balanced level of risk-taking propensity, creativity, and the ability to handle stress (Sarwoko & Nurfarida, 2021). Moreover, elevated levels of self-efficacy are vital qualities necessary for entrepreneurs (Kusumawijaya & Astuti, 2021). These attributes significantly contribute to an entrepreneur's success (Pattanayak & Kakati, 2023). Some of these qualities or characteristics can be transmitted from parents to other family members, fostering success in their entrepreneurial endeavours (Tan et al., 2019). This implies that an entrepreneur with robust self-efficacy within a family environment may influence others to follow suit.

The perpetuation of the entrepreneurial legacy within the family environment is often initiated by parents who are entrepreneurs (Le Thi Bao et al., 2020). This is evident in a study conducted within the Pakistani culture, where entrepreneur parents aspire for their children to engage in entrepreneurship, believing it offers greater freedom and financial rewards (Farrukh et al., 2017). Moreover, research provides evidence that entrepreneur parents continue to foster entrepreneurship within their lineage. For instance, in Turkey, parents have been instrumental in producing entrepreneurs across multiple generations through the transference of entrepreneurship cultures (Diken & Erdirençelebi, 2016). Likewise, in Nepal, it was discovered that the parental profession in entrepreneurship significantly influences their children's career choices, with those in business and agriculture, among other fields, often inspiring their offspring to follow a similar path (Pant, 2015). Therefore, the decision to become an entrepreneur is heavily influenced by the family environment, which transfers EI to the individual.

Entrepreneurial Intention (EI)

Generally, "intention" is defined as the state of mind that guides a person's action towards a specific behaviour (Uygun & Kasimoglu, 2013). Based on the TPB, intention is a predictor of future behaviour (Sesen, 2013). EI has garnered substantial research interest in entrepreneurship scholarship (Otache et al., 2021). It is also commonly described as the willingness to embark on an entrepreneurial venture (Nguyen, 2017). Consistent with this definition, Ahmed et al. (2017), as well as Sesen (2013), defined EI as a conscious and mental process that leads to a decision to initiate and manage a new business. Expanding on this definition, EI is referred to as an individual's self-acknowledged conviction to establish a new business venture and actively plan for its realisation in the future (Ngat & Tuyet, 2023).

Similarly, EI is an effective way to stimulate people's desire to engage in productive activities and undertake new ventures (Soomro et al., 2019). Accordingly, EI signifies an individual's decision to pursue entrepreneurship as a vocation, accompanied by the willingness to gather the necessary resources, assume associated risks, and initiate their own business (Karabulut, 2016). This means that EI is a major determinant in the decision of an individual to become an entrepreneur (Soni & Bakhru, 2021).

In essence, all the definitions and descriptions outlined emphasise that EI is a necessary condition for the development of entrepreneurship or the establishment of a business. This is supported by Ngat and Tuyet's (2023) assertion that EI leads individuals to pursue entrepreneurial projects or establish new business ventures driven by their self-interest. However, the inherent existence of a mere intention for a specific activity does not guarantee its actualisation; it requires manifestation. Hence, EI serves not only as a prerequisite for initiating a new venture but also wields influence over an individual's behaviour (Soni & Bakhru, 2021), particularly leading to entrepreneurial actions. Empirical evidence further confirms the significance of EI, with numerous studies investigating the factors that influence it (Ngat & Tuyet, 2023; Al Bati et al., 2022; Bellò Mattana & Loi, 2018), including the role of the family environment.

Various scholars have extensively documented the positive impact of family environment on the cultivation of EI (Boz & Ergeneli, 2014; Meroka, 2023). The family environment is recognised as a major force that moulds intention, providing support and guidance to children in shaping their decision-making processes and future choices (Puspasari, 2023). Thus, social support as a component of the non-physical environment of the family was reported as a significant factor that influenced the EIs of undergraduates from a university in Nigeria (Ilevbare et al., 2022).

Similarly, findings from the study carried out by Olofinyehun et al. (2022) indicate that family support influences students' intention to pursue entrepreneurship. Additionally, in Italy, support from both family and friends was identified as a predictor of EI (Molino et al., 2018). Although their research revealed a higher level of family support and self-efficacy among men, it also demonstrated that the relationship between this form of support and self-efficacy was more robust for women (Molino et al., 2018). According to the study, women perceived support from important people as crucial to the development of EI more than external characteristics such as self-efficacy (Molino et al., 2018). This corroborates a related finding that marital status or, more precisely, being married, is a significant determinant of self-employment (Molina, 2020).

Based on the analysis of the reviewed studies, it becomes clear that the family environment, along with its various components, plays a pivotal role in nurturing an individual's EI. This leads us to the central question: How does the family environment promote entrepreneurial intention? To respond to this question, we employed two notable theories in entrepreneurship research: TPB and SCT. These theories were used to analyse cases from three different countries, illuminating the ways in which the family environment promotes EI.

Theory of Planned Behaviour (TPB)

The framing of this chapter is rooted in the TPB, popularised by Ajzen (1991). The choice of TPB for this chapter is grounded in its widespread use in entrepreneurship research, particularly in the field of social and behavioural sciences, where it is employed to explain people's intentional behaviours (Acheampong & Tweneboah-Koduah, 2018; Henley et al. 2017). This choice is further supported by Pugh and Adkins (2020), who noted that the conceptualisation of human intentions to launch a business as depicted by some entrepreneurship scholars can be traced back to TPB.

According to TPB, behaviour is determined by one's intention to engage in that behaviour (Ajzen, 1991). TPB can be seen as an extension of the Theory of Reasoned Action (TRA), which was developed by Fishbein and Ajzen (1975). TRA posits that a person's intention to perform a specific behaviour is influenced by their attitude toward the behaviour (ATB), subjective norms (SNs), and perceived behavioural control (PBC) (Acheampong & Tweneboah-Koduah, 2018; Fayolle et al., 2006). In the TPB, three key constructs are identified as predictors of behavioural intentions: ATB, SN, and PBC (Ajzen, 1991).

ATB involves an individual's judgment regarding whether engaging in a particular behaviour is beneficial or detrimental. As noted by Sabah (2016), attitudes can be learned, and the more favourable a person's attitude, the stronger their intention to engage in that behaviour. This suggests that if an individual perceives an attitude as positive, they are more likely to act in that direction, whereas a negative attitude would lead to the opposite. Within the family environment, the influence of parents as role models can steer other members of the same household in a particular direction (Meroka, 2023).

On the other hand, SNs pertain to individuals' subjective judgements regarding whether they must or should engage in a particular behaviour. It involves the perception of the importance of certain actions based on the attitudes of people (Sabah, 2016). This implies that those in close proximity to an individual will either endorse or discourage certain behavioural expressions (Meroka 2023). Thus, the approval or disapproval of EIs within the family environment is necessitated by the person who occupies the leadership position in that household.

Social Cognitive Theory

The second theory employed to frame the chapter is the SCT introduced by Bandura (1986). As an extension of Social Learning Theory, the SCT postulates that learning takes place in a social context, with a dynamic and reciprocal interaction between individuals, their environment, as well as their behaviour. According to SCT, the environment causes behaviour, but behaviour also causes the environment (Bandura,

1986). This, Bandura refers to as the concept of reciprocal determinism, a situation where the world and the behaviour of an individual are mutually caused.

Accordingly, Bandura believes that the activities of individuals must be explained in relation to the reciprocal interaction between cognitive, behavioural, and environmental determinants (Bandura, 1986). The SCT posits that observation and imitation can be traced across various role models, which may include parents, teachers, friends, and even media icons (Bayrón, 2013). According to this theory, learning occurs when one person observes another with the intention of adopting a particular behaviour (Bayrón, 2013). Such imitation by the observer enhances their knowledge and, in turn, elevates their self-efficacy.

Self-efficacy is an individual's self-judgement in their ability to execute a task in a particular domain (Bandura, 1986). This suggests that individuals who have access to information about entrepreneurship are more likely to develop EIs and the belief in their capacity to carry out entrepreneurial tasks compared to those without similar education (Bayrón, 2013). Hence, the selection of the SCT as the second theory in this chapter is substantiated by the evidence that a family environment offering more education on entrepreneurship is in a favourable position to cultivate EI among its members by imparting knowledge within this domain, as demonstrated in the study by Meroka (2023).

CASE DESCRIPTION AND ANALYSIS

Cases of family environment from three different countries are analysed in the following section. These cases are based on empirical evidence on how the family environment fostered EIs. The first case analysis draws from the experiences of Chinese Indonesians, while the second and third cases focus on Turkey and Tunisia, respectively. The analysis primarily considers two constructs within the family environments: role modelling and support for autonomy. We begin this section with an examination of the experiences of Chinese Indonesians.

Case 1: Chinees Indonesian Experience

The Chinese Indonesians are a prominent ethnic group that plays a pivotal role in the nation's economy through their entrepreneurial spirit and skills (Tan et al., 2019). It is stated that about 60% of Indonesian monetary activities are contributed by Chinese Indonesians (Karsono & Suprapto, 2015). Additionally, data from Globe Asia August (GAA) in 2016 indicates that 60% of the top twenty conglomerate groups, ranked by revenues, are owned by Chinese Indonesians. As highlighted by Tan et al. (2019), this data underscores the economic importance of the Chinese

Indonesian community and emphasises the necessity of exploring the development of Chinese Indonesian family-owned small and medium-sized enterprises (SMEs) as a means to sustain the longevity of their businesses.

According to Mourougane (2012) and Yoshino and Wignaraja (2015), SMEs are responsible for providing 97% of the employment opportunities in the Indonesian economy, highlighting their crucial role in the nation. Furthermore, SMEs contribute approximately 57.8% to Indonesia's gross domestic product (GDP) (Yoshino & Wignaraja, 2015).

Consequently, this necessitated the need to carry out research on Chinese Indonesian family-owned SMEs (Tan et al., 2019). They explored and explained how predecessors (incumbents) of ethnic Chinese family SMEs in Indonesia, commonly referred to as Chinese Indonesian family SMEs, guide and facilitate the development of transgenerational entrepreneurship (Tan et al., 2019). Their study participants consisted of experts, incumbents, and successors of Chinese-Indonesian family SMEs.

Role Modelling. Role models can be drawn from two constructs, "role" which is the tendency to identify with others, or "role modelling" which is described as a psychological matching of cognitive skills between an observer and the person being observed (Bosma et al., 2012). From the Chinees Indonesian study, one notable finding that was brought to the fore was that of role modelling of the successor by the incumbent (Tan et al., 2019). Both the incumbent and successor highlighted this in their various comments. It was reported that the incumbent and their spouse actively instil their entrepreneurial spirit and attitude in the successor. This was evident in the remark made by a relative of the successor, who notes that the successor had inherited the incumbent's stubbornness and fierceness, exemplifying the impact of role modelling (Tan et al., 2019). As a result, the successor adopted the attitude of always looking out for business and investment opportunities.

Furthermore, in the process of modelling, the incumbent imparted essential competencies and entrepreneurial values to the successor. These included virtues such as honesty and diligence, which were deemed essential for the success of any business venture.

The influence of entrepreneurial values and competencies imparted by parental role models can be observed in individuals, both during their formative years and later stages of life, as noted by some scholars (Walter & Dohse, 2009). Supporting this idea is the outcome of an analysis conducted across eight German universities, which examined the EI of students. The analysis revealed a positive relationship between the presence of parental role models who were self-employed and the likelihood of their offspring becoming self-employed as well, with implications for personality traits such as openness in the individual (Chlosta et al., 2012).

The decision of children within a family to become entrepreneurs is often traceable to parental role models. In this case, where the successor learns from the incumbent, it best exemplifies the SN of the TPB, where a person's attitude towards an action is influenced by its perceived significance (Ajzen, 1991). Additionally, drawing from the implications of TPB, the closest person to the successor is the incumbent, who is in a position to endorse the successor's actions (Ajzen, 1991).

Furthermore, a study that explored the impact of the components of the TPB on the EI of young university graduates in Central and Eastern European countries, as well as developed European countries, revealed that social norms, especially coming from a family with a business background, are likely to stimulate the EI of individuals within these regions (Hartšenko & Küttim, 2019).

Support for Autonomy. The description of parental support for autonomy of their children or wards takes a dual dimension (Soenens & Vansteenkiste, 2005). First, it involves the perceived promotion of independence through educational practices, where parents encourage decision-making and freedom of expression in their children (Silk et al., 2003). Second, it encompasses the promotion of volitional functioning, where parents support their children's desire for psychological independence (Soenens & Vansteenkiste, 2005).

The Chinese Indonesian study revealed that parental support for autonomy also played a significant role in fostering EI. The comments from the incumbents indicated that each child was given a house to promote their independence. Children, including successors, tended to have a mindset of being independent and, if possible, supporting their parents financially (Tan et al., 2019). Allowing successors to make calculated mistakes and take risks as a way of testing their autonomy aligns with the idea that an individual's decision to engage in a particular behaviour is often influenced by the opinions and actions of others (Ajzen, 1991). This approach has also served to boost the self-efficacy of successors since they were allowed to operate based on the information at their disposal, which is a key component of Bandura's (1986) SCT. While making mistakes and subsequently correcting them, successors gain valuable information about the process, which, in turn, enhances their self-efficacy.

Case 2: Turkey Experience

The Turkey experience reports the findings of Diken and Erdirençelebi (2016), which aimed to address three objectives. Firstly, it explored the method of doing business by different generations in the same business. Secondly, it focused on the future strategies of entrepreneurs for their businesses, examining how this varied across different sectors. Lastly, it examined the policies followed by entrepreneurs in preparing the next generation to take over the business.

Several businesses were considered in their study, including agricultural tools and machinery manufacturing, tractor dealers, autogas systems, footwear production, spare parts, cold processing plant, hot rolling mill, office furniture manufacturing, household furniture, vegetable oil and food supplements, milk and milk products production, flour production, feed production, and construction materials. It is important to note that the study encompassed family members from the first and third generations.

Role Modelling. The findings of this study exemplify family role modelling, where the first generation passes on favourable attitudes and entrepreneurship cultures to the next generation. The study revealed a focus on decision-making processes and information transfer between generations, with an emphasis on steady growth and sustainability. They also focused on awareness together with sustainability.

The interviewed business groups prioritised qualities such as innovation, quality, awareness, long-term employment, and speed as essential characteristics for their businesses. They also recognised the importance of innovation and placed an emphasis on research and development (R&D). Furthermore, the decision-making approaches identified in the first generation, such as "moderate risk" or "calculated risk", were found to be adopted by the second and third generations (Diken & Erdirençelebi, 2016, p. 2400). This suggests the existence of an interface across the different generations, aligning with the principles of the SCT (Bandura, 1986), that learning takes place in a social context with dynamic and reciprocal interactions between individuals, their environment, and their behaviour. Additionally, the interest of the new generation in entrepreneurship was influenced during their childhood or teenage years when they were exposed to their parents' workplaces at an early age.

Support for Autonomy. In the transference of entrepreneurial culture to the next generation, it was found that both the behaviour of parents in the family, whether autocratic or democratic, and the creation of an organisational culture in the business were essential (Diken & Erdirençelebi, 2016). This implies that at some point in the business, either of the generation acts collectively or independently. The perspectives of all the interviewed business groups indicated that they viewed all the elements related to organisational culture positively. These elements include viewing business administration as a team effort, seeking consensus on important decisions, placing emphasis on group rather than the individual, creating values based on customers feedback, applying the same tactics in the market, and developing company policies from the perspectives of sellers. Other elements include the creation of policies that consider competitors' manoeuvres, maintaining flexible business operations that are open to change, fostering collaborative decision-making, supporting open communication channels, implementing cash budgets, focusing on return on investment, periodically examining assets converted from company capital, and evaluating business performance.

The actions of the first generation in the study were characterised by a deliberate approach and a reluctance to engage in highly risky activities across their four businesses. This approach stemmed from their awareness of a proportional relationship between profitability and risk. It is noteworthy that the first generation's approach suggests a lack of tolerance for autonomy and risk-taking. However, it was reported that subsequent generations were more willing to take risks and act independently of their competitors. In the following section, the third case is presented.

Case 3: Tunisian Experience

The main objective of the Tunisian case was to identify the role and importance of the family environment in shaping the EIs of young Tunisian students in a post-revolution context (Moussa & Kerkeni, 2021). The quantitative study involved surveying 297 final-year undergraduates from Tunisian universities. While several components of the family environment were assessed, the analysis focused on two specific constructs: role modelling and support for autonomy, as explained in the case description section.

Role Modelling. The Tunisian experience highlighted the significant impact of even limited exposure to entrepreneurship role models on the choice of an entrepreneurial career (Moussa & Kerkeni, 2021). The study also emphasised that engaging in discussions about business, work integration, and different interaction opportunities with entrepreneurship role models have a positive influence on the EI of individuals within a family circle (Moussa & Kerkeni, 2021). Boldureanu et al. (2020) further support this notion, suggesting that role models from a student's immediate environment, such as family members, tend to have a profound influence on the student, given their close proximity and strong personal connections (Meroka, 2023).

Support for Autonomy. The survey results indicated that parental support for autonomy, particularly the promotion of independence, was identified as an important factor in stimulating EI. Respondents perceived a strong emphasis on promoting independence and volitional functioning within their families. This was often associated with a democratic parenting style, which fosters autonomy (Moussa & Kerkeni, 2021). A similar emphasis on autonomy as a valuable motivator for entrepreneurs was found in a study conducted in Yemen (Al-Jubari et al., 2017). The study also confirmed that autonomy is a significant predictor of EI (Al-Jubari et al., 2017), and this relationship is mediated by ATB, SNs, and PBC, as proposed in the TPB (Ajzen, 1991). In particular, the SN comes into play as parents were willing and supportive of their children's independence, aligning with the perceived social pressure to engage in a particular behaviour (Ajzen, 1991).

From the analysis of the three cases, it is evident that the family environment is one of the major predictors of EI. The family, as the primary socialising agent in an individual's life, provides the foundational education and values that guide career choices (Wiani et al., 2018). When one or both parents are entrepreneurs, their children often find themselves drawn toward entrepreneurship. The family environment fosters positive discussions among relatives, which can serve as a motivating factor for developing EI (Samala et al., 2022).

Although there are several aspects of the family environment that foster the development of EI in individuals, in the cases analysed in this chapter, two constructs featured prominently. These include the presence of family role models and parental support for autonomy. The presence of family role models in the three cases confirm their importance as a valuable source of social capital (Meroka, 2023). Social capitals help in the identification of opportunities and sustain company performance (Bhagavatula et al., 2010), as evidenced in the Chinese Indonesian experience. On the other hand, the support for autonomy, as evidenced across all three cases, aligns with prior research indicating that fostering autonomy, alongside other parental practices, contributes to the development of entrepreneurial traits and intentions (Boz & Ergeneli, 2014). Corroborating this, some researchers have argued that autonomy is a significant predictor of EI (Al-Jubari et al., 2017).

CONCLUSION AND RECOMMENDATIONS

This chapter utilised a case approach to analyse the impact of the family environment on the promotion of EIs, employing the TPB and SCT as theoretical frameworks. The review centred on family environment, entrepreneurship, entrepreneurs, and EIs. Through the analysis of the three representative cases, it became evident that the presence of family role models significantly contributed to the development of EIs. it should be noted that this aspect was not universally embraced by all generations in the Turkish study; it was primarily associated with the first generation. Thus, it is concluded that the presence of entrepreneurial role models and support for autonomy within a family environment with entrepreneurs can indeed foster EIs.

The findings presented in this chapter, while insightful, are not exhaustive in their exploration of the family environment's impact on promoting EI. The chapter primarily focused on two key constructs – role modelling and support for autonomy – within the family environment. These findings underscore the importance of having entrepreneurial role models and fostering autonomy within a family environment as drivers of EIs.

Additionally, the methodological approach followed a secondary data generation method, and only three experiences from three countries were considered. This limitation suggests the need for further research that employs primary data collection methods to comprehensively assess the impact of the family environment, including all its components, in stimulating EI. Conducting research across various countries beyond the ones examined in this chapter would enhance the generalisability of the findings and provide a more comprehensive understanding of the topic.

REFERENCES

Acheampong, G., & Tweneboah-Koduah, E. Y. (2018). Does past failure inhibit future entrepreneurial intent? Evidence from Ghana. *Journal of Small Business and Enterprise Development*, *25*(5), 849–863. doi:10.1108/JSBED-03-2017-0128

Ahmed, T., Chandran, V. G. R., & Klobas, J. (2017). Specialized entrepreneurship education: Does it really matter? Fresh evidence from Pakistan. *International Journal of Entrepreneurial Behaviour & Research*, *23*(1), 4–19. doi:10.1108/IJEBR-01-2016-0005

Ajzen, I. (1991). The theory of planned behavior. *Organizational Behavior and Human Decision Processes*, *50*(2), 179–211. doi:10.1016/0749-5978(91)90020-T

Aktaş, R. (2019). Türkiye'de Girişimcilik. In M. Saygın (Ed.), *A current view of entrepreneurship and businesses* (pp. 24–27). Eğitim Yayınevi.

Al Bati, D. N., Ahmad, A., Al-Refai, A. M., & Aldweeri, R. (2022). Factors influencing student entrepreneurial intentions with the moderating role of COVID-19: A comparison study. *Journal of Positive School Psychology*, *6*(10), 1040–1064.

Al-Jubari, I., Hassan, A., & Hashim, J. (2017). The role of autonomy as a predictor of entrepreneurial intention among university students in Yemen. *International Journal of Entrepreneurship and Small Business*, *30*(3), 325–340. doi:10.1504/IJESB.2017.081950

Anil, B., & Azize, E. (2014). Women entrepreneurs' personality characteristics and parents' parenting style profile in Turkey. *Procedia: Social and Behavioral Sciences*, *109*, 92–97. doi:10.1016/j.sbspro.2013.12.425

Bandura, A. (1986). The explanatory and predictive scope of self-efficacy theory. *Journal of Social and Clinical Psychology*, *4*(3), 359–373. doi:10.1521/jscp.1986.4.3.359

Bayrón, C. E. (2013). Social cognitive theory, entrepreneurial self-efficacy and entrepreneurial intentions: Tools to maximize the effectiveness of formal entrepreneurship education and address the decline in entrepreneurial activity. *Griot*, *6*(1), 66–77.

Bellò, B., Mattana, V., & Loi, M. (2018). The power of peers: A new look at the impact of creativity, social context and self-efficacy on entrepreneurial intentions. *International Journal of Entrepreneurial Behaviour & Research*, *24*(1), 214–233. doi:10.1108/IJEBR-07-2016-0205

Bernardon, R., & Monticelli, J. (2015). Entrepreneurship between the 2nd and 4th generations of family businesses. In *ICSB World Conference Proceedings (ICSB 2015)*. International Council for Small Business (ICSB).

Bhagavatula, S., Elfring, T., Van Tilburg, A., & Van De Bunt, G. G. (2010). How social and human capital influence opportunity recognition and resource mobilization in India's handloom industry. *Journal of Business Venturing*, *25*(3), 245–260. doi:10.1016/j.jbusvent.2008.10.006

Bird, M., & Wennberg, K. (2016). Why family matters: The impact of family resources on immigrant entrepreneurs' exit from entrepreneurship. *Journal of Business Venturing*, *3*(1), 687–704. doi:10.1016/j.jbusvent.2016.09.002

Boldureanu, G., Ionescu, A. M., Bercu, A. M., Bedrule-Grigoruță, M. V., & Boldureanu, D. (2020). Entrepreneurship education through successful entrepreneurial models in higher education institutions. *Sustainability (Basel)*, *12*(3), 1267. doi:10.3390u12031267

Bosma, N., Hessels, J., Schutjens, V., Van Praag, M., & Verheul, I. (2012). Entrepreneurship and role models. *Journal of Economic Psychology*, *33*(2), 410–424. doi:10.1016/j.joep.2011.03.004

Bosma, N., & Kelley, D. (2019). *Global entrepreneurship monitor 2018/2019 global report*. https://www.gemconsortium.org/file/open?fileId=50213

Boz, A., & Ergeneli, A. (2014). Women entrepreneurs' personality characteristics and parents' parenting style profile in Turkey. *Procedia: Social and Behavioral Sciences*, *109*, 92–97. doi:10.1016/j.sbspro.2013.12.425

Cao, Z., & Shi, X. (2021). A systematic literature review of entrepreneurial ecosystems in advanced and emerging economies. *Small Business Economics*, *57*(1), 75–110. doi:10.100711187-020-00326-y

Chigunta, F. (2017). Entrepreneurship as a possible solution to youth unemployment in Africa. *Labor and Learning*, *10*(2), 433–451. doi:10.1007/978-981-287-032-2_19

Chlosta, S., Patzelt, H., Klein, S. B., & Dormann, C. (2012). Parental role models and the decision to become self-employed: The moderating effect of personality. *Small Business Economics*, *38*(1), 121–138. doi:10.100711187-010-9270-y

Diken, A., & Erdirençelebi, M. (2016). The role of parents in teaching entrepreneurship culture to their children in family businesses. *International Journal of Industrial and Systems Engineering*, *10*(7), 2423–2432.

Eurostat. (2020). *Eurostat Database* [data set]. European Union. https://ec.europa.eu/eurostat/data/database

Farrukh, M., Khan, A. A., Khan, M. S., Ramzani, S. R., & Soladoye, A. (2017). Entrepreneurial intentions: The role of family factors, personality traits and self-efficacy. *World Journal of Entrepreneurship, Management and Sustainable Development*, *13*(4), 303–317. doi:10.1108/WJEMSD-03-2017-0018

Fayolle, A., Gailly, B., & Lassas-Clerc, N. (2006). Assessing the impact of entrepreneurship education programmes: A new methodology. *Journal of European Industrial Training*, *30*(9), 701–720. doi:10.1108/03090590610715022

Fishbein, M., & Ajzen, I. (1975). A Bayesian analysis of attribution processes. *Psychological Bulletin*, *82*(2), 261–277. doi:10.1037/h0076477

Franco, M., & Prata, M. (2019). Influence of the individual characteristics and personality traits of the founder on the performance of family SMEs. *European Journal of International Management*, *13*(1), 41–68. doi:10.1504/EJIM.2019.096498

Georgescu, M. A., & Herman, E. (2020). The impact of the family background on students' entrepreneurial intentions: An empirical analysis. *Sustainability (Basel)*, *12*(11), 4775. doi:10.3390u12114775

Gieure, C., del Mar Benavides-Espinosa, M., & Roig-Dobón, S. (2020). The entrepreneurial process: The link between intentions and behavior. *Journal of Business Research*, *112*, 541–548. doi:10.1016/j.jbusres.2019.11.088

Global Asian August. (2016). *100 Top Groups. Globe Asia (Special Issue)*. Tanri Abeng.

Halabisky, D. (2021). *Untapped talent: Entrepreneurship can help address the youth unemployment challenge*. https://www.oecd-forum.org/posts/untapped-talent-entrepreneurship-can-help-address-the-youth-unemployment-challenge

Hartšenko, J., & Küttim, M. (2019). The entrepreneurial intentions of students in Central and Eastern European countries. *Research in Economics and Business: Central and Eastern Europe*, *11*(2), 64–84.

Henley, A., Contreras, F., Espinosa, J. C., & Barbosa, D. (2017). Entrepreneurial intentions of Colombian business students: Planned behaviour, leadership skills and social capital. *International Journal of Entrepreneurial Behaviour & Research, 23*(6), 1017–1032. doi:10.1108/IJEBR-01-2017-0031

Hutagalung, B., Dalimunthe, D. M., Pambudi, R., Hutagalung, A. Q., & Muda, I. (2017). The effect of entrepreneurship education and family environment towards students' entrepreneurial motivation. *International Journal of Economic Research, 14*(20), 331–348.

Ilevbare, F. M., Ilevbare, O. E., Adelowo, C. M., & Oshorenua, F. P. (2022). Social support and risk-taking propensity as predictors of entrepreneurial intention among undergraduates in Nigeria. *Asia Pacific Journal of Innovation and Entrepreneurship, 16*(2), 90–107. doi:10.1108/APJIE-02-2022-0010

Indaryani, M., Hidayah, M., & Lusianti, D. (2021). The effects of entrepreneurial education and family environment on the interest in enterprise through students' motivation of entrepreneurship. SSRN *Electronic Journal*, 1-15. https://doi.org/doi:10.2139/ssrn.3865920

Ismail, M., Ibrahim, A. F., Yaacob, M. R., Ibrahim, A. H., Zakaria, M. N., Razak, R. C., Yusoff, M. N. H., Guan, T. T., & Kamaruddin, A. N. (2018). Determine entrepreneurial characteristics using mobile. *International Journal of Interactive Mobile Technologies, 12*(1), 141–150. doi:10.3991/ijim.v12i1.7790

Jiang, J., Xu, J., Yin, X., & Hu, J. (2022). The impact of environment on college students' entrepreneurial intention based on the mediating effect of personality traits. *Frontiers in Psychology, 13*, 972992. doi:10.3389/fpsyg.2022.972992 PMID:36605283

Joseph, I. (2017). Factors influencing international student entrepreneurial intention in Malaysia. *American Journal of Industrial and Business Management*, *7*(4), 424–428. doi:10.4236/ajibm.2017.74030

Karabulut, A. T. (2016). Personality traits on entrepreneurial intention. *Procedia: Social and Behavioral Sciences, 229*, 12–21. doi:10.1016/j.sbspro.2016.07.109

Karsono, O. M. F., & Suprapto, W. (2015). The downfall of Chinese family businesses in East Java, Indonesia. *International Journal of Academic Research, 6*(6), 298–304.

Kerr, S. P., Kerr, W. R., & Xu, T. (2018). Personality traits of entrepreneurs: A review of recent literature. *Foundations and Trends® in Entrepreneurship, 14*(3), 279-356.

Khan, N., Aslam, R., Asad, M. M., Oad, L., & Almusharraf, N. M. (2022). Effects of WFH on educators' wellbeing: Mediating role of institutional head's support and moderating role of employees' self-efficacy at university level. *Journal of Professional Capital and Community*, *7*(3), 305–326. doi:10.1108/JPCC-10-2021-0063

Kirkwood, J. (2012). Family matters: Exploring the role of family in the new venture creation decision. *Journal of Small Business and Entrepreneurship*, *25*(2), 141–154. doi:10.1080/08276331.2012.10593565

Klofsten, M., Fayolle, A., Guerrero, M., Mian, S., Urbano, D., & Wright, M. (2019). The entrepreneurial university as driver for economic growth and social change - Key strategic challenges. *Technological Forecasting and Social Change*, *141*, 149–158. doi:10.1016/j.techfore.2018.12.004

Kusumawijaya, I. K., & Astuti, P. D. (2021). Mediating role of entrepreneurial competencies: Influence of personality traits on entrepreneurial intention. *Problems and Perspectives in Management*, *19*(3), 211–220. doi:10.21511/ppm.19(3).2021.18

Le Thi BaoQ.BlischkeJ.RoyM.SadikogluF.GwendolineA. (2020, February 11). *The role of family involvement in the entrepreneurial business*. doi:10.2139/ssrn.3783758

Lingappa, A. K., Shah, A., & Mathew, A. O. (2020). Academic, family, and peer influence on entrepreneurial intention of engineering students. *SAGE Open*, *10*(3). Advance online publication. doi:10.1177/2158244020933877

Mala, I. K., Pratikto, H., & Winarno, A. (2019). The effect of family environment, entrepreneurship education and self-efficacy on entrepreneurial intention in Pondok Pesantren at throughout Malang, Indonesia. *International Journal of Business, Economics, and Law*, *20*(5), 112–119.

Meroka, M. R. (2023). Role of the family in fostering student's entrepreneurial intention. In M. Mohiuddin, M. N. H. Reza, E. Hosseini, & S. Ed-Dafali (Eds.), *Entrepreneurship – New insights*. IntechOpen. doi:10.5772/intechopen.110026

Molina, J. A. (2020). Family and entrepreneurship: New empirical and theoretical results. *Journal of Family and Economic Issues*, *41*(1), 1–3. doi:10.100710834-020-09667-y

Molino, M., Dolce, V., Cortese, C. G., & Ghislieri, C. (2018). Personality and social support as determinants of entrepreneurial intention. Gender differences in Italy. *PLoS One*, *13*(6), e0199924. doi:10.1371/journal.pone.0199924 PMID:29953517

Mourougane, A. (2012). *Promoting SME development in Indonesia*. OECD Economics Department Working Papers, No. 995, OECD Publishing. doi:10.1787/18151973

Moussa, N. B., & Kerkeni, S. (2021). The role of family environment in developing the entrepreneurial intention of young Tunisian students. *Entrepreneurial Business and Economics Review*, *9*(1), 31–46. doi:10.15678/EBER.2021.090102

Muhtarom, M., & Suyatno, A. (2018). The influence of family environment and entrepreneurship learning on technopreneurship intentions of computer science management students. *Journal of Research and Community Service*, *4*(1), 1–8.

Mulyani, S. R., Sari, V. N., & Sari, M. W. (2019). The model of employee motivation and cooperative employee performance. *Polish Journal of Management Studies*, *20*(2), 379–390. doi:10.17512/pjms.2019.20.2.32

Ngat, T. T., & Tuyet, L. T. K. (2023). The factors affecting entrepreneurial intention with self confidence as a moderator-based on elderly people as an example. *International Journal of Professional Business Review*, *8*(6), e02125. doi:10.26668/businessreview/2023.v8i6.2125

Nguyen, C. (2017). Entrepreneurial intention of international business students in Viet Nam: A survey of the country joining the Trans-Pacific Partnership. *Journal of Innovation and Entrepreneurship*, *6*(1), 7. doi:10.118613731-017-0066-z

Noor, Y. M., Hong, L. M., Zakaria, A. N. B. I., Nik Mud, N. N. B., & Yunoh, M. N. M. (2019). The factors influencing small medium enterprise (SMEs) success in Kelantan. *International Journal of Innovation. Creativity and Change*, *6*(3), 55–64.

Olofinyehun, A., Egbetokun, A., & Adelowo, C. (2022). Pooled dataset on entrepreneurial characteristics of undergraduates in selected universities in Nigeria. *Data in Brief*, *40*, 107718. doi:10.1016/j.dib.2021.107718 PMID:34993285

Osunde, C. (2017). Family businesses and its impact on the economy. *Journal of Business & Financial Affairs*, *6*(1), 1–3. doi:10.4172/2167-0234.1000251

Otache, I., Umar, K., Audu, Y., & Onalo, U. (2021). The effects of entrepreneurship education on students' entrepreneurial intentions a longitudinal approach. *Education + Training*, *63*(7/8), 967–991. doi:10.1108/ET-01-2019-0005

Pant, S. K. (2015). Role of the family in entrepreneurship development in Nepali society. *Journal of Nepalese Business Studies*, *9*(1), 37–47. doi:10.3126/jnbs.v9i1.14592

Pattanayak, S., & Kakati, M. (2023). An empirical study on entrepreneurial traits and their impact on enterprise success. *Vilakshan-XIMB Journal of Management*, *20*(2), 277–291. doi:10.1108/XJM-09-2021-0249

Pratt, M. K. (2018). Entrepreneur (entrepreneurship). *TechTarget*. https://www.techtarget.com/searchcio/definition/entrepreneur#:~:text=An%20entrepreneur%20is%20an%20individual,need%20as%20an%20economic%20opportunity.

Pugh, G., & Adkins, P. (2020). Entrepreneurship education in China evidence from a preliminary. *Scoping Study University Students*, *12*(2), 305–326. doi:10.1108/JEEE-01-2019-0006

Puspasari, D. (2023). The influence of family environment and entrepreneurship education on student self-efficacy. *Journal of Entrepreneurship Education*, *26*(2), 1–9.

Rastiti, M. S., Widjaja, S. U. M., & Handayati, P. (2021). The role of self-efficacy in mediating the effect of entrepreneurship education, economic literacy and family environment on entrepreneurial intentions for vocational school students in Jember Regency. *South East Asia Journal of Contemporary Business, Economics and Law*, *24*(2), 26-42. https://seajbel.com/wp-content/uploads/2021/03/SEAJBEL24_511.pdf

Ratten, V., & Tajeddini, K. (2019). Entrepreneurship and sport business research: Synthesis and lessons: Introduction to the special journal issue. *International Journal of Sport Management and Marketing*, *19*(1), 1–7.

Sabah, S. (2016). Entrepreneurial intention: Theory of planned behaviour and the moderation effect of start-up experience. In M. Franco (Ed.), *Entrepreneurship – Practice-oriented perspectives*. IntechOpen. doi:10.5772/65640

Samala, A. D., Ganefri, G., Yulastri, A., Indarta, Y., Ranuharja, F., & Dewi, I. P. (2022). Entrepreneurial intentions for engineering students: Does entrepreneurship education and family environment matter? *Journal of Innovation in Educational and Cultural Research*, *3*(4), 590–606. doi:10.46843/jiecr.v3i4.300

Sandi, A., & Nurhayati, M. (2020). Effect of entrepreneurship education, family environment and self-efficacy on students entrepreneurship intention. In *4th International Conference on Management, Economics and Business (ICMEB 2019)* (pp. 9-12). Atlantis Press. 10.2991/aebmr.k.200205.003

Sarwoko, E., & Nurfarida, I. N. (2021). Entrepreneurial marketing: Between entrepreneurial personality traits and business performance. *Entrepreneurial Business and Economics Review*, *9*(2), 105–118. doi:10.15678/EBER.2021.090207

Sesen, H. (2013). Personality or environment? A comprehensive study on the entrepreneurial intentions of university students. *Education + Training*, *55*(7), 624–640. doi:10.1108/ET-05-2012-0059

Sharma, L. (2014). Impact of family capital and social capital on youth entrepreneurship – A study of Uttarakhand state, India. *Journal of Global Entrepreneurship Research*, *4*(1), 1–18. doi:10.118640497-014-0014-3

Sieger, P., & Minola, T. (2017). The family's financial support as a "poisoned gift": A family embeddedness perspective on entrepreneurial intentions. *Journal of Small Business Management*, *55*, 179–204. doi:10.1111/jsbm.12273

Silk, J. S., Morris, A. S., Kanaya, T., & Steinberg, L. (2003). Psychological control and autonomy granting: Opposite ends of a continuum or distinct constructs? *Journal of Research on Adolescence*, *13*(1), 113–128. doi:10.1111/1532-7795.1301004

Siregar, Z. A. (2020). The influence of family environment, entrepreneurship knowledge and entrepreneurship motivation on students' entrepreneurship interest of Islamic education management program of Universitas Islam Negeri Sumatera Utara. In *4th Padang International Conference on Education, Economics, Business and Accounting (PICEEBA-2 2019)* (pp. 566-574). Atlantis Press. 10.2991/aebmr.k.200305.120

Soenens, B., & Vansteenkiste, M. (2005). Antecedents and outcomes of self-determination in three life domains: The role of parents' and teachers' autonomy support. *Journal of Youth and Adolescence*, *34*(6), 589–604. doi:10.100710964-005-8948-y

Soni, A., & Bakhru, K. M. (2021). Personality traits and entrepreneurial intention among chartered accountancy students. *Problems and Perspectives in Management*, *19*(3), 136–147. doi:10.21511/ppm.19(3).2021.12

Soomro, M. A., Memon, M. S., & Bukhari, N. S. (2019). Entrepreneurial education and its impact on entrepreneurial intentions: A comparative analysis of business graduates of public and private universities of Sindh. *Pacific Business Review International*, *11*(6), 35–46.

Susanto, S. C. (2018). The influence of family environment, entrepreneurship education, and self-efficiency on student entrepreneurship interest. *Journal of Management and Business Start-ups*, *2*(3), 277–286.

Taha, K. A. S., Ramlan, S. N., & Noor, I. M. (2017). The factors affecting entrepreneurial intentions of university students in Malaysia. *International Journal of Business and Technopreneurship*, *7*(2), 189–202.

Tan, J. D., Supratikno, H., Pramono, R., Purba, J. T., & Bernarto, I. (2019). Nurturing transgenerational entrepreneurship in ethnic Chinese family SMEs: Exploring Indonesia. *Journal of Asia Business Studies, 13*(2), 294–325. doi:10.1108/JABS-04-2018-0132

Tantono, M., Ongkowijoyo, G., Hongdiyanto, C., & Hartono, W. (2022). Increasing students' entrepreneurial intention using internal and external factors through entrepreneurial self-efficacy. *Expert Journal of Business and Management, 10*(2), 65-76. https://business.expertjournals.com/23446781-1007/

United Nations. (2015). *United Nations Transforming Our World: The 2030 Agenda for Sustainable Development*. Division for Sustainable Development Goals.

Uygun, R., & Kasimoglu, M. (2013). The emergence of entrepreneurial intentions in indigenous entrepreneurs: The role of personal background on the antecedents of intentions. *International Journal of Business and Management, 8*(5), 24–41. doi:10.5539/ijbm.v8n5p24

Vodă, A. I., & Florea, N. (2019). Impact of personality traits and entrepreneurship education on entrepreneurial intentions of business and engineering students. *Sustainability (Basel), 11*(4), 1192. doi:10.3390u11041192

Walter, S. G., & Dohse, D. (2009). *The interplay between entrepreneurship education and regional knowledge potential in forming entrepreneurial intentions* (No. 1549). Kiel Working Paper. http://hdl.handle.net/10419/28376

Wiani, A., Ahman, E., & Machmud, A. (2018). Effect of family environment on interest in entrepreneurship students SMK in Subang Regency. *Oikos: Jurnal Ekonomi dan Pendidikan Ekonomi, 2*(2), 122-132. doi:10.23969/oikos.v2i2.1034

Wibowo, A. (2016). Adversity quetient, self-efficacy dan kesiapan kerja siswa kelas XII program keahlian multimedia SMKN 1 Kabupaten Jombang. *Persona: Jurnal Psikologi Indonesia, 5*(2).

Yoshino, N., & Wignaraja, G. (2015). SMEs internationalization and finance in Asia. Frontier and Developing Asia: Supporting Rapid and Inclusive Growth IMF-JICA Conference Tokyo (IMF-JICA 2015).

Zhou, M. J., Mu, W. Q., Li, F. G., Zhou, Y. X., Huang, D., Wang, K. X., & Zhang, J. (2021). Entrepreneur-region fit and entrepreneurial success in China: The effect of "Confucian" personality. *Frontiers in Psychology, 12*, 724939. doi:10.3389/fpsyg.2021.724939 PMID:34566808

Chapter 3
Family Processes, Entrepreneurial Resilience, and Socio-Economic Crisis:
Case of an Entertainment and Attraction Enterprise

Isaac Idowu Abe
SashBM LLC, USA

Eke Idi Chidi
https://orcid.org/0000-0003-1407-7706
Mangosuthu University of Technology, South Africa

EXECUTIVE SUMMARY

Resilience in entrepreneurship has been shown to mean more than the capacity of individuals to cope well under adversity. It is also the ability of the business to effectively navigate psychologically, socially, culturally, and physically, and turn hostile and uncertain situations into long-term opportunities. The aim of this chapter is to consider the possibilities of turning socio-economic adversity into opportunities through the functionality of family processes and entrepreneurial resilience. The chapter will examine the case of a successful entrepreneurial company that faced adversity during the pandemic and how the company turned adversity into opportunity. The strategies of the company are further analyzed from the lens of different theories that support her actions. Leadership flexibility in approach, techniques, and strategies emerged as a dominant factor for problem-solving in coping with family business during adverse socio-economic conditions. Stress and vulnerability in high-risk situations will foster growth and empower entrepreneurship in crisis.

DOI: 10.4018/978-1-6684-8748-8.ch003

1. INTRODUCTION

There are two distinct characteristic meanings of the word "crisis" from the Chinese context. One is that crisis represents menace, and the other is that it represents opportunity (Lopez-Garcia & Costa-Sanchez, 2021). From the Hindi perspective, crisis is an unstable situation of extreme danger or difficulty (Sarval, 2022). The two meanings have something in common, it is the danger that the instability of a situation causes high risks and uncertainty. Linguistically, it may not have been correct, but the apple has not fallen far from the tree: a crisis presents alternative outcomes for sharp and innovative minded entrepreneurs. After a crisis, a business will either die or get better (World Economic Forum 2023). Seeing the opportunities emerging from crisis is one thing but being able to seize the opportunities is another. Therefore, whether the crisis is in the short-term or protract; what an entrepreneur does during crisis is the standpoint of this chapter.

This chapter is construed in the context of the global socio-economic crisis that enveloped the world between the year 2020 and 2022 because of the COVID-19 pandemic which has upended every aspect of life including (personal) how people live and work, to the (professional) how entrepreneurial businesses interact with their customers. Several successful enterprise owners believed that the crisis has changed the way they do business, and it may continue for the next five years (McKinsey,2021). Other entrepreneurs are concerned that the crisis will have a perpetual impact on customers' needs and wants over a considerable period (McKinsey, 2021). This chapter seeks to establish the ability of the entrepreneurs to adapt to changes in the business environment and how they rebound after the experiences of adverse situations (Bullough, Renko, & Myatt, 2014). Furthermore, it explores the processes that entrepreneurs utilized to develop and deploy capabilities to adapt and respond to adversity (Garett & Zettel, 2021).

At the receiving end of the global crisis caused by the pandemic is the family. Several employees who belong to a family were told to work from home as measures to mitigate the effect of spreading the COVID-19 virus (Pew research centre, 2020). Entrepreneurship under the COVID-19 regulations was classified as non-essential, hence, shops and stores closed indefinitely until the government reversed its policy (Accenture 2020). Employees who were affected by the regulations were also told to remain at home with their families. On one end, most of these employees have either separated or divorced from spouses and consequently had no family or home to return to; on the other end, those who had families were not used to spending long hours at home together. That led to endless problems irreconcilable within the family unit. The residue of the policies, regulations, and decisions of organisations and governments fell on the lap of the family (Agrawal, Cantor, Sood, Whaley, 2022). Globally, the policies, regulations, and changes made to accommodate the pandemic situation have been reversed, but the effect on the family and businesses still lingers. This chapter considers the family as a dynamic system and the family processes as the functions that organize the family businesses and help it to cope more effectively with new crisis situations (Walsh, 1996).

Entrepreneurs face multiple risks in the process of doing business. The risks include bankruptcy, financial risk, competitive risks, environmental risks, reputational risks, political and economic risks (Lyapuntsova, Belozerova, Drozdova, Afanas'ev, & Okunkova, 2018). The process of identifying, evaluating, mitigating, and making opportunistic choices and strategies geared towards developing the business is referred to as entrepreneurship risk. Most studies on resilience now demonstrate that it is primarily the outcome of individuals interaction with their external environments and the processes that promote either well-being or protect the persons against the overwhelming effect of risks factors (Zautra, Arewasikporn, & Davis, 2010). Cognitively, it is understood as something acquired (Walsh, 2015). The risk processes can be in the form of individual's coping strategies or helpful assistance through family support, schools support or communities and social policies that makes resilience more likely to grow (Walsh, 2016). Entrepreneurial resilience is more than the capacity of individuals to cope well under adversity, but it is the ability of the business to effectively navigate psychologically, socially, culturally, and physically, and turning hostile and uncertain situations into long-term opportunities (Walsh, 2016).

It is well documented that several successful entrepreneurial businesses in the United States of America are owned by families. For example, Walmart, Disney, Hy-Vee, Herscend, Rockefeller foundation and a host of others are family owned or managed businesses etc. The unexpected disruption caused by the pandemic affected most of these businesses. Recently, several of these businesses have re-opened and others have locked their doors permanently. It is the firm aim of this chapter to examine the strategies, and theoretical ideas that one of these family businesses adopted during the COVID 19 crisis, and how it turned the socio-economic adversity into an opportunity. Therefore, we the chapter adopted a case study in discussing the subject matter.

2. LITERATURE

To accomplish the set objectives for this chapter, the review of extant literature on the key concepts of this chapter namely, socio-economic environment, entrepreneurial decision making, family processes and entrepreneurial resilience is presented in this section.

Socio-Economic Environment

Entrepreneurial activities play a significant role in the socio-economic development of a nation. Measures to promote economic growth and eradicate poverty are the recommendations to achieve sustainable development (Nguyen, 2016). The United Nations sustainable goals recommend that entrepreneurs follow three main developmental goals at the point of designing growth strategies. The goals are social inclusion, environmental protection, and economic development (Andito, Carillo- Hermosilla, Del-rio, Pontrandolfo, 2018). The relationship between the sustainable development goals and innovation dynamics became the concern of scholars Glavas and Mish, (2015); Kennedy et al (2016) and Andito et al (2018). Sustainable innovations were documented as a means through which organizations foster sustainable development. Entrepreneurs play a significant and critical role in the sustainable future of the state, through the changing competitive environment due to growing attention from researchers, companies, and government. The dynamics of the socio-economic environment has led to companies changing the way they think about technologies, products, processes, and business models. Enterprises are known to drive economic growth and job creation. Private enterprises account for significant percentage of all formal business entities and contributors to the Gross Domestic Product of nations. They also provide employment opportunities that drive economic sustainability (Surya, Hadijah, Suriana, Baharuddin, Fitriyah, Menne, & Rasyidi, 2020).

Entrepreneurial Decision Making in Times of Crises

Crisis creates economic shocks that disrupt enterprise activities. These disruptions have no regard for the levels of development attained by an economy or business enterprise. Disruption cuts across both the developed and the developing economies (Camuffo, Cordova, Gambardella & Spina, 2020). The role of entrepreneurship in recovery from crisis has generated lots of interest from scholars and practitioners, respectively. The body of knowledge is growing on the importance of entrepreneurial decision-making in times of uncertainty (Rapp, & Olbrich, 2020).

Recent developments in the discipline of entrepreneurship have resulted in a renewed interest in entrepreneurial action as a catalyst for economic recovery and sustainability in the post-disaster economic environments (Akinboye, & Morrish, 2022). Where an economic environment is engulfed by fear and danger of losing business, the uncertainty of restarting or reopening operations, coupled with additional vulnerability and risk beg for decision-making actions. According Bullough and Renko (2013), even at times of war and conditions of uncertainty, individuals and business leaders develop entrepreneurial intentions to allow them grow out of adversity. The belief individuals have in their entrepreneurial abilities and self-efficacy, which are the tools needed for entrepreneurial activity pushes them into entrepreneurial activities and possibly, resilience in the face of crises. Therefore, what appears as disaster may present new opportunities by disrupting the existing economic market. Entrepreneurial self-efficacy enhances effective recognition and exploitation of these opportunities (Miles, Lewis, Hall-Phillips, Morrish, Gilmore, & Kasouf, 2016).

Post-disaster environments are characterized by entrepreneurial activities that can lead to economic recovery. The environments are laced with hazardous conditions and uncertainty and low levels of motivation in making entrepreneurial decisions (Akinboye et al, 2022). These post-disaster entrepreneurial activities have been studied previously, but not much attention has been given to the entrepreneurial decisions that leads to success. The decision to take entrepreneurial actions in an uncertain and complex environment depends on specific environmental factors like motivation, self-perception and using decision making logics (Shepherd, & Osofero & Wincent,2022).

Entrepreneurial decisions have led to entrepreneurial actions that are effective in solving societal problems that result from disasters that range from unemployment, poverty, loss of earnings, and environmental ruin. Usually, crisis environments are characterized by negative emotions which impedes the decision-making actions of entrepreneurs. When such situation occurs, the hope of the entrepreneur is to exercise resilience through recognition and exploitation of opportunities in the environments and investigation of disaster recovery strategies that will assist them in their business recovery trajectory (Akinboye et al, 2022).

During the period of disaster, risk and uncertainties that are central to entrepreneurial process are heightened. Under these conditions, it is imperative for entrepreneurs to make logical decisions to manage the scarcity of resources and reduce the phobia of investors in the aftermath of crisis. However, the perceptions of individual and businesses differ between natural and man-made disasters. For example, victims of man-made disasters like terror attacks exhibit high risk discernments, while those from natural disasters like flood are surrounded with uncertainty. Therefore, it is important to evaluate the role of entrepreneurial decision-making with regards to the assessment of causation and effectuation during man-made and natural disasters (Shepherd, et al. 2022).

Family Processes and Resilience

The functions that underpin the way that families are organized are referred to as family process. These organized functions demand that the family adjusts to new needs and new conditions as the external environment dictates. According to Samani and Benhmanesh, (2011), the functions that makes up the family process construct are, communication skills, decision making, coping, problem solving, flexibility,, parenting, tolerance, planning, leadership, assertiveness, perspective taking, and self-presentation. However, the family members apply these functions to manipulate emotional cognitive and social events. These functions are key processes that enable individuals and families to effectively cope with new crisis (Walsh, Moore, Barber, & Opsteen, 2014). Over the years, researchers have attempted to identify these functions and have advanced the knowledge of family processes (Olson, 1993).

The concept of family resilience refers to the capacity of the family to function as a system built to withstand and rebound from adversity (Walsh, 1996, 2016a, & 2016b). The premise for this concept is found in the family systems theory which suggests that serious crises and persistent life challenging situations have significant effect on the whole family. Therefore, important family processes mediate adaptation for individual members, their relationships, and the family unit collectively.

Extending the knowledge of family processes as a functional unit, the concept of family resilience was presented to foster relational resilience of a family as a functional unit. The resiliency approach locates each family in relation to its challenges, constraints, and resources. The challenges may take the form of strains to normal life-cycle transitions, retirement, divorce, or remarriage, job loss, or untimely death of a family member or protracted strains of migration, or inner-city violence (Walsh, 1996). How families that own businesses deal with these challenges are crucial for the individual and business recovery (Walsh, 2020).

Resilience revolves from many recursive processes over a given time, which stems from family's approach to a threatened crisis through immediate disruptions and in the long-run adaptations. The processes involved in dealing with a set of challenges might be different from another. Relational or family resilience involves patterns organized to factor in communication and problem-solving processes, community resources, and affirmation of belief systems. However, it is important for family members to coherently make meaning of their crisis experience and build collaboration, competence, and confidence in surmounting family challenges. Therefore, due to the increasing family diversity and strains of social and economic upheaval, the family resilience processes have become relevant particularly to the times since families are prepared to meet uncertainty and future challenges with mutual support, flexibility and innovation needed for evolutionary hardiness in a changing world (Walsh 2020).

Entrepreneurial Resilience

Although the concept of resilience has increasingly become multi-disciplinary, much is still expected. Different dimensions of resilience have been studied by researchers, from health, psychology, and in the context of entrepreneurship (Corner, Singh, & Pavlovich, 2017; Bullough & Renko, 2013). In a health study, dimensions of hardness, resourcefulness, and optimism among Spanish entrepreneurs have been tested (Manzano & Ayala, 2013). Bullough et al (2013) investigated the psychological factors that drives entrepreneurial decisions during periods of adversity. The study revealed that entrepreneurial self-efficacy imbibed in business development training to build individual's belief in their entrepreneurial ability is instrumental to entrepreneurial resilience. Pursue of networking events, special lectures, and mentoring opportunities that model others who have been resilient during challenging times and agility in entrepreneurial pursuits, practicing business acumen are also attributed to proofs of resilience (Bullough, et al 2013).

Corner, Singh, and Pavlovich, (2017) in a study observed three distinct limitations associated with the knowledge of entrepreneurial resilience.

Firstly, the conceptualization of entrepreneurial resilience is not consistent with recent studies in psychology. The constructs needed to go beyond microprocesses (Leipold & Greve, 2009); rather than the focus being placed on the mechanisms that underlie resilience, for example, optimism, and hardness (Luthans & Vogelgesang, 2006). Secondly, the definition of entrepreneurial resilience lacks insight, as stability in emotional and psychological functioning, though it could unfold with time. Research on this concept has been based on a one-point measurement rather than on medium- or long-term dimension at the center of psychological constructs. For example, psychological studies have described typical patterns in functioning for two years after a traumatic event or loss (Bonanno, Bakker & Jussaume, 2011). One pattern is the description of resilience as a moderate disruption in functioning for a few months and the return to normal functioning (Parker &Ameen, 2018). And the other pattern is the severe or chronic disruptions in functioning that is not improving after two years of the event (Corner et al, 2017). The delayed and the recovery patterns fall in between. Thirdly, another limitation is that this chapter examines the decisions that are necessary for the survival of the family business although the pattern of disruption was not long and given the severity of the pandemic crisis (Fatoki, 2018). Peculiar case of a protracted crisis was the governmental regulations and conventions to the Covid-19 pandemic in South Africa which lasted in a near-total economic lockdown for over six hundred days. The trajectory threw many entrepreneurs and their entrepreneurial activities into jeopardy. A few entrepreneurs survived the fallout of this conundrum. Entrepreneurial resilience involves the potential for personal and relational transformation and positive development that can be forged out of adversity (Schafer, Kunzler, Kalisch, Tuscher & Lieb, 2022).

The case study examined in this chapter unpacks the practical interplay among entrepreneurship and family processes in a socioeconomic crisis.

3. CASE STUDY

The significant strength of resilience demonstrated by a family-controlled enterprise in the United States of America is noteworthy to the discussions of this chapter. The family enterprise was formed in 1950 (seventy-three years ago) by a couple entrepreneurs who were family members that pulled their resources together. The enterprise started in Georgia and had since spread to other states in the country. It owns several privately operated theme parks, tourist attractions and entertainment companies in the United States and Canada. This enterprise had about eleven thousand employees in her employment prior to the Covid-19 pandemic. The organization grew to become influential in the attraction and entertainment industry. In 2020, Covid-19 struck and governments globally, implemented stringent measures ranging from lockdowns to social distancing which forbade out and indoor entertainment and socializing. Therefore, due to the impact of the pandemic and its conventions, many of the enterprise's subsidiaries were forced to close operations temporarily between 2020 to 2021. The temporary closure resulted in total loss of revenue from all the concerned outlets. Th emerging problems, questions, and challenges called for leadership strategies, decisions, and changes in the objectives and goals of the organization.

Historical Background of the Enterprise

In this case study, aliases and pseudonyms will be used from time to time to protect the examined organization's reputation and confidentiality, In the beginning, two entrepreneurs namely H and M are husband and wife who visited an expansive cave in 1946 having heard that the original owner was looking to sell the cave. They negotiated a ninety-nine-year lease on the land in 1950 and became the owners. The family commenced the business by upgrading and improving the caves to attract more visitors. It led to a train being installed to move visitors around the cave from the lower part to the surface improving capacity and accessibility by 1959. Sixty-five thousand people visited the property each year generating over two hundred thousand dollars in revenue. The business expanded organically, so the couple created a small village close to the cave which was set in an 1880 mining town. The aim was to build a live in community with a general store, blacksmith store, ice cream parlor, authentic log cabins and a church. The village was named" SDC" in reference to the decision to give certain dollar incentives to patrons to promote the new business (attraction).

By 1964, the theme park attracted over 450,000 visitors at approximately three million dollars in revenues. At this point in time both SDC and the wonder cave were being operated by the couple's sons K and L). After multitude of successes, the brothers continued to expand their attractions, kept their Christian values at the heart of running the company.

By 1976, SDC attracted over 1.4 million annual visitors, employing over 800 members of staff. Hence, it was time for the business to expand away from its birthplace. The brothers' sites fell upon a park in pigeon forge Tennessee known as gold rush junction. They purchased the park for two million dollars in 1976 and renamed it Silver Dollar City. In the process the family found an opportunity to replicate what they had in another region. It was initially challenging; this ultimately discouraged the brothers from building more SDC parks keeping it to just two. As a result, the enterprise rather expanded into water park industry for the first time.

White water park in Branson Missouri opened in 1980 consisting of multiple waterslides rides and pools and the following years partially going further to open four more water parks. White water park in Oklahoma City grand prairie, Garland, and Atlanta. However, over the next two decades the four parks were gradually sold off to wet and wild premier parks and six flags. Despite this the brothers gained a greater appreciation for dealing with multiple properties in many states to assist in sustaining the growing business, they also created a board of six people, only two persons in the board belong to the original family that started the family business.

By including external opinions on major business decisions, the brothers hoped to ensure all developments were a positive move for the organisation. Although SDC in Tennessee was initially successful, the popularity of the park soared after they secured a deal with Dolly Parton, a well-known country artist at that time. Dolly was informed about the original SDC park in the early 1980s and after visiting was inspired to open a park of her own in Tennessee. Instead of accepting her proposition, the brothers offered her a partnership with her in Pigeon Forge Tennessee. That gave birth to Dollywood in 1986.

In the 90's the chain grew further with investments in new and exciting properties in Branson. They built the GTP together with Kenny Rogers, a four thousand seat theatre. This was followed by the GVS, an Ozark-themed shopping complex near the GTP and the debut of a second theatre in Pigeon Forge. However, overwhelming costs led to all three properties being sold in the years following. By 1995, the company had become a huge success gaining more than 100 million dollars in profit and attracting over 1.7 million visitors to their silver dollar city theme park. In 1998, they entered partnership with the State of Georgia to manage ae historical park located near the state capital. This was followed by the debut of Dolly splash country Dollywood's very own water park in 2001. The organisation also partnered with Ride the Ducks. An attraction that used amphibious World War 11 vehicles to take guests on water tours. They at the same time expanded the franchise to cities before acquiring the business in 2004. In 2017, it was then sold to a popular entertainment company. By this time also the business had seen a range of CEOs come and go from the chain.

As K was getting too old for the business role, they once again reached out to someone external from the family. Three CEOs have successfully run their tenures while the chain continued to expand, in 2019, they reached an agreement to operate and manage Callaway resort and gardens. As of 2020 the chain owns or operates over 25 different properties which employ 11,000 members of staff and attract 14 million visitors annually.

In the year 2020 by March the 16th, the enterprise had just opened Dollywood for season past holders and suddenly Disney announced an immediate closure of business operations. They are the leaders in the industry of family entertainment and attractions. After the shut down it became clear that serious and decisive actions will be needed. So, the CEO announce the closing of all franchises and properties.

Problem

According to the Global Association for the attraction industry (IAAPA) data on employment impact of the COVID-19 on the U.S. Attractions Industry (IAAPA, 2021). The industry faced its greatest crisis since the World War 11. Nearly all attraction parks in the world were closed to prevent the spread of the Covid-19 pandemic globally. During the pandemic, the challenges were that survival and success of the company was under immense pressure. Furthermore, business of all natures and sectors were completely shut down, and even when they were eventually opened months later, new safety protocols and regulations hampered the operations and capacity engagement was limited by staffing shortages, consumer reluctance and government restrictions. The limitations had severe effect on the industry in the United States with employment falling to levels not seen in decades. About seventy percent of the employees were laid off during the pandemic.

Organizational Culture and Goals

The examined organization rooted its business culture in the action of love. The community slogan is “love in action” which is used to describe how the organization wants people to perceive her and how owners and employees should behave and treat clients and each other. Their core business language is “leading with love”. The organization has nine defined behaviors and a purposeful structure that requires all employees in the organization to be trained to enable every employee to understand, align, and comply with the core culture of love.

The story was told about one of the hosts (an employee), who came across a family comprising a father and two children, who were obviously distraught. The host walked up to them to ask what was wrong and assured them that she was available to help them in every way possible, They family informed her that they did not come with enough money for the whole family to get in, and so their mom had to stay in the car. The employee knew immediately that this was the antithesis of what the organization was trying to achieve. Knowing that she had the organization's permission to lead with love, she took the family to the front gate, refunded their tickets, had the dad call his wife to meet with them at the front gate. Thereafter, the employee allowed them into the facility for free. Additionally, she refunded the money that they initially paid for ticket purchase so that they could have money to spend in entertaining themselves throughout the day. In this context, it could be said that the success of the company is not only in its generosity but also in the bold belief that in the demonstration of love lies the core strength of their business strategy..

Leadership Actions in Times of Crises

As the examined organization entered the beginning of the pandemic in 2020, the immediate challenge confronting the leadership was uncertainty about how long the pandemic will last. And for an organization whose operating setting depends on mass gatherings of people coming into a space where they could be close to each other, whether in a theme park, a water park, or dinner theatre or globetrotter game in an arena, the duration of the uncertainty was imperative. This drastically impacted the earnings of the organization and resulted in their income basically going down to ground zero. as there was no opportunity to make money.

Leadership effort at the time was not centered on endeavoring not to lose the enterprise but focused more on saving the family legacy. The legacy is about caring, taking care of people, and bringing families closer together. Their core value of leading with love was put to test, with respect to employees, clients, and stakeholders.

In the words of the chief executive, 'the first thing was to be upfront with the employees' by restating the obvious scenario to avoid creating a panic situation among them. Going out of business has never been to the advantage of anyone, so the leadership made their stand clear about the need to make real hard decisions to ensure the organization survived. Nevertheless, on the long run, they went from about 6600 employees to only 300, for the organization to survive. The second step was to ensure that the employees had money in their pockets to make it through the hard period of the pandemic. The stimulus packages of the Federal and State governments in the USA for unemployment were buffers as it was clear that there was going to be some cash for furloughed employees. But there were no health benefits attached to the stimulus packages so, the leadership took up the challenge to bridge the gap by paying the health benefits for all the furloughed employees in the organization.

Questions

The following salient questions were carved out by reason of the case study.

1. What is the situation of the family enterprise and your reaction to the organization's goals, cultures and vision that is under threat by the socio-economic crisis catalyzed by the pandemic?
2. What other possible actions could the leaders of this organization have taken to turn around the fortunes of the organization in the socio-economic adversity that they faced?
3. What were the opportunities open to the organization and consequences of not acting on them by the organization? List and briefly explain with respect to the implication on the family legacy, employees, and on the customers.
4. Are there any strategic actions that the organization should have taken to avoid laying off the number of employees that they did at the crucial time of the pandemic?
5. What are the general principles, models, and theories to follow in the establishing an organization's resilience in a socioeconomic crisis?

4. ANALYSIS OF THE CASE WITH PRINCIPLES, CONCEPTS, AND THEORIES

In response to the salient questions raised in this chapter, the following concepts and theories have been found to be suitable to both answer the question and give direction to the chapter.

Theory of Organizational Culture

The study of organizational culture is the concept that perceives the organization as a social phenomenon which possesses its own characteristics that differentiates it from an environment on one hand and from the individual aspirations and tendencies of its members on the other (Allaire & Firsirotu, 1984). Furthermore, the concept of organizational culture is useful in studying the processes of decay, adaptation, and radical change in complicated organizations. Hofstede (2011) upgraded the thinking of organizational culture in his study that demonstrated that organizations primarily and in value differ in their practices. The macro and micro analytic theories of organizational culture take the knowledge of culture further.

Macro analytic theories are concerned with understanding group culture, the functions of culture in maintaining a whole group or the conditions that makes group develop culturally. It largely deals with the rites and ceremonies of an organization. These rites are (rites of passage, degradation, renewal, and integration) and suggested that the rites fulfil both manifest, latent, and social functions (Trice & Beyer, 1984). It is also connected to the forms and content of culture that are interpreted as results of the needs of the company for efficiency. The content of an organizational culture results from the specific economic conditions that the organization members find themselves (Jones, 1983). Jones suggested that three types of culture may result, namely: production, professional, and bureaucratic. This culture may become the company's specific asset which can yield tremendous returns. The theories attempted to describe the purpose, functions and pattern of belief, language, and symbol in organizations. The element of culture presents organizations as stable and orderly and is regarded as resistant to explicit manipulation due to their natural and evolutionary features. Organizations in crisis situations need to examine the rites that the company observes to be able to cope with the unforeseen economic hardships associated with the crisis. Until the disruption of any sort, organizations with cultural efficiency are deemed orderly, stable, and successful.

Microanalytic theories are cultural values that reside within an individual and are understandable through the cognitive processes of learning, causal attribution, sense-making and by probing the unconscious mind (Kim, 2012). Existing works have been separated into two broad categories namely: psychological notions of attribution or social learning and the direction to the unconscious or underlying assumptions that offer meaning to the manifest nature of culture. The first category examined the disconnection between behaviours and attitudes.

Culture is the consolidation of what an individual has learnt about their organization, which is based on: observed results of past actions, and attempts to cope with failure and success as well as the need to avoid anxiety. Ultimately, this learning produces a few commonly shared beliefs. The pandemic introduced behaviors and attitudes that most employees may have found difficult to cope with knowing that it was not part of the culture of the organization. For example, the culture of assisting every customer may be reduced or withdrawn to be able to cope with the need for financial leverage that the company may be confronted with before eventually shutting down sites. The disruption of the pandemic set different tones, behaviours, and attitudes on the culture of organizations especially in the area of employees' uncertainty about the security of their jobs.

The cultural phenomena that contribute to failure and success of organizations were identified as power, role, task, and person. Power is a centralized form of rulership source such as is common in entrepreneurial organizations. Power characteristics are trust, and personal communication coupled with minimal bureaucracies, rules, and policies (Tear, Reader, Shorrock, & Kirwan, 2020). The role culture is the bureaucracy type that works with hospitals. Its strength is in the pillars, functions, and specialties

(Arigoni & Schofield, 2020). The task culture aims at gathering the right people with the right resources for job accomplishment. This may be in the form of committees, scheduling, and staffing issues (Govender, 2018). The person's culture is that which is directed at assisting and serving the individuals within an organization. The person is supported with the ultimate outcome of enhancing organizational goals (Joice, 2021). In the case studied in this chapter, employees needed to trust the decisions and actions of the employer, though some leadership steps may not favor them, but the actions were necessary for the survival of the company.

Kane-Urrabazo (2006) identified four building blocks for management to put in place, even when the cultures may seem to be predetermined. The onus of facilitating a positive work environment is the responsibility of the leadership of an organization. The following traits must be valued as success indicators, trustworthiness and trust, empowerment and delegation, consistency, and mentorship. Trustworthiness and trust are the outcomes of character and competence hence having integrity and honesty is not enough. Having confidence and believing in someone makes the difference. Trust includes the willingness to take risks due to the vulnerability to the actions of others. Trust refers to employees' faith in organization leadership and the confidence that organizational actions will benefit employees eventually (Brett& Michell, 2020). Empowerment is the process of enabling others to act or do something. The principle of empowerment contributes to employees' sense of worth. The tools that enhance empowerment are communication, positive interpersonal relationships, and commitment (Froner, 2017). Consistency means that organizational structure, mission statement, shared values, management philosophies and other principles must be congruent (aligned) with each other (Su, Chen, Cui, Yang & Ma, 2020). In connecting to the case study, it is imperative to infer that leadership sets the tone for the culture that an organization practices. The behaviours, character, disposition to work, interactions and relational successes depend on the organizational culture laid out by the leadership The leadership of a company must in times of crises, demonstrate the cultural ethos of the organization and use them as building blocks to be able to surmount above the crisis.

The Concept of Family Resilience

Family resilience is the ability to bounce back from crisis and challenges, Family resilience offers key processes that enable the family to surmount crisis and persistent stresses. Walsh (1996) documented that the resilience needed to weather the storm of adversity resides in the individual who is a product of a family. Furthermore, resilience can be found in families and family interventions, particularly when not viewed from the lens of dysfunctionality in families. Family resilience fosters a sense of coherence, collaboration, competence, and confidence that are important in coping and mastering adversity and conversely shaping members resilience. The way the family as a functional unit deal with crisis associated with adversity is critical. Many adaptive ways are possible, with more resilient families using various broad coping strategies, more effective problem-solving techniques, and more flexibility in dealing with internal and external life events (Walsh, 2021). Therefore, in coping with adverse situations the family resilience concept emphasizes the need for individuals or the family unit to be more flexible in approach, techniques, and strategies, to stay the business afloat in crisis.

According to Bonanno, Romero, and Klein, (2015) in a psychological study on the enhancement of emotional expression argued that the successful adaptation of enhancing and suppressing emotion depends not so much on any regulatory process, but on the ability to be flexible in enhancing or suppressing emotions as the case may demand. To reconcile enhancement and suppression of emotions, a study had indicated that the important element in successful adaptation depends on the coping strategies applied flexibly (Cheng, 2001). When flexibility is expressive, it is stable and protective (Westphal, Seivert & Bonanno, 2010). Where an individual, leader, or persons are highly stressed due to disruptions that affect their daily activities or operations, such a leader needs to be flexible in expressing their emotions (Westphal, et al, 2010).

The family resilience framework was developed to understand important variables that contribute to individual and leadership resilience in functional families. It helps to identify and target key family processes that can reduce stress and vulnerability in high-risk situations, foster business rebound and growth out of socio-economic crisis while empowering entrepreneurship to overcome protracted adversity (Walsh, 2015). The framework synthesizes key family processes within three domains of family functions, namely, family belief systems, organization patterns and communication processes (Walsh 1998). Family belief systems affect the way an individual views crisis, sufferings, and options (Wright, Watson, & Bell, 1996). Whether a personal tragedy or collective catastrophic event, adversity generates crisis and disruption of integration while resilience fosters shared, facilitative beliefs that increase the option for problem resolution, healing, and growth. Therefore, through an individual's belief system, affected persons are helped to make meaning of the crisis situations; facilitate a hopeful positive outcome; and offer spiritual anchorage.

The patterns of communication adopted by a family fosters resilience by providing clarity to a crisis, encouraging open emotional expression, and promoting collaborative problem-solving. In clear and consistent communication, ambiguous information is eliminated as much as possible; and all parties seek truth and speak truth to each other. Open communication that is supported by a climate of mutual trust, empathy and tolerance for differences allow members to share a wide range of feelings that can be created by a crisis (Afif, & Firsirotu, 2016). Creative brainstorming and resourcefulness in communication open new frontiers of possibilities for overcoming crisis, paving way for healing and growth out of a quagmire. Furthermore, resilient families set clear and unambiguous goals and take decisive steps towards achieving them (Giustiniano, eCunha, Simpson, Rego, & Clegg, 2020). Therefore, individuals and families do better when they become more resourceful and are able to shift from crisis reactive mode to proactive stance, in anticipation of a better prepared future.

The way an individual, family or enterprise organizes itself with resilience is demonstrated through their flexible structure, connectedness, and socio-economic resources. The discussion on resilience in this chapter centers on flexibility since it is a core element in the resilience process (Theiss, 2018).. However, in the aftermath of the major crisis and transitions, the ideal word to qualify a business' return to operations and possibly profitability would be "bounce back". A better metaphor for resilience will be "bouncing forward" by way of changing to meet new challenges (Walsh, 2002b). Enterprises often need support in navigating new terrain and in undergoing structural organization. With such occurrences like the COVID 19 pandemic, entrepreneurs must construct new sense of normality as they recreate relationships and reorganize patterns of interactions to fit in to the new conditions of post-pandemic.

Firm flexible authoritative leadership is most effective for enterprise functioning and well-being during period of crisis and uncertainty. It is imperative for leadership to provide nurturance, protection. and guidance through the period of turmoil and recovery. For instance, those employees affected by reason of the pandemic who are willing to come back to work for the organization should be considered first in demonstrating the strength of the leadership to showcase dependability and truth to the culture of the organization (Capler, 2021). In addition, creating a psychological buffer through providing counsel for employees who are traumatized and laid off during the shutdown is also a sign of leadership strength and prerogative. Such therapeutic efforts are directed towards empowering employees to take mastery over the challenges through the collaborative efforts of the leadership, families and therapists to assist affected persons.

Naturalistic Decision-Making (NDM)

The concept of decision making has changed the ways in which managers thought about their business-related actions (Pettigrew, 2014). The term decision indicates that the deciders have reached an end to series of deliberation and that the implementation of the needed actions has commenced or will soon commence. Entrepreneurial decision-making is of vital importance, and why certain decisions fail is crucial to the success of the business. The entrepreneur's decision-making process is largely influenced by the approach they adopt. The approaches may either be rational, emotional, or intuitive. For instance, the assumption of the traditional approach was that decision making was often unsuccessful due to a lack of recognition of uncertainties, time pressures, and unforeseen events on the part of decision makers. Therefore, NDM was introduced as a means by which leadership makes decisions despite uncertainty and the decisions are based on intuitive approach (De-Winnaar & Scholtz, 2018).

Four basic steps have been identified in the decision-making process namely, recognition of the present states, evaluation of the immediate options, selection of an action based on one's needs and re-evaluating the option based on the outcome (Beach & Lipshitz, 2017). But Lunenburg (2011) also identified six steps namely, identifying the problem, generating alternatives, evaluating alternatives, choosing an alternative, implementing the decision, and evaluating the decision effectiveness.

NDM offers decision makers the choice to make decisions under pressure without needing to compare options by presenting the concepts of situation assessment and mental simulation at the same time. Therefore, in the real case scenario NDM takes into consideration risks and uncertainties which disincentivize decision-makers from making actual decisions. Summarily, the NDM separates the concepts of risk and uncertainty (Zsambok, 2014).

By the concept of NDM the complexities involved in leadership decisions and actions that are deemed necessary and inevitable in a given pressure that an organization experience can be seen. The case study examined in this chapter presents various factors for assessment and decision areas that demanded the attention of the leadership during the Covid-19 pandemic.

Concept of Entrepreneurial Resilience

From the views of Kossek and Perrigino (2016), resilience is a multifaceted gestalt construct integrating resources that an individuals can draw on; namely: traits (that is, personality hardiness), capacities (i.e., developing capabilities and coping strategies), and processes (i.e., appraisal of feedback and experiences with adaptation) into a process model where these factors- plus contextual influences – interact to determine how individuals will successfully (or unsuccessfully) respond to stressors

Capabilities are developments necessary for a resilient response to adversity. These capabilities are skills, knowledge, and access to resources that can be leveraged when the need arises (Williams, Gruber, Sutcliffe, Shepherd & Zhao, 2017). The implication is that such capabilities may be dormant until needed, but they exist, and are measurable in the absence of adverse events. This implies that individuals/ entrepreneurs can respond to adverse conditions in a manner that promotes optimal performance because they have the factors necessary to act accordingly (Britt, Shen, Sinclair, Grossman & Klieger, 2016).

The resources on the other hand, are categorized as financial, physical, and informational resources, these factors have been identified as critical to resilience. For example, while capability endowments are trait based and acquired, financial capability endowments provide the resources needed to absorb shocks and manage crisis. Social resources are relational capability endowments which represent access to resources from a network of social support (Piprani, Jaafar & Mohezar, 2020). The entrepreneur needs to have the capability to access the available support. Without doubt, different social connections are crucial for resilience. For example, the support from family, work force, and the community (Britt et al. 2016), help individuals and organizations to remain resilient in crisis, as access to these resources provide instrumental, emotional and information support that the entrepreneur needs to get out of crisis.

Cognitive behavioral capabilities are entrepreneurial ability to direct attention to issues, process and understand challenges, and provide solutions the problems. The entrepreneur is expected to develop actions and behavioral routines to withstand crisis known as coping skills. In entrepreneurship research, it has been noted that entrepreneurs who use a combination of coping skills achieve better long-term well-being for the organization. Generally, entrepreneurs apply coping techniques that allow them to escape from problems even if it is temporary (Uys, Foo. & Song, 2013).

Recommendation

The following strategic interventions are recommended for the practitioners, families, entrepreneurs, and leaders of organizations who need to know what to do when faced with socio-economic crisis. If another pandemic occurs in the magnitude of the global Corona virus, what entrepreneurial leaders should do are as follows: First is the need for leaders of firms to be flexible in their leadership approach. Emphasizing on the need for leaders to shift from traditional to emerging leadership styles, Jordan, Wade & Yokoi (2022) postulated 7 strategies for the leader. Power sharer, visionary, adaptor, analyst, accelerator, prospector, and listener; as against power holder, tactician, constant, perfectionist, intuitionist, miner, and teller. Leaders who remain authentic will always motivate employees who are resistant to any form of technological advancement. Jordan et al (2022) further advised practicing leaders to find the right balance and be flexible at the same time in leadership style. Therefore, leadership flexibility demands a shift from the old manner of doing things to seeking strategic approaches to solving emerging problems.

Leadership must be willing to nurture, protect and guide organizations through hard times. The root of organizational resilience is in employee resilience. Through supports and care for employees tailored interests physically and mentally. Support employees' wellbeing, have a common purpose and adjust routines and processes to fit into the times the organization is passing through. According to Fernandez & Shaw, 2020, such a leader is similar to an academic leader who is known to have emotional intelligence and stability. The organization can rely on the leader because they place the interests of other above their own.

Strategically encourage employee wellness by providing buffer to counsel those in trauma during the period of adversity. This is usually done through an organizational culture that fosters supports and care for the employees. In a study Childs, Turner, Sneed & Berry (2022) investigated small retail leaders during times of crisis. The study revealed that they had resilient mindset, showing passion, agility, innovation, and relationship development. Encouraging employee wellness is an important tool to develop relationship among other tools.

Leadership collaborative effort should be towards empowering employees and their families during individual crisis or national disaster. Fernandez et al (2020) wrote that when leadership effort is towards collaboration and employee empowerment, leadership is a type of servant leadership. In crisis, this leadership style becomes more critical in that the leaders ets aside all biases to focus on solving the problems at hand carrying all stakeholders along.

Future Research

Lessons learnt from the invasion of the coronavirus pandemic according to public health leaders is that through the examination of the role and responsibility of the private sector, more needs to be done in supporting public health. Therefore, innovative, and collaborative partnerships need to be created to speed up responses to such crisis and promote and protect public health in the future (Kocsis, Roesler, & Totten, 2022). Milken Institute Center for Public Health requests for a new model of partnerships that focus on sustainable and systemic public impact. Opportunistic future areas to strengthen, protect and sustain public health may focus on human capital, logistics and data infrastructure.

Describing the unevenness in economic recovery globally, Michael Schlein (2022) reports that the global economic recovery is failing low-income people, families, and small businesses. To build a truly effective and inclusive recovery that will be sustainable, the realities of different people need to be considered. The hardest hit groups and businesses need empowerment in the areas that develop resilience. Therefore, the attention on recovery should be focused on inclusion, expansion of digital access and equity, and creating financial tools that build financial wellbeing.

Imperial College Business School (2022) in a collaboration with Asian Development Bank wrote on entrepreneurial resilience after the COVID-19, stating that although there has been considerable literature on the navigation of large businesses through the pandemic, less is known about how the smaller entrepreneurial businesses can increase their resilience against external shocks. Research is urgently needed that identifies effective strategies that assist entrepreneurs individually and as communities of entrepreneurship. This is an important gap in research for entrepreneurial directions, which scholars need to investigate further.

CONCLUSION

This chapter contributes to the literature of entrepreneurial businesses by examining a large family-based enterprise that survived the onslaught of the Covid-19 pandemic. The survival of the organization was informed by the demonstration of a strong organizational culture which derived from the family processes of the leadership, which kept both the leadership and the employees resilient during the difficult and uncertain time of the COVID-19 pandemic. Despite the pressure of the crisis, the organization needed to make informed decisions that considered her survival and the wellbeing of her employees. The organization demonstrated resilience by being able to use the tenets of her culture of love in action to contend the external environmental shocks created by the novel Covid-19 pandemic, following the order of national governments globally to close business operations, to isolate or keep social distances, and to sanitize hands frequently to prevent the extension of the virus. Both microanalytic and macro analytic cultures of the organization were instrumental to the resilience demonstrated in recovery of the organization during the crisis period.

Strategic factors of the family processes like leadership, communication skills, planning and flexibility have proven to be instrumental in repositioning the organization through a time of unprecedented crisis. The examination of different concepts and theories engaged in this chapter highlighted very crucial and salient thoughts of the leadership that fostered success through the hard times. Therefore, our case study took a hard knock through adversity and turned the same into success.

REFERENCES

Afifi, T. D., Merrill, A. F., & Davis, S. (2016). The theory of resilience and relational load. *Personal Relationships*, *23*(4), 663–683. doi:10.1111/pere.12159

Akinboye, A. K., & Morrish, S. C. (2022). Conceptualizing post-disaster entrepreneurial decision-making: Prediction and control under extreme environmental uncertainty. *International Journal of Disaster Risk Reduction*, *68*, 102703. doi:10.1016/j.ijdrr.2021.102703

Allaire, Y., & Firsirotu, M. E. (1984). Theories of organizational culture. *Organization Studies*, *5*(3), 193–226. doi:10.1177/017084068400500301

Andito, Carillo-Hermosilla, Del-rio, & Pontrandolfo. (2018). Sustaining innovation: Processes, strategies, and outcomes. *Corporate Social Responsibility and Environmental Management*, *25*(1), 106–109.

Arrigoni, G., Schofield, T., & Trujillo Pisanty, D. (2020). Framing collaborative processes of digital transformation in cultural organisations: From literary archives to augmented reality. *Museum Management and Curatorship*, *35*(4), 424–445. doi:10.1080/09647775.2019.1683880

Beach, L. R., & Lipshitz, R. (2017). Why classical decision theory is an inappropriate standard for evaluating and aiding most human decision making. In *Decision making in aviation* (pp. 85–102). Routledge. doi:10.4324/9781315095080-5

Bonanno, A., Bakker, H., Jussaume, R., Colfer, C. J. P., & Pfund, J. L. (2011). Decentering Biotechnology: Assemblages Built and Assemblages Masked. Burlington, VT: Ashgate.

Bonanno, G. A., Romero, S. A., & Klein, S. I. (2015). The temporal elements of psychological resilience: An integrative framework for the study of individuals, families, and communities. *Psychological Inquiry*, *26*(2), 139–169. doi:10.1080/1047840X.2015.992677

Brett, J. M., & Mitchell, T. (2020). Searching for trustworthiness: Culture, trust and negotiating new business relationships. *International Journal of Conflict Management*, *31*(1), 17–39. doi:10.1108/IJCMA-05-2019-0085

Britt, T. W., Shen, W., Sinclair, R. R., Grossman, M., & Klieger, D. (2016). How Much Do We Really Know About Employee Resilience? *Industrial and organizational psychology: Perspectives on science and practice*. http://my.siop.org/Publications/IOPFocalArticles

Bullough, A., Maija, R., & Tamara, M. (2014). The importance of resilience and self-efficacy for entrepreneurial in Froner, Y. A. (2017). International policies for sustainable development from cultural empowerment. *Journal of Cultural Heritage Management and Sustainable Development. Entrepreneurship Theory and Practice*, *38*(3), 473–499. doi:10.1111/etap.12006

Bullough, A., & Renko, M. (2013). Entrepreneurial resilience during challenging times. *Business Horizons*, *56*(3), 343–350. doi:10.1016/j.bushor.2013.01.001

Camuffo, A., Cordova, A., Gambardella, A., & Spina, C. (2020). A scientific approach to entrepreneurial decision making: Evidence from a randomized control trial. *Management Science*, *66*(2), 564–586. doi:10.1287/mnsc.2018.3249

Cantor, Sood, & Whaley. (2022). *The impact of the COVID 19 Pandemic and policy responses on excess mortality*. Academic Press.

Capler, J. (2021). Death by Authoritative Leadership and Micro-management. In When Leadership Fails: Individual, Group and Organizational Lessons from the Worst Workplace Experiences (pp. 49-57). Emerald Publishing Limited. doi:10.1108/978-1-80043-766-120211005

Cheng, C. (2001). Assessing coping flexibility in real-life and laboratory settings: A multimethod approach. *Journal of Personality and Social Psychology*, *80*(5), 814–833. doi:10.1037/0022-3514.80.5.814 PMID:11374752

Childs, M., Turner, T., Sneed, C., & Berry, A. (2022). A contingency theory approach to understanding small retail business continuity during Covid-19. *Family and Consumer Sciences Research Journal*, *50*(3), 216–230. doi:10.1111/fcsr.12434 PMID:35600319

Corner, P. D., Singh, S., & Pavlovich, K. (2017). Entrepreneurial resilience and venture failure. *International Small Business Journal*, *35*(6), 687–708. doi:10.1177/0266242616685604

De Winnaar, K., & Scholtz, F. (2020). Entrepreneurial decision-making: New conceptual perspectives. *Management Decision*, *58*(7), 1283–1300. doi:10.1108/MD-11-2017-1152

Fatoki, O. (2018). The impact of entrepreneurial resilience on the success of small and medium enterprises in South Africa. *Sustainability (Basel)*, *10*(7), 2527. doi:10.3390u10072527

Fernandez, A. A., & Shaw, G. P. (2020). Academic leadership in a time of crisis: The Coronavirus and COVID-19. *Journal of Leadership Studies*, *14*(1), 39–45. doi:10.1002/jls.21684

Froner, Y. A. (2017). International policies for sustainable development from cultural empowerment. *Journal of Cultural Heritage Management and Sustainable Development*, *7*(2), 208–223. doi:10.1108/JCHMSD-10-2016-0056

Garett & Zettel. (2021). *Washinton interscholastic activities association*. Cross Country Media. https://www.wiaa.com/conDocs/Con466/Cross%20Country%20Media%20Pack

Giustiniano, L., Cunha, M. P., Simpson, A. V., Rego, A., & Clegg, S. (2020). Resilient leadership as paradox work: Notes from COVID-19. *Management and Organization Review, 16*(5), 971–975. doi:10.1017/mor.2020.57

Govender, K. (2018). The Relationship Among Leadership, Organisation Culture, and Performance in the Public Service. *Advanced Science Letters, 24*(7), 4914–4917. doi:10.1166/asl.2018.11233

Hofstede, G. (2011). *National cultures, organizational cultures, and the role of management. In Values and ethics for the 21st century*. BBVA.

Imperial Business School. (2022). *Entrepreneurial resilience and recovery during and after COVID-19*. https://www.imperial.ac.uk/business-school/faculty-research/academic-areas/management-entrepreneur

International Association of Attraction Industry (IAAPA). (2021). https://www.bing.com/search?ptag=ICO37de9cc872970f6e&form=INCOH1&pc=1BDL&q=international%20association%20of%20attraction%20industries

Joice, K. (2021). Mothering in the frame: Cinematic microanalysis and the Pathogenic Mother, 1945–67. *History of the Human Sciences, 34*(5), 105–131. doi:10.1177/0952695120924266

Jordan, J., Wade, M., & Yokoi, T. (2022, Jan.). Finding the right balance-and flexibility-in your leadership style. *Harvard Business Review*.

Kane-Urrabazo, C. (2006). Management's role in shaping organizational culture. *Journal of Nursing Management, 14*(3), 188–194. doi:10.1111/j.1365-2934.2006.00590.x PMID:16600006

Kim, K. (2012). The role of culture in theories of the intergenerational transmission of violence. *Child & Family Social Work, 17*(4), 395–405. doi:10.1111/j.1365-2206.2011.00793.x

Kocsis, S. W., Roesler, A. R., & Totten, A. (2022). *Learning from COVID-19: Reimagining public -private partnerships in public health*. https://milkeninstitute.org/report/covid-19-public-private-partnerships?gclid=CjwKCAiAuOieBhAIEiw

Kossek, E. E., & Perrigino, M. B. (2016). Resilience: A review using a grounded integrated occupational approach. *Academy of Management Annals, 10*(1).

López-García, X., Costa-Sánchez, C., & Vizoso, Á. (2021). Journalistic fact-checking of information in pandemic: Stakeholders, hoaxes, and strategies to fight disinformation during the COVID-19 crisis in Spain. *International Journal of Environmental Research and Public Health, 18*(3), 1227. doi:10.3390/ijerph18031227 PMID:33573013

Lunenburg, F. C. (2010, September). The decision-making process. *National Forum of Educational Administration & Supervision Journal, 27*(4).

Luthans, F., Vogelgesang, G. R., & Lester, P. B. (2006). Developing the psychological capital of resiliency. *Human Resource Development Review*, *5*(1), 25–44. doi:10.1177/1534484305285335

Lyapuntsova, E., Belozerova, Y., Drozdova, I., Afanas'ev, G., & Okunkova, E. (2018). Entrepreneurial risks in the realities of the digital economy. In *MATEC Web of Conferences* (Vol. 251, p. 06032). EDP Sciences. 10.1051/matecconf/201825106032

Manzano García, G., & Ayala Calvo, J. C. (2013). Psychometric properties of Connor-Davidson Resilience Scale in a Spanish sample of entrepreneurs. *Psicothema*. PMID:23628541

McKinsey. (2021). *Business and work in a post-pandemic future*. https://www.mckinsey.com/featured-insights/coronavirus-leading-through-the-crisis

Miles, M. P., Lewis, G. K., Hall-Phillips, A., Morrish, S. C., Gilmore, A., & Kasouf, C. J. (2016). The influence of entrepreneurial marketing processes and entrepreneurial self-efficacy on community vulnerability, risk, and resilience. *Journal of Strategic Marketing*, *24*(1), 34–46. doi:10.1080/0965254X.2015.1035038

Nguyen, T. H. (2016). Impact of export on economic growth in Vietnam: Empirical research and recommendations. *International Business Management*, *13*(3), 45–52.

Olsen, D. C. (1993). *Integrative family therapy*. Fortress Press.

Parker, H., & Ameen, K. (2018). The role of resilience capabilities in shaping how firms respond to disruptions. *Journal of Business Research*, *88*, 535–541. doi:10.1016/j.jbusres.2017.12.022

Pew Research Centre. (2020). *How the Coronavirus outbreak has changed the way we work*. https://www.pewresearch.org/social-trends/2020/12/09/how-the-coronavirus-outbreak-has-and-hasnt-changed-the-way-americans-work/

Piprani, A. Z., Jaafar, N. I., & Mohezar Ali, S. (2020). Prioritizing resilient capability factors of dealing with supply chain disruptions: An analytical hierarchy process (AHP) application in the textile industry. *Benchmarking*, *27*(9), 2537–2563. doi:10.1108/BIJ-03-2019-0111

Rapp, D. J., & Olbrich, M. (2020). On entrepreneurial decision logics under conditions of uncertainty: An attempt to advance the current debate. *Journal of Innovation and Entrepreneurship*, *9*(1), 1–9. doi:10.118613731-020-00131-7

Samani, S., & Benhmanesh, Z. (2011). *Comparison between family processes and actions among ordinary and delinquent juvenile*.

Saryal, R. (2022). Ecological Crisis: The Self, State, and the Hindu Ethics. In Environmentalism Constitutionalism in the Anthropocene: Values, Principles and Actions. Academic Press.

Schäfer, S. K., Kunzler, A. M., Kalisch, R., Tüscher, O., & Lieb, K. (2022). Trajectories of resilience and mental distress to global major disruptions. *Trends in Cognitive Sciences*, *26*(12), 1171–1189. doi:10.1016/j.tics.2022.09.017 PMID:36302711

Schlein, M. (2022). *The economic impacts of the COVID19 crisis* (The World Bank Development Report 2022). https://www.worldbank.org/en/publication/wdr2022/brief/chapter-1-introduction-the-economic-impacts-

Shepherd, D. A., Osofero, M., & Wincent, J. (2022). A personal adversity model of justifying the costs of entrepreneurial action: The case of oil thieves in the Niger DELTA. *Journal of Business Venturing*, *37*(1), 106163. doi:10.1016/j.jbusvent.2021.106163

Su, T. S., Chen, C., Cui, X., Yang, C., & Ma, W. (2020). Consistency at different levels: A meta-analytic examination of organizational trust and performance. *Nankai Business Review International*, *11*(4), 537–567. doi:10.1108/NBRI-01-2020-0005

Surya, B., Hadijah, H., Suriani, S., Baharuddin, B., Fitriyah, A. T., Menne, F., & Rasyidi, E. S. (2020). Spatial Transformation of a New City in 2006–2020: Perspectives on the Spatial Dynamics, Environmental Quality Degradation, and Socio—Economic Sustainability of Local Communities in Makassar City, Indonesia. *Land (Basel)*, *9*(9), 324. doi:10.3390/land9090324

Tear, M. J., Reader, T. W., Shorrock, S., & Kirwan, B. (2020). Safety culture and power: Interactions between perceptions of safety culture, organisational hierarchy, and national culture. *Safety Science*, *121*, 550–561. doi:10.1016/j.ssci.2018.10.014

Theiss, J. A. (2018). Family communication and resilience. *Journal of Applied Communication Research*, *46*(1), 10–13. doi:10.1080/00909882.2018.1426706

Trice, H. M., & Beyer, J. M. (1984). Studying organizational cultures through rites and ceremonials. *Academy of Management Review*, *9*(4), 653–669. doi:10.2307/258488

Uy, M. A., Foo, M. D., & Song, Z. (2013). Joint effects of prior start-up experience and coping strategies on entrepreneurs' psychological well-being. *Journal of Business Venturing*, *28*(5), 583–597. doi:10.1016/j.jbusvent.2012.04.003

Walsh, A., Moore, A., Barber, A., & Opsteen, J. (2014). Educational role of nurse practitioners in a family practice centre: Perspectives of learners and nurses. *Canadian Family Physician Medecin de Famille Canadien*, *60*(6), e316–e321. PMID:24925966

Walsh, F. (1996). The concept of family resilience: Crisis and challenge. *Family Process*, *35*(3), 261–281. doi:10.1111/j.1545-5300.1996.00261.x PMID:9111709

Walsh, F. (1998). *Beliefs, spirituality, and transcendence: Keys to family resilience*. Academic Press.

Walsh, F. (2015). *Strengthening family resilience*. Guilford Publications.

Walsh, F. (2015). *Strengthening family resilience*. Guilford publications.

Walsh, F. (2016). Family resilience: A developmental systems framework. *European Journal of Developmental Psychology*, *13*(3), 313–324. doi:10.1080/17405629.2016.1154035

Walsh, F. (2016). Applying a family resilience framework in training, practice, and research: Mastering the art of the possible. *Family Process*, *55*(4), 616–632. doi:10.1111/famp.12260 PMID:27921306

Walsh, F. (2021). Family resilience: A dynamic systemic framework. In *Multisystemic Resilience* (pp. 255–270). Oxford University Press. doi:10.1093/oso/9780190095888.003.0015

Westphal, M., Seivert, N. H., & Bonanno, G. A. (2010). Expressive flexibility. *Emotion (Washington, D.C.)*, *10*(1), 92–100. doi:10.1037/a0018420 PMID:20141306

Williams, T. A., Gruber, D. A., Sutcliffe, K. M., Shepherd, D. A., & Zhao, E. Y. (2017). Organizational response to adversity: Fusing crisis management and resilience research streams. *The Academy of Management Annals*, *11*(2), 733–769. doi:10.5465/annals.2015.0134

World Economic Forum. (2023). *Global Risks: Today's Crisis*. Author.

Wright, L. M., Watson, W. L., & Bell, J. M. (1996). *Beliefs: The heart of healing in families and illness*. Basic Books.

Zautra, A. J., Arewasikporn, A., & Davis, M. C. (2010). Resilience: Promoting well-being through recovery, sustainability, and growth. *Research in Human Development*, *7*(3), 221–238. doi:10.1080/15427609.2010.504431

Zsambok, C. E. (2014). Naturalistic decision making: where are we now? In *Naturalistic decision making* (pp. 23–36). Psychology Press. doi:10.4324/9781315806129

Chapter 4
Fostering Psychological Safety for Team Effectiveness in Family Businesses:
Insights From Royal Savoy Hotel

Sulaiman Olusegun Atiku
https://orcid.org/0000-0001-9364-3774
Namibia University of Science and Technology, Namibia & Walter Sisulu University, South Africa

Funmilola Aderayo Soneye
Namibia University of Science and Technology, Namibia

Richmond Anane-Simon
https://orcid.org/0000-0003-2512-7772
Independent Researcher, Ghana

EXECUTIVE SUMMARY

This chapter examines the relationship between psychological safety and team effectiveness. Psychological safety is the perception and belief held by members of a team that interpersonal risk-taking is supported and encouraged in the workplace. A literature review was conducted to establish the relationships between psychological safety and employee engagement, satisfaction, performance, as well as team effectiveness in family businesses. The results showed that teams with a prominent level of psychological safety were significantly more effective than teams with a low level of psychological safety. Psychological safety has a significant effect on teams' performance and business effectiveness. This research holds that psychological safety is essential for team effectiveness and should be considered in building effective teams for innovative performance and sustainable competitive advantage in family businesses.

DOI: 10.4018/978-1-6684-8748-8.ch004

INTRODUCTION

Psychological safety refers to the belief held by members of a work team that one can freely express their opinions, challenge the status-quo, and raise concerns without fear of being victimised or ridiculed in the workplace. Psychological safety has been defined as a "shared belief held by members of a team that the team is safe for interpersonal risk-taking" (Edmondson, 1999, p. 4). It is a shared belief held by members of a team that the team is safe for risk-taking in the face of being seen as ignorant, imperfect, or vulnerable (Edmondson, 2019). The features of psychological safety are trust, respect, communication, collaboration, feedback, and support (Edmondson et al., 2004). Trust is essential for psychological safety, as it allows team members to feel comfortable sharing ideas and opinions without fear of judgement or criticism (Hershcovis, 2011). Respect is also necessary for psychological safety, as it enables team members to feel valued and respected for their contributions (Day et al., 2019). Communication is key for psychological safety, as it enables team members to discuss their ideas and opinions openly and honestly (O'Leary et al., 2012). Collaboration is important for psychological safety, as it allows team members to work together to solve problems and develop solutions (Harrison et al., 2020). Feedback is essential for psychological safety, as it allows team members to receive constructive criticism and feedback on their ideas and suggestions (Brockbank & McGill, 2018). Finally, support is necessary for psychological safety, as it allows team members to feel supported and encouraged to take risks and make mistakes (Baumeister et al., 2019).

Psychological safety is a critical component of successful teams and organisations, as it encourages employees to be open and honest about their thoughts, feelings, and ideas, which leads to greater creativity, collaboration, and productivity (Edmondson, 2019). To enhance creativity in a team setting, teams should encourage open dialogue and collaboration (Ling, 2020). This allows team members to share ideas and perspectives without fear of judgement. Teams should also provide time and space for creative thinking, such as through brainstorming sessions or hackathons (Kanter & Prahalad, 2017). Finally, teams should provide resources and feedback to help team members develop and refine their ideas (Keller, 2017). By implementing these strategies, teams can create an environment that encourages creative thinking and problem-solving capabilities in family business. A family business is a type of business organisation that is owned and operated by members of the same family. It is characterized by the involvement of family members in the management and decision-making processes of the business (Basco, 2017).

Family businesses can range from small, local enterprises to large multinational corporations. The unique feature of a family business is the intertwining of family dynamics and business operations, which can have both advantages and challenges.

Family businesses are driven by specific goals and values that are influenced by the family's vision, traditions, and long-term objectives (Basco, 2017). These goals often go beyond financial performance and include considerations such as preserving family legacy, maintaining family control, and ensuring the well-being of future generations. The goals of a family business shape its decision-making processes and can have a significant impact on its behaviour, performance, and sustainability (Basco, 2017). Trust is a crucial element in family businesses, as it affects the relationship between the business and its environment (Wang, 2016). Trust within the family and between family members and non-family employees can influence the ability of the business to adapt to environmental dynamism and develop dynamic capabilities (Wang, 2016). The unique dynamics of trust in family businesses can shape their ability to navigate and respond to changes in the business environment.

Succession planning and the dynamics of successor teams are important considerations in family businesses (Cater et al., 2016). Succession involves the transfer of leadership and ownership from one generation to the next. The dynamics of successor teams, which consist of family members who are being groomed to take over the business, can have a significant impact on the future success and continuity of the family business (Cater et al., 2016). Effective succession planning and the development of successor teams are crucial for ensuring a smooth transition and maintaining the family business's performance and competitiveness. Defining family businesses can be challenging due to the complex nature of the family-business relationship (Roffia et al., 2021). Researchers have sought to provide operational definitions and measures to distinguish family businesses from non-family businesses (Roffia et al., 2021). These definitions often consider factors such as the level of family involvement in the business, the presence of family ownership and control, and the influence of family values and goals on business operations.

Family businesses are significant contributors to the economy and society in many countries (Mahomed & Mtembu, 2021). They play a pivotal role in job creation, wealth generation, and community development. An atmosphere where team members can freely express their opinions, challenge the status-quo, and raise concerns without fear of being victimised or ridiculed is essential for cognitive engagement and innovative performance in family businesses. This means that the absence of psychological safety can be detrimental to employee engagement (Edmondson & Lei, 2014), talent retention (Lai, 2005; Liu & Hu, 2013) and operational effectiveness (George & Zhou, 2017; Kumar, 2018; Liu et al., 2019) in family businesses. An often-overlooked aspect of psychological safety is its potential to fuel skill development and innovation within family businesses. Drawing insight from Gardner et al. (2019), family businesses can create a nurturing environment that stimulates both soft and hard skills. Providing access to training courses, external workshops, and online resources not only contributes to personal and professional growth but also augments the business's internal capabilities.

In the context of family-operated businesses, psychological safety assumes additional layers of complexity. The presence of family members in key organisational roles and the permeation of familial values and traditions can markedly affect the prevailing level of psychological safety (Humphrey et al., 2021). Unique elements of family businesses—such as the juxtaposition of family and business systems, succession planning, and the integration of non-family employees—have significant implications for the establishment and preservation of psychological safety (Cater et al., 2016). Hence this chapter shall delve into the intricacies of psychological safety for team effectiveness in family businesses with the following specific objectives:

1) To examine the role of informal interactions in building team cohesion in family businesses.
2) To examine the impact of psychological safety on team performance in family businesses.

In summary, this chapter shall significantly contribute to the critical comprehension of psychological safety, team effectiveness, and their interplay in family businesses. This chapter shall expose organisations, especially family businesses to the essence of ensuring a psychologically safe environment as a bedrock for team effectiveness thereby nurturing resilient family businesses.

BACKGROUND

The concept of psychological safety, originally formulated by Amy Edmondson, is defined as a collective conviction among team members that the team environment is conducive to interpersonal risk-taking (Koopmann et al., 2016). This perception enables individuals within the team to freely express ideas, pose queries, and voice concerns without the apprehension of negative repercussions, such as mockery, punitive measures, or ostracization (O'Donovan & McAuliffe, 2020). The presence of psychological safety engenders a milieu of mutual trust, respect, and openness, elements that are indispensable for fostering effective collaboration, continuous learning, and innovation (Cauwelier et al., 2019). There exists a salient connection between psychological safety and the effectiveness of teams. Empirical studies demonstrate that teams exhibiting higher degrees of psychological safety are more inclined to engage in efficacious communication, cooperative problem-solving, and collaboration (Akan et al., 2020). The sense of psychological safety among team members encourages the uninhibited sharing of knowledge, expertise, and divergent perspectives, which collectively contribute to enhanced decision-making processes, creativity, and overall team performance (Cauwelier et al., 2019).

Psychological safety augments team cohesion, engenders trust, and elevates satisfaction levels among team members, thereby further enhancing team efficacy (Akan et al., 2020). Several theoretical frameworks elucidate the mechanisms by which psychological safety exerts its influence on team effectiveness. For instance, the Social Exchange Theory posits that heightened levels of psychological safety encourage positive social interactions among team members, such as information dissemination, mutual support, and assistance (Krawczyk-Bryłka et al., 2020). These constructive interactions instill a culture of reciprocity and collaboration within the team, thereby amplifying its effectiveness. Moreover, the Self-Determination Theory suggests that psychological safety satiates fundamental psychological requisites for autonomy, competence, and relatedness (Cole et al., 2016). The autonomy to articulate ideas and opinions nurtures competence, thereby elevating motivation and engagement, which in turn contributes to team effectiveness.

Additionally, the concept of psychological safety is intrinsically intertwined with other theoretical constructs such as trust, communication, and team learning. Trust constitutes a foundational aspect of psychological safety, underpinning the assumption that team members can depend on each other's positive intentions and behaviours (Sidani & Reese, 2020). Effective communication is integral for engendering and sustaining psychological safety, as it promotes open dialogue, active listening, and constructive feedback (Akan et al., 2020). Team learning is also facilitated by psychological safety, encouraging knowledge sharing, experiential reflection, and experimentation (Cauwelier et al., 2019).

Open communication, as indicated by Keller et al. (2018), is a cornerstone in this context. Encouraging employees to articulate their ideas and opinions freely generates a fertile ground for innovation. It is not merely about problem-solving but about allowing the space for innovative ideas to emerge and mature. The role of technology, as highlighted by Zhu et al. (2020), can be pivotal in modern family businesses. Whether it is leveraging data analytics for product development or automating routine processes, technology can be a significant enabler of innovation. As Harrison et al. (2019) suggest, data-driven insights can often lead to new products or methods that offer a competitive edge. Diversity and inclusion further enrich this innovative culture. According to Mannix & Neale (2005), a diverse workforce brings a variety of perspectives and problem-solving approaches. This diversity can be a catalyst for groundbreaking ideas and solutions, fostering a more robust and adaptable business model. The concept of teamwork and collaboration, as noted by Edmondson (2019), is essential for solving complex problems. When employees are encouraged to collaborate freely, the collective intelligence of the team often exceeds individual capabilities.

Furthermore, the role of incentives cannot be underestimated. Recognizing and rewarding creative thinking, as per Keller et al. (2018), can have a galvanizing effect on the entire organisation. Public acknowledgment or tangible rewards for innovation, as highlighted by Keller (2017), can spur further creativity and dedication among team members. Thus, the essence of fostering psychological safety in family businesses extends far beyond conflict resolution or open dialogues. It lays the groundwork for a culture of continuous learning, innovation, and overall business excellence.

Psychological safety and team building are essential elements of a successful organisation, being key to fostering trust, respect, collaboration, and creativity among team members (Layan, 2020). This creates an environment in which employees feel comfortable expressing their thoughts, ideas, and concerns without fear of judgement or criticism (Gonzalez, 2021). Team effectiveness, as delineated by Peralta et al. (2018), denotes a team's proficiency in realizing its stipulated goals and objectives. This notion is multifaceted, encompassing diverse dimensions such as task performance, interpersonal relations, communication, and collaborative dynamics (Buchler et al., 2018). Several determinants, ranging from the intrinsic attributes of teams to external influences, shape the efficacy of a team. One salient determinant is team composition, which is characterized by the collective attributes of team members, including their expertise, aptitude, and temperaments (Cheng et al., 2019). A body of research indicates that teams constituted by members with a plethora of skills, expertise, and backgrounds demonstrate superior performance, especially in realms of problem-solving and innovative endeavors (Kakar, 2017). Such diversity fosters a range of perspectives, facilitating comprehensive and inventive resolutions (Spedding, 2023).

Leadership style, notably transformational leadership, also significantly impacts team effectiveness. Leaders practicing this style invigorate and galvanize members towards maximizing their potential (Griggs et al., 2021). These transformational figures sculpt a cohesive vision, embolden members, and cultivate a milieu of trust and innovation (Leicht-Deobald et al., 2022). Team processes, including communication protocols, coordination methods, and decision-making mechanics, are pivotal for a team's efficacy. For instance, seamless communication is paramount for elucidating objectives, ameliorating conflicts, and engendering trust (Demir et al., 2019). Further, adept coordination ensures judicious resource allocation and task completion (Purwatiningsih & Faisal, 2022), while robust decision-making procedures, incorporating diverse viewpoints, underpin superior decision quality (Vlas et al., 2022). The external milieu, particularly organisational facets such as cultural ethos and logistical support, profoundly influences team efficacy. Organisations that foster a culture valorizing teamwork and continual learning invariably bolster team effectiveness (Cahyo & Rachmawati, 2021). Additionally, provisioning requisite logistical support—be it in the form of time, technological tools, or funding—enables teams to function optimally (McGuier et al., 2023). Institutional scaffolding, through training and feedback mechanisms, augments the competencies and motivation of team members (Salas et al., 2008).

Team cohesiveness and effectiveness are then able to be increased, as team members can challenge each other, experiment and try new ideas, and brainstorm and innovate (Gonzalez, 2021). This will lead to innovation, better problem solving, and higher job satisfaction, which will result in improved performance and success (Layan, 2020). It is thus paramount that team leaders create an environment in which this psychological safety is present by setting up team meetings to discuss projects, planning activities that allow team members to get to know each other and encouraging team members to give feedback to each other in a respectful manner (Gonzalez, 2021). Team members should also strive to create a culture of trust, where team members can openly discuss their ideas and concerns without fear of being criticized (Zhang & Bartlett, 2017). Team leaders in family businesses should set clear expectations to ensure that team members understand their core responsibilities and are encouraged to push boundaries and try new things (Layan, 2020). With these elements in place, family business is more likely to experience greater success.

LITERATURE

The Interplay of Psychological Safety and Employee Satisfaction

Psychological safety is an important workplace climate factor that has been linked to employee satisfaction (Moin et al., 2021). A myriad of scholarly research has delved into the intricate relationship between psychological safety and diverse facets of employee satisfaction, elucidating the underlying dynamics and implications. Liu et al. (2016) explored the detrimental impact of abusive supervision on both psychological safety and organisational identification. Their research underscored that psychological safety acts as a mediator between abusive supervision and organisational identification, elucidating its critical role in preserving employee alignment with their organisations. Kuo et al. (2019) provided insights into how psychological safety can enhance the correlation between proactive personality and job satisfaction. Their findings reinforced that, in environments characterized by psychological safety, employees with initiative-taking tendencies report heightened job satisfaction. Drawing on the theme of leadership, Wang et al. (2022) dissected the relationships between servant leadership, psychological safety, employee well-being, and creativity. Their results identified psychological safety as a bridge connecting servant leadership to employee well-being, which in turn influenced creativity. This pivotal role of psychological safety emphasizes its significance in fostering both employee wellness and innovation.

Erkutlu and Chafra (2016) emphasized the positive ramifications of a workplace culture embedded with psychological safety. Such a climate not only fosters feelings of comfort and autonomy but also culminates in elevated levels of employee well-being. Ding and Yu (2021) took a nuanced approach, examining how strengths-based leadership influenced employee psychological well-being. Their findings reinforced that the application of employee strengths mediated the relationship between this leadership style and psychological well-being, accentuating the crucial role of psychological safety in this equation. Additionally, Hasan and Kashif (2020) presented psychological safety as a precursor to both positive voicing and heightened psychological well-being among employees. Their findings further entrenched the idea that psychological safety is foundational in encouraging employee expression and overall wellness. In summation, the aforementioned studies collectively endorse the profound impact of psychological safety on employee satisfaction. A psychologically safe environment amplifies employee well-being, satisfaction, and innovation. Moreover, the role of psychological safety is instrumental in delineating the effects of varied leadership styles on employee outcomes. It behooves organisational leaders' especially family businesses to cultivate a psychologically safe atmosphere to bolster employee satisfaction and overall well-being.

Psychological Safety, Employee Engagement, and Job Satisfaction

Employee engagement is defined by the depth of emotional commitment, enthusiasm, and involvement an employee demonstrates towards both their specific tasks and the broader organisation they represent (Kumar, 2016). It represents a complex, multi-faceted construct that integrates various elements of an employee's attitudes and behaviours. This includes aspects like commitment, involvement, attachment, and the voluntary effort an employee might offer beyond their basic obligations (Gupta & Sharma, 2016). This state of engagement is marked by a positive, fulfilling work-related mindset, typified by vigor, dedication, and full immersion in tasks (Kossyva et al., 2022). Essentially, it conveys the depth of an employee's connection to their work, capturing their intrinsic motivation and their proactive stance in their roles (Bagyo, 2016). In today's ever-changing and competitive business environment, business organisations are constantly looking for ways to increase employee engagement and job satisfaction. One of the key factors in achieving these goals is providing employees with a psychologically safe work environment. Recent studies have shown that psychological safety is correlated with higher employee engagement and job satisfaction.

In a 2014 study conducted by Edmondson, a professor at Harvard Business School, it was found that teams with a higher level of psychological safety had higher rates of employee engagement (Edmondson & Lei, 2014). In this study, Edmondson specifically looked at the correlation between psychological safety and the level of effort employees were willing to put into their work. The results showed that employees in teams with higher levels of psychological safety were more likely to take risks and put more effort into their work. Another study conducted by Huang et al. (2015) found that psychological safety was correlated with higher levels of job satisfaction. In this study, the authors surveyed a large sample of employees in multiple industries. They found that employees who felt psychologically safe were more likely to be satisfied with their jobs. They also found that employees in teams with higher levels of psychological safety were more likely to be satisfied with their job security, their relationships with their co-workers, and their supervisors. Therefore, psychological safety is correlated with higher levels of employee engagement and job satisfaction. It has been found that teams with a higher level of psychological safety are more likely to have employees who are willing to take risks, put more effort into their work, and be satisfied with their job security, and relationships with co-workers, and supervisors.

Also, leadership stands out as a pivotal influencer of employee engagement. Leaders demonstrating humility and inclusiveness cultivate an atmosphere of psychological safety, subsequently elevating levels of engagement (Sun & Bunchapattanasakda, 2019; Baker & Cripe, 2018). Additionally, a leadership style that encourages participative decision-making resonates positively with employee engagement. Other determinants include the organisational culture, the specifics of job design, the broader work environment, and individual traits such as vitality and self-awareness (Sun & Bunchapattanasakda, 2019). Leaders should strive to create a culture of trust and psychological safety, where team members can be open and honest with each other without fear of being judged or criticised (Kumar, & Sharma, 2018). The ramifications of employee engagement are manifold and benefit both the individual and the organisation. Employees who are engaged typically exhibit heightened job satisfaction, demonstrate stronger organisational commitment, and proactively contribute towards organisational objectives (Alasadi et al., 2019). Such employees are also predisposed to optimal performance metrics, heightened creativity, and innovation (Sun & Bunchapattanasakda, 2019).

Empirical research underscores the positive correlations between engagement and performance, organisational allegiance, and constructive work behaviour. Furthermore, a robust engagement level correlates with improved job satisfaction, overall well-being, and increased retention rates (Book et al., 2019). To optimize levels of engagement, organisations can implement a range of strategies. This encompasses fostering an inclusive and supportive work atmosphere, championing employee participation, acknowledging and rewarding meritorious contributions, and ensuring transparent communication pathways (Dhanda, 2015). Effective talent management practices, such as comprehensive onboarding processes, opportunities for career advancement, and robust performance assessment systems, also play a pivotal role (Lenny & Sutawidjaya, 2019).

Aligning individual employee aspirations and values with the overarching organisational vision and principles is another key strategy to bolster engagement (Christianto, 2022). Psychological safety, employee engagement, and job satisfaction are interconnected factors that play a significant role in the workplace. Several other studies have explored the relationships between these variables, shedding light on their interplay and the outcomes they produce. One study by Walters and Diab (2016) examined the implications of humble leadership on psychological safety and follower engagement. The findings revealed that humble leadership positively influenced psychological safety, which in turn fully mediated the relationship between humble leadership and employee engagement. This study highlights the importance of psychological safety as a mediator between leadership behaviours and employee engagement. Another study by Chen et al. (2020) investigated the sequential mediation model of participative leadership, psychological safety, creative process engagement, and employee creativity. The results indicated that participative leadership positively influenced psychological safety, which further enhanced creative process engagement and ultimately led to increased employee creativity. This study emphasizes the role of psychological safety in facilitating employee engagement and creativity.

Furthermore, Kuo et al. (2019) proposed psychological safety as a moderator in the relationship between proactive personality and job satisfaction. The study found that employees with a proactive personality had greater job satisfaction, and psychological safety moderated this relationship. This suggests that a supportive and safe work environment enhances the positive effects of a proactive personality on job satisfaction. Moreover, a study by Chaudhary (2019) explored the impact of corporate social responsibility (CSR) perceptions on employee engagement through the psychological conditions of meaningfulness, safety, and availability. The findings revealed that CSR positively influenced employee engagement through these psychological conditions. This study highlights the role of psychological safety in mediating the relationship between CSR and employee engagement.

Research by Arasli et al. (2020) emphasized the role of psychological safety in promoting employee innovative behaviours. Employees who feel psychologically safe are more likely to engage in experimental trials, discuss failures with others, and learn from them. This study highlights the importance of psychological safety in fostering employee engagement and innovation. Furthermore, a study by Ma et al. (2019) examined the relationship between psychological contracts and job satisfaction. The findings revealed a positive relationship between the psychological contract and job satisfaction of employees. This study emphasizes the role of psychological factors, such as the psychological contract, in influencing job satisfaction. Moreover, a study by Wang et al. (2021) investigated the impact of coordination, psychological safety, and job security on employee performance. The findings indicated that coordination and psychological safety positively influenced employee performance, and job security moderated this relationship. This study emphasizes the role of psychological safety in enhancing employee performance and job satisfaction.

Furthermore, Prentice (2022) examined the relationship between supportive leadership, employee engagement, and job satisfaction. The findings indicated a positive relationship between employee engagement and job satisfaction, and that supportive leadership improved both employee engagement and job satisfaction. This study highlights the importance of supportive leadership in promoting employee engagement and job satisfaction. Moreover, a study by Igor and Haspolat (2016) investigated the relationship between job satisfaction and psychological well-being in different occupations. The findings revealed a positive relationship between job satisfaction and psychological well-being among different occupational groups. This study emphasizes the role of job satisfaction in promoting psychological well-being. Furthermore, a study by Noercahyo et al. (2021) analysed the role of employee engagement in the relationship between job satisfaction and organisational performance. The findings indicated that employee engagement mediated the relationship between job satisfaction and organisational performance. This study highlights the importance of employee engagement in driving organisational performance. In a nutshell, the interplay of psychological safety, employee engagement, and job satisfaction is crucial for creating a positive work environment and promoting employee well-being and performance. Psychological safety acts as a mediator or moderator in the relationship between leadership behaviours, proactive personality, CSR perceptions, and job satisfaction. It also plays a role in fostering employee engagement, creativity, innovation, and performance. Job satisfaction serves as an outcome of these factors and contributes to employee well-being and organisational performance. Organisations should prioritize creating a psychologically safe and supportive work environment to enhance employee engagement, job satisfaction, and overall organisational success.

Psychological Safety and Workforce Creativity

Psychological safety and workforce creativity are two important factors that can significantly impact the success and innovation of an organisation. Psychological safety refers to the perception of employees that they can take interpersonal risks without fear of negative consequences Edmondson and Lei (2014). It is a crucial element in creating an environment that fosters creativity and innovation (Frazier et al., 2016). On the other hand, workforce creativity is the ability of employees to generate new and valuable ideas, solutions, and products (Liu et al., 2016). Several studies have explored the interplay between psychological safety and workforce creativity. For example, Liu et al. (2016) found inconsistent relationships between psychological safety and employee creativity. They highlighted the importance of psychological safety in promoting creativity and identified abusive supervision as a potential barrier to creativity (Liu et al., 2016). Similarly, Wang et al. (2018) found mixed findings in the relationship between psychological safety and creativity. While psychological safety was identified as a predictor of creativity, it also interacted with other factors (Wang et al., 2018).

Other studies have examined the mediating role of psychological safety in the relationship between leadership styles and creativity. For instance, Chen et al. (2020) proposed a sequential mediation model linking participative leadership, psychological safety, creative process engagement, and employee creativity. They found that psychological safety played a crucial role in facilitating the relationship between participative leadership and employee creativity (Chen et al., 2020). Furthermore, the role of authentic leadership in promoting psychological safety and creativity has been investigated. Zeb et al. (2019) found that authentic leadership positively influenced employees' creativity through the mediating factors of team psychological safety and psychological capital (Zeb et al., 2019; Chaudhary & Panda, 2018) also found that authentic leadership positively influenced creativity through the mediating factors of psychological meaningfulness and work engagement (Chaudhary & Panda, 2018). Ethical leadership has also been linked to psychological safety and creativity. Wadei et al. (2020) found that ethical leadership positively influenced creative performance, and psychological safety mediated this relationship (Wadei et al., 2020). Similarly, Mehmood et al. (2021) found that entrepreneurial leadership positively influenced team creativity through the mediating factors of team psychological safety and knowledge sharing (Mehmood et al., 2021).

In addition to leadership styles, other factors have been found to influence the interplay between psychological safety and workforce creativity. For example, Lee et al. (2020) found that high-quality interpersonal relationships positively influenced psychological safety, which in turn positively influenced employees' creative work involvement (Lee et al., 2020). Moreover, individual characteristics and behaviours have also been explored about psychological safety and creativity. Choi et al. (2021) found that employees' proactive personality positively influenced their creative performance, and psychological safety served as a mediator in this relationship (Choi et al., 2021; Han et al., 2022) found that psychological empowerment mediated the relationship between psychological safety and creativity in project-based learning (Han et al., 2022). Other recent research into the effects of psychological safety on workforce creativity has shown that when psychological safety is established, teams are more likely to develop creative solutions to problems. For instance, one study found that teams with higher levels of psychological safety were more likely to generate innovative solutions to complex problems (George & Zhou, 2017).

Empirically, teams with higher levels of psychological safety were better able to use a variety of problem-solving strategies, leading to more creative solutions than teams with lower levels of psychological safety (George Zhou, 2017). Furthermore, psychological safety has been found to have an impact on the quality of creative work produced by teams. For instance, one study found that teams with higher levels of psychological safety were more likely to produce higher quality creative work (Liu et al., 2019). Overall, the interplay between psychological safety and workforce creativity is complex and influenced by various factors such as leadership styles, individual characteristics, and organisational culture. Psychological safety plays a crucial role in creating an environment that fosters creativity and innovation. Organisations need to promote psychological safety through effective leadership, high-quality interpersonal relationships, and supportive organisational practices to enhance workforce creativity.

Psychological Safety and Employee Performance

Several studies have shown that psychological safety has a positive impact on individual employee performance. For example, a study by Johnson et al. (2019) found that psychological safety was positively associated with employee job satisfaction, motivation, and job performance. They also found that psychological safety was associated with greater engagement in learning activities, suggesting that psychologically safe environments allow employees to take greater risks and take advantage of learning opportunities. Other studies have found that psychological safety has a positive effect on creativity, problem-solving, and decision-making (Muller et al., 2016; Kim et al., 2016). Additionally, psychological safety is associated with lower levels of burnout, which can improve work performance (Yin et al., 2018). Studies have found that psychologically safe environments promote better collaboration, mutual trust, and increased communication, which can lead to higher quality decisions and improved performance (Muller et al., 2016; Kim et al., 2016). Additionally, psychological safety is associated with greater team cohesion, which is important for successful teamwork (Taylor et al., 2017). A study by Yin et al. (2018) found that psychological safety was associated with lower levels of conflict and higher levels of job satisfaction, both of which can lead to improved team performance. Studies have found that psychologically safe workplaces are associated with higher levels of employee engagement and retention, which can lead to improved business performance (Johnson et al., 2019). Moreover, psychological safety is associated with increased innovation, creativity, and problem solving, which can result in improved business performance (Muller et al., 2016; Kim et al., 2016).

Psychological Safety and Organisational Commitment

Organisational commitment is a key element of operational effectiveness, as it is related to a range of outcomes such as job satisfaction, job performance, and organisational citizenship behaviour (Chen et al., 2017). Psychological safety is the sense of security and willingness to take risks in a workplace (Edmondson, 2019). Liang and Wang (2016) conducted a survey of 447 employees in a Taiwanese medical centre. Results showed that psychological safety was positively associated with organisational commitment. The authors also found that psychological safety had a mediating effect on the relationship between job insecurity and organisational commitment, as employees with a greater sense of psychological safety were less likely to be affected by job insecurity. Similarly, a study conducted by Zhang et al. (2017) with a sample of 315 Chinese employees showed that psychological safety had a positive relationship with organisational commitment, and that this relationship was mediated by job satisfaction. The authors concluded that providing a psychologically safe work environment could be an effective way to promote organisational commitment. Chen et al. (2018) investigated Chinese government organisation, the result showed that psychological safety was positively related to organisational commitment, and the relationship was mediated by trust in the organisation. The study further revealed that psychological safety is essential in promoting organisational commitment, the interventions aimed at increasing psychological safety could lead to higher levels of organisational commitment. Ma et al. (2020) examined the relationship between psychological safety and organisational commitment in a sample of 587 Chinese employees. The results showed that psychological safety was significantly related to organisational commitment, but the relationship was mediated by job satisfaction. Hence, a psychologically safe work environment could be an effective way to promote organisational commitment. Psychological safety is positively related to organisational commitment (Carmeli, & Freund, 2005), and this relationship is mediated by job satisfaction (Ma et al., 2020), trust in the organisation (Chen et al., 2018), and job insecurity (Liang & Wang, 2016). These findings indicate that interventions aimed at establishing a psychologically safe work environment could be an effective way to promote affective, normative and continuance commitment in family businesses.

Psychological Safety and Turnover Intentions

The first body of research to address the topic of psychological safety and turnover intentions is the work of Kahn (1990). In this seminal article, Kahn argued that psychological safety is an important determinant of an employee's level of commitment to their organisation. He suggested that a sense of psychological safety, in which employees feel psychologically supported and secure, is essential for maintaining commitment and engagement in a workplace. Moreover, Kahn argued that a lack of psychological safety can lead to turnover intentions. Subsequent research has confirmed the importance of psychological safety in predicting employee turnover intentions. Since Kahn's work, a large body of research has emerged on the topic of psychological safety and turnover intentions. For example, a study by Liao and colleagues (2005) found a positive relationship between psychological safety and higher levels of turnover intentions among employees. In the same vein, a study conducted by Liu and Hu (2013), showed that employees who experienced lower levels of psychological safety in the workplace were more likely to express intentions to leave their current employer.

Furthermore, research linking psychological safety to turnover intentions reveals that psychological safety is associated with higher levels of job satisfaction, work engagement, and commitment among employees (Shao et al., 2012). Moreover, a study by Chen et al, (2016) found that psychological safety was associated with increased creativity and innovation among employees. These studies suggest that psychological safety can have a positive effect on employee outcomes, in addition to its role in predicting turnover intentions. There is a growing body of research that examines the organisational factors that contribute to psychological safety in the workplace. For example, a study by Yang et al. (2018) found that organisational support, such as supervisor support and training, was associated with higher levels of psychological safety among employees. A study by Xiao et al. (2014) found that organisational culture, such as a culture of trust and respect, was associated with higher levels of psychological safety. Therefore, family businesses can take steps to foster a psychologically safe environment to enhance employee engagement and reduce turnover intentions.

The Link Between Psychological Safety and Organisational Outcomes

Psychological safety and organisational performance are deeply intertwined concepts in the realm of organisational studies. At its core, psychological safety pertains to the sense of trust and security that employees feel within their workplace. In contrast, organisational performance gauges the efficacy and results of an organisation. Several research pieces underscore this intrinsic connection. For instance, Blattner et al. (2019) highlighted that a robust sense of psychological safety among employees correlates with enhanced organisational performance. This includes notable upticks in job satisfaction, team dynamics, and commitment to the organisation's mission. Echoing these findings, Chmiel et al. (2018) unveiled a direct relationship between psychological safety and superior organisational results such as heightened employee retention, engagement, and profitability. Furthermore, Wayland et al. (2016) found a positive connection between psychological safety and innovative performance, employee engagement, and customer satisfaction. Diving deeper into team dynamics, Lee et al. (2012) explored how psychological safety influences team effectiveness. The study revealed that when teams operate within a psychologically safe environment, they experience superior collaboration, increased productivity, and heightened job satisfaction. In summary, there's substantial evidence suggesting that fostering psychological safety within the workplace can significantly enhance both individual and organisational outcomes. This suggests that businesses, including family-run ones, can benefit immensely from cultivating such an environment.

METHODOLOGY

The study employed a qualitative content analysis, a versatile method known for its capacity to function at various levels of abstraction and interpretation (Graneheim, Lindgren, & Lundman, 2017). Central to this approach is its emphasis on context, underlying meaning structures, unique individual cases, and the goal of simplifying complexity. It offers both descriptive and interpretative dimensions (Lindgren, Lundman & Graneheim, 2020). Notably, content analysis is valued for its sensitivity to content, flexibility in diverse research designs, and its applicability to a wide range of qualitative data (Kyngäs, 2019). Given these strengths, it was an apt choice for analysing the teaching case of the Royal Sovoy Hotel.

Data Source

The principal source of data is the case study titled "Royal Savoy Hotel (Case C) - Building Relationships to Create a High Performing Top Team at Royal Savoy Hotel," which was purchased from thecasecenter.org. The case study provided invaluable qualitative data, including interviews and reflections from key members of the Royal Savoy Hotel's senior team.

Qualitative Content Analysis

A detailed content analysis was conducted on the case. This involved:

- **Contextualization**: Understanding the background, organisational structure, and challenges facing the Royal Savoy Hotel.
- **Objective Analysis**: Identifying the primary goals behind the relationship-building workshop.
- **Action Analysis**: Examining the specific activities undertaken during the workshop.
- **Psychological Safety Parameters**: Scrutinizing how the activities and environment cultivated psychological safety among the team members.
- **Outcome Assessment**: Assessing the results and reflections of the workshop participants, with a focus on the shift towards a more collaborative and high-performing team.

Interpretation and Synthesis

After analyzing each component, the information was synthesized to create a cohesive narrative that aligned with the research objectives. This helped in interpreting the effectiveness of the relationship-building activities in fostering psychological safety and the resulting impact on team performance.

Ethical Considerations

Given that the case study was purchased, proper attribution and reference were given to the source as per the licensing agreement. The case was also summarized to avoid verbatim output.

Case Summary: Royal Savoy Hotel (Case C) - Building Relationships to Foster Team Cohesion

Background and Setting

The Royal Savoy Hotel, situated in Lausanne, Switzerland, is a luxury hotel business that recently underwent a renovation. The renovated hotel includes the historical building of 1909 paired with a new contemporary wing. The hotel's internal scenario was characterized by a top team that lacked a deep bond, due to frequent personnel changes as a result of the Covid 19 pandemic and a mix of new and tenured members.

Main Objectives

With an absence of a cohesive bond among the senior team, the primary aim was to foster stronger personal relationships among them, which in turn would promote a high-performing environment.

Actions and Activities

To tackle the challenge, a two-day workshop was organised at the Sannenmöser Hotel, a resort in the Bernese Alps (Switzerland). The workshop's focus was not strictly business; instead, it integrated both professional and personal activities. These activities included discussing strengths and improvement areas, sharing personal stories, and undertaking team-building exercises. Unique experiences, like breakfast, lunches, and pre-dining walks around offered an informal environment for the team members to bond.

Emphasis on Psychological Safety

The workshop was instrumental in fostering psychological safety. This was evident from the comfort level team members felt in sharing personal stories and their vulnerabilities. Such a safe environment is crucial for improved team collaboration, trust-building, and effective communication.

Outcomes and Reflections

Post the workshop, team members, including Hugli, Bauters, and Kropf,- the General Manager expressed their satisfaction and the value they derived. They felt that the workshop was an excellent beginning towards building profound personal relationships. They shared that they not only got to see each other in a different context but also learned more about their colleagues beyond the professional sphere. The positive outcomes included better communication, a sense of camaraderie, and a reduction in traditional conflicts common in hotel settings.

Reflecting on what they had experienced, Hugli- Spa Supervisor described the workshop:

The good thing is that everybody was new, because even if I have been here for five years, it is my first Head of Department position, so it is new for me too. It was good to see each other in a different place, another context. It was nice to know that colleagues are not thinking just of their department. It was good to feel that we were part of a team. Coming into the workshop, I did not know what to expect but when we left, everyone was relaxed and happy. It was interesting to get to know the team in a different environment. We meet every morning and discuss numbers and each of our departments, but there is nothing personal. At the workshop, I learned a lot about my colleagues.

Bauters -Director of Food and Beverages described:

I was happy to meet with the team outside of work and to spend time with Heads of Departments I do not work with at all like Revenue and Spa. It was great to spend quality time with them and we could bond over lunch and dinner. We went for a walk as well and spent time talking over a beer. Now, I feel that I could go to Gaby (Gabriella Hurmuzach, Revenue Manager), for example, and ask her opinion on certain topics unlike before. I feel that there is more collaboration and more communication.

Kropf-the General manager reflected:

Everyone opened up to each other and this is a good illustration of the team that we are trying to collectively build, where every member is working together. I can feel that. I feel a lot less conflict between team members, unlike the traditional conflicts you find in a hotel.

The General manager- Kropf, while recognizing the early stages of this transformation, felt that the team was moving towards becoming high-performing. He hoped to initiate a 360-degree feedback system later in the year to maintain this momentum.

QUALITATIVE CONTENT ANALYSIS

Context

The chapter revolves around the Royal Savoy, a luxury hotel in Lausanne, Switzerland. The narrative focuses on the challenges faced by hoteliers, particularly in the context of family-owned businesses where psychological safety is paramount for optimal team performance.

Objective

The primary objective at the Royal Savoy was to create a high-performing team at the senior level. The hotel, under the leadership of General Manager Kropf, felt the need to foster an environment where the senior management team could openly communicate, collaborate, and bond both professionally and personally.

Actions

- **Workshop at the Sannenmöser Hotel:** The senior team participated in an outdoor workshop designed to break the ice, facilitate open communication, and foster a sense of camaraderie.
- **Building Personal Relationships:** The activities were structured in a way to allow the team members to view each other beyond their professional roles.
- **Emphasis on Communication:** The team engaged in activities and discussions that shifted their focus from mere numbers and departmental goals to understanding and appreciating each other's narratives.

Psychological Safety and Its Importance

Psychological safety refers to an environment where individuals feel safe to express themselves without fear of negative repercussions. Within the context of the chapter:

- The workshop played a crucial role in promoting psychological safety. Team members were encouraged to be vulnerable, share personal stories, and discuss their fears and aspirations, paving the way for trust.
- Hugli's reflection showcased the importance of seeing colleagues beyond their professional roles, emphasizing the significance of human connections in a work environment.
- Bauters' newfound comfort in approaching Gabriella indicates the breaking down of hierarchical barriers and the creation of a space where open dialogue is encouraged.
- The decrease in traditional conflicts as observed by Kropf further underscores the benefits of fostering psychological safety.

Outcomes

- The workshop was successful in bridging gaps between various departments, leading to more cohesive teamwork.

- Personal bonds were strengthened, and the team started viewing each other as more than just colleagues.
- There was a noted reduction in traditional hotel conflicts, showcasing improved team dynamics.
- Plans for continuous development, such as the 360-degree feedback system, were conceived, indicating a future-focused approach.

Interpretation and Synthesis

Research Question 1: The role of informal interactions in building team cohesion

Findings:

- **Contextual Shift**: The workshop held outside the professional setting of the Royal Savoy Hotel enabled team members to see each other in a new light. Hugli mentioned that being in a different place helped them feel like a part of a team, and Bauters felt the informal setting helped deepen bonds with colleagues he rarely interacts with professionally.
- **Activities**: Activities like walks, lunches, and dinners provided an opportunity for genuine conversation and bonding. Bauters pointed out that he could now feel comfortable seeking opinions from colleagues he had not interacted with before.
- **Impact on Communication**: The informal interactions increased comfort and broke down professional barriers, resulting in more open communication channels among team members.

Research Question 2: Impact of psychological safety on team performance in family businesses

Findings:

- **Reduced Conflict**: Kropf noted that he felt a lot less conflict between team members after the workshop, indicating an increase in psychological safety, which is vital for high-performing teams.
- **Openness**: Hugli and Bauters both pointed out that team members felt free to share and discuss, indicating a level of psychological safety achieved through the workshop. Hugli expressed relief that colleagues were not just thinking about their departments, but the team as a whole.
- **Future Planning**: Kropf's plan to introduce a 360-degree survey reflects an effort to institutionalize psychological safety and open feedback

mechanisms within the team, showing the perceived importance of psychological safety in contributing to a high-performing senior team.

Findings are in line with existing research which posits that teams with high levels of psychological safety tend to be more effective than teams with low levels of psychological safety (Kumar, 2018). Also, the works of Forsyth et al., (2018) further indicate that the provision of feedback and support to team members is crucial to foster psychological safety in workplaces.

Practical Implications for Family Businesses

Drawing upon both the insights from the Royal Savoy case and relevant research, a set of practical implications for family businesses emerges:

- **Promote a Culture of Psychological Safety (Huff, 2019):** Family businesses should emphasize creating an environment underlined by psychological safety. Open conversations should be the norm, with employees confident in expressing ideas without apprehensions of judgment or backlash. Instituting an open-door policy can be an effective step towards this objective.
- **Leadership's Role in Setting a Positive Precedent (Huff, 2019):** Leadership within family businesses has a cardinal responsibility. They should champion the concept of psychological safety and its pivotal role in operational efficiency. Offering training sessions to create a safe and inclusive environment and setting a personal example in their behaviour are essential actions for leaders.
- **Fostering a Space for Risk-Taking and Feedback (Huff, 2019):** Family businesses, given their intimate nature, need to encourage an atmosphere where risk-taking is seen as a pathway to innovation and growth. Employees should be comfortable taking informed risks, learning from occasional failures, and providing candid feedback.
- **Strengthening Employee Engagement through Trust and Recognition (Kerr, 2019):** Building trust is foundational for family businesses. To elevate employee engagement, both business owners and team leaders should center their strategies on trust-building. Complementing this with genuine recognition and rewards for employee efforts can yield better team cohesion and performance.
- **Efficient Conflict Management:** In a domain where personal and professional lines often blur, it becomes essential for team leaders to swiftly and effectively manage conflicts. Addressing and resolving disputes promptly prevents them from festering and deteriorating the work environment.

- **Embracing Workshops and Activities for Enhanced Communication:** The Royal Savoy experience highlights the transformative power of workshops and team activities. Such interventions can break down communication barriers, foster open dialogues, and underscore the importance of personal relationships in a work setting. As the case suggests, understanding on a personal level can catalyze for a more collaborative and harmonious professional environment.

FUTURE AREAS OF RESEARCH

Future research should explore how psychological safety can be developed in family businesses using a qualitative approach to gather in-depth data from the family business owners and their family members, as well as various categories of employees working in family businesses operating in Africa or elsewhere globally. The employees' perceptions of the attitude and behaviour of family business owners towards constructive feedback from individual employees will contribute to family business research in Africa and/or globally.

CONCLUSION

In family businesses, where professional intricacies and familial ties seamlessly intersect, the emphasis on psychological safety emerges as paramount. This chapter underscores its pivotal role, especially as demonstrated in the case of the Royal Savoy. It is evident that fostering a psychologically safe environment yields multifaceted benefits, from heightened trust and collaboration to spurred creativity and improved decision-making. The qualitative analysis of the teaching case accentuates the significance of informal interactions in shaping team cohesion. Such interactions, imbued with psychological safety, profoundly influence the performance dynamics of senior teams in esteemed family establishments like the Royal Savoy Hotel. Encouragingly, the feedback and plans of such entities indicate a trajectory towards holistic excellence, characterized by psychological safety and robust interpersonal relationships. The family businesses seeking sustainable competitive advantages and cultivating psychological safety stand as a linchpin for enhancing engagement, innovation, and overall team efficacy.

REFERENCES

Agarwal, P., & Farndale, E. (2017). High-performance work systems and creativity implementation: The role of psychological capital and psychological safety. *Human Resource Management Journal, 27*(3), 440–458. doi:10.1111/1748-8583.12148

Akan, O., Jack, E., & Mehta, A. (2020). Concrescent conversation environment, psychological safety, and team effectiveness. *Team Performance Management, 26*(1/2), 29–51. doi:10.1108/TPM-07-2019-0079

Alasadi, R., Muhammed, S., Abidi, O., & Dzenopoljac, V. (2019). Impact of servant leadership on intrinsic and extrinsic job satisfaction. Leadership &Amp. *Leadership and Organization Development Journal, 40*(4), 472–484. doi:10.1108/LODJ-09-2018-0337

Ancona, D. G., Malone, T. W., Orlikowski, W. J., & Senge, P. M. (2007). In praise of the incomplete leader. *Harvard Business Review, 85*(9), 92–99. PMID:17345683

Anderson, C. B., Jacobson, J. W., & Kilduff, G. (2016). Psychological safety and engagement: The role of individual psychological characteristics. *The Leadership Quarterly, 27*(3), 461–473.

Arasli, H., Arasli, H., & Kole, E. (2020). Constructive leadership and employee innovative behaviours: A serial mediation model. *Sustainability (Basel), 12*(7), 2592. doi:10.3390u12072592

Bagyo, Y. (2016). The role of employee engagement in anticipating counterproductive work behaviour: A study of literature. *IOSR Journal of Business and Management, 18*(09), 141–147. doi:10.9790/487X-180904141147

Baker, S. R., & Cripe, S. M. (2018). Exploring the Role of Leaders and Team Members in Promoting Psychological Safety in Work Teams. *International Journal of Business and Management, 13*(1), 75–88.

Basco, R. (2017). "Where do you want to take your family firm?": A theoretical and empirical exploratory study of family business goals. *Business Research Quarterly, 20*(1), 28–44. doi:10.1016/j.brq.2016.07.001

Baumeister, R., Vohs, K., DeWall, N., & Zhang, L. (2019). Support as a fundamental of psychological safety at work. *Journal of Organizational Behavior, 40*(3), 393–417. doi:10.1002/job.2260

Blattner, M., Graf, S., & Blüthgen, N. (2019). Psychological safety and organisational effectiveness: A systematic review. *Journal of Organizational Behavior, 40*(5), 599–614.

Book, L., Gatling, A., & Kim, J. (2019). The effects of leadership satisfaction on employee engagement, loyalty, and retention in the hospitality industry. Journal of Human Resources in Hospitality &Amp. *Journal of Human Resources in Hospitality & Tourism*, *18*(3), 368–393. doi:10.1080/15332845.2019.1599787

Brockbank, A., & McGill, I. (2018). The crucial role of feedback in psychological safety. *The Academy of Management Perspectives*, *32*(2), 134–152. doi:10.5465/amp.2016.0126

Buchler, N., Fleur, C., Hoffman, B., Rajivan, P., Marusich, L., & Lightner, L. (2018). Cyber teaming and role specialization in a cyber security defense competition. *Frontiers in Psychology*, *9*, 2133. Advance online publication. doi:10.3389/fpsyg.2018.02133 PMID:30510527

Cahyo, M., & Rachmawati, R. (2021). *Cross-functional team effectiveness factors in technological-based service company: nsiapay*. doi:10.2991/aebmr.k.210831.114

Carmeli, A., & Freund, A. (2005). Psychological safety at work: Its impact on organisational commitment, job satisfaction, and turnover intentions. *The Leadership Quarterly*, *16*(1), 153–172.

Carmeli, A., Sheaffer, Z., Binyamin, G., Reiter-Palmon, R., & Shimoni, T. (2013). Transformational leadership and creative problem-solving: The mediating role of psychological safety and reflexivity. *The Journal of Creative Behavior*, *48*(2), 115–135. doi:10.1002/jocb.43

Cater, J. III, Kidwell, R., & Camp, K. (2016). Successor team dynamics in family firms. *Family Business Review*, *29*(3), 301–326. doi:10.1177/0894486516656255

Cauwelier, P., Ribiere, V., & Bennet, A. (2019). The influence of team psychological safety on team knowledge creation: A study with French and American engineering teams. *Journal of Knowledge Management*, *23*(6), 1157–1175. doi:10.1108/JKM-07-2018-0420

Chang, Y., Lin, H., Chien, Y., & Yen, W. (2018). Effects of creative components and creative behaviour on design creativity. *Thinking Skills and Creativity*, *29*, 23–31. doi:10.1016/j.tsc.2018.05.007

Chaudhary, R. (2019). Corporate social responsibility perceptions and employee engagement: Role of psychological meaningfulness, safety and availability. *Corporate Governance (Bradford)*, *19*(4), 631–647. doi:10.1108/CG-06-2018-0207

Choi, S., Ullah, S., & Kang, S. (2021). Proactive personality and creative performance: Mediating roles of creative self-efficacy and moderated mediation role of psychological safety. *Sustainability (Basel), 13*(22), 12517. doi:10.3390u132212517

Christianto, R. (2022). The influence of servant leadership and employee compensation on employee engagement through employee job satisfaction as an intervening variable at pt Indonesia power suralaya power generation unit. *Journal of Business and Behavioural Entrepreneurship, 5*(2), 118–128. doi:10.21009/JOBBE.005.2.14

Cole, M., Cox, J., & Stavros, J. (2016). Building collaboration in teams through emotional intelligence: Mediation by soar (strengths, opportunities, aspirations, and results). *Journal of Management & Organization, 25*(02), 263–283. doi:10.1017/jmo.2016.43

Dar, N., Ahmad, S., & Rahman, W. (2022). How and when overqualification improves innovative work behaviour: The roles of creative self-confidence and psychological safety. *Personnel Review, 51*(9), 2461–2481. doi:10.1108/PR-06-2020-0429

Day, C., Tan, J., & Huczynski, A. (2019). Respect in teams: Its impact on performance, psychological safety, and creativity. *International Journal of Human Resource Management, 30*(4), 680–699. doi:10.1080/09585192.2019.1567112

Demir, M., McNeese, N., She, M., & Cooke, N. (2019). Team coordination of team situation awareness in human-autonomy teaming. *Proceedings of the Human Factors and Ergonomics Society Annual Meeting, 63*(1), 146–147. doi:10.1177/1071181319631259

DeRue, D. S., Hollenbeck, J. R., Ilgen, D. R., Jundt, D. K., & Meyer, G. J. (2010). Psychological safety in teams: The role of transformational leadership and member satisfaction. *The Leadership Quarterly, 21*(5), 618–631.

Dhanda, U. (2015). Employee engagement: the key success factor. *International Journal of Research-Granthaalayah, 3*(5), 77-87. doi:10.29121/granthaalayah.v3.i5.2015.3017

Ding, H., & Yu, E. (2021). Strengths-based leadership and employee psychological well-being: A moderated mediation model. *Journal of Career Development, 49*(5), 1108–1121. doi:10.1177/08948453211018807

Edmondson, A. (1999). Psychological safety and learning behaviour in work teams. *Administrative Science Quarterly, 44*(2), 350–383. doi:10.2307/2666999

Edmondson, A. (2012). *Teaming: How organisations learn, innovate, and compete in the knowledge economy*. Jossey-Bass.

Edmondson, A. (2019). Psychological safety: The history, renaissance, and future of an interpersonal construct. *Annual Review of Organizational Psychology and Organizational Behavior*, *6*, 523–546. doi:10.1146/annurev-orgpsych-032519-050926

Edmondson, A. C., Kramer, R. M., & Cook, K. S. (2004). Psychological safety, trust, and learning in organisations: A group-level lens. *Trust and distrust in organisations: Dilemmas and approaches, 12*(2004), 239-272.

Edmondson, A. C., & Lei, Z. (2014). Psychological safety: The history, renaissance, and future of an interpersonal construct. *Annual Review of Organizational Psychology and Organizational Behavior*, *1*(1), 23–43. doi:10.1146/annurev-orgpsych-031413-091305

Forsyth, D. R., Mitchel, J., & Shepherd, K. (2018). Psychological safety and team effectiveness: A meta-analysis. *The Journal of Applied Psychology*, *103*(2), 158–178.

Frazier, M., Fainshmidt, S., Klinger, R., Pezeshkan, A., & Vracheva, V. (2016). Psychological safety: A meta-analytic review and extension. *Personnel Psychology*, *70*(1), 113–165. doi:10.1111/peps.12183

Fyhn, B., Bang, H., Sverdrup, T., & Schei, V. (2022). Safe among the unsafe: Psychological safety climate strength matters for team performance. *Small Group Research*. Advance online publication. doi:10.1177/10464964221121273

Gardner, T., Herman, A., & Yap, J. (2019). Exploring the impact of learning and development initiatives on employee engagement. *Human Resource Development Quarterly*, *30*(4), 577–605. doi:10.1002/hrdq.21290

George, D., & Zhou, J. (2017). The effects of psychological safety on team creativity: A meta-analysis. *Academy of Management Journal*, *60*(2), 488–509.

Gonzalez, M. (2021). *The Importance of Psychological Safety and Team Building in the Workplace*. Retrieved April 10, 2021, from https://blog.hubspot.com/marketing/psychological-safety-team-building

Graneheim, U., Lindgren, B., & Lundman, B. (2017). Methodological challenges in qualitative content analysis: A discussion paper. *Nurse Education Today*, *56*, 29–34. doi:10.1016/j.nedt.2017.06.002 PMID:28651100

Griggs, A., Rogers, J., Gisick, L., Lazzara, E., Keebler, J., & Cohen, T. (2021). Development of a team role behaviour observation tool: Insights and considerations for future research. *Proceedings of the Human Factors and Ergonomics Society Annual Meeting*, *65*(1), 122–127. doi:10.1177/1071181321651282

Gu, J., Chen, Z., Huang, Q., Liu, H., & Huang, S. (2016). A multilevel analysis of the relationship between shared leadership and creativity in inter-organisational teams. *The Journal of Creative Behavior*, *52*(2), 109–126. doi:10.1002/jocb.135

Guo, W., & Wang, D. (2017). Does joint decision-making foster team creativity? exploring the moderating and mediating effects. *Personnel Review*, *46*(8), 1590–1604. doi:10.1108/PR-03-2016-0055

Gupta, N., & Sharma, V. (2016). Exploring employee engagement—A way to better business performance. *Global Business Review*, *17*(3, suppl), 45S–63S. doi:10.1177/0972150916631082

Han, S., Liu, D., & Lv, Y. (2022). The influence of psychological safety on students' creativity in project-based learning: The mediating role of psychological empowerment. *Frontiers in Psychology*, *13*, 865123. Advance online publication. doi:10.3389/fpsyg.2022.865123 PMID:35572343

Harrison, D. A., Price, K. H., Gavin, J. H., & Florey, A. T. (2019). Leveraging technology for team creativity in the workplace. *Organizational Dynamics*, *48*(4), 274–284. doi:10.1016/j.orgdyn.2019.06.007

Harrison, D. A., Price, K. H., Gavin, J. H., & Florey, A. T. (2020). The power of psychological safety: A meta-analysis of team dynamics. *The Journal of Applied Psychology*, *105*(3), 557–581. doi:10.1037/apl0000444

Hasan, F., & Kashif, M. (2020). Psychological safety, meaningfulness and empowerment as predictors of employee well-being: A mediating role of promotive voice. *Asia-Pacific Journal of Business Administration*, *13*(1), 40–59. doi:10.1108/APJBA-11-2019-0236

Hershcovis, M. (2011). Incivility, social undermining, bullying…oh my! A call to reconcile constructs within workplace aggression research. *Journal of Organizational Behavior*, *32*(1), 629–647. doi:10.1002/job.689

Hirak, R., Peng, A., Carmeli, A., & Schaubroeck, J. (2012). Linking leader inclusiveness to work unit performance: The importance of psychological safety and learning from failures. *The Leadership Quarterly*, *23*(1), 107–117. doi:10.1016/j.leaqua.2011.11.009

Hong, J. S., & Lee, J. R. (2009). Psychological safety and organisational commitment: A study of Korean telecommunication. *International Journal of Human Resource Management*, *20*(10), 2095–2107.

Huang, C., & Hsieh, P. (2017). Inspiring creativity in teams: Perspectives of transactive memory systems. *Journal of Pacific Rim Psychology, 11*, e6. doi:10.1017/prp.2017.6

Huang, Y., Cheng, B., & Liu, J. (2015). Psychological safety and job satisfaction: An empirical study. *Applied Psychology, 64*(3), 468–494.

Huff, C. (2019). *Psychological Safety in the Workplace: What It Is and How to Create It*. The Muse. Retrieved from: https://www.themuse.com/advice/psychological-safety-in-the-workplace-what-it-is-and-how-to-create-it

Humphrey, R., Massis, A., Picone, P., Tang, Y., & Piccolo, R. (2021). The psychological foundations of management in family firms: Emotions, memories, and experiences. *Family Business Review, 34*(2), 122–131. doi:10.1177/08944865211012139

Işgör, İ., & Haspolat, N. (2016). Investigating the psychological well-being and job satisfaction levels in different occupations. *International Education Studies, 9*(12), 194. doi:10.5539/ies.v9n12p194

Javed, B., Khan, A., Bashir, S., & Arjoon, S. (2016). Impact of ethical leadership on creativity: The role of psychological empowerment. *Current Issues in Tourism, 20*(8), 839–851. doi:10.1080/13683500.2016.1188894

Javed, B., Naqvi, S., Khan, A., Arjoon, S., & Tayyeb, H. (2017). Impact of inclusive leadership on innovative work behaviour: The role of psychological safety. *Journal of Management &Amp. Organisation, 25*(1), 117–136. doi:10.1017/jmo.2017.3

Jha, S. (2019). Team psychological safety and team performance. *The International Journal of Organizational Analysis, 27*(4), 903–924. doi:10.1108/IJOA-10-2018-1567

Johnson, M., Dodgson, M., & Gann, D. (2019). Psychological safety and job performance: A study of banking professionals. *International Journal of Bank Marketing, 37*(3), 622–636.

Kahn, W. A. (1990). Psychological conditions of personal engagement and disengagement at work. *Academy of Management Journal, 33*(4), 692–724. doi:10.2307/256287

Kanter, R. M., & Prahalad, C. K. (2017). Collaborative advantage: The art of creative collaboration. *Harvard Business Review, 95*(11), 57–69.

Keller, R. T. (2017). Rewards for creative thinking. *Creativity Research Journal, 29*(2), 186–196.

Keller, R. T., Goldstein, M., & Davis, R. (2018). Creativity, innovation, and risk taking: A motivational perspective. *Human Resource Management Review*, *28*(3), 243–255. doi:10.1016/j.hrmr.2018.03.002

Kerr, M. (2019). Creating Psychological Safety in the Workplace. *Harvard Business Review*. Retrieved from: https://hbr.org/2019/06/creating-psychological-safety-in-the-workplace

Kessel, M., Kratzer, J., & Schultz, C. (2012). Psychological safety, knowledge sharing, and creative performance in healthcare teams. *Creativity and Innovation Management*, *21*(2), 147–157. doi:10.1111/j.1467-8691.2012.00635.x

Kim, B., Park, S., & Kim, T. (2019). The effect of transformational leadership on team creativity: Sequential mediating effect of employee's psychological safety and creativity. *Asian Journal of Technology Innovation*, *27*(1), 90–107. doi:10.1080/19761597.2019.1587304

Kim, T., & Park, H. J. (2012). The effect of psychological safety on work engagement: Focusing on the mediating role of job resources. *The Journal of Psychology*, *146*(3), 247–264.

Kim, T. H., Kim, Y. K., & Kim, M. S. (2016). Psychological safety and team performance: A study of knowledge-intensive teams. *Journal of Business Research*, *69*(11), 5347–5351.

Koopmann, J., Lanaj, K., Wang, M., Zhou, L., & Shi, J. (2016). Nonlinear effects of team tenure on team psychological safety climate and climate strength: Implications for average team member performance. *The Journal of Applied Psychology*, *101*(7), 940–957. doi:10.1037/apl0000097 PMID:26949818

Kossyva, D., Theriou, G., Aggelidis, V., & Sarigiannidis, L. (2022). Definitions and antecedents of engagement: A systematic literature review. *Management Research Review*, *46*(5), 719–738. doi:10.1108/MRR-01-2021-0043

Krawczyk-Bryłka, B., Stankiewicz, K., Ziemiański, P., & Tomczak, M. (2020). Effective collaboration of entrepreneurial teams—Implications for entrepreneurial education. *Education Sciences*, *10*(12), 364. doi:10.3390/educsci10120364

Kumar, M., & Sharma, R. (2018). Psychological Safety: A Literature Review. *International Journal of Business and Management*, *13*(1), 6–20.

Kumar, S. (2018). Psychological safety and team effectiveness: The mediating role of trust. *International Journal of Business and Behavioural Sciences*, *8*(3), 34–44.

Kumar, V., & Pansari, A. (2016). Competitive advantage through engagement. *JMR, Journal of Marketing Research, 53*(4), 497–514. doi:10.1509/jmr.15.0044

Kuo, C., Ye, Y., Chen, M., & Chen, L. (2019). Proactive personality enhances change in employees' job satisfaction: The moderating role of psychological safety. *Australian Journal of Management, 44*(3), 482–494. doi:10.1177/0312896218818225

Kyngäs, H. (2019). Qualitative Research and Content Analysis. *The Application of Content Analysis in Nursing Science Research.* . doi:10.1007/978-3-030-30199-6_1

Layan, S. (2020). *The Benefits of Psychological Safety and Team Building*. Retrieved April 10, 2021, from https://www.g2.com/hr/psychological-safety-and-team-building

Lee, H., Choi, J. N., & Kim, S. (2018). Does gender diversity help teams constructively manage status conflict? an evolutionary perspective of status conflict, team psychological safety, and team creativity. *Organizational Behavior and Human Decision Processes, 144*, 187–199. doi:10.1016/j.obhdp.2017.09.005

Lee, J. W., Choi, Y. S., & Choi, J. N. (2010). Psychological safety and trust in organisations. *The Journal of Psychology, 144*(3), 215–233.

Lee, K., Hyun, S., Park, H., & Kim, K. (2020). The antecedents and consequences of psychological safety in airline firms: Focusing on high-quality interpersonal relationships. *International Journal of Environmental Research and Public Health, 17*(7), 2187. doi:10.3390/ijerph17072187 PMID:32218262

Lee, P. C., Wu, Y. Y., Tsai, Y. P., & Chen, Y. J. (2012). The effects of psychological safety on team effectiveness: A study of software development teams in Taiwan. *IEEE Transactions on Software Engineering, 38*(3), 644–657.

Leicht-Deobald, U., Lam, C., Bruch, H., Kunze, F., & Wu, W. (2022). Team boundary work and team workload demands: Their interactive effect on team vigor and team effectiveness. *Human Resource Management, 61*(4), 465–488. doi:10.1002/hrm.22104

Li, Y., Cao, Y., & Li, D. (2015). *The mechanism of the impact of team climate and team psychological safety on team innovation performance.* doi:10.2991/msmi-15.2015.38

Liang, Y., & Wang, M. (2016). The moderating role of psychological safety on job insecurity and organisational commitment. *International Journal of Human Resource Management, 27*(1), 88–101. doi:10.1080/09585192.2015.1025158

Liao, H., Rupp, D. E., & Wu, A. (2005). The joint effects of psychological contract breach and organisational justice on employee turnover intentions. *The Journal of Applied Psychology, 90*(3), 534–543.

Lindgren, B., Lundman, B., & Graneheim, U. (2020). Abstraction and interpretation during the qualitative content analysis process. *International Journal of Nursing Studies, 108*, 103632. doi:10.1016/j.ijnurstu.2020.103632 PMID:32505813

Ling, Y. (2020). Unlocking creativity in teams: A review of the literature. *Creativity Research Journal, 32*(1), 48–63. doi:10.1080/10400419.2020.1727155

Liu, D., Li, Y., & Liu, Y. (2019). Effects of psychological safety on team creativity and creative work quality: The moderating role of team reflexivity. *Creativity Research Journal, 31*(1), 83–90.

Liu, W., Zhang, P., Liao, J., Hao, P., & Mao, J. (2016). Abusive supervision and employee creativity. *Management Decision, 54*(1), 130–147. doi:10.1108/MD-09-2013-0443

Liu, Y., & Hu, H. (2013). The role of psychological safety in predicting employees' turnover intentions. *Human Resource Management, 53*(2), 265–279.

Luksyte, A., & Spitzmueller, C. (2015). When are overqualified employees creative? it depends on contextual factors. *Journal of Organizational Behavior, 37*(5), 635–653. doi:10.1002/job.2054

Ma, L., Shao, Y., & Li, H. (2019). An empirical study on the relationship between psychological contract and job satisfaction of the cenozioc employees. *Open Journal of Social Sciences, 07*(10), 105–120. doi:10.4236/jss.2019.710010

Ma, X., Li, Y., Li, S., & Zou, S. (2020). The mediating role of job satisfaction in the relationship between psychological safety and organisational commitment. *International Journal of Environmental Research and Public Health, 17*(7), 2470. doi:10.3390/ijerph17072470 PMID:32260388

Madjar, N., & Ortiz-Walters, R. (2009). Trust in supervisors and trust in customers: Their independent, relative, and joint effects on employee performance and creativity. *Human Performance, 22*(2), 128–142. doi:10.1080/08959280902743501

Mahomed, Y., & Mtembu, V. (2021). Business succession in Indian family businesses in South Africa. *Journal of Economics and Behavioral Studies, 13*(3(J)), 73–80. doi:10.22610/jebs.v13i3(J).3182

Mannix, E., & Neale, M. (2005). What differences make a difference? The promise and reality of diverse teams in organisational settings. *Psychological Science in the Public Interest, 6*(2), 31–55. doi:10.1111/j.1529-1006.2005.00022.x PMID:26158478

McGuier, E., Kolko, D. J., Stadnick, N. A., Brookman-Frazee, L., Wolk, C. B., Yuan, C. T., Burke, C. S., & Aarons, G. A. (2023). Advancing research on teams and team effectiveness in implementation science: An application of the exploration, preparation, implementation, sustainment (epis) framework. *Implementation Research and Practice, 4*. Advance online publication. doi:10.1177/26334895231190855 PMID:37790168

Mehmood, M., Jian, Z., Akram, U., Akram, Z., & Tanveer, Y. (2021). Entrepreneurial leadership and team creativity: The roles of team psychological safety and knowledge sharing. *Personnel Review, 51*(9), 2404–2425. doi:10.1108/PR-07-2020-0517

Moin, M. F., Omar, M. K., Wei, F., Rasheed, M. I., & Hameed, Z. (2021). Green HRM and psychological safety: How transformational leadership drives follower's job satisfaction. *Current Issues in Tourism, 24*(16), 2269–2277. doi:10.1080/13683500.2020.1829569

Montag, T., Maertz, C. Jr, & Baer, M. (2012). A critical analysis of the workplace creativity criterion space. *Journal of Management, 38*(4), 1362–1386. doi:10.1177/0149206312441835

Muller, A., Turner, N., & van der Heijden, B. I. J. M. (2016). Psychological safety, risk taking and innovation in teams: An empirical study. *International Journal of Innovation Management, 20*(1), 1640001.

Newman, A., Donohue, R., & Eva, N. (2017). Psychological safety: A systematic review of the literature. *Human Resource Management Review, 27*(3), 521–535. doi:10.1016/j.hrmr.2017.01.001

Nielsen, K., & Einarsen, S. (2008). Perceived psychological safety and job satisfaction among offshore safety personnel. *Safety Science*. doi:10.21776/ub.jam.2021.019.02.06

Noercahyo, U., Maarif, M., & Sumertajaya, I. (2021). The role of employee engagement on job satisfaction and its effect on organisational performance. *Jurnal Aplikasi Manajemen, 19*(2), 296–309. doi:10.21776/ub.jam.2021.019.02.06

O'Donovan, R., & McAuliffe, E. (2020). A systematic review exploring the content and outcomes of interventions to improve psychological safety, speaking up and voice behaviour. *BMC Health Services Research, 20*(1), 101. Advance online publication. doi:10.118612913-020-4931-2 PMID:32041595

O'Donovan, R., & McAuliffe, E. (2020). Exploring psychological safety in healthcare teams to inform the development of interventions: Combining observational, survey and interview data. *BMC Health Services Research, 20*(1), 810. Advance online publication. doi:10.118612913-020-05646-z PMID:32867762

O'Leary, V. E., Jones, D. A., & Mitchell, R. (2012). Communication as a critical component of successful teams: A review and integration. In A. O'Leary-Kelly, J. E. Mathieu, & R. C. Richard (Eds.), *The Oxford Handbook of Organisational Psychology* (Vol. 2, pp. 476–497). Oxford University Press.

Pan, Y., Shang, Y., & Malika, R. (2020). Enhancing creativity in organisations: The role of the need for cognition. *Management Decision, 59*(9), 2057–2076. doi:10.1108/MD-04-2019-0516

Pattnaik, S., & Sahoo, R. (2020). Employee engagement, creativity and task performance: Role of perceived workplace autonomy. *South Asian Journal of Business Studies, 10*(2), 227–241. doi:10.1108/SAJBS-11-2019-0196

Peralta, C., Lourenço, P., Lopes, P., Baptista, C., & Pais, L. (2018). Team development: Definition, measurement and relationships with team effectiveness. *Human Performance, 31*(2), 97–124. doi:10.1080/08959285.2018.1455685

Prentice, S. (2022). Job satisfaction or employee engagement: Regardless of which comes first, supportive leadership improves them both. *Advances in Developing Human Resources, 24*(4), 275–285. doi:10.1177/15234223221112504

Purwatiningsih, Y., & Faisal, D. (2022). The influence of team cohesion and trust on team effectiveness in preventing tuberculosis. *Jurnal Administrasi Kesehatan Indonesia, 10*(2), 188–196. doi:10.20473/jaki.v10i2.2022.188-196

Rego, A., Sousa, F., Marques, C., & Cunha, M. (2012). Authentic leadership promoting employees' psychological capital and creativity. *Journal of Business Research, 65*(3), 429–437. doi:10.1016/j.jbusres.2011.10.003

Roffia, P., Moracchiato, S., Liguori, E., & Kraus, S. (2021). Operationally defining family smes: A critical review. *Journal of Small Business and Enterprise Development, 28*(2), 229–260. doi:10.1108/JSBED-11-2020-0399

Schein, E. (1993). On psychological safety and learning new behaviours in organisations. *Organizational Dynamics, 22*(2), 36–52.

Shao, R., Loi, R., & Lam, W. (2012). Psychological safety, job satisfaction, and performance: A meta-analysis. *Journal of Organizational Behavior, 33*(3), 486–509.

Sidani, Y., & Reese, S. (2020). Nancy dixon: Empowering the learning organisation through psychological safety. *The Learning Organization*, *27*(3), 259–266. doi:10.1108/TLO-01-2020-0015

Singh, M., & Sarkar, A. (2019). Role of psychological empowerment in the relationship between structural empowerment and innovative behaviour. *Management Research Review*, *42*(4), 521–538. doi:10.1108/MRR-04-2018-0158

Spedding, J., Brough, P., Hawkes, A. J., & Chan, X. W. (2023). The effective measurement of shared leadership: A multi-scale comparison. *Leadership and Organization Development Journal*, *44*(4), 564–581. doi:10.1108/LODJ-10-2021-0453

Sun, L., & Bunchapattanasakda, C. (2019). Employee engagement: A literature review. International. *Journal of Human Resource Studies*, *9*(1), 63. doi:10.5296/ijhrs.v9i1.14167

Sutawidjaya, A. (2019). Talent management in mediating competencies and motivation to improve employee's engagement. *International Journal of Economics and Business Administration*, *VII*(1), 140–152. doi:10.35808/ijeba/201

Suwandana, I. (2019). Role of transformational leadership mediation: Effect of emotional and communication intelligence towards teamwork effectiveness. *International Research Journal of Management It and Social Sciences*, *6*(2), 52–62. doi:10.21744/irjmis.v6n2.608

Taylor, R., Currie, G., & Henneberg, S. (2017). The impact of psychological safety on team performance: A longitudinal study. *The Leadership Quarterly*, *28*(3), 387–400.

Tremblay, D., Touati, N., Kilpatrick, K., Durand, M., Turcotte, A., Prady, C., Poder, T. G., Richard, P. O., Soldera, S., Berbiche, D., Généreux, M., Roy, M., Laflamme, B., Lessard, S., Landry, M., & Giordano, É. (2022). Building resilience in oncology teams: Protocol for a realist evaluation of multiple cases. *PLoS One*, *17*(5), e0268393. doi:10.1371/journal.pone.0268393 PMID:35551336

Vandekerkhof, P., Steijvers, T., Hendriks, W., & Voordeckers, W. (2017). Socio-emotional wealth separation and decision-making quality in family firm TMTs: The moderating role of psychological safety. *Journal of Management Studies*, *55*(4), 648–676. doi:10.1111/joms.12277

Vlas, R., Nguyen, H., & Vlas, C. (2022). A theoretical exploration of out-group versus in-group perspectives on the dynamics of team effectiveness. *Team Performance Management*, *28*(1/2), 45–60. doi:10.1108/TPM-09-2021-0070

Wadei, K., Chen, L., Frempong, J., & Appienti, W. (2020). The mediation effect of ethical leadership and creative performance: A social information processing perspective. *The Journal of Creative Behavior, 55*(1), 241–254. doi:10.1002/jocb.449

Walters, K., & Diab, D. (2016). Humble leadership: Implications for psychological safety and follower engagement. *Journal of Leadership Studies, 10*(2), 7–18. doi:10.1002/jls.21434

Wang, W., Kang, S., & Choi, S. (2022). Servant leadership and creativity: A study of the sequential mediating roles of psychological safety and employee well-being. *Frontiers in Psychology, 12*, 807070. Advance online publication. doi:10.3389/fpsyg.2021.807070 PMID:35185702

Wang, Y. (2016). Environmental dynamism, trust and dynamic capabilities of family businesses. *International Journal of Entrepreneurial Behaviour & Research, 22*(5), 643–670. doi:10.1108/IJEBR-11-2015-0234

Wang, Y., Ahmad, W., Arshad, M., Yin, H., Ahmed, B., & Ali, Z. (2021). Impact of coordination, psychological safety, and job security on employees' performance: The moderating role of coercive pressure. *Sustainability (Basel), 13*(6), 3175. doi:10.3390u13063175

Wang, Y., Liu, J., & Zhu, L. (2018). Humble leadership, psychological safety, knowledge sharing, and follower creativity: A cross-level investigation. *Frontiers in Psychology, 9*, 1727. Advance online publication. doi:10.3389/fpsyg.2018.01727 PMID:30283379

Wayland, R., Shore, L. M., & Ding, C. (2016). Psychological safety and organisational outcomes: A meta-analysis. *Journal of Organizational Behavior, 37*(1), 3–22.

Wu, C., Lv, H., He, L., & Cheng, T. (2022). *Research on the influence mechanism of psychological safety on leaders' ambidexterity based on experimental analysis.* doi:10.2991/assehr.k.220105.004

Xiao, Z., Liao, H., & Dai, S. (2014). Organisational culture, psychological safety, and knowledge sharing in a Chinese context. *Human Resource Management, 53*(5), 765–781.

Yang, Y., Jiang, Y., & Wan, K. (2018). The impact of organisational support on employees' psychological safety: A meta-analysis. *Human Resource Management Review, 28*(4), 551–564.

Yang, Y., Li, Z., Liang, L., & Zhang, X. (2019). Why and when paradoxical leader behaviour impact employee creativity: Thriving at work and psychological safety. *Current Psychology (New Brunswick, N.J.)*, *40*(4), 1911–1922. doi:10.100712144-018-0095-1

Yi, H., Hao, P., Yang, B., & Liu, W. (2016). How leaders' transparent behaviour influences employee creativity: The mediating roles of psychological safety and ability to focus attention. *Journal of Leadership & Organizational Studies*, *24*(3), 335–344. doi:10.1177/1548051816670306

Yin, Y., Chen, J., & Li, C. (2018). Psychological safety, conflict and team performance: A moderated mediation model. *International Journal of Manpower*, *39*(7), 1162–1178.

Younas, A., Wang, D., Javed, B., Rawwas, M., Abdullah, I., & Zaffar, M. (2018). Positive psychological states and employee creativity: The role of ethical leadership. *The Journal of Creative Behavior*, *54*(3), 567–581. doi:10.1002/jocb.391

Zeb, A., Abdullah, N., Hussain, A., & Safi, A. (2019). Authentic leadership, knowledge sharing, and employees' creativity. *Management Research Review*, *43*(6), 669–690. doi:10.1108/MRR-04-2019-0164

Zhang, X., & Bartlett, K. R. (2017). How Leaders and Team Members Create a Psychologically Safe Work Environment: A Multiple Case Study. *Journal of Business and Psychology*, *32*(3), 231–248.

Zhang, X., Qian, S., & Wang, Y. (2017). The mediating role of job satisfaction in the relationship between psychological safety and organisational commitment. *International Journal of Environmental Research and Public Health*, *14*(4), 427. doi:10.3390/ijerph14040427 PMID:28420149

Zhou, W., Zhu, Z., & Vredenburgh, D. (2020). Emotional intelligence, psychological safety, and team decision making. *Team Performance Management*, *26*(1/2), 123–141. doi:10.1108/TPM-10-2019-0105

Zhu, H., Schulte, M. A., & Thomas, J. (2020). Leveraging information technology to promote innovation in virtual teams. *Journal of Management Information Systems*, *37*(1), 54–81. doi:10.1080/07421222.2019.1708773

Chapter 5
Psychosocial Wellbeing of Entrepreneurs:
The Interplay of Business-Family Life Stressors and Social Support

Ethel Ndidiamaka Abe
https://orcid.org/0000-0003-1670-6801
SashBM LLC, USA

Doreen Mukuku
Varsity College, South Africa

Mercy Okoli
Durban University of Technology, South Africa

EXECUTIVE SUMMARY

Entrepreneurship engages every aspect of the entrepreneur's being in conducting work and engaging with family life. The entrepreneurial process, from beginning to completion, comprises transition stages, which are all distinctively stressful. Unlike people who are employees in the public or private sectors of any economy, the entrepreneur may not be able to draw boundaries between business life and family life as their business traverses both domains. These scholars argue that the resultant effect of the boundary-crossing activities of the entrepreneur will result in stress and conversely affect their psychosocial well-being. Amid their entrepreneurial activities and family responsibilities, the chaos unfolding opens the entrepreneur to needing balance. This chapter explores the role that business-family life strategies and social support could play in assisting entrepreneurs to achieve and maintain psychosocial well-being. The findings of the chapter from the review of extant literature will have practical and theoretical implications.

DOI: 10.4018/978-1-6684-8748-8.ch005

PROLOGUE

Rosetta is a hardworking entrepreneur that has led her social enterprise organisation for over six years. She has two children living with disabilities. She loves collaborating with people to solve challenging community problems and derives satisfaction when she accomplishes such challenging feats. She draws strength from making progress on such challenging tasks and demonstrates her best abilities during such occasions. In 2020, the Covid-19 pandemic struck with unprecedented challenges. The virus and its accompanying regulations of lockdown, social distancing, mask-wearing, and hand sanitisation brought tremendous stress on communities. Rosetta closed her office and asked her employees to go home and work remotely since the government had instructed that people obey the Covid-19 regulations. Nations waited for vaccination for several months as families were being devastated from loss of members, uncertain fears, sicknesses, and loss of income in most cases. Small businesses including Rosetta's suffered unprintable hardships ranging from loss of sponsors to loss of income leading to inability to pay bills.

As Rosetta watched her business, employees and the larger community suffer, all she could think of was how to help. For days and nights, she immersed herself in fruitless thoughts. When the government rolled out the COVID -19 vaccines, she worried about vaccination hesitations, and what to do to make vaccines available and acceptable to her community. For whole evenings including supper time and when in bed trying to fall asleep, she pondered on the challenges and how to solve them. She found herself feeling drained, tired, and in bad spirits every waking morning. Although those were not the first times that she found herself in similar mind situations, as she recalled the year before Covid-10 when she needed to convince a certain funder to extend the contractual period. She tried to piece all her documents and evidence together to convince her funder about the need to go on, but her laptop crashed two days to her meeting. Rosetta was so worried about completing the report and making a convincing presentation to the funder that she was absent minded throughout her daughter's choral evening. The cycle of worry, lack of appetite, sleeplessness, kicked in and she found herself grumpy, in bad moods, and drained through the next two days.

Members of her family, on seeing the challenges Rosetta faced and the effect on her wellbeing, decided to provide some of the funding needs of her enterprise. This somehow complicated her anxiety, uncertainty, and fear with respect to the result that accepting the family's financial resource would cause her enterprise. Torn between options, Rosetta decided to seek out a psychotherapist for professional assistance.

According to Wiklund, Nikolaev, Shir, Foo, and Bradley (2019), the well-being of entrepreneurs is gaining rising interest because of its linkage to meaningful results like organisational performance (Stephan, 2018) and satisfaction (Wach,

Stephan, & Georgievski, 2016). Unarguably, the line between the entrepreneurs and their companies cannot be clear, it is difficult for entrepreneurs to separate themselves physically and mentally from their companies. Therefore, this chapter also examines the way in which entrepreneurs detach and recover from their work and family stressors to maintain their well-being using Sonnentag and Fritz's (2015) stressor-detachment framework. The model suggests that entrepreneurs, by removing themselves mentally from their business when business time is over, plus, not giving thought to work in the evenings, reduce stress.

Questions for Discussions

1. What can be done to address start-up stressors?
2. Recommend remedies for family embeddedness -related stressors
3. Assist entrepreneurs in a volatile, uncertain, complex, and ambiguous global world to make sense of emerging stressors. What can they do to manage sudden emergencies like a pandemic in the future?

SECTION 1: THE ENTREPRENEURIAL PROCESS AND STRESS

Introduction

The entrepreneurial process is ambiguous. Ambiguity is a major source of stress (Chang & Hancock, 2003). The preliminary stages of entrepreneurship are froth with challenges and stress for start-up entrepreneurs. The entrepreneurial process includes the identification and development of prospects and related results (Shane & Venkataraman, 2000). The aim of this section is to investigate the origin of, and transformations in stressors that confront start-up entrepreneurs in the entrepreneurial process. Scholars have defined start-up businesses to mean different things. In this chapter, it is conceptualised as enterprises characteristically technology-based that have the propensity to achieve high growth and be successful in a highly risky environment. It should have been in operation for not more than five to ten years. Start-up does not include listed companies, acquisitions, and/or firms having more than eighty employees, and must not be generating more than twenty million dollars income, per annum.

Start-up entrepreneurs face diverse roles that engender stress. According to McGrath (1970), stress is a significant imbalance among the demands of an environment and the responsive capacity of the target entity. In addition, stress encompasses stressors, mental judgment, responsiveness to stress, and behavioural outcomes. The present chapter argues that stress and stressors are imperative underpinning factors in the entrepreneurial process. This section explains the implications of stress, business, and family-related stressors on the psychosocial well-being of an entrepreneur. vis-à-vis the entrepreneurial process.

The Entrepreneurial Process

The entrepreneurial process begins from the identification of a need through to ideation, opportunity analysis, planning, concept development and testing (Cohen, Hsu, & Shinnar, 2021), among others. Entrepreneurial and stress scholars introduced process frameworks to recognise the product or service that a firm wants to offer the identified target market and the cost of achieving these. Furthermore, process frameworks sought to describe the manner and reason behind the unfolding of processes with time (Van de Ven, 1992). Moroz and Hindle (2012) report that thirty-two different frameworks are recognised and considered in a thorough assessment.

The opportunity-driven new means-end model is one of the most useful process frameworks (Shane, 2003; Shane & Venkataraman, 2000). It theorizes the entrepreneurial process as comprising of the identification and development of prospects and their related results. Entrepreneurial prospects are circumstances wherein entrepreneurs propose and offer innovative commodities, services, material resources, and managing techniques at a profit. Hence, prospects occur in an empirical sense (Shane & Venkataraman, 2000). The materialisation of these prospects into a firm (prospect development) rest on the way that entrepreneurs perceive and interpret the prospects (prospect assessment), and the availability of needed resources in the environment (Edelman & Yli–Renko, 2010). Lastly, the environment and the entrepreneur's activities define the results of the development of the prospect (Gartner & Carter, 2003).

Stress

An entrepreneur is an innovatively creative individual who builds a new enterprise and plays the role of owner and director of the enterprise ((Wang & Richardson, 2021; Ko & Liu, 2021; Cunningham & Lischeron, 1991). This means that he manages the enterprise creation process in all its ramifications in an unpredictable environment. The way individuals interpret and react to the needs present in an environment is related to stress. The entrepreneur engages with two cognitive environments or domains of work (business) and life (i.e., family and others). With these come domain-specific stressors and their associated stress impacts in the business and life of the entrepreneur. Stress also arises from the incongruities among an individual's expectations and trait, capabilities to solve challenges, and realities (Kahn & Quinn, 1970).

In contrast to paid workers, the entrepreneurs' job is more difficult and complicated and entails excessive amounts of uncertainty, which makes it tremendously challenging and stressful (Cardon & Patel, 2015; Patzelt & Shepherd, 2011; Rauch, Fink & Hatak, 2018). These challenges increase by the entrepreneurs' immediate interface with their job outcomes, workers, family, and business. Furthermore, entrepreneurs face difficulty separating themselves psychologically, cognitively, or truly lawfully from their responsibility. The task of an entrepreneur is emotionally stressful: s/he must solve difficult problems, work under time strain, and swap between different duties (Frese, Chell, & Klandt, 2000). In addition, an entrepreneur's job can be psychologically difficult and exhausting due to disputes with clients, suppliers, and/ or workers (Lechat & Torres, 2017; Schonfeld & Mazzola, 2015). Such stressors are widespread among outstanding wealth-creating businesspersons like Elon Musk and for "normal" entrepreneurs (Aldrich & Ruef, 2018; Welter, Baker, Audretsch, & Gartner, 2017). The disruption of technology in the work-family domains and its implication on work-family boundaries constitute additional stressor to the entrepreneur.

Stress is a development that progresses with time and its process has been conceptualised as an outcome variable by predicting the effect of stress processes. Extant literature has proposed several conflicting stress process frameworks. While some scholars assume that stress has several causes, mediating effect, and result of stress processes. For instance, McGrath (1970) classifies four phases of the stress procedure. It commences with the circumstantial needs (stressors), that comprise tangible, mental, or cognitive demands. Nevertheless, the presence of needs does not of a necessity produce stress, but the way individuals experience stress is dependent on their perceptions about the needs and their ability to address such needs. Conversely, individuals perceive similar circumstances differently; while one person finds the circumstance stressful, another person may not. This dissimilarity in perceptions is a result of the cognitive evaluation of the stress procedure which could create a stress response (strain). In conclusion, the stress response could influence several behavioural outcomes including productivity. For instance, stress response of an entrepreneur could impair their ability to process information which conversely impairs the organisational productivity and the entrepreneur's well-being.

Stress is a part of entrepreneurship, resulting from substantial workloads and the extreme risks involved (Pratama, Nurlaila, & Nasution, 2023; Palmer, 1971), and the entrepreneur's desire for greater achievement (Xue, Qian, Qian, & Li, 2021; Bakracheva, et al., 2020; Brockhaus, 1982). High degrees of stress could result in nonattendance, mishaps, rise in cost of wellbeing and/ or decrease in performance (Musungwa & Kowe, 2022; Roberts, Lapidus, & Chonko, 1997; Crampton, Hodge, Jiterdra, & Price, 1995). The cost of challenges from business-related stress in the United States is over 10 percent of the Gross National Product (GNP) (Ivancevich

& Matteson, 1980). Paudel, In contemporary times, Khadka, Rai, and Singh, (2023) report that during the COVID-19 pandemic, business-related stressors among entrepreneurs in the tourism sector heightened and increased the level of psychosocial issues, including suicidal ideation.

The need for stress handling strategies, therefore, is important since it could result in undesirable outcomes for entrepreneurs and the nations. Extant investigations on stress management and reduction discovered that social support is a great remedy for lessening stress (Hou et al., 2020; Shao et al., 2020; Rahim, 1996; Chay, 1993). Also, Mack and McGee (2001) confirmed that social support palliates work and life stress. Furthermore, scholars extended the argument by asserting that people with strong internal locus of control are more efficient in utilising support resources, hence more capable of reducing the degree of anxiety resulting from stress (Giao, Vuong, & Tushar, 2020; Sandler & Lakey, 1982). Latack, Scholars also report that the capability to manage a situation could assist an individual in better dealing with (Demerouti & Bakker, 2023; Labrague & De los Santos, 2020; Kinicki & Prussia, 1995). Additionally, performance of complex and interesting tasks results in less stress (Menges, Tussing, Wihler, & Grant, 2017; Mack & McGee, 2001). And, working with adaptable guidelines and less stiff methods lessen degree of stress (Tomlin, Dalgleish-Warburton, & Lamph, 2020; Nasurdin, Ramaya, & Beng, 2006), although an organizational environment full of severe competition and absence of interaction is inclined to be incredibly stressful (Wong & Wong, 2002).

The following section discusses the identified business-related stressors.

SECTION 2: BUSINESS-RELATED STRESSORS

An entrepreneur is both cognitively (for e.g., regarding business) and emotionally (for e.g., regarding community or family) attached to his/her business. As entrepreneurs do not clearly separate themselves from their businesses cognitively and psychologically, this paper investigates the business-related stressors and their effect on entrepreneur's well-being. The likelihood that stressors have adverse implications (e.g., misunderstanding surrounding negotiations of remuneration) on the well-being of entrepreneurs exist (LePine et al., 2005). Hence, the business-related stressors that confront entrepreneurs can be classified into cognitive and emotional stressors. Wach et al. (2020) affirm that strong cognitive needs have a positive relationship while strong psychological needs have a negative association with the wellbeing of an entrepreneur at the family (personal) level. On the short run, however, a heightened prevalence of both cognitive and psychological stressors during working hours weakens the rate of an entrepreneur's well-being later in the

Chaudhary, R., & Panda, C. (2018). Authentic leadership and creativity. *International Journal of Productivity and Performance Management*, *67*(9), 2071–2088. doi:10.1108/IJPPM-02-2018-0082

Chen, A., & Hou, Y. (2016). The effects of ethical leadership, voice behaviour and climates for innovation on creativity: A moderated mediation examination. *The Leadership Quarterly*, *27*(1), 1–13. doi:10.1016/j.leaqua.2015.10.007

Chen, C., Liao, J., & Wen, P. (2013). Why does formal mentoring matter? the mediating role of psychological safety and the moderating role of power distance orientation in the Chinese context. *International Journal of Human Resource Management*, *25*(8), 1112–1130. doi:10.1080/09585192.2013.816861

Chen, L., Wadei, K., Bai, S., & Liu, J. (2020). Participative leadership and employee creativity: A sequential mediation model of psychological safety and creative process engagement. *Leadership and Organization Development Journal*, *41*(6), 741–759. doi:10.1108/LODJ-07-2019-0319

Chen, R., Guo, Y., & Yang, J. (2017). The influence of job insecurity on organisational commitment: The moderating role of psychological safety. *International Journal of Human Resource Management*, *28*(14), 2076–2092. doi:10.1080/09585192.2016.1257819

Chen, R., Yang, J., & Guo, Y. (2018). The mediating role of trust in the relationship between psychological safety and organisational commitment. *International Journal of Human Resource Management*, *29*(10), 1732–1748. doi:10.1080/09585192.2017.1337360

Chen, T., Li, F., & Leung, K. (2015). When does supervisor support encourage innovative behaviour? opposite moderating effects of general self-efficacy and internal locus of control. *Personnel Psychology*, *69*(1), 123–158. doi:10.1111/peps.12104

Chen, Y., Tsai, T. S., & Hsu, Y. (2016). Psychological safety, creativity, and innovation: A meta-analysis. *Journal of Organizational Behavior*, *37*(3), 459–483.

Cheng, Z., Yang, Y., Tan, C., Cheng, D., Cheng, A., & Zhuang, Y. (2019). *What makes a good team? A large-scale study on the effect of team composition in honor of kings*. doi:10.1145/3308558.3313530

Chmiel, A., Kaczmarczyk, M., & Bocian, K. (2018). Psychological safety and organisational performance: A systematic review. *Journal of Occupational and Organizational Psychology*, *91*(2), 205–225.

day by influencing the inability to detach from the day's work and rest well, thus resulting in restlessness at night and lack of energy for the next workday.

Uncertainty in entrepreneurship is a given because of the near absence of conclusive potentials, propositions, and environmental situations. Uncertainty is the hallmark of risks that harbour entrepreneurial opportunities. It is also a major precursor of stress procedures that create challenges to the entrepreneur. According to Mason (1968), the original source of stress is uncertainty as individuals infer that cause-effect interface exists in the choice of tactics to use in achieving determinate results. Hence, stress develops where a person is unsure of the tactics to choose, for instance, when the reality of an event is not what an individual expected.

In entrepreneurship, although the expectation of the entrepreneur is to resolve a problematic situation, provide a solution to a need, and/or make some profit, the strategy to use to achieve the certain outcome may not be easily determined. Stress develops in the process and to address the emerging stress, the entrepreneur can adapt his/her response (McGrath, 1970). For instance, adjusting one's mindset about uncertainty places one in the position to forecast the future results better and reduces the associated stress to uncertainty. Peters and McEwen (2015) agree that persistent and irresolvable uncertainty produces endless and disruptive mental stress reactions that result in depression, infarction, and cognitive weakening.

Psychological and physiological health challenges among entrepreneurs can also result from business-related psychosocial strain that result in immense costs to the economy, communities, and individuals. This is because, the vast number of employees globally are employed by entrepreneurial activities of small and medium size firms that often have smaller monetary and human capital when compared with bigger organisations. Hence, when the entrepreneur is unwell, the individual employees, communities that utilise the products/services of the firm as well as society at large, feel the pinch.

Notable governmental and systematic attention is being directed to the demands of psychosocial nature comprising of work content, workload, and the social environment (Eurofound & EU-OSHA, 2014). Scholars report that wellbeing-associated challenges and work-related health issues account for a considerable degree of absenteeism and inability to perform in Europe, resulting in socioeconomic concerns for people, communities, and the economy (OECD, 2018; Hassard, et al., 2014). For instance, Germany records that the rate of absence from work due to psychological illnesses has notably risen in the past four decades from 2% to almost 16% (Knieps, Pfaff, 2019; Marschall, et al, 2018). In financial terms, the OECD (2018) confirms that the direct and indirect costs of psychological illnesses in Europe is approximately 4.1% of the national GDP.

In this section, a summary of contemporary information on business-related stressors among entrepreneurs is identified. The psychosocial factors that influence the psychosocial wellbeing of entrepreneurs identified from the review of extant research are categorised as work *content and task*, *organization of work*, *social relations*, *working environment* and *new forms of work* (Schreibauer, Hippler, Burgess, Rieger, & Rind, 2020). Other psychosocial factors that have been severally investigated especially with respect to the business designs include job organisation, and job content and duty. The findings from the literature reveal the need for empirical evidence on psychosocial stressors and their effect on the wellbeing of entrepreneurs, especially with the new developments in the global work environment (for instance, the Covid-19 pandemic), and the digitization of business/entrepreneurial processes.

SECTION 3: FAMILY SUPPORT: EMBEDDEDNESS AND SOCIAL EXCHANGE RELATED STRESSORS

Extant literature shows the mutual advantages of family resources to an entrepreneur's business activities depending on the size of such resources that are accessible to the entrepreneur. The start-up activity for instance, has been found by two researchers to be mostly supported by family group capital (referred to as family support) which the start-up entrepreneur uses in preparation for the new business (Edelman, Manolova, Shirokova, & Tsukanova, 2016; Chang et al., 2009). In addition, Chua et al (2011) found that the involvement of a family in the start-up activity could be influential in acquiring debt financing for an enterprise.

Family Embeddedness in Entrepreneurship

In line with the *family embeddedness theory*, the responsibilities and connection of members of the family of an entrepreneur with respect to the enterprise can affect the total process of entrepreneurship from inception of the enterprise to the accomplishment of success (Sharma, 2004; Rogoff & Heck, 2003; Aldrich & Cliff, 2003). An important feature of the connectedness insertion is the capacity of the entrepreneur to totally exploit the resources offered by the members of his family to carry out his entrepreneurial activities. Classical examples of these resources are money, service, data, and knowledge (Dyer, Nenque, & Hill, 2014; Pearson, Carr & Shaw, 2008).

Scholars have analytically operationalised family embeddedness utilising various theoretical variables such as family investment (Chua, Chrisman, Kellermanns, & Wu, 2011; Chang, Memili, Chrisman, Kellermanns, & Chua, 2009), family assistance (Powell & Eddleston, 2013, 2017), or family bonds (Arregle, Batjargal, Hitt, Webb, Miller & Tsui, 2015). These scholars found that the family structure wields notable positive and negative influence on the process of entrepreneurship (for instance, the decision to commence a business) and results (productivity of the business, wellness).

With respect to the process of developing the enterprise, some studies suggest that family investment into an entrepreneur's business supports the entrepreneur to enlarge their social economic (Steier, 2007) and political (Ge, Carney, & Kellermanns, 2019) networks. Family resources (investment) has also been found to be helpful for migrant and serial entrepreneurs to commence business (Bird & Wennberg, 2016). In conclusion, literature confirms that family resources augment both enterprise performance (Cruz, Justo, & De Castro, 2012) and individual well-being (Powell & Eddleston, 2013, 2017).

On the contrary, scholars theorize that the interpersonal dimension of embeddedness as well underlines strong connections between people and conveys the prospect of mutuality and equity (Adler & Kwon, 2002; Granovetter, 1985). By way of these strong connections, entrepreneurs and the members of their family may create mutual responsibilities and expectations closely associated to both enterprise and non-enterprise activities (Aldrich & Cliff, 2003). In the situation where shared responsibilities and expectations are achieved, family embeddedness can result to disputes between family members and put the funds at risk, which could conversely have negative effect on the processes of the enterprise and its achievements (results). This can explain Rosetta's (*please see the prologue*) complicated feelings when her family offered financial support for her business.

Viewed from these empirical perspectives, scholars have provided evidence that the financial support offered by members of the family to an entrepreneur has negative association to an entrepreneur's decision to start-up a business (Edelman et al., 2016; Sieger & Minola, 2017), and that the embeddedness of family in business can interfere and weaken an enterprise's productivity (Au & Kwan, 2009; Arregle et al., 2015), and result in the consideration to exit entrepreneurship (Hsu, Wiklund, Anderson, & Coffey, 2016). Hence, to strengthen the reader's understanding of the two-sided influence of family funding (resources) on entrepreneurship, the social exchange concept is employed to bring clarity to the mutuality and equity in the interpersonal association among family members and the entrepreneur (Tereshina, 2023; Cropanzano & Mitchell, 2005).

Social Exchange in Entrepreneurship

In work environments, the social exchange concept (SEC) is operationalised to involve exchanges among two or more people depending on their standards and fairness (Cropanzano et al., 2017; Cropanzano & Mitchell, 2005) and refers to social or economic association with regards to traded resources and expected gains (Foa & Foa, 1980). Relationships that centre around economic trade-offs centrally require external gains of financial worth comprising the exchange of physical resources (for instance, money), while relationships that entail social exchange are centrally underpinned by internal or intangible gains that demonstrate emotive connections that involve the complementation of intrinsic resources (such as care, respect, affection) (Xu, Kellermanns, Jin, & Xi, 2020).

While respective associations can mutate with the level of trust growth among associates (Meyer, Stanley, Herscovitch, & Topolnytsky, 2002), clearly distinguishing them into categories of exchange permits the theoretical explanation about the way individuals begin social exchanges and how they profit from these association (Cropanzano & Mitchell, 2005). It is expected that a harmony among the categories of exchange association and the traded resources with respect to the value of the association will be achieved. For example, in a monetary association, where one person refuses to perform their economic responsibility in the association, the person (performer) or the recipient of the action or the two of them, may reassess the mutual agreement and reduce the level of their outlay in the association, leading to perceived reduction in well-being on both sides (Buunk & Schaufeli, 1999).

The exchange procedure commences in the same way irrespective of its category. The main party begins the activity positively or negatively (for instance, in rendering support) and the recipient responds excellently or awfully to the interaction (example well-being), and behaviourally (for instance, start-up actions) (Cropanzano et al., 2017). To illustrate this, the members of an entrepreneur's family could offer financial assistance or capital to him to support his need for financial resources to commence start-up activities (excellent actions). The entrepreneur could respond through interpersonal and behavioural actions in the light of their decision and background of the enterprise. Extant research demonstrates that financial support adversely associates to start-up entrepreneur's activities with respect to mutuality and justice (adverse behavioural responses) (Edelman et al, 2016). The factors leading to this outcome could be further investigated to understand why such excellent action as provision of financial support could lead to an unfavourable outcome. However, other investigations show that there is a positive connection between family support and well-being to the extent that entrepreneurs felt worthy and taken care of with respect to the family's show of emotional relationships and their own mental state of well-being (excellent interpersonal responses) (Marshall, Meek, Swab., & Markin, 2020; Powell & Eddleston, 2013).

From the theoretical distinction proposed by scholars, the social exchange among entrepreneurs and their family members in the entrepreneur's daily interactions are identifiable through the effect of the related stressors on the entrepreneur's firm-based activities or his well-being (Kollmann, Stockmann & Kensbock, 2019; Rauch et al., 2018). Stephan (2018) report that monetary and workload stressors which are the commonly investigated stressors are inherent in the process of entrepreneurship as entrepreneurial activities happen in exceptional environments that require extreme effort and time (Cardon & Patel, 2015), and monetary resources that are vital to the development and sustainability of enterprise (Shepherd, Wiklund, & Haynie, 2009). As these stressors seem to relate directly to monetary and social exchange connections, understanding the way that the entrepreneur's apparent support (good actions) from family members could influence their interpersonal responses (well-being) across the monetary and social contexts is necessary. Xu et al (2020) found that apparent support from family members has various controlling effects (stress-cushioning and stress-strengthening) on the relationships among stressors and well-being.

According to Schreibauer et al (2020), efforts by the German Government, to explain the empirical evidence relating to work-associated mental health using different theoretical frameworks accepted globally, excluded entrepreneurs. For families to effectively support an entrepreneur in conducting their entrepreneurial activities and mitigating the psychosocial effect of the challenges they face, they need to know the relevant business-related stressors confronting them. Hence there is a need for information, education, and attention as well as motivation and adjustment in the entrepreneurship-family support dimension (Rauch et al., 2018).

SECTION 4: IMPLICATIONS OF STRESSORS ON PSYCHOSOCIAL WELL-BEING OF ENTREPRENEURS

Using the view of the role theory, the entrepreneurs' effort to stabilise the multi-dimensional demands of their business and family has been classically interrogated (Biddle, 1986). The theory is underpinned by the hypothetical assumptions of insufficiency (Marks, 1977), and implies that individuals could derive benefits from constrained (and stable) quantity of resources like energy and time. Therefore, the higher the demands of performing a role the more the role conflict that a person must deal with. Entrepreneurs are confronted with work overload and insufficient time to perform the tasks or roles. Some of the roles they have in an enterprise include originating and leading business activities, identifying business opportunities, creating jobs and allocating employees their duties, identifying and addressing risks, forecasting changes in the environment of business, and developing strategic partnerships (Kuratko, Fisher, & Audretsch, 2021; Urbano, Audretsch, Aparicio, & Noguera, 2020). In addition to these, they also have roles to play in the family that include spousal roles, parenting roles, interpersonal roles among family and friends, and community engagement In the role theory, the notion of work-family conflict basically described as a type of inter-role discord wherein the role strains from the business and family terrains are mutually exclusive in some way is highlighted (Greenhouse & Beutell, 1985).

Interestingly, Jennings and McDougal (2007) observe that the discussion on the challenges of work-family conflict in the context of entrepreneurship is still unexploited. There is a general assumption that little, or no attention is given to research on entrepreneur's work-family conflict since they enjoy more independence and flexibility than employed personnel, which permits them to achieve better work-life balance than employees. However, Parasuraman et al (1996) postulate that, the entrepreneur's freedom is limited by their concern for the existence and economic achievement of the business. The implication is that deep concern for the enterprise reduces the entrepreneur's capacity to dedicate energy and time to the family. This adds to the frequency of work-life conflict, psychosocial stress, and consequently, impacts the entrepreneur's psychosocial wellbeing. This paper concurs to the observation and seeks to understand the influence that business-family conflict has on the psychosocial wellbeing of entrepreneurs.

Scholars believe that the entrepreneur's wellbeing is central to the existence of their businesses and increases their ability to identify opportunities and resilience (Wincent et al. 2008), entire business productivity (Stephan, 2018), and a success indicator (Wach et al., 2016). Considering the significance of wellbeing, it is imperative to examine the effects that stressors have on the psychosocial wellbeing of entrepreneurs.

The European Union had in 2008, highlighted the necessity for action on psychosocial stressors like poor work design, role ambiguity, and absence of supervisor and peer-support to lessen monetary and societal costs linked with job-related stress (Eurofound & EU-OSHA, 2014; McDaid, 2008). As psychosocial stressors constantly surpass the assets and coping capacities of individuals including entrepreneurs, perceived stress can occur (WHO, 2020), which could result to the occurrence of mental ill-health on the long run (Bonde, 2008; Madsen, Nyberg, Hanson, Ferrie, et al., 2017), and bodily or psychological diseases (Paridon, 2016; Yang, Haldeman, Lu, Baker, 2016).

The outcome of business-related psychosocial stress on entrepreneurs includes mental and physiological ill health leading to increased costs to the entrepreneur, family, economy, and the society at large (Schreibauer et al., 2020). It is important therefore, that future studies investigate rigorously, the present and emerging challenges in the entrepreneurial environment impacting on the psychosocial wellbeing of entrepreneurs. Some of the emerging challenges include those associated with technological advancement (of the 4th and 5th industrial revolution) and new diseases like the Covid-19 virus that led to a global pandemic.

SECTION 5: FAMILY SUPPORT AND PSYCHOSOCIAL WELL-BEING

The transactional theory links business-stressors to the environment and the individual entrepreneur's significant perception of those stressors as being influential in their well-being through the negative effect that it has on their personal resources (Lazarus, 1991). According to Abe, Abe, Fields, and Idris (2018), the way in which a person evaluates the situations in their environment to understand the implication on their wellness and determine how their ability to respond can be conceptualised. Lazarus (1991) further suggests that the connection between the individual and the environment need to be primarily determined. Thereafter, the applicable challenges that confronts the individual as well as the capacity of the individual to manage the stressors needs to be determined. Based on the transactional theory, this paper opines that individual entrepreneur is faced with domain specific stressors from the business and family spheres, and that social support has significant role to play in the equation.

Furthermore, through the *family embeddedness theory* and *social exchange theory*, this section examines the possible advantages and detriments of family support in the interface between entrepreneur's business and their family responsibilities and their psychosocial well-being. The assumption is that perceived social support significantly influences an entrepreneur's well-being in cognisance with the business and family life stressors. Xu, Kellermanns, Jin, and Xi (2020) provide evidence that strong degree of family support weakens the connection among finance-related stressors and well-being while strengthening the interface among business stressors and well-being.

The role that family plays in the process of entrepreneurship is vigorous from its positioning (embeddedness) in business and entrepreneurial activities or results (Jennings & McDougald, 2007; Sharma, 2004; Aldrich & Cliff, 2003). The family positioning perspective features the importance of the role of the family and interactions and concentrates on the interpersonal conversation processes among the entrepreneurs and their families (Aldrich & Kim, 2007; Aldrich & Cliff, 2003). In the conversation process, entrepreneurs, according to Aldrich and Cliff (2003) and Rogoff and Heck (2003), assemble some necessary funds from members of their family for the productivity of the enterprise (objective achievement) and themselves (subjective achievement), even as members of the family possibly derive monetary and social benefits.

Studies have over the years reported that certain family positioned activities such as provision of capital and family support create several outcomes for both the entrepreneur and the enterprise. Sieger and Minola (2017) report that the monetary capital or assistance offered by members of the family reduced the possibility of the entrepreneur to establish an enterprise, while Au and Kwan (2009) agree that it undermines entrepreneurial success. On the other hand, Hatak, and Zhou (2019), and Powell and Eddleston (2017) are of the opinion that monetary assistance or support offered to the entrepreneur by the family augments both the enterprise performance and the entrepreneur's well-being.

From the contradictory reports from extant literature, this chapter suggests that the nature of the interpersonal exchanges between the entrepreneur, his business, and the family (via support) and the stress process, could interfere with the psychosocial well-being of the entrepreneur. Uncertainty regarding the direction that the family support would go and the effect that it could have on family relationships can exacerbate the pressure on the entrepreneur's mental well-being.

From the entrepreneur's context, his relationship with family members is construed on two pillars, one on the economic and the other on the social exchange pillars, respectively. The economic pillar could become beneficial to the supply of the monetary or capital need of the entrepreneur and the family obtaining a repayment of their financial support to the entrepreneur. The social exchange pillar on the other hand supplies the communal and respect needs required to strengthen the reciprocal trust and responsibility between the entrepreneur and his family. Rauch, Fink, and Hatak (2018) agree that the context in which the economic and social exchanges occur between the entrepreneur and his family is often stressful. The present paper suggests that the interface between an entrepreneur, entrepreneurship, and the family happens in stressful contexts and can result in an adverse outcome to the entrepreneur's psychosocial well-being, although social support has been reported to result in positive outcomes in the entrepreneur's well-being (Kipkosgei, 2022; Semerci, 2016). The case of Rosetta in the prologue has also been supportably played out in the literature reviewed in this section.

SECTION 6: CONCLUSION AND RECOMMENDATIONS

This review shows that many psychosocial factors associated with entrepreneurship have been severally investigated from diverse dimensions. However, in agreement with Chirico (2017) observation, emerging work-stressors are yet to be sufficiently investigated by scholars. For instance, the rising mental health challenges among entrepreneurs post Covid-19 pandemic, social issues emanating from interpersonal disengagement at work, and stressors resulting from economic challenges (recession, spiked inflation rates, funding, and financing) have scarcely drawn the attention of scholars of entrepreneurship. Additionally, the emerging forms of work and work environments including remote working, expedited speed of digitization of work and work processes in the context of the contemporary times have highlighted the need for the scientific community to pay attention. Studies could investigate small and medium entrepreneurs from the wholesale and retail sector, finance sector, technical and automotive industry, non-profit and other social entrepreneurship sectors, as these appear to be inadequately represented in research.

Unfortunately, the literature on stressors is replete with investigations on work-related stressors, policies, and strategies and not psychosocial stressors. Psychosocial stress factors like the joint exposure to bodily and psychosocial stressors, uncertainty of earnings/success, intensity of entrepreneurial work and its high demand, heavy mental and emotional load associated with burnout, and challenges of achieving business-life balance need to be investigated.

Though governments of western and developed countries have promulgated policies and strategies to address work-related stressors, not much is known about policies and strategies to address the psychosocial challenges of entrepreneurs. Besides, these emerging psychosocial stressors could need dissimilar and further methods to manage entrepreneurs' psychosocial well-being, because work-associated stressors and psychosocial stress factors are not the same. Therefore, research for efficient and effective strategies to assist entrepreneurs to manage psychosocial stressors and improve and/or achieve psychosocial wellbeing is direly needed. In addition, seeing that the family is central to support needed by her members according to the extant literature, it is important that policies to strengthen the family to perform this function more effectively be looked into by governments and policy makers.

REFERENCES

Abe, E. N., Abe, I. I., Fields, Z., & Idris, G. O. (2018). Work-family stressors and work-family satisfaction: Effect of sense of coherence at a metropolitan municipality. *Journal of Economics and Behavioral Studies*, *10*(2 (J)), 74–88. doi:10.22610/jebs.v10i2(J).2218

Adler, P. S., & Kwon, S. W. (2002). Social capital: Prospects for a new concept. *Academy of Management Review*, *27*(1), 17–40. doi:10.2307/4134367

Aldrich, H. E., & Cliff, J. E. (2003). The pervasive effects of family on entrepreneurship: Toward a family embeddedness perspective. *Journal of Business Venturing*, *18*(5), 573–596. doi:10.1016/S0883-9026(03)00011-9

Aldrich, H. E., & Kim, P. H. (2007). Small worlds, infinite possibilities? How social networks affect entrepreneurial team formation and search. *Strategic Entrepreneurship Journal*, *1*(1-2), 147–165. doi:10.1002ej.8

Aldrich, H. E., & Ruef, M. (2018). Unicorns, gazelles, and other distractions on the way to understanding real entrepreneurship in the United States. *The Academy of Management Perspectives*, *32*(4), 458–472. doi:10.5465/amp.2017.0123

Arregle, J. L., Batjargal, B., Hitt, M. A., Webb, J. W., Miller, T., & Tsui, A. S. (2015). Family ties in entrepreneurs' social networks and new venture growth. *Entrepreneurship Theory and Practice*, *39*(2), 313–344. doi:10.1111/etap.12044

Au, K., & Kwan, H. K. (2009). Start–up capital and Chinese entrepreneurs: The role of family. *Entrepreneurship Theory and Practice*, *33*(4), 889–908. doi:10.1111/j.1540-6520.2009.00331.x

Bakracheva, M., Pavlov, D., Gudkov, A., Diaconescu, A., Kostov, A., Deneva, A., ... Blazheva, V. (2020). *The intergenerational family businesses as a stress management instrument for entrepreneurs*. Academic Press.

Biddle, B. J. (1986). Recent developments in role theory. *Annual Review of Sociology*, *12*(1), 67–92. doi:10.1146/annurev.so.12.080186.000435

Bird, M., & Wennberg, K. (2016). Why family matters: The impact of family resources on immigrant entrepreneurs' exit from entrepreneurship. *Journal of Business Venturing*, *31*(6), 687–704. doi:10.1016/j.jbusvent.2016.09.002

Bonde, J. P. E. (2008). Psychosocial factors at work and risk of depression: A systematic review of the epidemiological evidence. *Occupational and Environmental Medicine*, *65*(7), 438–445. doi:10.1136/oem.2007.038430 PMID:18417557

Brockhaus, R. H. (1982). *The psychology of the entrepreneur*. University of Illinois at Urbana-Champaign's Academy for Entrepreneurial Leadership Historical Research Reference in Entrepreneurship.

Cardon, M. S., & Patel, P. C. (2015). Is stress worth it? Stress-related health and wealth trade-offs for entrepreneurs. *Applied Psychology*, *64*(2), 379–420. doi:10.1111/apps.12021

Chang, E., & Hancock, K. (2003). Role stress and role ambiguity in new nursing graduates in Australia. *Nursing & Health Sciences*, *5*(2), 155–163. doi:10.1046/j.1442-2018.2003.00147.x PMID:12709171

Chang, E. P., Memili, E., Chrisman, J. J., Kellermanns, F. W., & Chua, J. H. (2009). Family social capital, venture preparedness, and start-up decisions: A study of Hispanic entrepreneurs in New England. *Family Business Review*, *22*(3), 279–292. doi:10.1177/0894486509332327

Chay, Y. W. (1993). Social support, individual differences, and well-being: A study of small business entrepreneurs and employees. *Journal of Occupational and Organizational Psychology*, *66*(4), 285–302. doi:10.1111/j.2044-8325.1993.tb00540.x

Chirico, F. (2017). The forgotten realm of the new and emerging psychosocial risk factors. *Journal of Occupational Health*, *59*(5), 433–435. doi:10.1539/joh.17-0111-OP PMID:28819083

Chua, J. H., Chrisman, J. J., Kellermanns, F., & Wu, Z. (2011). Family involvement and new venture debt financing. *Journal of Business Venturing*, *26*(4), 472–488. doi:10.1016/j.jbusvent.2009.11.002

Cohen, D., Hsu, D. K., & Shinnar, R. S. (2021). Identifying innovative opportunities in the entrepreneurship classroom: A new approach and empirical test. *Small Business Economics*, *57*(4), 1931–1955. doi:10.100711187-020-00387-z

Crampton, S. M., Hodge, J. W., Mishra, J. M., & Price, S. (1995). Stress and stress management. *S.A.M. Advanced Management Journal*, *60*(3), 10–24.

Cropanzano, R., & Mitchell, M. S. (2005). Social exchange theory: An interdisciplinary review. *Journal of Management*, *31*(6), 874–900. doi:10.1177/0149206305279602

Cruz, C., Justo, R., & De Castro, J. O. (2012). Does family employment enhance MSEs performance? Integrating socioemotional wealth and family embeddedness perspectives. *Journal of Business Venturing*, *27*(1), 62–76. doi:10.1016/j.jbusvent.2010.07.002

Demerouti, E., & Bakker, A. B. (2023). Job demands-resources theory in times of crises: New propositions. *Organizational Psychology Review*, *13*(3), 209–236. doi:10.1177/20413866221135022

Dyer, W. G., Nenque, E., & Hill, E. J. (2014). Toward a theory of family capital and entrepreneurship: Antecedents and outcomes. *Journal of Small Business Management*, *52*(2), 266–285. doi:10.1111/jsbm.12097

Edelman, L. F., Manolova, T., Shirokova, G., & Tsukanova, T. (2016). The impact of family support on young entrepreneurs' start-up activities. *Journal of Business Venturing*, *31*(4), 428–448. doi:10.1016/j.jbusvent.2016.04.003

Eurofound & EU-OSHA. (2014). *Psychosocial Risks in Europe: Prevalence and Strategies for Prevention*. Publications Office of the European Union.

Frese, M., Chell, E., & Klandt, H. (Eds.). (2000). *Psychological approaches to entrepreneurship*. Psychology Press.

Ge, J., Carney, M., & Kellermanns, F. (2019). Who fills institutional voids? Entrepreneurs' utilization of political and family ties in emerging markets. *Entrepreneurship Theory and Practice*, *43*(6), 1124–1147. doi:10.1177/1042258718773175

Giao, H. N. K., Vuong, B. N., & Tushar, H. (2020). The impact of social support on job-related behaviors through the mediating role of job stress and the moderating role of locus of control: Empirical evidence from the Vietnamese banking industry. *Cogent Business & Management*, *7*(1), 1841359. doi:10.1080/23311975.2020.1841359

Granovetter, M. (1985). Economic action and social structure: The problem of embeddedness. *American Journal of Sociology*, *91*(3), 481–510. doi:10.1086/228311

Hassard, J., Van den Broek, K., Flemming, D., Gründler, R., Dewe, P., Teoh, K., Cosemans, B., Cosmar, M., & Cox, T. (2014). *Calculating the Cost of Work-Related Stress and Psychosocial Risks: Literature Review*. Publications Office of the European Union.

Hatak, I., & Zhou, H. (2021). Health as human capital in entrepreneurship: Individual, extension, and substitution effects on entrepreneurial success. *Entrepreneurship Theory and Practice*, *45*(1), 18–42. doi:10.1177/1042258719867559

Hou, T., Zhang, T., Cai, W., Song, X., Chen, A., Deng, G., & Ni, C. (2020). Social support and mental health among health care workers during Coronavirus Disease 2019 outbreak: A moderated mediation model. *PLoS One*, *15*(5), e0233831. doi:10.1371/journal.pone.0233831 PMID:32470007

Hsu, D. K., Wiklund, J., Anderson, S. E., & Coffey, B. S. (2016). Entrepreneurial exit intentions and the business-family interface. *Journal of Business Venturing*, *31*(6), 613–627. doi:10.1016/j.jbusvent.2016.08.001

Ivancevich, J. M., & Matteson, M. T. (1980). *Stress and Work: A Managerial Perspective*. Scott. Foresman and Company.

Jennings, J. E., & McDougald, M. S. (2007). Work-family interface experiences and coping strategies: Implications for entrepreneurship research and practice. *Academy of Management Review*, *32*(3), 747–760. doi:10.5465/amr.2007.25275510

Kahn, R. L., & Quinn, R. P. (1970). Role stress: A framework for analysis. *Occupational mental health*, 50-115.

Kipkosgei, F. (2022). Perceived entrepreneurial stress and entrepreneurial resilience; the mediating role of the well-being of entrepreneurs and moderating role perceived online social support. *Merits*, *2*(1), 1–17. doi:10.3390/merits2010001

Knieps, F., & Pfaff, H. (2019). Mental Health, and Work: Figures, Data, Facts. BKK Health Report. MWV Medizinisch Wissenschaftliche Verlagsgesellschaft.

Ko, W. W., & Liu, G. (2021). The transformation from traditional nonprofit organizations to social enterprises: An institutional entrepreneurship perspective. *Journal of Business Ethics*, *171*(1), 15–32. doi:10.100710551-020-04446-z

Kuratko, D. F., Fisher, G., & Audretsch, D. B. (2021). Unraveling the entrepreneurial mindset. *Small Business Economics*, *57*(4), 1681–1691. doi:10.100711187-020-00372-6

Labrague, L. J., & De los Santos, J. A. A. (2020). COVID-19 anxiety among front-line nurses: Predictive role of organisational support, personal resilience, and social support. *Journal of Nursing Management*, *28*(7), 1653–1661. doi:10.1111/jonm.13121 PMID:32770780

Latack, J. C., Kinicki, A. J., & Prussia, G. E. (1995). An integrative process model of coping with job loss. *Academy of Management Review*, *20*(2), 311–342. doi:10.2307/258849

Lazarus, R. S. (1991). Progress on a cognitive-motivational-relational theory of emotion. *The American Psychologist*, *46*(8), 819–834. doi:10.1037/0003-066X.46.8.819 PMID:1928936

Lechat, T., & Torrès, O. (2017). Stressors and satisfactors in entrepreneurial activity: An event-based, mixed methods study predicting small business owners' health. *International Journal of Entrepreneurship and Small Business*, *32*(4), 537–569. doi:10.1504/IJESB.2017.087838

Mack, D. A., & McGee, J. E. (2001). *Occupational stress and the small business owner: The role of task complexity and social support.* In USASBE/SBIDA, 2001 Conference, Orlando, FL. Available at: http://usasbe. org/knowledge/proceedings/proceedingsDocs/USASBE2001proceedings-045. pdf

Madsen, I. E., Nyberg, S. T., Hanson, L. M., Ferrie, J. E., Ahola, K., Alfredsson, L., & ... IPD-Work Consortium. (2017). Job strain as a risk factor for clinical depression: Systematic review and meta-analysis with additional individual participant data. *Psychological Medicine*, *47*(8), 1342–1356. doi:10.1017/S003329171600355X PMID:28122650

Marks, S. R. (1977). Multiple roles and role strain: Some notes on human energy, time, and commitment. *American Sociological Review*, *42*(6), 921–936. doi:10.2307/2094577

Marschall, J., Hildebrandt, S., Zich, K., Tisch, T., Sorensen, J., & Nolting, H.-D. (2018). *DAK Health Report 2018*. DAK-Forschung.

Marshall, D. R., Meek, W. R., Swab, R. G., & Markin, E. (2020). Access to resources and entrepreneurial well-being: A self-efficacy approach. *Journal of Business Research, 120*, 203–212. doi:10.1016/j.jbusres.2020.08.015

Mason, J. W. (1968). A review of psychoendocrine research on the pituitary-adrenal cortical system. *Psychosomatic Medicine, 30*(5), 576–607. doi:10.1097/00006842-196809000-00020 PMID:4303377

McDaid, D. (2008). Mental Health in Workplace Settings. Consensus Paper. European Commission, Directorate General for Health, and Consumers.

McGrath, J. E. (1970). *Social and psychological factors of stress*. Holt, Rinehart, & Winston.

Menges, J. I., Tussing, D. V., Wihler, A., & Grant, A. M. (2017). When job performance is all relative: How family motivation energizes effort and compensates for intrinsic motivation. *Academy of Management Journal, 60*(2), 695–719. doi:10.5465/amj.2014.0898

Moroz, P. W., & Hindle, K. (2012). Entrepreneurship as a process: Toward harmonizing multiple perspectives. *Entrepreneurship Theory and Practice, 36*(4), 781–818. doi:10.1111/j.1540-6520.2011.00452.x

Musungwa, T., & Kowe, P. (2022). Effects of occupational health and safety management systems implementation in accident prevention at a Harare beverage company. *Cogent Engineering, 9*(1), 2124638. doi:10.1080/23311916.2022.2124638

Nasurdin, A. M., Ramayah, T., & Beng, Y. C. (2006). Organizational structure and organizational climate as potential predictors of job stress: Evidence from Malaysia. *International Journal of Commerce and Management, 16*(2), 116–128. doi:10.1108/10569210680000211

OECD & European Commission. (2018). *Health at a Glance: Europe 2018. State of Health in the EU Cycle*. OECD Publishing.

Palmer, M. (1971). The application of psychological testing to entrepreneurial potential. *California Management Review, 13*(3), 32–38. doi:10.2307/41164291

Paridon, H. (2016). *Psychosocial Demands in the Working World: A Literature Analysis on Health and Performance Relationships*. Initiative Gesundheit und Arbeit.

Patzelt, H., & Shepherd, D. A. (2011). Negative emotions of an entrepreneurial career: Self-employment and regulatory coping behaviors. *Journal of Business Venturing*, *26*(2), 226–238. doi:10.1016/j.jbusvent.2009.08.002

Paudel, R., Khadka, S., Rai, J., & Singh, R. (2023). Psychological impact of COVID-19 pandemic and lockdown among the population involved in tourism sector in Lakeside of Pokhara: A qualitative study. *Health Science Reports*, *6*(7), e1382. doi:10.1002/hsr2.1382 PMID:37396562

Pearson, A. W., Carr, J. C., & Shaw, J. C. (2008). Toward a theory of familiness: A social capital perspective. *Entrepreneurship Theory and Practice*, *32*(6), 949–969. doi:10.1111/j.1540-6520.2008.00265.x

Powell, G. N., & Eddleston, K. A. (2013). Linking family-to-business enrichment and support to entrepreneurial success: Do female and male entrepreneurs experience different outcomes? *Journal of Business Venturing*, *28*(2), 261–280. doi:10.1016/j.jbusvent.2012.02.007

Powell, G. N., & Eddleston, K. A. (2017). Family involvement in the firm, family-to-business support, and entrepreneurial outcomes: An exploration. *Journal of Small Business Management*, *55*(4), 614–631. doi:10.1111/jsbm.12252

Pratama, R., Nurlaila, N., & Nasution, M. L. I. (2023). The Influence of Workload, Work Stress, Organizational Culture, and Work Environment on Job Performance at Employees of PT. Bank Sumut Syariah Deli Serdang Area. *Indonesian Interdisciplinary Journal of Sharia Economics*, *6*(3), 1666–1686.

Rahim, A. (1996). Stress, strain, and their moderators: An empirical comparison of entrepreneurs and managers. *Journal of Small Business Management*, *34*(1), 46–58.

Rauch, A., Fink, M., & Hatak, I. (2018). Stress processes: An essential ingredient in the entrepreneurial process. *The Academy of Management Perspectives*, *32*(3), 340–357. doi:10.5465/amp.2016.0184

Rogoff, E. G., & Heck, R. K. Z. (2003). Evolving research in entrepreneurship and family business: Recognizing family as the oxygen that feeds the fire of entrepreneurship. *Journal of Business Venturing*, *18*(5), 559–566. doi:10.1016/S0883-9026(03)00009-0

Sandler, I. N., & Lakey, B. (1982). Locus of control as a stress moderator: The role of control perceptions and social support. *American Journal of Community Psychology*, *10*(1), 65–80. doi:10.1007/BF00903305 PMID:7102614

Schonfeld, I. S., & Mazzola, J. J. (2015). A qualitative study of stress in individuals self-employed in solo businesses. *Journal of Occupational Health Psychology, 20*(4), 501–513. doi:10.1037/a0038804 PMID:25705913

Schreibauer, E. C., Hippler, M., Burgess, S., Rieger, M. A., & Rind, E. (2020). Work-related psychosocial stress in small and medium-sized enterprises: An integrative review. *International Journal of Environmental Research and Public Health, 17*(20), 7446. doi:10.3390/ijerph17207446 PMID:33066111

Semerci, A. B. (2016). The effect of social support on job stress of entrepreneurs. *Academy of Entrepreneurship Journal, 22*(1), 41.

Shane, S., & Venkataraman, S. (2000). The promise of entrepreneurship as a field of research. *Academy of Management Review, 25*(1), 217–226. doi:10.5465/amr.2000.2791611

Shao, R., He, P., Ling, B., Tan, L., Xu, L., Hou, Y., Kong, L., & Yang, Y. (2020). Prevalence of depression and anxiety and correlations between depression, anxiety, family functioning, social support, and coping styles among Chinese medical students. *BMC Psychology, 8*(1), 1–19. doi:10.118640359-020-00402-8 PMID:32321593

Sharma, P. (2004). An overview of the field of family business studies: Current status and directions for the future. *Family Business Review, 17*(1), 1–36. doi:10.1111/j.1741-6248.2004.00001.x

Shepherd, D. A., Wiklund, J., & Haynie, J. M. (2009). Moving forward: Balancing the financial and emotional costs of business failure. *Journal of Business Venturing, 24*(2), 134–148. doi:10.1016/j.jbusvent.2007.10.002

Sieger, P., & Minola, T. (2017). The family's financial support as a "poisoned gift": A family embeddedness perspective on entrepreneurial intentions. *Journal of Small Business Management, 55*, 179–204. doi:10.1111/jsbm.12273

Steier, L. (2003). Variants of agency contracts in family-financed ventures as a continuum of familial altruistic and market rationalities. *Journal of Business Venturing, 18*(5), 597–618. doi:10.1016/S0883-9026(03)00012-0

Stephan, U. (2018). Entrepreneurs' mental health and well-being: A review and research agenda. *The Academy of Management Perspectives, 32*(3), 290–322. doi:10.5465/amp.2017.0001

Tereshina, D. (2023). Business as a gift: Family entrepreneurship and the ambiguities of sharing. In *Family Firms and Business Families in Cross-Cultural Perspective: Bringing Anthropology Back* (pp. 115–145). Springer International Publishing. doi:10.1007/978-3-031-20525-5_5

Tomlin, J., Dalgleish-Warburton, B., & Lamph, G. (2020). Psychosocial support for healthcare workers during the COVID-19 pandemic. *Frontiers in Psychology*, *11*, 1960. doi:10.3389/fpsyg.2020.01960 PMID:32849149

Urbano, D., Audretsch, D., Aparicio, S., & Noguera, M. (2020). Does entrepreneurial activity matter for economic growth in developing countries? The role of the institutional environment. *The International Entrepreneurship and Management Journal*, *16*(3), 1065–1099. doi:10.100711365-019-00621-5

Van de Ven, A. H. (1992). Suggestions for studying strategy process: A research note. *Strategic Management Journal*, *13*(S1), 169–188. doi:10.1002mj.4250131013

Wach, D., Stephan, U., Weinberger, E., & Wegge, J. (2021). Entrepreneurs' stressors and well-being: A recovery perspective and diary study. *Journal of Business Venturing*, *36*(5), 106016. doi:10.1016/j.jbusvent.2020.106016

Wang, Q., & Richardson, L. (2021). Race/ethnicity, place, and art and culture entrepreneurship in underserved communities. *Cities (London, England)*, *115*, 103243. doi:10.1016/j.cities.2021.103243

Welter, F., Baker, T., Audretsch, D. B., & Gartner, W. B. (2017). Everyday entrepreneurship—A call for entrepreneurship research to embrace entrepreneurial diversity. *Entrepreneurship Theory and Practice*, *41*(3), 311–321. doi:10.1111/etap.12258

Wiklund, J., Nikolaev, B., Shir, N., Foo, M. D., & Bradley, S. (2019). Entrepreneurship and well-being: Past, present, and future. *Journal of Business Venturing*, *34*(4), 579–588. doi:10.1016/j.jbusvent.2019.01.002

Wong, M. F., & Wong, M. P. (2002). Workplace stress: Causes, consequences, and why it concerns managers. *Akauntan Nasional*, *11*, 24–28.

Xu, F., Kellermanns, F. W., Jin, L., & Xi, J. (2020). Family support as social exchange in entrepreneurship: Its moderating impact on entrepreneurial stressors-well-being relationships. *Journal of Business Research*, *120*, 59–73. doi:10.1016/j.jbusres.2020.07.033 PMID:32834213

Xue, R., Qian, G., Qian, Z., & Li, L. (2021). Entrepreneurs' implicit and explicit achievement motives and their early international commitment. *MIR. Management International Review*, *61*(1), 91–121. doi:10.100711575-020-00436-5

Yang, H., Haldeman, S., Lu, M. L., & Baker, D. (2016). Low back pain prevalence and related workplace psychosocial risk factors: A study using data from the 2010 National Health Interview Survey. *Journal of Manipulative and Physiological Therapeutics*, *39*(7), 459–472. doi:10.1016/j.jmpt.2016.07.004 PMID:27568831

Chapter 6
The Influence of Family Dynamics on Entrepreneurial Intentions and Self-Efficacy

Taiwo Hassan Ajadi
University of KwaZulu-Natal, South Africa

Olalekan Adisa
University of Northampton, UK

Al-Amin Abba Dabo
University of Northampton, UK

Olushola Margaret Adisa
University of Zululand, South Africa

EXECUTIVE SUMMARY

This chapter explores the complex relationship between family dynamics and entrepreneurship, particularly in the context of evolving societal norms and the COVID-19 pandemic. It critically examines the role of parental influence, family support, and the family environment in shaping entrepreneurial intentions and self-efficacy. It also discusses the challenges and strategies that entrepreneurs face due to family dynamics, drawing on real-world case studies. The chapter provides a comprehensive theoretical framework that integrates various perspectives on how family interactions influence entrepreneurial decisions. It also highlights the practical implications of the findings and suggests areas for future research.

DOI: 10.4018/978-1-6684-8748-8.ch006

1.0 INTRODUCTION

Entrepreneurship stands as a formidable catalyst for economic growth and development, an arena replete with opportunities and challenges (McMullen, 2011). The fusion of individual intentions and capabilities invariably guides entrepreneurial aspirations, yet the profound role of family dynamics cannot be disregarded (Fouad et al., 2016). Paradoxically, families serve as both vital sources of support and potential wellsprings of conflict for entrepreneurs, significantly shaping their ambitions and impacting their decision-making processes. This duality underscores the imperative need for a comprehensive understanding of how family dynamics connect with entrepreneurship. This book chapter delves into the intricacies of this interplay and seeks to illuminate the profound influence of family dynamics on entrepreneurial intentions and self-efficacy.

1.1 Background of the Study

In recent years, the interconnection between family dynamics and entrepreneurship has garnered increasing attention in both academic research and the business realm. As societal norms evolve, there's a growing acknowledgement of the need to explore how family exerts its influence on entrepreneurial intentions and actions (Bertrand & Scholar, 2006). Moreover, the Coronavirus (COVID-19) pandemic, a seismic event reshaping global economic landscapes, has accelerated the adoption of entrepreneurial practices out of necessity, thus underscoring the crucial roles of family support and adaptability in entrepreneurial success (Wang et al., 2023). These contemporary trends underscore the timeliness and relevance of the current exploration.

Entrepreneurship, a dynamic cornerstone of economic growth, emerges not solely from individual intentions and capabilities but also from the profound familial and societal contexts that envelop it. To grasp the multifaceted nature of entrepreneurship (Brush et al., 2009), understanding the intricate interplay between family dynamics, entrepreneurial intentions and self-efficacy becomes paramount. This chapter delves into this complex relationship, aspiring to shed light on the family's role in the entrepreneurial journey, the impact of family dynamics on business success and the influence of societal norms on these dynamics (Loi et al., 2021).

1.2 Case Study: Sarah's Restaurant is Rejuvenated

Consider the case of Sarah, a determined entrepreneur who confronted the monumental hardships of the COVID-19 pandemic. Sarah was the proprietor of a small family restaurant, a beloved fixture in her community for years. When the pandemic struck, her business bore the brunt of severe impact, with lockdowns and restrictions precipitously diminishing her customer base. In the face of adversity, Sarah confronted difficult choices, including personnel layoffs and the adaptation of her business model to include takeout and delivery services. With unwavering determination, innovative thinking and the steadfast support of her family, Sarah not only sustained her restaurant but expanded her reach by establishing a robust online presence. Her journey stands as an inspiring example of an entrepreneur who, with family support and strategic adaptation, surmounted the challenges presented by an unprecedented crisis.

Sarah's case study unveils several critical facets of entrepreneurial intentions, family influence and self-efficacy:

1.2.1 Entrepreneurial Intentions

Vision and Commitment: Sarah's unwavering commitment and strong vision for her family restaurant exemplify her entrepreneurial intentions. Despite the severe challenges posed by the pandemic, she remained resolute in her commitment to her entrepreneurial endeavour.

Adaptability: Entrepreneurial intentions often necessitate the willingness to adapt to changing circumstances. Sarah's rapid recognition that her traditional restaurant model was no longer viable due to lockdown and restrictions exemplifies her flexibility and ability to pivot in response to adversity.

1.2.2 Family Influence

Emotional Support: Sarah's family played a pivotal role by providing essential emotional support during trying times. Their encouragement and unwavering belief in her abilities bolstered her confidence and determination to persevere, illustrating how family dynamics can positively influence an entrepreneur's resilience and self-efficacy.

Resource Sharing: The sphere of family influence extended beyond emotional support to practical assistance. Sarah's family members likely contributed resources, whether financial or through labour, to aid her in adapting the business model and establishing an online presence. This tangible resource sharing reflects the substantive role of family support in entrepreneurship.

1.2.3 Self-Efficacy

Problem-solving Skills: Sarah's adeptness in navigating the crisis and devising innovative solutions, such as offering takeout and delivery services, showcases her problem-solving skills. Her confidence in her capacity to address challenges and find solutions is indicative of a high level of self-efficacy.

Resilience: Self-efficacy entails the belief in overcoming setbacks and adversity. Sarah's resilience in the face of a severe business impact from the pandemic underscores her self-efficacy. She did not allow setbacks to deter her, persisting in her efforts to keep the restaurant afloat.

Online Presence: Sarah's success in establishing a robust online presence signifies her self-efficacy in adapting to the digital landscape. This achievement not only helped her retain her existing customer base but also extended her reach, showcasing her confidence in leveraging technology for business growth.

In Sarah's case, entrepreneurial intentions, family influence and self-efficacy intertwine as elements that collectively contributed to her ability to not only survive the challenges posed by the pandemic but also thrive and expand her business. Her story serves as a potent illustration of how these factors can harmoniously work together to support an entrepreneur during times of crisis and change.

1.3 Teaching Case Approach

To comprehensively address the research questions and provide practical insights, this chapter adopts a teaching case approach. By examining real-world scenarios, such as Sarah's entrepreneurial journey during the pandemic, readers will gain a deeper understanding of the intricate interplay between family dynamics, entrepreneurial intention and self-efficacy. This approach endeavours to bridge the gap between theory and practice, equipping readers with valuable knowledge to navigate the challenges and opportunities inherent in entrepreneurship within familial and societal contexts.

2.0 FAMILY DYNAMICS AND ENTREPRENEURSHIP

2.1 Parental Influence on Entrepreneurial Mindset and Self-Efficacy

Parental influence refers to the impact of parents' attitudes, beliefs and behaviours on their children's development, including their entrepreneurial mindset and self-efficacy. Parents can shape their children's mindset by fostering an environment that encourages risk-taking, creativity and a proactive approach to challenges. The concept of parental influence is a crucial factor that can significantly shape an individual's entrepreneurial intentions and self-efficacy.

Scholars who argue in favour of the influence of parents on entrepreneurial intentions and self-efficacy argue that early exposure to entrepreneurial values and behaviours within the family environment can have a profound and lasting impact. Liñán and Chen (2009) affirmed that parental support and encouragement can significantly boost an individual's self-efficacy in entrepreneurial endeavours. When parents promote a positive attitude toward entrepreneurship, provide guidance and share their entrepreneurial experiences, children are more likely to develop a strong entrepreneurial mindset. Furthermore, Krauss et al. (2019) demonstrated that parental influence can be especially influential in cultures with a strong tradition of family business ownership. In such contexts, parents often impart entrepreneurial skills, knowledge and values to their offspring from an early age, instilling a sense of self-efficacy and entrepreneurial drive.

However, critics contend that individual factors, such as education, personal experiences and external mentors, can override parental influence. The study by Arenius and Minniti (2005) highlights that while parental support can be a contributing factor, the impact of external influences and education can often be more pronounced in shaping entrepreneurial intentions. Additionally, Kautonen et al. (2015) argue that while parents may influence attitudes toward entrepreneurship, the actual transition from intention to entrepreneurial action is contingent on a variety of external factors, such as access to resources, market conditions and economic constraints. In this perspective, parental influence alone may not be a decisive factor in entrepreneurial success.

In conclusion, the role of parental influence in shaping entrepreneurial intentions and self-efficacy is a complex and multifaceted one. While there is evidence to suggest that parental support and encouragement can positively impact an individual's entrepreneurial mindset, the influence is not absolute and can be mediated by external factors and individual experiences. The debate over the significance of parental influence in entrepreneurship highlights the need to consider a holistic approach, taking into account the interplay of various factors, both internal and external, in shaping an individual's entrepreneurial aspirations and self-efficacy.

2.1.1 Case Study

Consider the case of Elon Musk, whose parents encouraged his curiosity and risk-taking behaviour from a young age. His father, an engineer, and his mother, a dietitian and model, supported his interests in technology and entrepreneurship. This parental influence played a crucial role in shaping Musk's entrepreneurial mindset, leading to the founding of companies like SpaceX and Tesla.

2.1.2 Critical Lessons

1. The Power of Role Models: Parents who are entrepreneurial themselves or support their children's entrepreneurial aspirations can serve as powerful role models, instilling a mindset of innovation and self-efficacy.
2. Balancing Support and Independence: Parents need to strike a balance between providing support and allowing their children to explore and learn from failures independently. Over-protectiveness can hinder the development of resilience.
3. Long-term Impact Parental Influence: This can have a long-lasting impact on an individual's entrepreneurial journey. Early experiences and lessons from parents can shape an individual's approach to entrepreneurship throughout their life.

2.2 Family Support in Entrepreneurial Ventures

Family support is often heralded as a vital factor in entrepreneurial success. This section of the book critically explores the extent to which family members engage in business activities and examines the arguments for and against such active involvement in entrepreneurial ventures. While family support is widely acknowledged, the complexities surrounding its implications merit scrutiny.

Family members' involvement in entrepreneurial ventures can vary widely, from moral support and advice to active participation in daily operations. In many cases, family members are engaged as co-founders, investors or employees. The extent of this involvement often depends on cultural, economic and individual factors.

2.2.1 Examples of Active Family Support

One notable example of substantial family support in entrepreneurship is the Koch family, owners of Koch Industries. The Koch family actively participates in managing one of the largest privately-owned companies in the United States, overseeing a conglomerate of businesses spanning various industries. Another illustration is the Disney family, whose entrepreneurial journey gave rise to the global media conglomerate, The Walt Disney Company. Their commitment, creativity and familial cooperation were instrumental in shaping the entertainment industry.

Advocates of family involvement emphasise its benefits. Active family support provides entrepreneurs with a solid foundation of trust, shared values and a long-term perspective. An article by Baudot et al. (2020) underscores the capacity of family businesses with engaged family members to maintain a sense of purpose, fostering sustainability and innovation. This argument posits that the shared commitment and emotional investment of family members can contribute positively to the entrepreneurial venture.

However, a counterargument against extensive family involvement posits that it can create challenges. Detractors argue that it may result in conflicts of interest, favouritism and a lack of professional management practices. Research by Zhao, Luo and Suh (2019) has shown that excessive family control can lead to inefficiency and resistance to change, hindering adaptability and competitiveness. This perspective suggests that the emotional ties among family members may sometimes limit objective decision-making and innovation.

In conclusion, family support in entrepreneurial ventures is a multifaceted issue with both advantages and disadvantages. While it can foster trust, shared values and a sense of purpose, it may also introduce complexities related to professionalism, conflicts of interest and resistance to change. The degree of family involvement should be carefully tailored to the specific needs of the business and the competencies of family members. Striking a balance between leveraging the benefits of family support and maintaining a structured, efficient and innovative entrepreneurial environment is essential.

2.2.2 Case Study

Consider the case of Steve Jobs, co-founder of Apple Inc. During the early stages of Apple, Jobs received financial support from his adoptive parents, allowing him and Steve Wozniak to start their business in the family garage. This support played a pivotal role in Apple's initial success.

2.2.3 Critical Lessons

1. Resource Mobilization: Family support, particularly in terms of financial assistance, can be a critical enabler for entrepreneurs. However, entrepreneurs should be cautious not to overly rely on family resources, as this can lead to complacency.
2. Emotional Resilience: Emotional support from family members can help entrepreneurs navigate the ups and downs of the entrepreneurial journey. It is crucial to maintain open lines of communication with family to manage stress effectively.
3. Alignment of Goals: Family members should align their expectations and goals with those of the entrepreneur. Misalignment can lead to conflicts and hinder progress.

2.3 Family Support

Family support in entrepreneurial ventures is a multifaceted concept encompassing emotional, financial and practical assistance. This critical examination delves into the profound significance of such support and navigates through real-life examples illustrating its positive influence on entrepreneurial decisions. However, it is equally crucial to acknowledge the potential drawbacks that can arise from family involvement in business matters.

2.3.1 Significance of Family Support

1. Emotional Support: Emotional backing from family members is a cornerstone of entrepreneurial resilience. It provides entrepreneurs with a psychological safety net that bolsters their self-confidence and determination to overcome challenges. Case in point, Elon Musk's unwavering commitment to his entrepreneurial endeavours, such as SpaceX and Tesla, is fortified by the emotional support of his family, particularly his brother Kimbal Musk (Musk & Nagelhout, 2015).
2. Financial Support: Financial assistance from family members can be a game-changer for aspiring entrepreneurs. In the case of Larry Page and Sergey Brin, co-founders of Google, family support in the form of loans enabled them to pursue their vision. Such financial backing can foster innovation and the exploration of high-risk, high-reward ventures (Zarrella, 2019).
3. Practical Support: Active involvement of family members in business activities often results in practical support, which ranges from sharing industry expertise to taking on key roles within the company. A compelling instance is the Walton family, whose strong involvement in Walmart's operations contributed significantly to the success of the retail giant. Their collective practical support played a pivotal role in Walmart's growth into an industry leader (Basker & Simcoe, 2018).

2.3.2 Positive Influence of Family Support

Family support has positively influenced entrepreneurial decisions in various ways, such as fostering innovation, promoting long-term commitment and facilitating resource mobilisation. The continuity of the Ford Motor Company under successive generations of the Ford family attests to the enduring influence of familial support on entrepreneurial legacies (Collins & Porras, 2019). Such cases highlight the lasting impact that family involvement can have on entrepreneurial ventures.

2.3.4 Potential Drawbacks of Family Support

Yet, it is essential to consider the potential downsides of family support. Excessive involvement or a lack of professional boundaries may lead to conflicts of interest and hinder objectivity. For instance, the Murdoch family's control over media conglomerates, such as News Corp, has faced scrutiny due to perceived conflicts between family interests and journalistic integrity (Shepherd & Haynie, 2009; Moreno, 2023). Additionally, family support can inadvertently lead to a culture of entitlement, inhibiting merit-based decision-making and stalling innovation (Ryan, 2020).

In conclusion, family support, encompassing emotional, financial and practical aspects, is a multifaceted force that can significantly shape entrepreneurial decisions. Numerous entrepreneurs, from Elon Musk to Larry Page, have benefitted from such support in their endeavours. However, the potential drawbacks, including conflicts of interest and a culture of entitlement, cannot be underestimated. Striking a balance between leveraging the advantages of family support and maintaining professional standards is essential for entrepreneurs seeking sustainable success.

2.3 Challenges Arising From Family Dynamics in Entrepreneurship

Entrepreneurs often grapple with challenges that stem from family dynamics, despite the invaluable support they may receive. This analysis uncovers the multifaceted nature of these challenges, drawing on real-world examples that illustrate how family-related issues can impede business success. It is essential to recognise these obstacles to entrepreneurship and the strategies employed to mitigate their impact.

2.3.1 Family Conflicts and Business Decisions

One significant challenge in family business dynamics is the potential for conflicts to emerge, affecting key business decisions. A glaring example is the Redstone family's longstanding feud over the control of ViacomCBS. Sumner Redstone's advanced age and health concerns led to a protracted legal battle among his family members, causing significant instability in the media conglomerate (Shepherd & Haynie, 2009; Alves, Gama & Augusto, 2021). Such conflicts can hinder strategic planning and divert resources away from core business activities.

2.3.2 Succession Planning and Leadership Transitions

Smooth leadership transitions are critical in family-owned businesses, but they often present substantial challenges. A pertinent case is that of IKEA, where Ingvar

Kamprad's passing sparked leadership conflicts among his family members. The absence of a clear succession plan and the lack of alignment among family shareholders resulted in considerable disruption and uncertainty within the company (Sharma, 2018; Smith, 2019). Family dynamics can obstruct the appointment of competent leaders, leading to potential leadership vacuums.

2.3.3 Overcoming Bias and Nepotism

Family businesses may face difficulties in dealing with issues of favouritism and nepotism. Although family members might be well-qualified, the perception of unfair advantages can harm employee morale and hinder business growth. In the case of the Mars family and their confectionery empire, allegations of nepotism have occasionally overshadowed their substantial business success (Whoriskey, 2019). Striking a balance between family involvement and promoting a meritocratic environment is a persistent challenge in such scenarios.

2.3.4 Intra-Family Rivalries

Entrepreneurial success often hinges on cohesive teamwork, but intra-family rivalries can fracture unity and collaboration. The Agnelli family, known for their involvement in the Fiat Group, has witnessed internal conflicts that occasionally spilt into the public domain (Ebhardt & Lepido, 2021). Such rivalries can disrupt strategic decision-making and lead to sub-optimal business outcomes.

Entrepreneurs navigating the intricate landscape of family dynamics in business face substantial challenges that can impact their ventures. The Redstone, IKEA, Mars and Agnelli cases exemplify the diverse challenges stemming from family conflicts, leadership transitions, bias and rivalries. While these challenges are formidable, entrepreneurs can adopt strategies, such as effective governance structures and succession planning, to mitigate their impact and pave the way for successful family businesses.

2.4 Strategies for Overcoming Family-Related Challenges in Entrepreneurship

Entrepreneurs, often entangled in complex family dynamics, must employ strategies to overcome the challenges that stem from these relationships. Adaptability and resilience are vital attributes for mitigating these challenges. This discussion explores the strategies entrepreneurs have employed and the resilience they have demonstrated in the face of family-related obstacles, exemplified through real-world case studies.

2.4.1 Establishing Clear Governance Structures

Entrepreneurs can overcome family-related challenges by establishing transparent governance structures within their businesses. A case in point is the Walton family, the heirs of Walmart, who have effectively employed governance mechanisms to avoid the conflicts that typically arise in family firms (Anderson, 2015). By delineating roles, responsibilities and decision-making processes, they have preserved business continuity.

2.4.2 Implementing Succession Planning

Smooth leadership transitions are paramount in family businesses. The Ambani family, behind India's Reliance Industries, exemplifies the importance of well-structured succession planning. Despite their substantial business empire, they have managed leadership changes with minimal disruptions by preparing the next generation (Gupta, 2021; Choudhury, 2021). Adequate succession planning ensures the sustained growth of the enterprise.

2.4.3 Engaging in Open Communication

Promoting open and honest communication among family members is a strategy to resolve conflicts and enhance collaboration. The Lee family, owners of the Samsung Group, have employed this approach by encouraging family members to communicate openly about their concerns and business matters (Lee & Rogoff, 1996). Effective communication can help avert misunderstandings and build consensus within the family enterprise.

2.4.4 Seeking External Expertise

Entrepreneurs facing family-related challenges may benefit from seeking external expertise to mediate or provide advisory services. The Rockefeller family, renowned for their philanthropic activities, has engaged external advisors to manage family dynamics and philanthropic initiatives (Lansberg, 1999; Handler, 2011). Leveraging external experts can provide an objective perspective and foster positive outcomes.

Overcoming family-related challenges in entrepreneurship requires astute strategies and a resilient mindset. Entrepreneurs can draw inspiration from the Walton, Ambani, Lee and Rockefeller families' successful applications of governance structures, succession planning, open communication and external expertise. Adaptability and resilience are foundational for managing family dynamics, ultimately ensuring the continued success of family businesses.

2.5 Family Environment as a Shaper of Entrepreneurial Mindset

The family environment, including communication patterns, values and conflicts, can shape an individual's entrepreneurial mindset and self-efficacy. A nurturing and supportive family environment can foster a mindset of innovation and confidence.

2.5.1 Case Study

Consider the case of the Walton family, the founders of Walmart. Their family environment emphasized hard work, frugality and a commitment to low prices. These values influenced Sam Walton's entrepreneurial approach and laid the foundation for the retail giant's success.

2.5.2 Critical Lessons

1. Values and Culture: Family values and culture can significantly influence entrepreneurial decisions and strategies. Entrepreneurs should align their ventures with their family's values to ensure long-term harmony.
2. Conflict Resolution: Addressing conflicts within the family environment is crucial. Unresolved conflicts can spill over into the business realm and negatively impact both family relationships and business success.
3. Adaptability: Entrepreneurs should be adaptable and open to evolving their mindset and strategies based on changing family dynamics and business needs.

In conclusion, parental influence, family support and the family environment are complex factors that can either empower or impede entrepreneurial endeavours. Entrepreneurs must navigate these dynamics carefully, recognising the potential benefits and challenges they present. Effective communication, alignment of goals and a balance between support and independence are key to harnessing the positive aspects of family dynamics while mitigating potential pitfalls.

3.0 THE CONTEMPORARY RELEVANCE: FAMILY DYNAMICS AND ENTREPRENEURSHIP

The contemporary relevance of the interplay between family dynamics and entrepreneurship is a topic of paramount importance in the rapidly evolving economic landscape. This section critically analyses the significance of family support and adaptability in entrepreneurial success, particularly in the context of evolving societal norms and the COVID-19 pandemic.

3.1 Evolving Societal Norms

Societal norms and values are not static; they continuously evolve, impacting various facets of life, including entrepreneurship. In recent years, there has been a noticeable shift towards recognising the influence of family dynamics on entrepreneurial intentions and actions (Bertrand & Scholar, 2006). This shift reflects a broader societal acknowledgement that individuals are not isolated agents in their entrepreneurial pursuits but are deeply rooted in their familial and cultural contexts. As entrepreneurship becomes increasingly intertwined with social and economic progress, understanding these evolving norms is crucial.

The critical lesson here is that entrepreneurs should be attuned to changing societal norms and values as they shape both opportunities and challenges in the entrepreneurial landscape. Adapting to these changes can be a strategic advantage, while disregarding them may result in missed opportunities or, conversely, conflict with societal expectations.

3.1.1 The Impact of the COVID-19 Pandemic

The COVID-19 pandemic has not only accelerated the adoption of entrepreneurial practices driven by necessity but has also underscored the indispensable role of family support and adaptability in entrepreneurial success (Wang et al., 2023). The pandemic brought unprecedented challenges, forcing entrepreneurs to confront economic uncertainties, lockdowns and disruptions in their businesses.

The case of Sarah, a resilient entrepreneur who managed to revitalise her family restaurant during the pandemic, exemplifies the importance of family dynamics. Her family's emotional support, resource sharing, problem-solving skills and resilience highlight the interplay between family influence and self-efficacy in the face of adversity.

A critical lesson derived from this scenario is that family support and adaptability are not just valuable in ordinary times but are essential lifelines during crises. Entrepreneurs who maintain strong bonds with their families and can leverage their support and resources are better equipped to weather unforeseen challenges.

3.2 Timeliness and Relevance of the Study

The current global economic landscape demands a deeper understanding of the intricate relationship between family dynamics, entrepreneurial intentions and self-efficacy (Brush et al., 2009). As entrepreneurship plays an increasingly pivotal role in economic growth and innovation, this understanding becomes a critical asset for aspiring and established entrepreneurs alike. The relevance of this study lies in its ability to provide actionable insights into navigating the multifaceted nature of entrepreneurship within familial and societal contexts.

Aspiring entrepreneurs, in particular, can draw inspiration from real-world cases like Sarah's, recognising that family support, adaptability and the ability to align their entrepreneurial aspirations with evolving societal norms can be key drivers of success.

In conclusion, the contemporary relevance of family dynamics in entrepreneurship is underscored by the evolving societal norms and the challenges posed by events like the COVID-19 pandemic. This section has elucidated the importance of understanding how family influences entrepreneurial intentions and actions in a rapidly changing world, emphasising the timely need for a comprehensive investigation into this complex relationship.

4.0 UNRAVELING THE COMPLEXITY: RESEARCH QUESTIONS AND PROBLEM STATEMENT

This section provides a critical analysis of the central research questions and problem statement that drive the exploration of family dynamics and entrepreneurship in the context of evolving societal norms, such as the COVID-19 pandemic.

4.1 Problem Statement

Entrepreneurship, a catalyst for economic development, is a multifaceted endeavour with a unique set of challenges (McMullen, 2011). While individual intentions and capabilities are undoubtedly influential in entrepreneurial pursuits, the role of family dynamics cannot be understated (Fouad et al., 2016). Families serve as both a source of support and a potential source of conflict for entrepreneurs, shaping their aspirations and influencing decision-making processes. This dichotomy highlights the need for a comprehensive understanding of how family dynamics impact entrepreneurship.

4.2 Research Questions

The research questions presented is important in guiding the exploration of this book chapter:

1. To what extent does family involvement and support influence an individual's entrepreneurial intentions and actions?

This question delves into the extent to which family, as a social support system, contributes to an individual's entrepreneurial journey. It recognises that family involvement can be both a driving force and a potential constraint. Research into this question can shed light on the nuanced ways in which family support affects entrepreneurial intentions and actions.

2. What challenges do entrepreneurs face due to family dynamics, and what strategies do they employ to overcome these challenges?

This question acknowledges that family dynamics are not always conducive to entrepreneurship and can pose significant challenges. It invites an exploration of the obstacles entrepreneurs encounter within their families and the strategies they employ to navigate these challenges. Understanding these challenges and strategies is essential for aspiring and existing entrepreneurs alike.

3. How do societal norms and values shape the relationship between family dynamics and entrepreneurship?

This question recognises that family dynamics are not isolated from the broader societal context. Societal norms and values can either reinforce or challenge familial influences on entrepreneurship. Investigating this aspect is crucial for comprehending the external forces that impact the interplay between family dynamics and entrepreneurial intentions.

4.3 The Influence of Societal Norms and Values on Family Dynamics in Entrepreneurship

Societal norms and values play a significant role in shaping family perspectives on entrepreneurship. These norms can either act as catalysts or obstacles for entrepreneurs within a family context. This analysis delves into the influence of societal norms and values on family dynamics, examining real-world cases where family dynamics were shaped by societal expectations and addressing potential conflicts between traditional norms and entrepreneurial aspirations.

4.3.1 Shaping Family Perspectives on Entrepreneurship

Societal norms and values have a profound impact on how families perceive entrepreneurial endeavours. In a study by Li and Nazrul (2021), Chinese families were found to place immense value on job security and stability, often viewing entrepreneurship with scepticism. This reflects a societal norm that favours traditional career paths. Such norms can influence family members' attitudes towards entrepreneurial intentions, with a potential reluctance to support these endeavours.

4.3.2 Cases of Societal Influence on Family Dynamics

The case of Fadil, an aspiring entrepreneur from a conservative Middle Eastern family, exemplifies how societal norms can affect family dynamics. Fadil's family adhered to a societal norm that expected young adults to follow established professional paths. His decision to pursue entrepreneurship was met with resistance from his family, who viewed it as unconventional and risky (Al-Saifi et al., 2021). This illustrates how societal norms can create conflicts within families when entrepreneurial aspirations deviate from traditional expectations.

4.3.3 Conflicts Between Traditional Norms and Entrepreneurial Aspirations

The clash between traditional norms and entrepreneurial aspirations can lead to conflicts within families. In a study by Chahal and Sharma (2020), Indian families facing societal expectations of secure, salaried jobs often experienced tension when younger family members sought entrepreneurial paths. Such conflicts highlight the challenge of navigating between traditional values and modern ambitions, potentially straining family relationships.

4.4 Navigating Societal Norms

Entrepreneurs often face the arduous task of navigating societal norms and family dynamics. The Amara family, from a close-knit African community, decided to establish a family bakery, which defied the common career paths of the community members. They succeeded by actively engaging with their community, aligning their entrepreneurial venture with community values, and thereby gaining acceptance (Hopp & Christian, 2012). This case exemplifies how entrepreneurs can adapt their ventures to align with societal norms, resulting in successful entrepreneurship within family dynamics.

Societal norms and values significantly influence family dynamics in entrepreneurship. While traditional norms may create conflicts and resistance, entrepreneurs have the opportunity to adapt their ventures to align with societal expectations. Real-life cases like Fadil and the Amara family demonstrate the multifaceted interplay between societal norms and family entrepreneurship, highlighting the need for entrepreneurs to navigate these influences strategically. The case study aims to put the problem into perspective.

4.4.1 Navigating Family Dynamics and Challenges in Entrepreneurship

Family dynamics can have a significant impact on the success of a business. Positive family dynamics, such as strong communication, mutual respect and shared values, can contribute to a supportive and nurturing environment for the business. On the other hand, negative family dynamics, such as conflicts, power struggles and lack of trust, can create a stressful and disruptive environment that can hinder the business's growth and success.

4.5 Some of the Impacts Include

Negative family dynamics can introduce substantial obstacles for family businesses. These challenges often manifest in the following ways:

- Disputes over resource allocation and leadership: Disagreements among family members regarding the distribution of resources or the assignment of leadership roles can instigate conflicts detrimental to the business (Rahim, 2023).
- Communication gaps: Avoidance of challenging conversations can lead to misunderstandings and a lack of trust within the family, which can negatively impact the business (Sue, 2016).
- Interpersonal tension: Divergent expectations for the business among family members can create friction and resentment, further complicating business operations (Hoover & Hoover, 2013).
- The decline in revenue and success: Negative family dynamics can significantly affect the business's performance. The family's systems and responses to disruptions can have profound effects on gross revenue and the owner's perceived success (Nose, Korunka & Frank, 2017).

These challenges, if not addressed, can lead to the disintegration of the family business. To mitigate these issues, family businesses may need to focus on enhancing communication, resolving conflicts and fostering a shared vision. Establishing decision-making processes that balance the business's needs with family members' expectations can also be beneficial (Rahim, 2023; Sue, 2016).

5.0 THEORETICAL FOUNDATIONS: UNDERSTANDING FAMILY DYNAMICS AND ENTREPRENEURSHIP

This review delves into various theoretical frameworks that shed light on the relationship between family dynamics, entrepreneurial intentions and self-efficacy. These frameworks provide distinct perspectives on how family interactions influence an individual's decision to embark on an entrepreneurial journey and their belief in their ability to succeed.

5.1 Abundance of Strange Attractors

The paper titled "Abundance of strange attractors" by Mora and Viana (1993) offers a unique mathematical framework that, while not initially designed for social sciences, holds relevance for understanding family dynamics. The authors investigate the complex dynamics of a family of diffeomorphisms of the plane. Within the context of entrepreneurial intentions, this framework metaphorically alludes to the intricate and multifaceted interactions within a family system. However, it is essential to recognise that this is primarily a mathematical model, and its direct application to social sciences would necessitate careful interpretation and adaptation.

5.1.1 Role of Self-Efficacy and Parental Influence

In their study, Rachmawan, Aprilianti-Lizar and Mangundjaya (2015) explore the relationship between self-efficacy and parental influence on entrepreneurial intention. While the theoretical framework is not explicitly stated, their work aligns with Bandura's Self-efficacy theory (2003). This theory posits that individuals' belief in their capabilities significantly impacts their motivation, behaviour and social environment. Here, self-efficacy emerges as a crucial factor shaping entrepreneurial intentions, overshadowing the influence of parents.

5.1.2 Family Tradition and Psychological Traits

The study by Altinay, Madanoglu, Daniele and Lashley (2012) investigate how family tradition and psychological traits influence entrepreneurial intention. Although the specific theoretical framework is not outlined, this study appears to draw from theories of personality and social influence. It suggests that familial influences extend beyond parental figures to encompass broader family traditions, impacting an individual's entrepreneurial mindset.

5.1.3 Familial Factors, Personality Traits, and Self-Efficacy

Akanbi and Alayande (2013) investigate the influence of familial factors, personality traits and self-efficacy on entrepreneurial behaviour. Although the explicit theoretical framework is not specified, it seems to encompass theories related to personality and social influence. This approach underscores the broader familial factors that can impact an individual's entrepreneurial intentions.

5.1.4 Influence of Individual/Psychological Factors and Social Norms

Peng, Lu and Kang's study (2013) focuses on the multifaceted influence on university students' entrepreneurial intentions. Their work draws from theories related to social norms, attitudes and self-efficacy. It considers the impact of family background and social environment factors on entrepreneurial intent. This framework encapsulates a wide range of individual, familial and social factors, providing a comprehensive understanding of entrepreneurial intentions.

In summary, these theoretical frameworks offer diverse perspectives on the influence of family dynamics on entrepreneurial intentions and self-efficacy. They underscore the importance of considering individual traits, familial factors and broader social influences. Integrating these perspectives in future research may contribute to a more comprehensive understanding of the intricate factors shaping entrepreneurial intentions and self-efficacy.

5.2 Societal Values and the Alignment of Family and Business Identities

Societal values play a pivotal role in shaping the relationship between family and entrepreneurship. They act as a silent yet profound influence on the alignment of family and business identities, either facilitating a harmonious integration or causing inherent conflicts.

5.2.1 Societal Values as Facilitators

Entrepreneurs who have successfully integrated societal values into their ventures often find that such alignment not only enhances their business identity but also fosters community acceptance (Morsing & Schultz, 2006). For example, socially responsible entrepreneurs like Anita Roddick, founder of The Body Shop (Pless, 2007), leveraged societal values related to environmental sustainability and ethical sourcing (Sasha, 2004). Her business thrived by embodying these values, aligning her family and business identity seamlessly. This alignment not only attracted a loyal customer base but also strengthened her familial bonds as her family actively participated in the venture (Andriof et al., 2017).

Likewise, the rise of impact-driven businesses reflects a deliberate embrace of societal values. Entrepreneurs like Blake Mycoskie, founder of TOMS, have successfully intertwined the societal value of giving back to the community with their business model (Sharma & Vredenburg, 1998; Malik et al., 2022). Mycoskie's "One for One" approach resonated with societal values of compassion and philanthropy, demonstrating that a family-oriented enterprise could harmoniously coexist with business practices that reflect societal concerns (Mycoskie, 2011).

5.2.2 Societal Values as Conflicting Forces

However, several entrepreneurs do not find it easy to align familial values with societal expectations (Hanson, Hessel & Danes, 2019; Stanwick & Stanwick, 1998). In certain cases, conflicts between familial traditions and societal values can arise, demanding entrepreneurs to make difficult choices. Such entrepreneurs often need to navigate the delicate balance between preserving their family's heritage and meeting the evolving demands of a society with shifting norms.

For instance, family-owned restaurants might face challenges when their traditional recipes clash with societal trends around health-consciousness (Smith & Johnson, 2019). In such cases, the family's commitment to preserving the authenticity of their cuisine can create conflicts with societal values promoting healthier eating. To adapt, these entrepreneurs must innovate while staying true to their family's heritage.

In conclusion, societal values profoundly impact the alignment of family and business identities for entrepreneurs. Entrepreneurs who successfully integrate societal values into their ventures can bolster both their familial bonds and their business ventures. Examples like The Body Shop and TOMS illustrate the potential for synergy between family values and societal concerns. Nonetheless, conflicts may arise, particularly when traditional family practices clash with contemporary societal values. These conflicts demand entrepreneurs to navigate a delicate balance between familial heritage and societal expectations.

5.3 Entrepreneurial Theories and Their Applications

Several theories have been used to discuss entrepreneurial intentions and self-efficacy in the literature. The prominent ones are the Theory of Planned Behavior (TPB), the Social Cognitive Theory (SCT) and the Regulatory Focus Theory (RF). These theories will be discussed concisely:

5.3.1 Theory of Planned Behavior

The TPB suggests that entrepreneurial intention is influenced by one's attitude, subjective norms and perceived behavioural control (Ajzen, 1991). Family dynamics and societal norms play essential roles in shaping these aspects. For example, a positive family attitude toward entrepreneurship may enhance an individual's attitude, thus positively affecting intentions (Krueger & Brazeal, 1994).

TPB posits that an individual's intention to engage in a behaviour (in this case, entrepreneurship) is determined by their attitude towards the behaviour, subjective norms and perceived behavioural control, which is closely related to self-efficacy. This theory has been applied in various studies to understand entrepreneurial intentions.

For instance, a study by Duong Cong Doanh and Tomasz Bernat (2019) used TPB to investigate the relationship between entrepreneurial self-efficacy and entrepreneurial intention among Vietnamese students, highlighting the indirect influence of subjective norms on entrepreneurial intention through entrepreneurial self-efficacy. The study also examined the role of subjective norms in shaping entrepreneurial intention. The authors found that subjective norms indirectly influence entrepreneurial intention through entrepreneurial self-efficacy, attitude toward entrepreneurship and perceived behavioural control (Doanh & Bernat, 2019).

5.3.2 Social Cognitive Theory (SCT)

SCT, developed by Bandura (1986), emphasised the role of observational learning, social experiences and reciprocal determinism in personality development. When applied to entrepreneurship, SCT posits that individuals learn from observing the experiences of family members (Krueger et al., 2000). This observational learning can significantly shape self-efficacy and entrepreneurial intentions. For instance, if an individual observes a family member succeeding in an entrepreneurial venture, this can boost their self-efficacy and intentions (Biraglia & Kadile, 2017).

The SCT is another theory that has been used to discuss entrepreneurial self-efficacy. SCT emphasises the role of observational learning, social experience and reciprocal determinism in the development of personality. A study by Biraglia and Kadile (2017) applied SCT to investigate the role of entrepreneurial passion and creativity as antecedents of entrepreneurial intentions. They found that entrepreneurial passion has a strong positive relationship with entrepreneurial intentions, even when entrepreneurial self-efficacy is introduced as a mediator (Biraglia & Kadile, 2017).

5.3.3 The Regulatory Focus Theory

RF Theory developed by Higgins (1997), suggests that the motivational context, whether promotion-focused or prevention-focused, influences behaviour. In the context of entrepreneurship, self-efficacy plays a crucial role in determining an individual's response to this motivational context (Piperopoulos & Dimov, 2015). Family dynamics can impact the alignment of an individual's regulatory focus. For example, a family that emphasises risk avoidance may create a prevention-focused environment, which may lead individuals with high self-efficacy to hesitate in pursuing entrepreneurship (Piperopoulos & Dimov, 2015).

RF Theory has been used to understand how the nature of an entrepreneurship course (whether theoretical) creates a distinct motivational frame for entrepreneurship in promotion or prevention terms. A study by Piperopoulos and Dimov (2015) found that higher self-efficacy is associated with lower entrepreneurial intentions in theoretically-oriented courses and higher entrepreneurial intentions in practically-oriented courses (Piperopoulos & Dimov, 2015).

5.3.4 Relationships Between TPB, SCT, and Regulatory Focus Theory

1. Theory of Planned Behavior (TPB)

TPB suggests that entrepreneurial intention is influenced by one's attitude, subjective norms and perceived behavioural control (Ajzen, 1991). Family dynamics and societal norms play essential roles in shaping these aspects. For example, a positive family attitude toward entrepreneurship may enhance an individual's attitude, thus positively affecting intentions (Krueger & Brazeal, 1994).

2. Social Cognitive Theory (SCT)

SCT, developed by Bandura (1986), emphasised the role of observational learning, social experiences and reciprocal determinism in personality development. When applied to entrepreneurship, SCT posits that individuals learn from observing the experiences of family members (Krueger et al., 2000). This observational learning can significantly shape self-efficacy and entrepreneurial intentions. For instance, if an individual observes a family member succeeding in an entrepreneurial venture, this can boost their self-efficacy and intentions (Biraglia & Kadile, 2017).

3. Regulatory Focus Theory

RF Theory, developed by Higgins (1997), suggests that the motivational context, whether promotion-focused or prevention-focused, influences behaviour. In the context of entrepreneurship, self-efficacy plays a crucial role in determining an individual's response to this motivational context (Piperopoulos & Dimov, 2015). Family dynamics can impact the alignment of an individual's regulatory focus. For example, a family that emphasises risk avoidance may create a prevention-focused environment, which may lead individuals with high self-efficacy to hesitate in pursuing entrepreneurship (Piperopoulos & Dimov, 2015).

These theories, when integrated, offer a comprehensive framework for understanding how entrepreneurial intentions are shaped by family dynamics, personal beliefs and societal values. They underscore the importance of considering family influences, individual self-efficacy and the motivational context in entrepreneurial decision-making (Ajzen, 1991; Bandura, 1986; Higgins, 1997). This integrated perspective provides valuable insights into the multifaceted nature of entrepreneurial intentions and how they are intertwined with the family's role and societal norms (Krueger et al., 2000; Krueger & Brazeal, 1994; Piperopoulos & Dimov, 2015).

5.4 Exploring Real-World Cases Where Family Dynamics Impact the Application of the Theories

5.4.1 Theory of Planned Behavior (TPB)

In a scenario, an individual called Sarah comes from a family that values job security and traditional career paths. In this family, entrepreneurial pursuits are not encouraged, and the subjective norm within her family is to have a stable job. According to TPB, Sarah's entrepreneurial intention might be negatively affected due to the subjective norms prevailing within her family. Despite her positive attitude towards entrepreneurship, her intention to start a business may be hindered by her family's beliefs.

5.4.2 Social Cognitive Theory (SCT)

Imagine a family where entrepreneurship is highly valued and several members have successfully started their businesses. Within this family, individuals grow up witnessing entrepreneurial success stories. One member, John, sees his older siblings and parents excel as entrepreneurs. According to SCT, John's observational learning and the positive experiences he observed within his family contribute to his high self-efficacy. John has a strong belief in his capabilities to succeed as an entrepreneur, and this significantly boosts his entrepreneurial intentions.

5.4.3 Regulatory Focus Theory (RF)

Consider a case where a family highly emphasises risk avoidance. They have experienced financial setbacks and failures in entrepreneurial ventures in the past. In this family, the motivational context leans toward prevention-focused goals, aiming to avoid risks. Sarah, from this family, has high self-efficacy but finds her family's emphasis on risk prevention challenging. RF theory is prevention-focused environment might create hesitancy in pursuing entrepreneurship, despite her self-efficacy. She's torn between her belief in her capabilities and her family's emphasis on avoiding risks.

These real-world examples illustrate how family dynamics can impact the application of the theories. TPB shows how subjective norms within a family can hinder entrepreneurial intentions. SCT demonstrates how positive family experiences can lead to high self-efficacy and boost intentions, while RF theory reveals how the family's emphasis on risk prevention can conflict with an individual's self-efficacy and affect their entrepreneurial decisions.

In these cases, it is evident how family dynamics interact with the theories, ultimately shaping an individual's entrepreneurial intentions, and highlighting the multifaceted nature of this process.

5.5 Gaps and Contradictions During the Application of the Theoretical Frameworks

1. **Complex Interplay of Family Dynamics:** The existing literature highlights the importance of self-efficacy, family factors and personality traits in influencing entrepreneurial intention (Rachmawan, Lizar & Mangundjaya, 2015; Şahin, Koçman, Karadağ & Tuncer, 2019). However, it often lacks a comprehensive understanding of how these factors interact and the potential contradictions among them. The complex interplay and potential contradictions are not well-explored (Farashah, 2015).
2. **Contextual Variations:** The studies often lack a cross-cultural perspective and findings may not be universally applicable. For example, the role of familial influence may differ between individualistic and collectivistic societies (Akanbi & Alayande, 2013; Supandi, Wulandari & Naufalin, 2022).
3. **Mediating Mechanisms:** The existing studies often do not delve into the underlying mechanisms explaining the relationships between self-efficacy, family dynamics and personality traits (Altinay, Madanoglu, Daniele & Lashley, 2012). Understanding the mediating mechanisms can provide a more holistic view of entrepreneurial intention (Turulja, Veselinović, Agić & Pašić-Mesihović, 2020).

4. **Longitudinal Studies:** Most of the referenced studies provide a snapshot of entrepreneurial intention at a given point in time. Longitudinal studies tracking individuals over time are required to assess the evolving influence of self-efficacy, family dynamics and personality traits on entrepreneurial intention (Mahfudzi & Fitri, 2022).

5.6 Future Research Directions Based on Theoretical Frameworks

Comprehensive Framework: Future research should aim to develop a comprehensive framework that integrates the roles of self-efficacy, family dynamics and personality traits in shaping entrepreneurial intention. This framework should consider the mediating mechanisms and how these factors interact in different contexts (Krueger & Brazeal, 1994).

Cross-cultural Analysis: Comparative studies across diverse cultural contexts can unveil how self-efficacy, family dynamics and personality traits manifest differently in entrepreneurial intention. This cross-cultural analysis should not only consider Western and non-Western contexts but also explore variations within regions and subcultures (Biraglia & Kadile, 2017).

Mediating Mechanisms: Research should focus on exploring the mediating mechanisms underlying the relationships between self-efficacy, family dynamics and personality traits. This could involve cognitive processes, emotional factors or the influence of social networks in shaping entrepreneurial intention (Piperopoulos & Dimov, 2015).

Longitudinal Studies: Longitudinal research designs can provide insights into how these factors influence changes in entrepreneurial intention over time. This would offer a more dynamic view of how self-efficacy, family dynamics and personality traits interact and evolve in the entrepreneurial decision-making process (Doanh & Bernat, 2019).

Interventions and Policies: Future research should also focus on practical applications. Understanding the complex dynamics can help in designing effective interventions, policies and educational programmes to foster entrepreneurial intention in individuals with varying self-efficacy levels and family backgrounds (Ajzen, 1991).

6.0 IMPLICATIONS AND FUTURE ENDEAVOURS

6.1 Practical Implications for This Study

- Entrepreneurs can benefit from leveraging the positive aspects of family dynamics, such as emotional, financial and practical support, while mitigating the potential pitfalls, such as conflicts, bias and rivalries.
- Entrepreneurs should be attuned to changing societal norms and values, as they can shape both opportunities and challenges in the entrepreneurial landscape.
- Adapting to these changes can be a strategic advantage, while disregarding them may result in missed opportunities or conflict with societal expectations.
- Entrepreneurs should be adaptable and resilient, especially in the face of crises, such as the COVID-19 pandemic. Family support and adaptability can be essential lifelines during such times, as exemplified by Sarah's case study. Sarah managed to revitalise her family restaurant during the pandemic by leveraging her family's emotional support, resource sharing and her problem-solving skills and resilience.

6.2 Future Research Questions

Future research studies could focus deeper into the empirical investigation of the relationship between family dynamics and entrepreneurship by addressing the following research questions:

1. How do family dynamics affect the development of entrepreneurial self-efficacy among university students?
2. How do family dynamics moderate the relationship between entrepreneurial self-efficacy and entrepreneurial intention?
3. How do societal norms and values mediate the relationship between family dynamics and entrepreneurial intention?

7.0 CONCLUSION

7.1 Summary of the Key Findings

Family dynamics, encompassing communication patterns, values and conflicts, can significantly shape an individual's entrepreneurial mindset and self-efficacy. A nurturing and supportive family environment can foster a mindset of innovation and confidence, while a stressful and disruptive family environment can hinder entrepreneurial aspirations and actions. Family support, particularly in terms of emotional, financial and practical assistance, is a multifaceted force that can significantly shape entrepreneurial decisions. Numerous entrepreneurs, from Elon Musk to Larry Page, have benefited from such support in their endeavours.

However, the potential drawbacks, including conflicts of interest and a culture of entitlement, cannot be underestimated. Striking a balance between leveraging the advantages of family support and maintaining professional standards is essential for entrepreneurs seeking sustainable success. Family dynamics are not isolated from the broader societal context. Societal norms and values can either reinforce or challenge familial influences on entrepreneurship, creating opportunities or obstacles for entrepreneurs. Understanding the intricate interplay between family dynamics, entrepreneurial intentions and self-efficacy is crucial for aspiring and established entrepreneurs alike.

The intricate relationship between family dynamics, entrepreneurial intention and self-efficacy underscores the importance of understanding these dynamics for entrepreneurs and policymakers. Entrepreneurs can benefit from leveraging the positive aspects of family dynamics, such as emotional, financial and practical support, while mitigating the potential pitfalls, such as conflicts, bias and rivalries. Entrepreneurs should also be attuned to changing societal norms and values as they can shape both opportunities and challenges in the entrepreneurial landscape. Adapting to these changes can be a strategic advantage, while disregarding them may result in missed opportunities or conflict with societal expectations.

Policymakers can also play a vital role in fostering a conducive environment for entrepreneurship, by providing support, incentives and education for entrepreneurs and their families. Policymakers should also be aware of the diverse needs and preferences of entrepreneurs from different family backgrounds and cultures, and tailor their policies accordingly.

7.2 Conclusion

This book chapter has explored the complex relationship between family dynamics and entrepreneurship, particularly in the context of evolving societal norms and the COVID-19 pandemic. It has critically examined the role of parental influence, family support and the family environment in shaping entrepreneurial intentions and self-efficacy. It has also discussed the challenges and strategies that entrepreneurs face due to family dynamics, drawing on real-world case studies. The chapter has provided a comprehensive theoretical framework that integrates various perspectives on how family interactions influence entrepreneurial decisions. It has also highlighted the practical implications of the findings and suggested areas for future research.

REFERENCES

Afonso Alves, C., Matias Gama, A. P., & Augusto, M. (2021). Family influence and firm performance: The mediating role of stewardship. *Journal of Small Business and Enterprise Development*, *28*(2), 185–204. doi:10.1108/JSBED-01-2019-0015

Al-Saifi. (2019). Entrepreneurship in the Arab Middle East: Exploring the Role of Culture and Context. *Journal of Business Research*, *94*, 172–182.

Alon, I., Jaffe, E., Prange, C., & Vianelli, D. (2020). *Global marketing: strategy, practice, and cases*. Routledge. doi:10.4324/9780429203343

Altinay, L., Madanoglu, M., Daniele, R., & Lashley, C. (2012). The influence of family tradition and psychological traits on entrepreneurial intention. *International Journal of Hospitality Management*, *31*(2), 489–499. doi:10.1016/j.ijhm.2011.07.007

Anderson, R. C. (2015). Family Business Governance: Maximizing Family and Business Potential. *Family Business Review*, *28*, 193–209.

Andjelkovic Pesic, M., & Dahlgaard, J. J. (2013). *Using the Balanced-Scorecard and the European Foundation for Quality Management Excellence model as a combined roadmap for diagnosing and attaining excellence*. Available: https://scholar.google.com/scholar?hl=en&as_sdt=0%2C5&q=Andjelkovic+Pesic%2C+M.%2C+%26+Dahlgaard%2C+J.+J.+%282013%29

Andriof, J., Waddock, S., Husted, B., & Rahman, S. S. (2017). *Unfolding stakeholder thinking: Theory, responsibility and engagement*. Routledge. doi:10.4324/9781351281843

Arenius, P., & Minniti, M. (2005). Perceptual variables and nascent entrepreneurship. *Small Business Economics*, *24*(3), 233–247. doi:10.100711187-005-1984-x

Astrachan, J. H., Klein, S. B., & Smyrnios, K. X. (2002). The F-PEC scale of family influence: A proposal for solving the family business definition problem. *Family Business Review*, *15*(1), 45–58. doi:10.1111/j.1741-6248.2002.00045.x

Au, K., Chiang, F.F.T., & Birtch, T.A. (2013). Incubating the next generation to venture: The case of a family business in Hong Kong. *Asia Pacific Journal of Management*, 30.

Bandura, A., & Locke, E. A. (2003). Negative self-efficacy and goal effects revisited. *The Journal of Applied Psychology*, *88*(1), 87–99. doi:10.1037/0021-9010.88.1.87 PMID:12675397

Basker, E. A. S. (2018). The Impact of Wal-Mart Supercenters on Grocery Prices and the Consumer Price Index. *Journal of Business & Economic Statistics*, *36*, 49–65.

Baudot, L., Johnson, J. A., Roberts, A., & Roberts, R. W. (2020). Is corporate tax aggressiveness a reputation threat? Corporate accountability, corporate social responsibility, and corporate tax behavior. *Journal of Business Ethics*, *163*(2), 197–215. doi:10.100710551-019-04227-3

Bignotti, A., & Le Roux, I. (2020). Which types of experience matter? The role of prior start-up experiences and work experience in fostering youth entrepreneurial intentions. *International Journal of Entrepreneurial Behaviour & Research*, *26*(6), 1181–1198. doi:10.1108/IJEBR-10-2019-0577

Biraglia, A., & Kadile, V. (2017). The role of entrepreneurial passion and creativity in developing entrepreneurial intentions: Insights from American homebrewers. *Journal of Small Business Management*, *55*(1), 170–188. doi:10.1111/jsbm.12242

Boyd, N. G., & Vozikis, G. S. (1994). The influence of self-efficacy on the development of entrepreneurial intentions and actions. *Entrepreneurship Theory and Practice*, *18*(4), 63–77. doi:10.1177/104225879401800404

Britannica. (2023). Walmart / History & Facts. *Encyclopedia Britannica*. Available: https://www.britannica.com/topic/Walmart

Cardella, G. M., Hernández-Sánchez, B. R., & Sanchez Garcia, J. C. (2020). Entrepreneurship and family role: A systematic review of a growing research. *Frontiers in Psychology*, *10*, 2939. doi:10.3389/fpsyg.2019.02939 PMID:31998192

Chahal, H., & Sharma, A. K. (2020). Family business in India: Performance, challenges and improvement measures. *Journal of New Business Ventures*, *1*(1-2), 9–30. doi:10.1177/2632962X20960824

Choudhury, D. (2021). Critical Evaluation of the Position of Women Directors in Corporate Boards. *Jus Corpus LJ*, *2*, 157.

Chua, J. H., Chrisman, J. J., & Sharma, P. (1999). Defining the family business by behavior. *Entrepreneurship Theory and Practice*, *23*(4), 19–39. doi:10.1177/104225879902300402

Collins, J. C., & Porras, J. (2005). *Built to last: Successful habits of visionary companies*. Random House.

Daszkiewicz, N., & Wach, K. (2014). Motives for going international and entry modes of family firms in Poland. *Journal of Intercultural Management*, *6*(2), 5–18. doi:10.2478/joim-2014-0008

Derné, S. (1994). Hindu men talk about controlling women: Cultural ideas as a tool of the powerful. *Sociological Perspectives*, *37*(2), 203–227. doi:10.2307/1389320

Doanh, D. C., & Bernat, T. (2019). Entrepreneurial self-efficacy and intention among Vietnamese students: A meta-analytic path analysis based on the theory of planned behavior. *Procedia Computer Science*, *159*, 2447–2460. doi:10.1016/j.procs.2019.09.420

Ebhardt, T. & Lepido, D. (2021). *Agnelli faces reckoning over bad bet as league dream dies*. Bloomberg.com.

Fitz-Koch, S., Cooper, S. & Discua Cruz, A. (2019). Entrepreneurship and rural family identity: Understanding portfolio development in a family farm business. The family business group phenomenon: Emergence and complexities, 353-383.

Ghosh, D. & Natarajan, P. (2019). *Indian Tech Start-up Ecosystem*. Academic Press.

Grant, S. (2004). *Narrating the body shop: A story about corporate identity*. University of Waikato.

Gubik, A. S., & Farkas, S. (2019). Entrepreneurial intention in the Visegrad countries. *Danube*, *10*(4), 347–368. doi:10.2478/danb-2019-0018

Gupta, S. (2019). Succession Planning in Family Businesses: Lessons from Reliance Industries. *Journal of Family Business Strategy*, *10*, 345–362.

Handler, W. C. (2011). The Role of External Advisors in Family Business: A Review and Extension. *Family Business Review*, *24*, 65–81.

Hanson, S. K., Hessel, H. M., & Danes, S. M. (2019). Relational processes in family entrepreneurial culture and resilience across generations. *Journal of Family Business Strategy*, *10*(3), 100263. doi:10.1016/j.jfbs.2018.11.001

Hernández-Linares, R., López-Fernández, M. C., García-Piqueres, G., Pina e Cunha, M., & Rego, A. (2023). How knowledge-based dynamic capabilities relate to firm performance: The mediating role of entrepreneurial orientation. *Review of Managerial Science*, 1–33. doi:10.100711846-023-00691-4

Hmieleski, K. M., & Baron, R. A. (2008). When does entrepreneurial self-efficacy enhance versus reduce firm performance? *Strategic Entrepreneurship Journal*, *2*(1), 57–72. doi:10.1002ej.42

Hoover, E. A., & Hoover, C. L. (2013). *Getting along in family business: The relationship intelligence handbook*. Routledge. doi:10.4324/9780203949757

Hopp, C. S., & Stephan, U. (2012). The influence of socio-cultural environments on the performance of nascent entrepreneurs: Community culture, motivation, self-efficacy and start-up success. *Entrepreneurship and Regional Development, 24*(9-10), 917–945. doi:10.1080/08985626.2012.742326

Jabbari, B., & Rouster, A. S. (2023). Family Dynamics. StatPearls Publishing LLC.

Kautonen, T., Van Gelderen, M., & Fink, M. (2015). Robustness of the theory of planned behavior in predicting entrepreneurial intentions and actions. *Entrepreneurship Theory and Practice*, *39*(3), 655–674. doi:10.1111/etap.12056

Khavul, S., Bruton, G. D., & Wood, E. (2009). Informal family business in Africa. *Entrepreneurship Theory and Practice*, *33*(6), 1219–1238. doi:10.1111/j.1540-6520.2009.00342.x

Kosuri, P., & Pantin, L. (2021). Nowhere to Run to, Nowhere to Hide. *Clinical Law Review*, *28*, 199.

Kurten, B. (2017). Poland's Transformation. Routledge.

Lansberg, I. (1999). *Succeeding Generations: Realizing the Dream of Families in Business.* Academic Press.

Lee, M.-S., & Rogoff, E. G. (1996). Research note: Comparison of small businesses with family participation versus small businesses without family participation: An investigation of differences in goals, attitudes, and family/business conflict. *Family Business Review*, *9*(4), 423–437. doi:10.1111/j.1741-6248.1996.00423.x

Li & Nazrul. (2021). Entrepreneurial Intentions and Family Support: A Study of Chinese University Students. *Journal of Entrepreneurship*, *13*, 2-23.

Li, Z., & Islam, A. A. (2021). Entrepreneurial intention in higher vocational education: An empirically-based model with implications for the entrepreneurial community. *SAGE Open*, *11*(4). doi:10.1177/21582440211059179

Li, Z., Mirko, C., D'Agostino, M. T., & Jin, J. (2023). Comparative analysis of the influence of Chinese urban and rural family cultures on household financial asset allocation. *Frontiers in Psychology*, *14*, 1119258. doi:10.3389/fpsyg.2023.1119258 PMID:36844357

Liñán, F., & Chen, Y. W. (2009). Development and cross–cultural application of a specific instrument to measure entrepreneurial intentions. *Entrepreneurship Theory and Practice*, *33*(3), 593–617. doi:10.1111/j.1540-6520.2009.00318.x

Luthans, F., & Ibrayeva, E. S. (2006). Entrepreneurial self-efficacy in Central Asian transition economies: Quantitative and qualitative analyses. *Journal of International Business Studies, 37*(1), 92–110. doi:10.1057/palgrave.jibs.8400173

Mahfudzi, A. A. B. & Fitri, R. (2022). *The Influence of Family Environment on Generation Z's Entrepreneurial Intention through Self-Efficacy*. Academic Press.

Malik, A., Sharma, P., Vinu, A., Karakoti, A., Kaur, K., Gujral, H. S., Munjal, S., & Laker, B. (2022). Circular economy adoption by SMEs in emerging markets: Towards a multilevel conceptual framework. *Journal of Business Research, 142*, 605–619. doi:10.1016/j.jbusres.2021.12.076

Miller, D., & Le Breton-Miller, I. (2005). *Managing for the long run: Lessons in competitive advantage from great family businesses*. Harvard Business Press.

Mora, L. & Viana, M. (1993). *Abundance of strange attractors*. Academic Press.

Morales-Gualdrón, S. T., & Roig, S. (2005). The new venture decision: An analysis based on the GEM project database. *The International Entrepreneurship and Management Journal, 1*(4), 479–499. doi:10.100711365-005-4774-7

Moreno, J. E. (2023). How Rupert Murdoch built his media empire. *The New York Times*. Available: https://www.nytimes.com/2023/09/21/business/rupert-murdoch-media-empire.html

Morsing, M., & Schultz, M. (2006). Corporate social responsibility communication: Stakeholder information, response and involvement strategies. *Business Ethics (Oxford, England), 15*(4), 323–338. doi:10.1111/j.1467-8608.2006.00460.x

Musk, E. & Nagelhout, R. (2015). *Elon Musk, AV2 by Weigl*. Academic Press.

Mycoskie, B. (2011). *Start something that matters*. Random House.

Negreira-Rey, M.-C., Vázquez-Herrero, J., & López-García, X. (2022). Blurring boundaries between journalists and tiktokers: Journalistic role performance on TikTok. *Media and Communication, 10*(1), 146–156. doi:10.17645/mac.v10i1.4699

Neneh, B. (2020). Entrepreneurial self-efficacy and a student's predisposition to choose an entrepreneurial career path: The role of self-perceived employability. *Education + Training, 62*(5), 559–580. doi:10.1108/ET-06-2019-0108

Newman, A., Obschonka, M., Schwarz, S., Cohen, M., & Nielsen, I. (2019). Entrepreneurial self-efficacy: A systematic review of the literature on its theoretical foundations, measurement, antecedents, and outcomes, and an agenda for future research. *Journal of Vocational Behavior, 110*, 403–419. doi:10.1016/j.jvb.2018.05.012

Nguyen, C. (2015). Entrepreneurial intention in Vietnam: same as everywhere? SSRN *Electronic Journal.* doi:10.2139/ssrn.3906124

Nosé, L., Korunka, C., Frank, H., & Danes, S. M. (2017). Decreasing the effects of relationship conflict on family businesses: The moderating role of family climate. *Journal of Family Issues, 38*(1), 25–51. doi:10.1177/0192513X15573869

Peng, Z., Lu, G., & Kang, H. (2013). Entrepreneurial intentions and its influencing factors: A survey of the university students in Xi'an China. *Creative Education, 3*(8), 95–100. doi:10.4236/ce.2012.38B021

Pieper, T. M., Klein, S. B., & Jaskiewicz, P. (2008). The impact of goal alignment on board existence and top management team composition: Evidence from family-influenced businesses. *Journal of Small Business Management, 46*(3), 372–394. doi:10.1111/j.1540-627X.2008.00249.x

Piperopoulos, P., & Dimov, D. (2015). Burst bubbles or build steam? Entrepreneurship education, entrepreneurial self-efficacy, and entrepreneurial intentions. *Journal of Small Business Management, 53*(4), 970–985. doi:10.1111/jsbm.12116

Pless, N. M. (2007). Understanding responsible leadership: Role identity and motivational drivers: The case of Dame Anita Roddick, founder of the Body Shop. *Journal of Business Ethics, 74*(4), 437–456. doi:10.100710551-007-9518-x

Rachmawan, A., Lizar, A. A., & Mangundjaya, W. L. (2015). The role of parent's influence and self-efficacy on entrepreneurial intention. *Journal of Developing Areas, 49*(3), 417–430. doi:10.1353/jda.2015.0157

Rahim, M. A. (2023). *Managing conflict in organizations.* Taylor & Francis. doi:10.4324/9781003285861

Ralat, J. R. (2020). *American Tacos: A History and Guide.* University of Texas Press. doi:10.7560/316528

Rosenkranz, C., & Wulf, T. (2019). Behavioral integration as a relational governance mechanism in family firms - The moderating role of family involvement in management. *Journal of Small Business Management, 57*(3), 801–819. doi:10.1111/jsbm.12325

Ryan, J. M. (2020). *Social consequences and cultural adaptations* (Vol. 2). Routledge. doi:10.4324/9781003142065

Sharma, S., & Vredenburg, H. (1998). Proactive corporate environmental strategy and the development of competitively valuable organizational capabilities. *Strategic Management Journal*, *19*(8), 729–753. doi:10.1002/(SICI)1097-0266(199808)19:8<729::AID-SMJ967>3.0.CO;2-4

Shen, L. (2015). *Meet Samsung's billionaire Lee family, South Korea's most powerful dynasty. Business Insider Online*. Business Insider.

Shepherd, D., & Haynie, J. M. (2009). Family business, identity conflict, and an expedited entrepreneurial process: A process of resolving identity conflict. *Entrepreneurship Theory and Practice*, *33*(6), 1245–1264. doi:10.1111/j.1540-6520.2009.00344.x

Sivathanu, B., & Pillai, R. (2020). An empirical study on entrepreneurial bricolage behavior for sustainable enterprise performance of startups: Evidence from an emerging economy. *Journal of Entrepreneurship in Emerging Economies*, *12*(1), 34–57. doi:10.1108/JEEE-01-2019-0009

Smith, A. (2019). The Impact of Family Dynamics on Leadership Succession in Family Business. *International Journal of Management Studies*, *10*, 56–78.

Smith. (2019). Navigating Culinary Authenticity and Health-Consciousness: Challenges Faced by Family-Owned Restaurants. *Journal of Culinary Entrepreneurship*, *3*, 112–128.

Stanwick, P. A., & Stanwick, S. D. (1998). The relationship between corporate social performance, and organizational size, financial performance, and environmental performance: An empirical examination. *Journal of Business Ethics*, *17*(2), 195–204. doi:10.1023/A:1005784421547

Stephan, U., & Pathak, S. (2016). Beyond cultural values? Cultural leadership ideals and entrepreneurship. *Journal of Business Venturing*, *31*(5), 505–523. doi:10.1016/j.jbusvent.2016.07.003

Stephan, U., & Uhlaner, L. M. (2010). Performance-based vs socially supportive culture: A cross-national study of descriptive norms and entrepreneurship. *Journal of International Business Studies*, *41*(8), 1347–1364. doi:10.1057/jibs.2010.14

Sue, D. W. (2016). *Race talk and the conspiracy of silence: Understanding and facilitating difficult dialogues on race*. John Wiley & Sons.

Sun, X., Lee, S.-H., & Phan, P. H. (2019). Family firm R&D investments in the 2007-2009 great recession. *Journal of Family Business Strategy*, *10*(4), 100244. doi:10.1016/j.jfbs.2018.02.004

Supandi, R., Wulandari, S. Z., & Naufalin, L. R. (2022). Influence of Family Circumstances, Peer Circumstances, and Entrepreneurial Learning on Entrepreneurial Interests with Self-Efficacy as Intervening Variables. *Journal of Economics Education and Entrepreneurship*, *3*(2), 140–150. doi:10.20527/jee.v3i2.5233

Turulja, L., Veselinovic, L., Agic, E., & Pasic-Mesihovic, A. (2020). Entrepreneurial intention of students in Bosnia and Herzegovina: What type of support matters? *Economic research-. Ekonomska Istrazivanja*, *33*(1), 2713–2732. doi:10.1080/1331677X.2020.1730216

Vătămănescu, E.-M., Gorgos, E.-A., Ghigiu, A. M., & Pătruț, M. (2019). Bridging intellectual capital and SMEs internationalization through the lens of sustainable competitive advantage: A systematic literature review. *Sustainability (Basel)*, *11*(9), 2510. doi:10.3390u11092510

Vershinina, N., Rodgers, P., Mcadam, M., & Clinton, E. (2019). Transnational migrant entrepreneurship, gender and family business. *Global Networks*, *19*(2), 238–260. doi:10.1111/glob.12225

Wennberg, K., Pathak, S., & Autio, E. (2013). How culture moulds the effects of self-efficacy and fear of failure on entrepreneurship. *Entrepreneurship and Regional Development*, *25*(9-10), 756–780. doi:10.1080/08985626.2013.862975

Whoriskey, P. (2019). Hershey, Nestle and Mars broke their pledges to end child labor in chocolate production. *Washington Post*. Available: https://www.washingtonpost.com/graphics/2019/business/hershey-nestle-mars-chocolate-child-labor-west-africa/

Youssef, A. B., Boubaker, S., Dedaj, B., & Carabregu-Vokshi, M. (2021). Digitalization of the economy and entrepreneurship intention. *Technological Forecasting and Social Change*, *164*, 120043. doi:10.1016/j.techfore.2020.120043

Yusuf, N., Jamjoom, Y. & Saci, K. (2023). Entrepreneurial orientation across gender in Saudi Arabia: evidence from the Adult Population Survey (APS) of Global Entrepreneurship Monitor (GEM). *Journal of Entrepreneurship in Emerging Economies*.

Zellweger, T., Sieger, P., & Halter, F. (2011). Should I stay or should I go? Career choice intentions of students with family business background. *Journal of Business Venturing*, *26*(5), 521–536. doi:10.1016/j.jbusvent.2010.04.001

Zhao, H., Seibert, S. E., & Hills, G. E. (2005). The mediating role of self-efficacy in the development of entrepreneurial intentions. *The Journal of Applied Psychology*, *90*(6), 1265–1272. doi:10.1037/0021-9010.90.6.1265 PMID:16316279

Zhu, F., Burmeister-Lamp, K., & Hsu, D. K. (2017). To leave or not? The impact of family support and cognitive appraisals on venture exit intention. *International Journal of Entrepreneurial Behaviour & Research*, *23*(3), 566–590. doi:10.1108/IJEBR-04-2016-0110

Chapter 7
Authentic Leadership, Entrepreneurial Self-Efficacy, and Family Values

Isaac Idowu Abe
SashBM LLC, USA

Ethel Ndidiamaka Abe
https://orcid.org/0000-0003-1670-6801
SashBM LLC, USA

EXECUTIVE SUMMARY

The case study of this chapter disposes of the notion of profit maximization as the major driving factor of an organization. There are other salient visions that should drive profit maximization. Making a profit becomes the means to an end, not an end. The aim of this chapter is to find the probable connector between entrepreneurial self-efficacy, strong family values, and the kind of leader who possesses these combinations. The knowledge search revealed that a strong interpersonal relationship between the authentic leader to all stakeholders in the organization and the response to the same from the stakeholders to the leader is key to the success of the organization and authentic leadership. Effective leadership performance is linked to high competencies, skills, characteristics, and behaviors in meeting an organization's strategic objectives. The leader must be willing to communicate with employees within and relate to the external stakeholders in holding high the flagship of leadership.

DOI: 10.4018/978-1-6684-8748-8.ch007

INTRODUCTION

The development of leadership abilities has been documented to be rooted in the leader's personal development, self-awareness, and their ability to transform goals and values into an effective influence (Northouse, 2019). It is important to understand the process individual goes through to comprehend themselves, their beliefs, and values. it was established that emerging leaders start their journey of leadership at different stages of self-awareness (Liu, Venkatesh, Murphy & Riggio, 2021). Leadership intentionality demands a primary understanding of these processes to achieve trust and deeper level of the follower's commitment. Therefore, a leader's grip in understanding the theoretical process becomes the immediate task of this discourse (Judge, Woodward, Gilham, Blom, Hoover, Schoeff, & Bellar 2021).

Entrepreneurial success and performance were traced to be positively linked with entrepreneurial self-efficacy (Norena-Chavez, & Guevara, 2020). An individual's level of self-efficacy is instrumental to set challenging goals, subsist towards the achievement of specific goals under volatile, difficult, and stressful conditions, and used to recover from persistent failure under adverse circumstances (Asebedo, & Payne, 2019). Self-efficacy is an individual's belief in their personal capability to accomplish a job or specific set of tasks (Bandura, 2000). Self-efficacy as a concept is the degree to which people perceive themselves as possessing the ability to perform effectively differing roles and tasks of entrepreneurship (Chen, Green, & Crick, 1998). Chen, Gully & Eden, (2004) documented that there is a positive association between general self-efficacy and performance. The attention of this chapter will be on the presence of entrepreneurial self-efficacy coupled with family values as instrumental variables to make an individual authentic leadership success. Several studies that confirm the positive relationships with self-efficacy will also be considered.

Successful family business is evidenced in the different relationships at work. The relationships are between the family business and employees, vendors, customers, and family. Emotionally, these relationships are attributed to family values that make the entrepreneurial businesses distinct (Minola, & Kammerlander, Kellermanns & Hoy 2021). Family firm institute (2021) identified five dimensions of the family values that helps to shape family business behavior. These values are deeply rooted and instrumental in driving the performance of family business decisions and actions that relate to strategy, innovation, corporate governance, stakeholder relations, corporate social responsibility, and effective management practices. The dimensions were derived from higher order values that comprised of openness to change, self enhancement, self-transcendence, and conservation (Schwartz, 1992).

In aligning family values to entrepreneurial self-efficacy coupled with sound leadership behavior, this chapter examined how these variables relate to the success of the family business. Perhaps in between the variables of this chapter lies a strong cord that binds the leader to his entrepreneurial self-efficacy and his family values. Finding the chord is the aim of this chapter. A quality, attitude, and behavior that is synonymous with the variables found in a successful leader.

The successful journey of an entrepreneurial leader over three decades that cannot be traced to specific qualities and virtues become unrelatable to the younger generation and therefore meaningless. Such learning becomes gainful if it can be applied with the hope of certainty of result and positive outcome. Our study is an entrepreneur who started his first job by picking potatoes for ten cents a bag. The man spent twenty-five years of his life finding his way to the top, only to give away reasonable percentage of the family fortune. Therefore, of interest to this chapter is the strong moral standard, honesty, honorableness, patterns of behavior, and integrity of a young man raised with nothing from the high school in Idaho, Utah United States.

LITERATURE REVIEW

Leadership theories have considered the need to not only understand how leaders direct and manage but the unique way they inspire their followers. In the 1920s Max Weber introduced the concept of charismatic leadership in consideration of the attitudes and behaviors of extraordinary leaders in exceptional situations (Yuki, 2010). The purpose was to understand unique and unusual responses of followers. Not long after, transformational leadership theory was developed significantly. The theory differentiated between transactional leadership behaviors and transformational leadership behaviors. Transformational leadership through the provision of insights, centred on the inspiration of extraordinary actions of followers with regards to the importance of ensuring the completion of tasks and outcomes (Chan, 2020). The intention is for the followers to subjugate their interest for the organization, and by motivating subordinates through activation of higher order needs. Higher order needs are social, esteem, and self-actualization needs that are generally satisfied internally within an individual. It is the final category of needs as postulated by Maslow's hierarchy of needs (Smith & Sweet, 2021). In the recent, examples of what is now referred to as neo-charismatic leadership theories are servant leadership, ethical leadership, and visionary leadership.

True leadership is moral authority, not formal authority (Goman, 2017). Leadership is a choice, not a position (Miki, 2019). The choice is to follow universal timeless principles, which will build trust and respect from the entire organization. Those with formal authority alone will lose this respect and trust (Covey, 2022). The behavior of individuals according to a set of rules, principles and values acknowledged collectively as basis for shared good. Examples of ethical leadership include integrity, respect, trust, fairness, transparency, and honesty. Integrity goes beyond honesty, honesty is telling the truth, conforming to reality, but integrity is conforming our reality to our words. Honesty and integrity are the basis of trustworthiness and reliable relationship between the leader and the follower (Kirkpatrick & Locke, 1991). Meanwhile, integrity is the link between word and action, while honesty is being trustful and not deceitful (Covey 2009). Therefore, a leader's personality qualities drive, motivation, honesty, self-confidence, cognitive ability, and knowledge are responsible for leadership (Freeman, Barnes & Long, 2021).

Daniel Kahneman 's psychological research threw limitations on ethical thinking, suggested improvement on ethical decision-making through the concept of bounded rationality due to the ethics domain struggle with bounded ethicality (Kahneman, 2020). At the turn of the millennium, criticism driven by corporate scandals revealed the dark side of charismatic leadership styles. Managerial misconduct, financial impropriety, and accountability crisis rocked many organizations and brought the morality of business executives under question (Einola & Alvesson, 2021). The limitations of ethical behavior gave room to search for a new narrative that is less heroic, more humble leadership concept, where leaders or individuals possess high standards of integrity, highly responsible and make principled decisions rather than short term success. Highly trusted by employees, peers, and stakeholders, with high team performance ability and relationally minded achieving organizational goals, mission, and vision. Authentic leadership traits are commitment to better themselves, cultivation of self-awareness, discipline, mission driven and faith inspiring; that is authentic leadership (Gavin, 2019). Walumbwa, Avolio, Gardner, Wernsing & Peterson (2008) described authentic leadership as "a pattern that draws upon and promotes both positive psychological capacities and a positive ethical climate, to foster greater self-awareness, an internalized moral perspective, balanced processing of information, and relational transparency on the part of leaders working with followers, fostering positive self-development."

Theory of Authentic Leadership

Covelli, & Mason (2017) in a book linking theory to practice on authentic leadership, wrote that the development of an authentic leader is influenced by the following factors: positive psychological capabilities, moral reasoning, and critical life events (Mason, 2017). Positive psychological capabilities are balanced cognitive reasoning and resilience. Balanced reasoning and resilience are the skills that allow a leader to surmount difficulties and challenges and view alternative strategies and consider objective information (Hinojosa, McCauley, Randolph-Seng, & Gardiner, 2014). Balanced processing are the decisions made while considering accounts of all opinions and significant information. The leaders that possess these traits often solicit views that challenge their own decisions (Alliyyani, Wong & Cummings 2018).

Moral reasoning is the decision-making process that is necessary to address moral and ethical dilemmas. Hardships and individual crises that are opportunities for growth are referred to as critical life events (Avolio, & Gardiner, 2005). The trajectory of an authentic leader is a life plagued with series of tragedies that are springboards for gaining self-awareness, life purpose discoveries that assist the authenticity in leadership (Shamir, & Eilam, 2005). It was documented that through life stories, leaders can develop self-discovery and concepts that justify and support their leadership role. Therefore, critical life events allow leaders to gain an increase and better sense of compassion and humanism, that assist leaders to relate with their followers. Positive psychology, moral reasoning and critical life events assist the growth of key characteristics of authentic leaders.

Authentic leadership theorists have identified five key characteristics of an authentic leader, which are: having a defined purpose (George, 2003), leading from the heart (Covelli & Mason, 2017), maintaining relationships (Alliyyani et al, 2018), being self-disciplined (George, 2003) and having strong values (Gardiner, Cogliser, Davis, &Dickens,2011). A prominent characteristic of the authentic leader is the belief that humans are the most important asset of an organization. The framing of human knowledge assists the leader to lead with purpose, while building authentic relationships. Authentic leaders will strive to grow their strengths and work to surmount challenges. The authentic leaders' personality traits are confidence, resilience, hopefulness, optimism, and high moral disposition. If these salient characteristics are undeveloped, authenticity cannot exist.

Neider & Schriesheim, (2011) drew the four-dimensional model of the concept of authentic leadership theories. These are self-awareness, relational transparency, internalized moral perspective, and balanced processing. Self-awareness is understanding how to make meaning of the world and allowing the process to affect self-image over time to create: awareness of strengths, weaknesses, multifaceted nature, and impact of self on others. Relational transparency is presenting self to others, promoting trust through disclosure, information sharing, and expression of true thoughts and feelings. Balanced processing is the objective analysis of relevant data for decision making; a willingness to consider opposing and challenging views of others over yours. Internalized moral perspectives have high moral standards, and strong moral values, making decisions based on those values (Neider & Schriesheim, 2011).

Family Values

Family values are of immense importance to parental structure. It is the factor that is at the base of a single joint activity of community of people connected by marriage, parenthood, relationship. Shiyanov & Kotova, (1999) identified two types of family values, self-sufficient and instrumental values. Self-sufficient values include social status and social importance of family, responsibility to the family, relatives and society, affection, respect and love for children, spouse, and parents. Instrumental values are values- attitudes, values-qualities, values- knowledge, and skills. These values occur in a parental home and are developed and implemented throughout an individual's life as basis of a family man personality (Valeeva, Koroleva, & Sakhapova, 2016).

Family values and family businesses are terms that are both inseparable and synergistic to the family relationships (Hougaz, 2015). Family relationships and family resources are increasingly crucial elements in the dynamics of family business. Family and business are interdependent and are not separable in principles, values, and obligations. Previous studies have suggested that the combination of business and family values are intertwining (Zhu, Thornhill, & Hsu, 2021). The argument was that a persistent commitment to values remains a considerable vice that family can bring to business. Family values have been conceptualized from different points. It is the moral and ethical traditional principles esteemed and passed on to others within the family like fidelity, honesty, truth, and faith (Ochiai, 2014). Therefore, the values are summed up in the form of family structure, function, roles, beliefs, attitudes, and ideals.

According to Matthew Erskine, (2021) in his analysis for Forbes, relationships with employees, vendors, customers, and family describes family values. Five perspectives of the family values are: family control and influence, identification of family members with the business, strong binding social ties both in and out of the business, intense emotional attachments by the family to the business and constant renewal of family bonds across multi-generational succession (Burckart, 2022). These values and their related behaviors are responsible for the success of family business, provided the results obtained are an openness to change (grounded on independence and freedom of choice), self-enhancement of owner-managers (through achievements and power), self-transcendence (by prioritizing the interest of others over self) and conservation (through tradition, conformity, and security) (Erskine, 2021).

Bryan Zitzman (2019) identified ten fundamental values of a strong family. These values are moral values (kindness, integrity, honesty, generosity, courage, patience, and justice). Personal conduct and social behavior (good listening, sharing and showing empathy), spiritual and religious values (young men and women of a particular faith follow specific guidelines for dating, marriage and parenting), family work ethic Achievement, welfarism, volunteerism) Educational values (reading together, investment in books,, visit museums, libraries and lectures collectively), family time, (a meal together daily, encouraging companionship, and maintaining the strong bond), family tradition (keeping the culture, participating in formal and informal rituals and observations), financial values (priorities on planning financial and economic resources), family health and fitness (cooking, hiking, biking and engaging in healthy recreational activities), and family entertainment (fun together, weekends together, and holidays together) (Zitzman, 2019).

Previous studies on family values have been elaborate on literature. The difficulty in the process of adaptation and acculturation through conflict among immigrants required adjustment and flexibility, but that family values were demonstrated when the immigrants integrate well (Nguyen & Williams 1989). Therefore, family values are determinant of the strength and weakness of a family through interpersonal interactions and integrations.

Entrepreneurial Self-Efficacy

An entrepreneur with a high self-efficacy is that individual whose ability to mobilize cognitive resources and plans the actions that generate successful outcome (Hawker, Merkouris, Youssef, & Dowling, 2021), more so, such has a high inclination to learn about entrepreneurial techniques and methods (Chen, Green, & Crick, 1998). Entrepreneurs' self-efficacy is a self-oriented, independent, and self-driven who believes in their ability to take certain risks and learn through entrepreneurial mechanisms and potential operating methods (Vaitoonkiat & Charoensukmongkol, 2020).

The idea of self- efficacy has been documented as a concept that plays an important role in the development of entrepreneurial intentions and actions (Vozikis, 1994). To take the knowledge further, Krueger and Brazeal, (1994) confirmed that by self-efficacy it is possible consider entrepreneurial potential. In examining the role of self-efficacy, it is a pivot variable in evaluating entrepreneurial behavior (Levander & Racuia, 2001), entrepreneurial activities (Markman, & Baron, 2001) and entrepreneurial optimism (Krueger & Dickson, 1994). A perceived high sense of self-efficacy is demonstrated when individuals regard tasks or situations as realizable opportunities (Bandura, 2001). Therefore, such is seen as strong with the feeling of control of the future (Brockhaus, Horwitz, 1986).

Conversely, entrepreneurs' sense of efficacy is weak in a particular field or discipline when the individual avoids difficult tasks or situations and perceives them as threat (Newman, Obschonka, Schwarz, Cohen & Nielsen, 2019). Expression of low aspiration and implication is reduced compared to the set goals. When confronted with difficulties they stumble on their personal failures, the obstacles, and the negative results of their acts rather than concentrate on getting more satisfactory results. The tendency is perceived in decrease efforts and ease of discouragement. Such individual is slow to find sense of efficacy after failure. The plurality of these characteristics minimizes the achievement appropriateness and exposes the entrepreneur to stress and depression. According to Erozkan (2013), interpersonal relations begin and develop with communication, the quality of communication direct interpersonal relationships, and that consequently affect how entrepreneurs feel about themselves.

Major Questions

Having highlighted salient issues in our discourse, the following questions have surfaced.

1. How does the family values affect the success of a family business?
2. What will make an entrepreneur who started at the lowest ebb of life and finds his/her way to the top give away most of the family fortunes to solve global problems?
3. How do leaders bring about change, involve, and motivate their employees to buy into the process of change?
4. Successful entrepreneurial decisions made are in the public domain, some of the decisions are viewed as opportunities or challenges, how does it affect the outcome?
5. Ethics and moral code of conduct are somewhat different around the world with different standards. What are the traits observed around the world that are similar and consistent in ethics?

CASE STUDY

Jon Meade Huntsman was called one of the world's greatest industrialist, philanthropist, and business leader, who wrote the book "Barefoot to Billionaire". Born to a poor family, hitchhiked to a big city ivy league school in a suit fit for Elvis Presley. He was raised with nothing from a small two room house in rural farm community Idaho in United States of American by his father a headmaster in a school who regarded himself as a successful man. He found his youthful days in Idaho to be a great school of ethics, having to love brothers and sisters and people of different races and backgrounds. A Jewish family sent him to Pennsylvania (university), and he has since given away five thousand scholarships. The family never ask anything of him other than" are you honest, have you done your best'. That set the tone and temperament that made him see the world from this same perspective.

He almost went bankrupt four times. Built a chemical empire worth billions of dollars. Seventy-five chemical manufacturing and research and development facilities in more than thirty countries bear his name. Adhesives, insulations, medical and aerospace products, plastic plates, Shampoos, and much more. Many of our most frequently used products are stocked with Huntsman's chemicals. In his world, deals are sealed with handshakes, promises, and a word is a bond notion of commitment that seems to hail from a different time. It sometimes confines those around him. He once conducted a multi-million-dollar deal on a cocktail napkin and could not understand why his lawyers were mortified. In many ways his characteristic charm is both a product of circumstance and a maker of it. His success is made possible from a perfect storm of self-determination, grit, and uncanny happenstance that began when he was summoned to his high school principal's office to find business tycoon Harold Zellerbach, of the crown Zellerbach paper company with a scholarship offer to the Wharton School of Business in Philadelphia.

Huntsman prescience with packaging that set him apart from his Wharton alumni. After a few years of graduating at the top of his class, he took a CEO position at a company called Dolco and proved administratively instrumental in helping the company develop a new form of egg packaging to replace the flimsy cardboard containers that offered eggs little protection. Using a chemical called polystyrene, it was lightweight, cheap to produce, and offered excellent insulation from both heat and cold. He realized that egg cartons were just the beginning. He left Dolco to start the Huntsman container company, Plasticware, like forks and plates, restaurant take-out containers that kept food warm for a long time. He turned this company into Huntsman Corporation, one of the largest petrochemical manufacturers in the world.

With the whole world in his hands, one who battles poverty for his entire childhood did something astonishing. He began to give it away. For Huntsman, philanthropy became an art form. He once dropped in on a homeless shelter and asked for the priest in charge. Handed him a check of a one million dollars. He has no plans to stop. Remarkably, he wants to give his fortune away, all of it to battle homelessness and settle an old score with a bitter enemy.

His entire life was summed up in gaining wealth to give it back to society. An example of that was demonstrated in that he was one of the nineteen people on earth who has given away of over a billion dollars.

To lots of luck and the ability to be surrounded with many talented and skilled people in different disciplines far better than him. Being a risk taker and putting everything on the line time and time again, because of his belief in himself, his team, the products they were manufacturing and the fun in doing those things. Knowing that if they were successful, they will make others successful, happy and bring back some of those heart aches and cracks in some people lives. It is all about learning with opportunities to keep driving and never give up. Lessons learnt on the way to achievement matters as we glide over time.

Academically, it does not matter the school, the grade, or the class to which an individual belongs. What matters is one's drive, one's intelligence with respect to quantitative areas of mathematics, or statistics mindset with which to out negotiate your opponent. Ability to be able to figure out far above opponents, the tools to negotiate acquisitions in business, what the numbers are and how to get the best side of the bargain without having to resort to financial experts. Our organizations have been blessed with competent persons who are rightly talented to handle things effectively. Especially those technological activities that relate to the systems of manufacturing and operations.

There are few entrepreneurs who believe in themselves, most people their ideas and dreams a shot for two to three years after which they throw in the towel by going to work for others. Their claim is that entrepreneurship is not working for them. As far as am concerned these are not true entrepreneurs. True entrepreneurs must truly forego almost everything, put a lot on the line, go through tremendous downswings and still come back fighting and swinging. Must know what it means to -pass through the valley of the shadow of death and keep a positive attitude that you are succeeding even though deep down you know the difference. One who instills energy and hope in others, by helping them regain their confidence.

Whoever refill the glass when it is half full knows that it is half full. "I always look at the good in what we are doing. The positive development of successful acquisitions, successful businesses, and so build on the successes, which may be 20, 25 or 30 percent of the total mix. To avoid concentrating on the negatives, build on the positive side of things.

From the great leaders he worked with in his early days, he learnt a great deal of information about what he will not want to do if given the opportunity to lead people. Through his closeness with President Nixon's administration, he earnt that sometimes we have role leaders who teaches by example what to do. He found that most of his leaders have though great examples of how to do the opposite or some aspect of what they are teaching that he did not want to pursue are picked up from their characteristics. President Nixon was a man of very fair mind, an intelligent man relationally. Through the president he found how to operate with an open mind towards others. He opened relationships with Soviet Union and China in 1971 and Reagan was able to capitalize on the relationship later to open new frontiers. But of course, there was also the negative, dubious side of things.

One of the things to know when borrowing a moral compass is to the difference between right or wrong, good, or bad. I know when someone wants me to do something that I do not want to do. I also know that I could get fired. People know when they are doing something that is not right. I do not believe we need to spend plenty of time debating on what is right or wrong. I have that approach and other have taught me that in schools through proper parentage. In his words "I wanted son s and daughters, wife, and family to be respected with an enormous example of strong moral values. I have chosen the path of strong moral standards, honorableness, honesty, and integrity. Being raised in a farm for me is a great school of ethics.

In his words, "as a young boy I share almost everything I got with my relatives who probably do not have enough or struggled to make ends meet. I will share the little I had that was not much, they will share the little they had that was not much with me. They will let me wear their peer of shoes and their one-dollar wristwatch to class which was a big deal for me. They will let me drive their old pick-up trucks when they taught me how to drive. We will always share what little we had. People who have the means and do not share with others are not my favorite companies. I enjoy sharing with brothers and sisters, people of all races and backgrounds''.

When he went to sign the giving pledge, he had an objection against one. In his opinion, these are friends that give generously towards different projects all over the world. In the giving pledge he gathered a group of forty-five Billionaires who are to give fifty percent of their fortunes away. He felt it was one of the most unusual things he ever heard. The objection came when one of the members in a meeting stood up and said he gave five hundred thousand the other day, another one stood up to counter the story that he gave a million sometime back and all these people are worth billions. So, he stood up from the back and said they should be ashamed of themselves to be giving five to ten percent of their earnings, or at the most fifty percent away. They should be giving eighty to ninety away. Knowing that even the ten percent left is still too much to take care of all their daily lives. The fact is that others need the money much more than them. So, he pleaded for eighty percent. It is all a part and parcel of who you are and your obligation to the people.

Inaugurating the Huntsman Business School Utah State University, he said "the world is changing dramatically, and business students must understand the role of emerging nations. They must study the volatility of currencies to comprehend financial commerce in a dynamic world. Hopefully, we will earnestly seek the most enriching seminars of study that will give our graduating students a jump starts on either Wall Street or Main Street, either in Toronto or Tremonton, either in Beijing or Pocatello. Surely the School of Business on this beautiful and unique campus should strive to teach not only the latest state of the art business practices, but the inculcation of ethics in all its forms to ensure that each graduate is a man or woman of unquestionable integrity. At the end of the day, our character, together with our charity, will determine our ultimate destiny. No matter what the business occasion may bring, no matter what your situation may be personally, if you are ethical and honorable in what you are doing, you will always come out ahead. No exercise is better for the human heart than reaching down and lifting another up. I am humbled that a rural boy could have his name on this school".

Huntsman was a four-time cancer survival himself does not want anyone to suffer from treating cancer. He wants to eradicate it. To do it, he founded the Huntsman Cancer Institute at the University of Utah, one of the most advanced cancer research and treatment organizations in the country. To date, Jon Huntsman has given away nearly 1.6 billion dollars. In a documentary on his passion towards research in Cancer revealed that his grandparents, and immediate parents died of the deadly disease. He was diagnosed with Prostate Cancer; therefore, he made up his mind to overcome the spread of the disease through research. In his contribution to the discovery. development, and eradication of the disease he contributed a hundred million dollars of the family fortune to medical research and fifty-one million dollars to create a research centre. He had focused the tremendous resources of his companies because he has never opened his companies to public shareholding. His company remained the largest privately owned petrol chemical business in the country (The Franklin Institute Awards, 2015).

As a man in his eighties, when asked how he wants to be remembered, he said "First I would like to be remembered as an honorable husband, as a fun and inciteful and loving father, far above else. Close to the two is someone who cares about fellow man and woman with equal feelings of love and concern irrespective of their background, faith, or religion. Someone who just love everybody the same. Jon Huntsman's nine children and twenty-seven grandchildren are his extraordinarily close friends. His dream was to guide them from the sufferings that surrounded his own childhood. Four of his sons and sons in law worked with him in some of the eighty-one facilities spread around the world. The family members remained the shareholders of the corporation. He kept the business private so they could move their money, direct their funds to courses that they believed in, like the funding of a cure for cancer. According to him, that is why the company was created and developed, and that explains the reason for our existence (Vintage Broadcasting System, 1996).

Admonishing people he said" Have the courage to be true to what you know is right. Have faith in yourself. You have great power in your soul every one of you to accomplish something great. The accumulation and use of wealth for the betterment of others is only one form of greatness. A righteous mother and father stand above all others. Obedient children are a blessing to a family, and a humble soul who loves the Lord can achieve great goodness." Quoting Dr Alfred C. Lane of the American Academy of Arts and Sciences, he said, "Faith keeps one true in the dark and humble in the spotlight".

Analysis of the Case

Dr Oliver Tearle in his literature writing had documented that the concept of being true to your self was first traced to William Shakespear's play "Hamlet" (Tearle, 2023). The phrase was used to describe how an individual must be loyal to his best interests first, and then take care of others. However, the modern age has given it a different meaning as it implies the sense of truth, self-ownership, and individuality. Another meaning of the term is that an individual can better judge himself if he/she has done what he/she could have done. Taking the meaning further, one must be honest in his/her ways and relations. The last is that one is expected to do the right thing. Sara L. Johnson, (2019) was of the view that the quality of being real or true in the concept of personal authenticity originated from the ancient Greek philosopher Socrates, who taught on the import of identity and staying true to that personality (Johnson, 2019). The case study of this chapter would have fitted to ethical leadership style, except that our major character demonstrated exceptional authenticity in the family business. Though the entrepreneur under investigation faced difficulties and challenges many times, he was consistent and resilient. Huntsman' was true to himself in his style of leadership due to his pattern of leadership behavior draws on the positive psychological capacities of the followers, fostering a positive ethical climate and self-development (Walumba, Avolio, Gardener, Wernsing, & Peterson, 2008).

Effect of Family Values on Family Business

Family values have been driven by structures, functions, roles, beliefs, attitudes, and ideals in different global cultures (Ochiai, 2014). However, our discourse is mindful of other family value variables other than those just mentioned that can affect the family businesses. These values run between parents and children who are the core of the family. The mechanisms between parent values and children's values have been categorized to include, occupational/social class influences, perceptions of similarity between parents and children, and parental behavior/ childbearing practices (Hitlin & Piliavin, 2004). Value transmission between parents and children can be intergenerational or intragenerational. The affective factors of family values (relational quality) are of more importance than the structural characteristics of family values (entrepreneurial decision-making styles) (Hougaz, 2015). However, our case study was an entrepreneur who had a close relationship with his children and grandchildren. Therefore, parental influence on value is strong from the testimonial of our case study.

Laura Hougaz (2015) on the role of values in family business, expressed the view that strong synergy exists between the family and the business, and both are not detachable; and that makes the subject difficult in terms of principles, values, and obligations. Studies on the subject have suggested that vital interdependence can arise from family values. Consistency in commitment to family values is of great importance to family business. Especially when the role of value is to strengthen the bond between family and business.

Russ Alan Prince, (2016) took a distinct position on the importance of family values in the family business. In a survey conducted it was revealed that 75% of the senior level family member executives surveyed clearly identified family values as determinant of the way business is managed. 90% of the family members attested to the fact that the values were crucial to the economic success and achievements of the businesses. According to Daniel Getrude of the firm's family office practice, in many of the extremely wealthy family businesses, family values play significant role in the strategies of the firm and in business decision making. Therefore, values are the principles upon which affluent and successful families run businesses and live their lives.

The scholarly discussion on family values and family businesses took a different dimension when Astrachan, Astrachan Campopiano & Bau (2020) in a study considered the need to include morality binding values such as religion, spirituality as essential factors for sustaining family business. The influence of these values on the formation and preservation of the family-owned businesses forms the basis for ethical behavior of the family firms in diverse geographic, cultural, and religious contexts. These values looped to shape the personal, professional character of individuals and their decision making and behavior in the business context (Wang & Hackett, 2016). Our case study revealed that the entrepreneur under consideration used his religious values as a root of influence to sustain both his relationship with his children and his firm. Suffice then to say that the value actions of our case study towards his family and the business suggest that values, principles, and norms are guided from the top of the organization (Astrachan et al, 2020).

Faith-Led Business Practices and Decision-Making

Considering the strong affinity that our case study towards philanthropy and organizational decisions to give most of the earned income away, suggests that his actions are deeply rooted in his religious beliefs. Two assumptions that explain his actions are processual perspective on the decision-making process and emergence and development of stewardship in the family business.

Kavas, Jarzabkowski & Nigam, (2020) in a study on the role of religion in business established three mechanisms as keys to the constitution of business activities. The first was that family imports religious practices as business culture; two was that family adheres to religious values as rational for business actions; and three, that family religious values define business restrictions by avoiding the evil eye. Using the concept of value rationality, Max Weber (1968) described the concept as "the conviction of actors that a binding or exigent value can be ascribed to the act: a conscious belief in the unconditional intrinsic value interpreted in ethical, aesthetic, religious or other terms of a specific act purely as such and independent of the outcome". The stamp of value rationality is the authenticity of the actor's commitments over their ultimate obligations. Guy Oakes, (2003) further explained that religion is the most dominant value sphere (Oakes, 2003).

The concept of value rationality in business suggests that value rational organizations are those which adhere to an absolute religious belief, and that prescribes the legitimacy of actions (Weber, 1968). However, religion is a dominant and shared meaning system that defines the nature of rationality. The shared dominant meaning system may prompt and guide people to take value rational actions in their business settings. Therefore, the study revealed that religious values assist people to constitute their business actions in ways that are ethical and value rational. Family business values derived from and reinforced by religion may both enable and constrain business activities in the firm (Kavas, Jarzabkowski, Nigam, 2020).

Carradus, Zozimo, & Discua, (2020) documented in a study that explored faith-led open systems of stewardship in family businesses. Using the autobiographies of six family business leaders who openly expressed their adherence to their faith. Riding on the stewardship theory proposed by Davis, & Schoorman, (1997) that "both psychological and situational mechanisms influence the behaviors of organizational actors. Stewards gain greater long-term utility from prosocial and collective behaviors than from economic, individualistic, and self-serving ones" (Neubaum, Thomas, & Dibrell, 2017). The study revealed that "the values, intentions, motivations and skills of the individual determine the actions and behaviors of the same individual solely or as part of a larger group"' (Pieper, & Klein, 2007). It is through relationship with God that faith-led practices emerge, and stewardship occurs and gains form over time. Collective goals in stewardship are achieved through personal power of the leader not by organizational power. The power stems from interpersonal relationships are built over time through sound communication, mutual trust, norms of reciprocity, gain recognizable by a knowledgeable leader, teamwork, and information exchange (Abe & Mason, 2016). Therefore, leaders can transform organizational practices with an understanding of what they expect from them as part of an extended spiritual family.

Leadership Commitment to Change and Motivation of Employees

Leadership failure in many organizations have been adduced to lack of efficiency and integrity of leaders; failure to incorporate human side of organizational change and collapse due to fraudulent practices by leaders (Trevino, den Nieuwenboer, & Kish-Gephart, 2014). Conversely, leaders must be true in factual sharing information, accept responsibility, avoid deceptive practices and lead by integrity and authenticity. Authentic leaders take decisions with utmost transparency and openness, involve followers in the decision-making process by encouraging their opinion and viewpoint in decisions that are based on true facts and figures after seeking due information from all relevant persons in the organization (Bakari, Hunjra & Niazi, (2017). In the context of planned organizational change, the burden for ethical and moral climate rests on the shoulders of the authentic leader.

The readiness for change in an organization is the degree to which organizational members are psychologically and behaviorally prepared to implement change in the firm. Armenakis, & Bedeian, (1999) proposed three step models that incorporated the elements of social learning theory. The first step is readiness, which means enhance readiness and decrease resistance. The second step is adoption and the third is institutionalization. Creating the readiness for change, making available incentives, and implementing the desired change through the application of leadership style to distil the behaviors where organization has reached the desired state. The mechanism applied by the leader to create a positive attitude by means of affecting previous beliefs and leading employees to enduring behaviors is best known as the theory of planned behavior. The pivot of the theory is that actual behavior is the function of intention which depends on attitude, subjective norm, and perceived behavioral control (Ajzen, 2002). Therefore, authentic leadership is readiness, commitment, and behavioral support (Bakari Hunjra, & Niazi, 2017).

The target of commitment is imperative where the focus of the leader is to take the organization from status quo to a new point of equilibrium. Commitment to change as defined by Herscovitch & Meyer (2002) as “a mindset that binds an individual to a course of action deemed necessary for the successful implementation of a change initiative”. This mindset may reflect affective commitment to change (supporting the change initiative based on the belief that change will bring benefits), continuous commitment to change (understanding that not supporting the change to incur unaffordable costs) and normative commitment to change (supporting the change based on a sense of obligation and duty). These three-step commitment to change is different from commitment to organization. The steps inform the commitment of both the leader and the followers to change in the organization. Only affective commitment to change was found positively significant among the behaviors (Bakari, Hunjra, & Niazi, 2017). Readiness enhances follower’s commitment to change through effective communication of the benefits of change (Appelbaum, Degbe, MacDonald & Nguyen-Quang, 2015). Therefore, the role of leaders is crucial in successful implementation of planned organizational changes.

Entrepreneurial Self-Efficacy

When an individual is a high achiever, the success of such is alluded to challenges turned into opportunities, the self-efficacy of such is viewed as high. Sometimes an entrepreneur can receive negative feedback, but in a constructive way utilize this feedback to enhance their performance and efficiency. Entrepreneurial self-efficacy operates under the premise that the leader beliefs in their proficiency to be successful (McGee, Peterson, Mueller & Sequeira, 2009). The leader should be self-responsible in all decision-making processes (Kumar & Sihag, 2012). Thus, entrepreneurship fosters a sense of confidence within the entrepreneur.

De Noble, Jung, & Ehrlich, (1999) on the association between entrepreneurial self-efficacy and entrepreneurial action described six dimensions including skills in risk and uncertainty management, innovation and product development, interpersonal and networking management, opportunity recognition, procurement and allocation of critical resources and development and maintenance of innovative environment. All the skills are positively associated with entrepreneurial intentions.

Using the intentionality model of entrepreneurship, Kumar, & Shukla, (2022) explored the mediating role of entrepreneurial self-efficacy on innovation, creativity, and proactivity of entrepreneurial intentions. Self-efficacy strongly predicted the intention of entrepreneurship. The study implied that entrepreneurs should be encouraged to be proactive, innovative, and creative for meaningful contribution to the economy and society. Training received by entrepreneurs elsewhere in the past either as public servants or administrative personnel in an organization can be utilized in the present firm. Therefore, personality development training of entrepreneurs should be encouraged to bring out the leader in them.

Behavioral decision approaches suggested that the effects of behavioral biases highly depend on the level of uncertainty in the decision environment (Thaler, 2018) When uncertainty is high, leaders tend to shift from rational models of decision-making, but as uncertainty is lessened, leaders tend to adopt more rational approaches to decision-making Lerner, Hunt & Dimov, 2018). Moreover, whether the decision-making is causal or effectual, self-efficacy has been instrumental in predicting a positive relationship.

Opportunities are regarded as gaps in the market that entrepreneurship has not tapped, and the unexplored opportunities are targets areas that leaders search for. The opportunities identified are dynamic processes that lead to continuously refined and reiterated (Schmitt, Rosing, & Zhang, 2018). Entrepreneurs' strife to constantly develop and change these ideas that form business opportunities. The ability to identify opportunities forms earlier conditions of being an entrepreneur through business performance and enterprise development. The ability increases to identify opportunities increases through the reflection of these abilities either when the business starts or development stage of the business. Therefore, active leadership vigilance about the environment is important for new ideas, collection of appropriate and effective information about new products or services in the market.

Hirsh, Mar & Peterson, (2012), in a framework for understanding uncertainty-related anxiety posited that uncertainty poses a critical challenge for entrepreneurs, such that leaders motivate followers to find ways to keep it at manageable levels. High Entrepreneurial self-efficacy was found to deal with increased uncertainty and overcome threat and anxiety. Whereas Schmitt Rosing, Zhang & Leatherbee, (2018) in a dynamic model of self-efficacy examined how dynamic fluctuations of perceived uncertainty are related to the number of business opportunities available to entrepreneurs. The changes embedded in perceived uncertainty initiate opportunity. This actively engages the entrepreneur with activities like experimentation with new approaches and processes, redesigning one's products or services and searching for new domains and new opportunities with respect to markets or products (Shahzadi, & Khurram, 2020). Therefore, uncertainty and opportunity are tools for business expansion for the entrepreneur.

Similar Global Ethical Leadership Practices

Ethical leadership traits have been described from the competencies of the leader. These competencies are the general qualities that enable an individual to perform their job separate from their own national as well as organizational culture, no matter what their educational or ethnic background is, what functional area their job description represents, or what organization they come from (Rickley, & Stackhouse, 202).

Previous studies have identified lists of global competency traits for effective global leaders Kim & McLean, (2015). Kakeman, Liang, Janati, Arab-Zozani, Mohaghegh, & Gholizadeh, (2020) in what was called MCAP framework competency identified evidence, resources, knowledge, communications, leadership and change as themes that emerged. Among the competencies identified by earlier scholars are global thinking, appreciation of cultural diversity, development of technological knowhow, partnership and alliance building, information sharing in leadership (Goldsmith, Bates & Davies, 2003). Other frameworks on leadership competencies emphasize core competencies that form fundamental characteristics (such as self-awareness and inquisitiveness) desired mental characteristics that guide a leader's action and behavior (like empathy, and cognitive skills), and desired behavioral competencies that include the important skills and knowledge associated with performance (e.g., networking skills). Emerging competencies are intercultural skills and awareness (Story & Barbuto, 2011), interpersonal awareness and skills (relationship management/ holistic competency) (Idowu, Ndidiamaka, 2018). Global mindset and knowledge (Kim. & McLean, 2015), change and vision (Yukl, 2006) Kim, J., & McLean, G.

N. (2015). An integrative framework for global leadership competency: Levels and dimensions. *Human Resource Development International*, *18*(3), 235-258.

Most of the studies on disposition/traits of global leaders proposed interpersonal competencies as a critical element for global leadership. Different terms have been used to describe it including close relationships (Campbell, Simpson, Kashy, & Fletcher, 2001), interpersonal skills (Bird, Mendenhall, Stevens, & Oddou 2010), interpersonal intelligence (Boyd, Moore, Williams, & Elbert, 2011), virtual team building skills (Huang, Ding, & Chen 2014), maintaining team emotional stability (Mobley & Dorfman, 2003). In his proposition on competency framework, Jokinen (2005) documented three dimensions of competencies, core, mental and behavioral competencies identified interpersonal skills and behavioral competencies between social skills and networking skills. Social skills are more informally enacted on a personal level, and networking skills relate to building formal relationships in the organization. Strong social skills and communication are important aspects of a leader's competency (Terrell & Rosenbusch, 2013).

Consolidating Our Thoughts

The decisions, attitudes, behaviours, and actions of our case study in leadership is rooted in specific concepts that were earlier discussed. These concepts alluded to the fact that certain actions of an actor are based on the specific convictions. For example, a leader that is religious will drive the family values along his own personal convictions. That is the concept of value rationality. It explains the rationale behind faith-led family businesses and practices. Same reasoning holds for the concept of stewardship, where the values, intentions, motivations, and skills of a leader is a strong determinant of the actions, behaviors of a larger group. Meanwhile the dominant influence is the leader's faith orientations and convictions. Therefore, our case study is a man whose religious convictions affect his style of leadership and entrepreneurial success.

At the core of the variables under consideration in this chapter is the recurrence of the word "interpersonal relationship". Which describes the strength of an authentic leader? The cord that holds communications, knowledge, resources, evidence, professionalism and change in an organization on one hand, family value structure, function, roles, beliefs, attitudes, and ideals on the other hand is interpersonal relationship. This relationship runs between the leader and the followers as a team at work, the same runs between the parents and their children at the family level. Stephen Covey, (2009) in a quote on everyday greatness documented that "the most important element we put into any goal or relationship is not what we say or what we do or what we have, but who we are.

In our case study, we heard Mr. Jon Huntsman made his sons leaders of the corporation, allowing all managerial decisions to be made at the family level. According to him "the objective is to bring the family to work and relate as members of one big family".

The leader's ability to balance the inputs and needs of followers while ensuring the collective goals are met comes to the fore. Regulate their own behavior and emotions. Ensure constituency between spoken words and actionable decisions from the heart that make for peace and balanced cognitive reasoning and resilience.

Recommendations

The attention of this discourse is drawn to global leadership competencies and efficiency tied to meeting the strategic objectives of an organization and improving interpersonal relationships within and outside the organization. The recommendations are according to the competencies identified towards organizational high performance. The assumption is that a leader is a high performing individual with success in managing many organizations. The following are the strategic recommendations visible in the circumstance of this case.

Leadership evidence is the development of high performing leaders who use their skills, characteristics, and behaviors to perform their roles effectively and help business meet strategic objectives. The evidence will be seen in human resource appraisals, application and evaluation of decision, and informed decision-making (Ismael & Shanmugam, 2021).

Clearly defined leadership knowledge that is encompassing and unlimited is needed, these are sets of skills attitudes and behaviors that a leader needs to be effective in various types of organizations. Knowledge needed is that which relates to both the environment and the organization in specific. The knowledge dimension may be political, social, religious, and economic in all ramifications (Guillory, 2022).

The leader should be resource oriented. Leadership resources are achieved through proper recruitment, retention of competent leaders internally and by external sourcing. Organizational resources are made available through operations, administration, and resource management. This is effective through staff, finance, and organizational management (Chadwick & Dabu, 2009).

Managing relationships within and outside the organization demand that the leadership should be willing to relate with all employees in the organization and outside the organization (Abe & Abe, 2021). The lifeblood of interpersonal relationships is communication (Abe, & Mason, 2016), whether the repairs of interpersonal conflict or social support relationships at work. Communication is manifested in relationship management and teamwork, communication, and personal quality of individuals (Abe, 2021).

The complexity of the management suggested that leadership competencies change over time and talent management strategies underpinned by integrated and formalized strategic Human Resource Management are important, given the instability that change may cause and the place of change in the organization. Change includes the organization's preparation in anticipation of change, the leader's personal involvement in the preparation for change, implementation and evaluation of change, and leaders' quality of change (Korbi, 2015).

The act of leading people and teams, leading organizations demand that the leader engage with competent employees that can take the organization to the next level through quality leadership (Hajiali, Budiandriani, Prihatin, & Sufri, 2022).

CONCLUSION

The evidence gathered from scholarly work on authentic leadership, family values and the interface of entrepreneurial self-efficacy suggested that workplace interpersonal relationships play a central and pivotal role in shapening the success of the leader. Leadership success may be characterized by the vertical relationships between a leader and his subordinates. The leader extends the relationship built with family to the workplace, thereby making the workplace an extension of the family. It was the aim of this chapter to search out the missing link between the variables that are pointers to the success of a leader. That gap is the interpersonal relationship of the organizational stakeholders. Stakeholder relationship becomes the web that ring organizational objectives to role players. This link revealed in this chapter can be further subjected to empirical analysis for authenticity and scholarly recognition.

REFERENCES

Abe, I. I. (2021). The Dynamics of Workplace Relationships, Employee Well-Being, and the Fourth Industrial Revolution: Perspectives of Workplace Relationships and Industry 4.0. In Future of Work, Work-Family Satisfaction, and Employee Well-Being in the Fourth Industrial Revolution (pp. 99-112). IGI Global.

Abe, I. I., & Abe, E. N. (2021). Leadership/Followership Interface and the Workplace of the Future: Who Leads? In Future of Work, Work-Family Satisfaction, and Employee Well-Being in the Fourth Industrial Revolution (pp. 69-80). IGI Global.

Abe, I. I., & Mason, R. B. (2016). *The role of individual interpersonal relationships on work performance in the South African retail sector*. Academic Press.

Ajzen, I. (2002). Perceived behavioral control, self-efficacy, locus of control, and the theory of planned behavior 1. *Journal of Applied Social Psychology, 32*(4), 665–683. doi:10.1111/j.1559-1816.2002.tb00236.x

Aliyyani, Wong, & Cummings. (2018). Antecedents, mediators, and outcomes of authentic leadership in healthcare: A systematic review. *PubMed, 83*, 34–64. PMID:29684833

Appelbaum, S. H., Degbe, M. C., MacDonald, O., & Nguyen-Quang, T. S. (2015). Organizational outcomes of leadership style and resistance to change (Part One). *Industrial and Commercial Training, 47*(2), 73–80. doi:10.1108/ICT-07-2013-0044

Armenakis, A. A., & Bedeian, A. G. (1999). Organizational change: A review of theory and research in the 1990s. *Journal of Management, 25*(3), 293–315. doi:10.1177/014920639902500303

Asebedo, S., & Payne, P. (2019). Market volatility and financial satisfaction: The role of financial self-efficacy. *Journal of Behavioral Finance, 20*(1), 42–52. doi:10.1080/15427560.2018.1434655

Avolio, B., & Gardner, W. L. (2005). Authentic leadership development: Getting to the root form of positive forms of leadership. *The Leadership Quarterly, 16*(3), 315–338. doi:10.1016/j.leaqua.2005.03.001

Bakari, H., Hunjra, A. I., & Niazi, G. S. K. (2017). How does authentic leadership influence planned organizational change? The role of employees' perceptions: Integration of theory of planned behavior and Lewin's three step model. *Journal of Change Management, 17*(2), 155–187. doi:10.1080/14697017.2017.1299370

Bandura, A. (2000). Exercise of human agency through collective efficacy. *Current Directions in Psychological Science, 9*(3), 75–78. doi:10.1111/1467-8721.00064

Bird, A., Mendenhall, M., Stevens, M. J., & Oddou, G. (2010). Defining the content domain of intercultural competence for global leaders. *Journal of Managerial Psychology, 25*(8), 810–828. doi:10.1108/02683941011089107

Boyd, B. L., Moore, L. L., Williams, J., & Elbert, C. D. (2011). Entry-level competencies needed for global leaders. *International Leadership Journal, 3*(1), 20–39.

Campbell, L., Simpson, J. A., Kashy, D. A., & Fletcher, G. J. (2001). Ideal standards, the self, and flexibility of ideals in close relationships. *Personality and Social Psychology Bulletin, 27*(4), 447–462. doi:10.1177/0146167201274006

Carradus, A., Zozimo, R., & Discua Cruz, A. (2020). Exploring a faith-led open-systems perspective of stewardship in family businesses. *Journal of Business Ethics*, *163*(4), 701–714. doi:10.100710551-019-04387-2

Chadwick, C., & Dabu, A. (2009). Human resources, human resource management, and the competitive advantage of firms: Toward a more comprehensive model of causal linkages. *Organization Science*, *20*(1), 253–272. doi:10.1287/orsc.1080.0375

Chan, S. C. (2020). Transformational leadership, self-efficacy, and performance of volunteers in non-formal voluntary service education. *Journal of Management Development*, *39*(7/8), 929–943. doi:10.1108/JMD-03-2020-0078

Chen, C. C., Greene, P. G., & Crick, A. (1998). Does entrepreneurial self-efficacy distinguish entrepreneurs from managers? *Journal of Business Venturing*, *13*(4), 295–316. doi:10.1016/S0883-9026(97)00029-3

Chen, G., Gully, S. M., & Eden, D. (2004). General self-efficacy and self-esteem: Toward theoretical and empirical distinction between correlated self-evaluations. *Journal of Organizational Behavior*, *25*(3), 375–395. doi:10.1002/job.251

Covelli, B. J., & Mason, I. (2017). Linking theory to practice: Authentic leadership. *Academy of Strategic Management Journal*, *16*(3), 1–10.

Covey, S. R. (2009). *Everyday greatness: Inspiration for a meaningful life*. Thomas Nelson.

Covey. (2022). *Trust and inspire: How truly great leaders unleash greatness in others*. CIO Summit of America New York. HMG Strategy. Hmgstrategy.com/resources.

Davis, J. H., Schoorman, F. D., & Donaldson, L. (1997). Toward a stewardship theory of management. *Academy of Management Review*, *22*(1), 20–47. doi:10.2307/259223

De Noble, A. F., Jung, D., & Ehrlich, S. B. (1999). Entrepreneurial self-efficacy: The development of a measure and its relationship to entrepreneurial action. *Frontiers of Entrepreneurship Research, 1999*(1), 73-87.

Einola, K., & Alvesson, M. (2021). The perils of authentic leadership theory. *Leadership*, *17*(4), 483–490. doi:10.1177/17427150211004059

Family Firm Institute. (2021). *Global conference Shaping futures: Evolve, Emerge, Engage*. Ffi.org/conference/2021-ff

Freeman, H., Barnes, L., & Long, W. R. (2021). *Leading Change Without Formal Authority: The ICC Model for the 21st Century*. Academic Press.

Gardner, W. L., Cogliser, C. C., Davis, K. M., & Dickens, M. P. (2011). Authentic leadership: A review of the literature and research agenda. *The Leadership Quarterly, 22*(6), 1120–1145. doi:10.1016/j.leaqua.2011.09.007

Gavin, M. (2019). Working industrially or professionally? What strategies should teacher unions use to improve teacher salaries in neoliberal times? *Labour & Industry: A Journal of the Social and Economic Relations of Work, 29*(1), 19-33.

George, B. (2003). *Authentic leadership: Rediscovering the secrets to creating lasting value* (Vol. 18). John Wiley & Sons.

Goldsmith, G. M., Bates, I. P., Davies, J. G., McRobbie, D., Webb, D. G., Wright, J., & Quinn, J. (2003). A pilot study to evaluate clinical competence in junior grade pharmacy practitioners. *Pharmacy Education, 3*(2), 127–134. doi:10.1080/15602210310001604044

Goman, C. K. (2017). *The power of collaborative leadership*. Institute for Management Studies. https://www.ims-online.com

Guillory, W. (2022). The Future Perfect Organization: Driven by Quantum-Thinking. *Innovative Leadership in Times of Compelling Changes: Strategies, Reflections and Tools*, 337-352.

Hajiali, I., Kessi, A. M. F., Budiandriani, B., Prihatin, E., & Sufri, M. M. (2022). Determination of Work Motivation, Leadership Style, Employee Competence on Job Satisfaction and Employee Performance. *Golden Ratio of Human Resource Management, 2*(1), 57–69. doi:10.52970/grhrm.v2i1.160

Herscovitch, L., & Meyer, J. P. (2002). Commitment to organizational change: Extension of a three-component model. *The Journal of Applied Psychology, 87*(3), 474–487. doi:10.1037/0021-9010.87.3.474 PMID:12090605

Hinojosa, A. S., McCauley, K. D., Randolph-Seng, B., & Gardner, W. L. (2014). Leader and follower attachment styles: Implications for authentic leader–follower relationships. *The Leadership Quarterly, 25*(3), 595–610. doi:10.1016/j.leaqua.2013.12.002

Hirsh, J. B., Mar, R. A., & Peterson, J. B. (2012). Psychological entropy: a framework for understanding uncertainty-related anxiety. *Psychological Review, 119*(2), 304. doi:10.1037/a0026767 PMID:22250757

Hougaz, L. (2015). *Entrepreneurs in family business dynasties: Stories of Italian-Australian family businesses over 100 Years*. Springer. doi:10.1007/978-3-319-13918-0

Huang, S., Ding, D., & Chen, Z. (2014). Entrepreneurial leadership and performance in C Chinese new ventures: A moderated mediation model of exploratory innovation, exploitative innovation, and environmental dynamism. *Creativity and Innovation Management*, *23*(4), 453–471. doi:10.1111/caim.12085

Idowu, A. I., & Ndidiamaka, A. E. (2018). The influence of supervisor/subordinate social support on employee performance in the South African retail sector. *The Journal of Business and Retail Management Research*, *12*(3). Advance online publication. doi:10.24052/JBRMR/V12IS03/ART-01

Ismael, A. M., & Shanmugam, K. (2022). Knowing your roots, enhancing oral proficiency of elementary students in Kurdistan using oral presentation as an alternative assessment in the family tree task. *Practitioner Research*, *4*(1), 35–51. doi:10.32890/pr2022.4.3

Jokinen, T. (2005). Global leadership competencies: A review and discussion. *Journal of European Industrial Training*, *29*(3), 199–216. doi:10.1108/03090590510591085

Judge, L. W., Woodward, S. C., Gillham, A. D., Blom, L. C., Hoover, D. L., Schoeff, M. A., Fox, B., Burt, T., & Bellar, D. M. (2021). Efficacy Sources that Predict Leadership Behaviors in Coaches of Athletes with Disabilities. *Journal of Human Kinetics*, *78*(1), 271–281. doi:10.2478/hukin-2021-0056 PMID:34025884

Kahneman D. (2020). *Thinking fast and slow*. Farrar, Straus, and Giroux. https//: amazon.com/Thinkingfastandslow

Kakemam, E., Liang, Z., Janati, A., Arab-Zozani, M., Mohaghegh, B., & Gholizadeh, M. (2020). Leadership and Management Competencies for Hospital Managers: A Systematic Review and Best-Fit Framework Synthesis. *Journal of Healthcare Leadership, 12*, 59–68.

Kavas, M., Jarzabkowski, P., & Nigam, A. (2020). Islamic family business: The constitutive role of religion in business. *Journal of Business Ethics*, *163*(4), 689–700. doi:10.100710551-019-04384-5

Kim, J., & McLean, G. N. (2015). An integrative framework for global leadership competency: Levels and dimensions. *Human Resource Development International*, *18*(3), 235–258. doi:10.1080/13678868.2014.1003721

Kirkpatrick, S. A., & Locke, E. A. (1991). Do traits matter. *The Academy of Management Executive*, *5*(2), 48–60.

Korbi, K. (2015). Leadership and strategic change. *The Journal of Organizational Management Studies*, *2015*, 1–32. doi:10.5171/2015.638847

Kumar, A., & Sihag, S. (2012). Traits of Entrepreneurs of Small-Scale Sector. *IUP Journal of Entrepreneurship Development, 9*(2).

Kumar, R., & Shukla, S. (2022). Creativity, proactive personality and entrepreneurial intentions: Examining the mediating role of entrepreneurial self-efficacy. *Global Business Review, 23*(1), 101–118. doi:10.1177/0972150919844395

Lerner, D. A., Hunt, R. A., & Dimov, D. (2018). Action! Moving beyond the intendedly rational logics of entrepreneurship. *Journal of Business Venturing, 33*(1), 52–69. doi:10.1016/j.jbusvent.2017.10.002

Liu, Z., Venkatesh, S., Murphy, S. E., & Riggio, R. E. (2021). Leader development across the lifespan: A dynamic experiences-grounded approach. *The Leadership Quarterly, 32*(5), 101382.

Mason, P. (2017). Identifying the barriers to female leadership in Paramedicine. *Irish Journal of Paramedicine, 2*(1). Advance online publication. doi:10.32378/ijp.v2i1.55

Matthew. (2021). Family values and success of the family business. *Forbes Money/ Wealth Management*. Forbes.com/sites/matthewerskine/2021/02/17family-values.

McGee, J. E., Peterson, M., Mueller, S. L., & Sequeira, J. M. (2009). Entrepreneurial self–efficacy: Refining the measure. *Entrepreneurship Theory and Practice, 33*(4), 965–988. doi:10.1111/j.1540-6520.2009.00304.x

Miki, M. (2019). How organisations waste real talent without realising. *Governance Directions, 71*(10), 591–594.

Minola, T., Kammerlander, N., Kellermanns, F. W., & Hoy, F. (2021). Corporate entrepreneurship and family business: Learning across domains. *Journal of Management Studies, 58*(1), 1–26. doi:10.1111/joms.12672

Mobley, W. H., & Dorfman, P. W. (2003). *Advances in global leadership*. JAI An imprint of Elsevier Science.

Neider, L. L., & Schriesheim, C. A. (2011). The authentic leadership inventory (ALI): Development and empirical tests. *The Leadership Quarterly, 22*(6), 1146–1164. doi:10.1016/j.leaqua.2011.09.008

Neubaum, D. O., Thomas, C. H., Dibrell, C., & Craig, J. B. (2017). Stewardship climate scale: An assessment of reliability and validity. *Family Business Review, 30*(1), 37–60. doi:10.1177/0894486516673701

Newman, A., Obschonka, M., Schwarz, S., Cohen, M., & Nielsen, I. (2019). Entrepreneurial self-efficacy: A systematic review of the literature on its theoretical foundations, measurement, antecedents and outcomes, and an agenda for future research. *Journal of Vocational Behavior, 110*, 403–419. doi:10.1016/j.jvb.2018.05.012

Norena-Chavez, D., & Guevara, R. (2020). *Entrepreneurial passion and self-efficacy as factors explaining innovative behavior: A Mediation Model.* Academic Press.

Northouse, P. (2019). *Leadership: Theory and Practice* (8th ed.). Sage.

Oakes, G. (2003). Max Weber on value rationality and value spheres: Critical remarks. *Journal of Classical Sociology, 3*(1), 27–45. doi:10.1177/1468795X03003001693

Ochiai, E. (2014). Leaving the West, rejoining the East? Gender and family in Japan's semi-compressed modernity. *International Sociology, 29*(3), 209–228. doi:10.1177/0268580914530415

Pieper, T. M., & Klein, S. B. (2007). The bulleye: A systems approach to modeling family firms. *Family Business Review, 20*(4), 301–319. doi:10.1111/j.1741-6248.2007.00101.x

Rickley, M., & Stackhouse, M. (2022). Global leadership effectiveness: A multilevel review and exploration of the construct domain. *Advances in Global Leadership, 14*, 87–123. doi:10.1108/S1535-120320220000014004

Schmitt, A., Rosing, K., Zhang, S. X., & Leatherbee, M. (2018). A dynamic model of entrepreneurial uncertainty and business opportunity identification: Exploration as a mediator and entrepreneurial self-efficacy as a moderator. *Entrepreneurship Theory and Practice, 42*(6), 835–859. doi:10.1177/1042258717721482

Schwartz, S. H. (1992). Universals in the content and structure of values: Theoretical advances and empirical tests in 20 countries. In Advances in experimental social psychology (Vol. 25, pp. 1–65). Academic Press. doi:10.1016/S0065-2601(08)60281-6

Shahzadi, K., & Khurram, S. (2020). Self-efficacy and innovative work behavior: The role of individual ambidexterity and formalization at workplace in Pakistan. *Journal of the Research Society of Pakistan, 57*(1), 31.

Shamir, B., & Eilam, G. (2005). "What's your story?" A life-stories approach to authentic leadership development. *The Leadership Quarterly, 16*(3), 395–417. doi:10.1016/j.leaqua.2005.03.005

Shiyanov, E. N., & Kotova, I. B. (1999). *Development of the person in training*. Academic Press.

Smith, C. M., & Sweet, J. (2021). Analyzing the Relationship between Maslow's Hierarchy of Needs and Consumer Spending Patterns. *Journal of Financial Service Professionals*, *75*(4).

Story, J. S., & Barbuto, J. E. Jr. (2011). Global mindset: A construct clarification and framework. *Journal of Leadership & Organizational Studies*, *18*(3), 377–384. doi:10.1177/1548051811404421

Terrell, S., & Rosenbusch, K. (2013). Global leadership development: What global organizations can do to reduce leadership risk, increase speed to competence, and build global leadership muscle. *People and Strategy*, *36*(1), 40.

Thaler, R. H. (2018). From cashews to nudges: The evolution of behavioral economics. *The American Economic Review*, *108*(6), 1265–1287. doi:10.1257/aer.108.6.1265

Treviño, L. K., Den Nieuwenboer, N. A., & Kish-Gephart, J. J. (2014). (Un) ethical behavior in organizations. *Annual Review of Psychology*, *65*(1), 635–660. doi:10.1146/annurev-psych-113011-143745 PMID:23834354

Valeeva, R. A., Korolyeva, N. E., & Sakhapova, F. K. (2016). Case-Study of the High School Student's Family Values Formation. *International Journal of Environmental and Science Education*, *11*(7), 1641–1649.

Walumbwa, F. O., Avolio, B. J., Gardner, W. L., Wernsing, T. S., & Peterson, S. J. (2008). Authentic leadership: Development and validation of a theory-based measure. *Journal of Management*, *34*(1), 89–126. doi:10.1177/0149206307308913

Weber, M. (1968). *On charisma and institution building* (Vol. 322). University of Chicago Press.

Yuki, G. (2010). *Leadership in Organizations* (7th ed.). State University of New York, Albany.

Yukl, G. (2006). Leadership in Organization (6th ed.). Pearson Prentice Hall.

Zhu, F., Thornhill, S., & Hsu, D.K. (2021). When owner family and community roles intertwine: Examining entrepreneurs' persistence decisions and the gender effect. *Journal of Small Business Management, 59*(sup1), S102-S133.

Zitzman B. E (2019). *What are family values and why are they important?* Beliefnet.com/love-family/family-values.aspx.

Chapter 8
Can Entrepreneurial Skills Development Mitigate Poverty Among Dropped Out High School Teenage Mothers in North-Central Nigeria?

Louis Okon Akpan
National Open University of Nigeria, Nigeria

EXECUTIVE SUMMARY

Recently, it was observed that a majority of girls dropped out of high schools due to early marriage, pregnancy, and poverty in North Central Zone of Nigeria. This led to the increase of out-of-school children which is now put at 12 million. Based on the conversation, the researcher seeks to examine whether entrepreneurial skills development do mitigate poverty among now teenage mothers in the zone. Two research questions guided the study. Furthermore, qualitative approach was used as research design for the study. Six focus groups were formed to elicit information for the study. Additionally, semi-structured interview was developed; thereafter, narrative analysis was adopted to analyse the data. It was discovered that teenage mothers were engaged in sewing and needle work, laali design, and mobile phone repairs. Similarly, it was also found that teenage mothers' acquisition of entrepreneurial skills has a great impact on their financial autonomy, poverty reduction, and improving the Nigerian economy.

DOI: 10.4018/978-1-6684-8748-8.ch008

INTRODUCTION

Nigeria is abundantly blessed with enormous human and natural resources. There is no part of the country where one particular natural resource or the other is not found. For instance, in Akwa Ibom state, there is crude oil, in Zamfara state gold is found, in Enugu state, there is abundant deposit of Iron Ore, more so, cassiterite is found in Plateau state, among others. In the area of human resource, Nigerians have excelled in various professions such as medicine, law, engineering, teaching, among others. Apparently, the success story of these Nigerians in various fields is a function of their doggedness in achieving their goals in the face of extreme hardship and unfriendly business environment. However, it is sad to say that most Nigerians who could not navigate this harsh situation are made to face abject poverty. In other words, most Nigerians go to bed every day without food because of high level of poverty. The few, who manage to eat one meal per day, do so from the position of extreme struggle and resilience (Ogbe, 2020). This chapter examines entrepreneurial skill development among high-school drop-out teenage mothers to understand its role in poverty mitigation in North Central Nigeria.

Background of the Study: Poverty in Nigeria

In addition, World Bank Report (2022) reports that every eight in ten Nigerians live below the national poverty line. This claim was corroborated by Uzoho (2022) who stated that Nigeria has maintained the infamous position as the poverty capital of the world, with over 93.9 million people currently living below the poverty line. This situation was further compounded by the recent outbreak of coronavirus 2019 (COVID-19) in the world which sent most families in Nigeria to unimaginable hardship and lack levels (Chitiga, Henseler, Mabugu, & Maisonnave, 2022). Andam, Edeh, Oboh, Pauw and Thurlow (2020) opine that during the COVID-19 outbreak, about 17 million more people fell into poverty in Nigeria, a country that already accounted for the highest absolute number of poor people in Sub-Saharan Africa. Farley (2020) postulate that COVID-19 has made females secondary school to servitude, prostitutes, street hawkers, among others on the ground of making ends meet. Similarly, Gichuna, Hassan, Sanders, Campbell, Mutonyi and Mwangi (2020) are of the view that women and girls suffered adversely during the COVID-19 pandemic because of increased poverty, Akanbi, Ope, Adeloye, Amoo, Iruonagbe and Omojola (2021) food insecurity, and unplanned pregnancies as well as reduced access to healthcare, water, and sanitation. These unfortunate situations eventually resulted in an alarming rate of school dropout among female teenagers.

In Nigeria, particularly in North Central Nigeria, millions of young teenage girls were forced to drop out of school due to early pregnancy occasioned by force early marriage (Okoli, Hajizadeh, Rahman, Velayutham & Khanam, 2022). Uyanga (2009) stated that the unfortunate situation has made these teenage girls become teenage mothers overnight, thereby putting them further into perpetual lack and poverty. To arrest this ugly trend among these vulnerable groups of people, the Ministry of Women Affairs, Non-Governmental Organisations (NGOs) and some religious bodies in Nigeria are orgainsing entrepreneurial skills so as to move them out of lack and poverty. However, one common question among Nigerians is whether entrepreneurial skills development mitigates attrition and poverty among high school teenage mothers in North Central Nigeria? In this context, the following questions are formulated to guide the study:

a) What kind of entrepreneurial skills training are high school dropout teenage mothers exposed to after dropping out of school?
b) What impact does entrepreneurial skills development have on teenage mothers' entrepreneurial activity after dropping out of school?

LITERATURE REVIEW

Theoretical Framework Underpinning the Study

The theoretical framework that underpins this study is the innovative theory of entrepreneurship developed by Schum-Peter in 1932. The concept of innovation is probably Schumpeter's most distinctive contribution to economics (Śledzik, 2013). However, this scholar conceptualised innovation from the perspective of introducing a new manufacturing process that has not yet been tested and commercially exploited or by introducing a new product with which the customers are not familiar and locating a new source of raw material or semi-finished product that was not exploited earlier, opening a new market, hitherto unexploited, where the company products were not sold earlier, developing a new combination of means of production (Upadhyay & Rawal, 2018). In fact, Wei, Liu and Sha (2019) sees innovation as nothing other than new combination of factor of production which unavoidably breaks the repetitious cycle of economic and market activities. Furthermore, Rae (2010) stated that an entrepreneur is the one who engages in creative activity. Therefore, the principal function of an entrepreneur is to reform or revolutionise the pattern of production by exploiting an invention, or Wei, Liu and Sha (2019) an untried technological possibility for producing a new commodity or producing an old one in a new way, by opening a new source of supply of materials or a new outlet for products, by reorganizing an industry and so on (Guerrero & Urbano, 2019). Innovation theory in education simply means doing things in a new way, requiring different approaches, processes, products, or strategies (Andam, Edeh, Oboh, Pauw & Thurlow, 2020). Optimal learning activity for livelihood sustenance occur when teenage mothers who dropped out of school engage in new entrepreneurial skills training to find the solution to their poverty situation, hence it relevance in the study under investigation.

The Entrepreneur and Entrepreneurship

Amitabh (2017) looks at entrepreneurship as a process of creating or developing a new business venture in order to make a profit. Similarly, Arogundade (2011) views the entrepreneur as a person who possesses the ability and innovation to develop a business where none exists. Therefore, an entrepreneur constantly engages with new markets and tries to figure out how to supply those markets efficiently to make a profit (Ogwu, 2023). Here, one would easily conclude that an entrepreneur can be considered as an innovator or creator of wealth. An entrepreneur does not engage in any business which does not generate profit (Kannampuzha & Hockerts, 2019). He/she usually takes risk to come up with a new product so as to maximise profit and create wealth. Entrepreneurship is a platform for youths to transform opportunities to business ventures towards creation of jobs and poverty reduction (Okehi, 2019).

Entrepreneurial Skills Development

Before now, the federal government of Nigeria has not made provisions to cater for the needs of teenage mothers who dropped out of school who were left on their own through the childbirth process resulting from their teenage pregnancies. Clearly, the government did not put in place any tangible plan to provide for the various needs of the participants. Therefore, they were exposed to all sorts of challenging issues ranging from hawking, drug abuse, servitude, prostitution, among others, for survival. Choji (2014) in his study on 'why we are on the streets*?' r*eported that teenage mothers who dropped out of secondary school comfortably competed with older women to offer their bodies to men. In another circumstance, Wildsmith, Manlove, Jekielek, Moore and Mincieli (2012, p.12) stated that "teenage mothers are less likely to finish their education and are more likely to bring up their child alone and in poverty" Primarolo and Merron (2010) went further to aver that children born from teenage mothers are likely at increased risk of poverty, low educational attainment, poor housing, poor health and have lower rates of economic activity in adult life. Notwithstanding the position held by Primarolo and Merron (2010), Wiggins et al. (2005) argued that teenage mothers were also significantly more likely than older mothers to be living on welfare benefits, experiencing unemployment, lacking in school and university qualifications and living in social housing.

However, in order to curtail the social ills from happening, the Federal government of Nigeria through the Federal Ministry of Women and Humanitarian Affairs in recent time introduced different intervention programmes to break the cycle of poverty which enveloping teenage mothers. In Kenya, Okore (2021) teenage mothers who dropped out of school was supported through engaging them in business management skills to enable to attain financial independent. Additionally, Primarolo and Merron (2010) have mentioned that Leicestershire Teenage Pregnancy Partnership (LTPP) in order reduce poverty among teenage mothers have place a high priority on supporting teenage parents into learning skills that will enable them to achieve above average level of participation of thirty-three per cent in Education, Employment and Training (EET) for mothers aged 16-19.

Challenges Facing Teenage Mothers' High School Dropped Out

Studies have shown that teenage mother faces lot of challenges ranging from (Zachry, 2005) stigmatisation, low self-esteem, poverty and rejection by family members. Stigmatisation is a sign of social unacceptability or rejection (Moonga, 2015). Stigmatisation is a process of enculturating discrimination against people judged to be abnormal, thereby creating insider and outsider social status (Ahmed, & Yola, 2021). Gillham (1997) opined that bias against teenage mothers often results in cruel social stigmatization. They are isolated from classes or sitting arrangement so as not to contaminate others (Moonga, 2015). Furthermore, a study carried out by Nkiruka (2020 indicated that most teenage mothers run away from school due to societal sigmatisation and seclusion.

Teenage mothers who dropped out of school always suffer from low self-esteem (Moonga, 2015). Huang, Roberts, Costeines and Kaufman (2019) reported that teenage mothers always feel bad about themselves. Low self-esteem causes teenage mothers to focus on their flaws rather than their strengths and always in doubt of their ability to achieve success (Pinquart & Gerke, 2019). In light of the above, Moonga (2015) submitted that low self-esteem resulted to teenage mothers realising their full potential in life hence fall into depression.

Poverty among teenage mothers is one of the strongest predictors of success which most of these girls do not cope well with (Moonga, 2015). Mokgabalone (1999), Rohmah, Yusuf, Hargono and Laksono (2020) reported that teenage pregnancy significantly disrupt schooling, which usually resulted to poverty among them. Similarly, Mwansa (2011) held that poverty is a plausible explanation of school disruption for teenage mothers which compelled most of them to school dropout.

Wanyama and Simatwa (2011) stated that teenage mothers suffer discrimination from family member or community. It was reported by Wanama and Simatwa that most community members see teenage mothers who dropped out of school as prostitutes. On the isssue of marriage, Bucknall and Bick (2019) opined that teenage mothers have difficulty getting married as they not or rarely accepted by young boys, rather, they were readily sex objects in the hands of elderly men. In line with above argument, Moonga (2015) submitted that old men take them for granted and sexually abuse them for small favours they sought from them.

Research Methodology

This study follows qualitative research approach. According to McBride, MacMillan, George, and Steiner (2019), qualitative approach is better in research because it enables researcher(s) to observe the complex cultural mechanisms that determine the patterns of transfers which cannot be understood or captured through conventional quantitative methods. Furthermore, qualitative research method is valuable in providing rich descriptions of complex phenomena; tracking unique or unexpected events (Morgan, 2022). Drawing from the above scholarly position, the researcher adopted the qualitative approach in order to have a better understanding of the problem and yield more complete evidence from the participants. Based on this approach, the researcher uses interpretive paradigms to make sense and also to understand the conversation in which participants narrated.

Population

The population of the study is the entire teenage mothers who dropped out from secondary schools in six states in north central zone of Nigeria. The states of the zone consist of Benue, Kogi, Kwara, Nasarawa, Niger, and Plateau. Similarly, all teenage mothers who dropped out of schools from the zone formed the population of this study. The researcher adopted purposive sampling technique to select the sample size. The choice of the sampling techniques is because the participants selected met the predetermined criteria for the study (Mthuli, Ruffin & Singh, 2022), which is teenage mothers who dropped out of schools and are engaged or engaging entrepreneurial skill development to start an entrepreneurial activity.

Purposive sampling technique was used to select sixty teenage mothers that dropped out of schools formed the sample size. In other words, ten participants were purposively selected from each of the six states of the zone, therefore, making the total of sixty participants. To elicit information from the participants, the researcher developed semi structured interview questions. In line with qualitative research, the researcher subjected the instrument to transferability and credibility (which is validity and reliability respectively in quantitative methods), and the instrument was found to answer the research questions developed.

The researcher reasoned that to engage all the participants in one-on-one interview will be very difficult to access and time-consuming because they are settled in different locations in their different states. Therefore, to address the challenges, a focus group interview was organised for the participants in each state. For clarity, Benue is focus group 1 (F.G.1) Kogi (F.G. 2), Kwara (F.G. 3), Nasarawa (F.G. 4) Niger (F. G. 5), and Plateau (F.G.6). During the focus group conversation, which was held in each state political capital, the researcher deployed audio tape recording and note-taking. According to Ngoasheng, Ngoepe and Marutha (2022), audio tape used during interview allow one to get everything the interviewee says word-for-word, while, note taking permits the researcher time to jot down important points which appear in non-verbal communication, hence its application in this study.

ETHICAL CONSIDERATIONS

This study involves teenage mothers, the participants' confidentiality and anonymity was adhered to strictly. Again, consent letter was drafted for the participants to sign for their willingness to take part in the study.

Data Analysis

Data collected from the field were transcribed manually. The choice of manual transcription is based on Tang's (2023) assertion that manual transcription allows the researcher to immerse in the data and provides justification for the dynamics that are often lost in completing audio-to-text transcription. After data transcription, it was coded, and the emerging themes were analysed using narrative analysis.

Findings

Research Question 1: What kind of entrepreneurial skills training were teenage mothers exposed to after being dropped out of school?

The themes that emerged from the first research questions are as follows; Sewing and Needle work, laali design and mobile phone repairs.

Sewing and Needle Work

Majority of the participants in all the focus groups reported that government and some religious organisations set up training centres where they (teenage mothers) are trained in sewing and needle work. A participant in F.G.3 specifically reported that her situation was pathetic immediately she discovered that she was pregnant in her second year of senior secondary school. She went further to state that she was forced to drop out of school and her parents who ought to have given her support made the matter worse by driving her out of their home. She narrated how she gave birth and raised the child under terrible condition. However, the situation changed for the better when she was introduced into sewing and needle work by a Non-Governmental Organisation (NGO) called Girls' Power Initiative. She concluded that her condition and her child's own have greatly improved. In her own words about how her condition and that of her child has improved, she declared:

I was always very sad the time was not engaged meaningfully. I was psychologically stressed and my parents always referred to me as a failure because I brought shame to the family. To make matter worst, my child's father did not help to care for our child. However, as soon as I was introduced into sewing and needle work by this organisation, I was able to stand on my own and care for my child.

In a similar manner, FG1 reported that aside from the religious bodies that assisted most teenage mothers by empowering them, Federal Ministry of Women Affairs also built some skills empowerment centres where most of the school dropped out teenage mothers are trained in needle works. The interviewer was quick to probe further by asking them the types of needlework they learned or are currently learning. In the reply, one of the participants in FG1 said.

"I glad to inform you that I am being trained on the making different types of handbags." Another participant still in the group declared, "Currently, I have designed different type of earrings, beads and necklaces for various celebrities in my community and I have made lot of money through this work."

From the above narrative, both religious bodies and Federal Ministry of Women Affairs set up skill empowerment centres in North Central Zone of Nigeria to empower teenage mothers who dropped out from school due to early marriage, pregnancy, poverty, among others.

Laali Design

Teenage mothers also stated that some of them who could not be trained on sewing and needle work decided to pick a different vocation. When the interviewer questioned those participants on the type of vocation others decided to specialise on, they responded in chorus*; "some of us have decided to choose Laali designing as a vocation."* The interviewer was compelled to ask the FG5 to explain how *Laali* look like. Instead of responding to the question asked, they handed over the picture that clearly showed a woman who was designed previously on *Laali (*see picture below).

Figure 1. Picture showing a woman' designed with Laali
Source: Picture from the participants of this study

Reacting to the above picture given by the FG5, the interviewer was quick to ask questions such as what is the cost for making Laali design, and on which occasion is the design made for? Responding, FG5 declared.

The amount charged for making one design is determined by the status of the client. If the client is rich monetarily, she will be charged to pay more. However, if she is an average client, she will be made to pay averagely. Most women used Laali on their wedding day or going on special occasion.

The above excerpt indicated that some of the teenage mothers who dropped out of school were empowered in Laali design. The interviewer was informed that laali design is often used during weddings and for special occasions such as Oba and Emir's (chieftaincy) coronation ceremonies. It was further stated that price for each design is a function of the client's social and economic status.

Mobile Phone Repairs

The issue of empowerment of the participants through training in mobile phone repair was equally raised. FGs 2 and 4 reported that when they were first informed by the officials of Ministry of Women Affairs that some teenage mothers will be trained in the area of mobile phone repair, they were a bit apprehensive because they were of the view that the job was only meant for men. However, they were so excited to later discover that mobile phone repair is not a male-dominated dominated job. Based on the narrative from these participants, the interviewer asked if they enjoy working as mobile phone repairers. In response to this question, FG 4 declared.

The simple truth is that repairing mobile phone for people is very interesting, because you meet all manners of people. Aside from that, we make a lot of money from the work.

Similarly, FG 6 believed that mobile phone repair is a very creative job in Nigeria today because there is no family where there is no mobile phone. In fact, the participants went on to say that there are at least three mobile phones in every family in the country, therefore, there are possibilities of these mobile phones getting spoiled due to poor handling by the owners. The spoiled phones are taken to the repairers by the owners for repairs. FG 6 concluded that in Nigeria today repairing damaged mobile phones is a viable money-making business which many people underestimated.

Research Question 2: What impact does entrepreneurial skills development have on teenage mothers' entrepreneurial activity after dropping out of school?

The themes that emerged from the second research question are teenage mothers' financial independence, poverty reduction and contribution to regional economy.

Teenage Mothers' Enjoyment of Financial Independence

The interviewer was reliably informed by all the focus groups that subjecting school dropped out teenage mothers to entrepreneurial skills development by the Federal Government of Nigeria via Ministry of Women Affairs and NGOs was the best thing to ever happen to them. They based their assertion on the fact that the skills acquired have significantly impacted their financial independence. FG1 and 2 specifically reported that all of them who were trained in one entrepreneurial skill or the other have enjoyed financial independence. The interviewer went further to ask for their explanation of the concept 'financial independence.' In response, FG1 declared:

Sir, what we mean by 'financial independence' is that all of us who specialised in one vocation or the other, we can comfortably feed and cloth ourselves and children without necessarily looking for any kind of financial assistance from our parents. In fact, most of us are now bread winners in our different homes.

In similar circumstance, FG3 and 5 narrated that they are extremely happy by the opportunity government provided to most of the teenage mothers who dropped out of school to pick up the pieces of their lives again after the society had written them off. They reported that their parents who usually spoke ill against them before, now praise them for providing food for all members of the family. The interviewer was informed by majority of the participants in FG6 that due to financial autonomy they are now enjoying their lives, most of them are planning to re-enrol in school to complete their educational programmes.

Poverty Reduction

The interviewer was also informed by all the focus groups that acquiring different skills is very advantageous because it has reduced poverty in their families. FG4 specifically narrated that before entrepreneurial skills acquisition, they found it extremely difficult to feed once a day. Moreover, they were often subjected to various verbal abuses by their parents and neighbours due to their (teenage mothers) inability to provide for the family what to eat. According to FG3 and 5, the acquisition of various skills has provided them money to solve their fundamental needs, which invariably reduced poverty in their families and conversely, communities.

In a similar reaction, FG1 declared:

Though, poverty cannot be eradicated in Nigeria because of some government policies. However, currently we can reasonably say that poverty in our families have been reduced by certain percentage due to our acquisition of different entrepreneurial skills. In fact, it is also possible for our family to eat at least two times a day, unlike before where to eat once was not feasible.

From the narrative, it can be observed that there was poverty reduction among teenage mothers' households due to their ability to work and earn a living legitimately. In fact, vocations engaged by these participants were able to provide money for their livelihood. Parents who hitherto saw the teenage mothers as 'never 'do well' people due to their inability to provide for themselves and family, suddenly saw them become 'saviours' based on the fact that they are now breadwinners to the family.

Contributing to Regional Economy

All the participants agreed that the acquisition of entrepreneurial skills has not only made them self-sufficient monetarily and reduced poverty in their families, rather, it also contributed significantly to the regional economy. FG 2 stated that most of the locally designed handbags produced by them are being sold overseas.

The interviewer was very curious to establish the authenticity of the participants' assertion, therefore, he asked how they know that their handbags are sold outside the country. In their response, they said:

We knew that our products (handbags) are shipped to countries such as South Africa, Botswana, Britain among others through some women who always patronised. They often tell us to improve the quality of the products because it is marketed outside the country.

FG 6 made the interviewer to understand that their products immensely contribute to Regional income, employment, productivity and entrepreneurial skill training. Additionally, FG 1 averred that their products are among the driver of economic growth in the region which ensures a paramount shift from groundnuts and onions export as a major source of government revenue to a service driven economy.

DISCUSSION

All the participants in this study agreed that they engaged in various vocations because of the ugly situations all of them found themselves, namely, falling pregnant as teenage girls and dropping out of school. It was discovered that these teenage mothers committed one mistake or the other which made them to drop out of school. Based on the foregoing, they were regarded by their parents and community as nuisance, therefore, to reclaim their lost image, teenage mothers were introduced into entrepreneurial skills such as sewing and needle work, laali design and mobile phone repairs by the Federal Ministry of Women Affairs and some NGOs. The essence of introducing teenage mothers to entrepreneurial skills development is to arrest the alarming rate of out of school children in Nigeria which is put at twelve million (Ogunode & Adanna, 2022). Furthermore, Aborisade (2019) supported the findings by saying that training teenage mothers on entrepreneurial skills provided or helped them to earn legitimate livelihood, therefore, quit prostitution.

From the second research question, it was discovered that teenage mothers benefited immensely by earning more money to themselves through the sales of their products to the public. In fact, it was found that teenage mothers were able to feed themselves and their wards from the proceeds of the handiwork. Furthermore, it was revealed that aside from having financial autonomy, hence, there was noticeable reduction in poverty in their household. Okolie, Ehiobuche, Igwe, Agha-Okoro and Onwe (2021) supported the findings when they said that rural Igbo women involvement in basket weaving enterprise significantly helps their families out of poverty. Mubecua and David (2019) had already stated that there is a positive relationship that exists between entrepreneurial skill development and poverty reduction. In order circumstance, in line with the findings which indicated that the teenage mothers' products contribute largely to the Nigeria economy. This finding is affirmation of Yunusa and Paul (2018) assertion who reported that girls' entrepreneurial skill revolution is effective tool for poverty reduction, employment generation and enhancement of Nigeria's economy.

CONCLUSION

The researcher wondered why teenage mothers who dropped out of high schools were regarded as nuisance by their parents and the society at large. The amazement is because most of them were redundant with no tangible means of livelihood. However, it was discovered that the Federal Government of Nigeria through Ministry of Women Affairs and NGOs introduced various skills acquisition centres to train them on various skills to be useful to themselves and the society. This compelled the researcher to question whether entrepreneurial skills development does mitigate poverty among teenage mothers who dropped out of school. The research found that these teenage mothers seized the opportunity provided by the government and NGOs to develop their skills on sewing, needle work, laali, and mobile phone repair skills. Similarly, based on the fact that they are meaningfully engaged skill wise, they are financially autonomous, they witnessed poverty reduction among their household and they also contribute immensely to Nigeria's economy.

RECOMMENDATIONS

Based on the findings, the following recommendations were reached.

a). Lack of adequate training on sex education by teenage mothers' parents was the cause of teenage pregnancy, therefore, they usually experiment unprotected sex on their own which led to unwanted pregnancy and eventual dropped out of school.

b). Federal, state and local governments should introduce counseling service for teenage mothers to support them emotionally during pregnancy and child's care.

c). Ministry of Education should ensure that teenage mothers who dropped out of school are encouraged to re-enroll and complete their education.

REFERENCES

Aborisade, R. A. (2019). Police abuse of sex workers in Nigeria: Evidence from a qualitative study. *Police Practice and Research, 20*(4), 405–419. doi:10.1080/15614263.2018.1500283

Akanbi, M. A., Ope, B. W., Adeloye, D. O., Amoo, E. O., Iruonagbe, T. C., & Omojola, O. (2021). Influence of socio-economic factors on prevalence of teenage pregnancy in Nigeria. *African Journal of Reproductive Health, 25*(5s), 138–146. PMID:37585778

Amitabh, S. (2017). *What is entrepreneurship?* Retrieved from http://www.paggu.com/entrep

Andam, K., Edeh, H., Oboh, V., Pauw, K., & Thurlow, J. (2020). Impacts of COVID-19 on food systems and poverty in Nigeria. In *Advances in food security and sustainability* (Vol. 5, pp. 145–173). Elsevier.

Arogundade, B. B. (2011). Entrepreneurship education: An imperative for sustainable development in Nigeria. *Journal of Emerging Trends in Educational Research and Policy Studies, 2*(1), 26–29.

Chitiga, M., Henseler, M., Mabugu, R. E., & Maisonnave, H. (2022). How COVID-19 pandemic worsens the economic situation of women in South Africa. *European Journal of Development Research, 34*(3), 1627–1644. doi:10.105741287-021-00441-w PMID:34421229

Choji, L. D. (2014). *Energy Demand And Economic Growth In Nigeria* [Doctoral dissertation]. Eastern Mediterranean University (EMU)-Doğu Akdeniz Üniversitesi (DAÜ).

Farley, M. (2020). Prostitution, the sex trade, and the COVID-19 pandemic. *Logos, 19*(1), 1–34.

Gichuna, S., Hassan, R., Sanders, T., Campbell, R., Mutonyi, M., & Mwangi, P. (2020). Access to Healthcare in a time of COVID-19: Sex Workers in Crisis in Nairobi, Kenya. *Global Public Health: An International Journal for Research, Policy and Practice, 15*(10), 1430–1442. doi:10.1080/17441692.2020.1810298 PMID:32816628

Guerrero, M., & Urbano, D. (2019). A research agenda for entrepreneurship and innovation: the role of entrepreneurial universities. *A research agenda for entrepreneurship and innovation*, 107-133.

McBride, K. A., MacMillan, F., George, E. S., & Steiner, G. Z. (2019). *The use of mixed methods in research.* Academic Press.

Mokgaabalone, M. B. (1999). Social- cultural conditions, teenage pregnancy and schooling disruptions: Themes from teachers and teenage in "poor rural" Schools. *South African Journal of Education, 19*(1), 191–237.

Moonga, G. M. (2015). *Challenges faced by teen mothers who re-entered School: A case of selected Schools on the Copper belt Province of Zambia* [Doctoral dissertation].

Morgan, H. (2022). Conducting a Qualitative Document Analysis. *Qualitative Report, 27*(1), 20–34.

Mthuli, S. A., Ruffin, F., & Singh, N. (2022). 'Define, Explain, Justify, Apply' (DEJA): An analytic tool for guiding qualitative research sample size. *International Journal of Social Research Methodology, 25*(6), 809–821. doi:10.1080/13645579.2021.1941646

Mubecua, M. A., & David, O. J. (2019). So far so good? Tracking the poverty eradication goal of SDGs in Kenya, Nigeria, and South Africa. *Journal of Public Affairs, 19*(4), e1964. doi:10.1002/pa.1964

Mwansa, A. (2011). *Re-entry to school after giving birth: An evaluation of the process used to design and implement policy in Zambia*. Create pathways to access, research monograph no.70.

Ngoasheng, C., Ngoepe, M., & Marutha, N. S. (2022). Sounds like a broken record: Preservation and access of audio-visual records at the South African broadcasting corporation radio. *Global Knowledge. Memory and Communication, 71*(4/5), 383–397. doi:10.1108/GKMC-11-2020-0185

OgbeA. (2020). The travails of women and girls in Northern Nigeria: A human rights issue. Available at SSRN 3599122.

Ogunode, N. J., & Adanna, C. M. (2022). An Analysis of Factors Responsible for High Out of School Children in Nigeria and Way Forward. *International Journal on Integrated Education, 5*(6), 194–202.

Ogwu, E. N. (2023). Challenges in implementing entrepreneurship education (ee) for youth's empowerment at the post-basic education level in Nigeria. *International Journal of Studies in Education, 16*(1), 209–219.

Okehi, F. (2019). Adopting new strategies in social entrepreneurial education: A panacea to the daunting challenges of the 21st century entrepreneurs (sociological approach). In M. A. Mkpa, Compendium of curriculum theorizing, development, designing & innovation in Nigeria (pp. 703-707). Owerri: C @ J Publishers.

Okoli, C. I., Hajizadeh, M., Rahman, M. M., Velayutham, E., & Khanam, R. (2022). Socioeconomic inequalities in teenage pregnancy in Nigeria: Evidence from Demographic Health Survey. *BMC Public Health*, *22*(1), 1–11. doi:10.118612889-022-14146-0 PMID:36096790

Okolie, U. C., Ehiobuche, C., Igwe, P. A., Agha-Okoro, M. A., & Onwe, C. C. (2021). Women entrepreneurship and poverty alleviation: Understanding the economic and socio-cultural context of the Igbo women's basket weaving enterprise in Nigeria. *Journal of African Business*, *22*(4), 448–467. doi:10.1080/15228916.2021.1874781

Olowu, D. I., Ichoku, H. E., & Nwosu, E. O. (2018). Spatial distribution of poverty in multiple dimensions in Delta State of Nigeria. *Journal of Economics and Allied Research*, *2*(2), 32–44.

Pinquart, M., & Gerke, D. C. (2019). Associations of parenting styles with self-esteem in children and adolescents: A meta-analysis. *Journal of Child and Family Studies*, *28*(8), 2017–2035. doi:10.100710826-019-01417-5

Primarolo, D & Merron, G. (2010). *Teenage Pregnancy Strategy: Beyond 2010*. Academic Press.

Rae, D. (2010). Universities and enterprise education: Responding to the challenges of the new era. *Journal of Small Business and Enterprise Development*, *17*(4), 591–606. doi:10.1108/14626001011088741

Rohmah, N., Yusuf, A., Hargono, R., & Laksono, A. D. (2020). Determinants of teenage pregnancy in Indonesia. *Indian Journal of Forensic Medicine Toxicology*, *14*(3), 2105–2110.

Schumpeter, J. A. (1932). *Capitalism, Socialism and Democracy* (3rd ed.). George Allen and Unwin.

Tang, R. (2023). Manual Transcription. In *Varieties of Qualitative Research Methods: Selected Contextual Perspectives* (pp. 295–302). Springer International Publishing. doi:10.1007/978-3-031-04394-9_47

Upadhyay, C. S., & Rawal, P. (2018). A critical study of Joseph A. Schumpeter's innovation theory of entrepreneurship. *International Journal of Creative Research Thoughts*, *6*(2), 1678–1686.

Uyanga, R. E. (2009). The Disadvantage in a Culturally Diversified Society: Focus on the Girl Child in Northern Nigeria. *The International Journal of Diversity in Organisations, Communities and Nations*, *8*(6), 1–8. doi:10.18848/1447-9532/CGP/v08i06/39672

Uzoho, M. (2022). *High level of Poverty in Nigeria*. Sage.

Wei, X., Liu, X., & Sha, J. (2019). How does the entrepreneurship education influence the students' innovation? Testing on the multiple mediation model. *Frontiers in Psychology*, *10*, 1557. doi:10.3389/fpsyg.2019.01557 PMID:31354574

Wiggins, M., Oakley, M., Austerberry, H., Clemens, F., & Elbourne, D. (2005). *Teenage parenthood and social exclusion: A multi-method study: Summary of report findings*. Social Science Research Unit, Institute of Education, University of London.

Wildsmith, E., Manlove, J., Jekielek, S., Moore, K. A., & Mincieli, L. (2012). Teenage childbearing among youth born to teenage mothers. *Youth & Society*, *44*(2), 258–283. doi:10.1177/0044118X11398366 PMID:31511752

Yunusa, A., & Paul, A. A. (2018). Assessment of the contributions of small scale enterprises to the development of the Nigerian economy. *Journal of Good Governance and Sustainable Development in Africa*, *4*(1), 37–47.

Zachry, E. M. (2005). Getting my education: Teen mothers experiences in school before and after motherhood. *Teachers College Record*, *107*(12), 2566–2598. doi:10.1111/j.1467-9620.2005.00629.x

Chapter 9
Succession and Survival Plan for Family Business:
Lessons Learnt From Houshi Ryokan's Family Business

Ayansola Olatunji Ayandibu
https://orcid.org/0000-0001-5870-2388
University of Zululand, South Africa

EXECUTIVE SUMMARY

This chapter explores the crucial aspect of succession planning and survival strategies for family businesses, drawing inspiration from the remarkable story of Houshi Ryokan, a traditional Japanese inn with a history spanning over a millennium. The chapter delves into the challenges faced by family-owned enterprises when transitioning leadership to the next generation and offers valuable insights into effective succession planning models. Finally, the chapter draws insightful lessons from Houshi Ryokan's family business journey, distilling key success factors and actionable strategies that can be applied by other family businesses seeking longevity and prosperity. By examining the exemplary case of Houshi Ryokan, this chapter provides invaluable insights for family business owners, managers, and advisors, offering practical guidance on navigating the complexities of succession planning and developing robust survival strategies to safeguard the legacy and prosperity of their enterprises.

DOI: 10.4018/978-1-6684-8748-8.ch009

INTRODUCTION

Family businesses have played a significant role in the global economy for centuries, and they continue to be a vital component of many societies today. These enterprises are unique in their nature, combining both family and business aspects to create a distinctive organizational structure (Hack-Polay, Igwe and Madichie, 2020). Family businesses are characterized by their ownership and management being closely connected to one or more families, with family members involved in the decision-making and operations of the business. This integration of family dynamics into the business realm brings about a set of distinct advantages and challenges that set family businesses apart from other types of enterprises.

In the intricate tapestry of business landscapes, few stories stand as timeless testaments to the power of succession and survival planning as that of Houshi Ryokan. Nestled in the heart of Japan, this iconic family-run inn has not only withstood the test of time but has thrived for over a millennium, seamlessly passing through generations with an unbroken lineage of family stewardship. As modern economies grapple with the intricate challenges of generational transitions and the preservation of familial legacies, the saga of Houshi Ryokan offers a profound wellspring of insights and wisdom.

This chapter embarks on a journey to uncover the invaluable lessons that the Houshi Ryokan legacy imparts to contemporary family businesses. From its humble origins in the eighth century to its current status as one of the world's oldest continuously operating inns, this chapter unveils the intricate strategies, cultural values, and adaptive practices that have enabled Houshi Ryokan to flourish through the ebb and flow of centuries.

Amidst the complexities of intergenerational dynamics, economic shifts, and evolving consumer preferences, this chapter delves into the principles that have steered Houshi Ryokan's ship through uncharted waters. It explores the seamless blending of tradition and innovation, the delicate balance between honouring heritage and embracing change, and the timeless significance of developing a deep sense of purpose within the family enterprise.

Furthermore, this chapter sheds light on the meticulous cultivation of leadership within the Houshi family, highlighting the significance of mentorship, education, and shared vision in ensuring a seamless transition from one generation to the next. By dissecting the nuanced interplay between family values and strategic foresight, readers gain profound insights into how to orchestrate a harmonious symphony of succession planning that preserves the essence of the past while embracing the opportunities of the future.

Drawing inspiration from Houshi Ryokan's journey, this chapter offers a treasure trove of actionable insights for family businesses navigating the intricate terrain of succession and survival planning. It underscores the significance of cultivating a resilient corporate DNA that stands firm in the face of challenges and adapts gracefully to changing times. As the world continues to witness the rise and fall of businesses, the tale of Houshi Ryokan's enduring legacy serves as a guiding light for all those seeking to ensure the perpetuity of their cherished family enterprises.

LITERATURE REVIEW

Definition of Family Business

A family business is generally defined as a commercial organization in which ownership and control are primarily concentrated within a family or a group of related individuals. While there is no universally accepted definition of a family business, various frameworks and criteria have been established to identify and classify these enterprises (Dyer Jr and Whetten, 2006).

One commonly used definition is based on the notion of "ownership and control." According to this perspective, a family business is one in which the majority of the ownership or control rights are held by members of a single family or multiple families who are related by blood, marriage, or adoption (Randerson, 2022). The family's involvement in the business is not limited to ownership but extends to management and decision-making roles as well. Family members may hold key positions in the company, such as executives or board members, and actively participate in shaping its strategic direction (Randerson, 2022).

Another criterion used to define family businesses is the intention to pass the business down through generations. In such cases, the family's long-term commitment to the enterprise is a defining characteristic. The preservation of family legacy and the desire to create opportunities for future generations are significant driving forces in these businesses This intergenerational focus often shapes the decision-making process, with a greater emphasis on sustainability, continuity, and the long-term impact of choices made (Czakon, Hajdas and Radomska, 2023).

Moreover, family businesses are often characterized by the presence of both family and business systems. The family system includes family members' relationships, values, and dynamics, while the business system refers to the organizational structure, strategies, and operations of the company. The integration of these two systems can create a unique set of opportunities and challenges, as the family's dynamics can influence the business and vice versa (Holt, Pearson, Carr and Barnett, 2017).

It is important to note that family businesses come in various sizes, ranging from small mom-and-pop stores to large multinational corporations. They operate in diverse industries and sectors, including manufacturing, retail, services, agriculture, and finance. The longevity and resilience of many family businesses have contributed significantly to their recognition as a distinct and important economic entity. The next section will explore the importance of Family Business (Patel, Pieper and Hair Jr, 2015).

Importance of Family Business

Family businesses has a great importance in the global economy and have a unique significance in various aspects. They are often characterized by the combination of family ties and business operations, which can create distinct advantages and challenges. Here are some key points highlighting the importance of family businesses:

Long-Term Vision and Commitment: Family businesses tend to have a long-term perspective, focusing on multi-generational success rather than short-term gains. This commitment to legacy and continuity allows them to make strategic decisions that may benefit the business over time, encouraging stability and sustainability (Magrelli, Rovelli, Benedetti, Überbacher and De Massis, 2022).

Strong Core Values: Family businesses often have well-defined core values that are deeply rooted in the family's heritage and traditions. These values can shape the company's culture, ethics, and decision-making processes, encouraging trust and loyalty among employees, customers, and stakeholders (Parada, Samara, Dawson, and Bonet, 2020).

Flexibility and Agility: Family businesses can be more agile in decision-making due to fewer layers of bureaucracy. They have the ability to respond quickly to market changes, adapt to new technologies, and seize emerging opportunities, allowing them to stay competitive in dynamic business environments (Zapata-Cantu, Sanguino, Barroso and Nicola-Gavrilă, 2023).

Employee Engagement and Development: Family businesses tend to bring a sense of belonging and personal investment among employees, as they are often seen as an extension of the family. This can lead to increased employee loyalty, motivation, and commitment, resulting in higher levels of productivity and overall organizational success (Rajan, Salunkhe and Kumar, 2023).

Community and Social Impact: Family businesses often have deep roots in their local communities. They contribute to job creation, economic development, and philanthropic initiatives, playing a significant role in supporting local economies and addressing social needs. Their long-standing presence can enhance the social fabric of communities (Leonidou, Eteokleous, Christodoulides, and Eduardsen, 2023).

Knowledge Transfer and Mentorship: In family businesses, knowledge and expertise are often passed down through generations, ensuring the preservation and transmission of industry-specific insights and best practices. Younger family members have the opportunity to learn from experienced predecessors, benefiting from their wisdom and mentorship (Mosolygó-Kiss, Heidrich, and Chandler, 2023).

Resilience and Adaptability: Family businesses have historically demonstrated resilience in times of economic uncertainty or crisis. The strong emotional bonds within the family unit, combined with a shared commitment to overcoming challenges, can help them navigate difficult situations and emerge stronger on the other side (Lin, and Wen, 2021).

Economic Contribution: Family businesses make a significant contribution to the global economy. According to various studies, they account for a substantial portion of the world's GDP and employment (Pieper, Kellermanns and Astrachan, 2021). Their operations span various sectors and industries, driving innovation, creating jobs, and generating wealth.

Despite the importance of family business discussed above, family businesses do have challenges too. Some challenges are discussed in the next section.

Challenges Faced by Family Businesses

Family businesses are a crucial component of the global economy, representing a significant proportion of companies worldwide. These businesses are characterized by their unique dynamics, which can present both advantages and challenges. While family businesses often enjoy a strong sense of identity, continuity, and shared values, they also face several distinct challenges that can impact their long-term success and sustainability. In this article, we will explore some of the common challenges faced by family businesses.

Succession Planning: One of the most critical challenges faced by family businesses is the issue of succession planning. Identifying and grooming the next generation of leaders within the family can be complex and emotionally charged. Balancing family dynamics, personal aspirations, and business needs can be a delicate task. It requires careful consideration of the qualifications, skills, and commitment of family members, as well as addressing potential conflicts and establishing a fair and transparent process for succession (Alkahtani, 2021).

Governance and Decision-Making: Family businesses often struggle with establishing effective governance structures and decision-making processes. In some cases, decision-making can be influenced by family dynamics, personal relationships, and emotions rather than purely business considerations (Steier, Chrisman and Chua, 2015). Striking the right balance between family interests and the long-term success of the business can be a challenge. Implementing clear policies, professional management practices, and independent boards can help mitigate this challenge, promoting transparency, accountability, and sound decision-making.

Conflict Resolution: Conflicts are inevitable in any business, but in a family business, they can be amplified due to the emotional ties among family members. Disputes can arise from differences in vision, goals, values, and expectations (Caputo, Marzi, Pellegrini and Rialti, 2018). The challenge lies in effectively managing and resolving these conflicts without letting them escalate and damage both personal relationships and the business itself. Family businesses can benefit from adopting formal conflict resolution mechanisms, such as family councils or outside mediators, to facilitate open communication, negotiation, and consensus-building.

Professionalization and Innovation: As family businesses grow and expand, they often face the challenge of professionalizing their operations and adapting to changes in the business environment. Moving from an informal, entrepreneurial structure to a more structured and professional organization can be a significant transition. It requires implementing formal processes, investing in talent development, embracing innovation, and embracing new technologies. The resistance to change and complacency can hinder the ability of family businesses to remain competitive and adapt to evolving market conditions (Cattaneo and Bassani, 2020).

Managing Family and Business Boundaries: Maintaining clear boundaries between family matters and business matters is essential for the success and harmony of family businesses. However, this can be challenging, as family relationships can often spill into the workplace, leading to conflicts of interest, favouritism, or blurred roles. Establishing clear policies, communication channels, and delineating family and business responsibilities can help manage these boundaries and create a professional and fair work environment (Bennedsen, Fan, Jian and Yeh, 2015).

Access to Capital and Resources: Family businesses may face difficulties in accessing external capital and resources, especially during periods of growth or economic uncertainty. External investors or lenders may be cautious about providing funding due to concerns about the influence of family dynamics on business decisions or the lack of formal governance structures (Gudmunson and Danes, 2013). Family businesses need to explore alternative financing options, build relationships with external stakeholders, and demonstrate their ability to separate personal and business interests to attract the necessary resources for growth and expansion.

Success and Legacy Sustainability: Family businesses often grapple with the challenge of ensuring the long-term sustainability of the business and preserving the family legacy across generations. In some cases, the next generation may not have the same level of commitment or interest in continuing the business, leading to potential succession crises (Muhumed, Bodolica, and Spraggon, 2017). Establishing a shared vision, instilling a strong sense of purpose and responsibility, and encouraging entrepreneurship among family members can help address this challenge. Additionally, implementing effective estate planning and wealth management strategies can ensure the smooth transition of ownership and assets.

Relevant Theories Underpinning Family Business

Family business is a distinct type of enterprise that is characterized by the involvement of multiple generations of a family in the ownership, management, and governance of the business. It is a unique organizational form that has received considerable attention from researchers and scholars across various disciplines. Over the years, several theories have been developed to understand the dynamics and complexities of family businesses, shedding light on the factors that influence their success, longevity, and unique challenges. In this response, we will explore some of the key theories underpinning family business and the authors associated with them.

Agency Theory: Agency theory posits that conflicts of interest arise in organizations when there is a separation between ownership and control. In the context of family businesses, agency theory examines the potential conflicts between family members who are the owners and those who are involved in the management and decision-making processes. The theory suggests that agency problems can arise when family members prioritize their individual interests over the best interests of the business. Agency theory has been influential in explaining issues such as the succession process, family control, and governance mechanisms in family businesses (Jensen and Meckling, 2019).

Resource-Based View (RBV): The resource-based view emphasizes the importance of unique and valuable resources possessed by firms that contribute to their competitive advantage. In the context of family businesses, RBV explores the distinctive resources and capabilities that arise from family involvement, such as family reputation, social networks, and long-term orientation. The theory suggests that these resources can provide family businesses with a competitive edge, enabling them to achieve sustainable growth and outperform their competitors (Barney and Arikan, 2005).

Socioemotional Wealth (SEW) Theory: Socioemotional wealth theory focuses on the unique non-financial goals and aspirations of family business owners. It argues that family businesses are driven not only by economic considerations but also by the desire to preserve and enhance socioemotional well-being, including family harmony, reputation, and legacy. According to SEW theory, family businesses may prioritize these socioemotional goals over maximizing financial returns. The theory sheds light on how family dynamics, values, and emotions influence strategic decisions, succession planning, and intergenerational transfers in family businesses (Chrisman, Sharma, Steier and Chua, 2013).

Stewardship Theory: Stewardship theory suggests that family businesses can benefit from the strong sense of stewardship and long-term orientation displayed by family members. According to this theory, family owners and managers are more likely to act in the best interests of the business due to their emotional attachment and commitment to preserving the family legacy. Stewardship theory emphasizes the positive aspects of family involvement, highlighting the potential for enhanced trust, cooperation, and long-term strategic decision-making in family businesses (Strand, Freeman and Hockerts, 2015).

Family Systems Theory: Family systems theory focuses on the interdependence and interactions among family members within the business context. It examines how family dynamics, relationships, and communication patterns influence the functioning and outcomes of the family business. Family systems theory emphasizes the need for effective communication, conflict management, and clear boundaries between family and business systems to ensure the success and sustainability of family businesses (Bequeath, 2014).

There are other theories related to family business, and there are several other perspectives and authors who have contributed to this field of study. The interdisciplinary nature of family business research has led to insights from various disciplines, including management, psychology, sociology, and economics, further enriching our understanding of the unique challenges and opportunities faced by family businesses.

Sustainable Development Goals (SDGs) Related to Family Business

The United Nations' Sustainable Development Goals (SDGs) are a set of 17 goals aimed at ending poverty, protecting the planet and ensuring peace and these goals are discussed below: There are some of these goals associated to family business(es)

No Poverty (SDG 1) - Family businesses contributes to ending poverty by creating jobs and generating income for families and communities. They can also help reduce poverty by providing access to essential goods and services and by supporting the development of local economies.

Decent Work and Economic Growth (SDG 8) - Family businesses provide decent work and support economic growth through their operations, investment, and employment practices. They can also promote inclusive and sustainable economic growth by providing training and development opportunities for employees, and by ensuring fair wages and working conditions.

Reduced Inequalities (SDG 10) - Family businesses play a role in reducing inequalities by creating a fair and inclusive economy that benefits all stakeholders. This can include ensuring equal opportunities for employees, fair treatment of suppliers, and supporting communities through corporate social responsibility initiatives.

Sustainable Cities and Communities (SDG 11) - Family businesses contributes to sustainable cities and communities by investing in sustainable infrastructure, reducing their environmental impact, and promoting sustainable consumption and production. This can include initiatives such as reducing waste and emissions, supporting renewable energy, and promoting sustainable transport and urban planning.

Responsible Consumption and Production (SDG 12) - Family businesses lead by example in promoting responsible consumption and production through sustainable practices and products. This can include reducing waste and emissions, using sustainable materials, and promoting environmentally friendly practices throughout their supply chain.

Climate Action (SDG 13) - Family businesses can help address the impacts of climate change by reducing their own carbon footprint and promoting sustainable solutions. This can include reducing energy use and emissions, investing in renewable energy, and promoting sustainable practices in their organisation.

Succession Planning Initiative of Houshi Ryokan Family Business

Houshi Ryokan stands as a testament to the meticulous art of family business succession planning, seamlessly passing down its legacy through generations. This venerable Japanese inn, renowned for its exceptional hospitality and serene ambiance, has perfected the delicate balance between preserving tradition and embracing innovation. The family's sagacious approach involves a gradual integration of the younger generation's ideas while upholding the time-honored customs that define the ryokan's identity. Through well-structured mentorship programs, immersive hands-on experiences, and a deep-rooted respect for ancestral wisdom, the torchbearers of Houshi Ryokan ardently learn the intricacies of hospitality management and cultural preservation. This seamless transition not only ensures the continuity of the ryokan's unparalleled service but also showcases a paragon of how family businesses can flourish when guided by strategic succession planning and a harmonious blend of heritage and modernity.

Case Study of Houshi Ryokan's Family Business

Houshi Ryokan is a traditional Japanese inn, or "ryokan," that has been in operation for over 1,300 years {Seki and Brooke, 2012). It is said to be the oldest continuously running ryokan in Japan, and is located in the city of Awazu, in Ishikawa Prefecture. Houshi Ryokan has been passed down through the generations of the same family, and has been a popular destination for both Japanese and international travelers seeking a taste of traditional Japanese culture and hospitality (Park and Park, 2021). Throughout its long history, Houshi Ryokan has played host to many famous guests, including historical figures, artists, and cultural luminaries, and has been featured in numerous books and articles about Japanese history and culture (Dodd, Anderson and Jack, 2013).

Houshi Ryokan is a famous Japanese inn that has been in business for over 1,300 years and is considered the oldest family-run business in the world (Dodd, Anderson and Jack, 2013). It provides valuable lessons for succession and survival planning in a family business:

Clear Succession Planning: Houshi Ryokan has a clear succession plan in place to ensure the smooth transfer of ownership and management from one generation to the next (Silva and Silva, 2014). This helps to avoid confusion and ensures the longevity of the business.

Houshi developed its succession plan through a comprehensive and forward-thinking process. First, they identified key leadership roles critical for their long-term success. They assessed the skills, experience, and potential of current employees to pinpoint potential successors for these roles. Houshi then focused on nurturing and developing these high-potential individuals through mentorship, training, and exposure to challenging projects, ensuring they were equipped with the necessary skills and knowledge. Additionally, the company followed a culture of continuous learning, allowing employees to grow and adapt. Regular reviews and feedback mechanisms were put in place to track progress and adjust the plan as needed. By integrating these strategies, Houshi ensured a seamless transition of leadership and a sustainable future for the organization (Chang, 2020).

Well succession plan has been put in place and the following were learnt based on this from the Houshi family business

Emphasize on family values: The inn has been passed down through 46 generations of the same family, and they place a strong emphasis on preserving their family values and traditions. This helps to maintain the unique character and identity of the business.

Focus on customer satisfaction: The inn prioritizes customer satisfaction, which has been a key factor in its longevity. By providing a high level of service and ensuring that guests have a memorable experience, the inn has maintained a loyal customer base.

Adaptability: Houshi Ryokan has been able to adapt to changing times and technology without losing its traditional essence. For instance, it has introduced modern amenities while preserving its historical architecture and traditional Japanese décor.

Employee loyalty: The inn values its employees and provides a stable work environment, which has helped to improve employee loyalty. This has contributed to the success of the business by ensuring that employees are committed to providing the highest level of service to guests.

Planning for Succession in Family Business

Succession planning is a critical process for any family business that aims to ensure a smooth transition of leadership and ownership from one generation to the next. It involves developing and implementing a comprehensive strategy to identify, groom, and prepare potential successors within the family to take over key roles and responsibilities in the business. Effective succession planning is vital for the long-term sustainability and continued success of the family business, as it minimizes disruptions, maintains stability, and preserves the core values and vision of the company (Estedadi and Hamidi, 2015).

Here are some key considerations and steps involved in planning for succession in a family business:

Start early and communicate openly: Succession planning should begin well in advance to provide sufficient time for grooming potential successors and addressing any challenges that may arise. Open and transparent communication among family members, stakeholders, and key employees is crucial to ensure everyone is aware of the succession plan and is aligned with the long-term goals of the business (Buckman, Jones and Buame, 2020).

Define the criteria for succession: Clearly outline the qualifications, skills, and competencies required for key leadership positions within the company. Identify the core values, vision, and mission of the business that the successors should embody (Matias and Franco, 2021). This will help in evaluating and selecting the most suitable candidates for future leadership roles.

Identify potential successors: Evaluate family members who have expressed interest and demonstrated capability to take on leadership roles. Assess their strengths, weaknesses, and developmental needs (Chirapanda, 2020). Consider external candidates if no suitable family members are available or qualified.

Provide training and development opportunities: Offer training, mentoring, and exposure to various aspects of the business to potential successors. This can include rotations across departments, participation in strategic planning, attending industry conferences, or pursuing advanced education and certifications. Investing in their professional growth will equip them with the necessary skills and knowledge to lead effectively (Habash and Baidoun, 2023).

Consider a gradual transition: A phased transition, where the successor initially works alongside the current leader or in a supporting role, allows for knowledge transfer, relationship building with stakeholders, and gaining hands-on experience (Qi and Wu, 2023). This gradual approach helps minimize disruption and ensures a smooth handover of responsibilities.

Establish a governance structure: Implement a governance structure that defines the roles, responsibilities, and decision-making processes for family members involved in the business (Renuka and Marath, 2023). This can include creating a family council, board of directors, or an advisory board comprising both family and independent members. Such structures provide a framework for effective decision-making, conflict resolution, and accountability.

Develop contingency plans: Succession planning should account for unforeseen circumstances such as sudden incapacitation or death of key family members. Having contingency plans in place, such as identifying backup successors or appointing interim leaders, ensures business continuity during times of crisis (Rodriguez Serna, Bowyer and Gregory, 2023).

Seek professional guidance: Engaging external advisors, such as lawyers, accountants, or business consultants with expertise in family business succession, can provide valuable insights and guidance throughout the planning process (Habash and Baidoun, 2023). They can help navigate complex legal, financial, and emotional considerations, and facilitate objective decision-making.

Culture of meritocracy: To maintain the long-term success of the family business, it is essential to prioritize merit-based decision-making rather than solely relying on family ties (Rafiei, Mehrtak, Amerzadeh, Rafiei, Moosavi and Kalhor, 2023). Encourage fair competition, recognize and reward performance, and promote a culture that values competence, innovation, and adaptability.

Review and adapt the plan: Succession planning is not a one-time event but an ongoing process. Regularly review and reassess the succession plan to ensure it remains relevant and aligned with the evolving needs of the business, market conditions, and family dynamics (Zapata-Cantu, Sanguino, Barroso and Nicola-Gavrilă, 2023). Adjust as necessary to address any changing circumstances or emerging challenges.

Building a Strong Family Culture in Family Business

Building a strong family culture in a family business is essential for its long-term success and harmony. A family business is unique because it involves the intersection of family dynamics and business operations. By establishing a strong family culture, you can create a sense of unity, shared values, and a clear vision that will guide the business and strengthen family relationships. In this response, we will explore various aspects of building a strong family culture in a family business and provide practical strategies to achieve this goal. Jahmurataj, Ramadani, Bexheti, Rexhepi, Abazi-Alili, and Krasniqi, (2023) discussed how to build a strong family culture.

Define and Communicate Core Values: The foundation of a strong family culture in a family business lies in defining and communicating core values. Core values reflect the fundamental beliefs and principles that guide the business and the family. Engage all family members in a collaborative process to identify and articulate these values. Once established, ensure that these values are consistently communicated and reinforced through various channels such as family meetings, employee training programs, and company documents.

Encourage Open Communication: Open and honest communication is vital in any business, but it becomes even more crucial in a family business where personal relationships can intersect with professional matters. Encourage open dialogue among family members and create platforms for regular communication, such as family meetings or retreats, where everyone can voice their opinions, concerns, and ideas. Active listening and respectful communication are essential to maintain harmony and resolve conflicts effectively.

Establish Clear Roles and Responsibilities: Clearly defining roles and responsibilities for family members within the business helps prevent confusion, overlapping responsibilities, and conflicts. Assigning positions based on individual strengths, skills, and interests can create a more efficient and harmonious work environment. It is also important to establish procedures for succession planning to ensure a smooth transition of leadership from one generation to the next.

Develop a Professional Work Environment: While it's essential to maintain strong family ties, it's equally important to facilitate a professional work environment within the family business. Set high standards for professionalism, including expectations for performance, accountability, and ethical behavior. Encourage family members to separate personal matters from business decisions and establish protocols for conflict resolution.

Invest in Education and Training: To build a strong family culture in a family business, it's crucial to invest in the education and training of family members involved in the business. Provide opportunities for professional development, both within the company and through external resources. Encourage family members to gain experience and knowledge outside the family business to bring fresh perspectives and ideas.

Encourage Collaboration and Teamwork: Promote a culture of collaboration and teamwork among family members and employees. Encourage cross-functional projects, intergenerational mentoring, and the sharing of knowledge and expertise. Emphasize the importance of working together towards common goals and demonstrate appreciation for the contributions of all team members.

Balance Family and Business Boundaries: Maintaining a healthy balance between family and business is critical for building a strong family culture. Clearly establish boundaries between family time and work time. Encourage family members to spend quality time together outside of work, engage in non-business activities, and nurture personal relationships. This balance helps prevent burnout, improves family cohesion, and strengthens the overall family culture.

Celebrate Achievements and Milestones: Recognize and celebrate achievements, milestones, and successes of both the business and family members. This acknowledgment can be in the form of public recognition, rewards, or family traditions. Celebrating accomplishments creates a positive atmosphere, motivates family members, and reinforces a sense of pride in both the family and the business.

Continuously Evaluate and Adapt: Building a strong family culture is an ongoing process that requires continuous evaluation and adaptation. Regularly assess the effectiveness of your family culture-building efforts and adjust as needed. Seek feedback from family members and employees to ensure that the culture aligns with their needs and aspirations. Embrace change and be willing to adjust.

Professionalizing the Family Business

Professionalizing the family business is a crucial step towards ensuring its long-term success and sustainability. Family businesses often face unique challenges due to the intertwining of family dynamics and business operations. Professionalizing the business involves implementing effective governance structures, developing clear strategies, and adopting modern management practices. This process helps create a solid foundation for growth, enhances operational efficiency, and minimizes conflicts within the family. Salimi, Della-Torre and Miniaci (2023), discussed further discussed the point below on professionalizing family business.

Establishing Governance Structures: Professionalizing a family business starts with establishing appropriate governance structures. It involves defining the roles and responsibilities of family members, creating a board of directors, and developing clear decision-making processes. By separating ownership and management roles, the family can bring in external expertise and ensure objective decision-making. Implementing governance mechanisms such as family councils, advisory boards, and regular family meetings can help promote transparency, accountability, and alignment of interests.

Defining a Clear Strategy: A well-defined strategy is essential for the long-term success of any business. In a family business, it is crucial to articulate a clear vision and mission statement that reflects both the family's values and the business's strategic direction. This process involves conducting a thorough analysis of the external market, identifying growth opportunities, and assessing the company's strengths and weaknesses. Developing a strategic plan with specific goals and key performance indicators (KPIs) provides a roadmap for the family business and ensures that decisions are aligned with the overall direction.

Professional Management: Professionalizing a family business often requires transitioning from a predominantly family-managed structure to a more professional management approach. This involves recruiting and retaining skilled professionals who bring expertise in areas such as finance, operations, marketing, and human resources. Implementing performance-based compensation systems and providing leadership development opportunities can help attract and motivate talented professionals. Additionally, introducing performance management practices, such as regular performance reviews and goal-setting, can enhance accountability and drive organizational excellence.

Implementing Formalized Processes and Systems: Family businesses can benefit from implementing formalized processes and systems to streamline operations and enhance efficiency. This includes establishing standardized procedures for financial management, budgeting, risk management, and reporting. Adopting modern technology solutions such as enterprise resource planning (ERP) systems, customer relationship management (CRM) software, and project management tools can improve productivity, data accuracy, and decision-making. By reducing reliance on informal systems, the business can achieve greater transparency, scalability, and professionalism.

Professional Development and Succession Planning: Succession planning is a critical aspect of professionalizing a family business. Developing a structured succession plan ensures a smooth transition of leadership and minimizes disruptions to the business. This involves identifying and grooming potential successors from within the family or considering external candidates. Providing training and mentorship programs to prepare the next generation for leadership roles can help them acquire the necessary skills and experience. Engaging external advisors and consultants in the succession planning process can bring objectivity and expertise to ensure the best outcome for the business.

Promoting a Culture of Innovation and Continuous Improvement: Professionalizing a family business requires developing a culture of innovation and continuous improvement. Encouraging creativity, embracing change, and promoting a learning mindset within the organization can drive innovation and adaptability. Regularly reviewing business processes, seeking feedback from customers and employees, and benchmarking against industry best practices can help identify areas for improvement. By prioritizing innovation and staying agile, family businesses can stay competitive in a rapidly evolving business landscape.

Communication and Conflict Resolution: Effective communication and conflict resolution are essential in professionalizing a family business. Open and transparent communication channels, both within the family and across the organization, brings trust and minimize misunderstandings. Establishing clear channels for conflict resolution, such as mediation or a designated family council, can help address disagreements in a constructive manner. Regular family meetings and forums for discussion create a platform for open dialogue, enabling the family to make collective decisions and resolve conflicts in the best interest of the business.

Building a strong Business Model: Professionalizing the family business requires a thorough examination and refinement of the business model. The business model serves as the foundation for how a company creates, delivers, and captures value. By professionalizing the business model, family businesses can enhance their competitiveness, adapt to changing market conditions, and drive sustainable growth.

Professionalizing a family business is a deliberate and ongoing process that involves implementing effective governance structures, developing clear strategies, adopting modern management practices, and nurturing a culture of professionalism. By embracing these practices, family businesses can position themselves for long-term success, ensure a smooth transition to the next generation, and overcome the unique challenges associated with family dynamics.

Succession Success Stories

There are numerous success stories of family businesses that have successfully navigated succession and continued to thrive. Here are a few notable examples:

Walmart: Walmart, one of the world's largest retail chains, was founded by Sam Walton in 1962. After his passing in 1992, his eldest son, S. Robson Walton, took over as Chairman of the Board. The Walton family has continued to play a significant role in the company's management, with several family members serving on the board (Bergdahl, 2004) Walmart has expanded globally and achieved tremendous success, becoming one of the most valuable companies in the world.

Ford Motor Company: Henry Ford established the Ford Motor Company in 1903. His son, Edsel Ford, succeeded him as the company's president in 1919. Despite facing challenges during the Great Depression, the Ford family managed to retain control of the company, and Henry Ford II, Edsel's son, took over leadership after World War II. Under Henry Ford II's guidance, the company experienced significant growth, introducing iconic vehicles like the Mustang and expanding into new markets (Ford, 2002) .

Samsung: Samsung, a South Korean conglomerate, was founded by Lee Byung-chul in 1938. After his passing in 1987, his son, Lee Kun-hee, took over as Chairman and played a pivotal role in transforming Samsung into a global technology leader. Lee Kun-hee's son, Lee Jae-yong, is now leading the company as Vice Chairman. Samsung has diversified its business into various sectors, including electronics, shipbuilding, and construction, achieving remarkable success (Park-Barjot, 2014).

The Estée Lauder Companies: Estée Lauder, an American cosmetics company, was founded by Estée and Joseph Lauder in 1946. The Lauders' sons, Leonard and Ronald, joined the company and helped expand its reach globally. The family-maintained control over the company, and subsequent generations, including William Lauder and Jane Lauder, have held key leadership positions {Koehn, 2014). The Estée Lauder Companies have grown into a multinational corporation with a portfolio of prestigious beauty brands.

Hermès: Hermès, a French luxury goods manufacturer, was established in 1837 by Thierry Hermès. Over the years, the business passed through multiple generations of the Hermès family. In the 20th century, Émile-Maurice Hermès, the third-generation family member, introduced iconic products and expanded the brand's offerings (Mase, 2020). Today, members of the Hermès family remain actively involved in the company, which is known for its high-quality leather goods, fashion, and accessories.

These success stories highlight the importance of effective succession planning, maintaining the vision and values of the founding generation, and adapting to changing market dynamics while preserving the legacy of the family business.

The Future of Family Business

The future of family businesses is subject to various trends and factors such as succession planning, digitalization, and globalization.

Succession planning: Family businesses face the challenge of passing on leadership and ownership to the next generation. Effective succession planning can ensure the smooth transfer of control and preserve the legacy of the business.

Digitalization: The integration of technology and digital processes is increasingly important for family businesses to remain competitive. This can include the adoption of digital marketing, e-commerce, and cloud-based systems.

Globalization: As markets become more connected and competition increases, family businesses may look to expand globally to access new customers and opportunities. This can bring new challenges, such as navigating different legal and cultural environments.

In conclusion, family businesses must be proactive in addressing these and other trends to ensure their long-term success. Some useful references on the topic include:

CONCLUSION

Family businesses hold a unique position in the global economy, combining the dynamics of entrepreneurship and the strength of familial bonds. Throughout history, they have played a vital role in shaping industries, creating jobs, and contributing to economic growth.

Family businesses bring a distinct set of values and principles to the table, such as long-term vision, commitment to quality, and a sense of loyalty to employees and customers. These businesses often prioritize sustainability and community engagement, recognizing the importance of leaving a positive legacy for future generations.

While family businesses face their fair share of challenges, such as succession planning and balancing family dynamics with business decisions, they have proven their resilience and adaptability over time. The ability to make quick decisions, improve innovation, and maintain a strong sense of purpose is deeply embedded within the fabric of family businesses.

Moreover, the strong bonds and shared history within a family business provide a solid foundation for trust and collaboration, encouraging a cohesive work environment.

This familial connection can lead to increased employee satisfaction, productivity, and a sense of belonging, ultimately benefiting both the business and its stakeholders.

As the world continues to evolve, family businesses must also adapt to changing market dynamics and embrace new technologies. Embracing innovation, seeking external expertise, and cultivating a culture of continuous learning will be crucial to their long-term success and sustainability.

In an era where corporate consolidation and impersonal transactions are prevalent, family businesses offer a refreshing alternative, emphasizing personalized service, integrity, and a commitment to customer relationships. These businesses have the ability to connect with their customers on a deeper level, often spanning generations, and create a sense of trust and loyalty that extends beyond mere transactions.

In conclusion, family businesses embody the spirit of entrepreneurship, resilience, and long-term thinking. Their unique blend of family values, business acumen, and community engagement positions them as key contributors to economic growth and societal well-being. As we move forward, let us recognize and celebrate the significant role that family businesses play in shaping our world and appreciate the enduring legacies they leave behind.

REFERENCES

Alkahtani, A. W. (2021). Family-owned businesses in Saudi Arabia: Challenges and solutions from a legal perspective. *Int. J. Contemp. Manag. Inf. Technol*, *1*(2), 16–22.

Barney, J. B., & Arikan, A. M. (2005). The resource-based view: Origins and implications. The Blackwell handbook of strategic management, 123-182. doi:10.1111/b.9780631218616.2006.00006.x

Bennedsen, M., Fan, J. P., Jian, M., & Yeh, Y. H. (2015). The family business map: Framework, selective survey, and evidence from Chinese family firm succession. *Journal of Corporate Finance*, *33*, 212–226. doi:10.1016/j.jcorpfin.2015.01.008

Bequeath, K. M. (2014). *Family-Firm Leadership: A Case Study of an Organizational Family-Firm Leadership According to Bowen's Family Systems Theory and Lewin's Systems Theory* [Doctoral dissertation]. Franklin Pierce University.

Bergdahl, M. (2004). *What I learned from Sam Walton: How to compete and thrive in a Wal-Mart World*. John Wiley & Sons.

Buckman, J., Jones, P., & Buame, S. (2020). Passing on the baton: A succession planning framework for family-owned businesses in Ghana. *Journal of Entrepreneurship in Emerging Economies*, *12*(2), 259–278. doi:10.1108/JEEE-11-2018-0124

Caputo, A., Marzi, G., Pellegrini, M. M., & Rialti, R. (2018). Conflict management in family businesses: A bibliometric analysis and systematic literature review. *International Journal of Conflict Management*, *29*(4), 519–542. doi:10.1108/IJCMA-02-2018-0027

Cattaneo, C., & Bassani, G. (2020). Professionalization and managerialization in family firms: A still open issue. *Management Controlling and Governance of Family Businesses: Theoretical Insights and Empirical Evidence from Italy*, 29-49.

Chang, Y. C. (2020). *Best Practices for Executive Leadership Succession Planning in Post-cultural Revolution China First-Generational Family Enterprises* [Doctoral dissertation]. Pepperdine University.

Chirapanda, S. (2020). Identification of success factors for sustainability in family businesses: Case study method and exploratory research in Japan. *Journal of Family Business Management*, *10*(1), 58–75.

Chrisman, J. J., Sharma, P., Steier, L. P., & Chua, J. H. (2013). The influence of family goals, governance, and resources on firm outcomes. *Entrepreneurship Theory and Practice*, *37*(6), 1249–1261. doi:10.1111/etap.12064

Czakon, W., Hajdas, M., & Radomska, J. (2023). Playing the wild cards: Antecedents of family firm resilience. *Journal of Family Business Strategy*, *14*(1), 100484. doi:10.1016/j.jfbs.2022.100484

Dodd, S. D., Anderson, A., & Jack, S. (2013). Being in time and the family owned firm. *Scandinavian Journal of Management*, *29*(1), 35–47. doi:10.1016/j.scaman.2012.11.006

Dyer, W. G. Jr, & Whetten, D. A. (2006). Family firms and social responsibility: Preliminary evidence from the S&P 500. *Entrepreneurship Theory and Practice*, *30*(6), 785–802. doi:10.1111/j.1540-6520.2006.00151.x

Estedadi, E., & Hamidi, K. (2015). The importance of succession planning in organizations. *Advanced Social Humanities and Management*, *2*(3), 41–47.

Ford, E. (2002). Henry Ford (1863-1947) and Edsel Ford (1893-1943). *Notable American Philanthropists: Biographies of Giving and Volunteering*, 92.

Gudmunson, C. G., & Danes, S. M. (2013). Family social capital in family businesses: A stocks and flows investigation. *Family Relations*, *62*(3), 399–414. doi:10.1111/fare.12017

Habash, N., & Baidoun, S. (2023). How to win the succession race: empirical analysis of Palestinian family businesses. *Journal of Entrepreneurship in Emerging Economies*.

Hack-Polay, D., Igwe, P. A., & Madichie, N. O. (2020). The role of institutional and family embeddedness in the failure of Sub-Saharan African migrant family businesses. *International Journal of Entrepreneurship and Innovation*, *21*(4), 237–249. doi:10.1177/1465750320909732

Holt, D. T., Pearson, A. W., Carr, J. C., & Barnett, T. (2017). Family firm (s) outcomes model: Structuring financial and nonfinancial outcomes across the family and firm. *Family Business Review*, *30*(2), 182–202. doi:10.1177/0894486516680930

Jahmurataj, V., Ramadani, V., Bexheti, A., Rexhepi, G., Abazi-Alili, H., & Krasniqi, B. A. (2023). Unveiling the determining factors of family business longevity: Evidence from Kosovo. *Journal of Business Research*, *159*, 113745. doi:10.1016/j.jbusres.2023.113745

Jensen, M. C., & Meckling, W. H. (2019). Theory of the firm: Managerial behavior, agency costs and ownership structure. In *Corporate governance* (pp. 77–132). Gower.

Koehn, N. (2014). Estee Lauder: self-definition and the modern cosmetics market. In Beauty and Business (pp. 221-256). Routledge.

Leonidou, L. C., Eteokleous, P. P., Christodoulides, P., & Eduardsen, J. S. (2023). A dynamic capabilities perspective to socially responsible family business: Implications on social-based advantage and market performance. *Journal of Business Research*, *155*, 113390. doi:10.1016/j.jbusres.2022.113390

Lin, Q., & Wen, J. J. (2021). Family Business, Resilience, and Ethnic Tourism in Yunnan, China. *Sustainability (Basel)*, *13*(21), 11799. doi:10.3390u132111799

Magrelli, V., Rovelli, P., Benedetti, C., Überbacher, R., & De Massis, A. (2022). Generations in family business: A multifield review and future research agenda. *Family Business Review*, *35*(1), 15–44. doi:10.1177/08944865211069781

Masè, S., & Masè, S. (2020). Art and Cross-Cultural Business. *Art and Business: Perspectives on Art-Based Management*, 99-112.

Matias, C., & Franco, M. (2021). The role of the family council and protocol in planning the succession process in family firms. *Journal of Family Business Management*, *11*(4), 440–461. doi:10.1108/JFBM-01-2020-0004

Mosolygó-Kiss, Á., Heidrich, B., & Chandler, N. (2023). Knowing me, knowing you: A study of the types of knowledge transferred during the succession process in intra-family takeover of family businesses in Hungary. *Journal for East European Management Studies*, *28*(1), 94–120. doi:10.5771/0949-6181-2023-1-94

Muhumed, Z., Bodolica, V., & Spraggon, M. (2017). Inside an African family business estate: The founder's legacy and the successor's dilemma. *Emerald Emerging Markets Case Studies*, *7*(3), 1–28. doi:10.1108/EEMCS-01-2017-0012

Parada, M. J., Samara, G., Dawson, A., & Bonet, E. (2020). Prosperity over time and across generations: The role of values and virtues in family businesses. *Journal of Organizational Change Management*, *33*(4), 639–654. doi:10.1108/JOCM-11-2018-0341

Park, Y. W., & Park, Y. J. (2021). Corporate Strategy for Corporate and Ecosystem Sustainability. *Corporate Social Responsibility and Entrepreneurship for Sustainability: Leading in the Era of Digital Transformation*, 71-79.

Park-Barjot, R. R. (2014). Samsung: An original case of knowledge transfer in economic organizations. *Entreprises et Histoire*, *75*(2), 91–101. doi:10.3917/eh.075.0091

Patel, V. K., Pieper, T. M., & Hair, J. F., Jr. (2015, October). Opportunities and challenges for family businesses pursuing global markets. In *Thriving in a New World Economy: Proceedings of the 2012 World Marketing Congress/Cultural Perspectives in Marketing Conference* (pp. 24-29). Cham: Springer International Publishing.

Pieper, T. M., Kellermanns, F. W., & Astrachan, J. H. (2021). Update 2021: Family businesses' contribution to the US economy. *Family Enterprise USA,* (704).

Qi, Y., & Wu, J. (2023). Performance feedback, succession process and innovative activities of family firms: Evidence from China. *Asian Business & Management*, *22*(2), 765–791. doi:10.105741291-022-00192-4

Rafiei, S., Mehrtak, M., Amerzadeh, M., Rafiei, S., Moosavi, S., & Kalhor, R. (2023). The relationship between succession and intellectual capital with entrepreneurship in hospitals. *BMC Health Services Research*, *23*(1), 1–8. doi:10.118612913-023-09435-2 PMID:37170204

Rajan, B., Salunkhe, U., & Kumar, V. (2023). Understanding customer engagement in family firms: A conceptual framework. *Journal of Business Research*, *154*, 113342. doi:10.1016/j.jbusres.2022.113342

Randerson, K. (2022). Conceptualizing family business social responsibility. *Technological Forecasting and Social Change*, *174*, 121225. doi:10.1016/j.techfore.2021.121225

Renuka, V. V., & Marath, B. (2023). Impact of effective governance structure on succession process in the family business: Exploring the mediating role of management succession planning. *Rajagiri Management Journal*, *17*(1), 84–97. doi:10.1108/RAMJ-06-2021-0048

Rodriguez Serna, L., Bowyer, D. M., & Gregory, S. K. (2023). Management control systems. A non-family stakeholder perspective on the critical success factors influencing continuous stakeholder support during businesses succession. *Journal of Small Business and Enterprise Development*, *30*(2), 290–310. doi:10.1108/JSBED-09-2021-0364

Salimi, M., Della Torre, E., & Miniaci, R. (2023). Why do firms adopt collective incentives? An analysis of family and non-family firms. *Employee Relations: The International Journal*.

Seki, A., & Brooke, E. H. (2012). *Ryokan: Japan's Finest Spas and Inns*. Tuttle Publishing.

Silva, P., & Silva, R. (2014). Family Business Transfer: The Importance of Continuing the Business. *Advances in Economics and Business*, *2*(5), 184–190. doi:10.13189/aeb.2014.020502

Steier, L. P., Chrisman, J. J., & Chua, J. H. (2015). Governance challenges in family businesses and business families. *Entrepreneurship Theory and Practice*, *39*(6), 1265–1280. doi:10.1111/etap.12180

Strand, R., Freeman, R. E., & Hockerts, K. (2015). Corporate social responsibility and sustainability in Scandinavia: An overview. *Journal of Business Ethics*, *127*(1), 1–15. doi:10.100710551-014-2224-6

Zapata-Cantu, L., Sanguino, R., Barroso, A., & Nicola-Gavrilă, L. (2023). Family business adapting a new digit al-based economy: Opportunities and challenges for future research. *Journal of the Knowledge Economy*, *14*(1), 408–425. doi:10.100713132-021-00871-1

Chapter 10
Knowledge Management in Family Firms:
Perspectives From Management Research

Nelson Andres Andrade-Valbuena
https://orcid.org/0000-0002-4873-8915
Universidad Católica de la Santísima Concepción, Chile

Sergio A. Olavarrieta Soto
University of Chile, Chile

Miguel Zapata Perez
University of Chile, Chile

EXECUTIVE SUMMARY

Knowledge management has received increasing attention from scholars. However, the understanding of this literature in the context of family firms remains fragmented. Different positions suggest that the inherent features of family businesses indicate the importance of considering the context. In this chapter, the authors aim to extend the understanding of knowledge management in the context of family firms. They achieve this by identifying the intellectual structure and evolution of the knowledge management corpus using bibliometric techniques applied to authors, universities, countries, and supranational regions. The analysis is complemented by the application of distance-based mapping techniques at the level of authors and publishers, enabling exploration of the historical dynamics and knowledge flows among management disciplines. The contribution of this chapter to the management literature lies in the provision of deep insights into this young and fertile stream of research, ultimately building bridges between both fields of research.

DOI: 10.4018/978-1-6684-8748-8.ch010

INTRODUCTION

Knowledge is the linchpin for cultivating sustainable competitive advantages within family firms (Bamel & Bamel, 2018). In addition to individual entrepreneurial skills in establishing enduring competitive edges, knowledge management significantly contributes to these organizations in terms of profitability, survival, and growth (Carayannis, Ferreira, & Fernandes, 2021). This is why knowledge management has evolved into the most strategically vital capability for family firms (Hatak & Roessl, 2013). Understanding the intricacies of knowledge management, from its inception to diffusion and effective utilization, has become a cornerstone of business research (Zack, 1999; Shahzad, Qu, Zafar, Rehman & Islam, 2020; Edwards, 2022). Over the years, knowledge management research has burgeoned, with exponential growth since its early beginnings in the early 1990s (Gaviria-Marin, Merigó, & Baier-Fuentes, 2019), resulting in a vast body of academic work (Gaviria-Marin, Merigo, & Popa, 2018). A simple search in the Web of Science database for "knowledge management" within the business and management categories yields around 5,000 academic products.

Researchers across various fields have increasingly turned to bibliometric techniques to categorize and rank extensive volumes of scholarly material and academic knowledge, providing comprehensive insights into diverse subjects (Andrade-Valbuena, Baier-Fuentes, & Gaviria-Marin, 2022). These techniques have been particularly useful in exploring complex research topics where multiple streams of knowledge converge, offering deeper insights into their commonalities (Andrade-Valbuena, Valenzuela-Fernández, & Merigó, 2022b). For instance, Vallaster, Kraus, Lindahl, and Nielsen (2019) delved into the ethical considerations inherent in entrepreneurial decision-making, utilizing performance indicators and statistical patterns to identify influential publications in this area. Lamboglia, Lavorato, Scornavacca, and Za (2021) mapped the conceptual structure of the body of knowledge at the intersection of auditing and technological absorption by examining publications, countries, and authors.

However, a comprehensive study that connects knowledge management and family firms, shedding light on the multifaceted nature of both research streams and their interplay, is conspicuously missing from the literature. While previous bibliometric endeavors have either analyzed knowledge management research (Fares, Chung, & Abbasi, 2021) or delved into family firms (Casillas & Acedo, 2007; Casprini, Dabic, Kotlar, & Pucci, 2020; Cisneros, Ibanescu, Keen, Lobato-Calleros, & Niebla-Zatarain, 2018), none have simultaneously examined both research streams. This chapter seeks to fill this gap by providing an overview of three decades of scientific production (1990-2020) that explores the multifaceted nature of knowledge management in family firms, offering insights into their connections.

Our chapter aims to expand the understanding of Knowledge Management in Family Firms research by employing bibliometric techniques to identify the intellectual structure and evolution of this corpus. We conduct a thorough performance analysis of research production, examining authors, universities, and countries, and highlighting statistical patterns within the scientific material. We complement this evaluation with a network-based analysis of authors and publishers to explore the dynamics and knowledge flows among the management disciplines comprising this corpus and its evolution over the three decades under consideration.

A bibliometric review of research literature on knowledge management in family firms enriches this book by providing evidence-based insights grounded in research outcomes within these organizations. It establishes connections between knowledge management and the interplay between family dynamics, societal influences, and firm operations (Su & Daspit, 2022). This chapter facilitates a deeper understanding of how knowledge management aligns with societal and cultural factors, especially considering the deep-rooted social context within which family firms are often studied (Kianto, Shujahat, Hussain, Nawaz & Ali, 2019). This alignment offers a broader perspective on how knowledge is shared, transferred, and preserved within familial and social systems, while also highlighting influential actors and papers in this research domain (Ghorbankhani & Rossi, 2022). Additionally, through science mapping techniques, this chapter aids readers in comprehending the interconnections among knowledge management research in family firms, presenting a comprehensive view of its collaborative research networks (Andrade-Valbuena, Valenzuela-Fernández & Merigó, 2022). By identifying key authors, we unveil the central network of researchers, their collaborations, and the underlying dynamics, a task that is challenging using alternative approaches (Andrade-Valbuena et al., 2022; Servantie, Cabrol, Guieu & Boissin, 2016). This chapter serves as a contextual framework for the case studies included in the book, providing readers with a broader context to understand the evolution of collaboration networks in knowledge management research in family firms and how these cases fit into the larger body of knowledge. It contributes to advancing the science of knowledge management and family firm research by analyzing three decades of scholarly outcomes in this field using scientific performance indicators and science mapping techniques.

The chapter is structured as follows: The first section provides an overview of the theoretical background, delving into Knowledge Management and its application in Family Firms. The second section outlines a two-step methodology that outlines research limitations and explains the bibliometric methods employed. Moving on to the third section, we present the results of a scientific performance analysis encompassing articles, authors, universities, and countries during the 1990-2020 period. Following that, we outline the co-citation and clustering analysis of authors, tracing the evolution of thematic relationships over three decades. Finally, the chapter concludes with discussions and conclusions.

THEORETICAL BACKGROUND

Knowledge Management

Knowledge Management (KM), despite emerging in the early 1990s, has deep historical roots spanning multiple disciplines like philosophy, computer science, economics, and accounting (Tzortzaki and Mihiotis, 2014; Gaviria-Marin, Merigó, & Baier-Fuentes, 2019). Its interdisciplinary nature has made it challenging to precisely define and delineate the scope of KM (Kakabadse, Kakabadse, & Kouzmin, 2003). Knowledge has been linked to various terms such as data, information, intelligence, skills, experiences, ideas, and perception (Liew, 2013).

The evolution of a KM definition has been categorized into three generations (Serenko, 2021). The first stage emphasized the strong connection between knowledge and individual experiences and information, with individuals being the primary source of knowledge (Nonaka 1994). The second stage expanded this concept, emphasizing the transformation of experiences into valuable knowledge involving individuals, teams, and organizational structures across all types of organizations (Nonaka & Takeuchi, 1995). Consequently, various individuals and groups within an organization play roles in the knowledge management process (Ling-hsing & Tung-Chin, 2015). The final stage views knowledge management as a process focused on enhancing performance by designing, implementing, maintaining, and improving systems that internalize personal knowledge within the organization (Glisby & Holden, 2003).

Ongoing research continues to explore KM's nature and dimensions (Ghorbankhani & Rossi, 2022; Engström, Johansson, Edh Mirzaei, Sollander, & Barry, 2023). This research primarily focuses on the evolution of KM processes, its connections to aspects like strategy and organizational culture (Lai, Wang, Ulhas, & Chang, 2022), learning, and information technologies for knowledge storage and exchange (Aviv, Hadar, & Levy, 2021), among others. These investigations aim to further our understanding of KM and its relevance in the ever-evolving landscape of organizational management.

Knowledge Management and Family Firms

Intellectual resources play a pivotal role in securing sustainable competitive advantages for contemporary businesses (Ballestar et al., 2020). Knowledge management, as evidenced in the literature, yields multifarious benefits, including the generation of competitive edges (Montgomery and Wenerfelt, 1997; Mahdi et al., 2019), the enhancement of business dynamics, fortification of business models (Bashir & Farooq, 2019), and the improvement of organizational structure and performance (Kogut and Zander, 1995; Song et al., 2019). Furthermore, it bolsters efficiency and worker productivity (Kianto et al., 2019), facilitating the creation and delivery of innovative products and services (Abbas & Sağsan, 2019).

A growing body of research has scrutinized the influence of knowledge management in Family Firms (Arzubiaga et al., 2022). Family Firms distinguish themselves by encompassing multiple family members as significant owners or managers, differentiating them from businesses founded by a sole founder with no familial involvement (Miller et al., 2007).

While there is an overlap in the literature between knowledge management in family and non-family businesses, contextual nuances hold significance (Anderson & Reeb, 2003; Villalonga & Amit, 2006; Chirico & Salvato, 2016; Cerchione et al., 2016). Family firms, driven by a desire for multi-generational longevity, emphasize the importance of passing down knowledge about the business's functioning and future prospects (Cabrera-Suárez et al., 2009). However, knowledge creation and transfer failures between generations have been identified as a cause of business collapse, with approximately two-thirds of family businesses failing to transition successfully (Barroso-Martínez et al., 2016; Chirico, 2008). Additionally, family firms face constraints on managerial and functional capabilities due to family members' involvement in operations and strategic decisions (Heck & Trent, 1999; Lumpkin et al., 2010). Often, these firms grapple with resource limitations and lack technological infrastructure, impacting their ability to manage information and knowledge flows (Price et al., 2013). These characteristics tend to result in risk aversion, potentially making family firms less innovative compared to their non-family counterparts (Allio, 2004; Carney, 2017).

The research landscape has evolved to address these specific challenges in family firms, with multiple calls for studies illuminating the intricate interplay between knowledge management and these enterprises (Su & Daspit, 2022; Arzubiaga et al., 2022; Belkhodja, 2022; Pütz & Werner, 2023). This indicates a burgeoning and promising area of research.

METHODOLOGY

Domain-based review articles encompass various types, such as structured reviews focusing on prevalent methods, theories, and constructs, bibliometric reviews, framework-based reviews, and hybrid reviews (Paul & Criado, 2020). Among these, bibliometric analyses stand out as they scrutinize a literature corpus using statistical results and qualitative indicators, including citations, co-citations, and the number of published papers, offering an objective perspective of a specific subject over time (Andrade-Valbuena, Merigó-Lindahl, Fernández & Alarcón, 2019). Unlike other systematic literature reviews, bibliometric types emphasize authors, affiliations, countries, citations, and co-citations, providing a comprehensive insight into research production within specific disciplines or subfields (Paul & Rosado-Serrano, 2019). This approach allows for the assessment of impact and influence at multiple levels, such as authors, institutions, countries, regions, and journals (Cobo, López-Herrera, Herrera-Viedma & Herrera, 2011).

The present book chapter falls into the bibliometric approach category, focusing on performance analysis and science mapping. Performance analyses offer a comprehensive overview of research production within specific disciplines or subjects, enabling the evaluation of their impact and influence across various levels of aggregation (e.g., authors, institutions, countries, regions, and journals) (Andrade-Valbuena et al., 2022; Laengle, Merigó, Modak & Yang, 2020; Zhou, Tijssen & Leydesdorff, 2016). Scientific mapping, within a specific area of knowledge, unveils its knowledge structure and dynamics (Zupic & Čater, 2015).

To ensure the validity and consistency of our exploration into Knowledge Management in Family Firms (KMFF), we followed a two-phase procedure, employing an integrative and generative approach (Post et al., 2020; Torraco, 2016). In the first phase, our focus was on delineating the scope and boundaries of the search. This involved constructing a robust database that effectively represents research on KMFF, consisting of several steps: (1) identifying key terms within the literature to create a foundational pool of articles through an initial search; (2) supplementing the terms based on a co-occurrence analysis of keywords in the initial pool of articles; (3) conducting a second search using the added keywords to further enrich the dataset; and (4) refining the dataset.

In the subsequent phase, we synthesized the findings from the initial stage, delving into the primary themes explored within the corpus. Figure 1 provides a visual representation of this comprehensive procedure.

Figure 1. Graphical representation of the systematic procedure followed

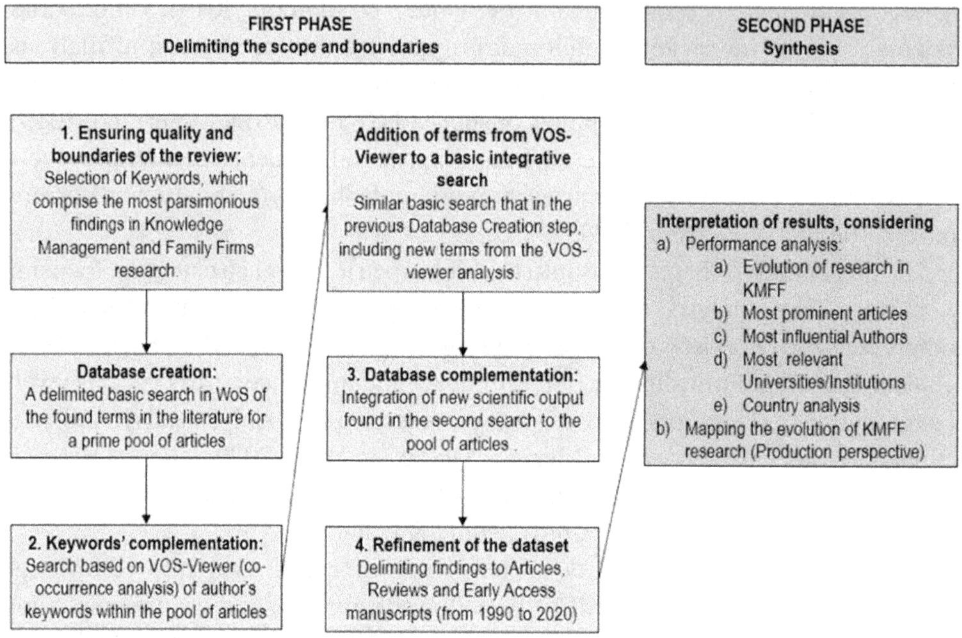

Delimitating the Corpus of Knowledge Management Research in Family Firms

A crucial aspect of conducting a comprehensive literature review is the meticulous selection of scientific output to include while excluding others, ensuring a judicious integration into the analyzed corpus (Paul & Criado, 2020). This process involves making thoughtful trade-offs and significant decisions. Our initial focus centered on the Web of Science (WoS) database, particularly the WoS core collection encompassing the Social Sciences Citation Index, Science Citation Index Expanded, and Emerging Sources Citation Index. This collection comprises over 500 journals falling within the Web of Science's Business and Management categories. Our primary interest lay in articles, reviews, and early access manuscripts within these categories, aiming to offer a thorough representation of scientific knowledge in the field of Knowledge Management in Family Firms (KMFF) research.

To initiate the research process from 1990 to 2020 in the Business and Management categories of WoS, with a managerial perspective in mind, we conducted a basic topic search. We chose 1990 as the starting point in our study, as existing literature points to this year as the inception of knowledge management as a distinct field of research (Nonaka 1994; Tzortzaki & Mihiotis, 2014; Gaviria Marin et al., 2019;

Serenko, 2021). The initial search utilized a compound basic search using the terms "family firm*" OR "family business*," representing the intersection of two major research themes: knowledge management and family firms.

To complement this search, we identified additional key terms through a visualization of similarities (VOS) mapping and clustering technique applied to the pool of articles retrieved in the previous step. Using the VOS-Viewer software version 1.6.4 (developed by van Eck & Waltman, 2017), we conducted a co-occurrence analysis of author keywords, leading to the identification of 87 key terms for the second-round search in the WoS database. Combining all these key terms with the "OR" command within each group resulted in acquiring 784 papers. Subsequently, we conducted a meticulous manual review of the full-text articles to ensure their relevance and suitability for our research, culminating in the final set of 349 papers that formed the basis for our subsequent analysis.

Bibliometric Methods

Two complementary approaches were employed to analyze the data: performance analysis and scientific mapping. Performance analysis utilized single and composite indicators, focusing on the number of publications and citations received over a specific period to gauge scientific impact (Mas-Tur et al., 2019). The H-Index, a composite measure based on the number of publications and citations, was employed to assess scientific performance (Hirsch & Buela-Casal, 2014).

Bibliometric mapping and clustering, grounded in network-graph techniques using VOS (Visualization of Similarities) of nodes and edges, were also utilized. Co-citation analysis was employed to uncover the structure, diffusion, and influence within the knowledge field (Servantie et al., 2016). Co-citation occurs when two articles are cited by a third publication, indicating thematic relationships and semantic dependencies. This analysis helps identify interconnected lines of research between authors, institutions, or countries (Kleminski, Kazienko & Kajdanowicz, 2022). Clustering analysis relied on fractional counting methodology, assigning authorship credit based on the number of authors for each publication (van Eck & Waltman, 2017).

RESULTS AND ANALYSIS

A General Overview of Knowledge Management Output Research in Family Firms: A Performance Analysis

General Citation Patterns

The distribution of the intellectual production of knowledge management research in family firms over time is shown below in Figure 2. As seen, the number of articles published on KMFF increased over the study period, almost following the tendency of intellectual production in business and management research. This subject of research received special attention among scholars in the last decade of the study period, when almost 60% of the total produced articles were published, which reflects the prominence that knowledge management has gained in these intellectual scenarios.

Figure 2. Total articles + reviews published in the WoS Business and Management category per year since 1990. Blue bars indicate the number of papers published per year, and red bars indicate the ratio (KMFF-TP/WoS-TP) x 10^6, where KMFF-TP is the total number of papers published related to KMFF and WoS-TP is the number of papers published in the WoS Business and Management category.

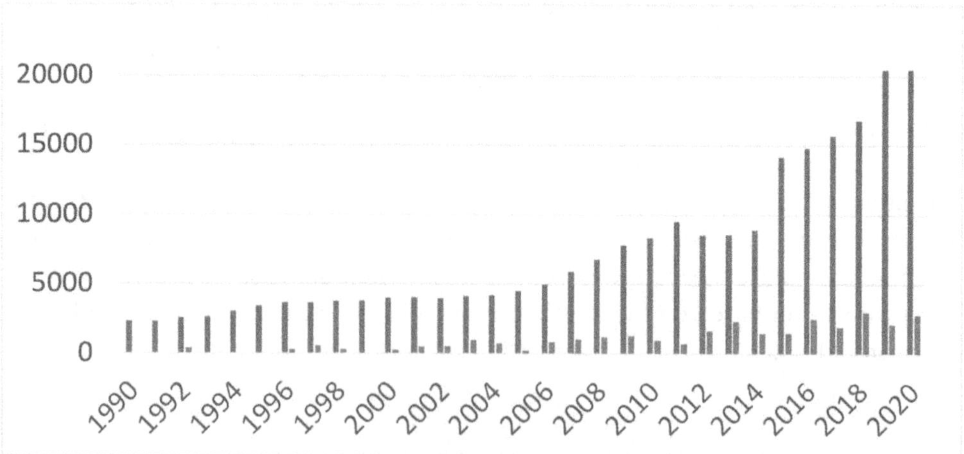

A significant bibliometric approach involves highlighting the most influential publications in Knowledge Management in Family Firms (KMFF) research. Table 1 presents the top 30 most cited publications since 1990, offering insights into the seminal works in this field. The first article by Adner & Helfat (2003) underscores the impact of diverse managerial decisions on business performance variance. They introduce the concept of dynamic managerial capabilities, supported by human, social, and cognitive capital, to elucidate this phenomenon. The second publication by Le Breton–Miller & Miller (2006) delves into the qualifying conditions that make family businesses more inclined to adopt long-term time horizons and investment policies. The third paper authored by Berman, Down, & Hill (2002) suggests that shared experience and collectively held tacit knowledge can positively affect performance, albeit with diminishing returns. Ultimately, the positive impact may diminish as knowledge ossification outweighs the benefits of collective knowledge. Notably, the literature review on technological innovation in family firms by De Massis, Frattini, & Lichtenthaler (2013) has garnered substantial attention in the academic community, receiving more than 30 citations annually. This signifies its significant influence on the direction of research in the field of knowledge management in family firms since its publication.

Table 1. Top 30 most cited papers on KMFF during the 1990-2020 period

R	Journal	KMFF-TC	Title	Author(s)	PY	C/Y
1	SMJ	563	Corporate Effects and Dynamic Managerial Capabilities	Adner, R; Helfat, CE	2003	33,12
2	ETP	349	Why Do Some Family Businesses Out-Compete? Governance, Long-Term Orientations, and Sustainable Capability	Le Breton-Miller, Isabelle; Miller, Danny	2006	24,93
3	AMJ	312	Tacit Knowledge as A Source of Competitive Advantage in The National Basketball Association	Berman, SL; Down, J; Hill, CWL	2002	17,33
4	AMAn	242	The Behavioral Theory of The Firm: Assessment and Prospects	Gavetti, Giovanni; Greve, Henrich R.; Levinthal, Daniel A.; et al.	2012	30,25
5	SBE	215	Gender Differences in Business Performance: Evidence from The Characteristics of Business Owners Survey	Fairlie, Robert W.; Robb, Alicia M.	2009	19,55
6	FBR	213	Family Involvement in Ownership and Management: Exploring Nonlinear Effects on Performance	Sciascia, Salvatore; Mazzola, Pietro	2008	17,75
7	FBR	212	Research on Technological Innovation in Family Firms: Present Debates and Future Directions	De Massis, Alfredo; Frattini, Federico; Lichtenthaler, Ulrich	2013	30,29
8	OS	208	Cognition and Renewal: Comparing CEO and Organizational Effects on Incumbent Adaptation to Technical Change	Eggers, J. P.; Kaplan, Sarah	2009	18,91
9	SMJ	197	Specificity of CEO Human Capital and Compensation	Harris, D; Helfat, C	1997	8,57
10	ETP	193	Entrepreneurial Founder Teams: Factors Associated with Member Entry and Exit	Ucbasaran, D; Lockett, A; Wright, M; et al.	2003	11,35
11	SMJ	183	Dynamic Managerial Capabilities: Configuration and Orchestration of Top Executives' Capabilities and The Firm's Dominant Logic	Kor, Yasemin Y.; Mesko, Andrea	2013	26,14
12	JMS	174	Dimensions of Social Capital and Firm Competitiveness Improvement: The Mediating Role of Information Sharing	Wu, Wei-Ping	2008	14,50
13	SMJ	171	Learning Across the Life Cycle: Experimentation and Performance Among the Hollywood Studio Heads	Miller, D; Shamsie, J	2001	9,00
14	FBR	162	Family Capital of Family Firms Bridging Human, Social, And Financial Capital	Danes, Sharon M.; Stafford, Kathryn; Haynes, George; et al.	2009	14,73
15	AMJ	162	When the Known Devil Is Better Than an Unknown God: An Empirical Study of The Antecedents and Consequences of Relay CEO Successions	Zhang, Y; Rajagopalan, N	2004	10,13
16	OS	161	Managerial Categorization of Competitors: Using Old Maps to Navigate New Environments	Reger, RK; Palmer, TB	1996	6,71
17	JBR	152	Knowledge Sharing and Technological Capabilities: The Moderating Role of Family Involvement	Zahra, Shaker A.; Neubaum, Donald O.; Larraneta, Barbara	2007	11,69
18	FBR	147	Knowledge Integration and Dynamic Organizational Adaptation in Family Firms	Chirico, Francesco; Salvato, Carlo	2008	12,25
19	JMS	145	CEO Experiences: Effects on The Choice of FDI Entry Mode	Herrmann, Pol; Datta, Deepak K.	2006	10,36
20	JSIS	141	Disruptive Technology: How Kodak Missed the Digital Photography Revolution	Lucas, Henry C., Jr.; Goh, Jie Mein	2009	12,82
21	JMS	139	The Effects of Family Firm Specific Sources of TMT Diversity: The Moderating Role of Information Exchange Frequency	Ling, Yan; Kellermanns, Franz W.	2010	13,90
22	ISBJl	126	Dynamic Capabilities and Trans-Generational Value Creation in Family Firms: The Role of Organizational Culture	Chirico, Francesco; Nordqvist, Mattias	2010	12,60

Continued on following page

Table 1. Continued

R	Journal	KMFF-TC	Title	Author(s)	PY	C/Y
23	ETP	120	Exploring the Entrepreneurial Behavior of Family Firms: Does the Stewardship Perspective Explain Differences?	Eddleston, Kimberly A.; Kellermanns, Franz W.; Zellweger, Thomas M.	2012	15,00
24	SMJ	120	The Effects of Board Human and Social Capital on Investor Reactions to New CEO Selection	Tian, Jie (Jenny); Haleblian, Jerayr (John); Rajagopalan, Nandini	2011	13,33
25	SBE	111	Trends in Family Business Research	Benavides-Velasco, Carlos A.; Quintana-Garcia, Cristina; Guzman-Parra, Vanesa F.	2013	15,86
26	SMJ	111	Firm Performance, Rent Appropriation, And the Strategic Resource Divestment Capability	Moliterno, Thomas P.; Wiersema, Margarethe F.	2007	8,54
27	JPIM	107	Technology Acquisition in Family and Nonfamily Firms: A Longitudinal Analysis of Spanish Manufacturing Firms	Kotlar, Josip; De Massis, Alfredo; Frattini, Federico; et al.	2013	15,29
28	IJHRM	106	In Search of The Changing Role of The Corporate Human Resource Function in The International Firm	Scullion, H; Starkey, K	2000	5,30
29	SBE	95	Organizational Learning and Entrepreneurship in Family Firms: Exploring the Moderating Effect of Ownership and Cohesion	Zahra, Shaker A.	2012	11,88
30	JBV	94	Buyouts, Information Asymmetry and The Family Management Dyad	Howorth, C; Westhead, P; Wright, M	2004	5,88

Abbreviations: R: Rank; KMFF-TC, total citations of the KMFF papers published; PY: Publication Year; C/Y average number of citations per year during the period.

Abbreviations of Journals: AMAn: Academy of Management Annals; AMJ: Academy of Management Journal; ETP: Entrepreneurship Theory and Practice; FBR: Family Business Review; IJHRM: The International Journal of Human Resource Management; ISBJ: International Small Business Journal; JBR: Journal of Business Research; JBV: Journal of Business Venturing; JFBM: Journal of Family Business Management; JFBS: Journal of Family Business Strategy; JFE: Journal of Financial Economics; JIBS: Journal of International Business Studies; JMS: Journal of Management Studies; JPIM: Journal of Product Innovation Management; JSIS: Journal of Strategic Information Systems ; OS: Organization Science; SMJ: Strategic Management Journal.

Most Prominent Authors

Prominent scholars often serve as authoritative figures in their respective domains, wielding substantial influence on research trajectories and the development of both theoretical and practical advancements (Podsakoff, MacKenzie, Podsakoff & Bachrach, 2008). Their contributions, characterized by rigorous methodologies and top-tier research, can serve as benchmarks for assessing research quality and adopting best practices to elevate impact and excellence (Nerur, Rasheed & Natarajan, 2008).

Recognizing these influential authors is paramount to enriching the overall impact of Knowledge Management in Family Firms (KMFF) research. Employing bibliometric techniques, Table 2 presents the 30 most prominent and influential authors in the KMFF domain. Authors are ranked based on their H-index, with ties broken by the number of KMFF articles published and then by the total number of citations received.

At the forefront of this list is Alfredo De Massis, who authored four of the top 30 most cited papers (Table 1), solidifying his status as a highly influential figure. Francesco Chirico, Mike Wright, and Maria Lopez-Fernandez stand out for their substantial focus on knowledge management in family businesses, with over 80% of their publications centered on this subject. In terms of prolificacy, Alfredo De Massis, Josip Kotlar, and Andrea Calabro lead the pack, consistently publishing at least one paper per year in KMFF research. These authors' contributions are instrumental in shaping and advancing the field.

Table 2 (a). Top 30 ranking of the most prominent researchers on KMFF

R	Author	H-KMFF	TP-KMFF	TC-KMFF	Country
1	De Massis, Alfredo	8	11	627	Italy
2	Chirico, Francesco	7	7	542	Sweden
3	Wright, M	5	5	505	UK
4	Kotlar, Josip	4	6	234	Italy
5	Frattini, Federico	4	5	442	Italy
6	Memili, Esra	4	5	125	USA
7	Calabro, Andrea	3	7	89	France
8	Sciascia, Savino	3	4	309	Italy
9	Danes, Sharon M	3	4	268	USA
10	Kellermanns, Franz W	3	4	266	Germany
11	Audretsch, David	3	4	143	Austria
12	Serrano-Bedia, Ana Maria	3	4	25	Spain
13	Lopez-Fernandez, Maria	3	4	22	Spain
14	Miller, Danny	3	3	537	Canada
15	Rajagopalan, Nandini	3	3	358	USA
16	Mazzola, Pietro	3	3	347	Italy
17	Westhead, Paul	3	3	323	UK
18	Zahra, Shaker A	3	3	259	USA
19	Salvato, Carlo	3	3	244	Italy
20	Fang, Hanqing	3	3	177	USA
21	Nordqvist, Mattias	3	3	154	Sweden
22	Boyd, Britta	3	3	115	Denmark
23	Chrisman, James J	3	3	100	USA
24	Ahrens, Jan-Philipp	3	3	48	Germany
25	Woywode, Michael	3	3	48	Germany
26	Duarte, A	2	5	14	Australia
27	Sanchez-Famoso, Valeriano	2	4	65	Spain
28	Daspit, Joshua J.	2	4	41	USA
29	Kok, Seng	2	1	8	Vietnam
30	Royer, Susanne	2	1	106	Germany

Table 2 (b). Top 30 ranking of the most prominent researchers on KMFF

Last Institution Registered	H	TP	TC	TP-KMFF5	TC-KMFF5	T30
Free University of Bozen-Bolzano	32	78	3168	8	262	4
Jonkoping University	19	36	1479	2	82	4
Imperial College	3	6	257	1	92	3
Polytechnic University of Milan	19	34	1411	5	157	2
Polytechnic University of Milan	26	85	589	3	123	3
University of North Carolina Greensboro	21	60	1642	2	24	0
IPAG Business School	15	42	1123	5	24	0
University of Turin	34	318	3920	0	0	2
University of Minnesota System	20	67	575	1	0	1
WHU Otto Beishe Sch Management	43	113	5966	2	17	2
Indiana Univ	72	326	21071	2	140	1
Universidad de Cantabria	10	39	294	4	25	0
Universidad de Cantabria	2	5	21	4	22	0
HEC Montreal	70	147	21441	0	0	2
University of Southern California	33	22	2548	0	0	3
PLANTA Ctr Ric Documentaz & Formaz	22	39	1666	0	0	2
Durham University	40	70	5620	0	0	1
University of Minnesota System	66	138	25402	1	11	2
Bocconi University	17	34	2177	1	55	3
Missouri University of Science & Technology	6	20	349	1	24	0
Jonkoping University	27	51	2825	1	9	1
University of Southern Denmark	7	11	172	0	0	1
Mississippi State University	44	104	8229	2	54	0
University of Mannheim	3	5	88	2	8	0
University of Mannheim	5	12	265	2	8	0
Curtin University	21	174	2147	5	14	0
University of Basque Country	4	20	101	3	19	0
Texas State University System	11	26	393	4	41	0
Royal Melbourne Institute of Technology (RMIT)	0	2	0	4	8	0
Univ Flensburg	4	11	145	0	0	1

Abbreviations: R: Ranking; H- KMFF is the H-Index based solely on KMFF papers; TC- KMFF and TP- KMFF are the total number of citations and papers, respectively, during the period from 1990-2020; TP- KMFF 5 and TC- KMFF5 are the total number of papers and citations in EO over the last 5 years; TP and TC are the total number of papers and citations of research in any given subject during the period, respectively; T30 is the number of papers ranked in the Top-30 list in Table 3.

Most Prominent Universities

Exploring the institutional landscape in Knowledge Management in Family Firms (KMFF) research is a valuable endeavor, providing insights into the most prominent and influential universities in the field. This knowledge aids researchers in making informed decisions and contributes significantly to the advancement of the field (Podsakoff, MacKenzie, Podsakoff, & Bachrach, 2008). It also helps researchers identify potential collaborators among these institutions, granting access to invaluable resources, data, and expertise that enhance their research efforts (Ferreira, Fernandes & Kraus, 2019).

Table 3 presents the top 30 universities in KMFF research, organized based on their H-index. Lancaster University and Mississippi State University emerge as the most prolific institutions in KMFF research, producing nearly double the average number of research outputs compared to other universities on the list. Among the top ten universities, the number of citations in KMFF research is relatively evenly distributed, with the University of Minnesota leading in this regard. Rice University and Witten/Herdecke University stand out for their significant concentration on KMFF research, contributing approximately 12% and 9% of their intellectual output to this topic, respectively. This is evident in the ratio of KMFF-focused papers to their total output. Notably, Rice University has garnered nearly 15% of its citations from its KMFF articles, while the Free University of Bozen-Bolzano has an even higher concentration of citations in this area, at almost 20%. An interesting observation is the balance between North American and Western European universities among the top 30 institutions in KMFF research. This suggests that a geographical analysis can provide valuable insights into the field's dynamics and global perspectives.

Table 3 (a). Top 30 ranking of the most prominent institutions in KMFF research

R	Universities	Country	H-KMFF	TP- KMFF
1	Lancaster University	England	8	12
2	Mississippi State University	USA	7	10
3	University of Minnesota	USA	7	8
4	University of Alberta	Canada	6	6
5	Universidad de Castilla-La Mancha	Spain	6	3
6	Politecnico di Milano	Italy	5	7
7	Free University of Bozen-Bolzano	Italy	5	6
8	University of Nottingham	England	5	6
9	Bocconi University	Italy	5	5
10	Jönköping International Business School	Sweden	5	5
11	Indiana University Bloomington	USA	4	5
12	Universidad de Cantabria	Spain	4	5
13	The University of North Carolina	USA	4	5
14	WHU	Germany	4	5
15	Rice University	USA	4	4
16	University of Innsbruck	Austria	4	4
17	Universität Mannheim	Germany	4	4
18	Nanyang Technological University	Singapore	3	5
19	Witten/Herdecke University	Germany	3	5
20	Kennesaw State University	USA	3	4
21	Pennsylvania State University	USA	3	4
22	Marche Polytechnic University	Italy	3	4
23	Chinese University of Hong Kong	Peoples' R. China	3	3
24	Erasmus University Rotterdam	Netherland	3	3
25	HEC Montréal	Canada	3	3
26	Iowa State University	USA	3	3
27	Edith Cowan University	Australia	2	4
28	Liverpool John Moores University	England	2	4
29	American University of Sharjah	U Arab Emirates	1	4
30	L'IPAG Business School	France	1	4

Table 3 (b). Top 30 ranking of the most prominent institutions in KMFF research

TC- KMFF	% KMFF /TP	TP	TC	H
433	7,6%	157	6908	43
387	10,8%	93	5201	34
574	6,5%	124	8867	48
553	4,3%	139	6882	44
42	2,1%	140	1899	21
458	3,2%	220	6814	47
151	10,9%	55	769	15
528	1,7%	343	11277	53
296	3,6%	137	5391	45
307	6,8%	74	4489	24
192	2,6%	191	13216	57
27	9,3%	54	846	15
134	9,3%	54	23393	67
229	4,5%	110	4058	32
327	11,8%	34	2122	17
49	4,6%	87	1874	21
271	6,1%	66	3977	25
114	3,1%	163	4500	35
86	13,9%	36	905	19
115	6,1%	66	2313	25
65	1,6%	256	12221	48
63	7,4%	54	506	14
202	2,2%	136	6943	40
83	1,1%	280	15178	62
378	2,6%	116	4856	36
277	2,9%	102	4872	32
14	4,0%	100	1820	23
14	5,4%	74	1141	14
12	8,2%	49	993	15
2	26,7%	15	66	5

Abbreviations: R: Ranking; H-KMFF is the H-Index based solely on KMFF papers; TC- KMFF and TP- KMFF are the total number of citations and papers, respectively, during the period from 1990-2020; TP- KMFF 5 and TC- KMFF5 are the total number of papers and citations in EO over the last 5 years; TP and TC are the total number of papers and citations of research in any given subject during the period, respectively; T30 is the number of papers ranked in the Top-30 list in Table 4.

Analysis by Country

To gain a broader perspective, we assessed the relative prominence of Knowledge Management in Family Firms (KMFF) research based on geographical boundaries. Table 4 presents the top 30 countries ranked by their H-Index in KMFF research. The United States stands out significantly in the 30 years of scientific publication on KMFF research, not only in terms of the sheer number of papers, nearly double that of the following countries on the list, but also in terms of citations. It's noteworthy that while only eight universities from the top 30 institutions (as shown in Table 3) are in the USA, the country's total intellectual production in this field is widely distributed across various institutions. The USA, Italy, England, and Spain collectively accounted for approximately 50% of the total paper production over the study period. However, the USA alone contributed to nearly 38% of the total citations for KMFF articles among the top 30 countries. Countries with the highest concentrations of KMFF research include Italy, Chile, and Spain, contributing 5.2%, 3.4%, and 3% of their intellectual production to this field, respectively.

Table 4 (a). Top-30 ranking of the most preponderant countries in KMFF research

R	Country	H-KMFF	TP- KMFF
1	USA	43	103
2	Italy	20	52
3	England	17	52
4	Spain	16	49
5	Germany	13	36
6	Canada	13	22
7	Peoples' R. of China	12	23
8	Sweden	9	13
9	France	8	23
10	Netherlands	7	9
11	Australia	6	14
12	Austria	6	8
13	Switzerland	6	6
14	Scotland	4	6
15	Denmark	4	5
16	Belgium	4	4
17	Finland	4	4
18	U Arab Emirates	3	7
19	Taiwan	3	7
20	Singapore	3	5
21	India	3	5
22	Russia	3	4
23	Chile	3	4
24	New Zealand	2	5
25	Brazil	2	4
26	Turkey	2	3
27	Vietnam	2	3
28	Colombia	2	3
29	Malaysia	2	3
30	Indonesia	2	3

Table 4 (b). Top-30 ranking of the most preponderant countries in KMFF research

TC- KMFF	% KMFF /TP	TP	TC	H
5948	1,4%	7532	458921	285
1615	5,2%	1005	21635	73
1366	1,3%	4056	132681	147
848	3,0%	1620	43836	95
905	2,5%	1423	40756	95
1048	1,6%	1382	62236	122
675	1,4%	1587	38839	87
513	1,8%	741	21260	67
820	2,3%	1022	26671	76
220	1,1%	854	35135	90
242	0,8%	1777	49541	99
112	2,8%	284	7595	41
580	1,4%	420	18209	62
46	1,5%	410	13402	57
139	1,0%	501	13012	58
147	1,3%	298	10917	59
126	0,5%	852	20795	69
43	3,0%	234	3255	24
42	0,9%	763	16902	59
114	1,7%	295	11292	59
44	0,5%	957	12150	48
25	1,5%	263	2178	24
23	3,4%	118	1895	25
34	1,3%	374	9852	48
45	0,5%	811	4574	34
85	1,1%	275	5187	37
29	2,8%	106	596	13
13	2,1%	146	909	15
13	0,7%	432	5484	35
8	1,7%	178	511	12

Abbreviations: R: Ranking; H-KMFF is the H-Index based solely on KMFF papers; TC- KMFF and TP- KMFF are the total number of citations and papers, respectively, during the period from 1990-2020; TP and TC are the total number of papers and citations of research in any given subject during the period, respectively.

Mapping Knowledge Management Research in Family Firms

In the preceding section, we presented general research performance results derived from bibliometric techniques. However, it's equally essential to explore academic material from a holistic perspective to identify collaboration structures and their underlying dynamics (Andrade-Valbuena, Baier-Fuentes, & Gaviria-Marin, 2022). This graphical representation serves to illustrate the interconnectedness of knowledge management research in family firms and offers a comprehensive view of collaborative networks (Andrade-Valbuena, Valenzuela-Fernández & Merigó, 2022). Recognizing key authors allows readers to unveil the central network of researchers and their collaborations, a task challenging to achieve through other means (Servantie, Cabrol, Guieu, & Boissin, 2016).

With this context in mind, the subsequent section of this chapter delves into three decades of intellectual production (1990-2020), focusing on authors and journals. This analysis is facilitated using Science Mapping techniques with the VOS Viewer (van Eck & Waltman, 2017). Science mapping encompasses domain analysis and visualization, involving graph or network visualization (Chen, 2017). This distance-based network analysis elucidates relationships between nodes and the number of citations within a graph (Orduña-Malea, & Costas, 2021). Nodes represent various elements, such as authors, universities, countries, and journals (Andrade Valbuena et al., 2018). The distance between two nodes signifies the strength of their relationship, with shorter distances indicating stronger affiliations (Van Eck & Waltman, 2010). Additionally, node size within the network reflects prominence based on the number of citations received during the specified period (van Eck & Waltman, 2017).

Co-Citation Analysis of Authors and Theoretical Dynamics During the 1990-2020 Period

This section focuses on identifying the core network of authors and their collaborations to understand the structure and dynamics of the research community and how it has evolved. Figure 3 presents co-citation analysis for the first decade (1990-2000) of KMFF research, offering insights into the nascent field's development.

The analysis reveals three distinct groups of authors during this period. In the lower right group, Randall Shuler and Hugh Scullion are prominent figures, primarily focused on human resource management subjects. In the center group, Coimbatore Krishnarao Prahalad and Oliver E. Williamson stand out, known for their knowledge-based perspectives on firms, corporate strategy, innovation, and transactions-cost economics.

The upper left group consists of multiple clusters: a blue cluster led by Glenn R. Carroll, Paul DiMaggio, and Walter Woody Powell, focusing on organizational identity and economic sociology; a yellow cluster led by Sydney Finkelstein, Henry Mintzberg, and Donald C. Hambrick, with a theoretical approach rooted in leadership; a green cluster led by Rhonda K. Reger and Jane Dutton, studying managerial cognition and behavioral strategy; and a blue cluster bridging the upper left clusters led by Kathleen M. Eisenhardt, Jeffrey Pfeffer, and Howard E. Aldrich. This bridging role highlights critical research areas that connect individual knowledge acquisition with organizational efforts. During this decade, the predominant theory emphasized the significant link between knowledge, personal experiences, and information acquired by individuals. As a result, individuals remained the central focus of research, with Nonaka's work in 1994 underscoring their role as the primary source of knowledge. The co-citation analysis reveals the foundational aspects within different management research subjects that shaped KMFF research during this formative period.

Figure 3. Bibliographic data map, based on a co-citation, fractional counting analysis from leading authors in the first decade (period 1990-2000) in KMFF research. Size variation-network visualization. Thresholds: 2 number of citations.

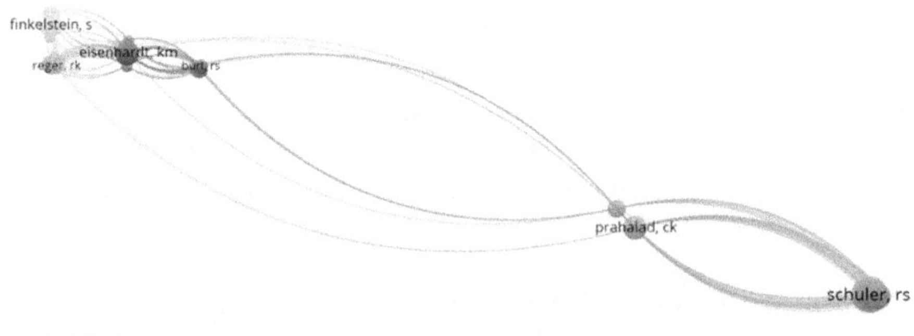

Figure 4 illustrates the co-citation analysis of authors in the second decade (2001-2010) of KMFF research, revealing five distinct clusters that characterized this period. The largest cluster, depicted in red, centered on family firm research. It featured prominent authors such as Pramodita Sharma and James Chrisman, along with specialists focusing on related topics. Notable contributors included Ikujiro

Nonaka in knowledge-based management and Shaker Zahra, Mike Wright, and Paul Westhead in entrepreneurship, small firm development, and innovation.

The second-largest cluster concentrated on strategy research, led by Danny Miller, who was the most cited author in this decade. Miller's work delved into key determinants of entrepreneurship, the firm life cycle, and the interplay of strategy, culture, and structure. The cluster also highlighted renowned theories like the resource-based view of the firm (Jay Barney) and related concepts involving capabilities (Kathleen Eisenhardt) and dynamic capabilities (David Teece), underscoring its theoretical significance in KMFF research.

The blue cluster emphasized theoretical approaches rooted in leadership, featuring authors like Donald Hambrick, Sydney Finkelstein, and Margarethe Wiersema. This period saw increased exploration of leadership-related aspects, including top management teams. Notably, theories such as organizational ecology (Michael Hannan) and organizational adaptation (Edward Zajac) were also present in this cluster, suggesting research integration between leadership and a firm's adaptation to its environment.

In contrast to the first decade, where managerial cognition was a significant focus, the second decade emphasized social concerns related to individuals' external environments. The yellow and purple clusters delved into the impact of family and community, social networks, and ownership and control of the firm. Scholars during this period recognized that relying solely on individual experiences was insufficient to understand organizational knowledge formation. As a result, theories were developed connecting various facets of the knowledge management process, encompassing individuals, teams, and groups within organizations. This period laid the theoretical foundation for organizational knowledge management itself.

Overall, this co-citation analysis illustrates the evolving landscape of KMFF research during the second decade, with shifting focal points and a deeper exploration of theoretical frameworks.

Figure 4. Bibliographic data map, based on a co-citation, fractional counting analysis from leading authors in the second decade (2001-2010 period) in KMFF research. Size variation-network visualization. Thresholds: 5 number of citations.

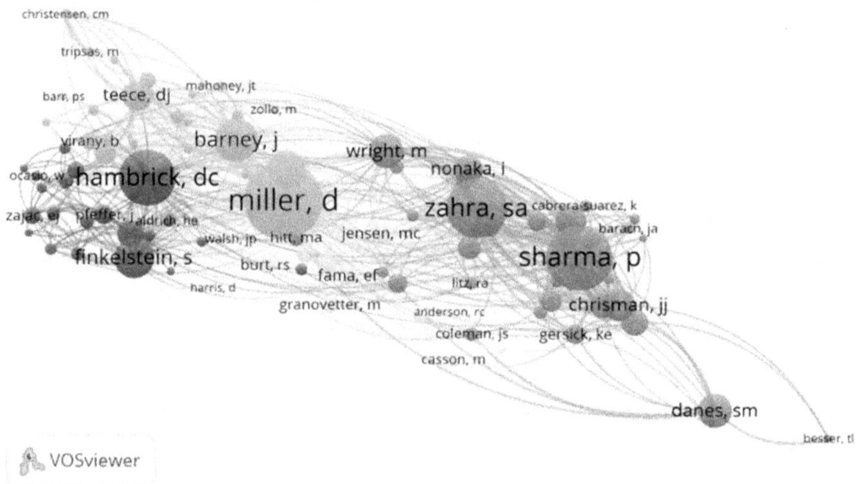

Figure 5 presents the co-citation analysis of authors in the last decade (2011-2020) of KMFF research, revealing three prominent clusters that characterized this period. The red cluster stands out as the largest and most influential, with a focus on entrepreneurial families and firm governance. Renowned authors such as Danny Miller, James Chrisman, and Isabelle Le Breton-Miller spearheaded research on these subjects in the last decade. This cluster encompassed various aspects within family firms and knowledge management, spanning innovation (e.g., Alfredo De Massis and Francesco Chirico), human resources, socioemotional wealth, and other elements, particularly within Ibero American family firms (Luis Gomez-Mejia). It also explored the intersection of strategic entrepreneurship (David Sirmon) and developments in family business education (Pramodita Sharma).

The second-largest cluster centered on entrepreneurship research, featuring notable scholars like Shaker Zahra, Tom Lumpkin, Johan Wiklund, and Jeffrey Covin. This cluster delved into the concept of entrepreneurial orientation, which garnered significant attention from scholars across different fields in this decade. It also incorporated models of organizational knowledge creation rooted in enduring wisdom (Ikujiro Nonaka), absorptive capabilities, and intellectual assets (William Cohen), as well as cognitive approaches (Scott Shane).

The green cluster emphasized perspectives in strategy research with a focus on firm resources and capabilities, featuring prominent authors from the last decade. However, scholars during this period seemed more oriented toward elucidating microfoundations in capabilities (e.g., Kathleen Eisenhardt and David Teece) and the Resource-Based View of the firm (e.g., Birger Wernerfelt, Constance Helfat, and Margaret Peteraf). Aspects related to leadership research, such as upper echelons theory (Donald C. Hambrick), organizational learning (James G. March), global strategy (Mike W. Peng), and international diversification (Michael A. Hitt), received less attention in this decade, although the dispersed nodes suggest inquiries into rather specific concerns.

This final phase of KMFF research revealed knowledge management as a multidisciplinary process, encompassing a series of steps aimed at enhancing performance by developing, implementing, maintaining, and improving systems that integrate individual knowledge within organizations. It highlighted the interdisciplinary nature of knowledge management, showcasing the influence of various research fields such as organizational theory, strategy, and culture. Additionally, it underscored the impact of disciplines like learning and information technologies in knowledge storage and exchange.

Figure 5. Bibliographic data map, based on co-citation, fractional counting analysis from leading authors in the third decade (period 2011-2020) in KMFF research. Size variation-network visualization. Thresholds: 25 number of citations.

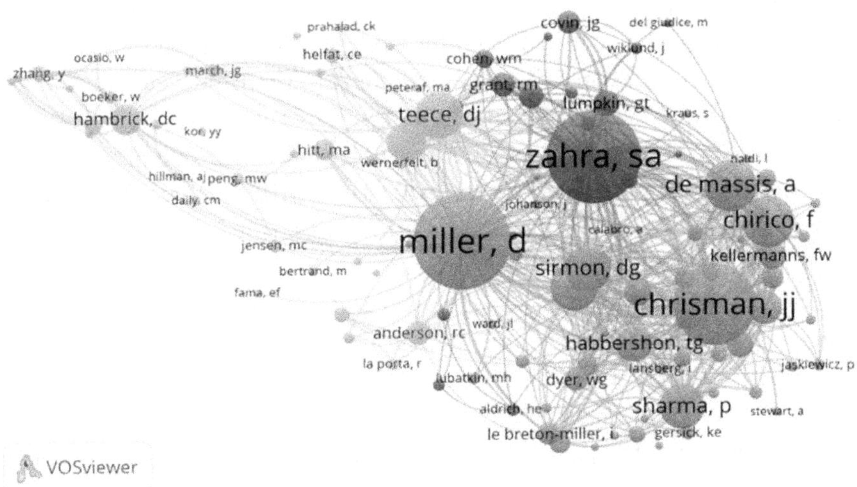

DISCUSSION AND CONCLUSIONS

Bibliometric methods have been instrumental in offering a comprehensive and longitudinal analysis of Knowledge Management in Family Firms (KMFF) research spanning three decades (1990-2020). Unlike other systematic literature reviews, bibliometric analyses delve into the intellectual structure and evolution of the corpus by emphasizing authors, affiliations, countries, citations, and co-citations. This approach provides a panoramic view of research production within specific disciplines or subjects, enabling assessment of impact and influence across various levels of aggregation.

In the context of a book chapter centered on "Cases on the Interplay Between Family, Society, and Entrepreneurship," a thorough bibliometric examination of KMFF research holds significant importance. Firstly, it aids in identifying the most influential contributors, including authors, universities, and countries, thereby assisting researchers, practitioners, and policymakers in making informed decisions and advancing the field. Knowledge of leading authors and institutions can facilitate collaboration opportunities, providing access to specialized resources, data, and expertise.

Secondly, comparing research productivity with that of renowned actors serves as a critical benchmark for evaluating academic work's quality and impact. This practice motivates researchers and institutions to strive for excellence and meet or exceed established standards, ultimately fostering a culture of academic rigor. Additionally, collaboration with esteemed actors enhances the credibility of research findings, as their reputation adds weight to the outcomes.

Thirdly, institutions and funding agencies can strategically allocate resources by identifying and supporting influential actors in KMFF research. Funding those with a substantial impact can drive advancements in the field, leading to a deeper understanding of knowledge management in family firms.

The results of this bibliometric analysis reveal a growing production of scientific outcomes, underscoring the increasing relevance of KMFF research among scholars. This growth is evident in the citation structure of published articles and the rising number of journals dedicated to this subject in the last decade.

However, it's essential to acknowledge certain limitations inherent to bibliometric techniques. For instance, performance indicators rely on full authorship assignment for each scientific product, which may not fully capture individual contributions. Additionally, co-citation analyses generate network maps based primarily on the strength of relations, potentially leading to skewed results. To address these concerns, a two-step methodology was employed in this chapter. Performance analysis combined simple and compounded indicators, while scientific mapping procedures utilized the fractional counting technique to provide a more accurate representation of the KMFF research landscape.

REFERENCES

Abbas, J., & Sağsan, M. (2019). Impact of knowledge management practices on green innovation and corporate sustainable development: A structural analysis. *Journal of Cleaner Production*, *229*, 611–620. doi:10.1016/j.jclepro.2019.05.024

Adner, R., & Helfat, C. E. (2003). Corporate effects and dynamic managerial capabilities. *Strategic Management Journal*, *24*(10), 1011–1025. doi:10.1002mj.331

Allio, M. K. (2004). Family businesses: Their virtues, vices, and strategic path. *Strategy and Leadership*, *32*(4), 24–33. doi:10.1108/10878570410576704

Anderson, R. C., & Reeb, D. M. (2003). Founding-family ownership and firm performance: Evidence from the S&P 500. *The Journal of Finance*, *58*(3), 1301–1328. doi:10.1111/1540-6261.00567

Andrade-Valbuena, N., Baier-Fuentes, H., & Gaviria-Marin, M. (2022). An Overview of Sustainable Entrepreneurship in Tourism, Destination, and Hospitality Research Based on the Web of Science. *Sustainability (Basel)*, *14*(22), 14944. doi:10.3390u142214944

Andrade-Valbuena, N. A., & Merigo, J. M. (2018). Outlining new product development research through bibliometrics: Analyzing journals, articles and researchers. *Journal of Strategy and Management*, *11*(3), 328–350. doi:10.1108/JSMA-08-2017-0061

Andrade-Valbuena, N. A., Merigó-Lindahl, J. M., Fernández, L. V., & Alarcón, C. N. (2019). Mapping leading universities in strategy research: Three decades of collaborative networks. *Cogent Business and Management*, *6*(1), 1–26. doi:10.1080/23311975.2019.1632569

Andrade-Valbuena, N. A., Merigo-Lindahl, J. M., & Olavarrieta, S. S. (2018). Bibliometric analysis of entrepreneurial orientation. *World Journal of Entrepreneurship, Management and Sustainable Development*, *15*(1), 45–69. doi:10.1108/WJEMSD-08-2017-0048

Andrade-Valbuena, N. A., Valenzuela-Fernández, L., & Merigó, J. M. (2022). Thirty-five years of strategic management research. A country analysis using bibliometric techniques for the 1987-2021 period. *Cuadernos de Gestión*, *22*(2), 7–22. doi:10.5295/cdg.211441na

Arzubiaga, U., De Massis, A., Kammerlander, N., & Hoy, F. (2022). Knowledge management in family firms: Opening the black box and suggestions for future research. *Journal of Knowledge Management*, *26*(2), 269–290. doi:10.1108/JKM-03-2022-924

Aviv, I., Hadar, I., & Levy, M. (2021). Knowledge management infrastructure framework for enhancing knowledge-intensive business processes. *Sustainability (Basel), 13*(20), 11387. doi:10.3390u132011387

Ballestar, M. T., Díaz-Chao, Á., Sainz, J., & Torrent-Sellens, J. (2020). Knowledge, robots and productivity in SMEs: Explaining the second digital wave. *Journal of Business Research, 108*, 119–131. doi:10.1016/j.jbusres.2019.11.017

Bamel, U. K., & Bamel, N. (2018). Organizational resources, KM process capability and strategic flexibility: A dynamic resource-capability perspective. *Journal of Knowledge Management, 22*(7), 1555–1572. doi:10.1108/JKM-10-2017-0460

Barroso-Martínez, A., Sanguino-Galván, R., & Bañegil-Palacios, T. M. (2016). Entrepreneurial Orientation and Knowledge Transfer: Analysis in Spanish family businesses. *Tourism & Management Studies, 12*(1), 211–219. doi:10.18089/tms.2016.12123

Bashir, M., & Farooq, R. (2019). The synergetic effect of knowledge management and business model innovation on firm competence: A systematic review. *International Journal of Innovation Science, 11*(3), 362–387. doi:10.1108/IJIS-10-2018-0103

Belkhodja, O. (2022). Managing knowledge resources in family firms: Opportunity or challenge? *Sustainability (Basel), 14*(9), 5087. doi:10.3390u14095087

Berman, S. L., Down, J., & Hill, C. W. (2002). Tacit knowledge as a source of competitive advantage in the National Basketball Association. *Academy of Management Journal, 45*(1), 13–31. doi:10.2307/3069282

Boyack, K. W., & Klavans, R. (2010). Co-citation analysis, bibliographic coupling, and direct citation: Which citation approach represents the research front most accurately? *Journal of the American Society for Information Science and Technology, 61*(12), 2389–2404. doi:10.1002/asi.21419

Cabrera-Suárez, K., de Saá-Pérez, P., & García-Almeida, D. (2009). The succession process from a resource-and knowledge-based view of the family firm. *Wiley Online Library, 14*(1), 37–46.

Cancino, C., Merigó, J., Urbano, D., & Amoros, J. (2020). Evolution of the entrepreneurship and innovation research in Ibero-America between 1986 and 2015. *Journal of Small Business Management*, 1–31.

Carayannis, E. G., Ferreira, J. J. M., & Fernandes, C. (2021). A prospective retrospective: Conceptual mapping of the intellectual structure and research trends of knowledge management over the last 25 years. *Journal of Knowledge Management*, *25*(8), 1977–1999. doi:10.1108/JKM-07-2020-0581

Carney, M. (2017). Corporate Governance and Competitive Advantage in Family–Controlled Firms. *Entrepreneurship Theory and Practice*, *29*(3), 249–265. doi:10.1111/j.1540-6520.2005.00081.x

Casillas, J. C., & Acedo, F. J. (2007). Evolution of the intellectual structure of family business literature: A bibliometric study of FBR. *Family Business Review*, *20*(2), 141–162. doi:10.1111/j.1741-6248.2007.00092.x

Casprini, E., Dabic, M., Kotlar, J., & Pucci, T. (2020). A bibliometric analysis of family firm internationalization research: Current themes, theoretical roots, and ways forward. *International Business Review*, *29*(5), 101715. doi:10.1016/j.ibusrev.2020.101715

Cerchione, R., Esposito, E., & Spadaro, M. R. (2016). A literature review on knowledge management in SMEs. *Knowledge Management Research and Practice*, *14*(2), 169–177. doi:10.1057/kmrp.2015.12

Chen, C. (2017). Science mapping: A systematic review of the literature. *Journal of Data and Information Science*, *2*(2), 1–40. doi:10.1515/jdis-2017-0006

Chirico, F. (2008). Knowledge Accumulation in Family Firms. *International Small Business Journal*, *26*(4), 433–462. doi:10.1177/0266242608091173

Chirico, F., & Salvato, C. (2016). Knowledge internalization and product development in family firms: When relational and affective factors matter. *Entrepreneurship Theory and Practice*, *40*(1), 201–229. doi:10.1111/etap.12114

Cisneros, L., Ibanescu, M., Keen, C., Lobato-Calleros, O., & Niebla-Zatarain, J. (2018). Bibliometric study of family business succession between 1939 and 2017: Mapping and analyzing authors' networks. *Scientometrics*, *117*(2), 919–951. doi:10.100711192-018-2889-1

Cobo, M. J., López-Herrera, A. G., Herrera-Viedma, E., & Herrera, F. (2011). Science mapping software tools: Review, analysis, and cooperative study among tools. *Journal of the American Society for Information Science and Technology*, *62*(7), 1382–1402. doi:10.1002/asi.21525

Dana, L. P., Kumar, S., Pandey, N., & Sureka, R. (2021). The Journal of Small Business Management: A bibliometric overview of 1996–2019. *Journal of Small Business Management, 59*(sup1), S215–S236.

De Massis, A., Frattini, F., & Lichtenthaler, U. (2013). Research on technological innovation in family firms: Present debates and future directions. *Family Business Review*, *26*(1), 10–31. doi:10.1177/0894486512466258

Edwards, J. S. (2022). Where knowledge management and information management meet: Research directions. *International Journal of Information Management*, *63*, 102458. doi:10.1016/j.ijinfomgt.2021.102458

Engström, A., Johansson, A., Edh Mirzaei, N., Sollander, K., & Barry, D. (2023). Knowledge creation in projects: An interactive research approach for deeper business insight. *International Journal of Managing Projects in Business*, *16*(1), 22–44. doi:10.1108/IJMPB-09-2021-0233

Fares, J., Chung, K. S. K., & Abbasi, A. (2021). Stakeholder theory and management: Understanding longitudinal collaboration networks. *PLoS One*, *16*(10), e0255658. doi:10.1371/journal.pone.0255658 PMID:34648505

Gaviria-Marin, M., Merigó, J. M., & Baier-Fuentes, H. (2019). Knowledge management: A global examination based on bibliometric analysis. *Technological Forecasting and Social Change*, *140*, 194–220. doi:10.1016/j.techfore.2018.07.006

Gaviria-Marin, M., Merigo, J. M., & Popa, S. (2018). Twenty years of the Journal of Knowledge Management: A bibliometric analysis. *Journal of Knowledge Management*, *22*(8), 1655–1687. doi:10.1108/JKM-10-2017-0497

Ghorbankhani, M., & Rossi, F. (2022). Intrinsic and strategic complementarity of research and knowledge transfer activities as determinants of knowledge transfer management: Evidence from public research organisations. *The Journal of Technology Transfer*, 1–27.

Glisby, M., & Holden, N. (2003). Contextual constraints in knowledge management theory: The cultural embeddedness of Nonaka's knowledge-creating company. *Knowledge and Process Management*, *10*(1), 29–36. doi:10.1002/kpm.158

Hatak, I. R., & Roessl, D. (2013). Relational Competence-Based Knowledge Transfer Within Intrafamily Succession. *Family Business Review*, *28*(1), 10–25. doi:10.1177/0894486513480386

Heck, R. K. Z., & Trent, E. S. (1999). The prevalence of family business from a household sample. *Family Business Review*, *12*(3), 209–219. doi:10.1111/j.1741-6248.1999.00209.x

Hirsch, J. E., & Buela-Casal, G. (2014). The meaning of the h-index. *International Journal of Clinical and Health Psychology*, *14*(2), 161–164. doi:10.1016/S1697-2600(14)70050-X

Kakabadse, N. K., Kakabadse, A., & Kouzmin, A. (2003). Reviewing the knowledge management literature: Towards a taxonomy. *Journal of Knowledge Management*, *7*(4), 75–91. doi:10.1108/13673270310492967

Kianto, A., Shujahat, M., Hussain, S., Nawaz, F., & Ali, M. (2019). The impact of knowledge management on knowledge worker productivity. *Baltic Journal of Management*, *14*(2), 178–197. doi:10.1108/BJM-12-2017-0404

Kleminski, R., Kazienko, P., & Kajdanowicz, T. (2022). Analysis of direct citation, co-citation and bibliographic coupling in scientific topic identification. *Journal of Information Science*, *48*(3), 349–373. doi:10.1177/0165551520962775

Laengle, S., Merigó, J. M., Modak, N. M., & Yang, J. B. (2020). Bibliometrics in operations research and management science: A university analysis. *Annals of Operations Research*, *294*(1–2), 769–813. doi:10.100710479-018-3017-6

Lamboglia, R., Lavorato, D., Scornavacca, E., & Za, S. (2021). Exploring the relationship between audit and technology. A bibliometric analysis. *Meditari Accountancy Research*, *29*(5), 1233–1260. doi:10.1108/MEDAR-03-2020-0836

Le Breton–Miller, I., & Miller, D. (2006). Why do some family businesses out–compete? Governance, long–term orientations, and sustainable capability. *Entrepreneurship Theory and Practice*, *30*(6), 731–746. doi:10.1111/j.1540-6520.2006.00147.x

Liew, A. (2013). DIKIW: Data, information, knowledge, intelligence, wisdom and their interrelationships. *Business Management Dynamics, 2*(10).

Ling-hsing, C., & Tung-Chin, L. (2015). The role of organizational culture in the knowledge management process. *Journal of Knowledge Management*, *19*(3), 433–455. doi:10.1108/JKM-08-2014-0353

Llanos-Herrera, G. R., & Merigo, J. M. (2019). Overview of brand personality research with bibliometric indicators. *Kybernetes*, *48*(3), 546–569. doi:10.1108/K-02-2018-0051

Lumpkin, G. T., Brigham, K. H., & Moss, T. W. (2010). Long-term orientation: Implications for the entrepreneurial orientation and performance of family businesses. *Entrepreneurship and Regional Development*, *22*(3–4), 241–264. doi:10.1080/08985621003726218

Mahdi, O. R., Nassar, I. A., & Almsafir, M. K. (2019). Knowledge management processes and sustainable competitive advantage: An empirical examination in private universities. *Journal of Business Research*, *94*, 320–334. doi:10.1016/j.jbusres.2018.02.013

Mas-Tur, A., Modak, N. M., Merigó, J. M., Roig-Tierno, N., Geraci, M., & Capecchi, V. (2019). Half a century of Quality & Quantity: A bibliometric review. *Quality & Quantity*, *53*(2), 981–1020. doi:10.100711135-018-0799-1

Miller, D., Le Breton-Miller, I., Lester, R. H., & Cannella, A. A. Jr. (2007). Are family firms really superior performers? *Journal of Corporate Finance*, *13*(5), 829–858. doi:10.1016/j.jcorpfin.2007.03.004

Nonaka, I. (1994). A dynamic theory of organizational knowledge creation. *Organization Science*, *5*(1), 14–37. doi:10.1287/orsc.5.1.14

Nonaka, I., & Takeuchi, H. (1995). The knowledge creating. Academic Press.

Orduña-Malea, E., & Costas, R. (2021). Link-based approach to study scientific software usage: The case of VOSviewer. *Scientometrics*, *126*(9), 8153–8186. doi:10.100711192-021-04082-y

Paul, J., & Criado, A. R. (2020). The art of writing literature review: What do we know and what do we need to know? *International Business Review*, *29*(4), 101717. doi:10.1016/j.ibusrev.2020.101717

Paul, J., & Rosado-Serrano, A. (2019). Gradual internationalization vs born-global/international new venture models: A review and research agenda. *International Marketing Review*, *36*(6), 830–858. doi:10.1108/IMR-10-2018-0280

Post, C., Sarala, R., Gatrell, C., & Prescott, J. E. (2020). Advancing Theory with Review Articles. *Journal of Management Studies*, *57*(2), 351–376. doi:10.1111/joms.12549

Price, D. P., Stoica, M., & Boncella, R. J. (2013). The relationship between innovation, knowledge, and performance in family and non-family firms: An analysis of SMEs. *Journal of Innovation and Entrepreneurship*, *2*(1), 14. doi:10.1186/2192-5372-2-14

Pütz, L., & Werner, A. (2023). Absorptive capacity in family firms: A systematic literature review. *Review of Managerial Science*, 1–56. doi:10.100711846-023-00651-y

Serenko, A. (2021). A structured literature review of scientometric research of the knowledge management discipline: A 2021 update. *Journal of Knowledge Management*, *25*(8), 1889–1925. doi:10.1108/JKM-09-2020-0730

Servantie, V., Cabrol, M., Guieu, G., & Boissin, J. P. (2016). Is international entrepreneurship a field? A bibliometric analysis of the literature (1989–2015). *Journal of International Entrepreneurship, 14*(2), 168–212.

Shahzad, M., Qu, Y., Zafar, A. U., Rehman, S. U., & Islam, T. (2020). Exploring the influence of knowledge management process on corporate sustainable performance through green innovation. *Journal of Knowledge Management*, *24*(9), 2079–2106. doi:10.1108/JKM-11-2019-0624

Shane, S., & Venkataraman, S. (2000). The promise of entrepreneurship as a field of research. *Academy of Management Review*, *25*(1), 217–226. doi:10.5465/amr.2000.2791611

Song, B., Li, Y., & Zhao, L. (2019). Complementary effect of knowledge management strategy on firm performance: Evidence from Chinese firms. *Sustainability (Basel)*, *11*(13), 3616. doi:10.3390u11133616

Su, E., & Daspit, J. (2022). Knowledge management in family firms: A systematic review, integrated insights and future research opportunities. *Journal of Knowledge Management*, *26*(2), 291–325.

Torraco, R. J. (2016). Writing Integrative Literature Reviews: Using the Past and Present to Explore the Future. *Human Resource Development Review*, *15*(4), 404–428. doi:10.1177/1534484316671606

Tzortzaki, A. M., & Mihiotis, A. (2014). A review of knowledge management theory and future directions. *Knowledge and Process Management*, *21*(1), 29–41. doi:10.1002/kpm.1429

Vallaster, C., Kraus, S., Lindahl, J., & Nielsen, A. (2019). Ethics and entrepreneurship: A bibliometric study and literature review. *Journal of Business Research*, *99*, 226–237. doi:10.1016/j.jbusres.2019.02.050

Van Eck, N., & Waltman, L. (2010). Software survey: VOSviewer, a computer program for bibliometric mapping. *Scientometrics, 84*(2), 523-538.

Van Eck, N. J., & Waltman, L. (2017). Citation-based clustering of publications using CitNetExplorer and VOSviewer. *Scientometrics*, *111*(2), 1053–1070. doi:10.100711192-017-2300-7 PMID:28490825

Villalonga, B., & Amit, R. (2006). How do family ownership, control and management affect firm value? *Journal of Financial Economics*, *80*(2), 385–417. doi:10.1016/j.jfineco.2004.12.005

Zack, M. H. (1999). Developing a knowledge strategy. *California Management Review*, *3*(3), 125–145. doi:10.2307/41166000

Zahra, S., & Dess, G. G. (2001). Entrepreneurship As a Field of Research: Encouraging Dialogue and Debate. *Academy of Management Review*, *26*(1), 8–10. doi:10.5465/amr.2001.4011916

Zhou, P., Tijssen, R., & Leydesdorff, L. (2016). University-industry collaboration in China and the USA: A bibliometric comparison. *PLoS One*, *11*(11), e0165277. doi:10.1371/journal.pone.0165277 PMID:27832084

Zupic, I., & Čater, T. (2015). Bibliometric Methods in Management and Organization. *Organizational Research Methods*, *18*(3), 429–472. doi:10.1177/1094428114562629

KEY TERMS AND DEFINITIONS

Bibliometrics: A quantitative method used to analyze and measure patterns, impact, and relationships within scientific literature. It focuses on aspects such as citations, authors, institutions, and publications.

Citation Patterns: Refer to the ways in which academic works, such as articles or papers, cite and reference other scholarly sources. They provide insights into the influence, connections, and impact of research.

Co-Citation Analysis: An exploration that involves identifying and analyzing the frequency with which two or more documents are cited together by other scholarly works. This reveals connections and relationships between those documents.

Corpus of Research: Refers to the collection of relevant academic papers, articles, and studies systematically gathered and analyzed to address a specific research question or topic.

Family Firms: Businesses where ownership and control are primarily held by one or more families. These companies are often managed and operated by family members across generations.

Knowledge Management: The process of capturing, organizing, storing, and sharing an organization's knowledge and information to enhance decision-making, innovation, and overall performance.

Systematic Literature Review: A rigorous and structured approach to identifying, analyzing, and synthesizing existing research on a specific topic. It provides a comprehensive overview of the current state of knowledge in the field.

VOS Network Analysis: A method that visualizes and analyzes relationships between research elements, such as authors, journals, or keywords. It uses network graphs to reveal patterns and connections in scholarly literature.

Chapter 11
Appraising the Influence of Social Support on Entrepreneurial Success and Sustainability

Olalekan Adisa
University of Northampton, UK

EXECUTIVE SUMMARY

This chapter critically explores the intricate relationship between social support and entrepreneurial success, examining the profound impact that various sociocultural norms and factors have on the experiences of entrepreneurs. It delves into the distinctive roles of both individualistic and collectivistic cultures in shaping the availability and utilization of social support. The chapter concludes by underscoring the profound influence of social support on entrepreneurial success and sustainability. It highlights a range of strategies for optimizing social support, including proactive network building, promoting inclusivity, managing reliance on social support, and effective time management. It concludes by examining the significant influence of cultural and societal norms on entrepreneurial activities, with suggestions on future research on how to integrate theories or develop new theoretical frameworks for a more comprehensive understanding of the dynamics between social support and entrepreneurship.

DOI: 10.4018/978-1-6684-8748-8.ch011

INTRODUCTION

Historically, the role of social support, especially from families, has been instrumental in entrepreneurial successes (Zhu, Burmeister-Lamp & Hsu, 2017). European and Asian economies, with their rich tapestry of family-run businesses, from the Medici dynasty in Renaissance Italy to the sprawling business chaebols in modern-day South Korea, underline the persistent and evolving influence of family in entrepreneurial pursuits (Cardella, Hernandez-Sanchez & Garcia, 2020).

The trend of familial involvement in business, while rooted in history, has metamorphosed over the ages. In earlier times, it was a matter of legacy and lineage, but contemporary family enterprises exhibit a blend of tradition and modern managerial practices.

The social cognitive theory emphasizes the role of learning from family, suggesting that entrepreneurship is often a skill honed within the family's ambit (Cardella, Hernandez-Sanchez & Garcia, 2020). The theory of planned behavior further elaborates, suggesting that family, as a significant 'subjective norm', heavily impacts entrepreneurial intentions. Lastly, the regulatory focus theory adds nuance, explaining how entrepreneurs, influenced by their familial backdrop, set goals that are either promotion-focused or prevention-focused (Zhu, Burmeister-Lamp & Hsu, 2017).

CASE STUDY

Case Study 1: The Tata Group (India)

One of Asia's most venerable business conglomerates, the Tata Group, offers a glimpse into the power of family dynamics and social support in the entrepreneurial journey. Founded by Jamsetji Tata in the late 19th century, the group faced several challenges, from colonial regulatory impediments to post-independence nationalization threats. Yet, with each generational transition, the conglomerate not only survived but thrived, thanks in no small measure to the family's cohesive vision and the emotional and strategic support they provided one another (Zhu, Burmeister-Lamp & Hsu, 2017).

The Tata journey aligns with the social cognitive theory, which underscores the importance of learning within a social context. The Tata heirs have often spoken of lessons imbibed from their predecessors, shaping their leadership styles and decisions. The theory of planned behavior also finds resonance here, with attitudes towards entrepreneurship being molded by familial norms and a long-standing legacy. The regulatory focus theory elucidates the Group's goal-setting tendencies, influenced heavily by its familial ethos and societal expectations.

Case Study 2: Donald Trump

Donald Trump's journey exemplifies the ebbs and flows of entrepreneurship. Faced with a series of business bankruptcies, Trump's ability to rebound each time is a testament to his resilience and the value of social support systems. His family played a pivotal role in providing not just financial backing but also the emotional sustenance needed to navigate such tumultuous times. This case affirms the propositions of the social cognitive theory, emphasizing the role of observational learning, reinforcements, and social reactions in shaping entrepreneurial behaviours (Kosuri & Pantin, 2021).

Moreover, Trump's trajectory aligns with the Theory of Planned Behavior, accentuating the connection between intentions and behaviours. These are shaped by a range of factors such as attitudes, subjective norms - in this case, family - and perceived behavioral control. His experiences also resonate with the Regulatory Focus Theory, which outlines how individuals pursue goals based on motivational concerns.

The case study above provides an apt transition into the increasing relevance of family dynamics in shaping entrepreneurial intentions and self-efficacy in the fast-paced economic landscape. Entrepreneurship is a vital engine for economic growth and innovation. Therefore, there are calls for a comprehensive grasp of the multifaceted factors that influence an individual's entrepreneurial aspirations and their belief in their ability to succeed. Among these factors, the role of family dynamics has emerged as particularly influential, receiving significant scholarly attention in recent years.

Family dynamics, which include elements such as parental influence, family support and the overall family environment, can significantly mold an individual's perspective towards entrepreneurship and their confidence in their entrepreneurial capabilities. However, the relationship between family dynamics and entrepreneurial intention and self-efficacy is intricate and multi-dimensional, necessitating a comprehensive investigation.

This chapter aims to delve into the fascinating intersection of family dynamics and entrepreneurship. The objectives of this chapter are threefold:

1. To explore the role of the family in the entrepreneurial process, including the extent of family involvement and support.
2. To examine the impact of family dynamics on the success of the business, including challenges faced and strategies used to overcome them.
3. To investigate the role of societal norms and values in shaping the relationship between family and entrepreneurship.

The structure of this chapter is as follows:

Initially, it will offer a comprehensive review of the existing literature on the influence of family dynamics on entrepreneurial intention and self-efficacy. This will encompass an examination of key theories and empirical studies in the field.

Subsequently, the chapter will present a series of case studies that exemplify the theories and concepts discussed in the literature review. These case studies will offer practical and teachable insights into how family dynamics can shape entrepreneurial intentions and self-efficacy in real-world contexts.

Finally, the chapter will discuss the implications of the literature and case studies for theory and practice and suggest areas for future research. By exploring the influence of family dynamics on entrepreneurial intention and self-efficacy, this chapter aims to contribute to the understanding of the personal and contextual factors that shape entrepreneurship.

Problem Statement

Historically, family-owned enterprises have been a cornerstone of global economic activity, especially prominent in European and Asian contexts. This deep-rooted tradition highlights the profound interplay between entrepreneurship and family dynamics. Despite entrepreneurship's acknowledged value to economic progress, the journey is laden with relational challenges stemming from family expectations and obligations, emotional tribulations of striking a balance between personal and professional realms and informational dilemmas pertaining to business acumen transfer within family-run ventures (Cardella, Hernandez-Sanchez & Garcia, 2020).

The interplay between family dynamics and entrepreneurial intentions has been studied extensively in the field of entrepreneurial research. However, there is a noticeable gap in understanding how varying familial interactions, roles and patterns directly influence an entrepreneur's intentions and eventual success (Zhu, Burmeister-Lamp & Hsu, 2017). Given the profound impact family can have on an individual's professional journey, there is an urgent need to dissect and comprehend these dynamics further. It became increasingly imperative to discern how family dynamics, laden with societal norms and historical expectations, impact entrepreneurial success and decision-making, as economies and societies evolved, and as entrepreneurial horizons broadened.

Research Questions

1. In what ways do family dynamics, bolstered by societal norms, affect an individual's propensity and confidence in undertaking entrepreneurial endeavours?

2. What unique challenges emerge from the confluence of family and business, and how are these navigated?
3. How do extant societal values and traditions mold the role of family in entrepreneurial ventures?

Family Dynamics and Entrepreneurial Intentions

Family dynamics refer to the patterns of interactions among family members and the rules that govern these behaviours. These dynamics can vary greatly from family to family, and understanding them can help improve family relationships, increase self-awareness and confidence, resolve conflicts healthily and provide a sense of security (Jabbari & Rouster, 2022). For example, family dynamics can include patterns of communication, roles, and responsibilities, problem-solving, decision-making and beliefs and values. These dynamics can be influenced by several factors such as family size, the level of parental control and the presence of any exceptional circumstances such as divorce, illness or disability (Jabbari & Rouster, 2022).

The Lee Family Business

The Lee family, based in Seoul, South Korea, has been in the textile business for three generations. With changing family dynamics over the decades, their business experienced fluctuations in growth. Youngest son Joon, after studying abroad, returned with intentions to diversify the business, but faced resistance from elder family members. This case examines how their family's communication patterns and roles influenced Joon's entrepreneurial intentions and the eventual direction the business took (Shen, 2015).

Family Dynamics in an Entrepreneurial Context

Family dynamics can play a pivotal role, for instance, a study by Bignotti and Le Roux (2016) found that entrepreneurship education and entrepreneurial characteristics per se do not positively influence entrepreneurial intentions. However, once interaction effects were introduced, entrepreneurship education moderated the influence of the need for achievement and family support on entrepreneurial intentions in a positive direction. In another study by Fitz-Koch, Cooper, and Discua Cruz (2019), they found that understanding the complexities and dynamics of family business groups begins with recognizing that the intentions and actions of business members are simultaneously actions and intentions of family members. This study shows that business groups can be the outcome of an emerging strategy that aligns with family members' identities as well as the context in which they operate.

In a different context, a study by Gubik (2019) found that the most important factors influencing attitudes towards entrepreneurship are identified and the entrepreneurial intentions towards entrepreneurship are determined, the fields of intervention targeting the creation of as many new and viable enterprises as possible can be defined. These studies suggest that family dynamics, including the level of family support and the alignment of family and business identities, can significantly influence entrepreneurial intentions. However, it's also important to note that other factors, such as entrepreneurship education and individual characteristics, can also play a role and may interact with family dynamics in complex ways.

The Role of Family in the Entrepreneurial Process

The family plays a crucial role in the entrepreneurial process. This role can be manifested in various ways, including the provision of financial support, emotional support and practical assistance. The family can also serve as a source of inspiration and role models for aspiring entrepreneurs. However, the role of the family in the entrepreneurial process is not always positive. In some cases, family dynamics can create obstacles and challenges for entrepreneurs. For instance, family conflicts can distract entrepreneurs from their business activities, and family responsibilities can limit the time and energy that entrepreneurs can devote to their businesses.

The Di Angelo Wineries

Hailing from the vineyards of Tuscany, Italy, the Di Angelo family boasts a legacy of fine wines. However, when Sofia Di Angelo decided to expand into the US market, she met with skepticism from her family, highlighting traditional methods. The case sheds light on how familial roles, responsibilities and emotional support, or lack thereof, can shape entrepreneurial processes (Pesic & Dalgaard, 2013).

Impact of Family Dynamics on Business Success

Family dynamics can have a significant impact on the success of a business. Positive family dynamics, such as persuasive communication, mutual respect, and shared values, can contribute to a supportive and nurturing environment for the business. On the other hand, negative family dynamics, such as conflicts, power struggles and lack of trust, can create a stressful and disruptive environment that can hinder the business's growth and success.

The Impacts Include

Negative family dynamics can introduce substantial obstacles for family businesses. These challenges often manifest in the following ways:

- Disputes over resource allocation and leadership: Disagreements among family members regarding the distribution of resources or the assignment of leadership roles can instigate conflicts detrimental to the business (Rahim, 2023).
- Communication gaps: Avoidance of challenging conversations can lead to misunderstandings and a lack of trust within the family, which can negatively impact the business (Sue, 2016).
- Interpersonal tension: Divergent expectations for the business among family members can create friction and resentment, further complicating business operations (Hoover & Hoover, 2013).
- The decline in revenue and success: Negative family dynamics can significantly affect the business's performance. The family's systems and responses to disruptions can have profound effects on gross revenue and the owner's perceived success (Nose, Korunka & Frank, 2017).

These challenges, if not addressed, can lead to the disintegration of the family business. To mitigate these issues, family businesses may need to focus on enhancing communication, resolving conflicts and fostering a shared vision. Establishing decision-making processes that balance the business's needs with family members' expectations can also be beneficial (Rahim, 2023; Sue, 2016).

The Chan Conundrum

The Chan family business in Hong Kong was a thriving electronics enterprise. However, unresolved disputes between siblings Helen and Richard over leadership roles and resource allocation led to a decline. Their case underscores the significant role family dynamics play in the success, or downfall, of a family business (Au, Chiang & Birtch, 2013).

ENTREPRENEURIAL INTENTIONS

In the context of entrepreneurial intentions, family dynamics refer to the influence of familial relationships, roles and interactions on an individual's aspiration and capability to initiate and manage a business. The concept of family dynamics is expansive and can include various aspects such as parental influence, family support, family business background and family values and norms (Vershinina, Rodgers, McAdam & Clinton, 2019).

One argument supporting the influence of family dynamics on entrepreneurial intentions posits that the family serves as a crucial socializing agent that shapes an individual's attitudes, behaviours, and intentions, including those related to entrepreneurship. For instance, Rachmawan, Lizar and Mangundjaya (2015) found that self-efficacy, nurtured within the family environment, has a positive and considerable influence on entrepreneurial intention. Similarly, Altinay, Madanoglu, Daniele and Lashley (2012) suggested that family entrepreneurial background and innovation influence the intention to start a new business.

Conversely, family dynamics may not always exert a positive influence on entrepreneurial intentions. For instance, Rachmawan et al. (2015) found that parental influence does not significantly influence entrepreneurial intention. This suggests that while the family environment can provide support and resources, it does not necessarily translate into a desire to engage in entrepreneurial activities.

Another counterargument is that the influence of family dynamics on entrepreneurial intentions is moderated or influenced by other factors. For example, Turulja, Veselinović, Agić and Pašić-Mesihović (2020) found that the negative relationship between the fear of failure and entrepreneurial intention is moderated by informal support, such as support from family and friends. This suggests that the influence of family dynamics on entrepreneurial intentions is not straightforward and is by individual psychological factors and external support systems.

Entrepreneurial Intentions: The Nguyen Tech Venture

Trang Nguyen, from Hanoi, Vietnam, comes from a family of traditional crafters. Despite her family's lack of understanding of the tech industry, Trang pursued her passion, influenced by her family's strong work ethic and values. The Nguyen case delves into the notion that while family might not always directly influence the entrepreneurial intentions in terms of the business domain, they do play a role in shaping the drive, ambition, and values of the entrepreneur (Nguyen, 2015).

SOCIETAL NORMS, VALUES, AND ENTREPRENEURSHIP

Societal norms and values can shape the relationship between family and entrepreneurship in significant ways. In societies that value entrepreneurship and view it as a desirable career path, families are more likely to encourage and support their members' entrepreneurial aspirations. Conversely, in societies that view entrepreneurship as risky or undesirable, families may discourage their members from pursuing entrepreneurial activities.

Entrepreneurial Ambitions in a Traditional Society

Background

Samira was born and raised in a conservative town in Northern India. Coming from a tight-knit community, societal norms played a significant role in shaping family decisions. As is typical in many parts of India, familial opinions, particularly those of elders, are often highly valued, and the broader society's view on specific roles can overshadow personal desires (Derne, 1994).

Dilemma

Samira was always enthusiastic about creating a start-up focused on eco-friendly products after her undergraduate studies in environmental science. She noticed a gap in the market for affordable, sustainable goods and felt she could create a niche. However, the society she lived in believed that young women, especially those of her age, should focus on marriage and family rather than the unpredictable world of entrepreneurship (Kanter, 1977).

While her friends from college, based in more urban settings, had their families' full support in pursuing start-ups, Samira's family was hesitant. They believed in the traditional path for women and feared the backlash from society, which might label her as "too ambitious" or "not focused on her primary duties."

Outcome

Against her family's wishes, Samira decided to move to Bengaluru, the start-up hub of India, to pursue her dream. With the challenges of being away from home and facing societal criticisms both from her hometown and peers, the journey was not easy. However, her passion and the mentorship she received in Bengaluru helped her navigate through the challenges.

Two years down the line, her start-up began to gain traction. As her success stories started appearing in local newspapers, the same societal norms that once looked down on her entrepreneurial ambitions began to celebrate her achievements. Witnessing her accomplishments, her family's perspective changed. They not only became supportive but also became her biggest cheerleaders.

Samira's journey demonstrates the profound influence societal norms can have on entrepreneurial aspirations, especially for women in traditionally conservative settings. It underscores the idea that while societal norms and values are significant, they can evolve and adapt with time and become success stories.

Discussion Questions

1. How do societal norms in various cultures influence entrepreneurial ambitions, especially for women?
2. What are the challenges faced by individuals who go against the societal grain to pursue their entrepreneurial dreams?
3. How can society play a role in fostering a more inclusive entrepreneurial ecosystem?

The Influence of Societal Norms and Values on Family Dynamics and Entrepreneurship

Societal norms and values significantly shape the entrepreneurial landscape within a family. These norms and values can either foster or hinder entrepreneurial activities within the family. For instance, in societies where entrepreneurship is highly valued and encouraged, family members are more likely to support and engage in entrepreneurial activities. Conversely, in societies where entrepreneurship is not highly valued or even discouraged, family members may be less supportive of entrepreneurial activities.

A study by Stephan and Uhlaner (2010) provides a compelling example of the role of societal norms and values in shaping the relationship between family and entrepreneurship. They conducted a cross-national study evaluating a framework relating cultural descriptive norms to entrepreneurship in a sample of 40 nations. The article identified two higher-order dimensions of culture - socially supportive culture (SSC) and performance-based culture (PBC) - and related them to entrepreneurship rates and associated supply-side and demand-side variables. Their findings provide dedicated support for a social capital/SSC and supply-side variable explanation of entrepreneurship rate (Stephan & Uhlaner, 2010).

Societal norms and values can also influence the types of entrepreneurial activities considered acceptable or desirable. For instance, certain types of businesses are considered more prestigious or acceptable than others by some societies. This could influence the types of entrepreneurial activities that individuals and families engage in (Stephan & Pathak, 2016).

Moreover, societal norms and values can also shape the family's attitudes and behaviours towards entrepreneurship. For instance, if a society values independence and risk-taking, families in that society may be more likely to encourage their members to pursue entrepreneurial activities. On the other hand, if a society values stability and security, families in that society may be more likely to discourage their members from pursuing entrepreneurial activities (Autio, Pathak & Wennberg, 2013).

In conclusion, societal norms and values play a crucial role in shaping the relationship between family dynamics and entrepreneurship. Understanding these societal influences is essential for developing effective strategies to promote entrepreneurship and support entrepreneurs. Future research could further explore this topic and provide more specific insight into the role of societal norms and values in shaping the relationship between family dynamics and entrepreneurship.

The Sharma Family and the Kowalski Family: Societal Perceptions and the Entrepreneurial Dream

Background

The Sharma family resides in Bengaluru (Bangalore), India - a city often touted as the Silicon Valley of India. Here, entrepreneurship is revered, with a robust startup ecosystem supported by government policies, abundant venture capital and a young, tech-savvy population (Ghosh & Natarjan, 2019). Societal norms in India, especially in its urban centres, have been shifting to view entrepreneurship as an aspirational career path (Sivathanu & Pillai, 2020).

Contrastingly, the Kowalski family hails from a small town near Warsaw, Poland. While Poland boasts a growing economy, traditional sectors like manufacturing dominate the landscape. In smaller towns, there is still a societal leaning towards pursuing stable jobs over entrepreneurial ventures, especially given Poland's tumultuous past with economic stability (Daszkiewicz & Wach, 2014).

Dilemma

Raj Sharma, a young engineer in India, has a passion for renewable energy. With India's push for sustainability and the country's favorable view of entrepreneurship, Raj's family is not only supportive but actively encourages him to launch his startup. His parents, while not entrepreneurs themselves, understand the changing societal landscape and believe in the merits of risk-taking in the modern economy (Sivathanu & Pillai, 2020).

Meanwhile, in Poland, Jakub Kowalski has a similar passion for sustainable energy solutions. However, the narrative here is different. His family, recalling economic hardships and valuing job security, fears the unpredictability of entrepreneurship (Kurten, 2018). They would rather Jakub secure a stable job with a multinational company than take a risk with a startup.

Outcome

Backed by his family's moral and sometimes financial support, Raj launches his renewable energy startup in Bengaluru. Leveraging the city's vast network of mentors, investors and fellow entrepreneurs, his business thrives. The Sharma family's encouragement, rooted in India's budding entrepreneurial culture, plays a crucial role in Raj's success.

On the other hand, Jakub faces an uphill battle. Despite his determination, the lack of family support affects his self-confidence. He juggles between a part-time job to finance his venture and working on his startup. Eventually, after a prolonged struggle and without adequate resources or support, Jakub puts his entrepreneurial dream on hold and takes up a full-time role in a multinational firm.

Discussion Questions

1. How do societal norms in different countries shape family dynamics regarding entrepreneurship?
2. How can young entrepreneurs navigate and possibly change deeply entrenched family views on entrepreneurship?
3. Can government policies and societal changes influence family perspectives on entrepreneurial ventures?

Influence of Family Dynamics on Entrepreneurship Intentions and Self-Efficacy Across Different Scenarios

The influence of family dynamics on entrepreneurship intentions and self-efficacy is a multifaceted topic that has been explored in various contexts, including Europe, the Asia, Europe, and Africa. This analysis will critically discuss the role of family dynamics in shaping entrepreneurial intentions and self-efficacy, supported by empirical evidence from two articles each.

China, the US, Southern Africa, Latin America, and Poland

Family dynamics can significantly shape an individual's entrepreneurial intentions and self-efficacy. According to a study published in Springer, family factors are recognized as important indicators in the establishment of a business (Alberto-Molina, 2020). The article presents five empirical examples that show connections between the gender variable in the family and the entrepreneurial decision, with important evidence for China, the US, Southern Africa, Latin America, and Poland. The article also provides a theoretical framework to understand the process of succession in family firms. In addition to these specific issues on entrepreneurship and self-employment, this article also includes other labor topics related to family variables, such as occupational gender segregation, maternal employment, mothers' work, family conflict and job insecurity (Yuan, Hu & Rong, 2021). The study suggests that businesses created by autonomous, family-motivated entrepreneurs have a higher chance of survival. This implies that the family environment can foster a sense of autonomy and motivation, which are crucial for entrepreneurial success.

Entrepreneurial activities are the outcome of various individual dispositional and environmental factors. A study conducted by Ahmed et al. (2021) aimed to investigate the impact of entrepreneurial self-efficacy on intentions through the mediating role of regret and moderation of family support. The study collected data through a questionnaire from 435 students of three large public sector universities at two points of time with an interval of four months. The findings suggest that self-efficacy influences entrepreneurial intentions through regret, while the absence of family support increases regret (Ahmed et al., 2021). As the family support is often perceived to be absent in the Pakistani entrepreneurial culture, the outcomes are distinctive. These findings add value in the existing literature by linking family support, self-efficacy and regret association, and their ultimate influence on entrepreneurial intentions (Ahmed et al., 2021).

The study further highlights several variables related to the family that influence entrepreneurship, including gender, age, marital status, parenthood and family income. For instance, it is reported that female self-employment is positively associated with the presence of children in the family. This suggests that family dynamics, such as having children, can influence women's entrepreneurial intentions and self-efficacy. Moreover, being married is a significant determinant of self-employment, especially among women. This indicates that marital status, a key aspect of family dynamics, can influence entrepreneurship intentions and self-efficacy.

Africa (South Africa)

The article by Bignotti and Le-Roux (2016), "Unravelling the conundrum of entrepreneurial intentions, entrepreneurship education, and entrepreneurial characteristics", investigated the individual and combined effect of entrepreneurship education and entrepreneurial characteristics on youth entrepreneurial intentions. The study found that entrepreneurship education and entrepreneurial characteristics per se do not influence entrepreneurial intentions positively. It also also discusses the importance of social networks, which include family networks, for entrepreneurs in a developing country context like South Africa. However, once interaction effects were introduced, entrepreneurship education moderated the influence of need for achievement and family support on entrepreneurial intentions in a positive direction.

In conclusion, family dynamics play a significant role in shaping entrepreneurship intentions and self-efficacy in Asia (China and Pakistan), Poland and the US, then Africa. Factors such as gender, age, marital status, parenthood and family income, entrepreneurial education, and entrepreneurial characteristics as well as the level of family support, can significantly influence an individual's entrepreneurial intentions and self-efficacy. However, it is important to note that the influence of family dynamics on entrepreneurship can vary depending on the specific context and cultural norms. Therefore, further research is needed to fully understand the complex relationship between family dynamics and entrepreneurship in diverse cultural contexts.

The Rodriguez Legacy: Balancing Tradition and Innovation in Mexico

Background

The Rodriguez family has been a prominent name in Guadalajara, Mexico, for generations. Starting with a small brick-and-mortar store selling traditional Mexican handicrafts in the early 1900s, the family business expanded into a chain of stores across the country. The family's entrepreneurial ventures have traditionally been in retail and real estate (Ralat, 2020).

Dilemma

Carlos Rodriguez, the youngest of the third generation, recently graduated from a university in the US with a degree in digital marketing. He recognized the global demand for authentic Mexican handicrafts and saw the potential of leveraging technology to tap into the international market through e-commerce. However, his vision for an online platform selling Mexican handicrafts was met with skepticism by the older members of the Rodriguez family. They believed in the traditional way of doing business, valuing face-to-face interactions, and fearing the unfamiliarity of the digital world (Hernández-Linares, López-Fernández, Garcia-Piqueres, Cunha & Rego, 2023).

Moreover, some family members doubted Carlos's self-efficacy due to his young age and perceived lack of experience in the "real world" of business. His cousins, who were of a similar age, were more inclined to follow the tried and tested path, seeing it as a safer option (Morales-Gualdron & Roig, 2005). This created tension at family meetings where they discussed the future of the business.

Outcome

Carlos, determined to prove the potential of his idea and backed by a few supportive family members, started a small online platform using his savings. The initial months were challenging, but as international orders started pouring in, the business began to thrive. Recognizing the success and potential of the e-commerce model, the older generation began to acknowledge the changing business landscape. They offered to invest in Carlos's venture to expand it further. With the combined resources and knowledge of both the traditional and modern aspects of business, the Rodriguez family successfully merged their brick-and-mortar legacy with the digital age, reaching customers worldwide.

Carlos's journey not only transformed the family's business but also brought about a change in their mindset. The older generation realized the importance of adapting to changing times, while the younger members witnessed the value of resilience, innovation and bridging generational gaps for entrepreneurial success.

Discussion Questions

1. How do family dynamics influence the entrepreneurial intentions of younger members in multi-generational businesses?
2. How can the generational gaps in family businesses be addressed to ensure growth and adaptation to changing business environments?
3. What role does self-efficacy play in determining the success of young entrepreneurs in traditional family settings?

ENTREPRENEURIAL SELF-EFFICACY (ESE)

The concept of "entrepreneurial self-efficacy" (ESE) is a significant topic in entrepreneurship research. It refers to an individual's belief in their ability to successfully perform entrepreneurial tasks and roles. This belief is a key determinant of entrepreneurial intentions and actions (Neneh, 2020). Zhao, Seibert, and Hills (2005) conducted a study that highlighted the mediating role of self-efficacy in the development of students' intentions to become entrepreneurs. They found that self-efficacy fully mediated the effects of perceived learning from entrepreneurship-related courses, previous entrepreneurial experience, and risk propensity on entrepreneurial intentions. However, they also found that gender played no mediating role with self-efficacy but had a direct effect such that women reported lower entrepreneurial career intentions.

Piperopoulos and Dimov (2015) examined the relationship between students' self-efficacy beliefs and entrepreneurial intentions in the context of entrepreneurship courses. They found that higher self-efficacy was associated with lower entrepreneurial intentions in theoretically oriented courses and higher entrepreneurial intentions in oriented courses. This suggests that the nature of the entrepreneurship course, whether (theoretically or oriented) can influence the relationship between self-efficacy and entrepreneurial intentions.

Hmieleski and Baron (2008) explored the effects of ESE on firm performance and found that these effects were moderated by dispositional optimism and environmental dynamism. In dynamic environments, the effects of high ESE on firm performance were positive when combined with moderate optimism, but negative when combined with high optimism. In stable environments, the effects of self-efficacy were weak and were not moderated by optimism.

Newman, Obschonka, Schwarz, Cohen, and Nielsen (2019) conducted a systematic review of the literature on ESE, highlighting its theoretical foundations, measurement, antecedents, and outcomes. They suggested the need to consider alternative theoretical perspectives to improve understanding of how ESE influences outcomes at various levels of analysis. They also identified a need to examine the factors which drive short-term fluctuations and long-term changes in ESE and to investigate whether ESE can be treated as a collective-level phenomenon.

Luthans and Ibrayeva (2006) examined the self-efficacy of entrepreneurs in the transition economies of Kazakhstan and Kyrgyzstan. They found that their self-efficacy had a direct and mediating impact on performance. This study contributes to a better understanding of successful entrepreneurial practices in countries undergoing the complicated process of transition to a market economy.

JOURNEY OF ENTREPRENEURIAL SELF-BELIEF: LI MING AND SOFIA RODRIGUEZ

Case 1: Li Ming's Transformation Through Entrepreneurship Education

Background

Li Ming is a final year business student in Shanghai, China. China has rapidly evolved into an entrepreneurial powerhouse, spurred by supportive government policies, technological advancements, and significant market potential (Mirko, D'Agostino & Jin, 2023). However, Li Ming, despite being technically sound, has always been apprehensive about starting her own venture.

Journey

During her final year, Li enrolls in an intensive entrepreneurship course, a curriculum infused with not only theory but also real-world challenges and mentorship. The course requires students to develop a business plan, pitch it to real investors and receive feedback from successful entrepreneurs (Zhao, Seibert & Hills, 2005).

Throughout the course, Li Ming's perception changes; she starts believing in her abilities to navigate the entrepreneurial world, understand market dynamics and build a viable business model. This development in her ESE significantly shapes her intention to launch her startup upon graduation.

Outcome

Post-graduation, Li Ming takes the leap, bolstered by her heightened ESE. She successfully launches a fintech startup, attributing much of her success and confidence to the entrepreneurship course.

Case 2: Sofia Rodriguez and Her Venture in a Dynamic Landscape

Background

Sofia Rodriguez from Santiago, Chile, a Latin American nation known for its thriving startup ecosystem, particularly in technology and innovation sectors (Khavul, Bruton & Wood, 2009), had always been an optimist. With a dream of making a mark in the e-commerce space, she launched her venture amid rapid technological changes and fierce competition.

Journey

Sofia's high ESE and optimism were her driving forces. Even in challenging times, such as facing planning issues or dealing with unsatisfied customers, her intrinsic belief in her abilities ensured she found solutions. She continuously adapted, learning from mistakes, and seeking mentorship from industry veterans (Boyd & Vizikis, 1994).

Sofia's resilience, coupled with her high ESE, ensured her team remained motivated. Her optimism became infectious, leading to a positive organisational culture.

Outcome

Despite facing multiple challenges typical in a dynamic e-commerce environment, Sofia's firm outperformed several competitors. Her steadfast belief in her entrepreneurial abilities, backed by optimism, played a pivotal role in her firm's success and longevity in the market.

Discussion Questions

1. How does entrepreneurial education impact an individual's ESE and subsequently their entrepreneurial intentions?
2. How can entrepreneurs maintain elevated levels of ESE in rapidly changing environments?
3. How does an entrepreneur's ESE influence their team and overall firm performance?

CASE STUDIES REVIEW

The article "The influence of family tradition and psychological traits on entrepreneurial intention" by Altinay, Madanoglu, Daniele and Lashley (2012) suggests that self-efficacy has a significant positive influence on entrepreneurial intention, but parental influence does not significantly affect entrepreneurial intention. The study suggests that developing self-efficacy through training, coaching, and mentoring can enhance entrepreneurial intention.

"The influence of family tradition and psychological traits on entrepreneurial intention" by Altinay, Madanoglu, Daniele and Lashley (2012): This article suggests that family entrepreneurial background and innovation influence the intention to start a new business. It also found a positive relationship between tolerance of ambiguity and risk-taking propensity and a negative relationship between locus of control and risk-taking propensity.

"The effects of demographic, cognitive and institutional factors on the development of entrepreneurial intention: Toward a socio-cognitive model of entrepreneurial career" by Farashah (2015): This study found that entrepreneurial self-efficacy beliefs and entrepreneurial career outcome expectations are significantly correlated with entrepreneurial intention. It also found that mastery experience, exposure to a role model, social persuasion through media and fear of failure are significant sources of ESE.

"Familial factors, personality traits and self-efficacy as determinants of entrepreneurial intention among vocational based college of education students in

Oyo State, Nigeria" by Akanbi and Alayande (2013): This study found that familial factors, certain personality traits (extraversion, agreeableness, conscientiousness, neuroticism, openness) and self-efficacy significantly contribute to the prediction of entrepreneurial intention.

"Influence of Family Circumstances, Peer Circumstances and Entrepreneurial Learning on Entrepreneurial Interests with Self-Efficacy as Intervening Variables" by Supandi, Wulandari and Naufalin (2022): This study suggests that family environment, peer environment and entrepreneurship learning directly affect entrepreneurial interest and self-efficacy.

"Influence of Family Environment on Generation Z's Entrepreneurial Intention through Self-efficacy" by Mahfudzi and Fitri (2022): This study found that the family environment has a positive and significant effect on entrepreneurial intention through self-efficacy in Generation Z. It suggests that the family environment plays a crucial role in shaping the entrepreneurial intention of the younger generation.

"Big five personality traits, ESE and entrepreneurial intention: A configurational approach" by Şahin, Koçman, Karadağ and Tuncer (2019): This research suggests that an elevated level of entrepreneurial intention can be realized through multiple configurations of the big five personality traits and ESE. It highlights the importance of personal characteristics in shaping entrepreneurial intentions.

"Entrepreneurial intention of students in Bosnia and Herzegovina: what type of support matters?" by Turulja, Veselinović, Agić and Pašić-Mesihović (2020): This study found that informal support, perceived as support from family and friends, exerts a significant positive influence on entrepreneurial intentions. It also found that fear of failure has a significant adverse impact on entrepreneurial intentions, but this negative relationship is dampened by informal support.

There is a strong correlation between self-efficacy and entrepreneurial intention. This is a recurring theme in the studies by Rachmawan, Lizar and Mangundjaya (2015), Farashah (2015), Akanbi and Alayande (2013), Supandi, Wulandari and Naufalin (2022), Mahfudzi and Fitri (2022) and Şahin, Koçman, Karadağ and Tuncer (2019). These studies suggest that self-efficacy, which refers to an individual's belief in their ability to succeed in specific situations or accomplish a task, plays a significant role in fostering entrepreneurial intention. It also implies that interventions aimed at enhancing self-efficacy, such as training, coaching, and mentoring, could potentially boost entrepreneurial intention.

Furthermore, the role of family and parental influence on entrepreneurial intention, however, appears to be more nuanced. While Rachmawan, Lizar and Mangundjaya (2015) found that parental influence does not significantly affect entrepreneurial intention, other studies such as those by Altinay, Madanoglu, Daniele and Lashley (2012), Akanbi and Alayande (2013), Supandi, Wulandari and Naufalin (2022) and Mahfudzi and Fitri (2022) suggest that family environment and familial factors can have a significant impact on entrepreneurial intention. These differences might be due to differences in the specific familial factors examined in these studies, or they might reflect cultural or contextual differences between the populations studied.

Alternatively, personality traits also emerge as a significant factor in entrepreneurial intention. The studies by Altinay, Madanoglu, Daniele and Lashley (2012), Akanbi and Alayande (2013) and Şahin, Koçman, Karadağ and Tuncer (2019) all highlight the role of various personality traits, including tolerance of ambiguity, risk-taking propensity, the big five personality traits (extraversion, agreeableness, conscientiousness, neuroticism, openness) and locus of control, in shaping entrepreneurial intention.

Moreover, the study by Turulja, Veselinović, Agić and Pašić-Mesihović (2020) introduces the concept of informal support, such as support from family and friends, as a significant positive influence on entrepreneurial intentions. This study also highlights the role of fear of failure, suggesting that while it can harm entrepreneurial intentions this effect can be mitigated by informal support.

In summary, these articles collectively suggest that entrepreneurial intention is influenced by a complex interplay of factors including self-efficacy, familial influences, personality traits and informal support. Further research could explore these relationships in more detail, potentially leading to more effective interventions to foster entrepreneurial intention.

Gaps Identified in the Literature

The existing literature indicates that self-efficacy, family influence and personality traits significantly contribute to entrepreneurial intention. However, there are notable gaps in the literature, particularly regarding the influence of cultural factors and the impact of various types of family dynamics on entrepreneurial intention. These areas could be explored in future research.

Furthermore, there is a need to establish a link that connects family dynamics to entrepreneurial intentions, especially in Generation Z. While many studies focus on individual traits or broader social influences, the specific role of family dynamics warrants further exploration. Additionally, understanding how various aspects of the family environment influence self-efficacy, which in turn impacts entrepreneurial intentions, could be a valuable area of research (Mahfudzi & Fitri, 2022; Supandi, Wulandari & Naufalin, 2022).

In terms of ESE, one potential gap in the existing literature that this chapter could address is the role of specific types of self-efficacy in entrepreneurial intention. While self-efficacy is a general construct, examining the role of specific types of self-efficacy (e.g., financial self-efficacy, social self-efficacy) in entrepreneurial intention could be beneficial. Another potential gap is the role of cultural factors in shaping entrepreneurial intentions, as most existing studies focus on individual and family factors (Farashah, 2015; Şahin, Koçman, Karadağ & Tuncer, 2019).

The study by Rachmawan, Aprilianti-Lizar and Mangundjaya (2015) focused on the role of self-efficacy and parental influence on entrepreneurial intentions, finding that self-efficacy has a significant positive influence on entrepreneurial intention. However, it does not delve deeply into the specific aspects of family dynamics that might influence entrepreneurial intention, leaving room for further research in this area (Rachmawan et al., 2015).

The study by Altinay, Madanoglu, Daniele and Lashley (2012) suggests that family dynamics, specifically family entrepreneurial tradition, can have a significant impact on entrepreneurial intention. However, the study is limited to the hospitality industry and may not be generalisable to other sectors (Altinay et al., 2012).

Rachmawan, Aprilianti-Lizar and Mangundjaya (2015) investigated the role of self-efficacy and parental influence on entrepreneurial intention. The study provided a comprehensive view of the factors influencing entrepreneurial intention, including family dynamics. However, it did not focus specifically on family dynamics, indicating a gap in the literature (Rachmawan et al., 2015).

Lastly, the study by Akanbi and Alayande (2013) explored the influence of familial factors, personality traits and self-efficacy on entrepreneurial behavior among College of Education students. The study provided a nuanced view of the role of family dynamics in entrepreneurial intention, but it is limited to a specific population (vocational-based College of Education students in Oyo State, Nigeria), indicating a need for further research in diverse populations (Akandi & Alayande, 2013).

Review of Theoretical Frameworks

The studies on family dynamics, entrepreneurial intentions and self-efficacy have used various theoretical frameworks. Below are some key findings from the reviews:

The first theoretical framework reviewed was the paper titled "Abundance of strange attractors" by Mora and Viana (1993), which provides a theoretical framework for understanding the dynamics of a family of diffeomorphisms of the plane. The authors performed a numerical study of this family and detected a non-trivial attractor with a highly intricate geometric structure. This theoretical framework could be relevant for understanding family dynamics in the context of the influence of the family environment on Generation Z's entrepreneurial intention. It could provide a mathematical model for understanding the complex interactions and influences within a family system. However, it is important to note that this is a mathematical model and its application to social sciences would require careful interpretation and adaptation.

For entrepreneurial self-efficacy, the reviewed article "The Role of Parent's Influence and Self-Efficacy on Entrepreneurial Intention" by Rachmawan, Aprilianti-Lizar and Mangundjaya (2015), found that self-efficacy has a positive and considerable influence on entrepreneurial intention, while parental influence does not significantly affect entrepreneurial intentions. The theoretical framework of this study is not explicitly stated, but it seems to draw on Bandura's self-efficacy theory (2003), which posits that an individual's belief in their capabilities to execute tasks affects their motivation, behavior and social environment.

"The Influence of Family Tradition and Psychological Traits on Entrepreneurial Intention" by Altinay, Madanoglu, Daniele and Lashley (2012) investigates the influence of family tradition and psychological traits on entrepreneurial intention. The theoretical framework underpinning this study is not explicitly presented. but the chapter draws from theories of personality and social influence.

"The Effects of Demographic, Cognitive and Institutional Factors on the Development of Entrepreneurial Intention: Toward a Socio-Cognitive Model of Entrepreneurial Career" by Farashah (2015) examines the effects of a range of factors on the development of entrepreneurial intention, based on the Social Cognitive Career Theory. The study found that entrepreneurial self-efficacy beliefs and entrepreneurial career outcome expectations are significantly correlated with entrepreneurial intention.

"The article Familial Factors, Personality Traits and Self-efficacy as Determinants of Entrepreneurial Intention Among Vocational Based College of Education Students in Oyo State, Nigeria" by Akanbi and Alayande (2013) explored the influence of familial factors, personality traits and self-efficacy on entrepreneurial behavior among College of Education students. The theoretical framework of this study is also not explicitly stated, but it appears to draw on theories of personality and social influence.

The article by Peng, Lu and Kang (2013) titled "The Influence of Individual/Psychological Factors, Family Background Factors and Social Environment Factors on University Student's Entrepreneurial Intentions" provides an analysis of the entrepreneurial intentions of university students in Xi'an, China, and the factors that influence them. The theoretical framework of this study appears to draw on theories of social norms, attitudes, and self-efficacy in influencing entrepreneurial intentions. The study also considers the influence of family background and social environment factors, which aligns with the broader literature on the multifaceted influences on entrepreneurial intentions.

In summary, the paper "Abundance of strange attractors" by Mora and Viana (1993) provides a new perspective on family dynamics and their influence on entrepreneurial intentions. The article by Rachmawan, Aprilianti-Lizar and Mangundjaya (2015) directly addresses the role of self-belief in shaping behavior. Both papers by Altinay, Madanoglu, Daniele and Lashley (2012) and Akanbi and

Alayande (2013) address the role of individual traits and social factors in shaping behavior. In his article, Farashah (2015) focused on the Social Cognitive Career Theory which provided a robust framework for studying entrepreneurial intentions, as it considers both individual and contextual factors. Finally, the paper by Peng, Lu and Kang (2013) appears to draw on theories of social norms, attitudes and self-efficacy. This framework is also highly relevant to the study of entrepreneurial intentions, as it considers a wide range of individual, familial and social factors.

In conclusion, these theoretical frameworks offer a range of perspectives on the influence of family dynamics on entrepreneurial intentions and self-efficacy. They highlight the importance of considering both individual traits and social factors, as well as the complex interactions between these factors. Future research could benefit from integrating these perspectives to develop a more comprehensive understanding of the factors influencing entrepreneurial intentions and self-efficacy.

Entrepreneurial Theories and Their Applications

Several theories have been used to discuss entrepreneurial intentions and self-efficacy in the literature. The prominent ones are the Theory of Planned Behavior, the Social Cognitive Theory and the Regulatory Focus Theory.

Theory of Planned Behavior

The Theory of Planned Behavior (TPB) posits that an individual's intention to engage in a behavior (in this case, entrepreneurship) is determined by their attitude towards the behavior, subjective norms, and perceived behavioral control, which is closely related to self-efficacy. This theory has been applied in numerous studies to understand entrepreneurial intentions. For instance, a study by Doanh and Bernat in 2019 used TPB to investigate the relationship between ESE and entrepreneurial intention among Vietnamese students, highlighting the indirect influence of subjective norms on entrepreneurial intention through ESE. The study also examined the role of subjective norms in shaping entrepreneurial intention. The authors found that subjective norms indirectly influence entrepreneurial intention through ESE, attitude toward entrepreneurship and perceived behavioral control (Doanh & Bernat, 2019).

Another study by Thomas Zellweger, Philipp Sieger and Frank Halter (2011) also applied TPB to explore how intentional founders, successors and employees differ in terms of locus of control and ESE as well as independence and innovation motives (Zellweger, Sieger & Halter, 2011).

The Social Cognitive Theory

The Social Cognitive Theory (SCT) is another theory used to discuss ESE. SCT emphasizes the role of observational learning, social experience, and reciprocal determinism in the development of personality. A study by Biraglia and Kadile in 2017 applied SCT to investigate the role of entrepreneurial passion and creativity as antecedents of entrepreneurial intention. They found that entrepreneurial passion has a strong positive relationship with entrepreneurial intention, even when ESE is introduced as a mediator (Biraglia & Kadile, 2017).

The Regulatory Focus Theory

Regulatory Focus Theory has been used to understand how the nature of an entrepreneurship course (whether theoretically or oriented) creates a distinct motivational frame for entrepreneurship in promotion or prevention terms. A study by Piperopoulos and Dimov in 2015 found that higher self-efficacy is associated with lower entrepreneurial intentions in theoretically oriented courses and higher entrepreneurial intentions in oriented courses (Piperopoulos & Dimov, 2015).

These theories provide a useful framework for understanding the roles of self-efficacy in entrepreneurial intentions and could be used to guide future research in this area.

Implication and Future Research

While this and other existing literature provide valuable insights into the role of ESE, there are still gaps that need to be addressed. For instance, more research is needed to understand the negative or curvilinear effects of ESE, the effects of ESE on outcomes outside of entrepreneurial contexts and the developmental precursors of ESE in childhood, adolescence, and early adulthood. Additionally, more research is needed to improve the measurement and research design of studies on ESE.

CONCLUSION

The exploration of family dynamics and their influence on entrepreneurial intentions and self-efficacy in this chapter has revealed a complex interplay of factors. Family dynamics, encompassing parental influence, family support, family business background and family values and norms, play a significant role in shaping entrepreneurial intentions. However, the influence of these dynamics is not uniform and can be shaped by societal norms and values.

The case studies reviewed in this chapter highlight the multifaceted nature of these influences and the need for further research to understand them better. Future research could delve deeper into the specific aspects of family dynamics that influence entrepreneurial intention and could explore these dynamics in diverse populations and sectors.

The theoretical frameworks reviewed in this chapter provide a foundation for understanding the complex interactions and influences within a family system. However, these frameworks need to be applied and interpreted carefully, considering the complexity of human behavior and interactions.

In conclusion, this chapter underscores the importance of understanding family dynamics in the context of entrepreneurship. It suggests that enhancing communication, resolving conflicts, and fostering a shared vision within families could potentially support the development of entrepreneurial intentions and self-efficacy. Furthermore, it highlights the need for entrepreneurship education and societal support for entrepreneurship.

REFERENCES

Alon, I., Jaffe, E., Prange, C., & Vianelli, D. (2020). *Global marketing: strategy, practice, and cases*. Routledge. doi:10.4324/9780429203343

Altinay, L., Madanoglu, M., Daniele, R., & Lashley, C. (2012). The influence of family tradition and psychological traits on entrepreneurial intention. *International Journal of Hospitality Management*, *31*(2), 489–499. doi:10.1016/j.ijhm.2011.07.007

Andjelkovic Pesic, M., & Dahlgaard, J. J. (2013). *Using the Balanced-Scorecard and the European Foundation for Quality Management Excellence model as a combined roadmap for diagnosing and attaining excellence*. https://scholar.google.com/scholar?hl=en&as_sdt=0%2C5&q=Andjelkovic+Pesic%2C+M.%2C+%26+Dahlgaard%2C+J.+J.+%282013%29

Au, K., Chiang, F. F. T., Birtch, T. A., & Ding, Z. (2013). Incubating the next generation to venture: The case of a family business in Hong Kong. *Asia Pacific Journal of Management*, *30*(3), 30. doi:10.100710490-012-9331-7

Bandura, A., & Locke, E. A. (2003). Negative self-efficacy and goal effects revisited. *The Journal of Applied Psychology*, *88*(1), 87–99. doi:10.1037/0021-9010.88.1.87 PMID:12675397

Bignotti, A., & Le Roux, I. (2020). Which types of experience matter? The role of prior start-up experiences and work experience in fostering youth entrepreneurial intentions. *International Journal of Entrepreneurial Behaviour & Research*, *26*(6), 1181–1198. doi:10.1108/IJEBR-10-2019-0577

Biraglia, A., & Kadile, V. (2017). The role of entrepreneurial passion and creativity in developing entrepreneurial intentions: Insights from American homebrewers. *Journal of Small Business Management*, *55*(1), 170–188. doi:10.1111/jsbm.12242

Boyd, N. G., & Vozikis, G. S. (1994). The influence of self-efficacy on the development of entrepreneurial intentions and actions. *Entrepreneurship Theory and Practice*, *18*(4), 63–77. doi:10.1177/104225879401800404

Cardella, G. M., Hernández-Sánchez, B. R., & Sanchez Garcia, J. C. (2020). Entrepreneurship and family role: A systematic review of a growing research. *Frontiers in Psychology*, *10*, 2939. doi:10.3389/fpsyg.2019.02939 PMID:31998192

Daszkiewicz, N., & Wach, K. (2014). Motives for going international and entry modes of family firms in Poland. *Journal of Intercultural Management*, *6*(2), 5–18. doi:10.2478/joim-2014-0008

Derné, S. (1994). Hindu men talk about controlling women: Cultural ideas as a tool of the powerful. *Sociological Perspectives*, *37*(2), 203–227. doi:10.2307/1389320

Doanh, D. C., & Bernat, T. (2019). Entrepreneurial self-efficacy and intention among Vietnamese students: A meta-analytic path analysis based on the theory of planned behavior. *Procedia Computer Science*, *159*, 2447–2460. doi:10.1016/j.procs.2019.09.420

Fitz-Koch, S., Cooper, S., & Discua Cruz, A. (2019). Entrepreneurship and rural family identity: Understanding portfolio development in a family farm business. *The family business group phenomenon: Emergence and complexities*, 353-383.

Ghosh, D., & Natarajan, P. (2019). *Indian Tech Start-up Ecosystem*. Academic Press.

Gubik, A. S., & Farkas, S. (2019). Entrepreneurial intention in the Visegrad countries. *Danube*, *10*(4), 347–368. doi:10.2478/danb-2019-0018

Hernández-Linares, R., López-Fernández, M. C., García-Piqueres, G., Pina e Cunha, M., & Rego, A. (2023). How knowledge-based dynamic capabilities relate to firm performance: The mediating role of entrepreneurial orientation. *Review of Managerial Science*, 1–33. doi:10.100711846-023-00691-4

Hmieleski, K. M., & Baron, R. A. (2008). When does entrepreneurial self-efficacy enhance versus reduce firm performance? *Strategic Entrepreneurship Journal*, *2*(1), 57–72. doi:10.1002ej.42

Hoover, E. A., & Hoover, C. L. (2013). *Getting along in family business: The relationship intelligence handbook*. Routledge. doi:10.4324/9780203949757

Jabbari, B., & Rouster, A. S. (2023). Family Dynamics. StatPearls Publishing LLC.

Khavul, S., Bruton, G. D., & Wood, E. (2009). Informal family business in Africa. *Entrepreneurship Theory and Practice*, *33*(6), 1219–1238. doi:10.1111/j.1540-6520.2009.00342.x

Kosuri, P., & Pantin, L. (2021). Nowhere to Run to, Nowhere to Hide. *Clinical Law Review*, *28*, 199.

Kurten, B. (2017). Poland's Transformation. Routledge.

Li, Z., Mirko, C., D'Agostino, M. T., & Jin, J. (2023). Comparative analysis of the influence of Chinese urban and rural family cultures on household financial asset allocation. *Frontiers in Psychology*, *14*, 1119258. doi:10.3389/fpsyg.2023.1119258 PMID:36844357

Luthans, F., & Ibrayeva, E. S. (2006). Entrepreneurial self-efficacy in Central Asian transition economies: Quantitative and qualitative analyses. *Journal of International Business Studies*, *37*(1), 92–110. doi:10.1057/palgrave.jibs.8400173

Mahfudzi, A. A. B., & Fitri, R. (2022). *The Influence of Family Environment on Generation Z's Entrepreneurial Intention through Self-Efficacy*. Academic Press.

Mora, L., & Viana, M. (1993). *Abundance of strange attractors*. Academic Press.

Morales-Gualdrón, S. T., & Roig, S. (2005). The new venture decision: An analysis based on the GEM project database. *The International Entrepreneurship and Management Journal*, *1*(4), 479–499. doi:10.100711365-005-4774-7

Neneh, B. (2020). Entrepreneurial self-efficacy and a student's predisposition to choose an entrepreneurial career path: The role of self-perceived employability. *Education + Training*, *62*(5), 559–580. doi:10.1108/ET-06-2019-0108

Newman, A., Obschonka, M., Schwarz, S., Cohen, M., & Nielsen, I. (2019). Entrepreneurial self-efficacy: A systematic review of the literature on its theoretical foundations, measurement, antecedents, and outcomes, and an agenda for future research. *Journal of Vocational Behavior*, *110*, 403–419. doi:10.1016/j.jvb.2018.05.012

Nguyen, C. (2015). Entrepreneurial intention in vietnam: same as everywhere? SSRN *Electronic Journal*. doi:10.2139/ssrn.3906124

Nosé, L., Korunka, C., Frank, H., & Danes, S. M. (2017). Decreasing the effects of relationship conflict on family businesses: The moderating role of family climate. *Journal of Family Issues*, *38*(1), 25–51. doi:10.1177/0192513X15573869

Peng, Z., Lu, G., & Kang, H. (2013). Entrepreneurial intentions and its influencing factors: A survey of the university students in Xi'an China. *Creative Education*, *3*(08), 95–100. doi:10.4236/ce.2012.38B021

Piperopoulos, P., & Dimov, D. (2015). Burst bubbles or build steam? Entrepreneurship education, entrepreneurial self-efficacy, and entrepreneurial intentions. *Journal of Small Business Management*, *53*(4), 970–985. doi:10.1111/jsbm.12116

Rachmawan, A., Lizar, A. A., & Mangundjaya, W. L. (2015). The role of parent's influence and self-efficacy on entrepreneurial intention. *Journal of Developing Areas*, *49*(3), 417–430. doi:10.1353/jda.2015.0157

Rahim, M. A. (2023). *Managing conflict in organizations*. Taylor & Francis. doi:10.4324/9781003285861

Ralat, J. R. (2020). *American Tacos: A History and Guide*. University of Texas Press. doi:10.7560/316528

Shen, L. (2015). Meet Samsung's billionaire Lee family, South Korea's most powerful dynasty. *Business Insider*. https://www.businessinsider.com/lee-family-power-war-for-samsung-scandals-and-bribes-2015-6

Sivathanu, B., & Pillai, R. (2020). An empirical study on entrepreneurial bricolage behavior for sustainable enterprise performance of startups: Evidence from an emerging economy. *Journal of Entrepreneurship in Emerging Economies*, *12*(1), 34–57. doi:10.1108/JEEE-01-2019-0009

Stephan, U., & Pathak, S. (2016). Beyond cultural values? Cultural leadership ideals and entrepreneurship. *Journal of Business Venturing*, *31*(5), 505–523. doi:10.1016/j.jbusvent.2016.07.003

Stephan, U., & Uhlaner, L. M. (2010). Performance-based vs socially supportive culture: A cross-national study of descriptive norms and entrepreneurship. *Journal of International Business Studies*, *41*(8), 1347–1364. doi:10.1057/jibs.2010.14

Sue, D. W. (2016). *Race talk and the conspiracy of silence: Understanding and facilitating difficult dialogues on race*. John Wiley & Sons.

Sun, X., Lee, S.-H., & Phan, P. H. (2019). Family firm R&D investments in the 2007-2009 great recession. *Journal of Family Business Strategy, 10*(4), 100244. doi:10.1016/j.jfbs.2018.02.004

Supandi, R., Wulandari, S. Z., & Naufalin, L. R. (2022). Influence of Family Circumstances, Peer Circumstances, and Entrepreneurial Learning on Entrepreneurial Interests with Self-Efficacy as Intervening Variables. *Journal of Economics Education and Entrepreneurship, 3*(2), 140–150. doi:10.20527/jee.v3i2.5233

Turulja, L., Veselinovic, L., Agic, E., & Pasic-Mesihovic, A. (2020). Entrepreneurial intention of students in Bosnia and Herzegovina: What type of support matters? *Ekonomska Istrazivanja, 33*(1), 2713–2732. doi:10.1080/1331677X.2020.1730216

Vătămănescu, E.-M., Gorgos, E.-A., Ghigiu, A. M., & Pătruț, M. (2019). Bridging intellectual capital and SMEs internationalization through the lens of sustainable competitive advantage: A systematic literature review. *Sustainability (Basel), 11*(9), 2510. doi:10.3390u11092510

Vershinina, N., Rodgers, P., McAdam, M., & Clinton, E. (2019). Transnational migrant entrepreneurship, gender and family business. *Global Networks, 19*(2), 238–260. doi:10.1111/glob.12225

Wennberg, K., Pathak, S., & Autio, E. (2013). How culture moulds the effects of self-efficacy and fear of failure on entrepreneurship. *Entrepreneurship and Regional Development, 25*(9-10), 756–780. doi:10.1080/08985626.2013.862975

Zellweger, T., Sieger, P., & Halter, F. (2011). Should I stay or should I go? Career choice intentions of students with family business background. *Journal of Business Venturing, 26*(5), 521–536. doi:10.1016/j.jbusvent.2010.04.001

Zhao, H., Seibert, S. E., & Hills, G. E. (2005). The mediating role of self-efficacy in the development of entrepreneurial intentions. *The Journal of Applied Psychology, 90*(6), 1265–1272. doi:10.1037/0021-9010.90.6.1265 PMID:16316279

Zhu, F., Burmeister-Lamp, K., & Hsu, D. K. (2017). To leave or not? The impact of family support and cognitive appraisals on venture exit intention. *International Journal of Entrepreneurial Behaviour & Research, 23*(3), 566–590. doi:10.1108/IJEBR-04-2016-0110

Chapter 12
Empirical Investigation for Assessing the Causality of Entrepreneurship Ecosystem With Entrepreneurial Behavior and Attitudes Across Countries

Ajay Kumar Singh
https://orcid.org/0000-0003-0429-0925
Department of Economics, School of Liberal Arts and Management, DIT University, Dehradun, India

Bhim Jyoti
Department of Seed Science and Technology, College of Forestry, Veer Chandra Singh Garhwali Uttarakhand University of Horticulture and Forestry, Ranichauri, India

EXECUTIVE SUMMARY

This chapter measures the causal association of the entrepreneurship ecosystem (EE) with entrepreneurial behavior and attitudes (EBA) in 47 countries using log-linear regression equations. Entrepreneurship ecosystem index (ENECIN) and entrepreneurial behavior and attitudes index (ENBEATIN) are used as representative variables for EE and EBA, respectively, in regression analysis while ENECIN and ENBEATIN are the composite indexes of 12 and 11 indicators, respectively, using

DOI: 10.4018/978-1-6684-8748-8.ch012

principal component analysis. These indicators are reported as key determinants of EE and EBA as per the global entrepreneurship monitor (GEM). There was a high level of diversity in EE and EBA across countries. EE has a positive impact on EBA and vice versa. The causation of EE and EBA with control variables is detected using the Granger causality test. The findings of this chapter are beneficial for global policymakers to implement appropriate policies to reinforce EE and EBA.

1. INTRODUCTION

Entrepreneurship is an operating system of economic players and governments who start new businesses, ventures, and start-ups to produce goods and services (Singh & Jyoti, 2023c). It works as the creativity of products and knowledge, enhancing social-economic development and technological advancement (Rafiei et al., 2022). Entrepreneurship helps to make potential changes in society through creating job opportunities, increasing the profit of businessmen, maintaining the network of people (Rafiei et al., 2022), and increasing the number of self-employed people (de Rocha et al., 2021). Entrepreneurship emerged as an engine of economic growth (de Rocha et al., 2021). The entrepreneurship ecosystem (EE) is a network of various elements (i.e., social-economic, technology, government, physical infrastructure, and markets) that create business opportunities.

Entrepreneurship ecosystem (EE) is the set of elements—individuals, organizations or institutions, research organizations, business development cells, technology transfer offices, marketing, and government initiatives—that stimulate an individual to be an entrepreneur (Karimi & Ataei, 2022). EE is favorable to increasing the growth of business in numerous ways (Doran et al., 2018; Ilić et al., 2020; Gao & Qin, 2022; Singh & Kumar, 2022). EE makes significant changes in the market in terms of innovation and innovative products and encourages perfect competition. EE also works as a motivator and strengthens social information and human skills (Karimi & Ataei, 2022). The concept of EE emerged as a basis for designing entrepreneurship policies in the areas of technologies and business sectors (Singh & Jyoti, 2023c).

EE is a significant driver in increasing the intention of an individual or group of people to make investments in the product market (de Rocha et al., 2021). EE also increases the desirability of economic agents to be entrepreneurs and businessmen. An entrepreneur has the innovative ability to create a new venture, business, or start-up (Baluku et al., 2021). EE is helpful to enhance the investment abilities and economic returns of entrepreneurs (Rafiei et al., 2022). EE, therefore, nurtures a conducive ecosystem that meets the needs of consumers and producers in the product markets. Earlier evidence specified that the EE is positive for creating jobs, new markets, accelerating innovation, perfect competition, infrastructure, discovery of new goods and services, and industrial development (Bashir & Akhtar, 2016; Singh & Ashraf, 2020; Ali & Jabeen, 2020; Arbabian & Zamani, 2022; Sharma et al., 2023).

EE is efficient at reducing monopolies in the market, increasing significant changes in the market, maintaining the price stability of products, and creating a market-based economy (Arbabian & Zamani, 2022). Foreign direct investment (FDI), money flow, financial stability and development, foreign trade, and exports of goods improve due to an increase in EE (Hameli et al., 2021; Sharma et al., 2023). The EE leads to increased economic development and growth (Arbabian & Zamani, 2022). EE and economic development have a positive and bi-directional causal association (Singh et al., 2023a; Sharma et al., 2023). Also, factors promoting EE help to sustain economic growth and development (Mirjana et al., 2018; Ilić et al., 2020; Wang et al., 2022).

Science and technological development (S&TD) help to create or discover new technology, intellectual knowledge, innovation, and industrial designs for the development of products (Ashraf & Singh, 2019; Singh & Kumar, 2022b; Paranata et al., 2023). S&TD is fruitful in creating intellectual property for researchers that can be protected through strict IPR regimes (Singh et al., 2020a). S&TD and IPR regimes have a positive impact on the entrepreneurship ecosystem (EE). EE is a crucial driver for increasing the growth of the manufacturing sector. EE is worthy of financial inclusion and development (Sharma et al., 2023). Previous studies focused their investigations on the implication of the EE on economic growth, economic development, social development, sustainable development, financial development, digitalization, and S&TD (Ashraf & Singh, 2020; Singh & Ashraf, 2020; Singh & Jyoti, 2023a).

Singh et al. (2022a); Singh et al. (2023a, 2023b) investigated the impact of the green entrepreneurship ecosystem on social, economic, environmental, and sustainable development. Entrepreneurial activities are helpful to creating employment growth and increasing social-economic change (Uvarova et al., 2021). Entrepreneurial activity may be useful to increase the economic, ecological, and social dimensions of sustainable development (Volkmann et al., 2019). Most studies explored the impact of economic development, digitalization, science and technology, IPRs, innovation, financial development, financial inclusion, and FDI on EE (Singh et al., 2019b; Uvarova et al., 2021; Singh & Kumar, 2022a; Jyoti & Singh, 2023). The process of entrepreneurship is determined by economic, financial, non-economic, and digital processes (Mirjana et al., 2018; Bouarir et al., 2023).

Entrepreneurial behavior and attitudes (EBA) are also essential to nurturing a favorable entrepreneurial ecosystem. EBA is an ecosystem in which economic agents try to be self-employed by creating their own ventures and start-ups. EBA is a crucial drive to increase the intention of people to be businessmen. Entrepreneurial ecosystems create a foundation for the growth of enterprises (Volkmann et al.,

2019) and contribute to nurturing the entrepreneurial ecosystem (EE). While the entrepreneurial ecosystem is determined by physical infrastructure, government policies, entrepreneurship education, and new rules in the business sector (Paranata et al., 2023). The entrepreneurial ecosystem is directly and indirectly associated with resources, policies, and financial development (Wu et al., 2021). Investors, business planners, start-up creators, and financial granters are the players in the entrepreneurial ecosystem.

The EBA creates a platform for EE (Zabelina et al., 2019). EE depends on self-efficacy, creativity, entrepreneurial skills, and improvisation, which also increase the entrepreneurial mindset of people (Jalam & Adamu, 2022). Wang et al. (2022) examined the significance of entrepreneurial self-efficacy in the digital economy. Entrepreneurial skills have a direct impact on EE (Karimi & Ataei, 2022). An appropriate EE also enhances EBA. Henceforth, EE and EBA have a positive and bi-directional causal association with each other's (Singh & Jyoti, 2023c). Entrepreneurial behavior and its associated indicators are significantly linked with the entrepreneurial ecosystem (Wu et al., 2021). Entrepreneurs' aspirations have a direct influence on entrepreneurial behavior (Wang et al., 2022). Entrepreneurial behavior is an inclusion of risk-taking, innovation, and forward-looking behavior in an individual (Wu et al., 2021).

Entrepreneurial behavior helps to create possibilities and develop ideas into action with regards to new business (Wang et al., 2022). It is the ability of a person to identify a plan for developing a business or enterprise. Therefore, EE and EBA have significant interlinkage with each other. Entrepreneurs' activities and plans are useful to increase the entrepreneurial ecosystem (Elnadi & Gheith, 2021; Wu et al., 2021). Extensive studies determined the factors affecting the entrepreneurship ecosystem (EE) at the macro level. EBA is a crucial driver of EE, while EE is also supportive of increasing EBA. Attitude is defined in terms of people's interest, intention, and motivation to transform a venture into a business (Anjum et al., 2022).

Most studies explained the significance of EBA in the EE and the importance of the EE to promote EBA (Wu et al., 2021). Despite that, existing researchers could not pay more attention to observing the causal association between EE and EBA across countries. Hence, this chapter has a significant contribution to existing literature that assesses the answers to the following research questions:

- What are the different indicators of EE and EBA?
- What may be the integrated approach for measuring the EE and EBA?
- Is there a causal association between EE and EBA?
- Which indicators are beneficial to increasing EE and EBA?
- What must be an integrated policy to increase EE and EBA?

This chapter accomplishes the following objectives to achieve the answers to the aforementioned research questions:

- To develop the entrepreneurship ecosystem index (*ENECIN*) and entrepreneurial behavior and attitudes index (*ENBEATIN*) as a composition of 12 indicators and 11 indicators, respectively, as suggested by GEM using the PCA method.
- To analyze the impact of EE on EBA and vice versa using log-linear regression models.
- To assess the causation of EE with EBA using a Granger causality test.
- To provide practical policy implications to improve the EE and EBA in developed and developing countries.

2. REVIEW OF LITERATURE

Existing studies examined the determinants and factors affecting the entrepreneurship ecosystem (EE) across countries (Singh & Kumar, 2022a). Most studies concluded that economic development is a vital determinant of EE (Singh et al., 2023c). Past studies have also given crucial attention to examining the impact of foreign trade, trade openness, population growth, money supply, bank rate, and ICT imports and exports on EE (Singh & Kumar, 2022a; Sabra & Shreteh, 2021). These underlined indicators are divided into four groups, i.e., financial, institutional, economic, and framework conditions (Arbabian & Zamani, 2022). Existing studies also analyze the influence of these groups of factors on EE. For instance, Singh and Ashraf (2020) emphasized the role of economic development in promoting EE across countries.

Human capital, markets, finance, culture, and government policies are also the main components of EE (Karimi & Ataei, 2022). The impact of green entrepreneurship on environmental sustainability and sustainable development has been detected to be significant (Domańska et al., 2018; Singh et al., 2022a; Zeng & Ren, 2022; Singh et al., 2023a). Galindo-Martín et al. (2020) explained the role of social entrepreneurship and green innovation in sustainable development. Moya-Clemente et al. (2019) reviewed the consequences of the SDGs on sustainable entrepreneurship. Previous researchers also used diverse indicators like total early-stage and total entrepreneurial activity, business density rate, business ownership, new business registration, and annual growth in registered business for the EE (Adusei, 2016; Dvouletý, 2017; Doran et al., 2018; Hameli et al., 2021).

The number of company formations is also used to explore the association of EE with economic growth (Chen, 2014). Audretsch et al. (2015) considered new firm start-ups to assess their impact on economic growth. The number of newly established firms also infers the progress of EE (Zaki & Rashid, 2016). Rusu and Roman (2017) reported that the inflation rate, foreign direct investments, access to finance, and total tax have a significant impact on entrepreneurial activity. Entrepreneurial knowledge and skills are supportive for reducing the unemployment rate in developing countries (Jalam & Adamu, 2022). Erken et al. (2018) investigated the impact of GDP per capita, R&D capital, technological catch-up, human capital, and labour participation on business ownership rates in 20 OECD countries.

Most studies also assessed the impact of several macro-level indicators on the entrepreneurship ecosystem index (EEI). Ashraf and Singh (2019) noticed a positive impact of high-technology, merchandise trade, and R&D expenditures on the entrepreneurship creativity development index. Singh and Ashraf (2020) observed the impact of economic development, foreign direct net outflows, the self-employed, education expenditure, fixed telephone subscribers, high-technology exports, merchandise trade, R&D expenditure, innovation, inflation, GDP deflator, and individuals using the internet on EEI. The global competitiveness index (GCI) is also adopted as a representative variable for EE in regression analysis (Bashir & Akhtar, 2016). Tasnim and ibne Afzal (2018) adopted the GCI to assess its interconnection with economic development across countries.

Singh and Kumar (2022a) found a positive impact of economic development, business density rate, foreign direct investment net inflows (FDINI), individuals using the internet, and market exchange rate on EE across countries. Arbabian and Zamani (2022) identified the impact of human capital on entrepreneurship as giving more focus on financial development in 17 countries. Sharma et al. (2023) observed the impact of the global financial inclusion index, gross domestic product, inflation, ease of doing business score, employers total, individuals using the internet, population growth, profit tax, wage, and salaried workers on the global entrepreneurship index across countries. Entrepreneurial activities also help to increase the motivation level of people to be self-employed and solely depend on financial development (Hameli et al., 2021).

Entrepreneurship ecosystem (EE) and entrepreneurial activities are indispensable drivers to increase the intention of economic agents to be self-employed. The motivation of economic agents to be self-employed creates entrepreneurial activities. Entrepreneurial activities also work as an essential driver to nurture a favorable EE. The inclusive entrepreneurship ecosystem (IEE) provides equal opportunities to all people to start their businesses without any barriers. IEE, therefore, plays an essential role in increasing entrepreneurial behavior and intention. The entrepreneurial intention of people is determined by their environmental, social, and educational characteristics (de Rocha et al., 2021). Mirjana et al. (2018) also explored the determinants of entrepreneurial intentions in Slovenia, and this study reported that personal attitude towards entrepreneurship, subjective norms, and perceived behavior have a crucial influence on entrepreneurial intentions.

Entrepreneurial attitudes also play a positive role in increasing economic growth (Doran et al., 2018). Zabelina et al. (2019) analyzed the students' entrepreneurial attitudes towards business, investments, saving, and consumption using exploratory and confirmatory factor analyses. de Rocha et al. (2021) detected the role of universities in creating entrepreneurial skills among the students in Brazil. The findings reported that entrepreneurial behavior and intention among students increase when universities adopt the culture of EE. EBA depends on the availability of credit for entrepreneurs, entrepreneurial training, entrepreneurial learning, entrepreneurial education, entrepreneurial skills, entrepreneurial opportunities, work experience, perceived opportunities, social networking, expectation to earn profit, family background, and stability of their venture in the market (Wu et al., 2022; Gao & Qin, 2022).

Emotional intelligence and the entrepreneurship ecosystem (EE) are useful to increase students' ability to develop entrepreneurial skills (Karimi & Ataei, 2022). Local environmental conditions also determine entrepreneurial behavior (Fredin & Lidén, 2020). EE has a positive impact on social and emotional intelligence and mediators' impact on entrepreneurial skills (Karimi & Ataei, 2022). EE may be imperative to increase EBA. Numerous studies have observed factors affecting entrepreneurial behavior, attitudes, intentions, mindset, and ecosystem in different countries (Fredin & Lidén, 2020; Wu et al., 2021). Most scholars recognized the perceptions of people, students, and entrepreneurs to understand their entrepreneurial intentions towards the entrepreneurial ecosystem (Mirjana et al., 2018; Amofah & Saladrigues, 2021; Wu et al., 2021, 2022).

The entrepreneurship ecosystem (EE) is the integration of self-efficacy, creativity, entrepreneurial skills, and improvisation. Jalam and Adamu (2022) observed the implications of the EE on the entrepreneurial mindset of students. Paranata et al. (2023) emphasized that self-efficacy, business opportunities, and role models help to develop an enterprise. Entrepreneurial self-efficacy and entrepreneurial ecosystem are useful determinants of entrepreneurial intentions and behavior and EE (Elnadi & Gheith, 2021; Gao & Qin, 2022). Entrepreneurial self-efficacy has a positive association with entrepreneurial intention (Wu et al., 2022). Entrepreneurial intention is the desirability of an individual person to start their own venture or business (Anjum et al., 2022). Entrepreneurial self-efficacy improves the interlinkage between entrepreneurship education and intention (Wu et al., 2022).

Wu et al. (2021) emphasized that entrepreneurial willingness is a prime necessity for entrepreneurial behavior and intention. Ali and Jabeen (2020) estimated the factors affecting the establishment of start-ups to understand the entrepreneurial behavior of people in India. Entrepreneurship attitudes, subjective norms, and perceived behavior have a significant impact on establishing start-ups. Paranata et al. (2023) also determined the factors affecting start-up business initiatives in Indonesia. Prathap et al. (2020) argued that entrepreneurial training and credit availability help to increase the entrepreneurial intention of microfinance clients to search for business prospects in India. Elnadi and Gheith (2021) suggested that entrepreneurial self-efficacy plays a key role in increasing the entrepreneurial intentions of students in higher education in Saudi Arabia. Amofah and Saladrigues (2021) investigated the impact of entrepreneurship education on the entrepreneurial intentions of students in Spain.

Wu et al. (2021) analyze the entrepreneurial behavior and intention of students towards entrepreneurial activity in China. Gao and Qin (2022) also explored the participation of entrepreneurship competitions to increase entrepreneurial knowledge, ability, and intention in higher educational institutions in China. Entrepreneurial competition and entrepreneurial self-efficacy derived from entrepreneurial education have a positive influence on entrepreneurial intention or behavior. Khuong and Van (2022) reported that the entrepreneurial ecosystem is correlated with start-up success in Vietnam. Rafiei et al. (2022) explained the impact of business attitude on entrepreneurial behavior in postgraduate students in Iran. It found an insignificant impact of gender, education level, and age on entrepreneurial behavior and a significant impact of business attitude on entrepreneurial behavior.

Bouarir et al. (2023) observed the factors affecting the entrepreneurial intent and behavior of 148 women in Morocco. It is reported that entrepreneurial intent helps to increase entrepreneurial behavior. Entrepreneurial intent is significantly associated with entrepreneurial attitude, education, and business opportunities. Few studies have examined the impact of entrepreneurial attitudes on per capita GDP (Doran et al., 2018). The above-mentioned literature infers that there are multiple factors that may be used for the EE and entrepreneurial behavior and attitudes (EBA). The present chapter used secondary data to examine the determinants of EE and EBA and the causal associations among them across countries. Hence, the above-mentioned variables cannot be used for said empirical investigation due to the unavailability of data across counties in this chapter.

The Global Entrepreneurship Monitor (GEM) collects data on various indicators associated with EE and EBA across countries. Ilić et al. (2020) also used these indicators to explain the entrepreneurial behavior and attitudes of entrepreneurs in Slovenia and Croatia using GEM data. Singh and Jyoti (2023c) also applied similar indicators in the domain of EBA to explore the health of entrepreneurial behavior and attitudes.

3. METHODOLOGY

3.1. Inclusion of Countries and Time Period

The prime aim of this chapter is to develop the entrepreneurship ecosystem index (*ENECIN*) and entrepreneurial behavior and attitudes index (*ENBEATIN*) across countries. This study, therefore, considers only those countries that had data related to *ENECIN* and *ENBEATIN* between 2006 and 2022. The statistics of identified indicators related to *ENECIN* and *ENBEATIN* are available for 47 countries on the website of the Global Entrepreneurship Monitor (GEM). Accordingly, 47 countries are compiled into a panel of dependent and independent variables for statistical analysis. The segregation of these countries into high-income, upper-middle-income, lower-income, and low-income groups is explained in Table 1.

Table 1. List of comprised countries

Income Group of Countries		
High	**Upper Middle**	**Lower**
Australia, Austria, Belgium, Canada, Chile, Croatia, Denmark, Finland, France, Germany, Greece, Hungary, Ireland, Israel, Italy, Japan, Latvia, Netherlands, Norway, Poland, Portugal, Singapore, Slovenia, South Korea, Spain, Sweden, Switzerland, United Arab Emirates, United Kingdom, United States and Uruguay	Argentina, Brazil, China, Colombia, Ecuador, Jamaica, Jordan, Malaysia, Mexico, Peru, Russia, South Africa, Thailand, and Turkey	India and Indonesia

3.2. Data Sources

The data on factors associated with EE and EBA is taken from GEM. The information on other explanatory variables is taken from the world development indicators (the World Bank).

3.3. Data Analysis

3.3.1. Creation of ENECIN and ENATBEIN

Previous studies observed the impact of macro- and micro-level factors on the entrepreneurship ecosystem (EE) using different indicators such as business density rate, firms' formation, new business registration, and start-up rate (Acs, 2006; Domańska et al., 2018; Ashraf & Singh, 2019; Jyoti & Singh 2020; Hameli et al., 2021; Khuong & Van, 2022; Sharma et al., 2023). Most studies claimed that one specific indicator may be irrational to expose the progress of EE (Singh & Jyoti, 2021). Another group of researchers has developed various indexes, such as the entrepreneurship ecosystem development index (Ashraf & Singh, 2019), and the green entrepreneurship index (Singh et al., 2022a) to avoid the drawbacks of past studies. Accordingly, these indexes are used as useful indicators for EE in regression analysis. Existing researchers used estimated indexes as dependent and independent variables to explore their association among them (Singh & Jyoti, 2021; Singh & Jyoti, 2023a).

Ashraf and Singh (2019); Singh and Ashraf (2020); Amorós et al. (2021); Singh & Jyoti (2023a) developed the entrepreneurship ecosystem index, which is the integration of 12 factors in the domain of entrepreneurial framework conditions recommended by the GEM. Szerb et al. (2013) created a global entrepreneurship development index (GEDI) to measure the health of entrepreneurship. Singh and Ashraf (2020) also developed EEI as a composition of 12 factors proposed by GEM. This chapter also uses 12 indicators to create an entrepreneurship ecosystem index (*ENECIN*) for 47 selected countries. The following equation is applied to develop *ENECI:*

$$(ENECIN)_{ct} = W_{1,t} \times (NS\_BaScEnEdTr)_{ct} + W_{2,t} \times (NS\_CoProIn)_{ct} + W_{3,t} \times (NS\_CuSoNo)_{ct} + W_{4,t} \times (NS\_FiEn)_{ct} + W_{5,t} \times (NS\_GoPr)_{ct} + W_{6,t} \times (NS\_GoSuPo)_{ct} + W_{7,t} \times (NS\_\text{InMrDy})_{ct} + W_{8,t} \times (NS\_\text{InMrOp})_{ct} + W_{9,t} \times (NS\_PhSeIn)_{ct} + W_{10,t} \times (NS\_PoScEnEdTr)_{ct} + W_{11,t} \times (NS\_ReDeTr)_{ct} + W_{12,t} \times (NS\_TaBu)_{ct} \quad (1)$$

Here, *ENECIN* is the entrepreneurship ecosystem index; *NS* is the normalization score of respective variables; $W_1, W_2, \ldots, W_{12}$ are the weights of associated variables; t is time; and c is cross-sectional country in equation (1). The summary of *BaScEnEdTr*; *CoProIn*; *CuSoNo*; *FiEn*; *GoPr*; *GoSuPo*; *InMrDy*; *InMrOp*; *PhSeIn*; *PoScEnEdTr*; *ReDeTr*; and *TaBu* is presented in Table: 2. The entrepreneurship ecosystem index (*ENECIN*) is defined as a composite index of 12 indicators that explain the relative performance of the entrepreneurship ecosystem in 47 countries in this chapter.

Past literature used different indicators such as entrepreneurial behavior, entrepreneurial intention, entrepreneurial self-efficacy, and entrepreneurial skills to explore the EBA of entrepreneurs using primary data (Doran et al., 2018; Zabelina et al., 2019; Fredin & Lidén, 2020; Amofah & Saladrigues, 2021; Wu et al., 2022). Most studies applied structural equation modeling and factor component analysis to describe the factors affecting the entrepreneurial intentions of students in different countries (Elnadi & Gheith, 2021). Jyoti and Singh (2020) analyzed the determinants of start-up ecosystems in Gujarat. Age, education level, entrepreneurial skills, entrepreneurial training, business team, and early-stage firms are the determinants of EBA.

Entrepreneurial behavior and attitudes cannot be explained by a specific indicator. Doran et al. (2018) applied 14 different indicators of the entrepreneurship ecosystem (EE) to explain the impact of entrepreneurial attitudes on per capita GDP. GEM provides data on 15 indicators that describe the progress of EBA across countries. Ilić et al. (2020) also used these indicators to explain the progress of EBA in Slovenia and Croatia. Singh & Jyoti (2023c) also applied EBA-related indicators to explore their association with EE. Though, the statistics of 11 indicators associated with EBA were available for 47 countries during 2000–2022. Thus, this chapter used 11 indicators to develop a country-wise entrepreneurial behavior and attitude index (*ENBEATIN*). Here, *ENBEATIN* is defined as an integrated index of 11 indicators that measure the comparative performance of 47 countries in the EBA. The *ENBEATIN* is created as:

$$(ENBEATIN)_{ct} = W_{1,t} \times (NS\_BuSeSe)_{ct} + W_{2,t} \times (NS\_EnGoCaCh)_{ct} + W_{3,t} \times (NS\_EnIn)_{ct} + W_{4,t} \times (NS\_EsBuOw)_{ct} + W_{5,t} \times (NS\_FeFaRa)_{ct} + W_{6,t} \times (NS\_FeMaTEA)_{ct} + W_{7,t} \times (NS\_HiJoCrEx)_{ct} + W_{8,t} \times (NS\_HiSuEn)_{ct} + W_{9,t} \times (NS\_PeOp)_{ct} + W_{10,t} \times (NS\_PeCa)_{ct} + W_{11,t} \times (NS\_ToEaStEnAc)_{ct} \quad (2)$$

Here, *ENBEATIN* is the entrepreneurial behavior and attitudes index; W_1, W_2, ..., W_{12} are the weights of associated variables; t is time; and c is cross-sectional country in equation (2). The descriptions of *BuSeSe*; *EnGoCaCh*; *EnIn*; *EsBuOw*; *FeFaRa*; *FeMaTEA*; *HiJoCrEx*; *HiSuEn*; *PeOp*; *PeCa*; and *ToEaStEnAc* are given in Table: 2. The PCA technique is employed to create *ENECIN* and *ENBEATIN* in this chapter.

Table 2. Indicators of EE and EBA

Entrepreneurship Ecosystem		Entrepreneurial Behavior & Attitudes	
Indicators	**Symbol**	**Indicators**	**Symbol**
Basic school entrepreneurial education and training	*BaScEnEdTr*	Business Services Sector	BuSeSe
Commercial and professional infrastructure	*CoProIn*	Entrepreneurship as a good career choice	EnGoCaCh
Cultural and social norms	*CuSoNo*	Entrepreneurial intentions	EnIn
Financing for entrepreneurs	*FiEn*	Established business ownership	*EsBuOw*
Governmental programs	*GoPr*	Fear of failure rate	*FeFaRa*
Governmental support and policies	*GoSuPo*	Female/Male TEA	*FeMaTEA*
Internal market dynamics	*InMrDy*	High job creation expectation	*HiJoCrEx*
Internal market openness	*InMrOp*	High status to successful entrepreneurs	*HiSuEn*
Physical and services infrastructure	*PhSeIn*	Perceived capabilities	*PeCa*
Post school entrepreneurial education and training	*PoScEnEdTr*	Perceived opportunities	*PeOp*
R&D transfer	*ReDeTr*	Total early-stage entrepreneurial activity	*ToEaStEnAc*
Taxes and bureaucracy	*TaBu*		

Source: GEM; Ashraf and Singh (2019); Ilić et al. (2020); Singh and Ashraf, (2020); Singh and Jyoti (2023a).

3.3.2. Hypothetical Framework of Principal Components Analysis (PCA)

The PCA is a viable method to integrate multiple indicators in an index estimation (de Rocha et al., 2021; Ma & Zhu, 2022; Singh & Kumar, 2022c; Singh & Jyoti, 2023c). The technique reduces the dimensionality of variables in a set of variables. It helps to make a linear combination of variables in a set of simultaneous equations. The technique measures the coefficient of variation in the group of variables that has the largest contribution. It is useful to regulate the latent variables among the variables. It converts numerous variables into a final index (Doran et al., 2018). The PCA method is adopted to create *ENECIN* and *ENBEATIN* using the below process:

Standardization Form (*SF*) *of Variables:* SF transforms all values of a particular variable between 0 and 1 across countries or entities (Wu et al., 2022). Hence, it makes a comparison across countries in a specific variable. The *SF* of all indicators is derived as follows:

$$(SF)_{ict} = \{[(AcVa)_{ict} - (MiVa)_{ict}]/[(MaVa)_{ict} - (MiVa)_{ict}]\} \quad (3)$$

Here, *SF* is the standardization form of the corresponding variable; *AcVa*, *MiVa* and *MaVa* are the actual, minimum, and maximum values, respectively, for a specific variable across countries; *i* is the ith indicator; *c* is the cross-sectional country; and *t* is the time period in equation (3).

Variance matrix: It measures the proportion of variation of a specific variable in the group of variables (Singh et al., 2023b).

Eigenvector and Eigenvalues: Co-variance among the variables is observed through the statistical values of the eigenvector and eigenvalues. Eigenvectors determine the future space, and eigenvalues measure the magnitude of co-variance among the variables (Doran et al., 2018).

Validity Test: The KMO test is also applied to check the validity of PCA results (Wu et al., 2021; Singh et al., 2022a; Singh & Kumar, 2022a; Singh et al., 2023b).

Weights Estimation for Variables: The weight of respective variables is estimated as per the statistical values of eigenvalues and existing variance across indicators.

Final Index: It is the linear sum of the *SF* of the respective variables, which is also multiplied by their weights (Singh et al., 2022a; Singh et al., 2023b).

3.3.3. Formulation of Regression Equations

Previous studies used estimated indexes as dependent variables (*DV*s) and independent variables (*IV*s) in the regression analysis (Domańska et al., 2018; Tasnim & ibne Afzal, 2018; Galindo-Martín et al., 2020). Moya-Clemente et al. (2019) observed the impact of the SDG index on sustainable entrepreneurship in OECD countries. Galindo-Martín et al. (2020) used the environmental performance index and the human development index to assess their association with social entrepreneurship and green innovation in OECD countries. Sharma et al. (2023) investigated the impact of the financial inclusion index on global entrepreneurship index scores across countries. Singh et al. (2020b) and Singh et al. (2021) attempted to assess the interaction of sustainable development with its supportive indicators by estimating different indexes.

Aly (2020) used the human capital index and the digital evolution index to assess their impact on labour productivity and employment rates across developing countries using linear regression equations. Jio and Sun (2021) observed the impact of the digital economy development index on urban entrepreneurship in China. Amorós et al. (2021) compiled GEM data and the human development index to explore their impact on poverty in developing countries. Singh and Kumar (2022c) also analyze the interconnection among sustainable development and its key drivers using different indexes. Singh et al. (2023b) detected a causal relationship between the green entrepreneurship index and the global sustainable development index.

Jyoti & Singh (2023) examined the causal relationship between the information and communication index (*ICTI*) and economic development.

Singh & Jyoti (2023a, 2023b) also used the *ICTI* index as a dependent and independent variable in regression analysis. The above-mentioned empirical literature indicates that estimated indexes can be used as dependent and independent variables to examine the interconnection among them. Hence, this chapter used the entrepreneurship ecosystem index (*ENECIN*) and entrepreneurial behavior and attitudes index (*ENBEATIN*) as dependent and independent variables in regression equations to observe their causal relationship. Accordingly, two regression equations are formulated in this chapter. In the first regression equation, *ENECIN* is considered a dependent variable (*DV*), while *ENBEATIN* is applied as an independent variable (*IV*).

GDP per capita (constant 2015 US$) (Singh & Ashraf, 2020), employment to population ratio (15+% of total), foreign direct investment net inflows (% of GDP) (Rusu & Roman, 2017), inflation GDP deflator (annual%) (Rusu & Roman, 2017; Singh & Ashraf, 2020), manufacturing value added (% of GDP), population growth (annual%) (Sabra & Shreteh, 2021), scientific and technical journal articles (Paranata et al., 2023), GDP per person employed (constant 2017 PPP $), and unemployment total (% of total labor force) (Rusu & Roman, 2017; Aly, 2020) are comprised as control variables in the first equation. While log-linear regression is adopted to estimate the regression coefficients of the mentioned *IV*s with *ENECI*. The following regression equation is used:

$$\begin{aligned}\ln(ENECIN)_{ct} &= \alpha_0 + \alpha_1 \ln(ENBEATIN)_{ct} + \alpha_2 \ln(grdoprpeca)_{ct} + \alpha_3 \ln(empora)_{ct} + \alpha_4 \ln(fodiinnein)_{ct} \\ &+ \alpha_5 \ln(ingrdoprde)_{ct} + \alpha_6 \ln(mavaad)_{ct} + \alpha_7 \ln(pogran)_{ct} + \alpha_8 \ln(sctejoar)_{ct} \\ &+ \alpha_9 \ln(grdoprpeem)_{ct} + \alpha_{10} \ln(unto)_{ct} + \mu_{ct}\end{aligned} \tag{4}$$

Here, *ENECIN* is the entrepreneurship ecosystem index; *ENBEATIN* is the entrepreneurial behavior and attitudes index; *ln* is the natural *log* of corresponding variables; *c* is a specific country; *t* is time; is the constant coefficient; are the coefficients of *IV*s; and is the error term in equation (4). The description of all variables is given in Table 3.

Table 3. Summary of dependent and independent variables

Variables	Code	Units
Entrepreneurship ecosystem index	*ENECIN*	Number
Entrepreneurial behavior & attitudes index	*ENBEATIN*	Number
Compulsory education duration (years)	*coedudu*	Years
Employment to population ratio, 15+, total (%)	*empora*	%
Final consumption expenditure (% of GDP)	*ficoex*	%
Foreign direct investment, net inflows (% of GDP)	*fodiinnein*	%
GDP per capita (constant 2015 US$)	*grdoprpeca*	US$
Individuals using the Internet (% of population)	*inusin*	%
Inflation GDP deflator (annual %)	*ingrdoprde*	%
Manufacturing value added (% of GDP)	*mavaad*	%
Mobile cellular subscriptions (per 100 people)	*mocesu*	Number
Population growth (annual %)	*pogran*	%
Scientific and technical journal articles	*sctejoar*	Number
Vulnerable employment, total (% of total employment)	*vuemto*	%
GDP per person employed (constant 2017 PPP $)	*grdoprpeem*	PPP $
Self-employed total (% of total employment)	*seemto*	%
Unemployment total (% of total labour force)	*unto*	%

In the 2nd equation, *ENBEATIN* and *ENECIN* are applied as *DV* and *IV*, respectively. While compulsory education duration (years), inflation GDP deflator (annual %) (Singh & Ashraf, 2020), mobile cellular subscriptions (per 100 people), population growth (annual %) (Sabra & Shreteh, 2021), vulnerable employment total (% of total employment) (Aly, 2020), self-employed total (% of total employment) (Singh & Ashraf, 2020; de Rocha et al., 2021), unemployment total (% of total labour force) (Aly, 2020), individuals using the internet (% of population) (Singh & Ashraf, 2020; Singh & Kumar, 2022a; Sharma et al., 2023), and final consumption expenditure (% of GDP) are applied as control variables. The model is adopted in a following form:

$$\ln(ENBEATIN)_{ct} = \beta_0 + \beta_1 \ln(ENECIN)_{ct} + \beta_2 \ln(coedudu)_{ct} + \beta_3 \ln(ingrdoprde)_{ct} + \beta_4 \ln(mocesu)_{ct} + \beta_5 \ln(pogran)_{ct} + \beta_6 \ln(vuemto)_{ct} + \beta_7 \ln(seemto)_{ct} + \beta_8 \ln(unto)_{ct} + \beta_9 \ln(inusin)_{ct} + \beta_{10} \ln(ficoex)_{ct} + \eta_{ct} \quad (5)$$

Here, β_0 is the constant-term; $\beta_1, \beta_2, \beta_3, \ldots, \beta_{10}$ are the coefficients of associated *IV*s; and η_{ct} is the error-term in equation (5). The clarification of all variables is presented in Table: 3.

3.3.4. Robustness Test and Selection of Consistent Model

The empirical investigation of this chapter compiles two *DV*s and different *IV*s in the panel data of 47 countries. These countries have high diversity in *DV*s and *IV*s. So, country-wise panels have multi-correlation among the variables, autocorrelation, cross-sectional independence, and groupwise heteroskedasticity (Dahmani et al., 2022). The results of different tests like the Wooldridge test, Pesaran's test, and the Modified Wald test provide confirmation that the country-wise data is not free from the mentioned statistical issues. Then, the coefficients of *IV*s with *DV*s in equations (4) and (5) are estimated using linear regression-correlated panels corrected standard errors. This model is suggested by several researchers to avoid the presence of autocorrelation, cross-sectional independence, and groupwise heteroskedasticity in the panel data analysis (Ashraf & Singh, 2019; Jyoti & Singh, 2023).

3.3.5. Causality of EE and EBA With Explanatory Variables

The conceptual review argued that the entrepreneurship ecosystem (EE) helps to increase entrepreneurial behavior and attitudes (EBA), and EBA helps to improve EE. This chapter, therefore, also examines the causality of EE and EBA with explanatory variables. The Granger causality test is used to detect the causality between *DV*s and *IV*s. Evans (2019) also used the Granger casualty test to observe the causality between two different variables. Singh et al. (2023a) also used the Granger causality test to examine the causal association of the green entrepreneurship ecosystem with economic development. This chapter assumes that EBA is caused to improve EE and EE is caused to increase EE. Therefore, the causal association of EE with EBA is estimated as:

$$\left(eneci\right)_{ct} = \lambda_0 + \sum\nolimits_{j=1}^{p} \lambda_{1,j} \left(eneci\right)_{c,t-j} + \sum\nolimits_{j=0}^{p} \lambda_{2,j} \left(enbeatin\right)_{c,t-j} + \delta_{ct} \qquad (6)$$

Here, j_s are various lagged of *ENECIN* and *ENBEATIN*; *t* is time; is fixed effect; λ_1 and λ_2 are the vectors of coefficients of respective lags of *ENECIN* and *ENBEATIN*, respectively; is error term in equation (6). If λ_1 and λ_2 are statistically significant, that shows a causation between EE and EBA. The causal relationship of EE and EBA with other control variables is also identified using the above-mentioned process.

The proposed descriptive and regression analyses are completed using STATA and SPSS statistical software.

4. RESULTS AND DISCUSSION

4.1. Relative Progress of Factor-Driven, Efficiency-Driven, and Innovative-Driven Countries in EE and EBA

Figure 1. Relative progress of factor, efficiency, and innovative-driven countries
Source: Estimated by authors.

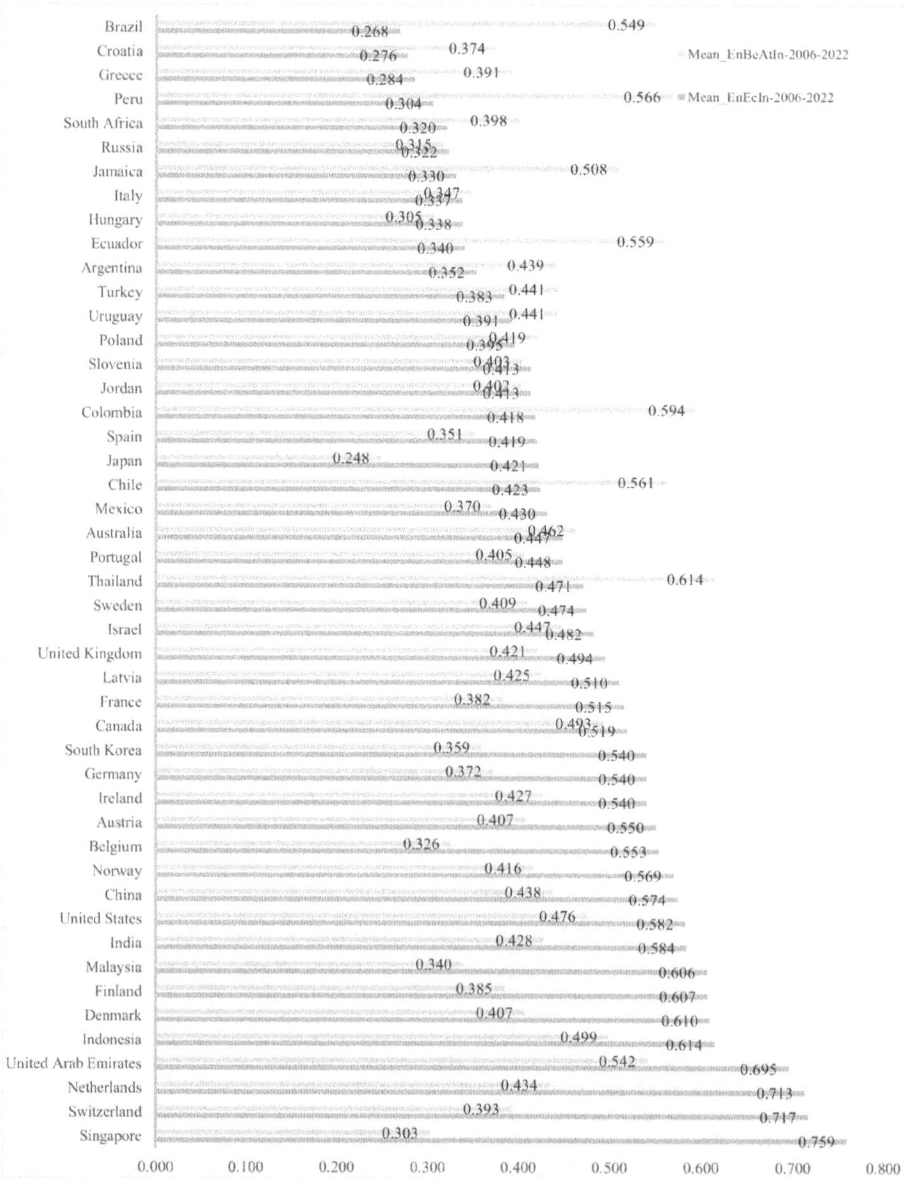

Table 4. Ranking of across countries as per the estimated values of ENECIN and ENBEATIN

Stage of Development	Country	Mean_*ENECIN* (2006-2022)		Mean_*ENBEATIN* (2006-2022)	
		Value	Rank	Value	Rank
Efficiency-driven	Indonesia	0.614	5	0.499	9
	China	0.574	11	0.438	17
	Thailand	0.471	24	0.614	1
	Mexico	0.430	27	0.370	38
	Colombia	0.418	31	0.594	2
	Jordan	0.413	32	0.402	30
	Ecuador	0.340	38	0.559	5
	Jamaica	0.330	41	0.508	8
	Russia	0.322	42	0.315	44
	South Africa	0.320	43	0.398	31
	Peru	0.304	44	0.566	3
	Brazil	0.268	47	0.549	6
Factor-driven	India	0.584	9	0.428	19

Continued on following page

Table 4. Continued

Stage of Development	Country	Mean_*ENECIN* (2006-2022)		Mean_*ENBEATIN* (2006-2022)	
		Value	Rank	Value	Rank
Innovation-driven	Singapore	0.759	1	0.303	46
	Switzerland	0.717	2	0.393	32
	Netherlands	0.713	3	0.434	18
	UAE	0.695	4	0.542	7
	Denmark	0.610	6	0.407	27
	Finland	0.607	7	0.385	34
	United States	0.582	10	0.476	11
	Norway	0.569	12	0.416	24
	Ireland	0.540	15	0.427	20
	Germany	0.540	16	0.372	37
	South Korea	0.540	17	0.359	39
	France	0.515	19	0.382	35
	United Kingdom	0.494	21	0.421	22
	Israel	0.482	22	0.447	13
	Sweden	0.474	23	0.409	25
	Portugal	0.448	25	0.405	28
	Japan	0.421	29	0.248	47
	Spain	0.419	30	0.351	40
	Slovenia	0.413	33	0.403	29
	Italy	0.337	40	0.347	41
	Greece	0.284	45	0.391	33
	Belgium	0.553	13	0.326	43
	Austria	0.550	14	0.407	26
	Canada	0.519	18	0.493	10
	Australia	0.447	26	0.462	12

Continued on following page

Table 4. Continued

Stage of Development	Country	Mean_*ENECIN* (2006-2022)		Mean_*ENBEATIN* (2006-2022)	
		Value	Rank	Value	Rank
Transition from 2nd stage to 3rd stage	Malaysia	0.606	8	0.340	42
	Latvia	0.510	20	0.425	21
	Chile	0.423	28	0.561	4
	Poland	0.395	34	0.419	23
	Uruguay	0.391	35	0.441	14
	Turkey	0.383	36	0.441	15
	Argentina	0.352	37	0.439	16
	Hungary	0.338	39	0.305	45
	Croatia	0.276	46	0.374	36

Source: Author's estimation.

The World Economic Forum (WEF) segregated global countries into three categories (i.e., factor-driven, efficiency-driven, and innovation-driven). As per the estimated values of *ENECIN* and *ENBEATIN*, the relative progress of the undertaken countries is given below:

Factor-driven countries: This is the first or initial stage of a country in which the livelihood security of a large population depends on the agricultural sector. Thus, at this stage, a country also has a huge unskilled labour force in all sectors. India is a factor-driven country, and it has 9th and 19th positions in the entrepreneurship ecosystem (EE) and entrepreneurial behavior and attitudes (EBA) among the 57 countries (Table: 4). India has taken several policy steps to increase EE. Therefore, India could improve its position in EE and EBA.

Efficiency-driven countries: This is the second stage of the development of a country. In this stage, the development of a country starts to shift from the agricultural sector to the industrial sector. Indonesia, China, Thailand, Mexico, Colombia, Jordan, Ecuador, Russia, South Africa, Peru, and Brazil are the efficiency-driven countries (Table: 4). Indonesia and China have 1st and 2nd positions in EE and EBA, respectively, in efficiency-driven countries. China has taken several policy initiatives in higher academic institutions to create students' start-ups. Therefore, China could improve its position in EE and EBA. Thailand and Colombia have 1st and 2nd positions in the EBA. Ecuador, Jamaica, Russia, South Africa, Peru, and Brazil have poor positions in EE. Mexico, Russia, and South Africa could not increase their positions in EBA. There is a reported a high diversity in EE and EBA in efficiency-driven countries.

Table 5. Relative position of across countries in EE and EBA

Values of *ENECIN* and *ENBEATIN*	Comparative Position of Countries in EE	Comparative Position of Countries in EBA
Best position (if values are more than 0.60)	Singapore, Switzerland, Netherlands, United Arab Emirates, Indonesia, Denmark, Finland and Malaysia	Thailand
Better position (if values lie between 0.50–0.60)	India, United States, China, Norway, Belgium, Austria, Ireland, Germany, South Korea, Canada, France and Latvia	Colombia, Peru, Chile, Ecuador, Brazil, United Arab Emirates and Jamaica
Average position (if values lie between 0.40–0.49)	United Kingdom, Israel, Sweden, Thailand, Portugal, Australia, Mexico, Chile, Japan, Spain, Colombia, Jordan and Slovenia	Indonesia, Canada, United States, Australia, Israel, Uruguay, Turkey, Argentina, China, Netherlands, India, Ireland, Latvia, United Kingdom, Poland, Norway, Sweden, Austria, Denmark, Portugal, Slovenia and Jordan
Poorest position (if values are less than 0.40)	Poland, Uruguay, Turkey, Argentina, Ecuador, Hungary, Italy, Jamaica, Russia, South Africa, Peru, Greece, Croatia and Brazil	South Africa, Switzerland, Greece, Finland, France, Croatia, Germany, Mexico, South Korea, Spain, Italy, Malaysia, Belgium, Russia, Hungary, Singapore and Japan

Source: Author's estimation.

Innovation-driven countries: This is the third stage of the economic development of a country. In this stage, the efficiency of inputs in the production sector increases due to an increase in human skills, innovation, science, and technological development. Innovative-driven countries produce highly innovative products and increase their position in the international market. Singapore, Switzerland, and the Netherlands have the 1st, 2nd, and 3rd positions in EE in the innovation-driven countries (Table: 4). Most innovation-driven countries like the United Arab Emirates, Denmark, Finland, the United States, Norway, Ireland, Germany, South Korea, France, Austria, and Canada have better-performing countries in EE.

The United Kingdom, Israel, Sweden, Portugal, Japan, Spain, Slovenia, and Australia have good performers in the EE. Italy and Greece have poor performance in EE. Moreover, Singapore, Switzerland, Finland, Germany, South Korea, France, Japan, Spain, Italy, Greece, and Belgium have poor positions in EBA. The United Arab Emirates (UAE) has a better performance in EBA. Remaining innovation-driven countries have good positions in EBA.

Transition of Countries from 2nd Stage to 3rd Stage: Malaysia, Latvia, Chile, Poland, Uruguay, Turkey, Argentina, Hungary, and Croatia are being transferred from 2nd stage to 3rd stage of development (Table: 4). These countries have diversity in EE and EBA. Malaysia has the best position in EE, while it is in a poor position in EBA. Latvia has a better position in EE, and it has a good position in EBA. Most transitioning countries (except Malaysia, Hungary, and Croatia) have good positions in EBA. Chile has the best performance in the EBA. Figure: 1 also infers the comparison across countries in terms of efficiency and innovative-driven countries. The relative positions of 47 countries as per the estimated values of *ENECIN* and *ENBEATIN* are given in Table: 5.

4.2. Discussion on Regression Results

The center measure of the *DV*s and *IV*s is presented in Table: 6. The mean values of most variables are very large. Moreover, as per the skewness values of most variables, more than 1 indicates that these variables are not in the normal forms. This chapter, therefore, consider the *log* form of all variables in the regression equations.

Table 6. Centre measures of the variables

Variables	Minimum	Maximum	Mean	Standard Deviation	Skewness	Kurtosis
ENECIN	0.04	0.99	0.47	0.16	0.19	2.99
ENBEATIN	0.11	0.73	0.43	0.10	0.29	3.27
coedudu	6.00	16.41	10.47	2.17	0.00	2.74
empora	32.03	80.55	56.88	8.36	-0.27	3.79
ficoex	35.90	107.35	74.03	10.36	-0.53	4.89
fodiinnein	0.00	106.60	5.32	9.09	5.23	41.26
grdoprpeca	948	88967	26935	20951	0.74	2.69
inusin	2.39	100.00	65.10	24.33	-0.75	2.59
ingrdoprde	0.00	54.15	4.21	5.49	4.12	27.65
mavaad	5.49	34.65	15.19	5.70	0.98	3.84
mocesu	7.81	221.31	112.60	27.74	-0.11	4.81
pogran	0.00	18.13	0.97	1.40	7.53	77.01
sctejoar	94	669744	40418	81548	4.19	22.37
vuemto	0.34	82.97	19.56	16.64	1.56	5.06
grdoprpeem	9468	215522	74067	36139	0.23	2.61
seemto	2.94	84.37	23.77	16.54	1.41	4.58
unto	0.25	29.81	7.43	4.64	1.84	7.23

Source: Author's estimation.

The mean values of variance inflation factors (*VIF*) are found at 5.91 and 8.34 for the *IV*s in Tables 7 and 7, respectively. The estimates indicate *IV*s do not have multi-correlation. The statistically significant F-values under the *Ramsey RESET test* specify that the functional forms of regression equations are correctly defined. Statistically significant F-values under the Wooldridge test recommended that country-wise panel data have autocorrelation. The results of Pesaran's test also claimed that there is a presence of cross-sectional dependency across countries. Finally, the modified Wald test also indicates the presence of groupwise heteroskedasticity in the panel data.

The dependency of the entrepreneurship ecosystem index (*ENECIN*) on the entrepreneurial behavior and attitudes index (*ENBEATIN*) and other variables is estimated through regression coefficients (Table: 7). The dependency of the entrepreneurial behavior and attitudes index on the entrepreneurship ecosystem index and control variables is also observed through regression coefficients (Table: 8). The positive coefficient of *ENECIN* with *ENBEATIN* suggests that the entrepreneurship ecosystem (EE) increases as EBA increases. Also, the positive coefficient of *ENBEATIN* with *ENECIN* infers that EBA is likely to improve as EE increases. There is a positive causality between EE and EBA across countries. EE is projected to improve by 0.07% due to a 1% increase in EBA. EBA is predicted to increase by 0.03% as EE increases by 1%.

Table 7. Regression coefficients of ENECIN with explanatory variables

Number of observations						799
Number of countries						47
observations per country						17
R-squared						0.2635
Wald Chi^2						1113.51
Prob > Chi^2						0.000
Mean VIF						5.91
Ramsey RESET test using powers of the fitted values of *ln(ENECIN)* [*F*-Value]						10.76*
Ramsey RESET test using powers of the independent variables [*F*-Value]						7.96*
Wooldridge test for autocorrelation [*F*- Value]						17.881*
Pesaran's test of cross-sectional independence						2.935*
Modified Wald test for groupwise heteroskedasticity [Chi^2]						2432.72*
ln (ENECIN) [DV]	*Reg. Coef.*	*Std. Err.*	*z*	*P>|z|*	[95% Conf. Interval]	
ln (ENBEATIN)	0.0766	0.0626	1.22	0.221	-0.0462	0.1993
ln(grdoprpeca)	0.0374	0.0432	0.87	0.387	-0.0473	0.1222
ln(empora)	0.5547	0.1424	3.89	0.000	0.2755	0.8338
ln(fodiinnein)	0.0555	0.0102	5.43	0.000	0.0354	0.0755
ln(ingrdoprde)	-0.0003	0.0113	-0.02	0.981	-0.0225	0.0220
ln(mavaad)	0.1763	0.0243	7.260	0.000	0.1287	0.2238
ln(pogran)	0.0573	0.0118	4.870	0.000	0.0342	0.0803
ln(sctejoar)	0.0401	0.0129	3.110	0.002	0.0148	0.0653
ln(grdoprpeem)	0.1347	0.0689	1.960	0.051	-0.0003	0.2697
ln(unto)	-0.0237	0.0337	-0.700	0.482	-0.0898	0.0423
Con. Coef.	-5.6826	0.9406	-6.040	0.000	-7.5262	-3.8391

Source: Author's estimation.

Per capita income plays a positive role in increasing EE. Hence, per capita gross domestic product showed a positive influence on EE. GDP per person employed measures the per capita output of all production activities. Hence, this variable helps to increase per capita income. Accordingly, the EE also increases as GDP per person employed increases. The estimate infers that EE increases by 0.13% as GDP per person employed increases by 1%. Employment opportunities are also effective in increasing per capita income. The positive coefficient of employment to population ratio with *ENECIN* infers that EE is projected to be improved by 0.55% as the employment population ratio increases by 1%. EE and EBA are expected to decline as the unemployment rate increase. Vulnerable employment is also responsible for reducing EBA.

Table 8. Regression coefficients of ENBEATIN with explanatory variables

Number of observations						798
Number of countries						47
Observations per country						16
R-squared						0.2656
Wald Chi^2						323.42
Prob > Chi^2						0.000
Mean VIF						8.34
Ramsey RESET test using powers of the fitted values of *logENECIN* [*F*-Value]						1.34*
Ramsey RESET test using powers of the independent variables [*F*-Value]						10.74*
Wooldridge test for autocorrelation [*F*- Value]						83.888*
Pesaran's test of cross-sectional independence						21.173*
Modified Wald test for groupwise heteroskedasticity [Chi^2]						1352.59*
ln(ENBEATIN) [DV]	*Reg. Coef.*	*Std. Err.*	*z*	*P>|z|*	[95% Conf. Interval]	
ln(ENECIN)	0.0358	0.0152	2.350	0.019	0.0060	0.0657
ln(coedudu)	0.1711	0.0366	4.680	0.000	0.0994	0.2429
ln(ingrdoprde)	0.0253	0.0075	3.350	0.001	0.0105	0.0400
ln(mocesu)	-0.0105	0.0280	-0.370	0.709	-0.0654	0.0445
ln(pogran)	0.0417	0.0063	6.620	0.000	0.0293	0.0540
ln(vuemto)	-0.2899	0.0432	-6.710	0.000	-0.3745	-0.2053
ln(seemto)	0.4810	0.0637	7.550	0.000	0.3561	0.6058
ln(unto)	-0.0888	0.0119	-7.480	0.000	-0.1120	-0.0655
ln(inusin)	0.0427	0.0147	2.900	0.004	0.0139	0.0714
ln(ficoex)	0.3318	0.0434	7.640	0.000	0.2467	0.4169
Con. Coef.	-3.2879	0.2911	-11.290	0.000	-3.8585	-2.7174

Source: Author's estimation.

The prime intention of EBA is to increase self-employment (de Rocha et al., 2021). The positive coefficient of self-employment with *ENBEATIN* infers that EBA is likely to increase by 0.48% due to an increase in self-employment by 1%. The technical skills of people increase as their level of education increases. In this chapter, compulsory education duration is used to capture the influence of education level on EBA. The positive coefficient of compulsory education with *ENBEATIN* approved that EBA increases as the level of education increases. It also seems that EBA is projected to increase by 0.17% as compulsory education duration increases by 1%.

Population growth creates demand for goods and services in the domestic market. Hence, it also cultivates a positive environment for the business sector and encourages new entrepreneurs to start new ventures to meet the rising demand for products among the growing population. For instance, China and India have large populations. Therefore, both countries have greater possibilities for nurturing a conducive ecosystem for new entrepreneurs. The empirical results also claimed a positive impact of annual population growth on *ENECIN* and *ENBEATIN*. EE and EBA are likely to increase by 0.012% and 0.06%, respectively, due to a 1% increase in annual population growth.

The growth and development of new ventures and start-ups depend on technological advancement and technology transfer. Scientific and technical journal articles are an important way to disseminate technical information among scientists, industrial delegates, and the manufacturing sector. Accordingly, it discovers new ideas, knowledge, and skills to provide social-economic services to consumers. Hence, technological development is a useful determinant of EE. The empirical association of scientific and technical research articles with *ENECIN* appeared positive and statistically significant. The estimate indicates that technological development helps to create EE. EE is to be increased by 0.04% as technological development increases by 1%.

The role of the manufacturing sector in GDP is useful for creating EE. The coefficient of manufacturing value added with EE is positive and statistically significant. EE may increase by 0.18% due to a 1% increase in the share of manufacturing value added to GDP. FDI also creates huge opportunities to increase capital formation, business development, money flow, knowledge and technological transfer, employment opportunities, and foreign trade. EE increases due to a rise in foreign direct investment net inflows (FDINI). EE is likely to be improved by 0.06% as the contribution of FDINI increases by 1%. Real income, purchasing power, investment, saving, and consumption by people decline due to the rise in inflation. Consequently, inflation has an adverse impact on EE and EBA. The result also indicates that EE and EBA are adversely affected due to the increase in inflation GDP deflator.

EBA is positively associated with final consumption expenditure. The result showed that EBA increased by 0.33% as final consumption expenditure increased by 1%. The impact of individuals using the internet on *ENBEATIN* is found to be positive and statistically significant. The estimate indicates that digitalization helps to increase EBA. EBA may increase by 0.04% as digitalization increases by 1%. Mobile cellular subscriptions produce a negative and statistically insignificant impact on EBA.

4.3. Causal Association Between Dependent and Independent Variables

The causation of *ENECIN* with *IV*s is presented in Table - 8. The estimate infers that EE has a causal association with EBA, GDP per capita, foreign direct investment net inflows, manufacturing value added, population growth, scientific and technical journal articles, GDP per person employed, and unemployment rate. Hence, the progress of EE depends on the above-mentioned variables, which can be useful for its further prediction.

Table 9. Causation of entrepreneurship ecosystem index with explanatory variables

DV	**Entrepreneurship Ecosystem Index (*ENECIN*)**			
Hypothesis	**H_0: Independent Variables Does Not Granger-Cause *ENECIN*.** **H_1: Independent Variables Does Granger-Cause *ENECIN* for at Least One Panel**			
Indicators	*W*-**Bar**	*Z*-**Bar**	*Z*-**Bar Tilde**	*Conclusion*
ENBEATIN	2.5603	7.5636[a]	4.8967[a]	H_0: Rejected
grdoprpeca	2.4478	7.0186[a]	4.4973[a]	H_0: Rejected
empora	1.5848	2.8351[a]	1.4316	H_0: Accepted
fodiinnein	1.7220	3.5001[a]	1.9190[c]	H_0: Rejected
ingrdoprde	1.3133	1.5189	0.4672	H_0: Accepted
mavaad	3.0187	9.7862[a]	6.5253[a]	H_0: Rejected
pogran	2.0129	4.9103[a]	2.9523[a]	H_0: Rejected
sctejoar	2.4397	6.9791[a]	4.4684[a]	H_0: Rejected
grdoprpeem	3.0099	9.7434[a]	6.4940[a]	H_0: Rejected
unto	3.0386	9.8825[a]	6.5959[a]	H_0: Rejected

Source: Author's estimation.

EBA does not have a causal association with EE. EBA has a causal relationship with mobile cellular subscriptions, population growth, vulnerable employment, self-employed total, unemployment rate, individuals using the internet, and final consumption expenditure. These variables, therefore, may be useful in the forecasting of EBA.

Table 10. Causation of entrepreneurial behavior and attitudes index with explanatory variables

DV	**Entrepreneurial Behavior & Attitudes Index (*ENBEATIN*)**			
Hypothesis	**H_0: Independent Variables Does Not Granger-Cause *ENBEATIN*. H_1: Independent VARIABLES DOES GRANGER-CAUSE *ENBEATIN* for at Least One Panel.**			
Indicators	***W*-Bar**	***Z*-Bar**	***Z*-Bar Tilde**	*Conclusion*
ENECIN	1.1581	0.7662	0.0844	H_0: Accepted
ingrdoprde	1.3544	1.7179[c]	0.6130	H_0: Accepted
mocesu	2.9276	9.3442[a]	6.2015[a]	H_0: Rejected
pogran	2.0543	5.1111[a]	3.0995[a]	H_0: Rejected
vuemto	2.2500	6.0594[a]	3.7944[a]	H_0: Rejected
seemto	2.0258	4.9725[a]	2.9979[a]	H_0: Rejected
unto	2.2528	6.0732[a]	3.8045[a]	H_0: Rejected
inusin	3.0519	9.9468[a]	6.6431[a]	H_0: Rejected
ficoex	1.8130	3.9414[a]	2.2423[b]	H_0: Rejected

Source: Author's estimation. **Note:** [a], [b] and [c] indicate that coefficients are statistically significant at 1%, 5% and 10% significance level, respectively.

5. CONCLUSION

The results based on the entrepreneurship ecosystem index (*ENECIN*) and entrepreneurial behavior and attitudes index (*ENBEATIN*) indicate that across countries have high diversity in the mentioned indicators. Singapore, Switzerland, and the Netherlands have values of *ENECIN* greater than 0.70. Hence, these countries have the best performance in the entrepreneurship ecosystem (EE). These countries have an average position in entrepreneurial behavior and attitudes (EBA). The estimates also reported that most countries (except the United Arab Emirates) have high values of *ENECIN*, while these countries have low values of *ENBEATIN*. The highest value of *ENBEATIN* for Thailand indicates that this country has the best position in EBA. Peru, Chile, Ecuador, Brazil, the United Arab Emirates, and Jamaica have good positions in the EBA.

Indonesia, Canada, the United States, Australia, Israel, Uruguay, Turkey, Argentina, China, the Netherlands, India, Ireland, Latvia, the United Kingdom, Poland, Norway, Sweden, Austria, Denmark, Portugal, Slovenia, and Jordan have average positions in the EBA. The remaining countries have poor positions in the EBA. Furthermore, the results infer that there is a reported high diversity in EE and EBA in efficiency-driven and innovation-driven countries.

The entrepreneurship ecosystem (EE) helps to enhance entrepreneurial behavior and attitudes (EBA). EBA also plays a positive role in increasing EE. EBA has a causal relationship with EE, however, EE does not have any causation with EBA. Therefore, the authors found a one-way causal association between EE and EBA. EE is to be improved as GDP per capita, employment to population ratio, foreign direct investment net inflow, manufacturing value added, population growth, technological advancement, and GDP per person employed increase. Inflation and the unemployment rate have a negative impact on EE. EBA is likely to improve as compulsory education duration, population growth, self-employment, digitalization, and final consumption expenditure increase. EBA may decline due to an increase in inflation, GDP deflator, unemployment rate, and mobile cellular subscriptions.

6. POLICY IMPLICATIONS

The creation of more employment helps to enhance the income and purchasing power of people. It would be positive to create demand for goods and services in the market and increase consumption expenditures. Further, rising demand for goods and services will create a positive ecosystem for the business sector to increase production. Level of employment has a significant contribution to increase EE and EBA. The global countries should control high unemployment rates and inflation to avoid the occurrence of an economic crisis. FDI is useful to create physical infrastructure, money flow, job opportunities, and business ecosystems. The developing countries should adopt policies to increase FDI. The global countries should also implement policies to increase the growth of the manufacturing sector. Extensive investment in the R&D sector helps to increase technological development and meet the technological requirements of business sectors. R&D will promote technology transfer and commercialization from research institutions to industrial fields.

The global countries should create adequate institutional infrastructure, culture, and self-efficacy to increase the intention of people to be entrepreneurs. Entrepreneurship education and academic entrepreneurship may be constructive ways to increase EBA. Entrepreneurial knowledge, skill development, and entrepreneurial education may be creative ways to increase EE and EBA. Promotion of women's entrepreneurship may be a significant initiative to increase EE and EBA in developing countries. Business practitioners should also provide training to students to increase their entrepreneurial skills. The government should be providing incentives for scientific staff, creating more technology transfer activities, facilitating more finance for entrepreneurs, and increasing private investment in business activities to promote EE.

The developing economies should strengthen small-scale enterprises (SMEs) to create a favorable EE. A favorable ecosystem for SMEs also changes the EBA of entrepreneurs. This initiative would work as a significant driver to increase the number of self-employed people. Provisions to provide entrepreneurship education to youth and skilled workers create a conducive EE. Education and training for entrepreneurship at the elementary and secondary levels would be positive for increasing EE. The policy initiatives would promote academic entrepreneurship and tech-based start-ups in developing economies. Further, it would assist in maintaining the collaboration of research organizations with existing industries. It is essential to increase public research funding to discover more technologies for new business and manufacturing sectors in developing economies.

Technology transfer and commercialization are essential to creating EE. Therefore, developing economies should pay attention to increasing technology transfer and commercialization to reinforce their positions in EE and EBA. Technology transfer and exchange would also enhance innovation and create a smooth network among the small and large firms within a country and across countries. Access to finance is also useful to increase an individual's intentions towards business activities. The government needs to provide extensive funding to the business community to increase EE and EBA. The government must provide management assistance and training for new entrepreneurs to create an appropriate EE.

7. LIMITATION AND SCOPE FOR FURTHER RESEARCH

The findings of this chapter are based on secondary data in the areas of entrepreneurship ecosystem (EE) and entrepreneurial behavior and attitudes (EBA) across countries. Therefore, the results may be unreliable as compared to the previous studies that used primary data. The present chapter compiles indicators associated with EE and EBA for 47 countries that exhibit diversity in numerous ways. Also, these countries have high diversity in social-economic, cultural, government policies, geographical location, and human skills. While the stated variables are not included in the empirical analysis of this chapter. Existing researchers can detect the long-run and short-run relationship between EE and EBA using ARDL and VECM models. Further research can be devoted to examining the impact of EE and EBA on social, economic, technological, and environmental development.

REFERENCES

Acs, Z. (2006). How is entrepreneurship good for economic growth? *Innovations: Technology, Governance, Globalization*, *1*(1), 97-107. http://www.mitpressjournals.org/doi/pdf/10.1162/itgg.2006.1.1.97

Adusei, M. (2016). Does entrepreneurship promote economic growth in Africa? *African Development Review*, *28*(2), 201–214. doi:10.1111/1467-8268.12190

Ali, J., & Jabeen, Z. (2020). Understanding entrepreneurial behavior for predicting start-up intention in India: Evidence form global entrepreneurship monitor (GEM) data. *Journal of Public Affairs*, *22*(1), 1–11. doi:10.1002/pa.2399

Aly, H. (2020). Digital transformation, development, and productivity in developing countries: Is artificial intelligence a cure or a blessing? *Review of Economics and Political Science*, *7*(4), 1–19. doi:10.1108/REPS-11-2019-0145

Amofah, K., & Saladrigues, R. (2021). Impact of attitude towards entrepreneurship education and role models on entrepreneurial intention. *Journal of Innovation and Entrepreneurship*, *11*(36), 1–30. doi:10.118613731-022-00197-5

Amorós, J. E., Ramírez, L. M., Rodríguez-Aceves, L., & Ruiz, L. E. (2021). Revisiting poverty and entrepreneurship in developing countries. *Journal of Developmental Entrepreneurship*, *26*(2), 1–23. doi:10.1142/S1084946721500084

Anjum, T., Amoozegar, A., Farrukh, M., & Heidler, P. (2022). Entrepreneurial intentions among business students: The mediating role of attitude and the moderating role of university support. *Education + Training*, *65*(4), 1–20. doi:10.1108/ET-01-2021-0020

Arbabian, S., & Zamani, Z. (2022). The interactive effect of financial development and human capital on entrepreneurship in selected countries. *Journal of Development and Capital*, *8*(1), 1–21. doi:10.22103/jdc.2022.19537.1249

Ashraf, S. N., & Singh, A. K. (2019). Does entrepreneurship ecosystem have a long-term relationship with economic Growth in selected economies? A statistical investigation. In S. Misra, S. Shukla, & G. Batthini (Eds.), *Proceedings of the 13th Biennial Conference on Entrepreneurship Organized by EDII Ahmedabad* (pp. 176–187). Bookwell Publishing House. http://library.ediindia.ac.in:8181/xmlui/handle/123456789/7903

Audretsch, D. B., Belitski, M., & Desai, S. (2015). Entrepreneurship and economic development in cities. *The Annals of Regional Science*, *55*(1), 33–60. doi:10.100700168-015-0685-x

Baluku, M. M., Nansubuga, F., Otto, K., & Horn, L. (2021). Risk aversion, entrepreneurial attitudes, intention, and entry among young people in Uganda and Germany: A gendered analysis. *Journal of Entrepreneurship and Innovation in Emerging Economies*, *7*(1), 31–59. doi:10.1177/2393957520960567

Bashir, H. A., & Akhtar, A. (2016). The role of innovative entrepreneurship in economic development: A study of G20 countries. *Management Studies and Economic System, 2*(2), 91-100. https://www.msaes.org/article_44797_6f698044d22cf862ec02dd49aafaf42c.pdf

Bouarir, H., Diani, A., Boubker, O., & Rharzouz, J. (2023). Key determinants of women's entrepreneurial intention and behaviour: The role of business opportunity recognition and need for achievement. *Administrative Sciences, 13*(33), 1–19. doi:10.3390/admsci13020033

Chen, C. C. (2014). Entrepreneurship, economic growth, and employment: A case study of Taiwan. *Hitotsubashi Journal of Economics*, *55*(1), 71–88. https://www.jstor.org/stable/43296271

Dahmani, M., Mabrouki, M., & Youssef, A. B. (2022). ICT, trade openness and economic growth in Tunisia: What is going wrong? *Economic Change and Restructuring*, *55*(1), 2317–2336. doi:10.100710644-022-09388-2

de Rocha, A. K. L., de Moraes, G. H. S. M., & Fischer, B. (2021). The role of university environment in promoting entrepreneurial behavior: Evidence from heterogeneous regions in Brazil. *Innovation & Management Review*, *19*(1), 39–61. doi:10.1108/INMR-08-2020-0112

Domańska, A., Żukowska, B., & Zajkowski, R. (2018). Green entrepreneurship as a connector among social, environmental, and economic pillars of sustainable development. Why some countries are more agile? *Problemy Ekorozwoju, 13*(2), 67-76. https://ekorozwoj.pollub.pl/no26/i.pdf

Doran, J., McCarthy, N., & O'Connor, M. (2018). The role of entrepreneurship in stimulating economic growth in developed and developing countries. *Cogent Economics & Finance*, *6*(1), 1–14. doi:10.1080/23322039.2018.1442093

Dvouletý, O. (2017). Relationship between unemployment and entrepreneurship dynamics in the Czech Regions: A panel var approach. *Acta Universitatis Agriculturae et Silviculturae Mendelianae Brunensis*, *65*(102), 987–995. doi:10.11118/actaun201765030987

Elnadi, M., & Gheith, M. H. (2021). Entrepreneurial ecosystem, entrepreneurial self-efficacy, and entrepreneurial intention in higher education: Evidence from Saudi Arabia. *International Journal of Management Education, 19*(1), 100458. Advance online publication. doi:10.1016/j.ijme.2021.100458

Erken, H., Donselaar, P., & Thurik, R. (2018). Total factor productivity and the role of entrepreneurship. *The Journal of Technology Transfer*, *43*(1), 1493–1521. doi:10.100710961-016-9504-5

Evans, O. (2019). Information and communication technologies and economic development in Africa in the short and long run. *International Journal of Technology Management & Sustainable Development*, *18*(2), 127–146. doi:10.1386/tmsd_00002_1

Fredin, S., & Lidén, A. (2020). Entrepreneurial ecosystems: Towards a systemic approach to entrepreneurship? *Geografisk Tidskrift*, *120*(2), 87–97. doi:10.1080/00167223.2020.1769491

Galindo-Martín, M. A., Castaño-Martínez, M. S., & Méndez-Picazo, M. T. (2020). The relationship between green innovation, social entrepreneurship, and sustainable development. *Sustainability (Basel)*, *12*(11), 1–19. doi:10.3390u12114467

Gao, Y., & Qin, X. (2022). Entrepreneurship education and entrepreneurial intention of Chinese college students: Evidence from a moderated multi-mediation model. *Frontiers in Psychology*, *13*(1), 1–12. doi:10.3389/fpsyg.2022.1049232 PMID:36524159

Hameli, A., Kampouris, L., Machaal, A. K., & Mertzanis, C. (2021). Financial development, institutions, Gender and Entrepreneurship in the United Arab Emirates. *Asian Journal of Empirical Research*, *11*(2), 11–22. doi:10.18488/journal.1007.2021.112.11.22

Ilić, M, Ranković, M., Janić, L., & Mitić, B. (2020). Indicators of entrepreneurial behavior and attitudes for entrepreneurs of Slovenia and Croatia, in 2018/2019. *Journal of Economic Development, Environment and People*, *9*(1), 6-16. doi:.v8i4.641 doi:10.26458/jedep

Jalam, M. U., & Adamu, M. (2022). Relationship between entrepreneurship ecosystems and entrepreneurial mindset development among students. *International Journal of Intellectual Discourse*, *5*(3), 1–13. https://ijidjournal.org/index.php/ijid/article/view/271

Jio, S., & Sun, Q. (2021). Digital economic development and its impact on economic growth in China: Research based on the perspective of sustainability. *Sustainability (Basel)*, *13*(18), 1–18. doi:10.3390u131810245

Jyoti, B., & Singh, A. K. (2020). Characteristics and determinants of new start-ups in Gujarat, India. *Entrepreneurship Review*, *1*(2), 1-25. doi:.v1i2.154 doi:10.38157/entrepreneurship-review

Jyoti, B., & Singh, A. K. (2023). Does digitalization have a causal relationship with economic development? An experience from a country-wise panel data statistical analysis. In R. S. Nazlı & G. Sari (Eds.), Handbook of Research on Perspectives on Society and Technology Addiction (pp. 34-61). IGI Global. doi:10.4018/978-1-6684-8397-8.ch003

Karimi, H., & Ataei, P. (2022). The effect of entrepreneurship on entrepreneurial skills of agriculture students: The mediation role of social intelligence and emotional intelligence (The case of Zabol University, Iran). *Current Psychology (New Brunswick, N.J.)*, *42*(1), 23250–23264. doi:10.100712144-022-03479-z PMID:35854700

Khuong, M. N., & Van, N. T. (2022). The influence of entrepreneurial ecosystem on entrepreneurs' perceptions and business success. *Gadjah Mada International Journal of Business, 24*(2), 198-222. https://search.informit.org/doi/abs/10.3316/informit.491830241767765

Maheshwari, G., Kha, K. L., & Arokiasamy, A. R. A. (2022). *Factors affecting students' entrepreneurial intentions: a systematic review (2005 – 2022) for future directions in theory and practice*. Management Review Quarterly. doi:10.100711301-022-00289-2

Mirjana, P. B., Ana, A., & Marjana, M. S. (2018). Examining determinants of entrepreneurial intentions in Slovenia: Applying the theory of planned behaviour and an innovative cognitive style. *Ekonomska Istrazivanja*, *31*(1), 1453–1471. doi:10.1080/1331677X.2018.1478321

Moya-Clemente, I., Ribes-Giner, G., & Pantoja-Díaz, O. (2019). Configurations of sustainable development goals that promote sustainable entrepreneurship over time. *Sustainable Development (Bradford)*, *28*(4), 572–584. doi:10.1002d.2009

Paranata, A., Pahrudin, Muzayyanah, S., & Trinh, T. H. (2023). Identification of factors influencing entrepreneurial behavior: Unveiling start-up business initiatives in Indonesia. *Humanities & Social Sciences Communications*, *10*(407), 1–11. doi:10.105741599-023-01896-4

Prathap, S. K., & Sreelakshmi, C. C. (2020). Entrepreneurial learning and microcredit as triggers of micro-entrepreneurship in India. *Small Enterprises Development, Management & Extension Journal*, *47*(3), 194–212. doi:10.1177/09708464211037533

Rafiei, S., Alizadeh, A., Aziziani, L., Borojeni, F. H., Vahdati, F., & Nejatifar, Z. (2022). The impact of business attitude on entrepreneurial behavior in postgraduate students: A cross-sectional study during the COVID-19 pandemic. *Journal of Health Reports and Technology*, *8*(1), 1–6. doi:10.5812/jhrt.119118

Rusu, V. D., & Roman, A. (2017). Entrepreneurial activity in the EU: An empirical evaluation of its determinants. *Sustainability (Basel)*, *9*(10), 1–16. doi:10.3390u9101679

Sabra, M. M., & Shreteh, D. (2021). The nexus relationship between entrepreneurship and economic growth dynamic: Evidence from selected MENA countries. *Information Economics and Policy*, *2*(35), 56–75. doi:10.33111/iep.eng.2021.35.03

Sharma, A., Das, N., & Singh, S. P. (2023). Causal association of entrepreneurship ecosystem and financial inclusion. *Heliyon, 9*(3), 1-13. doi: .2023.e14596 doi:10.1016/j.heliyon

Singh, A. K., Arya, A. K., & Jyoti, B. (2019b). A conceptual review on economic, business, intellectual property rights and science & technology related activities in Asian economies. *JNNCE Journal of Engineering & Management*, *3*(2), 1–22.

Singh, A. K., & Ashraf, S. N. (2020). Association of entrepreneurship ecosystem with economic growth in selected countries. *Journal of Entrepreneurship. Business Economics (Cleveland, Ohio)*, *8*(2), 36–92. http://scientificia.com/index.php/JEBE/article/view/138

Singh, A. K., Issac, J., & Narayanan, K. G. S. (2019a). Measurement of environmental sustainability index and its association with socio-economic indicators in selected Asian economies: An empirical investigation. *International Journal of Environment and Sustainable Development*, *18*(1), 57–100. doi:10.1504/IJESD.2019.098641

Singh, A. K., & Jyoti, B. (2021). Further research direction for indicators of technology entrepreneurship ecosystem, technology start-ups ecosystem and technology-business incubators: A conceptual review. *Dimensions International Journal of Management ICFAI Business School (IBS) Mumbai, 7*(1), 14-33.

Singh, A. K., & Jyoti, B. (2023a). Does digitalization have a bi-directional causal relationship with the entrepreneurship ecosystem? Evidence from a country-wise panel data analysis. In Y. Ramakrishna & L. Indiran (Eds.), *Handbook of Research on Designing Sustainable Strategies to Develop Entrepreneurial Intention* (pp. 178–172). IGI Global. doi:10.4018/978-1-6684-8781-5.ch007

Singh, A. K., & Jyoti, B. (2023b). Empirical evidence from a different income group countries on the interdependency between digitalization and economic development. In P. O. de Pablos & X. Zhang (Eds.), 5G, Artificial Intelligence, and Next Generation Internet of Things: Digital Innovation for Green and Sustainable Economies (pp. 44-85). IGI Global. doi:10.4018/978-1-6684-8634-4.ch003

Singh, A. K., & Jyoti, B. (2023c). Relative performance of entrepreneurship ecosystem for selected countries using a composite Z-score technique of index estimation. *Eurasian Journal of Management & Social Sciences*, *4*(2).

Singh, A. K., Jyoti, B., Kumar, S., & Lenka, S. K. (2021). Assessment of global sustainable development, environmental sustainability, economic development, and social development index in selected economies. *International Journal of Sustainable Development and Planning*, *16*(1), 123–138. doi:10.18280/ijsdp.160113

Singh, A. K., Jyoti, B., & Mishra, V. K. (2023d). Policy implications from selected countries for a sustainable future of the society through green entrepreneurship and economic development. In Entrepreneurship Ecosystems and Their Opportunities and Challenges (pp. 129-162). IGI Global. doi:10.4018/978-1-6684-7140-1.ch006

Singh, A. K., & Kumar, S. (2022a). Factors influencing entrepreneurship ecosystem and economic development: Evidence from cross-sectional country-wise imbalanced panel data analysis. *The IUP Journal of Entrepreneurship Development*, *19*(3), 24–47.

Singh, A. K., & Kumar, S. (2022b). Expert's perception on technology transfer and commercialization, and intellectual property rights in India: Evidence from selected research organizations. *Journal of Management, Economics, and Industrial Organization*, *6*(1), 1–33. doi:10.31039/jomeino.2022.6.1.1

Singh, A. K., & Kumar, S. (2022c). Exploring the impact of sustainable development on social-economic, and science and technological development in selected countries: A panel data analysis. *Society & Sustainability*, *4*(1), 55–83. doi:10.38157s.v4i1.405

Singh, A. K., Kumar, S., & Jyoti, B. (2022b). Influence of climate change on agricultural sustainability in India: A state-wise panel data analysis. *Asian Journal of Agriculture*, *6*(1), 15–27. doi:10.13057/asianjagric/g060103

Singh, A. K., Kumar, S., & Jyoti, B. (2023c). Does entrepreneurship ecosystem have a causal relationship with economic development? A country-wise imbalanced panel data investigation. In H. Magd, S. A. Khan, N. D. Nte, & M. Sarim (Eds.), *Entrepreneurship and Economic Sustainability* (pp. 1–15). Prestige Publishers.

Singh, A. K., Kumar, S., & Sharma, A. K. (2023a). Does green entrepreneurship ecosystem have causal association with economic development? Evidence from country-wise panel data investigation. *Journal of International Business Research*, *22*(2), 1–18. https://www.abacademies.org/articles/Does-Green-Entrepreneurship-Ecosystem-have-1544-0230-22-2-191.pdf

Singh, A. K., Kumar, S., Sharma, A. K., & Sinha, S. (2022a). Does green entrepreneurship have an association with sustainable development and its components? Evidence from a country-wise panel data investigation. In M. Magd, D. Singh, D. Spicer, & R. T. Syed (Eds.), *International Perspectives on Value Creation and Sustainability Through Social Entrepreneurship* (pp. 132–172). IGI Global. doi:10.4018/978-1-6684-4666-9.ch008

Singh, A. K., Sharma, A. K., & Jyoti, B. (2023e). Does economic development have a causal relationship with environmental degradation? Experience from different income group countries. In G. Sart (Ed.), *Considerations on Education for Economic, Social, and Environmental Sustainability* (pp. 300–333). IGI Global. doi:10.4018/978-1-6684-8356-5.ch015

Singh, A. K., Sharma, S. K., & Lenka, S. K. (2023b). Causality between green entrepreneurship and sustainable development: A cross-country analysis using ARDL model. *The IUP Journal of Applied Economics*, *22*(1), 5–38.

Singh, A. K., Singh, B., & Ashraf, S. N. (2020a). Implications of intellectual property protection, and science and technological development in the manufacturing sector in selected economies. *Journal of Advocacy, Research and Education, 7*(1), 16-35. https://oaji.net/articles/2021/1704-1615668997.pdf

Singh, A. K., Singh, B. J., & Negi, V. (2020b). Does sustainable development have a causal relationship with environmental development? Evidence from a country-wise panel data analysis. *International Journal of Technology Management & Sustainable Development*, *19*(2), 147–171. doi:10.1386/tmsd_00020_1

Szerb, L., Aidis, R., & Acs, Z. J. (2013). The comparison of the global entrepreneurship monitor and the global entrepreneurship and development index methodologies. *Foundations and Trends R in Entrepreneurship, 9*(1), 1-142. doi:10.1561/0300000046

Tasnim, N., & Afzal, M. N. I. (2018). An empirical investigation of country level efficiency and national systems of entrepreneurship using data envelopment analysis (DEA) and the TOBIT model. *Journal of Global Entrepreneurship Research*, *8*(37), 1–17. doi:10.118640497-018-0138-y

Uvarova, I., Mavlutova, I., & Atstaja, D. (2021). Development of the green entrepreneurial mindset through modern entrepreneurship education. *IOP Conference Series. Earth and Environmental Science*, *628*(1), 1–13. doi:10.1088/1755-1315/628/1/012034

Volkmann, C., Fischter, K., Klofsten, M., & Audretsch, D. B. (2019). Sustainable entrepreneurial ecosystems: An emerging field of research. *Small Business Economics*, *1*(1), 1–9. doi:10.100711187-019-00253-7

Wang, Y., Zhou, H., Zhang, Y., & Sun, X. R. (2022). Role of entrepreneurial behaviour in achieving sustainable digital economy. *Frontiers in Public Health, 10*(1), 1–13. doi:10.3389/fpubh.2022.829289 PMID:35284394

Wu, L., Jiang, S., Wang, X., Yu, L., Wang, Y., & Pan, H. (2022). Entrepreneurship education and entrepreneurial intentions of college students: The mediating role of entrepreneurial self-efficacy and the moderating role of entrepreneurial competition experience. *Frontiers in Psychology, 12*(1), 1–9. doi:10.3389/fpsyg.2021.727826 PMID:35069312

Wu, P., Chen, H., Yang, D., & Sun, D. (2021). Nature or nurture: Influencing factors of entrepreneurial behaviour from the perspective of university entrepreneurial ecosystem. *Academic Journal of Business & Management, 3*(6), 9–17. doi:10.25236/AJBM.2021.030602

Zabelina, E., Deyneka, O., & Tsiring, D. (2019). Entrepreneurial attitudes in the structure of students' economic minds. *International Journal of Entrepreneurial Behaviour & Research, 25*(8), 1621–1633. doi:10.1108/IJEBR-04-2018-0224

Zaki, I. M., & Rashid, N. H. (2016). Entrepreneurship impact on economic growth in emerging countries. *The Business and Management Review, 7*(2), 31-39. https://cberuk.com/cdn/conference_proceedings/conference_40058.pdf

Zeng, J., & Ren, J. (2022). How does green entrepreneurship affect environmental improvement? Empirical findings from 293 enterprises. *The International Entrepreneurship and Management Journal, 18*(1), 409–434. doi:10.100711365-021-00780-4

Compilation of References

Abbas, J., & Sağsan, M. (2019). Impact of knowledge management practices on green innovation and corporate sustainable development: A structural analysis. *Journal of Cleaner Production, 229*, 611–620. doi:10.1016/j.jclepro.2019.05.024

Abe, E. N. (2015). *The connection between work-life balance (WLB) and a sense of coherence (SOC) at a municipality in the South African public sector* [Doctoral dissertation].

Abe, I. I. (2021). The Dynamics of Workplace Relationships, Employee Well-Being, and the Fourth Industrial Revolution: Perspectives of Workplace Relationships and Industry 4.0. In Future of Work, Work-Family Satisfaction, and Employee Well-Being in the Fourth Industrial Revolution (pp. 99-112). IGI Global.

Abe, I. I., & Abe, E. N. (2021). Leadership/Followership Interface and the Workplace of the Future: Who Leads? In Future of Work, Work-Family Satisfaction, and Employee Well-Being in the Fourth Industrial Revolution (pp. 69-80). IGI Global.

Abe, I. I., & Mason, R. B. (2016). *The role of individual interpersonal relationships on work performance in the South African retail sector*. Academic Press.

Abe, E. N., Abe, I. I., Fields, Z., & Idris, G. O. (2018). Work-family stressors and work-family satisfaction: Effect of sense of coherence at a metropolitan municipality. *Journal of Economics and Behavioral Studies, 10*(2 (J)), 74–88. doi:10.22610/jebs.v10i2(J).2218

Aborisade, R. A. (2019). Police abuse of sex workers in Nigeria: Evidence from a qualitative study. *Police Practice and Research, 20*(4), 405–419. doi:10.1080/15614263.2018.1500283

Acheampong, G., & Tweneboah-Koduah, E. Y. (2018). Does past failure inhibit future entrepreneurial intent? Evidence from Ghana. *Journal of Small Business and Enterprise Development, 25*(5), 849–863. doi:10.1108/JSBED-03-2017-0128

Acs, Z. (2006). How is entrepreneurship good for economic growth? *Innovations: Technology, Governance, Globalization, 1*(1), 97-107. http://www.mitpressjournals.org/doi/pdf/10.1162/itgg.2006.1.1.97

Adler, P. S., & Kwon, S. W. (2002). Social capital: Prospects for a new concept. *Academy of Management Review, 27*(1), 17–40. doi:10.2307/4134367

Adner, R., & Helfat, C. E. (2003). Corporate effects and dynamic managerial capabilities. *Strategic Management Journal*, *24*(10), 1011–1025. doi:10.1002mj.331

Adusei, M. (2016). Does entrepreneurship promote economic growth in Africa? *African Development Review*, *28*(2), 201–214. doi:10.1111/1467-8268.12190

Afifi, T. D., Merrill, A. F., & Davis, S. (2016). The theory of resilience and relational load. *Personal Relationships*, *23*(4), 663–683. doi:10.1111/pere.12159

Afonso Alves, C., Matias Gama, A. P., & Augusto, M. (2021). Family influence and firm performance: The mediating role of stewardship. *Journal of Small Business and Enterprise Development*, *28*(2), 185–204. doi:10.1108/JSBED-01-2019-0015

Agarwal, P., & Farndale, E. (2017). High-performance work systems and creativity implementation: The role of psychological capital and psychological safety. *Human Resource Management Journal*, *27*(3), 440–458. doi:10.1111/1748-8583.12148

Ahmed, T., Chandran, V. G. R., & Klobas, J. (2017). Specialized entrepreneurship education: Does it really matter? Fresh evidence from Pakistan. *International Journal of Entrepreneurial Behaviour & Research*, *23*(1), 4–19. doi:10.1108/IJEBR-01-2016-0005

Ajzen, I. (1991). The theory of planned behavior. *Organizational Behavior and Human Decision Processes*, *50*(2), 179–211. doi:10.1016/0749-5978(91)90020-T

Ajzen, I. (2002). Perceived behavioral control, self-efficacy, locus of control, and the theory of planned behavior 1. *Journal of Applied Social Psychology*, *32*(4), 665–683. doi:10.1111/j.1559-1816.2002.tb00236.x

Akanbi, M. A., Ope, B. W., Adeloye, D. O., Amoo, E. O., Iruonagbe, T. C., & Omojola, O. (2021). Influence of socio-economic factors on prevalence of teenage pregnancy in Nigeria. *African Journal of Reproductive Health*, *25*(5s), 138–146. PMID:37585778

Akan, O., Jack, E., & Mehta, A. (2020). Concrescent conversation environment, psychological safety, and team effectiveness. *Team Performance Management*, *26*(1/2), 29–51. doi:10.1108/TPM-07-2019-0079

Akinboye, A. K., & Morrish, S. C. (2022). Conceptualizing post-disaster entrepreneurial decision-making: Prediction and control under extreme environmental uncertainty. *International Journal of Disaster Risk Reduction*, *68*, 102703. doi:10.1016/j.ijdrr.2021.102703

Aktaş, R. (2019). Türkiye'de Girişimcilik. In M. Saygın (Ed.), *A current view of entrepreneurship and businesses* (pp. 24–27). Eğitim Yayınevi.

Al Bati, D. N., Ahmad, A., Al-Refai, A. M., & Aldweeri, R. (2022). Factors influencing student entrepreneurial intentions with the moderating role of COVID-19: A comparison study. *Journal of Positive School Psychology*, *6*(10), 1040–1064.

Alasadi, R., Muhammed, S., Abidi, O., & Dzenopoljac, V. (2019). Impact of servant leadership on intrinsic and extrinsic job satisfaction. Leadership &Amp. *Leadership and Organization Development Journal*, *40*(4), 472–484. doi:10.1108/LODJ-09-2018-0337

Aldrich, H. E., & Cliff, J. E. (2003). The pervasive effects of family on entrepreneurship: Toward a family embeddedness perspective. *Journal of Business Venturing*, *18*(5), 573–596. doi:10.1016/S0883-9026(03)00011-9

Aldrich, H. E., & Kim, P. H. (2007). Small worlds, infinite possibilities? How social networks affect entrepreneurial team formation and search. *Strategic Entrepreneurship Journal*, *1*(1-2), 147–165. doi:10.1002ej.8

Aldrich, H. E., & Ruef, M. (2018). Unicorns, gazelles, and other distractions on the way to understanding real entrepreneurship in the United States. *The Academy of Management Perspectives*, *32*(4), 458–472. doi:10.5465/amp.2017.0123

Ali, J., & Jabeen, Z. (2020). Understanding entrepreneurial behavior for predicting start-up intention in India: Evidence form global entrepreneurship monitor (GEM) data. *Journal of Public Affairs*, *22*(1), 1–11. doi:10.1002/pa.2399

Aliyyani, Wong, & Cummings. (2018). Antecedents, mediators, and outcomes of authentic leadership in healthcare: A systematic review. *PubMed*, *83*, 34–64. PMID:29684833

Al-Jubari, I., Hassan, A., & Hashim, J. (2017). The role of autonomy as a predictor of entrepreneurial intention among university students in Yemen. *International Journal of Entrepreneurship and Small Business*, *30*(3), 325–340. doi:10.1504/IJESB.2017.081950

Alkahtani, A. W. (2021). Family-owned businesses in Saudi Arabia: Challenges and solutions from a legal perspective. *Int. J. Contemp. Manag. Inf. Technol*, *1*(2), 16–22.

Allaire, Y., & Firsirotu, M. E. (1984). Theories of organizational culture. *Organization Studies*, *5*(3), 193–226. doi:10.1177/017084068400500301

Allio, M. K. (2004). Family businesses: Their virtues, vices, and strategic path. *Strategy and Leadership*, *32*(4), 24–33. doi:10.1108/10878570410576704

Alon, I., Jaffe, E., Prange, C., & Vianelli, D. (2020). *Global marketing: strategy, practice, and cases*. Routledge. doi:10.4324/9780429203343

Al-Saifi. (2019). Entrepreneurship in the Arab Middle East: Exploring the Role of Culture and Context. *Journal of Business Research*, *94*, 172–182.

Altinay, L., Madanoglu, M., Daniele, R., & Lashley, C. (2012). The influence of family tradition and psychological traits on entrepreneurial intention. *International Journal of Hospitality Management*, *31*(2), 489–499. doi:10.1016/j.ijhm.2011.07.007

Aly, H. (2020). Digital transformation, development, and productivity in developing countries: Is artificial intelligence a cure or a blessing? *Review of Economics and Political Science*, *7*(4), 1–19. doi:10.1108/REPS-11-2019-0145

Amacha, E., & Dastane, O. (2017). Sustainability Practices as Determinants of Financial Performance: A Case of Malaysian Corporations. *The Journal of Asian Finance, Economics and Business*, *4*(2), 55–68.

Amitabh, S. (2017). *What is entrepreneurship?* Retrieved from http://www.paggu.com/entrep

Amofah, K., & Saladrigues, R. (2021). Impact of attitude towards entrepreneurship education and role models on entrepreneurial intention. *Journal of Innovation and Entrepreneurship*, *11*(36), 1–30. doi:10.118613731-022-00197-5

Amorós, J. E., Ramírez, L. M., Rodríguez-Aceves, L., & Ruiz, L. E. (2021). Revisiting poverty and entrepreneurship in developing countries. *Journal of Developmental Entrepreneurship*, *26*(2), 1–23. doi:10.1142/S1084946721500084

Ancona, D. G., Malone, T. W., Orlikowski, W. J., & Senge, P. M. (2007). In praise of the incomplete leader. *Harvard Business Review*, *85*(9), 92–99. PMID:17345683

Andam, K., Edeh, H., Oboh, V., Pauw, K., & Thurlow, J. (2020). Impacts of COVID-19 on food systems and poverty in Nigeria. In *Advances in food security and sustainability* (Vol. 5, pp. 145–173). Elsevier.

Anderson, C. B., Jacobson, J. W., & Kilduff, G. (2016). Psychological safety and engagement: The role of individual psychological characteristics. *The Leadership Quarterly*, *27*(3), 461–473.

Anderson, R. C. (2015). Family Business Governance: Maximizing Family and Business Potential. *Family Business Review*, *28*, 193–209.

Anderson, R. C., & Reeb, D. M. (2003). Founding-family ownership and firm performance: Evidence from the S&P 500. *The Journal of Finance*, *58*(3), 1301–1328. doi:10.1111/1540-6261.00567

Andersson, M., & Noseleit, F. (2011). Start-ups and employment dynamics within and across sectors. *Small Business Economics*, *36*(4), 461–483. doi:10.100711187-009-9252-0

Andito, Carillo-Hermosilla, Del-rio, & Pontrandolfo. (2018). Sustaining innovation: Processes, strategies, and outcomes. *Corporate Social Responsibility and Environmental Management*, *25*(1), 106–109.

Andjelkovic Pesic, M., & Dahlgaard, J. J. (2013). *Using the Balanced-Scorecard and the European Foundation for Quality Management Excellence model as a combined roadmap for diagnosing and attaining excellence*. Available: https://scholar.google.com/scholar?hl=en&as_sdt=0%2C5&q=Andjelkovic+Pesic%2C+M.%2C+%26+Dahlgaard%2C+J.+J.+%282013%29

Andjelkovic Pesic, M., & Dahlgaard, J. J. (2013). *Using the Balanced-Scorecard and the European Foundation for Quality Management Excellence model as a combined roadmap for diagnosing and attaining excellence*. https://scholar.google.com/scholar?hl=en&as_sdt=0%2C5&q=Andjelkovic+Pesic%2C+M.%2C+%26+Dahlgaard%2C+J.+J.+%282013%29

Andrade-Valbuena, N. A., & Merigo, J. M. (2018). Outlining new product development research through bibliometrics: Analyzing journals, articles and researchers. *Journal of Strategy and Management, 11*(3), 328–350. doi:10.1108/JSMA-08-2017-0061

Andrade-Valbuena, N. A., Merigó-Lindahl, J. M., Fernández, L. V., & Alarcón, C. N. (2019). Mapping leading universities in strategy research: Three decades of collaborative networks. *Cogent Business and Management, 6*(1), 1–26. doi:10.1080/23311975.2019.1632569

Andrade-Valbuena, N. A., Merigo-Lindahl, J. M., & Olavarrieta, S. S. (2018). Bibliometric analysis of entrepreneurial orientation. *World Journal of Entrepreneurship, Management and Sustainable Development, 15*(1), 45–69. doi:10.1108/WJEMSD-08-2017-0048

Andrade-Valbuena, N. A., Valenzuela-Fernández, L., & Merigó, J. M. (2022). Thirty-five years of strategic management research. A country analysis using bibliometric techniques for the 1987-2021 period. *Cuadernos de Gestión, 22*(2), 7–22. doi:10.5295/cdg.211441na

Andrade-Valbuena, N., Baier-Fuentes, H., & Gaviria-Marin, M. (2022). An Overview of Sustainable Entrepreneurship in Tourism, Destination, and Hospitality Research Based on the Web of Science. *Sustainability (Basel), 14*(22), 14944. doi:10.3390u142214944

Andriof, J., Waddock, S., Husted, B., & Rahman, S. S. (2017). *Unfolding stakeholder thinking: Theory, responsibility and engagement.* Routledge. doi:10.4324/9781351281843

Anekwe, I. R., Ndubuisi-Okolo, P & Nwanah, C. P. (2020). *Entrepreneurship Management: A Panacea for Social Economic Development in Nigeria.* Academic Press.

Anil, B., & Azize, E. (2014). Women entrepreneurs' personality characteristics and parents' parenting style profile in Turkey. *Procedia: Social and Behavioral Sciences, 109*, 92–97. doi:10.1016/j.sbspro.2013.12.425

Anjum, T., Amoozegar, A., Farrukh, M., & Heidler, P. (2022). Entrepreneurial intentions among business students: The mediating role of attitude and the moderating role of university support. *Education + Training, 65*(4), 1–20. doi:10.1108/ET-01-2021-0020

Appelbaum, S. H., Degbe, M. C., MacDonald, O., & Nguyen-Quang, T. S. (2015). Organizational outcomes of leadership style and resistance to change (Part One). *Industrial and Commercial Training, 47*(2), 73–80. doi:10.1108/ICT-07-2013-0044

Arasli, H., Arasli, H., & Kole, E. (2020). Constructive leadership and employee innovative behaviours: A serial mediation model. *Sustainability (Basel), 12*(7), 2592. doi:10.3390u12072592

Arbabian, S., & Zamani, Z. (2022). The interactive effect of financial development and human capital on entrepreneurship in selected countries. *Journal of Development and Capital, 8*(1), 1–21. doi:10.22103/jdc.2022.19537.1249

Arenius, P., & Minniti, M. (2005). Perceptual variables and nascent entrepreneurship. *Small Business Economics, 24*(3), 233–247. doi:10.100711187-005-1984-x

Armenakis, A. A., & Bedeian, A. G. (1999). Organizational change: A review of theory and research in the 1990s. *Journal of Management*, *25*(3), 293–315. doi:10.1177/014920639902500303

Arogundade, B. B. (2011). Entrepreneurship education: An imperative for sustainable development in Nigeria. *Journal of Emerging Trends in Educational Research and Policy Studies*, *2*(1), 26–29.

Arregle, J. L., Batjargal, B., Hitt, M. A., Webb, J. W., Miller, T., & Tsui, A. S. (2015). Family ties in entrepreneurs' social networks and new venture growth. *Entrepreneurship Theory and Practice*, *39*(2), 313–344. doi:10.1111/etap.12044

Arrigoni, G., Schofield, T., & Trujillo Pisanty, D. (2020). Framing collaborative processes of digital transformation in cultural organisations: From literary archives to augmented reality. *Museum Management and Curatorship*, *35*(4), 424–445. doi:10.1080/09647775.2019.1683880

Arzubiaga, U., De Massis, A., Kammerlander, N., & Hoy, F. (2022). Knowledge management in family firms: Opening the black box and suggestions for future research. *Journal of Knowledge Management*, *26*(2), 269–290. doi:10.1108/JKM-03-2022-924

Asebedo, S., & Payne, P. (2019). Market volatility and financial satisfaction: The role of financial self-efficacy. *Journal of Behavioral Finance*, *20*(1), 42–52. doi:10.1080/15427560.2018.1434655

Ashraf, S. N., & Singh, A. K. (2019). Does entrepreneurship ecosystem have a long-term relationship with economic Growth in selected economies? A statistical investigation. In S. Misra, S. Shukla, & G. Batthini (Eds.), *Proceedings of the 13th Biennial Conference on Entrepreneurship Organized by EDII Ahmedabad* (pp. 176–187). Bookwell Publishing House. http://library.ediindia.ac.in:8181/xmlui/handle/123456789/7903

Ashton, T. S. (1939). An eighteenth-century industrialist: Peter Stubs of Warrington, 1756-1806 (No. 13). Manchester University Press.

Astrachan, J., & Carey, M. (1994). *Family Businesses in the United States Economy*. Paper presented to the Center for the Study of Taxation, Washington, DC.

Astrachan, J. H., Klein, S. B., & Smyrnios, K. X. (2002). The F-PEC scale of family influence: A proposal for solving the family business definition problem. *Family Business Review*, *15*(1), 45–58. doi:10.1111/j.1741-6248.2002.00045.x

Atems, B., & Shand, G. (2018). An empirical analysis of the relationship between entrepreneurship and income inequality. *Small Business Economics*, *51*(4), 905–922. doi:10.100711187-017-9984-1

Au, K., Chiang, F.F.T., & Birtch, T.A. (2013). Incubating the next generation to venture: The case of a family business in Hong Kong. *Asia Pacific Journal of Management*, 30.

Audretsch, D. B., Belitski, M., & Desai, S. (2015). Entrepreneurship and economic development in cities. *The Annals of Regional Science*, *55*(1), 33–60. doi:10.100700168-015-0685-x

Audretsch, D., & Fritsch, M. (2003). Linking entrepreneurship to growth: The case of West Germany. *Industry and Innovation*, *10*(1), 65–73. doi:10.1080/1366271032000068104

Au, K., Chiang, F. F. T., Birtch, T. A., & Ding, Z. (2013). Incubating the next generation to venture: The case of a family business in Hong Kong. *Asia Pacific Journal of Management, 30*(3), 30. doi:10.100710490-012-9331-7

Au, K., & Kwan, H. K. (2009). Start–up capital and Chinese entrepreneurs: The role of family. *Entrepreneurship Theory and Practice, 33*(4), 889–908. doi:10.1111/j.1540-6520.2009.00331.x

Aviv, I., Hadar, I., & Levy, M. (2021). Knowledge management infrastructure framework for enhancing knowledge-intensive business processes. *Sustainability (Basel), 13*(20), 11387. doi:10.3390u132011387

Avolio, B., & Gardner, W. L. (2005). Authentic leadership development: Getting to the root form of positive forms of leadership. *The Leadership Quarterly, 16*(3), 315–338. doi:10.1016/j.leaqua.2005.03.001

Bagyo, Y. (2016). The role of employee engagement in anticipating counterproductive work behaviour: A study of literature. *IOSR Journal of Business and Management, 18*(09), 141–147. doi:10.9790/487X-180904141147

Bakari, H., Hunjra, A. I., & Niazi, G. S. K. (2017). How does authentic leadership influence planned organizational change? The role of employees' perceptions: Integration of theory of planned behavior and Lewin's three step model. *Journal of Change Management, 17*(2), 155–187. doi:10.1080/14697017.2017.1299370

Baker, S. R., & Cripe, S. M. (2018). Exploring the Role of Leaders and Team Members in Promoting Psychological Safety in Work Teams. *International Journal of Business and Management, 13*(1), 75–88.

Bakracheva, M., Pavlov, D., Gudkov, A., Diaconescu, A., Kostov, A., Deneva, A., ... Blazheva, V. (2020). *The intergenerational family businesses as a stress management instrument for entrepreneurs*. Academic Press.

Ballestar, M. T., Díaz-Chao, Á., Sainz, J., & Torrent-Sellens, J. (2020). Knowledge, robots and productivity in SMEs: Explaining the second digital wave. *Journal of Business Research, 108*, 119–131. doi:10.1016/j.jbusres.2019.11.017

Baluku, M. M., Nansubuga, F., Otto, K., & Horn, L. (2021). Risk aversion, entrepreneurial attitudes, intention, and entry among young people in Uganda and Germany: A gendered analysis. *Journal of Entrepreneurship and Innovation in Emerging Economies, 7*(1), 31–59. doi:10.1177/2393957520960567

Bamel, U. K., & Bamel, N. (2018). Organizational resources, KM process capability and strategic flexibility: A dynamic resource-capability perspective. *Journal of Knowledge Management, 22*(7), 1555–1572. doi:10.1108/JKM-10-2017-0460

Bandura, A. (1986). The explanatory and predictive scope of self-efficacy theory. *Journal of Social and Clinical Psychology, 4*(3), 359–373. doi:10.1521/jscp.1986.4.3.359

Bandura, A. (2000). Exercise of human agency through collective efficacy. *Current Directions in Psychological Science*, *9*(3), 75–78. doi:10.1111/1467-8721.00064

Bandura, A., & Locke, E. A. (2003). Negative self-efficacy and goal effects revisited. *The Journal of Applied Psychology*, *88*(1), 87–99. doi:10.1037/0021-9010.88.1.87 PMID:12675397

Barney, J. B., & Arikan, A. M. (2005). The resource-based view: Origins and implications. The Blackwell handbook of strategic management, 123-182. doi:10.1111/b.9780631218616.2006.00006.x

Barroso-Martínez, A., Sanguino-Galván, R., & Bañegil-Palacios, T. M. (2016). Entrepreneurial Orientation and Knowledge Transfer: Analysis in Spanish family businesses. *Tourism & Management Studies*, *12*(1), 211–219. doi:10.18089/tms.2016.12123

Basco, R. (2017). "Where do you want to take your family firm?": A theoretical and empirical exploratory study of family business goals. *Business Research Quarterly*, *20*(1), 28–44. doi:10.1016/j.brq.2016.07.001

Bashir, H. A., & Akhtar, A. (2016). The role of innovative entrepreneurship in economic development: A study of G20 countries. *Management Studies and Economic System, 2*(2), 91-100. https://www.msaes.org/article_44797_6f698044d22cf862ec02dd49aafaf42c.pdf

Bashir, M., & Farooq, R. (2019). The synergetic effect of knowledge management and business model innovation on firm competence: A systematic review. *International Journal of Innovation Science*, *11*(3), 362–387. doi:10.1108/IJIS-10-2018-0103

Basker, E. A. S. (2018). The Impact of Wal-Mart Supercenters on Grocery Prices and the Consumer Price Index. *Journal of Business & Economic Statistics*, *36*, 49–65.

Bates, T. (1985). Entrepreneur Human Capital Endowments and Minority Business Viability. *The Journal of Human Resources*, *20*(4), 540–554. doi:10.2307/145683

Bates, T. (1990). Entrepreneur Human Capital Inputs and Small Business Longevity. *The Review of Economics and Statistics*, *72*(4), 551–559. doi:10.2307/2109594

Baudot, L., Johnson, J. A., Roberts, A., & Roberts, R. W. (2020). Is corporate tax aggressiveness a reputation threat? Corporate accountability, corporate social responsibility, and corporate tax behavior. *Journal of Business Ethics*, *163*(2), 197–215. doi:10.100710551-019-04227-3

Baumeister, R., Vohs, K., DeWall, N., & Zhang, L. (2019). Support as a fundamental of psychological safety at work. *Journal of Organizational Behavior*, *40*(3), 393–417. doi:10.1002/job.2260

Bayrón, C. E. (2013). Social cognitive theory, entrepreneurial self-efficacy and entrepreneurial intentions: Tools to maximize the effectiveness of formal entrepreneurship education and address the decline in entrepreneurial activity. *Griot*, *6*(1), 66–77.

Beach, L. R., & Lipshitz, R. (2017). Why classical decision theory is an inappropriate standard for evaluating and aiding most human decision making. In *Decision making in aviation* (pp. 85–102). Routledge. doi:10.4324/9781315095080-5

Belkhodja, O. (2022). Managing knowledge resources in family firms: Opportunity or challenge? *Sustainability (Basel), 14*(9), 5087. doi:10.3390u14095087

Bellò, B., Mattana, V., & Loi, M. (2018). The power of peers: A new look at the impact of creativity, social context and self-efficacy on entrepreneurial intentions. *International Journal of Entrepreneurial Behaviour & Research, 24*(1), 214–233. doi:10.1108/IJEBR-07-2016-0205

Bennedsen, M., Fan, J. P., Jian, M., & Ych, Y. H. (2015). The family business map: Framework, selective survey, and evidence from Chinese family firm succession. *Journal of Corporate Finance, 33*, 212–226. doi:10.1016/j.jcorpfin.2015.01.008

Bequeath, K. M. (2014). *Family-Firm Leadership: A Case Study of an Organizational Family-Firm Leadership According to Bowen's Family Systems Theory and Lewin's Systems Theory* [Doctoral dissertation]. Franklin Pierce University.

Bergdahl, M. (2004). *What I learned from Sam Walton: How to compete and thrive in a Wal-Mart World.* John Wiley & Sons.

Berman, S. L., Down, J., & Hill, C. W. (2002). Tacit knowledge as a source of competitive advantage in the National Basketball Association. *Academy of Management Journal, 45*(1), 13–31. doi:10.2307/3069282

Bernardon, R., & Monticelli, J. (2015). Entrepreneurship between the 2nd and 4th generations of family businesses. In *ICSB World Conference Proceedings (ICSB 2015).* International Council for Small Business (ICSB).

Bhagavatula, S., Elfring, T., Van Tilburg, A., & Van De Bunt, G. G. (2010). How social and human capital influence opportunity recognition and resource mobilization in India's handloom industry. *Journal of Business Venturing, 25*(3), 245–260. doi:10.1016/j.jbusvent.2008.10.006

Bhatt, B., Qureshi, I., & Riaz, S. (2019). Social entrepreneurship in non-munificent institutional environments and implications for institutional work: Insights from China. *Journal of Business Ethics, 154*(3), 605–630. doi:10.100710551-017-3451-4

Biddle, B. J. (1986). Recent developments in role theory. *Annual Review of Sociology, 12*(1), 67–92. doi:10.1146/annurev.so.12.080186.000435

Bignotti, A., & Le Roux, I. (2020). Which types of experience matter? The role of prior start-up experiences and work experience in fostering youth entrepreneurial intentions. *International Journal of Entrepreneurial Behaviour & Research, 26*(6), 1181–1198. doi:10.1108/IJEBR-10-2019-0577

Biraglia, A., & Kadile, V. (2017). The role of entrepreneurial passion and creativity in developing entrepreneurial intentions: Insights from American homebrewers. *Journal of Small Business Management, 55*(1), 170–188. doi:10.1111/jsbm.12242

Bird, A., Mendenhall, M., Stevens, M. J., & Oddou, G. (2010). Defining the content domain of intercultural competence for global leaders. *Journal of Managerial Psychology, 25*(8), 810–828. doi:10.1108/02683941011089107

Bird, M., & Wennberg, K. (2016). Why family matters: The impact of family resources on immigrant entrepreneurs' exit from entrepreneurship. *Journal of Business Venturing*, *3*(1), 687–704. doi:10.1016/j.jbusvent.2016.09.002

Blattner, M., Graf, S., & Blüthgen, N. (2019). Psychological safety and organisational effectiveness: A systematic review. *Journal of Organizational Behavior*, *40*(5), 599–614.

Boldureanu, G., Ionescu, A. M., Bercu, A. M., Bedrule-Grigoruţă, M. V., & Boldureanu, D. (2020). Entrepreneurship education through successful entrepreneurial models in higher education institutions. *Sustainability (Basel)*, *12*(3), 1267. doi:10.3390u12031267

Bonanno, A., Bakker, H., Jussaume, R., Colfer, C. J. P., & Pfund, J. L. (2011). Decentering Biotechnology: Assemblages Built and Assemblages Masked. Burlington, VT: Ashgate.

Bonanno, G. A., Romero, S. A., & Klein, S. I. (2015). The temporal elements of psychological resilience: An integrative framework for the study of individuals, families, and communities. *Psychological Inquiry*, *26*(2), 139–169. doi:10.1080/1047840X.2015.992677

Bonde, J. P. E. (2008). Psychosocial factors at work and risk of depression: A systematic review of the epidemiological evidence. *Occupational and Environmental Medicine*, *65*(7), 438–445. doi:10.1136/oem.2007.038430 PMID:18417557

Book, L., Gatling, A., & Kim, J. (2019). The effects of leadership satisfaction on employee engagement, loyalty, and retention in the hospitality industry. Journal of Human Resources in Hospitality &Amp. *Journal of Human Resources in Hospitality & Tourism*, *18*(3), 368–393. doi:10.1080/15332845.2019.1599787

Bosma, N., & Kelley, D. (2019). *Global entrepreneurship monitor 2018/2019 global report*. https://www.gemconsortium.org/file/open?fileId=50213

Bosma, N., Hessels, J., Schutjens, V., Van Praag, M., & Verheul, I. (2012). Entrepreneurship and role models. *Journal of Economic Psychology*, *33*(2), 410–424. doi:10.1016/j.joep.2011.03.004

Boswell, J. (1972). *The Rise and Decline of Small Firms*. Allen and Unwin.

Bouarir, H., Diani, A., Boubker, O., & Rharzouz, J. (2023). Key determinants of women's entrepreneurial intention and behaviour: The role of business opportunity recognition and need for achievement. *Administrative Sciences*, *13*(33), 1–19. doi:10.3390/admsci13020033

Boyack, K. W., & Klavans, R. (2010). Co-citation analysis, bibliographic coupling, and direct citation: Which citation approach represents the research front most accurately? *Journal of the American Society for Information Science and Technology*, *61*(12), 2389–2404. doi:10.1002/asi.21419

Boyd, B. L., Moore, L. L., Williams, J., & Elbert, C. D. (2011). Entry-level competencies needed for global leaders. *International Leadership Journal*, *3*(1), 20–39.

Boyd, N. G., & Vozikis, G. S. (1994). The influence of self-efficacy on the development of entrepreneurial intentions and actions. *Entrepreneurship Theory and Practice, 18*(4), 63–77. doi:10.1177/104225879401800404

Brett, J. M., & Mitchell, T. (2020). Searching for trustworthiness: Culture, trust and negotiating new business relationships. *International Journal of Conflict Management, 31*(1), 17–39. doi:10.1108/IJCMA-05-2019-0085

Bristow, D. K. (2000). *Composition of US stock exchanges firms.* Unpublished study of the Directors Institute, Los Angeles, UCLA.

Britannica. (2023). Walmart / History & Facts. *Encyclopedia Britannica*. Available: https://www.britannica.com/topic/Walmart

Britt, T. W., Shen, W., Sinclair, R. R., Grossman, M., & Klieger, D. (2016). How Much Do We Really Know About Employee Resilience? *Industrial and organizational psychology: Perspectives on science and practice.* http://my.siop.org/Publications/IOPFocalArticles

Brockbank, A., & McGill, I. (2018). The crucial role of feedback in psychological safety. *The Academy of Management Perspectives, 32*(2), 134–152. doi:10.5465/amp.2016.0126

Brockhaus, R. H. (1982). *The psychology of the entrepreneur.* University of Illinois at Urbana-Champaign's Academy for Entrepreneurial Leadership Historical Research Reference in Entrepreneurship.

Brooks, D. B. (1990). Beyond catch phrases: What does sustainable development really mean? *The IDRC Reports / International Development Research Centre, 18*(4), 1–2.

Buchler, N., Fleur, C., Hoffman, B., Rajivan, P., Marusich, L., & Lightner, L. (2018). Cyber teaming and role specialization in a cyber security defense competition. *Frontiers in Psychology, 9*, 2133. Advance online publication. doi:10.3389/fpsyg.2018.02133 PMID:30510527

Buckman, J., Jones, P., & Buame, S. (2020). Passing on the baton: A succession planning framework for family-owned businesses in Ghana. *Journal of Entrepreneurship in Emerging Economies, 12*(2), 259–278. doi:10.1108/JEEE-11-2018-0124

Bullough, A., Maija, R., & Tamara, M. (2014). The importance of resilience and self-efficacy for entrepreneurial in Froner, Y. A. (2017). International policies for sustainable development from cultural empowerment. *Journal of Cultural Heritage Management and Sustainable Development. Entrepreneurship Theory and Practice, 38*(3), 473–499. doi:10.1111/etap.12006

Bullough, A., & Renko, M. (2013). Entrepreneurial resilience during challenging times. *Business Horizons, 56*(3), 343–350. doi:10.1016/j.bushor.2013.01.001

Cabrera-Suárez, K., de Saá-Pérez, P., & García-Almeida, D. (2009). The succession process from a resource-and knowledge-based view of the family firm. *Wiley Online Library, 14*(1), 37–46.

Cahyo, M., & Rachmawati, R. (2021). *Cross-functional team effectiveness factors in technological-based service company: nsiapay.* doi:10.2991/aebmr.k.210831.114

Campbell, L., Simpson, J. A., Kashy, D. A., & Fletcher, G. J. (2001). Ideal standards, the self, and flexibility of ideals in close relationships. *Personality and Social Psychology Bulletin*, *27*(4), 447–462. doi:10.1177/0146167201274006

Camuffo, A., Cordova, A., Gambardella, A., & Spina, C. (2020). A scientific approach to entrepreneurial decision making: Evidence from a randomized control trial. *Management Science*, *66*(2), 564–586. doi:10.1287/mnsc.2018.3249

Cancino, C., Merigó, J., Urbano, D., & Amoros, J. (2020). Evolution of the entrepreneurship and innovation research in Ibero-America between 1986 and 2015. *Journal of Small Business Management*, 1–31.

Cantor, Sood, & Whaley. (2022). *The impact of the COVID 19 Pandemic and policy responses on excess mortality*. Academic Press.

Cao, Z., & Shi, X. (2021). A systematic literature review of entrepreneurial ecosystems in advanced and emerging economies. *Small Business Economics*, *57*(1), 75–110. doi:10.100711187-020-00326-y

Capler, J. (2021). Death by Authoritative Leadership and Micro-management. In When Leadership Fails: Individual, Group and Organizational Lessons from the Worst Workplace Experiences (pp. 49-57). Emerald Publishing Limited. doi:10.1108/978-1-80043-766-120211005

Caputo, A., Marzi, G., Pellegrini, M. M., & Rialti, R. (2018). Conflict management in family businesses: A bibliometric analysis and systematic literature review. *International Journal of Conflict Management*, *29*(4), 519–542. doi:10.1108/IJCMA-02-2018-0027

Carayannis, E. G., Ferreira, J. J. M., & Fernandes, C. (2021). A prospective retrospective: Conceptual mapping of the intellectual structure and research trends of knowledge management over the last 25 years. *Journal of Knowledge Management*, *25*(8), 1977–1999. doi:10.1108/JKM-07-2020-0581

Cardella, G. M., Hernández-Sánchez, B. R., & Sanchez Garcia, J. C. (2020). Entrepreneurship and family role: A systematic review of a growing research. *Frontiers in Psychology*, *10*, 2939. doi:10.3389/fpsyg.2019.02939 PMID:31998192

Cardone, G. (2022). *Before I had everything, I almost lost everything. Here's the story of how I faced lawsuits, loans, and some of the biggest challenges in my life*. https://gctv.com/almost-lost-everything/

Cardone, G. (2023b). *Grant Cardone on Learning from the 2008 Crash & Preparing for This One (Part 1)*. https://www.youtube.com/watch?v=ElE_MgDmrbY

CardoneG. (2023a). *About*. https://grantcardone.com/about/

CardoneG. (2023c). https://wikibio.in/grant-cardone/#f+71761+1+1

Cardon, M. S., & Patel, P. C. (2015). Is stress worth it? Stress-related health and wealth trade-offs for entrepreneurs. *Applied Psychology*, *64*(2), 379–420. doi:10.1111/apps.12021

Carmeli, A., & Freund, A. (2005). Psychological safety at work: Its impact on organisational commitment, job satisfaction, and turnover intentions. *The Leadership Quarterly*, *16*(1), 153–172.

Carmeli, A., Sheaffer, Z., Binyamin, G., Reiter-Palmon, R., & Shimoni, T. (2013). Transformational leadership and creative problem-solving: The mediating role of psychological safety and reflexivity. *The Journal of Creative Behavior*, *48*(2), 115–135. doi:10.1002/jocb.43

Carney, M. (2017). Corporate Governance and Competitive Advantage in Family–Controlled Firms. *Entrepreneurship Theory and Practice*, *29*(3), 249–265. doi:10.1111/j.1540-6520.2005.00081.x

Carradus, A., Zozimo, R., & Discua Cruz, A. (2020). Exploring a faith-led open-systems perspective of stewardship in family businesses. *Journal of Business Ethics*, *163*(4), 701–714. doi:10.100710551-019-04387-2

Carree, M. A., & Thurik, A. R. (2008). The lag structure of the impact of business ownership on economic performance in OECD countries. *Small Business Economics*, *30*(1), 101–110. doi:10.100711187-006-9007-0

Carree, M., Van Stel, A., Thurik, R., & Wennekers, S. (2002). Economic development and business ownership: An analysis using data of 23 OECD countries in the period 1976–1996. *Small Business Economics*, *19*(3), 271–290. doi:10.1023/A:1019604426387

Casillas, J. C., & Acedo, F. J. (2007). Evolution of the intellectual structure of family business literature: A bibliometric study of FBR. *Family Business Review*, *20*(2), 141–162. doi:10.1111/j.1741-6248.2007.00092.x

Casprini, E., Dabic, M., Kotlar, J., & Pucci, T. (2020). A bibliometric analysis of family firm internationalization research: Current themes, theoretical roots, and ways forward. *International Business Review*, *29*(5), 101715. doi:10.1016/j.ibusrev.2020.101715

Cater, J. III, Kidwell, R., & Camp, K. (2016). Successor team dynamics in family firms. *Family Business Review*, *29*(3), 301–326. doi:10.1177/0894486516656255

Cattaneo, C., & Bassani, G. (2020). Professionalization and managerialization in family firms: A still open issue. *Management Controlling and Governance of Family Businesses: Theoretical Insights and Empirical Evidence from Italy*, 29-49.

Cauwelier, P., Ribiere, V., & Bennet, A. (2019). The influence of team psychological safety on team knowledge creation: A study with French and American engineering teams. *Journal of Knowledge Management*, *23*(6), 1157–1175. doi:10.1108/JKM-07-2018-0420

Cerchione, R., Esposito, E., & Spadaro, M. R. (2016). A literature review on knowledge management in SMEs. *Knowledge Management Research and Practice*, *14*(2), 169–177. doi:10.1057/kmrp.2015.12

Chadwick, C., & Dabu, A. (2009). Human resources, human resource management, and the competitive advantage of firms: Toward a more comprehensive model of causal linkages. *Organization Science*, *20*(1), 253–272. doi:10.1287/orsc.1080.0375

Chahal, H., & Sharma, A. K. (2020). Family business in India: Performance, challenges and improvement measures. *Journal of New Business Ventures*, *1*(1-2), 9–30. doi:10.1177/2632962X20960824

Chandler, A. (1990). *Entrepreneurship and Economic Growth*. Harvard University Press.

Chang, Y. C. (2020). *Best Practices for Executive Leadership Succession Planning in Post-cultural Revolution China First-Generational Family Enterprises* [Doctoral dissertation]. Pepperdine University.

Chang, E. P., Memili, E., Chrisman, J. J., Kellermanns, F. W., & Chua, J. H. (2009). Family social capital, venture preparedness, and start-up decisions: A study of Hispanic entrepreneurs in New England. *Family Business Review*, *22*(3), 279–292. doi:10.1177/0894486509332327

Chang, E., & Hancock, K. (2003). Role stress and role ambiguity in new nursing graduates in Australia. *Nursing & Health Sciences*, *5*(2), 155–163. doi:10.1046/j.1442-2018.2003.00147.x PMID:12709171

Chang, Y., Lin, H., Chien, Y., & Yen, W. (2018). Effects of creative components and creative behaviour on design creativity. *Thinking Skills and Creativity*, *29*, 23–31. doi:10.1016/j.tsc.2018.05.007

Chan, S. C. (2020). Transformational leadership, self-efficacy, and performance of volunteers in non-formal voluntary service education. *Journal of Management Development*, *39*(7/8), 929–943. doi:10.1108/JMD-03-2020-0078

Chaudhary, R. (2019). Corporate social responsibility perceptions and employee engagement: Role of psychological meaningfulness, safety and availability. *Corporate Governance (Bradford)*, *19*(4), 631–647. doi:10.1108/CG-06-2018-0207

Chaudhary, R., & Panda, C. (2018). Authentic leadership and creativity. *International Journal of Productivity and Performance Management*, *67*(9), 2071–2088. doi:10.1108/IJPPM-02-2018-0082

Chay, Y. W. (1993). Social support, individual differences, and well-being: A study of small business entrepreneurs and employees. *Journal of Occupational and Organizational Psychology*, *66*(4), 285–302. doi:10.1111/j.2044-8325.1993.tb00540.x

Chen, A., & Hou, Y. (2016). The effects of ethical leadership, voice behaviour and climates for innovation on creativity: A moderated mediation examination. *The Leadership Quarterly*, *27*(1), 1–13. doi:10.1016/j.leaqua.2015.10.007

Chen, C. (2017). Science mapping: A systematic review of the literature. *Journal of Data and Information Science*, *2*(2), 1–40. doi:10.1515/jdis-2017-0006

Chen, C. C. (2014). Entrepreneurship, economic growth, and employment: A case study of Taiwan. *Hitotsubashi Journal of Economics*, *55*(1), 71–88. https://www.jstor.org/stable/43296271

Chen, C. C., Greene, P. G., & Crick, A. (1998). Does entrepreneurial self-efficacy distinguish entrepreneurs from managers? *Journal of Business Venturing, 13*(4), 295–316. doi:10.1016/S0883-9026(97)00029-3

Chen, C., Liao, J., & Wen, P. (2013). Why does formal mentoring matter? the mediating role of psychological safety and the moderating role of power distance orientation in the Chinese context. *International Journal of Human Resource Management, 25*(8), 1112–1130. doi:10.1080/09585192.2013.816861

Cheng, Z., Yang, Y., Tan, C., Cheng, D., Cheng, A., & Zhuang, Y. (2019). *What makes a good team? A large-scale study on the effect of team composition in honor of kings.* doi:10.1145/3308558.3313530

Chen, G., Gully, S. M., & Eden, D. (2004). General self-efficacy and self-esteem: Toward theoretical and empirical distinction between correlated self-evaluations. *Journal of Organizational Behavior, 25*(3), 375–395. doi:10.1002/job.251

Cheng, C. (2001). Assessing coping flexibility in real-life and laboratory settings: A multimethod approach. *Journal of Personality and Social Psychology, 80*(5), 814–833. doi:10.1037/0022-3514.80.5.814 PMID:11374752

Chen, L., Wadei, K., Bai, S., & Liu, J. (2020). Participative leadership and employee creativity: A sequential mediation model of psychological safety and creative process engagement. *Leadership and Organization Development Journal, 41*(6), 741–759. doi:10.1108/LODJ-07-2019-0319

Chen, R., Guo, Y., & Yang, J. (2017). The influence of job insecurity on organisational commitment: The moderating role of psychological safety. *International Journal of Human Resource Management, 28*(14), 2076–2092. doi:10.1080/09585192.2016.1257819

Chen, R., Yang, J., & Guo, Y. (2018). The mediating role of trust in the relationship between psychological safety and organisational commitment. *International Journal of Human Resource Management, 29*(10), 1732–1748. doi:10.1080/09585192.2017.1337360

Chen, T., Li, F., & Leung, K. (2015). When does supervisor support encourage innovative behaviour? opposite moderating effects of general self-efficacy and internal locus of control. *Personnel Psychology, 69*(1), 123–158. doi:10.1111/peps.12104

Chen, Y., Tsai, T. S., & Hsu, Y. (2016). Psychological safety, creativity, and innovation: A meta-analysis. *Journal of Organizational Behavior, 37*(3), 459–483.

Chigunta, F. (2017). Entrepreneurship as a possible solution to youth unemployment in Africa. *Labor and Learning, 10*(2), 433–451. doi:10.1007/978-981-287-032-2_19

Childs, M., Turner, T., Sneed, C., & Berry, A. (2022). A contingency theory approach to understanding small retail business continuity during Covid-19. *Family and Consumer Sciences Research Journal, 50*(3), 216–230. doi:10.1111/fcsr.12434 PMID:35600319

Chirapanda, S. (2020). Identification of success factors for sustainability in family businesses: Case study method and exploratory research in Japan. *Journal of Family Business Management, 10*(1), 58–75.

Chirico, F. (2008). Knowledge Accumulation in Family Firms. *International Small Business Journal*, *26*(4), 433–462. doi:10.1177/0266242608091173

Chirico, F. (2017). The forgotten realm of the new and emerging psychosocial risk factors. *Journal of Occupational Health*, *59*(5), 433–435. doi:10.1539/joh.17-0111-OP PMID:28819083

Chirico, F., & Salvato, C. (2016). Knowledge internalization and product development in family firms: When relational and affective factors matter. *Entrepreneurship Theory and Practice*, *40*(1), 201–229. doi:10.1111/etap.12114

Chitiga, M., Henseler, M., Mabugu, R. E., & Maisonnave, H. (2022). How COVID-19 pandemic worsens the economic situation of women in South Africa. *European Journal of Development Research*, *34*(3), 1627–1644. doi:10.105741287-021-00441-w PMID:34421229

Chlosta, S., Patzelt, H., Klein, S. B., & Dormann, C. (2012). Parental role models and the decision to become self-employed: The moderating effect of personality. *Small Business Economics*, *38*(1), 121–138. doi:10.100711187-010-9270-y

Chmiel, A., Kaczmarczyk, M., & Bocian, K. (2018). Psychological safety and organisational performance: A systematic review. *Journal of Occupational and Organizational Psychology*, *91*(2), 205–225.

Choi, S., Ullah, S., & Kang, S. (2021). Proactive personality and creative performance: Mediating roles of creative self-efficacy and moderated mediation role of psychological safety. *Sustainability (Basel)*, *13*(22), 12517. doi:10.3390u132212517

Choji, L. D. (2014). *Energy Demand And Economic Growth In Nigeria* [Doctoral dissertation]. Eastern Mediterranean University (EMU)-Doğu Akdeniz Üniversitesi (DAÜ).

Choudhury, D. (2021). Critical Evaluation of the Position of Women Directors in Corporate Boards. *Jus Corpus LJ*, *2*, 157.

Chrisman, J. J., Sharma, P., Steier, L. P., & Chua, J. H. (2013). The influence of family goals, governance, and resources on firm outcomes. *Entrepreneurship Theory and Practice*, *37*(6), 1249–1261. doi:10.1111/etap.12064

Christianto, R. (2022). The influence of servant leadership and employee compensation on employee engagement through employee job satisfaction as an intervening variable at pt Indonesia power suralaya power generation unit. *Journal of Business and Behavioural Entrepreneurship*, *5*(2), 118–128. doi:10.21009/JOBBE.005.2.14

Chua, J. H., Chrisman, J. J., Kellermanns, F., & Wu, Z. (2011). Family involvement and new venture debt financing. *Journal of Business Venturing*, *26*(4), 472–488. doi:10.1016/j.jbusvent.2009.11.002

Chua, J. H., Chrisman, J. J., & Sharma, P. (1999). Defining the family business by behavior. *Entrepreneurship Theory and Practice*, *23*(4), 19–39. doi:10.1177/104225879902300402

Cisneros, L., Ibanescu, M., Keen, C., Lobato-Calleros, O., & Niebla-Zatarain, J. (2018). Bibliometric study of family business succession between 1939 and 2017: Mapping and analyzing authors' networks. *Scientometrics, 117*(2), 919–951. doi:10.100711192-018-2889-1

Cobo, M. J., López-Herrera, A. G., Herrera-Viedma, E., & Herrera, F. (2011). Science mapping software tools: Review, analysis, and cooperative study among tools. *Journal of the American Society for Information Science and Technology, 62*(7), 1382–1402. doi:10.1002/asi.21525

Cohen, D., Hsu, D. K., & Shinnar, R. S. (2021). Identifying innovative opportunities in the entrepreneurship classroom: A new approach and empirical test. *Small Business Economics, 57*(4), 1931–1955. doi:10.100711187-020-00387-z

Cole, M., Cox, J., & Stavros, J. (2016). Building collaboration in teams through emotional intelligence: Mediation by soar (strengths, opportunities, aspirations, and results). *Journal of Management & Organization, 25*(02), 263–283. doi:10.1017/jmo.2016.43

Collins, J. C., & Porras, J. (2005). *Built to last: Successful habits of visionary companies.* Random House.

Constantinidis, C., Lebègue, T., El Abboubi, M., & Salman, N. (2019). How families shape women's entrepreneurial success in Morocco: An intersectional study. *International Journal of Entrepreneurial Behaviour & Research, 25*(8), 1786–1808. doi:10.1108/IJEBR-12-2017-0501

Corner, P. D., Singh, S., & Pavlovich, K. (2017). Entrepreneurial resilience and venture failure. *International Small Business Journal, 35*(6), 687–708. doi:10.1177/0266242616685604

Covelli, B. J., & Mason, I. (2017). Linking theory to practice: Authentic leadership. *Academy of Strategic Management Journal, 16*(3), 1–10.

Covey. (2022). *Trust and inspire: How truly great leaders unleash greatness in others.* CIO Summit of America New York. HMG Strategy. Hmgstrategy.com/resources.

Covey, S. R. (2009). *Everyday greatness: Inspiration for a meaningful life.* Thomas Nelson.

Crampton, S. M., Hodge, J. W., Mishra, J. M., & Price, S. (1995). Stress and stress management. *S.A.M. Advanced Management Journal, 60*(3), 10–24.

Cropanzano, R., & Mitchell, M. S. (2005). Social exchange theory: An interdisciplinary review. *Journal of Management, 31*(6), 874–900. doi:10.1177/0149206305279602

Cruz, C., Justo, R., & De Castro, J. O. (2012). Does family employment enhance MSEs performance? Integrating socioemotional wealth and family embeddedness perspectives. *Journal of Business Venturing, 27*(1), 62–76. doi:10.1016/j.jbusvent.2010.07.002

Czakon, W., Hajdas, M., & Radomska, J. (2023). Playing the wild cards: Antecedents of family firm resilience. *Journal of Family Business Strategy, 14*(1), 100484. doi:10.1016/j.jfbs.2022.100484

Dahl, M., & Reichstein, T. (2005). *Are You Experienced? Prior Experience and the Survival of New Organizations.* Aalborg: DRUID Working Paper, 05-01.

Dahmani, M., Mabrouki, M., & Youssef, A. B. (2022). ICT, trade openness and economic growth in Tunisia: What is going wrong? *Economic Change and Restructuring*, *55*(1), 2317–2336. doi:10.100710644-022-09388-2

Dana, L. P., Kumar, S., Pandey, N., & Sureka, R. (2021). The Journal of Small Business Management: A bibliometric overview of 1996–2019. *Journal of Small Business Management*, *59*(sup1), S215–S236.

Dar, N., Ahmad, S., & Rahman, W. (2022). How and when overqualification improves innovative work behaviour: The roles of creative self-confidence and psychological safety. *Personnel Review*, *51*(9), 2461–2481. doi:10.1108/PR-06-2020-0429

Daszkiewicz, N., & Wach, K. (2014). Motives for going international and entry modes of family firms in Poland. *Journal of Intercultural Management*, *6*(2), 5–18. doi:10.2478/joim-2014-0008

Davis, J. H., Schoorman, F. D., & Donaldson, L. (1997). Toward a stewardship theory of management. *Academy of Management Review*, *22*(1), 20–47. doi:10.2307/259223

Day, C., Tan, J., & Huczynski, A. (2019). Respect in teams: Its impact on performance, psychological safety, and creativity. *International Journal of Human Resource Management*, *30*(4), 680–699. doi:10.1080/09585192.2019.1567112

De Massis, A., Frattini, F., & Lichtenthaler, U. (2013). Research on technological innovation in family firms: Present debates and future directions. *Family Business Review*, *26*(1), 10–31. doi:10.1177/0894486512466258

De Noble, A. F., Jung, D., & Ehrlich, S. B. (1999). Entrepreneurial self-efficacy: The development of a measure and its relationship to entrepreneurial action. *Frontiers of Entrepreneurship Research*, *1999*(1), 73-87.

de Rocha, A. K. L., de Moraes, G. H. S. M., & Fischer, B. (2021). The role of university environment in promoting entrepreneurial behavior: Evidence from heterogeneous regions in Brazil. *Innovation & Management Review*, *19*(1), 39–61. doi:10.1108/INMR-08-2020-0112

De Winnaar, K., & Scholtz, F. (2020). Entrepreneurial decision-making: New conceptual perspectives. *Management Decision*, *58*(7), 1283–1300. doi:10.1108/MD-11-2017-1152

Demerouti, E., & Bakker, A. B. (2023). Job demands-resources theory in times of crises: New propositions. *Organizational Psychology Review*, *13*(3), 209–236. doi:10.1177/20413866221135022

Demir, M., McNeese, N., She, M., & Cooke, N. (2019). Team coordination of team situation awareness in human-autonomy teaming. *Proceedings of the Human Factors and Ergonomics Society Annual Meeting*, *63*(1), 146–147. doi:10.1177/1071181319631259

Derné, S. (1994). Hindu men talk about controlling women: Cultural ideas as a tool of the powerful. *Sociological Perspectives*, *37*(2), 203–227. doi:10.2307/1389320

DeRue, D. S., Hollenbeck, J. R., Ilgen, D. R., Jundt, D. K., & Meyer, G. J. (2010). Psychological safety in teams: The role of transformational leadership and member satisfaction. *The Leadership Quarterly*, *21*(5), 618–631.

Dhanda, U. (2015). Employee engagement: the key success factor. *International Journal of Research-Granthaalayah, 3*(5), 77-87. doi:10.29121/granthaalayah.v3.i5.2015.3017

Diken, A., & Erdirençelebi, M. (2016). The role of parents in teaching entrepreneurship culture to their children in family businesses. *International Journal of Industrial and Systems Engineering*, *10*(7), 2423–2432.

Ding, H., & Yu, E. (2021). Strengths-based leadership and employee psychological well-being: A moderated mediation model. *Journal of Career Development*, *49*(5), 1108–1121. doi:10.1177/08948453211018807

Doanh, D. C., & Bernat, T. (2019). Entrepreneurial self-efficacy and intention among Vietnamese students: A meta-analytic path analysis based on the theory of planned behavior. *Procedia Computer Science*, *159*, 2447–2460. doi:10.1016/j.procs.2019.09.420

Dodd, S. D., Anderson, A., & Jack, S. (2013). Being in time and the family owned firm. *Scandinavian Journal of Management*, *29*(1), 35–47. doi:10.1016/j.scaman.2012.11.006

Domańska, A., Żukowska, B., & Zajkowski, R. (2018). Green entrepreneurship as a connector among social, environmental, and economic pillars of sustainable development. Why some countries are more agile? *Problemy Ekorozwoju, 13*(2), 67-76. https://ekorozwoj.pollub.pl/no26/i.pdf

Doran, J., McCarthy, N., & O'Connor, M. (2018). The role of entrepreneurship in stimulating economic growth in developed and developing countries. *Cogent Economics & Finance*, *6*(1), 1–14. doi:10.1080/23322039.2018.1442093

Drucker, P. F. (1985). *Innovation and Entrepreneurship. Practice and Principles*. Heinemman.

Dvouletý, O. (2017). Relationship between unemployment and entrepreneurship dynamics in the Czech Regions: A panel var approach. *Acta Universitatis Agriculturae et Silviculturae Mendelianae Brunensis*, *65*(102), 987–995. doi:10.11118/actaun201765030987

Dyer, W. G. Jr, & Whetten, D. A. (2006). Family firms and social responsibility: Preliminary evidence from the S&P 500. *Entrepreneurship Theory and Practice*, *30*(6), 785–802. doi:10.1111/j.1540-6520.2006.00151.x

Dyer, W. G., Nenque, E., & Hill, E. J. (2014). Toward a theory of family capital and entrepreneurship: Antecedents and outcomes. *Journal of Small Business Management*, *52*(2), 266–285. doi:10.1111/jsbm.12097

Ebhardt, T. & Lepido, D. (2021). *Agnelli faces reckoning over bad bet as league dream dies*. Bloomberg.com.

Edelman, L. F., Manolova, T., Shirokova, G., & Tsukanova, T. (2016). The impact of family support on young entrepreneurs' start-up activities. *Journal of Business Venturing*, *31*(4), 428–448. doi:10.1016/j.jbusvent.2016.04.003

Edmondson, A. C., Kramer, R. M., & Cook, K. S. (2004). Psychological safety, trust, and learning in organisations: A group-level lens. *Trust and distrust in organisations: Dilemmas and approaches, 12*(2004), 239-272.

Edmondson, A. (1999). Psychological safety and learning behaviour in work teams. *Administrative Science Quarterly*, *44*(2), 350–383. doi:10.2307/2666999

Edmondson, A. (2012). *Teaming: How organisations learn, innovate, and compete in the knowledge economy*. Jossey-Bass.

Edmondson, A. (2019). Psychological safety: The history, renaissance, and future of an interpersonal construct. *Annual Review of Organizational Psychology and Organizational Behavior*, *6*, 523–546. doi:10.1146/annurev-orgpsych-032519-050926

Edwards, J. S. (2022). Where knowledge management and information management meet: Research directions. *International Journal of Information Management*, *63*, 102458. doi:10.1016/j.ijinfomgt.2021.102458

Einola, K., & Alvesson, M. (2021). The perils of authentic leadership theory. *Leadership*, *17*(4), 483–490. doi:10.1177/17427150211004059

El Ebrashi, R. (2013). Social entrepreneurship theory and sustainable social impact. *Social Responsibility Journal*, *9*(2), 188–209. doi:10.1108/SRJ-07-2011-0013

Elkington, J. (1997). The triple bottom line. *Environmental management: Readings and cases, 2*, 49-66.

Elnadi, M., & Gheith, M. H. (2021). Entrepreneurial ecosystem, entrepreneurial self-efficacy, and entrepreneurial intention in higher education: Evidence from Saudi Arabia. *International Journal of Management Education*, *19*(1), 100458. Advance online publication. doi:10.1016/j.ijme.2021.100458

Engström, A., Johansson, A., Edh Mirzaei, N., Sollander, K., & Barry, D. (2023). Knowledge creation in projects: An interactive research approach for deeper business insight. *International Journal of Managing Projects in Business*, *16*(1), 22–44. doi:10.1108/IJMPB-09-2021-0233

Erken, H., Donselaar, P., & Thurik, R. (2018). Total factor productivity and the role of entrepreneurship. *The Journal of Technology Transfer*, *43*(1), 1493–1521. doi:10.100710961-016-9504-5

Estedadi, E., & Hamidi, K. (2015). The importance of succession planning in organizations. *Advanced Social Humanities and Management*, *2*(3), 41–47.

Eurofound & EU-OSHA. (2014). *Psychosocial Risks in Europe: Prevalence and Strategies for Prevention*. Publications Office of the European Union.

Eurostat. (2020). *Eurostat Database* [data set]. European Union. https://ec.europa.eu/eurostat/data/database

Evans, O. (2019). Information and communication technologies and economic development in Africa in the short and long run. *International Journal of Technology Management & Sustainable Development, 18*(2), 127–146. doi:10.1386/tmsd_00002_1

Family Firm Institute. (2021). *Global conference Shaping futures: Evolve, Emerge, Engage.* Ffi.org/conference/2021-ff

Fang, Z., Razzaq, A., Mohsin, M., & Irfan, M. (2022). Spatial spillovers and threshold effects of internet development and entrepreneurship on green innovation efficiency in China. *Technology in Society, 68*, 101844. doi:10.1016/j.techsoc.2021.101844

Fares, J., Chung, K. S. K., & Abbasi, A. (2021). Stakeholder theory and management: Understanding longitudinal collaboration networks. *PLoS One, 16*(10), e0255658. doi:10.1371/journal.pone.0255658 PMID:34648505

Farley, M. (2020). Prostitution, the sex trade, and the COVID-19 pandemic. *Logos, 19*(1), 1–34.

Farrukh, M., Khan, A. A., Khan, M. S., Ramzani, S. R., & Soladoye, A. (2017). Entrepreneurial intentions: The role of family factors, personality traits and self-efficacy. *World Journal of Entrepreneurship, Management and Sustainable Development, 13*(4), 303–317. doi:10.1108/WJEMSD-03-2017-0018

Fatoki, O. (2018). The impact of entrepreneurial resilience on the success of small and medium enterprises in South Africa. *Sustainability (Basel), 10*(7), 2527. doi:10.3390u10072527

Fayolle, A., Gailly, B., & Lassas-Clerc, N. (2006). Assessing the impact of entrepreneurship education programmes: A new methodology. *Journal of European Industrial Training, 30*(9), 701–720. doi:10.1108/03090590610715022

Fernandez, A. A., & Shaw, G. P. (2020). Academic leadership in a time of crisis: The Coronavirus and COVID-19. *Journal of Leadership Studies, 14*(1), 39–45. doi:10.1002/jls.21684

Fishbein, M., & Ajzen, I. (1975). A Bayesian analysis of attribution processes. *Psychological Bulletin, 82*(2), 261–277. doi:10.1037/h0076477

Fitz-Koch, S., Cooper, S. & Discua Cruz, A. (2019). Entrepreneurship and rural family identity: Understanding portfolio development in a family farm business. The family business group phenomenon: Emergence and complexities, 353-383.

Fitz-Koch, S., Cooper, S., & Discua Cruz, A. (2019). Entrepreneurship and rural family identity: Understanding portfolio development in a family farm business. *The family business group phenomenon: Emergence and complexities*, 353-383.

Folke, C. (2006). Resilience: The emergence of a perspective for social–ecological systems analyses. *Global Environmental Change, 16*(3), 253–267. doi:10.1016/j.gloenvcha.2006.04.002

Ford, E. (2002). Henry Ford (1863-1947) and Edsel Ford (1893-1943). *Notable American Philanthropists: Biographies of Giving and Volunteering*, 92.

Forouharfar, A., Rowshan, S. A., & Habibollah Salarzehi, H. (2019). The Relationship between Social Entrepreneurship and Sustainable Development from the Social Expertsâ Points of View. *Quarterly Journal of Environmental Education and Sustainable Development*, *7*(4), 70–82.

Forsyth, D. R., Mitchel, J., & Shepherd, K. (2018). Psychological safety and team effectiveness: A meta-analysis. *The Journal of Applied Psychology*, *103*(2), 158–178.

Franco, M., & Prata, M. (2019). Influence of the individual characteristics and personality traits of the founder on the performance of family SMEs. *European Journal of International Management*, *13*(1), 41–68. doi:10.1504/EJIM.2019.096498

Frazier, M., Fainshmidt, S., Klinger, R., Pezeshkan, A., & Vracheva, V. (2016). Psychological safety: A meta-analytic review and extension. *Personnel Psychology*, *70*(1), 113–165. doi:10.1111/peps.12183

Fredin, S., & Lidén, A. (2020). Entrepreneurial ecosystems: Towards a systemic approach to entrepreneurship? *Geografisk Tidskrift*, *120*(2), 87–97. doi:10.1080/00167223.2020.1769491

Freeman, H., Barnes, L., & Long, W. R. (2021). *Leading Change Without Formal Authority: The ICC Model for the 21st Century*. Academic Press.

Frese, M., Chell, E., & Klandt, H. (Eds.). (2000). *Psychological approaches to entrepreneurship*. Psychology Press.

Fritsch, M. (1996). Turbulence and growth in West Germany: A comparison of evidence by regions and industries. *Review of Industrial Organization*, *11*(2), 231–251. doi:10.1007/BF00157669

Fritsch, M., & Mueller, P. (2008). The effect of new business formation on regional development over time: The case of Germany. *Small Business Economics*, *30*(1), 15–29. doi:10.100711187-007-9067-9

Froner, Y. A. (2017). International policies for sustainable development from cultural empowerment. *Journal of Cultural Heritage Management and Sustainable Development*, *7*(2), 208–223. doi:10.1108/JCHMSD-10-2016-0056

Fyhn, B., Bang, H., Sverdrup, T., & Schei, V. (2022). Safe among the unsafe: Psychological safety climate strength matters for team performance. *Small Group Research*. Advance online publication. doi:10.1177/10464964221121273

Gagné, M., Marwick, C., Brun de Pontet, S., & Wrosch, C. (2021). Family business succession: What's motivation got to do with it? *Family Business Review*, *34*(2), 154–167. doi:10.1177/0894486519894759

Galindo-Martín, M. A., Castaño-Martínez, M. S., & Méndez-Picazo, M. T. (2020). The relationship between green innovation, social entrepreneurship, and sustainable development. *Sustainability (Basel)*, *12*(11), 1–19. doi:10.3390u12114467

Gao, Y., & Qin, X. (2022). Entrepreneurship education and entrepreneurial intention of Chinese college students: Evidence from a moderated multi-mediation model. *Frontiers in Psychology*, *13*(1), 1–12. doi:10.3389/fpsyg.2022.1049232 PMID:36524159

Gardner, T., Herman, A., & Yap, J. (2019). Exploring the impact of learning and development initiatives on employee engagement. *Human Resource Development Quarterly*, *30*(4), 577–605. doi:10.1002/hrdq.21290

Gardner, W. L., Cogliser, C. C., Davis, K. M., & Dickens, M. P. (2011). Authentic leadership: A review of the literature and research agenda. *The Leadership Quarterly*, *22*(6), 1120–1145. doi:10.1016/j.leaqua.2011.09.007

Garett & Zettel. (2021). *Washinton interscholastic activities association*. Cross Country Media. https://www.wiaa.com/conDocs/Con466/Cross%20Country%20Media%20Pack

Gavin, M. (2019). Working industrially or professionally? What strategies should teacher unions use to improve teacher salaries in neoliberal times? *Labour & Industry: A Journal of the Social and Economic Relations of Work, 29*(1), 19-33.

Gaviria-Marin, M., Merigó, J. M., & Baier-Fuentes, H. (2019). Knowledge management: A global examination based on bibliometric analysis. *Technological Forecasting and Social Change*, *140*, 194–220. doi:10.1016/j.techfore.2018.07.006

Gaviria-Marin, M., Merigo, J. M., & Popa, S. (2018). Twenty years of the Journal of Knowledge Management: A bibliometric analysis. *Journal of Knowledge Management*, *22*(8), 1655–1687. doi:10.1108/JKM-10-2017-0497

Ge, J., Carney, M., & Kellermanns, F. (2019). Who fills institutional voids? Entrepreneurs' utilization of political and family ties in emerging markets. *Entrepreneurship Theory and Practice*, *43*(6), 1124–1147. doi:10.1177/1042258718773175

George, B. (2003). *Authentic leadership: Rediscovering the secrets to creating lasting value* (Vol. 18). John Wiley & Sons.

George, D., & Zhou, J. (2017). The effects of psychological safety on team creativity: A meta-analysis. *Academy of Management Journal*, *60*(2), 488–509.

Georgescu, M. A., & Herman, E. (2020). The impact of the family background on students' entrepreneurial intentions: An empirical analysis. *Sustainability (Basel)*, *12*(11), 4775. doi:10.3390u12114775

Gerschenkron, A. (1962b). Social Attitudes, Entrepreneurship, and Economic Development: A Comment. *Explorations in Entrepreneurial History, 6*, 245-72.

Gerschenkron, A. (1966). The Modernization of Entrepreneurship. InWeiner, M. (Ed.), *Modernization: The Dynamics of Growth*. Basic Books.

Gerschenkron, A. (1962a). *Economic Backwardness in Historical Perspective*. Belknap Press.

Ghorbankhani, M., & Rossi, F. (2022). Intrinsic and strategic complementarity of research and knowledge transfer activities as determinants of knowledge transfer management: Evidence from public research organisations. *The Journal of Technology Transfer*, 1–27.

Ghosh, D. & Natarajan, P. (2019). *Indian Tech Start-up Ecosystem*. Academic Press.

Ghosh, D., & Natarajan, P. (2019). *Indian Tech Start-up Ecosystem*. Academic Press.

Giao, H. N. K., Vuong, B. N., & Tushar, H. (2020). The impact of social support on job-related behaviors through the mediating role of job stress and the moderating role of locus of control: Empirical evidence from the Vietnamese banking industry. *Cogent Business & Management*, *7*(1), 1841359. doi:10.1080/23311975.2020.1841359

Gibb, A. (2004). *Effective Policies for Small Business. A Guide for the Policy Review Process and Strategic Plans for Micro, Small and Medium Enterprise Development. OECD/United Nations Industrial Development Organization*. UNIDO.

Gichuna, S., Hassan, R., Sanders, T., Campbell, R., Mutonyi, M., & Mwangi, P. (2020). Access to Healthcare in a time of COVID-19: Sex Workers in Crisis in Nairobi, Kenya. *Global Public Health: An International Journal for Research, Policy and Practice*, *15*(10), 1430–1442. doi:10.1080/17441692.2020.1810298 PMID:32816628

Gieure, C., del Mar Benavides-Espinosa, M., & Roig-Dobón, S. (2020). The entrepreneurial process: The link between intentions and behavior. *Journal of Business Research*, *112*, 541–548. doi:10.1016/j.jbusres.2019.11.088

Giustiniano, L., Cunha, M. P., Simpson, A. V., Rego, A., & Clegg, S. (2020). Resilient leadership as paradox work: Notes from COVID-19. *Management and Organization Review*, *16*(5), 971–975. doi:10.1017/mor.2020.57

Glisby, M., & Holden, N. (2003). Contextual constraints in knowledge management theory: The cultural embeddedness of Nonaka's knowledge-creating company. *Knowledge and Process Management*, *10*(1), 29–36. doi:10.1002/kpm.158

Global Asian August. (2016). *100 Top Groups. Globe Asia (Special Issue)*. Tanri Abeng.

Global Reporting Index (GRI). (2019). *Sustainability reporting guidelines*. Available: https://www.globalreporting.org/Pages/default.aspx

Godley, A. (2001). *Jewish immigrant entrepreneurship in New York and London, 1880-1914*. Palgrave. doi:10.1057/9780333993866

Goel, S., & Jones, R. J. III. (2016). Entrepreneurial exploration and exploitation in family business: A systematic review and future directions. *Family Business Review*, *29*(1), 94–120. doi:10.1177/0894486515625541

Goldsmith, G. M., Bates, I. P., Davies, J. G., McRobbie, D., Webb, D. G., Wright, J., & Quinn, J. (2003). A pilot study to evaluate clinical competence in junior grade pharmacy practitioners. *Pharmacy Education*, *3*(2), 127–134. doi:10.1080/15602210310001604044

Goman, C. K. (2017). *The power of collaborative leadership*. Institute for Management Studies. https://www.ims-online.com

Gonzalez, M. (2021). *The Importance of Psychological Safety and Team Building in the Workplace*. Retrieved April 10, 2021, from https://blog.hubspot.com/marketing/psychological-safety-team-building

Goodland, R., & Daly, H. (1996). Environmental sustainability: Universal and non-negotiable. *Ecological Applications*, *6*(4), 1002–1017. doi:10.2307/2269583

Govender, K. (2018). The Relationship Among Leadership, Organisation Culture, and Performance in the Public Service. *Advanced Science Letters*, *24*(7), 4914–4917. doi:10.1166/asl.2018.11233

Graneheim, U., Lindgren, B., & Lundman, B. (2017). Methodological challenges in qualitative content analysis: A discussion paper. *Nurse Education Today*, *56*, 29–34. doi:10.1016/j.nedt.2017.06.002 PMID:28651100

Granovetter, M. (1985). Economic action and social structure: The problem of embeddedness. *American Journal of Sociology*, *91*(3), 481–510. doi:10.1086/228311

Grant, S. (2004). *Narrating the body shop: A story about corporate identity*. University of Waikato.

Griggs, A., Rogers, J., Gisick, L., Lazzara, E., Keebler, J., & Cohen, T. (2021). Development of a team role behaviour observation tool: Insights and considerations for future research. *Proceedings of the Human Factors and Ergonomics Society Annual Meeting*, *65*(1), 122–127. doi:10.1177/1071181321651282

Growth, A. (2012). *Sustainability or growth? Why not both?* https://www.businessinsider.com/grant-cardone-on-why-companies-fail-2012-4

Gubik, A. S., & Farkas, S. (2019). Entrepreneurial intention in the Visegrad countries. *Danube*, *10*(4), 347–368. doi:10.2478/danb-2019-0018

Gudmunson, C. G., & Danes, S. M. (2013). Family social capital in family businesses: A stocks and flows investigation. *Family Relations*, *62*(3), 399–414. doi:10.1111/fare.12017

Guerrero, M., & Urbano, D. (2019). A research agenda for entrepreneurship and innovation: the role of entrepreneurial universities. *A research agenda for entrepreneurship and innovation*, 107-133.

Guillory, W. (2022). The Future Perfect Organization: Driven by Quantum-Thinking. *Innovative Leadership in Times of Compelling Changes: Strategies, Reflections and Tools*, 337-352.

Gu, J., Chen, Z., Huang, Q., Liu, H., & Huang, S. (2016). A multilevel analysis of the relationship between shared leadership and creativity in inter-organisational teams. *The Journal of Creative Behavior*, *52*(2), 109–126. doi:10.1002/jocb.135

Guo, W., & Wang, D. (2017). Does joint decision-making foster team creativity? exploring the moderating and mediating effects. *Personnel Review*, *46*(8), 1590–1604. doi:10.1108/PR-03-2016-0055

Gupta, N., & Sharma, V. (2016). Exploring employee engagement—A way to better business performance. *Global Business Review*, *17*(3, suppl), 45S–63S. doi:10.1177/0972150916631082

Gupta, S. (2019). Succession Planning in Family Businesses: Lessons from Reliance Industries. *Journal of Family Business Strategy*, *10*, 345–362.

Habash, N., & Baidoun, S. (2023). How to win the succession race: empirical analysis of Palestinian family businesses. *Journal of Entrepreneurship in Emerging Economies*.

Hack-Polay, D., Igwe, P. A., & Madichie, N. O. (2020). The role of institutional and family embeddedness in the failure of Sub-Saharan African migrant family businesses. *International Journal of Entrepreneurship and Innovation*, *21*(4), 237–249. doi:10.1177/1465750320909732

Hajiali, I., Kessi, A. M. F., Budiandriani, B., Prihatin, E., & Sufri, M. M. (2022). Determination of Work Motivation, Leadership Style, Employee Competence on Job Satisfaction and Employee Performance. *Golden Ratio of Human Resource Management*, *2*(1), 57–69. doi:10.52970/grhrm.v2i1.160

Halabisky, D. (2021). *Untapped talent: Entrepreneurship can help address the youth unemployment challenge*. https://www.oecd-forum.org/posts/untapped-talent-entrepreneurship-can-help-address-the-youth-unemployment-challenge

Halis Akder, A. (1994). *A Means to Closing Gaps: Disaggregated Human Development Index*. Human Development Report Office.

Hamel, G., & Valikangas, L. (2004). The quest for resilience. *icade. Revista de la Facultad de Derecho (Montevideo)*, (62), 355–358.

Hameli, A., Kampouris, L., Machaal, A. K., & Mertzanis, C. (2021). Financial development, institutions, Gender and Entrepreneurship in the United Arab Emirates. *Asian Journal of Empirical Research*, *11*(2), 11–22. doi:10.18488/journal.1007.2021.112.11.22

Hamilton, E., Cruz, A. D., & Jack, S. (2017). Re-framing the status of narrative in family business research: Towards an understanding of families in business. *Journal of Family Business Strategy*, *8*(1), 3–12. doi:10.1016/j.jfbs.2016.11.001

Handler, W. C. (2011). The Role of External Advisors in Family Business: A Review and Extension. *Family Business Review*, *24*, 65–81.

Hannah, L. (1984). Entrepreneurs and the Social Sciences. *Economica*, *51*(203), 219–234. doi:10.2307/2554542

Han, S., Liu, D., & Lv, Y. (2022). The influence of psychological safety on students' creativity in project-based learning: The mediating role of psychological empowerment. *Frontiers in Psychology*, *13*, 865123. Advance online publication. doi:10.3389/fpsyg.2022.865123 PMID:35572343

Hanson, S. K., Hessel, H. M., & Danes, S. M. (2019). Relational processes in family entrepreneurial culture and resilience across generations. *Journal of Family Business Strategy*, *10*(3), 100263. doi:10.1016/j.jfbs.2018.11.001

Harrison, D. A., Price, K. H., Gavin, J. H., & Florey, A. T. (2019). Leveraging technology for team creativity in the workplace. *Organizational Dynamics*, *48*(4), 274–284. doi:10.1016/j.orgdyn.2019.06.007

Harrison, D. A., Price, K. H., Gavin, J. H., & Florey, A. T. (2020). The power of psychological safety: A meta-analysis of team dynamics. *The Journal of Applied Psychology*, *105*(3), 557–581. doi:10.1037/apl0000444

Hartšenko, J., & Küttim, M. (2019). The entrepreneurial intentions of students in Central and Eastern European countries. *Research in Economics and Business: Central and Eastern Europe*, *11*(2), 64–84.

Hasan, F., & Kashif, M. (2020). Psychological safety, meaningfulness and empowerment as predictors of employee well-being: A mediating role of promotive voice. *Asia-Pacific Journal of Business Administration*, *13*(1), 40–59. doi:10.1108/APJBA-11-2019-0236

Hassard, J., Van den Broek, K., Flemming, D., Gründler, R., Dewe, P., Teoh, K., Cosemans, B., Cosmar, M., & Cox, T. (2014). *Calculating the Cost of Work-Related Stress and Psychosocial Risks: Literature Review*. Publications Office of the European Union.

Hatak, I. R., & Roessl, D. (2013). Relational Competence-Based Knowledge Transfer Within Intrafamily Succession. *Family Business Review*, *28*(1), 10–25. doi:10.1177/0894486513480386

Hatak, I., & Zhou, H. (2021). Health as human capital in entrepreneurship: Individual, extension, and substitution effects on entrepreneurial success. *Entrepreneurship Theory and Practice*, *45*(1), 18–42. doi:10.1177/1042258719867559

Heck, R. K., Danes, S. M., Fitzgerald, M. A., Haynes, G. W., Jasper, C. R., Schrank, H. L., . . . Winter, M. (2006). The family's dynamic role within family business entrepreneurship. Handbook of research on family business, 80-105.

Heck, R. K. Z., & Trent, E. S. (1999). The prevalence of family business from a household sample. *Family Business Review*, *12*(3), 209–219. doi:10.1111/j.1741-6248.1999.00209.x

Henley, A., Contreras, F., Espinosa, J. C., & Barbosa, D. (2017). Entrepreneurial intentions of Colombian business students: Planned behaviour, leadership skills and social capital. *International Journal of Entrepreneurial Behaviour & Research*, *23*(6), 1017–1032. doi:10.1108/IJEBR-01-2017-0031

Hernández-Linares, R., López-Fernández, M. C., García-Piqueres, G., Pina e Cunha, M., & Rego, A. (2023). How knowledge-based dynamic capabilities relate to firm performance: The mediating role of entrepreneurial orientation. *Review of Managerial Science*, 1–33. doi:10.100711846-023-00691-4

Herscovitch, L., & Meyer, J. P. (2002). Commitment to organizational change: Extension of a three-component model. *The Journal of Applied Psychology*, *87*(3), 474–487. doi:10.1037/0021-9010.87.3.474 PMID:12090605

Hershcovis, M. (2011). Incivility, social undermining, bullying…oh my! A call to reconcile constructs within workplace aggression research. *Journal of Organizational Behavior*, *32*(1), 629–647. doi:10.1002/job.689

Hinojosa, A. S., McCauley, K. D., Randolph-Seng, B., & Gardner, W. L. (2014). Leader and follower attachment styles: Implications for authentic leader–follower relationships. *The Leadership Quarterly*, *25*(3), 595–610. doi:10.1016/j.leaqua.2013.12.002

Hirak, R., Peng, A., Carmeli, A., & Schaubroeck, J. (2012). Linking leader inclusiveness to work unit performance: The importance of psychological safety and learning from failures. *The Leadership Quarterly*, *23*(1), 107–117. doi:10.1016/j.leaqua.2011.11.009

Hirsch, J. E., & Buela-Casal, G. (2014). The meaning of the h-index. *International Journal of Clinical and Health Psychology*, *14*(2), 161–164. doi:10.1016/S1697-2600(14)70050-X

Hirsh, J. B., Mar, R. A., & Peterson, J. B. (2012). Psychological entropy: a framework for understanding uncertainty-related anxiety. *Psychological Review*, *119*(2), 304. doi:10.1037/a0026767 PMID:22250757

Hmieleski, K. M., & Baron, R. A. (2008). When does entrepreneurial self-efficacy enhance versus reduce firm performance? *Strategic Entrepreneurship Journal*, *2*(1), 57–72. doi:10.1002ej.42

Hofstede, G. (2011). *National cultures, organizational cultures, and the role of management. In Values and ethics for the 21st century*. BBVA.

Holt, D. T., Pearson, A. W., Carr, J. C., & Barnett, T. (2017). Family firm (s) outcomes model: Structuring financial and nonfinancial outcomes across the family and firm. *Family Business Review*, *30*(2), 182–202. doi:10.1177/0894486516680930

Hong, J. S., & Lee, J. R. (2009). Psychological safety and organisational commitment: A study of Korean telecommunication. *International Journal of Human Resource Management*, *20*(10), 2095–2107.

Hoover, E. A., & Hoover, C. L. (2013). *Getting along in family business: The relationship intelligence handbook*. Routledge. doi:10.4324/9780203949757

Hopp, C. S., & Stephan, U. (2012). The influence of socio-cultural environments on the performance of nascent entrepreneurs: Community culture, motivation, self-efficacy and start-up success. *Entrepreneurship and Regional Development*, *24*(9-10), 917–945. doi:10.1080/08985626.2012.742326

Hougaz, L. (2015). *Entrepreneurs in family business dynasties: Stories of Italian-Australian family businesses over 100 Years*. Springer. doi:10.1007/978-3-319-13918-0

Hou, T., Zhang, T., Cai, W., Song, X., Chen, A., Deng, G., & Ni, C. (2020). Social support and mental health among health care workers during Coronavirus Disease 2019 outbreak: A moderated mediation model. *PLoS One*, *15*(5), e0233831. doi:10.1371/journal.pone.0233831 PMID:32470007

Hsu, D. K., Wiklund, J., Anderson, S. E., & Coffey, B. S. (2016). Entrepreneurial exit intentions and the business-family interface. *Journal of Business Venturing*, *31*(6), 613–627. doi:10.1016/j.jbusvent.2016.08.001

Huang, C., & Hsieh, P. (2017). Inspiring creativity in teams: Perspectives of transactive memory systems. *Journal of Pacific Rim Psychology*, *11*, e6. doi:10.1017/prp.2017.6

Huang, S., Ding, D., & Chen, Z. (2014). Entrepreneurial leadership and performance in C Chinese new ventures: A moderated mediation model of exploratory innovation, exploitative innovation, and environmental dynamism. *Creativity and Innovation Management*, *23*(4), 453–471. doi:10.1111/caim.12085

Huang, Y., Cheng, B., & Liu, J. (2015). Psychological safety and job satisfaction: An empirical study. *Applied Psychology*, *64*(3), 468–494.

Huff, C. (2019). *Psychological Safety in the Workplace: What It Is and How to Create It*. The Muse. Retrieved from: https://www.themuse.com/advice/psychological-safety-in-the-workplace-what-it-is-and-how-to-create-it

Humphrey, R., Massis, A., Picone, P., Tang, Y., & Piccolo, R. (2021). The psychological foundations of management in family firms: Emotions, memories, and experiences. *Family Business Review*, *34*(2), 122–131. doi:10.1177/08944865211012139

Hutagalung, B., Dalimunthe, D. M., Pambudi, R., Hutagalung, A. Q., & Muda, I. (2017). The effect of entrepreneurship education and family environment towards students' entrepreneurial motivation. *International Journal of Economic Research*, *14*(20), 331–348.

Idowu, A. I., & Ndidiamaka, A. E. (2018). The influence of supervisor/subordinate social support on employee performance in the South African retail sector. *The Journal of Business and Retail Management Research*, *12*(3). Advance online publication. doi:10.24052/JBRMR/V12IS03/ART-01

Ilevbare, F. M., Ilevbare, O. E., Adelowo, C. M., & Oshorenua, F. P. (2022). Social support and risk-taking propensity as predictors of entrepreneurial intention among undergraduates in Nigeria. *Asia Pacific Journal of Innovation and Entrepreneurship*, *16*(2), 90–107. doi:10.1108/APJIE-02-2022-0010

Ilić, M, Ranković, M., Janić, L., & Mitić, B. (2020). Indicators of entrepreneurial behavior and attitudes for entrepreneurs of Slovenia and Croatia, in 2018/2019. *Journal of Economic Development, Environment and People*, *9*(1), 6-16. doi:.v8i4.641 doi:10.26458/jedep

Imperial Business School. (2022). *Entrepreneurial resilience and recovery during and after COVID-19*. https://www.imperial.ac.uk/business-school/faculty-research/academic-areas/management-entrepreneur

Indaryani, M., Hidayah, M., & Lusianti, D. (2021). The effects of entrepreneurial education and family environment on the interest in enterprise through students' motivation of entrepreneurship. SSRN *Electronic Journal*, 1-15. https://doi.org/ doi:10.2139/ssrn.3865920

International Association of Attraction Industry (IAAPA). (2021). https://www.bing.com/search?ptag=ICO37de9cc872970f6e&form=INCOH1&pc=1BDL&q=international%20association%20of%20attraction%20industries

Işgör, İ., & Haspolat, N. (2016). Investigating the psychological well-being and job satisfaction levels in different occupations. *International Education Studies*, *9*(12), 194. doi:10.5539/ies.v9n12p194

Ismael, A. M., & Shanmugam, K. (2022). Knowing your roots, enhancing oral proficiency of elementary students in Kurdistan using oral presentation as an alternative assessment in the family tree task. *Practitioner Research*, *4*(1), 35–51. doi:10.32890/pr2022.4.3

Ismail, M., Ibrahim, A. F., Yaacob, M. R., Ibrahim, A. H., Zakaria, M. N., Razak, R. C., Yusoff, M. N. H., Guan, T. T., & Kamaruddin, A. N. (2018). Determine entrepreneurial characteristics using mobile. *International Journal of Interactive Mobile Technologies*, *12*(1), 141–150. doi:10.3991/ijim.v12i1.7790

Ivancevich, J. M., & Matteson, M. T. (1980). *Stress and Work: A Managerial Perspective*. Scott. Foresman and Company.

Jabbari, B., & Rouster, A. S. (2023). Family Dynamics. StatPearls Publishing LLC.

Jabbari, B., & Rouster, A. S. (2023). Family Dynamics. StatPearls Publishing LLC.

Jahmurataj, V., Ramadani, V., Bexheti, A., Rexhepi, G., Abazi-Alili, H., & Krasniqi, B. A. (2023). Unveiling the determining factors of family business longevity: Evidence from Kosovo. *Journal of Business Research*, *159*, 113745. doi:10.1016/j.jbusres.2023.113745

Jalam, M. U., & Adamu, M. (2022). Relationship between entrepreneurship ecosystems and entrepreneurial mindset development among students. *International Journal of Intellectual Discourse*, *5*(3), 1–13. https://ijidjournal.org/index.php/ijid/article/view/271

Javed, B., Khan, A., Bashir, S., & Arjoon, S. (2016). Impact of ethical leadership on creativity: The role of psychological empowerment. *Current Issues in Tourism*, *20*(8), 839–851. doi:10.1080/13683500.2016.1188894

Javed, B., Naqvi, S., Khan, A., Arjoon, S., & Tayyeb, H. (2017). Impact of inclusive leadership on innovative work behaviour: The role of psychological safety. *Journal of Management &Amp. Organisation*, *25*(1), 117–136. doi:10.1017/jmo.2017.3

Jenks, L. H. (1944). Railroads as an Economic Force in American Development. *The Journal of Economic History, 4, 18-20.* doi:10.1017/S002205070008400X

Jennings, J. E., & McDougald, M. S. (2007). Work-family interface experiences and coping strategies: Implications for entrepreneurship research and practice. *Academy of Management Review*, *32*(3), 747–760. doi:10.5465/amr.2007.25275510

Jensen, M. C., & Meckling, W. H. (2019). Theory of the firm: Managerial behavior, agency costs and ownership structure. In *Corporate governance* (pp. 77–132). Gower.

Jha, S. (2019). Team psychological safety and team performance. *The International Journal of Organizational Analysis*, *27*(4), 903–924. doi:10.1108/IJOA-10-2018-1567

Jiang, J., Xu, J., Yin, X., & Hu, J. (2022). The impact of environment on college students' entrepreneurial intention based on the mediating effect of personality traits. *Frontiers in Psychology*, *13*, 972992. doi:10.3389/fpsyg.2022.972992 PMID:36605283

Jilenga, M. T. (2017). Social enterprise and economic growth: A theoretical approach and policy recommendations. *International Journal of Academic Research in Accounting, Finance and Management Sciences*, *7*(1), 41–49.

Jio, S., & Sun, Q. (2021). Digital economic development and its impact on economic growth in China: Research based on the perspective of sustainability. *Sustainability (Basel)*, *13*(18), 1–18. doi:10.3390u131810245

Johnson, M., Dodgson, M., & Gann, D. (2019). Psychological safety and job performance: A study of banking professionals. *International Journal of Bank Marketing*, *37*(3), 622–636.

Joice, K. (2021). Mothering in the frame: Cinematic microanalysis and the Pathogenic Mother, 1945–67. *History of the Human Sciences*, *34*(5), 105–131. doi:10.1177/0952695120924266

Jokinen, T. (2005). Global leadership competencies: A review and discussion. *Journal of European Industrial Training*, *29*(3), 199–216. doi:10.1108/03090590510591085

Jones, G., & Wadhwani, R. D. (2006). *Entrepreneurship and business history: Renewing the research agenda* (Vol. 7). Harvard Business School.

Jordan, J., Wade, M., & Yokoi, T. (2022, Jan.). Finding the right balance-and flexibility-in your leadership style. *Harvard Business Review*.

Joseph, I. (2017). Factors influencing international student entrepreneurial intention in Malaysia. *American Journal of Industrial and Business Management*, *7*(4), 424–428. doi:10.4236/ajibm.2017.74030

Judge, L. W., Woodward, S. C., Gillham, A. D., Blom, L. C., Hoover, D. L., Schoeff, M. A., Fox, B., Burt, T., & Bellar, D. M. (2021). Efficacy Sources that Predict Leadership Behaviors in Coaches of Athletes with Disabilities. *Journal of Human Kinetics*, *78*(1), 271–281. doi:10.2478/hukin-2021-0056 PMID:34025884

Jyoti, B., & Singh, A. K. (2020). Characteristics and determinants of new start-ups in Gujarat, India. *Entrepreneurship Review*, *1*(2), 1-25. doi:.v1i2.154 doi:10.38157/entrepreneurship-review

Jyoti, B., & Singh, A. K. (2023). Does digitalization have a causal relationship with economic development? An experience from a country-wise panel data statistical analysis. In R. S. Nazlı & G. Sari (Eds.), Handbook of Research on Perspectives on Society and Technology Addiction (pp. 34-61). IGI Global. doi:10.4018/978-1-6684-8397-8.ch003

Kahn, R. L., & Quinn, R. P. (1970). Role stress: A framework for analysis. *Occupational mental health*, 50-115.

Kahneman D. (2020). *Thinking fast and slow*. Farrar, Straus, and Giroux. https//: amazon.com/ Thinkingfastandslow

Kahn, W. A. (1990). Psychological conditions of personal engagement and disengagement at work. *Academy of Management Journal, 33*(4), 692–724. doi:10.2307/256287

Kakabadse, N. K., Kakabadse, A., & Kouzmin, A. (2003). Reviewing the knowledge management literature: Towards a taxonomy. *Journal of Knowledge Management, 7*(4), 75–91. doi:10.1108/13673270310492967

Kakemam, E., Liang, Z., Janati, A., Arab-Zozani, M., Mohaghegh, B., & Gholizadeh, M. (2020). Leadership and Management Competencies for Hospital Managers: A Systematic Review and Best-Fit Framework Synthesis. *Journal of Healthcare Leadership, 12*, 59–68.

Kane-Urrabazo, C. (2006). Management's role in shaping organizational culture. *Journal of Nursing Management, 14*(3), 188–194. doi:10.1111/j.1365-2934.2006.00590.x PMID:16600006

Kanter, R. M., & Prahalad, C. K. (2017). Collaborative advantage: The art of creative collaboration. *Harvard Business Review, 95*(11), 57–69.

Karabulut, A. T. (2016). Personality traits on entrepreneurial intention. *Procedia: Social and Behavioral Sciences, 229*, 12–21. doi:10.1016/j.sbspro.2016.07.109

Karimi, H., & Ataei, P. (2022). The effect of entrepreneurship on entrepreneurial skills of agriculture students: The mediation role of social intelligence and emotional intelligence (The case of Zabol University, Iran). *Current Psychology (New Brunswick, N.J.), 42*(1), 23250–23264. doi:10.100712144-022-03479-z PMID:35854700

Karsono, O. M. F., & Suprapto, W. (2015). The downfall of Chinese family businesses in East Java, Indonesia. *International Journal of Academic Research, 6*(6), 298–304.

Kautonen, T., Van Gelderen, M., & Fink, M. (2015). Robustness of the theory of planned behavior in predicting entrepreneurial intentions and actions. *Entrepreneurship Theory and Practice, 39*(3), 655–674. doi:10.1111/etap.12056

Kavas, M., Jarzabkowski, P., & Nigam, A. (2020). Islamic family business: The constitutive role of religion in business. *Journal of Business Ethics, 163*(4), 689–700. doi:10.100710551-019-04384-5

Keller, R. T. (2017). Rewards for creative thinking. *Creativity Research Journal, 29*(2), 186–196.

Keller, R. T., Goldstein, M., & Davis, R. (2018). Creativity, innovation, and risk taking: A motivational perspective. *Human Resource Management Review, 28*(3), 243–255. doi:10.1016/j.hrmr.2018.03.002

Kerr, M. (2019). Creating Psychological Safety in the Workplace. *Harvard Business Review*. Retrieved from: https://hbr.org/2019/06/creating-psychological-safety-in-the-workplace

Kerr, S. P., Kerr, W. R., & Xu, T. (2018). Personality traits of entrepreneurs: A review of recent literature. *Foundations and Trends® in Entrepreneurship, 14*(3), 279-356.

Kessel, M., Kratzer, J., & Schultz, C. (2012). Psychological safety, knowledge sharing, and creative performance in healthcare teams. *Creativity and Innovation Management*, *21*(2), 147–157. doi:10.1111/j.1467-8691.2012.00635.x

Khan, N. U., Li, S., Safdar, M. N., & Khan, Z. U. (2019). The role of entrepreneurial strategy, network ties, human and financial capital in new venture performance. *Journal of Risk and Financial Management*, *12*(1), 41. doi:10.3390/jrfm12010041

Khan, N., Aslam, R., Asad, M. M., Oad, L., & Almusharraf, N. M. (2022). Effects of WFH on educators' wellbeing: Mediating role of institutional head's support and moderating role of employees' self-efficacy at university level. *Journal of Professional Capital and Community*, *7*(3), 305–326. doi:10.1108/JPCC-10-2021-0063

Khavul, S., Bruton, G. D., & Wood, E. (2009). Informal family business in Africa. *Entrepreneurship Theory and Practice*, *33*(6), 1219–1238. doi:10.1111/j.1540-6520.2009.00342.x

Khuong, M. N., & Van, N. T. (2022). The influence of entrepreneurial ecosystem on entrepreneurs' perceptions and business success. *Gadjah Mada International Journal of Business, 24*(2), 198-222. https://search.informit.org/doi/abs/10.3316/informit.491830241767765

Kianto, A., Shujahat, M., Hussain, S., Nawaz, F., & Ali, M. (2019). The impact of knowledge management on knowledge worker productivity. *Baltic Journal of Management*, *14*(2), 178–197. doi:10.1108/BJM-12-2017-0404

Kim, B., Park, S., & Kim, T. (2019). The effect of transformational leadership on team creativity: Sequential mediating effect of employee's psychological safety and creativity. *Asian Journal of Technology Innovation*, *27*(1), 90–107. doi:10.1080/19761597.2019.1587304

Kim, J., & McLean, G. N. (2015). An integrative framework for global leadership competency: Levels and dimensions. *Human Resource Development International*, *18*(3), 235–258. doi:10.1080/13678868.2014.1003721

Kim, K. (2012). The role of culture in theories of the intergenerational transmission of violence. *Child & Family Social Work*, *17*(4), 395–405. doi:10.1111/j.1365-2206.2011.00793.x

Kim, T. H., Kim, Y. K., & Kim, M. S. (2016). Psychological safety and team performance: A study of knowledge-intensive teams. *Journal of Business Research*, *69*(11), 5347–5351.

Kim, T., & Park, H. J. (2012). The effect of psychological safety on work engagement: Focusing on the mediating role of job resources. *The Journal of Psychology*, *146*(3), 247–264.

Kipkosgei, F. (2022). Perceived entrepreneurial stress and entrepreneurial resilience; the mediating role of the well-being of entrepreneurs and moderating role perceived online social support. *Merits*, *2*(1), 1–17. doi:10.3390/merits2010001

Kirkpatrick, S. A., & Locke, E. A. (1991). Do traits matter. *The Academy of Management Executive*, *5*(2), 48–60.

Kirkwood, J. (2012). Family matters: Exploring the role of family in the new venture creation decision. *Journal of Small Business and Entrepreneurship*, *25*(2), 141–154. doi:10.1080/08276331.2012.10593565

Kleminski, R., Kazienko, P., & Kajdanowicz, T. (2022). Analysis of direct citation, co-citation and bibliographic coupling in scientific topic identification. *Journal of Information Science*, *48*(3), 349–373. doi:10.1177/0165551520962775

Klofsten, M., Fayolle, A., Guerrero, M., Mian, S., Urbano, D., & Wright, M. (2019). The entrepreneurial university as driver for economic growth and social change - Key strategic challenges. *Technological Forecasting and Social Change*, *141*, 149–158. doi:10.1016/j.techfore.2018.12.004

Knieps, F., & Pfaff, H. (2019). Mental Health, and Work: Figures, Data, Facts. BKK Health Report. MWV Medizinisch Wissenschaftliche Verlagsgesellschaft.

Kocsis, S. W., Roesler, A. R., & Totten, A. (2022). *Learning from COVID-19: Reimagining public -private partnerships in public health*. https://milkeninstitute.org/report/covid-19-public-private-partnerships?gclid=CjwKCAiAuOieBhAIEiw

Koehn, N. (2014). Estee Lauder: self-definition and the modern cosmetics market. In Beauty and Business (pp. 221-256). Routledge.

Koopmann, J., Lanaj, K., Wang, M., Zhou, L., & Shi, J. (2016). Nonlinear effects of team tenure on team psychological safety climate and climate strength: Implications for average team member performance. *The Journal of Applied Psychology*, *101*(7), 940–957. doi:10.1037/apl0000097 PMID:26949818

Korbi, K. (2015). Leadership and strategic change. *The Journal of Organizational Management Studies*, *2015*, 1–32. doi:10.5171/2015.638847

Kossek, E. E., & Perrigino, M. B. (2016). Resilience: A review using a grounded integrated occupational approach. *Academy of Management Annals, 10*(1).

Kossyva, D., Theriou, G., Aggelidis, V., & Sarigiannidis, L. (2022). Definitions and antecedents of engagement: A systematic literature review. *Management Research Review*, *46*(5), 719–738. doi:10.1108/MRR-01-2021-0043

Kosuri, P., & Pantin, L. (2021). Nowhere to Run to, Nowhere to Hide. *Clinical Law Review*, *28*, 199.

Ko, W. W., & Liu, G. (2021). The transformation from traditional nonprofit organizations to social enterprises: An institutional entrepreneurship perspective. *Journal of Business Ethics*, *171*(1), 15–32. doi:10.100710551-020-04446-z

Krawczyk-Bryłka, B., Stankiewicz, K., Ziemiański, P., & Tomczak, M. (2020). Effective collaboration of entrepreneurial teams—Implications for entrepreneurial education. *Education Sciences*, *10*(12), 364. doi:10.3390/educsci10120364

Kumar, A., & Sihag, S. (2012). Traits of Entrepreneurs of Small-Scale Sector. *IUP Journal of Entrepreneurship Development, 9*(2).

Kumar, M., & Sharma, R. (2018). Psychological Safety: A Literature Review. *International Journal of Business and Management, 13*(1), 6–20.

Kumar, R., & Shukla, S. (2022). Creativity, proactive personality and entrepreneurial intentions: Examining the mediating role of entrepreneurial self-efficacy. *Global Business Review, 23*(1), 101–118. doi:10.1177/0972150919844395

Kumar, S. (2018). Psychological safety and team effectiveness: The mediating role of trust. *International Journal of Business and Behavioural Sciences, 8*(3), 34–44.

Kumar, V., & Pansari, A. (2016). Competitive advantage through engagement. *JMR, Journal of Marketing Research, 53*(4), 497–514. doi:10.1509/jmr.15.0044

Kuo, C., Ye, Y., Chen, M., & Chen, L. (2019). Proactive personality enhances change in employees' job satisfaction: The moderating role of psychological safety. *Australian Journal of Management, 44*(3), 482–494. doi:10.1177/0312896218818225

Kuratko, D. F., Fisher, G., & Audretsch, D. B. (2021). Unraveling the entrepreneurial mindset. *Small Business Economics, 57*(4), 1681–1691. doi:10.100711187-020-00372-6

Kurten, B. (2017). Poland's Transformation. Routledge.

Kusumawijaya, I. K., & Astuti, P. D. (2021). Mediating role of entrepreneurial competencies: Influence of personality traits on entrepreneurial intention. *Problems and Perspectives in Management, 19*(3), 211–220. doi:10.21511/ppm.19(3).2021.18

Kyngäs, H. (2019). Qualitative Research and Content Analysis. *The Application of Content Analysis in Nursing Science Research.* . doi:10.1007/978-3-030-30199-6_1

Labrague, L. J., & De los Santos, J. A. A. (2020). COVID-19 anxiety among front-line nurses: Predictive role of organisational support, personal resilience, and social support. *Journal of Nursing Management, 28*(7), 1653–1661. doi:10.1111/jonm.13121 PMID:32770780

Laengle, S., Merigó, J. M., Modak, N. M., & Yang, J. B. (2020). Bibliometrics in operations research and management science: A university analysis. *Annals of Operations Research, 294*(1–2), 769–813. doi:10.100710479-018-3017-6

Lamboglia, R., Lavorato, D., Scornavacca, E., & Za, S. (2021). Exploring the relationship between audit and technology. A bibliometric analysis. *Meditari Accountancy Research, 29*(5), 1233–1260. doi:10.1108/MEDAR-03-2020-0836

Landes, D. (1949). French Entrepreneurship and Industrial Growth in the Nineteenth Century. *Journal of Economic History, 9, 45-61.* doi:10.1017/S002205070009032X

Landes, D. S. (2003). *The unbound Prometheus: technological change and industrial development in Western Europe from 1750 to the present.* Cambridge University Press. doi:10.1017/CBO9780511819957

Lansberg, I. (1999). *Succeeding Generations: Realizing the Dream of Families in Business.* Academic Press.

Larsson, M., Milestad, R., Hahn, T., & Von Oelreich, J. (2016). The resilience of a sustainability entrepreneur in the Swedish food system. *Sustainability (Basel), 8*(6), 550. doi:10.3390u8060550

Latack, J. C., Kinicki, A. J., & Prussia, G. E. (1995). An integrative process model of coping with job loss. *Academy of Management Review, 20*(2), 311–342. doi:10.2307/258849

Layan, S. (2020). *The Benefits of Psychological Safety and Team Building*. Retrieved April 10, 2021, from https://www.g2.com/hr/psychological-safety-and-team-building

Lazarus, R. S. (1991). Progress on a cognitive-motivational-relational theory of emotion. *The American Psychologist, 46*(8), 819–834. doi:10.1037/0003-066X.46.8.819 PMID:1928936

Le Breton–Miller, I., & Miller, D. (2006). Why do some family businesses out–compete? Governance, long–term orientations, and sustainable capability. *Entrepreneurship Theory and Practice, 30*(6), 731–746. doi:10.1111/j.1540-6520.2006.00147.x

Le Thi BaoQ.BlischkeJ.RoyM.SadikogluF.GwendolineA. (2020, February 11). *The role offamily involvement in the entrepreneurial business.* doi:10.2139/ssrn.3783758

Lechat, T., & Torrès, O. (2017). Stressors and satisfactors in entrepreneurial activity: An event-based, mixed methods study predicting small business owners' health. *International Journal of Entrepreneurship and Small Business, 32*(4), 537–569. doi:10.1504/IJESB.2017.087838

Lee, H., Choi, J. N., & Kim, S. (2018). Does gender diversity help teams constructively manage status conflict? an evolutionary perspective of status conflict, team psychological safety, and team creativity. *Organizational Behavior and Human Decision Processes, 144*, 187–199. doi:10.1016/j.obhdp.2017.09.005

Lee, J. W., Choi, Y. S., & Choi, J. N. (2010). Psychological safety and trust in organisations. *The Journal of Psychology, 144*(3), 215–233.

Lee, K., Hyun, S., Park, H., & Kim, K. (2020). The antecedents and consequences of psychological safety in airline firms: Focusing on high-quality interpersonal relationships. *International Journal of Environmental Research and Public Health, 17*(7), 2187. doi:10.3390/ijerph17072187 PMID:32218262

Lee, M.-S., & Rogoff, E. G. (1996). Research note: Comparison of small businesses with family participation versus small businesses without family participation: An investigation of differences in goals, attitudes, and family/business conflict. *Family Business Review, 9*(4), 423–437. doi:10.1111/j.1741-6248.1996.00423.x

Lee, P. C., Wu, Y. Y., Tsai, Y. P., & Chen, Y. J. (2012). The effects of psychological safety on team effectiveness: A study of software development teams in Taiwan. *IEEE Transactions on Software Engineering, 38*(3), 644–657.

Leicht-Deobald, U., Lam, C., Bruch, H., Kunze, F., & Wu, W. (2022). Team boundary work and team workload demands: Their interactive effect on team vigor and team effectiveness. *Human Resource Management, 61*(4), 465–488. doi:10.1002/hrm.22104

Leonidou, L. C., Eteokleous, P. P., Christodoulides, P., & Eduardsen, J. S. (2023). A dynamic capabilities perspective to socially responsible family business: Implications on social-based advantage and market performance. *Journal of Business Research, 155*, 113390. doi:10.1016/j.jbusres.2022.113390

Lerner, D. A., Hunt, R. A., & Dimov, D. (2018). Action! Moving beyond the intendedly rational logics of entrepreneurship. *Journal of Business Venturing, 33*(1), 52–69. doi:10.1016/j.jbusvent.2017.10.002

Li & Nazrul. (2021). Entrepreneurial Intentions and Family Support: A Study of Chinese University Students. *Journal of Entrepreneurship, 13*, 2-23.

Li, Y., Cao, Y., & Li, D. (2015). *The mechanism of the impact of team climate and team psychological safety on team innovation performance*. doi:10.2991/msmi-15.2015.38

Liang, Y., & Wang, M. (2016). The moderating role of psychological safety on job insecurity and organisational commitment. *International Journal of Human Resource Management, 27*(1), 88–101. doi:10.1080/09585192.2015.1025158

Liao, H., Rupp, D. E., & Wu, A. (2005). The joint effects of psychological contract breach and organisational justice on employee turnover intentions. *The Journal of Applied Psychology, 90*(3), 534–543.

Liew, A. (2013). DIKIW: Data, information, knowledge, intelligence, wisdom and their interrelationships. *Business Management Dynamics, 2*(10).

Liñán, F., & Chen, Y. W. (2009). Development and cross–cultural application of a specific instrument to measure entrepreneurial intentions. *Entrepreneurship Theory and Practice, 33*(3), 593–617. doi:10.1111/j.1540-6520.2009.00318.x

Lindgren, B., Lundman, B., & Graneheim, U. (2020). Abstraction and interpretation during the qualitative content analysis process. *International Journal of Nursing Studies, 108*, 103632. doi:10.1016/j.ijnurstu.2020.103632 PMID:32505813

Lingappa, A. K., Shah, A., & Mathew, A. O. (2020). Academic, family, and peer influence on entrepreneurial intention of engineering students. *SAGE Open, 10*(3). Advance online publication. doi:10.1177/2158244020933877

Ling-hsing, C., & Tung-Chin, L. (2015). The role of organizational culture in the knowledge management process. *Journal of Knowledge Management, 19*(3), 433–455. doi:10.1108/JKM-08-2014-0353

Ling, Y. (2020). Unlocking creativity in teams: A review of the literature. *Creativity Research Journal, 32*(1), 48–63. doi:10.1080/10400419.2020.1727155

Linnenluecke, M. K., Griffiths, A., & Winn, M. (2012). Extreme weather events and the critical importance of anticipatory adaptation and organizational resilience in responding to impacts. *Business Strategy and the Environment*, *21*(1), 17–32. doi:10.1002/bse.708

Lin, Q., & Wen, J. J. (2021). Family Business, Resilience, and Ethnic Tourism in Yunnan, China. *Sustainability (Basel)*, *13*(21), 11799. doi:10.3390u132111799

Liu, D., Li, Y., & Liu, Y. (2019). Effects of psychological safety on team creativity and creative work quality: The moderating role of team reflexivity. *Creativity Research Journal*, *31*(1), 83–90.

Liu, W., Zhang, P., Liao, J., Hao, P., & Mao, J. (2016). Abusive supervision and employee creativity. *Management Decision*, *54*(1), 130–147. doi:10.1108/MD-09-2013-0443

Liu, Y., & Hu, H. (2013). The role of psychological safety in predicting employees' turnover intentions. *Human Resource Management*, *53*(2), 265–279.

Liu, Z., Venkatesh, S., Murphy, S. E., & Riggio, R. E. (2021). Leader development across the lifespan: A dynamic experiences-grounded approach. *The Leadership Quarterly*, *32*(5), 101382.

Li, Z., & Islam, A. A. (2021). Entrepreneurial intention in higher vocational education: An empirically-based model with implications for the entrepreneurial community. *SAGE Open*, *11*(4). doi:10.1177/21582440211059179

Li, Z., Mirko, C., D'Agostino, M. T., & Jin, J. (2023). Comparative analysis of the influence of Chinese urban and rural family cultures on household financial asset allocation. *Frontiers in Psychology*, *14*, 1119258. doi:10.3389/fpsyg.2023.1119258 PMID:36844357

Llanos-Herrera, G. R., & Merigo, J. M. (2019). Overview of brand personality research with bibliometric indicators. *Kybernetes*, *48*(3), 546–569. doi:10.1108/K-02-2018-0051

López-García, X., Costa-Sánchez, C., & Vizoso, Á. (2021). Journalistic fact-checking of information in pandemic: Stakeholders, hoaxes, and strategies to fight disinformation during the COVID-19 crisis in Spain. *International Journal of Environmental Research and Public Health*, *18*(3), 1227. doi:10.3390/ijerph18031227 PMID:33573013

Luksyte, A., & Spitzmueller, C. (2015). When are overqualified employees creative? it depends on contextual factors. *Journal of Organizational Behavior*, *37*(5), 635–653. doi:10.1002/job.2054

Lumpkin, G. T., Brigham, K. H., & Moss, T. W. (2010). Long-term orientation: Implications for the entrepreneurial orientation and performance of family businesses. *Entrepreneurship and Regional Development*, *22*(3–4), 241–264. doi:10.1080/08985621003726218

Lunenburg, F. C. (2010, September). The decision-making process. *National Forum of Educational Administration & Supervision Journal, 27*(4).

Luthans, F., & Ibrayeva, E. S. (2006). Entrepreneurial self-efficacy in Central Asian transition economies: Quantitative and qualitative analyses. *Journal of International Business Studies*, *37*(1), 92–110. doi:10.1057/palgrave.jibs.8400173

Luthans, F., Vogelgesang, G. R., & Lester, P. B. (2006). Developing the psychological capital of resiliency. *Human Resource Development Review*, *5*(1), 25–44. doi:10.1177/1534484305285335

Lyapuntsova, E., Belozerova, Y., Drozdova, I., Afanas'ev, G., & Okunkova, E. (2018). Entrepreneurial risks in the realities of the digital economy. In *MATEC Web of Conferences* (Vol. 251, p. 06032). EDP Sciences. 10.1051/matecconf/201825106032

Mack, D. A., & McGee, J. E. (2001). *Occupational stress and the small business owner: The role of task complexity and social support.* In USASBE/SBIDA, 2001 Conference, Orlando, FL. Available at: http://usasbe. org/knowledge/proceedings/proceedingsDocs/USASBE2001proceedings-045. pdf

Madjar, N., & Ortiz-Walters, R. (2009). Trust in supervisors and trust in customers: Their independent, relative, and joint effects on employee performance and creativity. *Human Performance*, *22*(2), 128–142. doi:10.1080/08959280902743501

Madsen, I. E., Nyberg, S. T., Hanson, L. M., Ferrie, J. E., Ahola, K., Alfredsson, L., & ... IPD-Work Consortium. (2017). Job strain as a risk factor for clinical depression: Systematic review and meta-analysis with additional individual participant data. *Psychological Medicine*, *47*(8), 1342–1356. doi:10.1017/S003329171600355X PMID:28122650

Magrelli, V., Rovelli, P., Benedetti, C., Überbacher, R., & De Massis, A. (2022). Generations in family business: A multifield review and future research agenda. *Family Business Review*, *35*(1), 15–44. doi:10.1177/08944865211069781

Mahdi, O. R., Nassar, I. A., & Almsafir, M. K. (2019). Knowledge management processes and sustainable competitive advantage: An empirical examination in private universities. *Journal of Business Research*, *94*, 320–334. doi:10.1016/j.jbusres.2018.02.013

Maheshwari, G., Kha, K. L., & Arokiasamy, A. R. A. (2022). *Factors affecting students' entrepreneurial intentions: a systematic review (2005 – 2022) for future directions in theory and practice*. Management Review Quarterly. doi:10.100711301-022-00289-2

Mahfudzi, A. A. B. & Fitri, R. (2022). *The Influence of Family Environment on Generation Z's Entrepreneurial Intention through Self-Efficacy*. Academic Press.

Mahfudzi, A. A. B., & Fitri, R. (2022). *The Influence of Family Environment on Generation Z's Entrepreneurial Intention through Self-Efficacy*. Academic Press.

Mahomed, Y., & Mtembu, V. (2021). Business succession in Indian family businesses in South Africa. *Journal of Economics and Behavioral Studies*, *13*(3(J)), 73–80. doi:10.22610/jebs.v13i3(J).3182

Ma, L., Shao, Y., & Li, H. (2019). An empirical study on the relationship between psychological contract and job satisfaction of the cenozioc employees. *Open Journal of Social Sciences*, *07*(10), 105–120. doi:10.4236/jss.2019.710010

Mala, I. K., Pratikto, H., & Winarno, A. (2019). The effect of family environment, entrepreneurship education and self-efficacy on entrepreneurial intention in Pondok Pesantren at throughout Malang, Indonesia. *International Journal of Business, Economics, and Law, 20*(5), 112–119.

Malik, A., Sharma, P., Vinu, A., Karakoti, A., Kaur, K., Gujral, H. S., Munjal, S., & Laker, B. (2022). Circular economy adoption by SMEs in emerging markets: Towards a multilevel conceptual framework. *Journal of Business Research, 142*, 605–619. doi:10.1016/j.jbusres.2021.12.076

Mannix, E., & Neale, M. (2005). What differences make a difference? The promise and reality of diverse teams in organisational settings. *Psychological Science in the Public Interest, 6*(2), 31–55. doi:10.1111/j.1529-1006.2005.00022.x PMID:26158478

Manyaka, S. J. (2015). Social entrepreneurship: A solution for transforming the disadvantaged community of Nellmapius. *Hervormde Teologiese Studies, 71*(3), 1–7. doi:10.4102/hts.v71i3.2821

Manzano García, G., & Ayala Calvo, J. C. (2013). Psychometric properties of Connor-Davidson Resilience Scale in a Spanish sample of entrepreneurs. *Psicothema*. PMID:23628541

Marks, S. R. (1977). Multiple roles and role strain: Some notes on human energy, time, and commitment. *American Sociological Review, 42*(6), 921–936. doi:10.2307/2094577

Marschall, J., Hildebrandt, S., Zich, K., Tisch, T., Sorensen, J., & Nolting, H.-D. (2018). *DAK Health Report 2018*. DAK-Forschung.

Marshall, D. R., Meek, W. R., Swab, R. G., & Markin, E. (2020). Access to resources and entrepreneurial well-being: A self-efficacy approach. *Journal of Business Research, 120*, 203–212. doi:10.1016/j.jbusres.2020.08.015

Masè, S., & Masè, S. (2020). Art and Cross-Cultural Business. *Art and Business: Perspectives on Art-Based Management*, 99-112.

Masocha, R., & Fatoki, O. (2018). The impact of coercive pressures on sustainability practices of small businesses in South Africa. *Sustainability (Basel), 10*(9), 3032. doi:10.3390u10093032

Mason, J. W. (1968). A review of psychoendocrine research on the pituitary-adrenal cortical system. *Psychosomatic Medicine, 30*(5), 576–607. doi:10.1097/00006842-196809000-00020 PMID:4303377

Mason, P. (2017). Identifying the barriers to female leadership in Paramedicine. *Irish Journal of Paramedicine, 2*(1). Advance online publication. doi:10.32378/ijp.v2i1.55

Mas-Tur, A., Modak, N. M., Merigó, J. M., Roig-Tierno, N., Geraci, M., & Capecchi, V. (2019). Half a century of Quality & Quantity: A bibliometric review. *Quality & Quantity, 53*(2), 981–1020. doi:10.100711135-018-0799-1

Matias, C., & Franco, M. (2021). The role of the family council and protocol in planning the succession process in family firms. *Journal of Family Business Management, 11*(4), 440–461. doi:10.1108/JFBM-01-2020-0004

Matthew. (2021). Family values and success of the family business. *Forbes Money/Wealth Management.* Forbes.com/sites/matthewerskine/2021/02/17family-values.

Ma, X., Li, Y., Li, S., & Zou, S. (2020). The mediating role of job satisfaction in the relationship between psychological safety and organisational commitment. *International Journal of Environmental Research and Public Health, 17*(7), 2470. doi:10.3390/ijerph17072470 PMID:32260388

McBride, K. A., MacMillan, F., George, E. S., & Steiner, G. Z. (2019). *The use of mixed methods in research.* Academic Press.

McDaid, D. (2008). Mental Health in Workplace Settings. Consensus Paper. European Commission, Directorate General for Health, and Consumers.

McGee, J. E., Peterson, M., Mueller, S. L., & Sequeira, J. M. (2009). Entrepreneurial self–efficacy: Refining the measure. *Entrepreneurship Theory and Practice, 33*(4), 965–988. doi:10.1111/j.1540-6520.2009.00304.x

McGrath, J. E. (1970). *Social and psychological factors of stress.* Holt, Rinehart, & Winston.

McGuier, E., Kolko, D. J., Stadnick, N. A., Brookman-Frazee, L., Wolk, C. B., Yuan, C. T., Burke, C. S., & Aarons, G. A. (2023). Advancing research on teams and team effectiveness in implementation science: An application of the exploration, preparation, implementation, sustainment (epis) framework. *Implementation Research and Practice, 4.* Advance online publication. doi:10.1177/26334895231190855 PMID:37790168

McKinsey. (2021). *Business and work in a post-pandemic future.* https://www.mckinsey.com/featured-insights/coronavirus-leading-through-the-crisis

Mehmood, M., Jian, Z., Akram, U., Akram, Z., & Tanveer, Y. (2021). Entrepreneurial leadership and team creativity: The roles of team psychological safety and knowledge sharing. *Personnel Review, 51*(9), 2404–2425. doi:10.1108/PR-07-2020-0517

Menges, J. I., Tussing, D. V., Wihler, A., & Grant, A. M. (2017). When job performance is all relative: How family motivation energizes effort and compensates for intrinsic motivation. *Academy of Management Journal, 60*(2), 695–719. doi:10.5465/amj.2014.0898

Meroka, M. R. (2023). Role of the family in fostering student's entrepreneurial intention. In M. Mohiuddin, M. N. H. Reza, E. Hosseini, & S. Ed-Dafali (Eds.), *Entrepreneurship – New insights.* IntechOpen. doi:10.5772/intechopen.110026

Miki, M. (2019). How organisations waste real talent without realising. *Governance Directions, 71*(10), 591–594.

Miles, M. P., Lewis, G. K., Hall-Phillips, A., Morrish, S. C., Gilmore, A., & Kasouf, C. J. (2016). The influence of entrepreneurial marketing processes and entrepreneurial self-efficacy on community vulnerability, risk, and resilience. *Journal of Strategic Marketing, 24*(1), 34–46. doi:10.1080/0965254X.2015.1035038

Miller, D., & Le Breton-Miller, I. (2005). *Managing for the long run: Lessons in competitive advantage from great family businesses*. Harvard Business Press.

Miller, D., Le Breton-Miller, I., Lester, R. H., & Cannella, A. A. Jr. (2007). Are family firms really superior performers? *Journal of Corporate Finance*, *13*(5), 829–858. doi:10.1016/j.jcorpfin.2007.03.004

Minola, T., Kammerlander, N., Kellermanns, F. W., & Hoy, F. (2021). Corporate entrepreneurship and family business: Learning across domains. *Journal of Management Studies*, *58*(1), 1–26. doi:10.1111/joms.12672

Mirjana, P. B., Ana, A., & Marjana, M. S. (2018). Examining determinants of entrepreneurial intentions in Slovenia: Applying the theory of planned behaviour and an innovative cognitive style. *Ekonomska Istrazivanja*, *31*(1), 1453–1471. doi:10.1080/1331677X.2018.1478321

Mobley, W. H., & Dorfman, P. W. (2003). *Advances in global leadership*. JAI An imprint of Elsevier Science.

Moin, M. F., Omar, M. K., Wei, F., Rasheed, M. I., & Hameed, Z. (2021). Green HRM and psychological safety: How transformational leadership drives follower's job satisfaction. *Current Issues in Tourism*, *24*(16), 2269–2277. doi:10.1080/13683500.2020.1829569

Mokgaabalone, M. B. (1999). Social- cultural conditions, teenage pregnancy and schooling disruptions: Themes from teachers and teenage in "poor rural" Schools. *South African Journal of Education*, *19*(1), 191–237.

Molina, J. A. (2020). Family and entrepreneurship: New empirical and theoretical results. *Journal of Family and Economic Issues*, *41*(1), 1–3. doi:10.100710834-020-09667-y

Molino, M., Dolce, V., Cortese, C. G., & Ghislieri, C. (2018). Personality and social support as determinants of entrepreneurial intention. Gender differences in Italy. *PLoS One*, *13*(6), e0199924. doi:10.1371/journal.pone.0199924 PMID:29953517

Montag, T., Maertz, C. Jr, & Baer, M. (2012). A critical analysis of the workplace creativity criterion space. *Journal of Management*, *38*(4), 1362–1386. doi:10.1177/0149206312441835

Moonga, G. M. (2015). *Challenges faced by teen mothers who re-entered School: A case of selected Schools on the Copper belt Province of Zambia* [Doctoral dissertation].

Mora, L. & Viana, M. (1993). *Abundance of strange attractors*. Academic Press.

Mora, L., & Viana, M. (1993). *Abundance of strange attractors*. Academic Press.

Morales-Gualdrón, S. T., & Roig, S. (2005). The new venture decision: An analysis based on the GEM project database. *The International Entrepreneurship and Management Journal*, *1*(4), 479–499. doi:10.100711365-005-4774-7

Morck, R., & Yeung, B. (2002). *Family control and the rent-seeking society*. Paper presented at the 2002 Theories of the Family Enterprise Conference, Wharton Business School, Philadelphia, PA.

Moreno, J. E. (2023). How Rupert Murdoch built his media empire. *The New York Times*. Available: https://www.nytimes.com/2023/09/21/business/rupert-murdoch-media-empire.html

Morgan, H. (2022). Conducting a Qualitative Document Analysis. *Qualitative Report*, *27*(1), 20–34.

Moroz, P. W., & Hindle, K. (2012). Entrepreneurship as a process: Toward harmonizing multiple perspectives. *Entrepreneurship Theory and Practice*, *36*(4), 781–818. doi:10.1111/j.1540-6520.2011.00452.x

Morsing, M., & Schultz, M. (2006). Corporate social responsibility communication: Stakeholder information, response and involvement strategies. *Business Ethics (Oxford, England)*, *15*(4), 323–338. doi:10.1111/j.1467-8608.2006.00460.x

Mosolygó-Kiss, Á., Heidrich, B., & Chandler, N. (2023). Knowing me, knowing you: A study of the types of knowledge transferred during the succession process in intra-family takeover of family businesses in Hungary. *Journal for East European Management Studies*, *28*(1), 94–120. doi:10.5771/0949-6181-2023-1-94

Mourougane, A. (2012). *Promoting SME development in Indonesia*. OECD Economics Department Working Papers, No. 995, OECD Publishing. doi:10.1787/18151973

Moussa, N. B., & Kerkeni, S. (2021). The role of family environment in developing the entrepreneurial intention of young Tunisian students. *Entrepreneurial Business and Economics Review*, *9*(1), 31–46. doi:10.15678/EBER.2021.090102

Moya-Clemente, I., Ribes-Giner, G., & Pantoja-Díaz, O. (2019). Configurations of sustainable development goals that promote sustainable entrepreneurship over time. *Sustainable Development (Bradford)*, *28*(4), 572–584. doi:10.1002d.2009

Mthuli, S. A., Ruffin, F., & Singh, N. (2022). 'Define, Explain, Justify, Apply'(DEJA): An analytic tool for guiding qualitative research sample size. *International Journal of Social Research Methodology*, *25*(6), 809–821. doi:10.1080/13645579.2021.1941646

Mubecua, M. A., & David, O. J. (2019). So far so good? Tracking the poverty eradication goal of SDGs in Kenya, Nigeria, and South Africa. *Journal of Public Affairs*, *19*(4), e1964. doi:10.1002/pa.1964

Muhtarom, M., & Suyatno, A. (2018). The influence of family environment and entrepreneurship learning on technopreneurship intentions of computer science management students. *Journal of Research and Community Service*, *4*(1), 1–8.

Muhumed, Z., Bodolica, V., & Spraggon, M. (2017). Inside an African family business estate: The founder's legacy and the successor's dilemma. *Emerald Emerging Markets Case Studies*, *7*(3), 1–28. doi:10.1108/EEMCS-01-2017-0012

Muller, A., Turner, N., & van der Heijden, B. I. J. M. (2016). Psychological safety, risk taking and innovation in teams: An empirical study. *International Journal of Innovation Management*, *20*(1), 1640001.

Mulyani, S. R., Sari, V. N., & Sari, M. W. (2019). The model of employee motivation and cooperative employee performance. *Polish Journal of Management Studies*, *20*(2), 379–390. doi:10.17512/pjms.2019.20.2.32

Muralidharan, E., & Pathak, S. (2018). Sustainability, transformational leadership, and social entrepreneurship. *Sustainability (Basel)*, *10*(2), 1–22. doi:10.3390u10020567

Musk, E. & Nagelhout, R. (2015). *Elon Musk, AV2 by Weigl*. Academic Press.

Musungwa, T., & Kowe, P. (2022). Effects of occupational health and safety management systems implementation in accident prevention at a Harare beverage company. *Cogent Engineering*, *9*(1), 2124638. doi:10.1080/23311916.2022.2124638

Mwansa, A. (2011). *Re-entry to school after giving birth: An evaluation of the process used to design and implement policy in Zambia*. Create pathways to access, research monograph no.70.

Mycoskie, B. (2011). *Start something that matters*. Random House.

Narva, R. L. (2001). Heritage and tradition in family business: how family-controlled enterprises connect the experience of their past to the promise of their future. In G. K. McCann & N. Upton (Eds.), *Destroying Myths and Creating Value in Family Business* (pp. 29–38). Stetson University.

Nasurdin, A. M., Ramayah, T., & Beng, Y. C. (2006). Organizational structure and organizational climate as potential predictors of job stress: Evidence from Malaysia. *International Journal of Commerce and Management*, *16*(2), 116–128. doi:10.1108/10569210680000211

Negreira-Rey, M.-C., Vázquez-Herrero, J., & López-García, X. (2022). Blurring boundaries between journalists and tiktokers: Journalistic role performance on TikTok. *Media and Communication*, *10*(1), 146–156. doi:10.17645/mac.v10i1.4699

Neider, L. L., & Schriesheim, C. A. (2011). The authentic leadership inventory (ALI): Development and empirical tests. *The Leadership Quarterly*, *22*(6), 1146–1164. doi:10.1016/j.leaqua.2011.09.008

Neneh, B. (2020). Entrepreneurial self-efficacy and a student's predisposition to choose an entrepreneurial career path: The role of self-perceived employability. *Education + Training*, *62*(5), 559–580. doi:10.1108/ET-06-2019-0108

Neubauer, F., & Lank, A. G. (2016). *The family business: Its governance for sustainability*. Springer.

Neubaum, D. O., Thomas, C. H., Dibrell, C., & Craig, J. B. (2017). Stewardship climate scale: An assessment of reliability and validity. *Family Business Review*, *30*(1), 37–60. doi:10.1177/0894486516673701

Neumann, T. (2021). The impact of entrepreneurship on economic, social and environmental welfare and its determinants: A systematic review. *Management Review Quarterly*, *71*(3), 553–584. doi:10.100711301-020-00193-7

Newman, A., Donohue, R., & Eva, N. (2017). Psychological safety: A systematic review of the literature. *Human Resource Management Review*, *27*(3), 521–535. doi:10.1016/j.hrmr.2017.01.001

Newman, A., Obschonka, M., Schwarz, S., Cohen, M., & Nielsen, I. (2019). Entrepreneurial self-efficacy: A systematic review of the literature on its theoretical foundations, measurement, antecedents, and outcomes, and an agenda for future research. *Journal of Vocational Behavior, 110*, 403–419. doi:10.1016/j.jvb.2018.05.012

Ngat, T. T., & Tuyet, L. T. K. (2023). The factors affecting entrepreneurial intention with self confidence as a moderator-based on elderly people as an example. *International Journal of Professional Business Review, 8*(6), e02125. doi:10.26668/businessreview/2023.v8i6.2125

Ngoasheng, C., Ngoepe, M., & Marutha, N. S. (2022). Sounds like a broken record: Preservation and access of audio-visual records at the South African broadcasting corporation radio. *Global Knowledge. Memory and Communication, 71*(4/5), 383–397. doi:10.1108/GKMC-11-2020-0185

Nguyen, C. (2015). Entrepreneurial intention in Vietnam: same as everywhere? SSRN *Electronic Journal.* doi:10.2139/ssrn.3906124

Nguyen, C. (2017). Entrepreneurial intention of international business students in Viet Nam: A survey of the country joining the Trans-Pacific Partnership. *Journal of Innovation and Entrepreneurship, 6*(1), 7. doi:10.118613731-017-0066-z

Nguyen, T. H. (2016). Impact of export on economic growth in Vietnam: Empirical research and recommendations. *International Business Management, 13*(3), 45–52.

Nielsen, K., & Einarsen, S. (2008). Perceived psychological safety and job satisfaction among offshore safety personnel. *Safety Science*. doi:10.21776/ub.jam.2021.019.02.06

Nonaka, I., & Takeuchi, H. (1995). The knowledge creating. Academic Press.

Nonaka, I. (1994). A dynamic theory of organizational knowledge creation. *Organization Science, 5*(1), 14–37. doi:10.1287/orsc.5.1.14

Noor, Y. M., Hong, L. M., Zakaria, A. N. B. I., Nik Mud, N. N. B., & Yunoh, M. N. M. (2019). The factors influencing small medium enterprise (SMEs) success in Kelantan. *International Journal of Innovation. Creativity and Change, 6*(3), 55–64.

Norena-Chavez, D., & Guevara, R. (2020). *Entrepreneurial passion and self-efficacy as factors explaining innovative behavior: A Mediation Model*. Academic Press.

Northouse, P. (2019). *Leadership: Theory and Practice* (8th ed.). Sage.

Nosé, L., Korunka, C., Frank, H., & Danes, S. M. (2017). Decreasing the effects of relationship conflict on family businesses: The moderating role of family climate. *Journal of Family Issues, 38*(1), 25–51. doi:10.1177/0192513X15573869

O'Donovan, R., & McAuliffe, E. (2020). A systematic review exploring the content and outcomes of interventions to improve psychological safety, speaking up and voice behaviour. *BMC Health Services Research, 20*(1), 101. Advance online publication. doi:10.118612913-020-4931-2 PMID:32041595

O'Donovan, R., & McAuliffe, E. (2020). Exploring psychological safety in healthcare teams to inform the development of interventions: Combining observational, survey and interview data. *BMC Health Services Research*, *20*(1), 810. Advance online publication. doi:10.118612913-020-05646-z PMID:32867762

O'Leary, V. E., Jones, D. A., & Mitchell, R. (2012). Communication as a critical component of successful teams: A review and integration. In A. O'Leary-Kelly, J. E. Mathieu, & R. C. Richard (Eds.), *The Oxford Handbook of Organisational Psychology* (Vol. 2, pp. 476–497). Oxford University Press.

Oakes, G. (2003). Max Weber on value rationality and value spheres: Critical remarks. *Journal of Classical Sociology*, *3*(1), 27–45. doi:10.1177/1468795X03003001693

Obraztsova, O., & Chepurenko, A. (2010). *Entrepreneurship and socio-economic development in cross-countries analysis. In Strategic Entrepreneurship: The promise for future entrepreneurship, family business and SME research.* KMU Verlag HSG.

Ochiai, E. (2014). Leaving the West, rejoining the East? Gender and family in Japan's semi-compressed modernity. *International Sociology*, *29*(3), 209–228. doi:10.1177/0268580914530415

OECD & European Commission. (2018). *Health at a Glance: Europe 2018. State of Health in the EU Cycle*. OECD Publishing.

OgbeA. (2020). The travails of women and girls in Northern Nigeria: A human rights issue. Available at SSRN 3599122.

Ogunode, N. J., & Adanna, C. M. (2022). An Analysis of Factors Responsible for High Out of School Children in Nigeria and Way Forward. *International Journal on Integrated Education*, *5*(6), 194–202.

Ogwu, E. N. (2023). Challenges in implementing entrepreneurship education (ee) for youth's empowerment at the post-basic education level in Nigeria. *International Journal of Studies in Education*, *16*(1), 209–219.

Okehi, F. (2019). Adopting new strategies in social entrepreneurial education: A panacea to the daunting challenges of the 21st century entrepreneurs (sociological approach). In M. A. Mkpa, Compendium of curriculum theorizing, development, designing & innovation in Nigeria (pp. 703-707). Owerri: C @ J Publishers.

Okoli, C. I., Hajizadeh, M., Rahman, M. M., Velayutham, E., & Khanam, R. (2022). Socioeconomic inequalities in teenage pregnancy in Nigeria: Evidence from Demographic Health Survey. *BMC Public Health*, *22*(1), 1–11. doi:10.118612889-022-14146-0 PMID:36096790

Okolie, U. C., Ehiobuche, C., Igwe, P. A., Agha-Okoro, M. A., & Onwe, C. C. (2021). Women entrepreneurship and poverty alleviation: Understanding the economic and socio-cultural context of the Igbo women's basket weaving enterprise in Nigeria. *Journal of African Business*, *22*(4), 448–467. doi:10.1080/15228916.2021.1874781

Okpara, F. O. (2000). *Entrepreneurship: Test and Cases*. Precision Printers and Publishers.

Olofinyehun, A., Egbetokun, A., & Adelowo, C. (2022). Pooled dataset on entrepreneurial characteristics of undergraduates in selected universities in Nigeria. *Data in Brief*, *40*, 107718. doi:10.1016/j.dib.2021.107718 PMID:34993285

Olowu, D. I., Ichoku, H. E., & Nwosu, E. O. (2018). Spatial distribution of poverty in multiple dimensions in Delta State of Nigeria. *Journal of Economics and Allied Research*, *2*(2), 32–44.

Olsen, D. C. (1993). *Integrative family therapy*. Fortress Press.

Orduña-Malea, E., & Costas, R. (2021). Link-based approach to study scientific software usage: The case of VOSviewer. *Scientometrics*, *126*(9), 8153–8186. doi:10.100711192-021-04082-y

Osunde, C. (2017). Family businesses and its impact on the economy. *Journal of Business & Financial Affairs*, *6*(1), 1–3. doi:10.4172/2167-0234.1000251

Otache, I., Umar, K., Audu, Y., & Onalo, U. (2021). The effects of entrepreneurship education on students' entrepreneurial intentions a longitudinal approach. *Education + Training*, *63*(7/8), 967–991. doi:10.1108/ET-01-2019-0005

Palmer, M. (1971). The application of psychological testing to entrepreneurial potential. *California Management Review*, *13*(3), 32–38. doi:10.2307/41164291

Pant, S. K. (2015). Role of the family in entrepreneurship development in Nepali society. *Journal of Nepalese Business Studies*, *9*(1), 37–47. doi:10.3126/jnbs.v9i1.14592

Pan, Y., Shang, Y., & Malika, R. (2020). Enhancing creativity in organisations: The role of the need for cognition. *Management Decision*, *59*(9), 2057–2076. doi:10.1108/MD-04-2019-0516

Parada, M. J., Samara, G., Dawson, A., & Bonet, E. (2020). Prosperity over time and across generations: The role of values and virtues in family businesses. *Journal of Organizational Change Management*, *33*(4), 639–654. doi:10.1108/JOCM-11-2018-0341

Paranata, A., Pahrudin, Muzayyanah, S., & Trinh, T. H. (2023). Identification of factors influencing entrepreneurial behavior: Unveiling start-up business initiatives in Indonesia. *Humanities & Social Sciences Communications*, *10*(407), 1–11. doi:10.105741599-023-01896-4

Paridon, H. (2016). *Psychosocial Demands in the Working World: A Literature Analysis on Health and Performance Relationships*. Initiative Gesundheit und Arbeit.

Park, Y. W., & Park, Y. J. (2021). Corporate Strategy for Corporate and Ecosystem Sustainability. *Corporate Social Responsibility and Entrepreneurship for Sustainability: Leading in the Era of Digital Transformation*, 71-79.

Park-Barjot, R. R. (2014). Samsung: An original case of knowledge transfer in economic organizations. *Entreprises et Histoire*, *75*(2), 91–101. doi:10.3917/eh.075.0091

Parker, H., & Ameen, K. (2018). The role of resilience capabilities in shaping how firms respond to disruptions. *Journal of Business Research*, *88*, 535–541. doi:10.1016/j.jbusres.2017.12.022

Patel, V. K., Pieper, T. M., & Hair, J. F., Jr. (2015, October). Opportunities and challenges for family businesses pursuing global markets. In *Thriving in a New World Economy: Proceedings of the 2012 World Marketing Congress/Cultural Perspectives in Marketing Conference* (pp. 24-29). Cham: Springer International Publishing.

Pattanayak, S., & Kakati, M. (2023). An empirical study on entrepreneurial traits and their impact on enterprise success. *Vilakshan-XIMB Journal of Management*, *20*(2), 277–291. doi:10.1108/XJM-09-2021-0249

Pattnaik, S., & Sahoo, R. (2020). Employee engagement, creativity and task performance: Role of perceived workplace autonomy. *South Asian Journal of Business Studies*, *10*(2), 227–241. doi:10.1108/SAJBS-11-2019-0196

Patzelt, H., & Shepherd, D. A. (2011). Negative emotions of an entrepreneurial career: Self-employment and regulatory coping behaviors. *Journal of Business Venturing*, *26*(2), 226–238. doi:10.1016/j.jbusvent.2009.08.002

Paudel, R., Khadka, S., Rai, J., & Singh, R. (2023). Psychological impact of COVID-19 pandemic and lockdown among the population involved in tourism sector in Lakeside of Pokhara: A qualitative study. *Health Science Reports*, *6*(7), e1382. doi:10.1002/hsr2.1382 PMID:37396562

Paul, J., & Criado, A. R. (2020). The art of writing literature review: What do we know and what do we need to know? *International Business Review*, *29*(4), 101717. doi:10.1016/j.ibusrev.2020.101717

Paul, J., & Rosado-Serrano, A. (2019). Gradual internationalization vs born-global/international new venture models: A review and research agenda. *International Marketing Review*, *36*(6), 830–858. doi:10.1108/IMR-10-2018-0280

Pearson, A. W., Carr, J. C., & Shaw, J. C. (2008). Toward a theory of familiness: A social capital perspective. *Entrepreneurship Theory and Practice*, *32*(6), 949–969. doi:10.1111/j.1540-6520.2008.00265.x

Peng, Z., Lu, G., & Kang, H. (2013). Entrepreneurial intentions and its influencing factors: A survey of the university students in Xi'an China. *Creative Education*, *3*(8), 95–100. doi:10.4236/ce.2012.38B021

Peralta, C., Lourenço, P., Lopes, P., Baptista, C., & Pais, L. (2018). Team development: Definition, measurement and relationships with team effectiveness. *Human Performance*, *31*(2), 97–124. doi:10.1080/08959285.2018.1455685

Pew Research Centre. (2020). *How the Coronavirus outbreak has changed the way we work.* https://www.pewresearch.org/social-trends/2020/12/09/how-the-coronavirus-outbreak-has-and-hasnt-changed-the-way-americans-work/

Pieper, T. M., Kellermanns, F. W., & Astrachan, J. H. (2021). Update 2021: Family businesses' contribution to the US economy. *Family Enterprise USA,* (704).

Pieper, T. M., & Klein, S. B. (2007). The bulleye: A systems approach to modeling family firms. *Family Business Review*, *20*(4), 301–319. doi:10.1111/j.1741-6248.2007.00101.x

Pieper, T. M., Klein, S. B., & Jaskiewicz, P. (2008). The impact of goal alignment on board existence and top management team composition: Evidence from family-influenced businesses. *Journal of Small Business Management*, *46*(3), 372–394. doi:10.1111/j.1540-627X.2008.00249.x

Pinquart, M., & Gerke, D. C. (2019). Associations of parenting styles with self-esteem in children and adolescents: A meta-analysis. *Journal of Child and Family Studies*, *28*(8), 2017–2035. doi:10.100710826-019-01417-5

Piperopoulos, P., & Dimov, D. (2015). Burst bubbles or build steam? Entrepreneurship education, entrepreneurial self-efficacy, and entrepreneurial intentions. *Journal of Small Business Management*, *53*(4), 970–985. doi:10.1111/jsbm.12116

Piprani, A. Z., Jaafar, N. I., & Mohezar Ali, S. (2020). Prioritizing resilient capability factors of dealing with supply chain disruptions: An analytical hierarchy process (AHP) application in the textile industry. *Benchmarking*, *27*(9), 2537–2563. doi:10.1108/BIJ-03-2019-0111

Pless, N. M. (2007). Understanding responsible leadership: Role identity and motivational drivers: The case of Dame Anita Roddick, founder of the Body Shop. *Journal of Business Ethics*, *74*(4), 437–456. doi:10.100710551-007-9518-x

Post, C., Sarala, R., Gatrell, C., & Prescott, J. E. (2020). Advancing Theory with Review Articles. *Journal of Management Studies*, *57*(2), 351–376. doi:10.1111/joms.12549

Powell, G. N., & Eddleston, K. A. (2013). Linking family-to-business enrichment and support to entrepreneurial success: Do female and male entrepreneurs experience different outcomes? *Journal of Business Venturing*, *28*(2), 261–280. doi:10.1016/j.jbusvent.2012.02.007

Powell, G. N., & Eddleston, K. A. (2017). Family involvement in the firm, family-to-business support, and entrepreneurial outcomes: An exploration. *Journal of Small Business Management*, *55*(4), 614–631. doi:10.1111/jsbm.12252

Poza, E. J. (2013). *Family business*. Cengage Learning.

Pratama, R., Nurlaila, N., & Nasution, M. L. I. (2023). The Influence of Workload, Work Stress, Organizational Culture, and Work Environment on Job Performance at Employees of PT. Bank Sumut Syariah Deli Serdang Area. *Indonesian Interdisciplinary Journal of Sharia Economics*, *6*(3), 1666–1686.

Prathap, S. K., & Sreelakshmi, C. C. (2020). Entrepreneurial learning and microcredit as triggers of micro-entrepreneurship in India. *Small Enterprises Development, Management & Extension Journal*, *47*(3), 194–212. doi:10.1177/09708464211037533

Pratt, M. K. (2018). Entrepreneur (entrepreneurship). *TechTarget*. https://www.techtarget.com/searchcio/definition/entrepreneur#:~:text=An%20entrepreneur%20is%20an%20individual,need%20as%20an%20economic%20opportunity.

Preisendörfer, P., & Voss, T. (1990). Organizational Mortality of Small Firms: The Effects of Entrepreneurial Age and Human Capital. *Organization Studies*, *11*(1), 107–112. doi:10.1177/017084069001100109

Prentice, S. (2022). Job satisfaction or employee engagement: Regardless of which comes first, supportive leadership improves them both. *Advances in Developing Human Resources*, *24*(4), 275–285. doi:10.1177/15234223221112504

Price, D. P., Stoica, M., & Boncella, R. J. (2013). The relationship between innovation, knowledge, and performance in family and non-family firms: An analysis of SMEs. *Journal of Innovation and Entrepreneurship*, *2*(1), 14. doi:10.1186/2192-5372-2-14

Primarolo, D & Merron, G. (2010). *Teenage Pregnancy Strategy: Beyond 2010*. Academic Press.

Pugh, G., & Adkins, P. (2020). Entrepreneurship education in China evidence from a preliminary. *Scoping Study University Students*, *12*(2), 305–326. doi:10.1108/JEEE-01-2019-0006

Purwatiningsih, Y., & Faisal, D. (2022). The influence of team cohesion and trust on team effectiveness in preventing tuberculosis. *Jurnal Administrasi Kesehatan Indonesia*, *10*(2), 188–196. doi:10.20473/jaki.v10i2.2022.188-196

Puspasari, D. (2023). The influence of family environment and entrepreneurship education on student self-efficacy. *Journal of Entrepreneurship Education*, *26*(2), 1–9.

Pütz, L., & Werner, A. (2023). Absorptive capacity in family firms: A systematic literature review. *Review of Managerial Science*, 1–56. doi:10.100711846-023-00651-y

Qi, Y., & Wu, J. (2023). Performance feedback, succession process and innovative activities of family firms: Evidence from China. *Asian Business & Management*, *22*(2), 765–791. doi:10.105741291-022-00192-4

Rachmawan, A., Lizar, A. A., & Mangundjaya, W. L. (2015). The role of parent's influence and self-efficacy on entrepreneurial intention. *Journal of Developing Areas*, *49*(3), 417–430. doi:10.1353/jda.2015.0157

Rae, D. (2010). Universities and enterprise education: Responding to the challenges of the new era. *Journal of Small Business and Enterprise Development*, *17*(4), 591–606. doi:10.1108/14626001011088741

Rafiei, S., Alizadeh, A., Aziziani, L., Borojeni, F. H., Vahdati, F., & Nejatifar, Z. (2022). The impact of business attitude on entrepreneurial behavior in postgraduate students: A cross-sectional study during the COVID-19 pandemic. *Journal of Health Reports and Technology*, *8*(1), 1–6. doi:10.5812/jhrt.119118

Rafiei, S., Mehrtak, M., Amerzadeh, M., Rafiei, S., Moosavi, S., & Kalhor, R. (2023). The relationship between succession and intellectual capital with entrepreneurship in hospitals. *BMC Health Services Research*, *23*(1), 1–8. doi:10.118612913-023-09435-2 PMID:37170204

Rahim, A. (1996). Stress, strain, and their moderators: An empirical comparison of entrepreneurs and managers. *Journal of Small Business Management*, *34*(1), 46–58.

Rahim, M. A. (2023). *Managing conflict in organizations*. Taylor & Francis. doi:10.4324/9781003285861

Rahman, H. (2009). Network deployment for social benefits in developing countries. In *Encyclopedia of Multimedia Technology and Networking* (2nd ed., pp. 1048–1054). IGI Global. doi:10.4018/978-1-60566-014-1.ch141

Rajan, B., Salunkhe, U., & Kumar, V. (2023). Understanding customer engagement in family firms: A conceptual framework. *Journal of Business Research*, *154*, 113342. doi:10.1016/j.jbusres.2022.113342

Ralat, J. R. (2020). *American Tacos: A History and Guide*. University of Texas Press. doi:10.7560/316528

Randerson, K. (2022). Conceptualizing family business social responsibility. *Technological Forecasting and Social Change*, *174*, 121225. doi:10.1016/j.techfore.2021.121225

Rapp, D. J., & Olbrich, M. (2020). On entrepreneurial decision logics under conditions of uncertainty: An attempt to advance the current debate. *Journal of Innovation and Entrepreneurship*, *9*(1), 1–9. doi:10.118613731-020-00131-7

Rastiti, M. S., Widjaja, S. U. M., & Handayati, P. (2021). The role of self-efficacy in mediating the effect of entrepreneurship education, economic literacy and family environment on entrepreneurial intentions for vocational school students in Jember Regency. *South East Asia Journal of Contemporary Business, Economics and Law, 24*(2), 26-42. https://seajbel.com/wp-content/uploads/2021/03/SEAJBEL24_511.pdf

Ratten, V., & Tajeddini, K. (2019). Entrepreneurship and sport business research: Synthesis and lessons: Introduction to the special journal issue. *International Journal of Sport Management and Marketing*, *19*(1), 1–7.

Rauch, A., Fink, M., & Hatak, I. (2018). Stress processes: An essential ingredient in the entrepreneurial process. *The Academy of Management Perspectives*, *32*(3), 340–357. doi:10.5465/amp.2016.0184

Rego, A., Sousa, F., Marques, C., & Cunha, M. (2012). Authentic leadership promoting employees' psychological capital and creativity. *Journal of Business Research*, *65*(3), 429–437. doi:10.1016/j.jbusres.2011.10.003

Renuka, V. V., & Marath, B. (2023). Impact of effective governance structure on succession process in the family business: Exploring the mediating role of management succession planning. *Rajagiri Management Journal*, *17*(1), 84–97. doi:10.1108/RAMJ-06-2021-0048

Rickley, M., & Stackhouse, M. (2022). Global leadership effectiveness: A multilevel review and exploration of the construct domain. *Advances in Global Leadership*, *14*, 87–123. doi:10.1108/S1535-120320220000014004

Rodriguez Serna, L., Bowyer, D. M., & Gregory, S. K. (2023). Management control systems. A non-family stakeholder perspective on the critical success factors influencing continuous stakeholder support during businesses succession. *Journal of Small Business and Enterprise Development*, *30*(2), 290–310. doi:10.1108/JSBED-09-2021-0364

Roffia, P., Moracchiato, S., Liguori, E., & Kraus, S. (2021). Operationally defining family smes: A critical review. *Journal of Small Business and Enterprise Development*, *28*(2), 229–260. doi:10.1108/JSBED-11-2020-0399

Rogoff, E. G., & Heck, R. K. Z. (2003). Evolving research in entrepreneurship and family business: Recognizing family as the oxygen that feeds the fire of entrepreneurship. *Journal of Business Venturing*, *18*(5), 559–566. doi:10.1016/S0883-9026(03)00009-0

Rohmah, N., Yusuf, A., Hargono, R., & Laksono, A. D. (2020). Determinants of teenage pregnancy in Indonesia. *Indian Journal of Forensic Medicine Toxicology*, *14*(3), 2105–2110.

Rosenkranz, C., & Wulf, T. (2019). Behavioral integration as a relational governance mechanism in family firms - The moderating role of family involvement in management. *Journal of Small Business Management*, *57*(3), 801–819. doi:10.1111/jsbm.12325

Rusu, V. D., & Roman, A. (2017). Entrepreneurial activity in the EU: An empirical evaluation of its determinants. *Sustainability (Basel)*, *9*(10), 1–16. doi:10.3390u9101679

Ryan, J. M. (2020). *Social consequences and cultural adaptations* (Vol. 2). Routledge. doi:10.4324/9781003142065

Sabah, S. (2016). Entrepreneurial intention: Theory of planned behaviour and the moderation effect of start-up experience. In M. Franco (Ed.), *Entrepreneurship – Practice-oriented perspectives*. IntechOpen. doi:10.5772/65640

Sabra, M. M., & Shreteh, D. (2021). The nexus relationship between entrepreneurship and economic growth dynamic: Evidence from selected MENA countries. *Information Economics and Policy*, *2*(35), 56–75. doi:10.33111/iep.eng.2021.35.03

Salimi, M., Della Torre, E., & Miniaci, R. (2023). Why do firms adopt collective incentives? An analysis of family and non-family firms. *Employee Relations: The International Journal*.

Samala, A. D., Ganefri, G., Yulastri, A., Indarta, Y., Ranuharja, F., & Dewi, I. P. (2022). Entrepreneurial intentions for engineering students: Does entrepreneurship education and family environment matter? *Journal of Innovation in Educational and Cultural Research*, *3*(4), 590–606. doi:10.46843/jiecr.v3i4.300

Samani, S., & Benhmanesh, Z. (2011). *Comparison between family processes and actions among ordinary and delinquent juvenile.*

Sandi, A., & Nurhayati, M. (2020). Effect of entrepreneurship education, family environment and self-efficacy on students entrepreneurship intention. In *4th International Conference on Management, Economics and Business (ICMEB 2019)* (pp. 9-12). Atlantis Press. 10.2991/aebmr.k.200205.003

Sandler, I. N., & Lakey, B. (1982). Locus of control as a stress moderator: The role of control perceptions and social support. *American Journal of Community Psychology, 10*(1), 65–80. doi:10.1007/BF00903305 PMID:7102614

Santos, F. M. (2012). A positive theory of social entrepreneurship. *Journal of Business Ethics, 111*(3), 335–351. doi:10.100710551-012-1413-4

Sarango-Lalangui, P., Álvarez-García, J., & del Río-Rama, M. D. L. C. (2018). Sustainable practices in small and medium-sized enterprises in Ecuador. *Sustainability (Basel), 10*(6), 2105. doi:10.3390u10062105

Sarwoko, E., & Nurfarida, I. N. (2021). Entrepreneurial marketing: Between entrepreneurial personality traits and business performance. *Entrepreneurial Business and Economics Review, 9*(2), 105–118. doi:10.15678/EBER.2021.090207

Saryal, R. (2022). Ecological Crisis: The Self, State, and the Hindu Ethics. In Environmentalism Constitutionalism in the Anthropocene: Values, Principles and Actions. Academic Press.

Sauvé, S., Bernard, S., & Sloan, P. (2016). Environmental sciences, sustainable development and circular economy: Alternative concepts for trans-disciplinary research. *Environmental Development, 17*, 48–56. doi:10.1016/j.envdev.2015.09.002

Sawyer, J. (1954). The Social Basis of the American System of Manufacturing. *The Journal of Economic History, 14*(4), 361–379. doi:10.1017/S0022050700077007

Schäfer, S. K., Kunzler, A. M., Kalisch, R., Tüscher, O., & Lieb, K. (2022). Trajectories of resilience and mental distress to global major disruptions. *Trends in Cognitive Sciences, 26*(12), 1171–1189. doi:10.1016/j.tics.2022.09.017 PMID:36302711

Schein, E. (1993). On psychological safety and learning new behaviours in organisations. *Organizational Dynamics, 22*(2), 36–52.

Schlein, M. (2022). *The economic impacts of the COVID19 crisis* (The World Bank Development Report 2022). https://www.worldbank.org/en/publication/wdr2022/brief/chapter-1-introduction-the-economic-impacts-

Schmitt, A., Rosing, K., Zhang, S. X., & Leatherbee, M. (2018). A dynamic model of entrepreneurial uncertainty and business opportunity identification: Exploration as a mediator and entrepreneurial self-efficacy as a moderator. *Entrepreneurship Theory and Practice, 42*(6), 835–859. doi:10.1177/1042258717721482

Schonfeld, I. S., & Mazzola, J. J. (2015). A qualitative study of stress in individuals self-employed in solo businesses. *Journal of Occupational Health Psychology, 20*(4), 501–513. doi:10.1037/a0038804 PMID:25705913

Schreibauer, E. C., Hippler, M., Burgess, S., Rieger, M. A., & Rind, E. (2020). Work-related psychosocial stress in small and medium-sized enterprises: An integrative review. *International Journal of Environmental Research and Public Health, 17*(20), 7446. doi:10.3390/ijerph17207446 PMID:33066111

Schumpeter, J. (1942). *Capitalism, Socialism, and Democracy*. Harper and Brothers.

Schumpeter, J. A. (1932). *Capitalism, Socialism and Democracy* (3rd ed.). George Allen and Unwin.

Schwartz, S. H. (1992). Universals in the content and structure of values: Theoretical advances and empirical tests in 20 countries. In Advances in experimental social psychology (Vol. 25, pp. 1–65). Academic Press. doi:10.1016/S0065-2601(08)60281-6

Seki, A., & Brooke, E. H. (2012). *Ryokan: Japan's Finest Spas and Inns*. Tuttle Publishing.

Semerci, A. B. (2016). The effect of social support on job stress of entrepreneurs. *Academy of Entrepreneurship Journal*, *22*(1), 41.

Serenko, A. (2021). A structured literature review of scientometric research of the knowledge management discipline: A 2021 update. *Journal of Knowledge Management*, *25*(8), 1889–1925. doi:10.1108/JKM-09-2020-0730

Servantie, V., Cabrol, M., Guieu, G., & Boissin, J. P. (2016). Is international entrepreneurship a field? A bibliometric analysis of the literature (1989–2015). *Journal of International Entrepreneurship, 14*(2), 168–212.

Sesen, H. (2013). Personality or environment? A comprehensive study on the entrepreneurial intentions of university students. *Education + Training*, *55*(7), 624–640. doi:10.1108/ET-05-2012-0059

Shahzadi, K., & Khurram, S. (2020). Self-efficacy and innovative work behavior: The role of individual ambidexterity and formalization at workplace in Pakistan. *Journal of the Research Society of Pakistan*, *57*(1), 31.

Shahzad, M., Qu, Y., Zafar, A. U., Rehman, S. U., & Islam, T. (2020). Exploring the influence of knowledge management process on corporate sustainable performance through green innovation. *Journal of Knowledge Management*, *24*(9), 2079–2106. doi:10.1108/JKM-11-2019-0624

Shamir, B., & Eilam, G. (2005). "What's your story?" A life-stories approach to authentic leadership development. *The Leadership Quarterly*, *16*(3), 395–417. doi:10.1016/j.leaqua.2005.03.005

Shane, S., & Venkataraman, S. (2000). The promise of entrepreneurship as a field of research. *Academy of Management Review*, *25*(1), 217–226. doi:10.5465/amr.2000.2791611

Shan, S., Jia, Y., Zheng, X., & Xu, X. (2018). Assessing relationship and contribution of China's technological entrepreneurship to socio-economic development. *Technological Forecasting and Social Change*, *135*, 83–90. doi:10.1016/j.techfore.2017.12.022

Shao, R., He, P., Ling, B., Tan, L., Xu, L., Hou, Y., Kong, L., & Yang, Y. (2020). Prevalence of depression and anxiety and correlations between depression, anxiety, family functioning, social support, and coping styles among Chinese medical students. *BMC Psychology*, *8*(1), 1–19. doi:10.118640359-020-00402-8 PMID:32321593

Shao, R., Loi, R., & Lam, W. (2012). Psychological safety, job satisfaction, and performance: A meta-analysis. *Journal of Organizational Behavior, 33*(3), 486–509.

Shapiro, J. P., & Gross, S. J. (2008). *Ethical educational leadership in turbulent times*. Routledge.

Sharma, A., Das, N., & Singh, S. P. (2023). Causal association of entrepreneurship ecosystem and financial inclusion. *Heliyon, 9*(3), 1-13. doi: .2023.e14596 doi:10.1016/j.heliyon

Sharma, L. (2014). Impact of family capital and social capital on youth entrepreneurship – A study of Uttarakhand state, India. *Journal of Global Entrepreneurship Research, 4*(1), 1–18. doi:10.118640497-014-0014-3

Sharma, P. (2004). An overview of the field of family business studies: Current status and directions for the future. *Family Business Review, 17*(1), 1–36. doi:10.1111/j.1741-6248.2004.00001.x

Sharma, S., & Vredenburg, H. (1998). Proactive corporate environmental strategy and the development of competitively valuable organizational capabilities. *Strategic Management Journal, 19*(8), 729–753. doi:10.1002/(SICI)1097-0266(199808)19:8<729::AID-SMJ967>3.0.CO;2-4

Shen, L. (2015). Meet Samsung's billionaire Lee family, South Korea's most powerful dynasty. *Business Insider*. https://www.businessinsider.com/lee-family-power-war-for-samsung-scandals-and-bribes-2015-6

Shen, L. (2015). *Meet Samsung's billionaire Lee family, South Korea's most powerful dynasty. Business Insider Online*. Business Insider.

Shepherd, D. A., Osofero, M., & Wincent, J. (2022). A personal adversity model of justifying the costs of entrepreneurial action: The case of oil thieves in the Niger DELTA. *Journal of Business Venturing, 37*(1), 106163. doi:10.1016/j.jbusvent.2021.106163

Shepherd, D. A., Wiklund, J., & Haynie, J. M. (2009). Moving forward: Balancing the financial and emotional costs of business failure. *Journal of Business Venturing, 24*(2), 134–148. doi:10.1016/j.jbusvent.2007.10.002

Shepherd, D., & Haynie, J. M. (2009). Family business, identity conflict, and an expedited entrepreneurial process: A process of resolving identity conflict. *Entrepreneurship Theory and Practice, 33*(6), 1245–1264. doi:10.1111/j.1540-6520.2009.00344.x

Shiyanov, E. N., & Kotova, I. B. (1999). *Development of the person in training*. Academic Press.

Sidani, Y., & Reese, S. (2020). Nancy dixon: Empowering the learning organisation through psychological safety. *The Learning Organization, 27*(3), 259–266. doi:10.1108/TLO-01-2020-0015

Sieger, P., & Minola, T. (2017). The family's financial support as a "poisoned gift": A family embeddedness perspective on entrepreneurial intentions. *Journal of Small Business Management, 55*, 179–204. doi:10.1111/jsbm.12273

Silk, J. S., Morris, A. S., Kanaya, T., & Steinberg, L. (2003). Psychological control and autonomy granting: Opposite ends of a continuum or distinct constructs? *Journal of Research on Adolescence, 13*(1), 113–128. doi:10.1111/1532-7795.1301004

Silva, P., & Silva, R. (2014). Family Business Transfer: The Importance of Continuing the Business. *Advances in Economics and Business, 2*(5), 184–190. doi:10.13189/aeb.2014.020502

Simmel, G. (1908). The Stranger. In K. H. Wolff (Ed.), *The Sociology of Georg Simmel*. The Free Press.

Singh, A. K., & Jyoti, B. (2021). Further research direction for indicators of technology entrepreneurship ecosystem, technology start-ups ecosystem and technology-business incubators: A conceptual review. *Dimensions International Journal of Management ICFAI Business School (IBS) Mumbai, 7*(1), 14-33.

Singh, A. K., & Jyoti, B. (2023b). Empirical evidence from a different income group countries on the interdependency between digitalization and economic development. In P. O. de Pablos & X. Zhang (Eds.), 5G, Artificial Intelligence, and Next Generation Internet of Things: Digital Innovation for Green and Sustainable Economies (pp. 44-85). IGI Global. doi:10.4018/978-1-6684-8634-4.ch003

Singh, A. K., Jyoti, B., & Mishra, V. K. (2023d). Policy implications from selected countries for a sustainable future of the society through green entrepreneurship and economic development. In Entrepreneurship Ecosystems and Their Opportunities and Challenges (pp. 129-162). IGI Global. doi:10.4018/978-1-6684-7140-1.ch006

Singh, A. K., Singh, B., & Ashraf, S. N. (2020a). Implications of intellectual property protection, and science and technological development in the manufacturing sector in selected economies. *Journal of Advocacy, Research and Education, 7*(1), 16-35. https://oaji.net/articles/2021/1704-1615668997.pdf

Singh, A. K., Arya, A. K., & Jyoti, B. (2019b). A conceptual review on economic, business, intellectual property rights and science & technology related activities in Asian economies. *JNNCE Journal of Engineering & Management, 3*(2), 1–22.

Singh, A. K., & Ashraf, S. N. (2020). Association of entrepreneurship ecosystem with economic growth in selected countries. *Journal of Entrepreneurship. Business Economics (Cleveland, Ohio), 8*(2), 36–92. http://scientificia.com/index.php/JEBE/article/view/138

Singh, A. K., Issac, J., & Narayanan, K. G. S. (2019a). Measurement of environmental sustainability index and its association with socio-economic indicators in selected Asian economies: An empirical investigation. *International Journal of Environment and Sustainable Development, 18*(1), 57–100. doi:10.1504/IJESD.2019.098641

Singh, A. K., & Jyoti, B. (2023a). Does digitalization have a bi-directional causal relationship with the entrepreneurship ecosystem? Evidence from a country-wise panel data analysis. In Y. Ramakrishna & L. Indiran (Eds.), *Handbook of Research on Designing Sustainable Strategies to Develop Entrepreneurial Intention* (pp. 178–172). IGI Global. doi:10.4018/978-1-6684-8781-5.ch007

Singh, A. K., & Jyoti, B. (2023c). Relative performance of entrepreneurship ecosystem for selected countries using a composite Z-score technique of index estimation. *Eurasian Journal of Management & Social Sciences*, *4*(2).

Singh, A. K., Jyoti, B., Kumar, S., & Lenka, S. K. (2021). Assessment of global sustainable development, environmental sustainability, economic development, and social development index in selected economies. *International Journal of Sustainable Development and Planning*, *16*(1), 123–138. doi:10.18280/ijsdp.160113

Singh, A. K., & Kumar, S. (2022a). Factors influencing entrepreneurship ecosystem and economic development: Evidence from cross-sectional country-wise imbalanced panel data analysis. *The IUP Journal of Entrepreneurship Development*, *19*(3), 24–47.

Singh, A. K., & Kumar, S. (2022b). Expert's perception on technology transfer and commercialization, and intellectual property rights in India: Evidence from selected research organizations. *Journal of Management, Economics, and Industrial Organization*, *6*(1), 1–33. doi:10.31039/jomeino.2022.6.1.1

Singh, A. K., & Kumar, S. (2022c). Exploring the impact of sustainable development on social-economic, and science and technological development in selected countries: A panel data analysis. *Society & Sustainability*, *4*(1), 55–83. doi:10.38157s.v4i1.405

Singh, A. K., Kumar, S., & Jyoti, B. (2022b). Influence of climate change on agricultural sustainability in India: A state-wise panel data analysis. *Asian Journal of Agriculture*, *6*(1), 15–27. doi:10.13057/asianjagric/g060103

Singh, A. K., Kumar, S., & Jyoti, B. (2023c). Does entrepreneurship ecosystem have a causal relationship with economic development? A country-wise imbalanced panel data investigation. In H. Magd, S. A. Khan, N. D. Nte, & M. Sarim (Eds.), *Entrepreneurship and Economic Sustainability* (pp. 1–15). Prestige Publishers.

Singh, A. K., Kumar, S., & Sharma, A. K. (2023a). Does green entrepreneurship ecosystem have causal association with economic development? Evidence from country-wise panel data investigation. *Journal of International Business Research*, *22*(2), 1–18. https://www.abacademies.org/articles/Does-Green-Entrepreneurship-Ecosystem-have-1544-0230-22-2-191.pdf

Singh, A. K., Kumar, S., Sharma, A. K., & Sinha, S. (2022a). Does green entrepreneurship have an association with sustainable development and its components? Evidence from a country-wise panel data investigation. In M. Magd, D. Singh, D. Spicer, & R. T. Syed (Eds.), *International Perspectives on Value Creation and Sustainability Through Social Entrepreneurship* (pp. 132–172). IGI Global. doi:10.4018/978-1-6684-4666-9.ch008

Singh, A. K., Sharma, A. K., & Jyoti, B. (2023e). Does economic development have a causal relationship with environmental degradation? Experience from different income group countries. In G. Sart (Ed.), *Considerations on Education for Economic, Social, and Environmental Sustainability* (pp. 300–333). IGI Global. doi:10.4018/978-1-6684-8356-5.ch015

Singh, A. K., Sharma, S. K., & Lenka, S. K. (2023b). Causality between green entrepreneurship and sustainable development: A cross-country analysis using ARDL model. *The IUP Journal of Applied Economics*, *22*(1), 5–38.

Singh, A. K., Singh, B. J., & Negi, V. (2020b). Does sustainable development have a causal relationship with environmental development? Evidence from a country-wise panel data analysis. *International Journal of Technology Management & Sustainable Development*, *19*(2), 147–171. doi:10.1386/tmsd_00020_1

Singh, M., & Sarkar, A. (2019). Role of psychological empowerment in the relationship between structural empowerment and innovative behaviour. *Management Research Review*, *42*(4), 521–538. doi:10.1108/MRR-04-2018-0158

Siregar, Z. A. (2020). The influence of family environment, entrepreneurship knowledge and entrepreneurship motivation on students' entrepreneurship interest of Islamic education management program of Universitas Islam Negeri Sumatera Utara. In *4th Padang International Conference on Education, Economics, Business and Accounting (PICEEBA-2 2019)* (pp. 566-574). Atlantis Press. 10.2991/aebmr.k.200305.120

Sivathanu, B., & Bhise, P. V. (2016). *Challenges for Social Entrepreneurship.* Available online: http://www.ijaiem.org/ RATMIG2013/MGT%2025%20Challenges%20for%20Social %20 Entrepreneurship.pdf

Sivathanu, B., & Pillai, R. (2020). An empirical study on entrepreneurial bricolage behavior for sustainable enterprise performance of startups: Evidence from an emerging economy. *Journal of Entrepreneurship in Emerging Economies*, *12*(1), 34–57. doi:10.1108/JEEE-01-2019-0009

Smith. (2019). Navigating Culinary Authenticity and Health-Consciousness: Challenges Faced by Family-Owned Restaurants. *Journal of Culinary Entrepreneurship*, *3*, 112–128.

Smith, A. (2019). The Impact of Family Dynamics on Leadership Succession in Family Business. *International Journal of Management Studies*, *10*, 56–78.

Smith, C. M., & Sweet, J. (2021). Analyzing the Relationship between Maslow's Hierarchy of Needs and Consumer Spending Patterns. *Journal of Financial Service Professionals*, *75*(4).

Smith, M. S. (2006). *The Emergence of Modern Business Enterprise in France, 1800- 1930.* Harvard University Press.

Social Sustainability Policy. (2016). *A city for all: Towards a socially just and resilient Sydney.* Available at: http://www.cityofsydney.nsw.gov.au/__data/assets/pdf_file/0 005/262346/Social-Sustainability-Policy.pdf

Soenens, B., & Vansteenkiste, M. (2005). Antecedents and outcomes of self-determination in three life domains: The role of parents' and teachers' autonomy support. *Journal of Youth and Adolescence*, *34*(6), 589–604. doi:10.100710964-005-8948-y

Sombart, W. (1911). *The Jews and Modern Capitalism*. Transaction Books.

Song, B., Li, Y., & Zhao, L. (2019). Complementary effect of knowledge management strategy on firm performance: Evidence from Chinese firms. *Sustainability (Basel)*, *11*(13), 3616. doi:10.3390u11133616

Soni, A., & Bakhru, K. M. (2021). Personality traits and entrepreneurial intention among chartered accountancy students. *Problems and Perspectives in Management*, *19*(3), 136–147. doi:10.21511/ppm.19(3).2021.12

Soomro, M. A., Memon, M. S., & Bukhari, N. S. (2019). Entrepreneurial education and its impact on entrepreneurial intentions: A comparative analysis of business graduates of public and private universities of Sindh. *Pacific Business Review International*, *11*(6), 35–46.

Spedding, J., Brough, P., Hawkes, A. J., & Chan, X. W. (2023). The effective measurement of shared leadership: A multi-scale comparison. *Leadership and Organization Development Journal*, *44*(4), 564–581. doi:10.1108/LODJ-10-2021-0453

Stanwick, P. A., & Stanwick, S. D. (1998). The relationship between corporate social performance, and organizational size, financial performance, and environmental performance: An empirical examination. *Journal of Business Ethics*, *17*(2), 195–204. doi:10.1023/A:1005784421547

Steier, L. (2003). Variants of agency contracts in family-financed ventures as a continuum of familial altruistic and market rationalities. *Journal of Business Venturing*, *18*(5), 597–618. doi:10.1016/S0883-9026(03)00012-0

Steier, L. P., Chrisman, J. J., & Chua, J. H. (2015). Governance challenges in family businesses and business families. *Entrepreneurship Theory and Practice*, *39*(6), 1265–1280. doi:10.1111/etap.12180

Stenn, T. L. (2016). *Social entrepreneurship as sustainable development: Introducing the sustainability lens*. Springer.

Stephan, U. (2018). Entrepreneurs' mental health and well-being: A review and research agenda. *The Academy of Management Perspectives*, *32*(3), 290–322. doi:10.5465/amp.2017.0001

Stephan, U., & Pathak, S. (2016). Beyond cultural values? Cultural leadership ideals and entrepreneurship. *Journal of Business Venturing*, *31*(5), 505–523. doi:10.1016/j.jbusvent.2016.07.003

Stephan, U., & Uhlaner, L. M. (2010). Performance-based vs socially supportive culture: A cross-national study of descriptive norms and entrepreneurship. *Journal of International Business Studies*, *41*(8), 1347–1364. doi:10.1057/jibs.2010.14

Story, J. S., & Barbuto, J. E. Jr. (2011). Global mindset: A construct clarification and framework. *Journal of Leadership & Organizational Studies*, *18*(3), 377–384. doi:10.1177/1548051811404421

Strand, R., Freeman, R. E., & Hockerts, K. (2015). Corporate social responsibility and sustainability in Scandinavia: An overview. *Journal of Business Ethics*, *127*(1), 1–15. doi:10.100710551-014-2224-6

Su, E., & Daspit, J. (2022). Knowledge management in family firms: A systematic review, integrated insights and future research opportunities. *Journal of Knowledge Management*, *26*(2), 291–325.

Sue, D. W. (2016). *Race talk and the conspiracy of silence: Understanding and facilitating difficult dialogues on race*. John Wiley & Sons.

Sulphey, M. M., & Alkahtani, N. (2017). Economic security and sustainability through social entrepreneurship: the current Saudi scenario. *Journal of Security and Sustainability Issues, 6*(3).

Sun, L., & Bunchapattanasakda, C. (2019). Employee engagement: A literature review. International. *Journal of Human Resource Studies*, *9*(1), 63. doi:10.5296/ijhrs.v9i1.14167

Sun, X., Lee, S.-H., & Phan, P. H. (2019). Family firm R&D investments in the 2007-2009 great recession. *Journal of Family Business Strategy*, *10*(4), 100244. doi:10.1016/j.jfbs.2018.02.004

Supandi, R., Wulandari, S. Z., & Naufalin, L. R. (2022). Influence of Family Circumstances, Peer Circumstances, and Entrepreneurial Learning on Entrepreneurial Interests with Self-Efficacy as Intervening Variables. *Journal of Economics Education and Entrepreneurship*, *3*(2), 140–150. doi:10.20527/jee.v3i2.5233

Surya, B., Hadijah, H., Suriani, S., Baharuddin, B., Fitriyah, A. T., Menne, F., & Rasyidi, E. S. (2020). Spatial Transformation of a New City in 2006–2020: Perspectives on the Spatial Dynamics, Environmental Quality Degradation, and Socio—Economic Sustainability of Local Communities in Makassar City, Indonesia. *Land (Basel)*, *9*(9), 324. doi:10.3390/land9090324

Susanto, S. C. (2018). The influence of family environment, entrepreneurship education, and self-efficiency on student entrepreneurship interest. *Journal of Management and Business Start-ups*, *2*(3), 277–286.

Su, T. S., Chen, C., Cui, X., Yang, C., & Ma, W. (2020). Consistency at different levels: A meta-analytic examination of organizational trust and performance. *Nankai Business Review International*, *11*(4), 537–567. doi:10.1108/NBRI-01-2020-0005

Sutawidjaya, A. (2019). Talent management in mediating competencies and motivation to improve employee's engagement. *International Journal of Economics and Business Administration*, *VII*(1), 140–152. doi:10.35808/ijeba/201

Suwandana, I. (2019). Role of transformational leadership mediation: Effect of emotional and communication intelligence towards teamwork effectiveness. *International Research Journal of Management It and Social Sciences*, *6*(2), 52–62. doi:10.21744/irjmis.v6n2.608

Szerb, L., Aidis, R., & Acs, Z. J. (2013). The comparison of the global entrepreneurship monitor and the global entrepreneurship and development index methodologies. *Foundations and Trends R in Entrepreneurship, 9*(1), 1-142. doi:10.1561/0300000046

Taha, K. A. S., Ramlan, S. N., & Noor, I. M. (2017). The factors affecting entrepreneurial intentions of university students in Malaysia. *International Journal of Business and Technopreneurship, 7*(2), 189–202.

Tang, R. (2023). Manual Transcription. In *Varieties of Qualitative Research Methods: Selected Contextual Perspectives* (pp. 295–302). Springer International Publishing. doi:10.1007/978-3-031-04394-9_47

Tan, J. D., Supratikno, H., Pramono, R., Purba, J. T., & Bernarto, I. (2019). Nurturing transgenerational entrepreneurship in ethnic Chinese family SMEs: Exploring Indonesia. *Journal of Asia Business Studies, 13*(2), 294–325. doi:10.1108/JABS-04-2018-0132

Tantono, M., Ongkowijoyo, G., Hongdiyanto, C., & Hartono, W. (2022). Increasing students' entrepreneurial intention using internal and external factors through entrepreneurial self-efficacy. *Expert Journal of Business and Management, 10*(2), 65-76. https://business.expertjournals.com/23446781-1007/

Tasnim, N., & Afzal, M. N. I. (2018). An empirical investigation of country level efficiency and national systems of entrepreneurship using data envelopment analysis (DEA) and the TOBIT model. *Journal of Global Entrepreneurship Research, 8*(37), 1–17. doi:10.118640497-018-0138-y

Taylor, R., Currie, G., & Henneberg, S. (2017). The impact of psychological safety on team performance: A longitudinal study. *The Leadership Quarterly, 28*(3), 387–400.

Tear, M. J., Reader, T. W., Shorrock, S., & Kirwan, B. (2020). Safety culture and power: Interactions between perceptions of safety culture, organisational hierarchy, and national culture. *Safety Science, 121*, 550–561. doi:10.1016/j.ssci.2018.10.014

Tereshina, D. (2023). Business as a gift: Family entrepreneurship and the ambiguities of sharing. In *Family Firms and Business Families in Cross-Cultural Perspective: Bringing Anthropology Back* (pp. 115–145). Springer International Publishing. doi:10.1007/978-3-031-20525-5_5

Terrell, S., & Rosenbusch, K. (2013). Global leadership development: What global organizations can do to reduce leadership risk, increase speed to competence, and build global leadership muscle. *People and Strategy, 36*(1), 40.

Thaler, R. H. (2018). From cashews to nudges: The evolution of behavioral economics. *The American Economic Review, 108*(6), 1265–1287. doi:10.1257/aer.108.6.1265

Theiss, J. A. (2018). Family communication and resilience. *Journal of Applied Communication Research, 46*(1), 10–13. doi:10.1080/00909882.2018.1426706

Tomlin, J., Dalgleish-Warburton, B., & Lamph, G. (2020). Psychosocial support for healthcare workers during the COVID-19 pandemic. *Frontiers in Psychology, 11*, 1960. doi:10.3389/fpsyg.2020.01960 PMID:32849149

Torraco, R. J. (2016). Writing Integrative Literature Reviews: Using the Past and Present to Explore the Future. *Human Resource Development Review*, *15*(4), 404–428. doi:10.1177/1534484316671606

Tremblay, D., Touati, N., Kilpatrick, K., Durand, M., Turcotte, A., Prady, C., Poder, T. G., Richard, P. O., Soldera, S., Berbiche, D., Généreux, M., Roy, M., Laflamme, B., Lessard, S., Landry, M., & Giordano, É. (2022). Building resilience in oncology teams: Protocol for a realist evaluation of multiple cases. *PLoS One*, *17*(5), e0268393. doi:10.1371/journal.pone.0268393 PMID:35551336

Treviño, L. K., Den Nieuwenboer, N. A., & Kish-Gephart, J. J. (2014). (Un) ethical behavior in organizations. *Annual Review of Psychology*, *65*(1), 635–660. doi:10.1146/annurev-psych-113011-143745 PMID:23834354

Trice, H. M., & Beyer, J. M. (1984). Studying organizational cultures through rites and ceremonials. *Academy of Management Review*, *9*(4), 653–669. doi:10.2307/258488

Turulja, L., Veselinovic, L., Agic, E., & Pasic-Mesihovic, A. (2020). Entrepreneurial intention of students in Bosnia and Herzegovina: What type of support matters? *Economic research-. Ekonomska Istrazivanja*, *33*(1), 2713–2732. doi:10.1080/1331677X.2020.1730216

Tzortzaki, A. M., & Mihiotis, A. (2014). A review of knowledge management theory and future directions. *Knowledge and Process Management*, *21*(1), 29–41. doi:10.1002/kpm.1429

United Nations. (2015). *United Nations Transforming Our World: The 2030 Agenda for Sustainable Development*. Division for Sustainable Development Goals.

Upadhyay, C. S., & Rawal, P. (2018). A critical study of Joseph A. Schumpeter's innovation theory of entrepreneurship. *International Journal of Creative Research Thoughts*, *6*(2), 1678–1686.

Urbano, D., Audretsch, D., Aparicio, S., & Noguera, M. (2020). Does entrepreneurial activity matter for economic growth in developing countries? The role of the institutional environment. *The International Entrepreneurship and Management Journal*, *16*(3), 1065–1099. doi:10.100711365-019-00621-5

Uvarova, I., Mavlutova, I., & Atstaja, D. (2021). Development of the green entrepreneurial mindset through modern entrepreneurship education. *IOP Conference Series. Earth and Environmental Science*, *628*(1), 1–13. doi:10.1088/1755-1315/628/1/012034

Uyanga, R. E. (2009). The Disadvantage in a Culturally Diversified Society: Focus on the Girl Child in Northern Nigeria. *The International Journal of Diversity in Organisations, Communities and Nations*, *8*(6), 1–8. doi:10.18848/1447-9532/CGP/v08i06/39672

Uygun, R., & Kasimoglu, M. (2013). The emergence of entrepreneurial intentions in indigenous entrepreneurs: The role of personal background on the antecedents of intentions. *International Journal of Business and Management*, *8*(5), 24–41. doi:10.5539/ijbm.v8n5p24

Uy, M. A., Foo, M. D., & Song, Z. (2013). Joint effects of prior start-up experience and coping strategies on entrepreneurs' psychological well-being. *Journal of Business Venturing*, *28*(5), 583–597. doi:10.1016/j.jbusvent.2012.04.003

Uzoho, M. (2022). *High level of Poverty in Nigeria*. Sage.

Valeeva, R. A., Korolyeva, N. E., & Sakhapova, F. K. (2016). Case-Study of the High School Student's Family Values Formation. *International Journal of Environmental and Science Education*, *11*(7), 1641–1649.

Vallaster, C., Kraus, S., Lindahl, J., & Nielsen, A. (2019). Ethics and entrepreneurship: A bibliometric study and literature review. *Journal of Business Research*, *99*, 226–237. doi:10.1016/j.jbusres.2019.02.050

Van de Ven, A. H. (1992). Suggestions for studying strategy process: A research note. *Strategic Management Journal*, *13*(S1), 169–188. doi:10.1002mj.4250131013

Van Eck, N., & Waltman, L. (2010). Software survey: VOSviewer, a computer program for bibliometric mapping. *Scientometrics*, *84*(2), 523-538.

Van Eck, N. J., & Waltman, L. (2017). Citation-based clustering of publications using CitNetExplorer and VOSviewer. *Scientometrics*, *111*(2), 1053–1070. doi:10.100711192-017-2300-7 PMID:28490825

Vandekerkhof, P., Steijvers, T., Hendriks, W., & Voordeckers, W. (2017). Socio-emotional wealth separation and decision-making quality in family firm TMTs: The moderating role of psychological safety. *Journal of Management Studies*, *55*(4), 648–676. doi:10.1111/joms.12277

Vaswani, J. (2023). *Grant Cardone Net Worth: Why He Is So Successful?* https://schemaninja.com/grant-cardone-net-worth/

Vătămănescu, E.-M., Gorgos, E.-A., Ghigiu, A. M., & Pătruț, M. (2019). Bridging intellectual capital and SMEs internationalization through the lens of sustainable competitive advantage: A systematic literature review. *Sustainability (Basel)*, *11*(9), 2510. doi:10.3390u11092510

Vershinina, N., Rodgers, P., Mcadam, M., & Clinton, E. (2019). Transnational migrant entrepreneurship, gender and family business. *Global Networks*, *19*(2), 238–260. doi:10.1111/glob.12225

Villalonga, B., & Amit, R. (2006). How do family ownership, control and management affect firm value? *Journal of Financial Economics*, *80*(2), 385–417. doi:10.1016/j.jfineco.2004.12.005

Vlas, R., Nguyen, H., & Vlas, C. (2022). A theoretical exploration of out-group versus in-group perspectives on the dynamics of team effectiveness. *Team Performance Management*, *28*(1/2), 45–60. doi:10.1108/TPM-09-2021-0070

Vodă, A. I., & Florea, N. (2019). Impact of personality traits and entrepreneurship education on entrepreneurial intentions of business and engineering students. *Sustainability (Basel)*, *11*(4), 1192. doi:10.3390u11041192

Volkmann, C., Fischter, K., Klofsten, M., & Audretsch, D. B. (2019). Sustainable entrepreneurial ecosystems: An emerging field of research. *Small Business Economics*, *1*(1), 1–9. doi:10.100711187-019-00253-7

Wach, D., Stephan, U., Weinberger, E., & Wegge, J. (2021). Entrepreneurs' stressors and well-being: A recovery perspective and diary study. *Journal of Business Venturing*, *36*(5), 106016. doi:10.1016/j.jbusvent.2020.106016

Wadei, K., Chen, L., Frempong, J., & Appienti, W. (2020). The mediation effect of ethical leadership and creative performance: A social information processing perspective. *The Journal of Creative Behavior*, *55*(1), 241–254. doi:10.1002/jocb.449

Walker, B., Holling, C. S., Carpenter, S. R., & Kinzig, A. (2004). Resilience, adaptability and transformability in social–ecological systems. *Ecology and Society*, *9*(2), 1–18. doi:10.5751/ES-00650-090205

Walsh, F. (1998). *Beliefs, spirituality, and transcendence: Keys to family resilience*. Academic Press.

Walsh, A., Moore, A., Barber, A., & Opsteen, J. (2014). Educational role of nurse practitioners in a family practice centre: Perspectives of learners and nurses. *Canadian Family Physician Medecin de Famille Canadien*, *60*(6), e316–e321. PMID:24925966

Walsh, F. (1996). The concept of family resilience: Crisis and challenge. *Family Process*, *35*(3), 261–281. doi:10.1111/j.1545-5300.1996.00261.x PMID:9111709

Walsh, F. (2015). *Strengthening family resilience*. Guilford Publications.

Walsh, F. (2016). Applying a family resilience framework in training, practice, and research: Mastering the art of the possible. *Family Process*, *55*(4), 616–632. doi:10.1111/famp.12260 PMID:27921306

Walsh, F. (2016). Family resilience: A developmental systems framework. *European Journal of Developmental Psychology*, *13*(3), 313–324. doi:10.1080/17405629.2016.1154035

Walsh, F. (2021). Family resilience: A dynamic systemic framework. In *Multisystemic Resilience* (pp. 255–270). Oxford University Press. doi:10.1093/oso/9780190095888.003.0015

Walter, S. G., & Dohse, D. (2009). *The interplay between entrepreneurship education and regional knowledge potential in forming entrepreneurial intentions* (No. 1549). Kiel Working Paper. http://hdl.handle.net/10419/28376

Walters, K., & Diab, D. (2016). Humble leadership: Implications for psychological safety and follower engagement. *Journal of Leadership Studies*, *10*(2), 7–18. doi:10.1002/jls.21434

Walumbwa, F. O., Avolio, B. J., Gardner, W. L., Wernsing, T. S., & Peterson, S. J. (2008). Authentic leadership: Development and validation of a theory-based measure. *Journal of Management*, *34*(1), 89–126. doi:10.1177/0149206307308913

Wang, Q., & Richardson, L. (2021). Race/ethnicity, place, and art and culture entrepreneurship in underserved communities. *Cities (London, England)*, *115*, 103243. doi:10.1016/j.cities.2021.103243

Wang, W., Kang, S., & Choi, S. (2022). Servant leadership and creativity: A study of the sequential mediating roles of psychological safety and employee well-being. *Frontiers in Psychology, 12*, 807070. Advance online publication. doi:10.3389/fpsyg.2021.807070 PMID:35185702

Wang, Y. (2016). Environmental dynamism, trust and dynamic capabilities of family businesses. *International Journal of Entrepreneurial Behaviour & Research, 22*(5), 643–670. doi:10.1108/IJEBR-11-2015-0234

Wang, Y., Ahmad, W., Arshad, M., Yin, H., Ahmed, B., & Ali, Z. (2021). Impact of coordination, psychological safety, and job security on employees' performance: The moderating role of coercive pressure. *Sustainability (Basel), 13*(6), 3175. doi:10.3390u13063175

Wang, Y., Liu, J., & Zhu, L. (2018). Humble leadership, psychological safety, knowledge sharing, and follower creativity: A cross-level investigation. *Frontiers in Psychology, 9*, 1727. Advance online publication. doi:10.3389/fpsyg.2018.01727 PMID:30283379

Wang, Y., Zhou, H., Zhang, Y., & Sun, X. R. (2022). Role of entrepreneurial behaviour in achieving sustainable digital economy. *Frontiers in Public Health, 10*(1), 1–13. doi:10.3389/fpubh.2022.829289 PMID:35284394

Ward, J. (2016). *Keeping the family business healthy: How to plan for continuing growth, profitability, and family leadership*. Springer.

Wayland, R., Shore, L. M., & Ding, C. (2016). Psychological safety and organisational outcomes: A meta-analysis. *Journal of Organizational Behavior, 37*(1), 3–22.

Weber, M. (1904). *The Protestant Ethic and the Spirit of Capitalism*. Scribner.

Weber, M. (1968). *On charisma and institution building* (Vol. 322). University of Chicago Press.

Wei, X., Liu, X., & Sha, J. (2019). How does the entrepreneurship education influence the students' innovation? Testing on the multiple mediation model. *Frontiers in Psychology, 10*, 1557. doi:10.3389/fpsyg.2019.01557 PMID:31354574

Welter, F., Baker, T., Audretsch, D. B., & Gartner, W. B. (2017). Everyday entrepreneurship—A call for entrepreneurship research to embrace entrepreneurial diversity. *Entrepreneurship Theory and Practice, 41*(3), 311–321. doi:10.1111/etap.12258

Wennberg, K., Pathak, S., & Autio, E. (2013). How culture moulds the effects of self-efficacy and fear of failure on entrepreneurship. *Entrepreneurship and Regional Development, 25*(9-10), 756–780. doi:10.1080/08985626.2013.862975

Westphal, M., Seivert, N. H., & Bonanno, G. A. (2010). Expressive flexibility. *Emotion (Washington, D.C.), 10*(1), 92–100. doi:10.1037/a0018420 PMID:20141306

Whoriskey, P. (2019). Hershey, Nestle and Mars broke their pledges to end child labor in chocolate production. *Washington Post*. Available: https://www.washingtonpost.com/graphics/2019/business/hershey-nestle-mars-chocolate-child-labor-west-africa/

Wiani, A., Ahman, E., & Machmud, A. (2018). Effect of family environment on interest in entrepreneurship students SMK in Subang Regency. *Oikos: Jurnal Ekonomi dan Pendidikan Ekonomi, 2*(2), 122-132. doi:10.23969/oikos.v2i2.1034

Wibowo, A. (2016). Adversity quetient, self-efficacy dan kesiapan kerja siswa kelas XII program keahlian multimedia SMKN 1 Kabupaten Jombang. *Persona: Jurnal Psikologi Indonesia, 5*(2).

Wiener, M. (1981). English Culture and the Decline of the Industrial Spirit: 1850– 1980. New York: Cambridge University Press.

Wiener, M. (Ed.). (1966). Modernization: The Dynamics of Growth. New York: Basic Books.

Wiggins, M., Oakley, M., Austerberry, H., Clemens, F., & Elbourne, D. (2005). *Teenage parenthood and social exclusion: A multi-method study: Summary of report findings*. Social Science Research Unit, Institute of Education, University of London.

Wiklund, J., Nikolaev, B., Shir, N., Foo, M. D., & Bradley, S. (2019). Entrepreneurship and well-being: Past, present, and future. *Journal of Business Venturing, 34*(4), 579–588. doi:10.1016/j.jbusvent.2019.01.002

Wildsmith, E., Manlove, J., Jekielek, S., Moore, K. A., & Mincieli, L. (2012). Teenage childbearing among youth born to teenage mothers. *Youth & Society, 44*(2), 258–283. doi:10.1177/0044118X11398366 PMID:31511752

Williams, T. A., Gruber, D. A., Sutcliffe, K. M., Shepherd, D. A., & Zhao, E. Y. (2017). Organizational response to adversity: Fusing crisis management and resilience research streams. *The Academy of Management Annals, 11*(2), 733–769. doi:10.5465/annals.2015.0134

Wilson, C. H. (1955). The Entrepreneur in the Industrial Revolution. *Explorations in Entrepreneurial History, 7*(3), 129–145.

Winter, M., Danes, S. M., Koh, S.-K., Fredericks, K., & Paul, J. J. (2004). Tracking family businesses and their owners over time: Panel attrition, manager departure, and business demise. *Journal of Business Venturing, 19*(4), 535–559. doi:10.1016/S0883-9026(03)00061-2

Winter, M., Fitzgerald, M. A., Heck, R. K. Z., Haynes, G. W., & Danes, S. M. (1998). Revisiting the study of family businesses: Methodological challenges, dilemmas, and alternative approaches. *Family Business Review, 11*(3), 239–252. doi:10.1111/j.1741-6248.1998.00239.x

Winter, M., Puspitawati, H., Heck, R. K. Z., & Stafford, K. (1993). Time-management strategies used by households with home-based work. *Journal of Family and Economic Issues, 14*(1), 69–92. doi:10.1007/BF01013430

Wong, M. F., & Wong, M. P. (2002). Workplace stress: Causes, consequences, and why it concerns managers. *Akauntan Nasional, 11*, 24–28.

World Economic Forum. (2023). *Global Risks: Today's Crisis*. Author.

Wright, L. M., Watson, W. L., & Bell, J. M. (1996). *Beliefs: The heart of healing in families and illness*. Basic Books.

Wu, C., Lv, H., He, L., & Cheng, T. (2022). *Research on the influence mechanism of psychological safety on leaders' ambidexterity based on experimental analysis*. doi:10.2991/assehr.k.220105.004

Wu, L., Jiang, S., Wang, X., Yu, L., Wang, Y., & Pan, H. (2022). Entrepreneurship education and entrepreneurial intentions of college students: The mediating role of entrepreneurial self-efficacy and the moderating role of entrepreneurial competition experience. *Frontiers in Psychology*, *12*(1), 1–9. doi:10.3389/fpsyg.2021.727826 PMID:35069312

Wu, P., Chen, H., Yang, D., & Sun, D. (2021). Nature or nurture: Influencing factors of entrepreneurial behaviour from the perspective of university entrepreneurial ecosystem. *Academic Journal of Business & Management*, *3*(6), 9–17. doi:10.25236/AJBM.2021.030602

Xiao, Z., Liao, H., & Dai, S. (2014). Organisational culture, psychological safety, and knowledge sharing in a Chinese context. *Human Resource Management*, *53*(5), 765–781.

Xue, R., Qian, G., Qian, Z., & Li, L. (2021). Entrepreneurs' implicit and explicit achievement motives and their early international commitment. *MIR. Management International Review*, *61*(1), 91–121. doi:10.100711575-020-00436-5

Xu, F., Kellermanns, F. W., Jin, L., & Xi, J. (2020). Family support as social exchange in entrepreneurship: Its moderating impact on entrepreneurial stressors-well-being relationships. *Journal of Business Research*, *120*, 59–73. doi:10.1016/j.jbusres.2020.07.033 PMID:32834213

Yang, H., Haldeman, S., Lu, M. L., & Baker, D. (2016). Low back pain prevalence and related workplace psychosocial risk factors: A study using data from the 2010 National Health Interview Survey. *Journal of Manipulative and Physiological Therapeutics*, *39*(7), 459–472. doi:10.1016/j.jmpt.2016.07.004 PMID:27568831

Yang, Y., Jiang, Y., & Wan, K. (2018). The impact of organisational support on employees' psychological safety: A meta-analysis. *Human Resource Management Review*, *28*(4), 551–564.

Yang, Y., Li, Z., Liang, L., & Zhang, X. (2019). Why and when paradoxical leader behaviour impact employee creativity: Thriving at work and psychological safety. *Current Psychology (New Brunswick, N.J.)*, *40*(4), 1911–1922. doi:10.100712144-018-0095-1

Yi, H., Hao, P., Yang, B., & Liu, W. (2016). How leaders' transparent behaviour influences employee creativity: The mediating roles of psychological safety and ability to focus attention. *Journal of Leadership & Organizational Studies*, *24*(3), 335–344. doi:10.1177/1548051816670306

Yin, Y., Chen, J., & Li, C. (2018). Psychological safety, conflict and team performance: A moderated mediation model. *International Journal of Manpower*, *39*(7), 1162–1178.

Ylijoki, O. H., & Henriksson, L. (2017). Tribal, proletarian and entrepreneurial career stories: Junior academics as a case in point. *Studies in Higher Education*, *42*(7), 1292–1308. doi:10.1080/03075079.2015.1092129

Yoshino, N., & Wignaraja, G. (2015). SMEs internationalization and finance in Asia. Frontier and Developing Asia: Supporting Rapid and Inclusive Growth IMF-JICA Conference Tokyo (IMF-JICA 2015).

Younas, A., Wang, D., Javed, B., Rawwas, M., Abdullah, I., & Zaffar, M. (2018). Positive psychological states and employee creativity: The role of ethical leadership. *The Journal of Creative Behavior*, *54*(3), 567–581. doi:10.1002/jocb.391

Youssef, A. B., Boubaker, S., Dedaj, B., & Carabregu-Vokshi, M. (2021). Digitalization of the economy and entrepreneurship intention. *Technological Forecasting and Social Change*, *164*, 120043. doi:10.1016/j.techfore.2020.120043

Yuki, G. (2010). *Leadership in Organizations* (7th ed.). State University of New York, Albany.

Yukl, G. (2006). Leadership in Organization (6th ed.). Pearson Prentice Hall.

Yunusa, A., & Paul, A. A. (2018). Assessment of the contributions of small scale enterprises to the development of the Nigerian economy. *Journal of Good Governance and Sustainable Development in Africa*, *4*(1), 37–47.

Yusuf, N., Jamjoom, Y. & Saci, K. (2023). Entrepreneurial orientation across gender in Saudi Arabia: evidence from the Adult Population Survey (APS) of Global Entrepreneurship Monitor (GEM). *Journal of Entrepreneurship in Emerging Economies*.

Zabelina, E., Deyneka, O., & Tsiring, D. (2019). Entrepreneurial attitudes in the structure of students' economic minds. *International Journal of Entrepreneurial Behaviour & Research*, *25*(8), 1621–1633. doi:10.1108/IJEBR-04-2018-0224

Zachry, E. M. (2005). Getting my education: Teen mothers experiences in school before and after motherhood. *Teachers College Record*, *107*(12), 2566–2598. doi:10.1111/j.1467-9620.2005.00629.x

Zack, M. H. (1999). Developing a knowledge strategy. *California Management Review*, *3*(3), 125–145. doi:10.2307/41166000

Zahra, S., & Dess, G. G. (2001). Entrepreneurship As a Field of Research: Encouraging Dialogue and Debate. *Academy of Management Review*, *26*(1), 8–10. doi:10.5465/amr.2001.4011916

Zaki, I. M., & Rashid, N. H. (2016). Entrepreneurship impact on economic growth in emerging countries. *The Business and Management Review*, *7*(2), 31-39. https://cberuk.com/cdn/conference_proceedings/conference_40058.pdf

Zapata-Cantu, L., Sanguino, R., Barroso, A., & Nicola-Gavrilă, L. (2023). Family business adapting a new digit al-based economy: Opportunities and challenges for future research. *Journal of the Knowledge Economy*, *14*(1), 408–425. doi:10.100713132-021-00871-1

Zautra, A. J., Arewasikporn, A., & Davis, M. C. (2010). Resilience: Promoting well-being through recovery, sustainability, and growth. *Research in Human Development*, *7*(3), 221–238. doi:10.1080/15427609.2010.504431

Zeb, A., Abdullah, N., Hussain, A., & Safi, A. (2019). Authentic leadership, knowledge sharing, and employees' creativity. *Management Research Review*, *43*(6), 669–690. doi:10.1108/MRR-04-2019-0164

Zellweger, T., Sieger, P., & Halter, F. (2011). Should I stay or should I go? Career choice intentions of students with family business background. *Journal of Business Venturing*, *26*(5), 521–536. doi:10.1016/j.jbusvent.2010.04.001

Zeng, J., & Ren, J. (2022). How does green entrepreneurship affect environmental improvement? Empirical findings from 293 enterprises. *The International Entrepreneurship and Management Journal*, *18*(1), 409–434. doi:10.100711365-021-00780-4

Zhang, D. D., & Swanson, L. A. (2014). Linking social entrepreneurship and sustainability. *Journal of Social Entrepreneurship*, *5*(2), 175–191. doi:10.1080/19420676.2014.880503

Zhang, X., & Bartlett, K. R. (2017). How Leaders and Team Members Create a Psychologically Safe Work Environment: A Multiple Case Study. *Journal of Business and Psychology*, *32*(3), 231–248.

Zhao, H., Seibert, S. E., & Hills, G. E. (2005). The mediating role of self-efficacy in the development of entrepreneurial intentions. *The Journal of Applied Psychology*, *90*(6), 1265–1272. doi:10.1037/0021-9010.90.6.1265 PMID:16316279

Zhou, M. J., Mu, W. Q., Li, F. G., Zhou, Y. X., Huang, D., Wang, K. X., & Zhang, J. (2021). Entrepreneur-region fit and entrepreneurial success in China: The effect of "Confucian" personality. *Frontiers in Psychology*, *12*, 724939. doi:10.3389/fpsyg.2021.724939 PMID:34566808

Zhou, P., Tijssen, R., & Leydesdorff, L. (2016). University-industry collaboration in China and the USA: A bibliometric comparison. *PLoS One*, *11*(11), e0165277. doi:10.1371/journal.pone.0165277 PMID:27832084

Zhou, W., Zhu, Z., & Vredenburgh, D. (2020). Emotional intelligence, psychological safety, and team decision making. *Team Performance Management*, *26*(1/2), 123–141. doi:10.1108/TPM-10-2019-0105

Zhu, F., Thornhill, S., & Hsu, D.K. (2021). When owner family and community roles intertwine: Examining entrepreneurs' persistence decisions and the gender effect. *Journal of Small Business Management, 59*(sup1), S102-S133.

Zhu, F., Burmeister-Lamp, K., & Hsu, D. K. (2017). To leave or not? The impact of family support and cognitive appraisals on venture exit intention. *International Journal of Entrepreneurial Behaviour & Research*, *23*(3), 566–590. doi:10.1108/IJEBR-04-2016-0110

Zhu, H., Schulte, M. A., & Thomas, J. (2020). Leveraging information technology to promote innovation in virtual teams. *Journal of Management Information Systems*, *37*(1), 54–81. doi:10.1080/07421222.2019.1708773

Zitzman B. E (2019). *What are family values and why are they important?* Beliefnet.com/love-family/family-values.aspx.

Zsambok, C. E. (2014). Naturalistic decision making: where are we now? In *Naturalistic decision making* (pp. 23–36). Psychology Press. doi:10.4324/9781315806129

Zupic, I., & Čater, T. (2015). Bibliometric Methods in Management and Organization. *Organizational Research Methods*, *18*(3), 429–472. doi:10.1177/1094428114562629

About the Contributors

Ethel Ndidiamaka Abe is a co-founder and the CEO of Sash Business Management South Africa, and SashBM LLC. in the United States of America. She is an experienced management consultant, and editor of a peer-reviewed book titled, Future of Work, Work-Family Satisfaction, and Employee Well-Being in the Fourth Industrial Revolution published in 2021. The quality of this book has been acknowledged by Scopus and PsycINFO, two leading indexing databases in the industry which will only list books that are of top quality, demonstrate a rigorous observance of ethical publishing, and make a meaningful impression on the research community. Both Scopus and PsycINFO have listed the book within their database in a year's time. Ethel is a scholar at the top of her field, a business coach, an entrepreneurial mentor, and an international speaker. Please see her Google scholar citations. Dr. Abe holds a doctoral degree in Management and Entrepreneurship from the University of KwaZulu-Natal, Durban South Africa, a Master of Business Administration degree, as well as a Bachelor of Science (Hons) degree in Business Administration from the Ahmadu Bello University, Zaria, Nigeria. She is an accredited domestic relationship counselor, moderator, and assessor of learning outcomes, curriculum developer, data analyst, and team builder, among others.

Isaac Idowu Abe (Ph.D.) is the chairperson of SashBM LLC United States and Sash Business Management South Africa, a professional management consultant and a researcher and postdoctoral fellow at the University of KwaZulu-Natal. He holds a Ph.D. in Business/Leadership Studies from the Graduate school of Business, University of KwaZulu-Natal. His research interests are in Leadership, interpersonal relationship at work, social exchange, Business management and entrepreneurship development. Dr. Abe lectures Business Ethics, marketing, management and leadership modules. He has published articles in peer- reviewed journals. Dr. Abe has presented papers in academic conferences in South Africa, United Kingdom, Canada and the United States of America. His support has seen many Masters and Honors student through their academic projects.

* * *

Olalekan Ismaila Adisa is an accomplished Senior Lecturer with over 14 years experience of in teaching and research in Nigeria, South Africa, and the United Kingdom. He has made significant contributions to the fields of Project Management, Public Administration, Political Science, International Business, Logistics and Supply Chain Management, and the MBA program. With a profound passion for teaching, learning, and research, Dr. Adisa has become a recognized authority in the academic and professional community. Dr Adisa holds a Ph.D. in Political Science from the University of KwaZulu-Natal South Africa and three master's degrees from the University of Lagos (Nigeria), the University of Ibadan(Nigeria), and the University of Northampton (UK). He has conducted groundbreaking research across disciplines in leading journals globally. His research has been instrumental in advancing our understanding of African and global economy, poverty, demography, international development and entrepreneurship, business management, and globalization and has been published in numerous prestigious journals. Throughout his career, Dr. Adisa has demonstrated a strong commitment to education and has been actively involved in teaching and mentoring the next generation of scholars. He has taught a wide range of courses in Project Management, International Business, and International Logistics Management and has supervised several successful graduate students. As one of the authors of the book chapter titled "The Influence of Family Dynamics on Entrepreneurial Intentions and Self-efficacy," published by IGI Global, Dr. Adisa brings together years of expertise and a wealth of knowledge to contribute to the collective understanding of The Influence of Family Dynamics on Entrepreneurial Intentions and Self-efficacy. Their comprehensive insights and innovative perspectives are invaluable to the academic and professional community. Dr. Adisa is a sought-after speaker at national and international conferences and has received multiple awards and accolades for his outstanding contributions to the field. He is a dedicated researcher, educator, and advocate for the advancement of knowledge in Business Management, Logistics and Supply Management, Project Management, and International Politics. In addition to his professional achievements, Dr. Adisa is an avid soccer fan and enjoys traveling and adventures. He believes in the importance of work-life balance and strives to lead a fulfilling and meaningful life both inside and outside the academic world. For more information about Dr Adisa, you can find him on LinkedIn.

Taiwo Hassan Ajadi is a budding academic researcher trained at the University of KwaZulu-Natal, where he has made significant contributions to the field of green Human Resource Management and now entrepreneurship. With a profound passion for business and organization management, Ajadi has become a recognized authority in the academic and professional community. Ajadi holds a Ph.D. in Human Resource Management from UKZN, where they conducted ground-breaking research on 'The Place of human resource in developing workplace green behavior model for eThekwini Municipality Durban, South Africa'. This research has been instrumental in advancing our understanding of the concept of green human resource management activities across public sector organizations and has been published in numerous prestigious journals. Throughout his career, Dr. Ajadi has demonstrated a strong commitment to education and has been actively involved in teaching and mentoring the next generation of scholars. They have taught a wide range of courses in human resource management and have supervised several successful graduate students. As one of the authors of the book chapter titled "The Influence of Family Dynamics on Entrepreneurial Intentions and Self-efficacy," in the book "Cases on the interplay between Family, Entrepreneurship, and Society" published by IGI Global, Ajadi brings together years of expertise and a wealth of knowledge to contribute to the collective understanding of the Influence of Family Dynamics on Entrepreneurial Intentions and Self-efficacy. Their comprehensive insights and innovative perspectives are invaluable to the academic and professional community. Ajadi is a sought-after speaker at national and international conferences and has received multiple awards and accolades for their outstanding contributions to the field. He is a dedicated researcher, educator, and advocate for the advancement of knowledge in Organizational and Business Management. In addition to their professional achievements, Ajadi is an avid technology enthusiast exploring the world of artificial intelligence (AI) possibilities and enjoys engaging in sports activities and watching mystery, action, and adventure movies. He also believes in the importance of work-life balance and strives to lead a fulfilling and meaningful life both inside and outside the academic world. For more information about Ajadi, you can find Dr. Ajadi on LinkedIn.

Louis Okon Akpan is a seasoned scholar interested in qualitative research. He began his academic journey at the University of Calabar where he obtained a Bachelor of Science Education (B.Sc./Ed.) in Geography Education. Dr. Okon holds three master's degrees in Climatology, Comparative Education, and Commerce (Leadership). He obtained his Ph.D. in Comparative Education from the University of KwaZulu-Natal, South Africa. Louis belongs to several academic associations including the World Association of Academics and Researchers, the International Society of Comparative Education, Science, and Technology, and the Association of Nigerian Geographers. His research interests include education for disadvantaged people, gender and sexuality education, and inclusive education. He has published widely in national and international peer-reviewed journals.

Richmond Anane-Simon is a corporate executive, researcher, activist in civil society, and critical thinker with experience working for the government, for-profit companies, and non-profit organizations. He possesses outstanding research, entrepreneurial/intrapreneurial, and leadership skills that are crucial for corporate success. His areas of interest in research include strategic management, sustainability, entrepreneurship, and technological innovation. His current positions include managing partner at Eco Electric Africa Limited and advisory board member of Naturopaths Without Borders USA.

Nelson A. Andrade-Valbuena is an Associate Professor at the Faculty of Economics and Business Administration, Universidad Católica de la Santísima Concepción. Dr. Andrade holds a PhD in Management from the University of Chile (Chile), a Master's degree in Business Administration (MBA) from Università Degli Studi Guglielmo Marconi (Italy), and a Bachelor's degree in Business Administration from EAN University (Colombia). He serves as an Associate Editor at Revista Estudios de Administración and has numerous publications in journals, books, and conference proceedings. His research has been featured in journals such as Technological Forecasting and Social Change, Journal of Business Research, World Journal of Entrepreneurship, Management and Sustainable Development, Journal of Strategy and Management, among others. Currently, his research interests encompass innovation, entrepreneurship, and strategic management.

Sulaiman Olusegun Atiku is a Professor of Human Resources at Harold Pupkewitz Graduate School of Business (HP-GSB), Namibia University of Science and Technology, Namibia. He is a pragmatic researcher specializing in Strategic Human Resource Management. His current research area of interest includes Human Capital Formation for the Fourth Industrial Revolution, and Human Resource Management Practices for Promoting Sustainability. He has over 15 years' experience in Higher Education. A native of Lagos, Sulaiman graduated from the University of KwaZulu-Natal with a PhD degree in Human Resource Management. His Master of Science degree was awarded in Human Resources and Industrial Relations at Lagos State University, Nigeria. His Bachelor of Science (Honours) degree was also awarded at Lagos State University in the field of Industrial Relations and Personnel Management. He has lectured several courses in his field home/abroad and published many scholarly articles in international journals. He is a member of International Labour and Employment Relations Association (ILERA), Nigerian Institute of Management (NIM), and Institute of People Management (IPM) South Africa.

Ayansola Ayandibu holds a BSc Hons in Accounting, Master of Business Administration, and a PhD. in Leadership Studies (Strategy, Innovation, and Entrepreneurship). He worked in the corporate environment for 8 years in Nigeria before relocating to South Africa. In 2012, Dr Ayandibu worked for Lieutenant Consulting, in Midrand, Johannesburg as an accountant/economist. He lectured at the University of KwaZulu-Natal from February 2013 to January 2021 in the discipline of Management and Entrepreneurship. Dr Ayandibu has lectured Accounting, Management, and Entrepreneurship modules at thc University of KwaZulu-Natal. He has also published articles in accredited journals, published book chapters, and edited a book on entrepreneurship. Dr. Ayandibu has attended international conferences at the University of London, UK, Harvard University (USA), and Ryerson University, Toronto Canada. He lectures Banking and Financial Management modules. Dr Ayandibu has supervised several honours students, master's and PhD candidates. Dr. Ayansola Ayandibu is a member of the South African Institute of Management (SAIM), South African Institute of Management Scientists (SAIMS), South African Institute of Business Accountants (SAIBA), and Institute of Chartered Economists of Nigeria (ICEN).

Chidi Idi Eke is a senior researcher at the Mangosuthu University of Technology, Durban, South Africa. As a scholar at the apex of his career, he has teaching experience that spans eight years as well as proficient mastery of applied research using the pragmatic mixed-method research approach. Dr. Eke holds a doctorate (Ph.D.) in Management studies from the University of KwaZulu Natal. In addition to his academic career, he has founded and managed several companies including Noble Global Security Company, a risk management company, where he was the CEO, of Vivid Data Limited – he acted as director of operations, and Kia-fronting Foundation (KFF), a Non-Profit Organisation. He is the Chairperson of KFF which focuses on providing remedial and structured interventions against Gender Based Violence as well as initiatives addressing refugee issues. He has created community development platforms that enable impact positively on communities in South Africa and Nigeria. Dr. Eke combines his academic and industry experiences in managing people and organizations. He has published articles in internationally accredited and high-impact journals. Chidi is a Member of the Senate of Richfield Graduate Institute of Technology, Durban, and a Committee member on Curriculum, Innovation, Design, and Development (CIDD) at the same institution.

Bhim Jyoti has been working with V.C.S.G., UUHF, College of Forestry, Ranichauri, Tehri Garhwal, Uttarakhand, India as Assistant Professor of Seed and Technology. She received MSc in Seed and Technology from CCS University Meerut and PhD in Seed and Technology from G. B. Pant University of Agriculture, Pantnagar, Uttarakhand. She has published several research articles in the seed and technology, plant growth, seed vigour, genetic variability, Biotechnological approaches, climate change and agricultural productivity.

Dagogo William Legg-Jack is a Postdoctoral Research Fellow at Walter Sisulu University, Nelson Mandela Drive, Mthatha, Eastern Cape, South Africa. He obtained his PhD in Technology Education, and has served as a teacher in high schools in Nigeria, where he taught Technology-based subject. He has also functioned as a lecturer in the Department of Metal Work Technology, School of Secondary Education (Technical), Federal College of Education (Technical), Omoku, Rivers State, Nigeria for several years. In South Africa, he has also served as a lecturer in the Department of Technology Education, at the University of KwaZulu-Natal. Dr Legg-Jack's research project supervision experience spans across different levels of higher education institutions namely, the NigerianCertificate of Education (NCE) in Federal College of Education (Technical), Omoku, and Bachelor of Education (B. Ed) of the same institution in affiliation with the University of Nigeria, Nssuka. Moreover, he has participated in seminars and conferences both within and outside South Africa and has published articles in peer-reviewed journals that focus on skills development, poverty reduction as well as wealth creation.

Doreen Mukuku is the Programme Manager for School of Management at The IIE's Varsity College Sandton Campus, in Johannesburg. She currently lectures International Business Management and Contemporary Management and Innovation to Bachelor of Commerce Honours students. Doreen also supervises Bachelor of Commerce Honours research students' research projects. Her research interests are in the broad areas of Business Management and Teaching and Learning initiatives especially in Private Tertiary Institutions.

Clever Ndebele is currently the Senior Director: Learning and Teaching at Walter Sisulu University. He has extensive experience in higher education studies with more than 10 years' experience at senior management level in the area of teaching and learning at several universities in South Africa. Has participated in several (NRF) research projects on academic staff development in collaboration with other universities and has also been involved in Teaching Development Grant National collaborative projects (namely PGDHE for educational development practitioners and PGDHE for academics). He is also a member of the CHE National Standards and Reviews Committee and the CHE Peer Advisory Group on Reconceptualising Teaching and Learning (RELATE). Prof Ndebele currently oversees academic staff development and student academic support and coordinates the University Capacity Development Programme, the New Generation of Academics Programme, National

Siyaphumelela Student Success project and Future Professors Programme at Walter Sisulu University.

Mercy Okoli is Post-doctoral research fellow, Faculty of Management Sciences, Durban University of Technology. Her experience centers around Doctoral Research Supervision Experiences, Higher Education Teaching and Learning, Learning experiences in the First Industrial Revolution, Women Empowerment and Entrepreneurship. Recently, being a panelist member of the Faculty of Management Sciences Research Defense has also broadened her research horizons.

Sergio Olavarrieta is the Vice President of Economic and Financial Affairs, and Associate Professor of Marketing and Strategy of the University of Chile. His research and teaching interests include Strategic Management, Marketing, Branding and Strategy in Higher Education having published in prestigious journals such as: Journal of the Academy of Marketing Science, Journal of Business Research, Journal of Strategic Marketing, International Marketing Review, and participates in several Editorial Boards including ACADEMIA, RAE, Estudios Gerenciales. Professor Olavarrieta has held several senior executive positions including: Former Dean of the Universidad Diego Portales Business School, former Dean of the Graduate School of Business and Economics, former ViceDean of Faculty of Economics and Business at the University of Chile. He also has served in several academic associations: Past President of the Business Association of Latin American Studies (BALAS) and of the Chilean Association of Business Schools (ASFAE-Chile) and as President of the Academic Committee of the Latin American Council of Business Schools (CLADEA).

Ajay K. Singh is working as an Assistant Professor (Economics) in the School of Liberal Arts & Management, DIT University Dehradun. He did Post-Doctorate Research with EDI of India, Ahmedabad, Gujarat (India). He received MPhil (Economics) from Devi Ahilya University Indore (India), and PhD (Economics) from IIT Indore (India). He has published research papers in the area of climate change and agricultural productivity, assessment of food security; estimation of GFSI, assessment of environmental sustainability index and its association with socio-economic indicators; implications of entrepreneurship ecosystem on economic development; and implications of digitalization on economic development at national and global level.

Funmilola Aderayo Soneye studies Public Management at the Faculty of Commerce, Human Sciences, and Education at the Namibia University of Science and Technology. Her interest lies in researching contemporary issues in public management and proposing plausible frameworks for sustainable public governance and development in Industry 5.0. ''Fostering Psychological Safety for Team Effectiveness in Family Businesses:Insights from Savoy Hotel'' is her first published scholarly work. She is interested in conducting more research on sustainable entrepreneurship and probing different pathways towards the sustainability of public enterprises in developing countries.

Miguel Ángel Zapata Pérez currently works as a Study Engineer in the Department of Institutional Analysis at the University of the Americas (Chile). He holds a Bachelor's degree in Economics and a Master's in Economic Analysis from the University of Chile (Chile), and a Master's in Economics from the University of Groningen (The Netherlands). His professional experience and academic knowledge converge in his current role, where he is dedicated to studying and promoting the benefits of higher education for young individuals. He also maintains a keen interest in economic analysis focused on strategic management.

Index

A

Actions 2, 19, 36, 40-41, 44-45, 57, 60-61, 66-70, 72-74, 81, 101, 103, 105, 131-132, 147, 158-160, 171, 174, 176, 183-184, 188, 195-196, 200, 290, 300, 311
Authors 92, 97, 163, 166, 233-234, 250-252, 255, 257, 261-262, 271-276, 279, 284-285, 306, 308, 332, 344

B

Bibliometrics 277, 281, 284
Business-Family Life 122

C

Challenges 3, 6, 9, 11, 13, 17, 19, 21, 24-25, 27, 32-33, 35, 52, 62, 64, 66, 70, 72, 74, 85, 100, 102, 111, 123-126, 128, 132-136, 146-149, 152-160, 162, 165, 171-172, 174, 179, 185-186, 189, 194, 198, 214, 216, 224-225, 227-231, 233-234, 237, 239-240, 242-245, 248-249, 254, 287-292, 294-295, 302-303, 351
Citation Patterns 258, 284
Co-Citation Analysis 257, 271-274, 278, 284
Corpus of Research 284
Countries 4, 7, 15, 23, 27-28, 31, 34, 40, 42, 44, 47, 50, 86, 136, 144, 175, 190, 208, 221, 250-252, 255, 257, 268-271, 276, 297, 301, 311, 315-316, 318-327, 330, 332-333, 335-338, 341, 343-347, 350-353
COVID-19 Pandemic 1, 10, 18, 22, 24, 58, 63-64, 66, 73, 76, 123, 127, 129, 135, 142, 144, 146-147, 157-159, 171-172, 211, 223, 349
Crises 1, 10, 24, 60-62, 67, 70, 138, 158, 171, 186, 233

D

Development 1-8, 10-12, 19, 22-32, 35-36, 38, 40, 43, 45, 47-48, 50, 52-53, 56, 60, 63, 75, 77-78, 80-81, 83, 86, 88, 104, 107, 109-111, 115, 118-119, 124-126, 132, 147, 149, 151, 159, 166-167, 171, 173-176, 179-181, 183, 185, 188, 190-191, 193, 195, 198-201, 203-204, 206-213, 215, 219, 221-226, 230, 232, 234-235, 238, 240-241, 249, 261, 271, 273, 277, 279, 282-283, 300, 302-303, 307, 309-311, 314, 316-320, 323-324, 327-328, 330, 335-336, 341, 344-352

E

Economic Development 4, 8, 23, 26-27, 29-30, 60, 159, 230, 317, 319-320, 328, 330, 336, 346-352
Employee Engagement 84, 86, 91-94, 97-99, 105, 107-108, 110-112, 117-119, 230
Employee Performance 53, 84, 94, 96, 116, 205-206
Entrepreneurial Decision-Making 60-61, 72, 76, 78, 168, 170, 194, 251

Entrepreneurial Intentions 34, 48-51, 53-56, 60, 143, 146-150, 158-161, 163-169, 172, 174, 176, 178, 181, 188, 198, 207, 287-293, 297-301, 303-311, 313-314, 320-322, 324, 346, 349, 353
Entrepreneurial Process 50, 61, 122, 124-125, 142, 179, 288, 291
Entrepreneurial Resilience 5, 57, 59, 62-63, 73, 75, 77-79, 139, 153
Entrepreneurial Success 6, 20, 28, 56, 135, 139, 142, 147, 150-151, 155, 157-158, 168, 183, 200, 286, 289, 298, 300
Entrepreneurs 1-4, 6, 8, 11-14, 16, 22-25, 29, 34-39, 43-44, 46-49, 51, 56, 58-61, 63-64, 72-74, 76, 80, 82, 122-139, 142-147, 151-161, 164-165, 168, 171-172, 176, 188-189, 191, 198-199, 204-205, 207, 209, 224, 286-287, 291, 296-298, 300-303, 316, 318, 321-322, 324, 341, 345, 348-349
Entrepreneurship 1-13, 15, 19-33, 35-37, 39-43, 45-60, 63, 71, 74, 76-77, 81, 110, 122, 124, 126, 128-131, 133-144, 146-151, 154-164, 166-169, 171-180, 183, 191, 198, 204, 207-208, 212-213, 223-226, 233, 244-249, 261, 273-274, 276-279, 281-284, 286-291, 294-302, 304, 308-325, 327-328, 330, 335, 338, 342-353
Entrepreneurship Ecosystem 315-321, 323-325, 328, 330, 335, 338, 342-346, 350-351
Entrepreneurship Intentions 297-299

F

Family 1-2, 4-10, 13-14, 19-23, 25, 27, 29-31, 33-47, 49-59, 61-68, 70-72, 74, 76, 78-82, 86-91, 97-98, 104-108, 113, 116, 118-120, 122-127, 129-139, 141-144, 146-163, 165-182, 184, 187-189, 192-194, 196, 200-202, 204-209, 214, 217, 219-220, 225, 228-259, 261-262, 265, 268, 271-284, 287-300, 303-314, 321
Family Business 5, 29-31, 33, 57, 63, 65, 85-86, 90, 106-108, 113, 137, 142-143, 150, 154, 162, 173-176, 179-180, 183-184, 187, 189, 194-196, 205-208, 229-242, 244-249, 257, 261, 274, 279-281, 290, 292-293, 299, 309-312, 314
Family Dynamics 5, 85, 146-149, 154-164, 166-172, 176, 179, 228, 231-232, 234, 239-240, 242, 244, 252, 287-293, 295-300, 305-310, 312
Family Environments 42
Family Firms 108, 113, 144, 156, 174, 178, 195, 208, 246-248, 250-259, 262, 265, 268, 271, 274-280, 282-284, 298, 311
Family Processes 57, 59, 61-63, 71, 76, 81
Family Values 21, 86, 157, 165, 182-184, 187-189, 194-195, 200, 202, 207, 209, 228, 237, 245, 293, 309
Foreign Direct Investment 317, 320, 328, 341-342, 344

G

Generation 44-47, 86, 110, 156, 173, 177, 184, 222, 227-228, 231, 233, 235-237, 239, 242, 244, 253, 299-300, 304-306, 310, 312, 350

H

Houshi Ryokan 227-229, 235-237

I

Interpersonal Risk-Taking 84-85, 87

J

Job Satisfaction 90-94, 96-99, 107-108, 110, 113, 115-118, 121, 205

K

Knowledge Management 108, 250-259, 262, 265, 268, 271, 273-283, 285

L

Leadership 7, 24, 26, 31-33, 41, 51, 57, 62,

64, 67, 70-76, 78-79, 86, 89-96, 103, 105, 107-110, 112-114, 117-121, 137, 154-156, 162, 178-179, 182-186, 194, 196-197, 199-209, 227-228, 236-239, 241-246, 272-273, 275, 277, 287, 292, 313

M

Medium 29, 53, 78, 128, 136, 210

N

Networking Theory 6, 20

P

Population Growth 319-320, 328-329, 341-342, 344
Poverty Reduction 213, 219-220, 222
Psychological Safety 84-121, 153

R

Regulatory Focus Theory 165, 167, 169, 287-288, 308-309
Resilience 5-6, 8-10, 13, 18-19, 21-22, 24, 26, 28-30, 33, 57, 59, 61-64, 68, 70-83, 119, 133, 139-140, 148-149, 151-153, 155-156, 158, 171, 175, 185-186, 201, 211, 230-231, 244-247, 288, 300, 302
Resource-Based View 233, 245, 273, 275

S

Self-Efficacy 5, 22, 37, 39-40, 42, 44, 48-50, 52, 54, 56, 61, 63, 77, 80, 109-110, 141, 146-151, 157-158, 163-178, 180-184, 188, 198-199, 202-204, 207-208, 288-289, 293, 297-301, 303-314, 318, 321-322, 324, 344, 347, 353
Self-Efficacy Theory 48, 163, 307
Small 8, 15, 22-23, 25-29, 31-32, 43, 48-49, 52-53, 55, 64, 75, 78, 85, 111, 118, 123, 128, 136, 138, 140, 142-143, 147, 173-174, 176, 178, 189, 209-210, 215, 225-226, 229, 249, 261, 273, 278-280, 287, 296, 299-300, 311, 313, 345, 349, 352
Social Capital 12, 36, 47, 51, 55, 136-137, 142, 246, 295
Social Support 40, 51-52, 74, 122, 127, 134-135, 138-140, 142-143, 160, 201, 206, 286-288
Societal Norms 146-147, 157-161, 166-168, 171-172, 286, 288-289, 293-297, 309
Society 1-3, 8, 11-13, 21-22, 25, 28, 31, 33, 53, 86, 110-111, 128, 133, 165, 187, 190, 198, 208, 220, 222, 225-226, 276, 278-279, 294-296, 316, 349, 351
Socio-Cognitive Model 303, 307
Sociocultural Norms 286
Stressors 73, 122, 124-129, 131-136, 140, 144
Succession Planning 86-87, 154-156, 175, 227-228, 231, 234-239, 241-242, 244-246, 249
Supranational Regions 250
Survival Strategies 227
Sustainability 1, 5-6, 9-13, 18-22, 24-26, 29-33, 45, 49-50, 56, 60, 78, 81, 83, 86, 107, 110, 120, 132, 151, 164, 180, 223, 229-231, 233-234, 237, 240, 244-249, 277-278, 283, 286, 296, 314, 319, 348, 350-352
Systematic Literature Review 49, 114, 180, 246, 283, 285, 314
Systems Theory 9, 62, 234, 245

T

Team Dynamics 99, 104, 108, 112
Team Effectiveness 84, 87-89, 99, 107-108, 111, 114-115, 117-119
Teenage Mothers 210-222, 226
Theoretical Frameworks 47, 88, 132, 163-164, 169-170, 273, 286, 306, 308, 310
Theory of Planned Behavior 48, 165-168, 175-176, 197, 203, 287-288, 308, 311

U

Universities 43, 46, 53, 55, 223, 225, 250,

252, 265, 268, 271, 276-277, 282, 298, 321

V

VOS Network Analysis 285

W

Wellbeing 8, 12, 23, 52, 74-76, 122-123, 126-127, 129, 133, 136

www.ingramcontent.com/pod-product-compliance
Lightning Source LLC
LaVergne TN
LVHW081249011026
849162LV00005BA/1108